WITHDRAWN
UTSA Libraries

RUSSIAN FOREIGN POLICY IN TRANSITION

Concepts and Realities

RUSSIAN FOREIGN POLICY IN TRANSITION

Concepts and Realities

Edited by:
Andrei Melville
and
Tatiana Shakleina

Central European University Press
Budapest   New York

Published in 2005 by
Central European University Press

An imprint of the
Central European University Share Company
Nádor utca 11, H-1051 Budapest, Hungary
Tel: +36-1-327-3138 or 327-3000
Fax: +36-1-327-3183
E-mail: ceupress@ceu.hu
Website: www.ceupress.com

400 West 59th Street, New York NY 10019, USA
Tel: +1-212-547-6932
Fax: +1-646-557-2416
E-mail: mgreenwald@sorosny.org

ISBN 963 7326 17 0 cloth

Library of Congress Cataloging-in-Publication Data

Russian foreign policy in transition : concepts and realities / [edited by] Andrei Melville and
Tatiana Shakleina.—1st ed.
    p. cm.
    Includes index.
1. Russia (Federation)—Foreign relations—Sources. I. Melville, A. I. (Andrei Iurevich) II. Shakleina,
Tatiana

DK510.764.R867 2005
327.47'009'049—dc22

2005007264

Printed in Hungary by
Akadémiai Nyomda, Martonvásár

Table of Contents

PART 2: STATEMENTS

PART 3: ANALYSIS

Introduction

Andrei Melville with Tatiana Shakleina

From a broad historical perspective, a 10–15 year spell of time is not very long. However, if this time span happens to embrace profound changes in the social and political spheres, considerable shifts in public values, and transformational processes on a global scale, then the period can certainly be regarded as of special significance.

The last decade of the 20th century and the beginning of the 21st century can be seen as just such a period of dramatic social perturbations. The collapse of communism, the disintegration of the bipolar world order, the downfall of the Soviet state system, and Russia's proclaimed reorientation towards freedom and democracy are among the world's most momentous events. The deep transformations in question are of special importance for Russia. Indeed, these changes have affected more than just specific aspects of Russia's domestic and foreign policies. They have had an impact on the very essence of Russian self-consciousness and self-identity, and upon common beliefs in the country's role and place in the world.

The scale and nature of the changes happening beneath our very eyes in Russian domestic and foreign policy can be adequately appreciated only by carrying out impartial and thorough analysis. Naturally, first and foremost, any researcher has to examine the actual transformations—whether in Russia's domestic or foreign policy—giving due regard to detail, on the one hand, and the broad context of the ongoing developments, on the other. However, familiarity with these policies as they are specifically represented and justified in strategic documents, the presentations of political leaders and state officials, and in the writings of scholars and analysts may prove to be no less important and insightful for scholarly and practical purposes. As a matter of fact, this is precisely what we had in mind when we embarked on this anthology, which deals with the Russian foreign policy outlook in the crucial period of 1991–2004.[1]

---

1 The Russian-language reader *Foreign Policy and Security of Contemporary Russia* was published in 2002 (Moscow, ROSSPEN).

After the collapse of the USSR and the end of the Cold War, Russia faced essentially new domestic conditions and an unprecedentedly complicated international situation. Having lost its previous geostrategic, economic, military, political and ideological potential and been left to deal with the "hybrid" unbalanced and decentralized political system, the "personalism" of the Yeltsin epoch, the institutional disintegration (as compared to Soviet times) of its foreign policy mechanism, and growing competition among new interest groups, the country and its people also faced an acute crisis of identity on both the international arena and in the sphere of its national interests. Determined as they were by the ruling elites' "subjective" choices, rather than by the "objective" reality flowing from the country's geopolitical situation and historical traditions, the interests in question turned into a site of disputes, disagreements, and tense conflicts among various political and ideological postures.

What follows is a tentative sketch of the key milestones of the developments.

Essentially romantic and full of illusions, the stance assumed by the radical wing of the Russian "Westernizers" of the early 1990s (in the foreign policy sphere, until approximately 1994, this group was represented by what one might call the "early" Russian Foreign Minister A. Kozyrev) matter-of-factly assumed that Russia would be immediately included in the civilized community of Western nations. Of course, this stance was countered by powerful forces striving for the communist and national-imperial restoration. However, neither before nor since has this type of unconditional pro-Western orientation commanded as much influence in Russian political discourse.

The splits in the Russian political class became deeper, and there was a more thorough review of foreign policy priorities in the wake of Russia's failed expectations and ruptured illusions with regard to "alliance with" and "accession to" the West, its injured ambitions, the internal critical tendencies in the economic and social spheres, political instability, as well as its growing disappointment over NATO enlargement, conflicts in the former Yugoslavia, failure of the "CIS project," US warnings of impending withdrawal from the ABM Treaty, etc. Of course these developments have been analyzed in the writings of experts and reflected in the practice of foreign policy. The foreign policy of the Primakov period was (appointed Foreign Minister in January 1996) quite clearly marked by its orientation towards constructing the anti-American international axis in the *Realpolitik* style, and was welcomed by a considerable part of the Russian elite, becoming conceptually embodied in the idea of "multipolarity," while—on a practical level—it led to attempts to create counterbalances to US dominance in the form of various axes: Russia-China-India-Western Europe-Japan, etc. The conceptual errors further aggravated the failures in the foreign policy. The consolidation of the leftist and nationalist opposition, combined with the rise of the radical state imperial instincts in a considerable section of the Russian bureaucracy in the 1990s, proved to be an additional critical factor. It must be admitted, though, that this factor emerged largely as a result of the increasingly evident US "arrogance of power" and the West's general condescending treatment of Russia as a "disciple."

It appears that Putin's pro-American/pro-Western (anti-terrorist in terms of its initial motives, and yet embracing a far larger sphere in terms of its consequences) "revolution" after September 11, 2001 marked a radical turn by Russian foreign policy towards a new agenda, with recognition of global realities and essentially new threats, a cure for the imperial "phantom-limb pains," and redefinition of national priorities in favor of internal tasks of economic and socio-political modernization. As V. Putin's public utterances showed, the President's course in the foreign policy sphere was distinctively based on an awareness that—contrary to expectations—the post-Cold War world had become more unstable, more unpredictable and more dangerous, especially in light of the new threats posed by international terrorism, the proliferation of weapons of mass destruction, the growth of transnational criminal activities, and the escalation of regional conflicts, including some waged by frustrated "might-have-been" states. Therefore, the cardinal national project that Russia was to embark on was formulated as a stark dilemma: either to undertake a systemic (primarily economic but also socio-political) modernization and become involved in the worldwide globalization processes, or lag hopelessly behind and become a "third-rate" state.

Has everything been done in Russia (as well as in the West) to resolve the dilemma? At present, it is hard to come up with a definite answer to this question. And there are a number of reasons why.

First of all, one can not rule out a possible aggravation of the tension between the increasingly distinct autocratic tendencies in domestic policy, and the impulse in foreign policy that is essentially modernizing in terms of its aims, and pro-Western in terms of its orientation.

What remains unresolved is also the issue of institutionalizing the new type of "limited partnership" relations with the West, and transforming declarations made at the highest level into specific procedures and institutions that can function virtually routinely.

Besides, it remains unclear to what extent and how efficiently Russia can overcome the great-power ambitions that persist in the minds of a considerable section of the Russian political elite, but that are neither adequately supported by any substantial resources, nor compatible with relevant tendencies in global development.

Apparently, the West has not fully determined its policy towards Russia either. In particular, neither the USA, nor the European Union seems to have accepted the idea of integration with the Russian Federation. With the exception of some areas of common interests, Russia has moved onto the periphery of the West's interests.

As a matter of fact, the Russian reaction to these developments, which has become increasingly distinct since the start of Putin's second presidential term, appears more explicable. Refraining from confrontation and international crises or conflicts, and aware that it is fated to remain "outside the West" in the foreseeable future and merely involved in superficial interaction with it, Russia is increasingly inclined to assume the posture of an "independent variable" in today's international "equation." Russia strives to determine and accentuate its own independent place in world politics without committing itself to other (particularly, more powerful) international players. "Pragmatism, economic efficiency, priority of national interests" (V. Putin's expression!) is the credo of the foreign policy conducted by Russia today.

Hence Russia's tendency to depart from ideological and confrontational "multipolarity" and move towards a pragmatic "multi-vector" course in its foreign policy, prioritizing the development of—economically beneficial—links and relations with the USA, the EU, European countries, as well as with Asian partners, including China, India and the countries of the Asia-Pacific region. Hence also the pointedly regional, rather than global, priorities in Russia's foreign policy today, with the CIS standing out among these priorities. However, this stance is no longer dictated by the illusory mission to integrate the post-Soviet space with the Russian Federation, but rather by a clearly defined economic interest, namely to safeguard preferential conditions for the spread of Russian capital into the CIS countries (the "liberal empire" declared by A. Chubais, who represents the extreme version of this posture).

As we can see, there is a multitude of unresolved issues and quite tangible challenges that Russia's foreign policy is facing today. No doubt, discussions, disputes and conflicts over these and other issues will continue. There is no point in trying to predict the possible outcome of these debates, but their nature in itself is an indication of the tragectory of Russia's transformation (despite all the setbacks) over the period 1991–2004.

Our anthology comprises three parts. The *first* part includes some of the main official documents of the Russian Federation (agreements, charters, doctrines, conceptions, declarations, etc.) that either directly determine the strategic orientation of its activities in the sphere of foreign policy, or have a direct bearing on this orientation. The *second* part contains public statements and articles by the Russian political leaders: from President Putin to the ministers of foreign affairs and defense. Finally, the *third* part comprises articles written by well-known Russian scholars and analysts that deal with the key issues of Russia's foreign policy and give an idea of the debates ongoing within the Russian academic community.

We would like to believe that the materials we have included (in the limited space of this anthology) can give a fairly extensive and valid idea of how Russian foreign policy has taken shape, evolved and what conceptual foundations it has proceeded from in the period since the end of the Cold War and the collapse of communism. We leave it to our readers to make their own judgements on where we did and did not succeed in carrying out this project.

PART 1
Documents

"Belovezhskiie Agreements"

Agreement on the Establishment of the Commonwealth of Independent States (1991)

["Belovezhskiie Agreements" consist of four documents: "Declaration by Heads of State of the Republic of Belarus, the RSFSR, Ukraine"; "Agreement on the Establishment of the Commonwealth of Independent States"; Declaration by Governments of Belarus, the Russian Federation and Ukraine on Coordination of Economic Policy"; "Protocol to the Agreement on the Establishment of the Commonwealth of Independent States signed on December 8, 1991 in the city of Minsk by the Republic of Belarus, the Russian federation (RSFSR), Ukraine"]

We, the Republic of Belarus, the Russian Federation (RSFSR), and Ukraine, as founding states of the Union of Soviet Socialist Republics, who signed the Union Agreement of 1922, hereinafter referred to as the High Contracting Parties, state that the Union of Soviet Socialist Republics, as a subject of international law and a geopolitical reality, hereby terminates its existence.

Based on the historical affinity of our peoples and the ties that have formed between them, taking into consideration the bilateral accords concluded between the High Contracting Parties,

striving to build democratic law-based states,

intending to develop our relations on the basis of mutual recognition and respect for state sovereignty, the inherent right to self-determination, the principles of equality and non-interference in internal affairs, rejection of the use of force and of economic or any other methods of pressure, resolution of disputes by means of negotiations, and other commonly recognized principles and norms of international law,

believing that further development and strengthening of relations of friendship, good-neighborliness and mutually beneficial cooperation between our states meets the fundamental national interests of their peoples and serves peace and security, *confirming* our commitment to the goals and principles of the Charter of the United Nations, the Helsinki Final Act, as well as other documents of the Conference on Security and Cooperation in Europe,

pledging to observe the generally accepted international norms on human rights and the rights of peoples, have agreed upon the following:

ARTICLE 1

The High Contracting Parties hereby establish the Commonwealth of Independent States.

ARTICLE 2

The High Contracting Parties hereby guarantee their citizens, irrespective of their nationality or other differences, equal rights and freedoms. Each of the High Contracting Parties guarantees the citizens of the other Parties, as well as stateless persons residing in its territory, irrespective of their nationality or other differences, civil, political, economic, and cultural rights and freedoms in accordance with the generally recognized international norms concerning human rights.

ARTICLE 3

The High Contracting Parties, wishing to facilitate the expression, preservation and development of the ethnic, cultural, linguistic and religious originality of national minorities residing in their territories and of their established unique ethno-cultural regions, take them under their protection.

ARTICLE 4

The High Contracting Parties shall develop equal and mutually beneficial cooperation of their peoples and states in the spheres of politics, economics, culture, education, health care, environmental protection, science, and trade, in humanitarian and other areas, shall facilitate broad exchange of information, and conscientiously and meticulously observe mutual obligations.

The Parties believe it necessary that they conclude agreements on cooperation in the aforementioned areas.

ARTICLE 5

The High Contracting Parties shall acknowledge and respect the territorial integrity of each other and the inviolability of existing borders under the framework of the Commonwealth. They shall guarantee the openness of borders, freedom of movement for citizens and for the transfer of information within the Commonwealth.

ARTICLE 6

The member states of the Commonwealth will cooperate in ensuring international peace and security, undertaking effective measures to reduce armaments and military expenditure. They will strive for the elimination of all nuclear weapons, general and full disarmament under strict international control.

The Parties will respect one another's striving to achieve the status of a non-nuclear zone and neutral state.

The member states of the Commonwealth will preserve and support, under a joint command, the common military and strategic space, including united control over nuclear weapons, which shall be carried out as stipulated by a special agreement.

They shall also provide joint guarantees of necessary conditions for the placement, functioning, material and social support for strategic military forces. The Parties shall undertake to conduct a coordinated policy with regard to the issues pertinent to social defense and pension support for military personnel and their families.

ARTICLE 7

The High Contracting Parties hereby recognize that the sphere of their joint activities carried out on an equal basis through common coordinating institutions of the Commonwealth includes:
- coordination of their foreign policy activities;
- cooperation in forming and developing a common economic space, common European and Eurasian markets, and in the sphere of customs policy;
- cooperation in developing communications and transport systems;
- cooperation in the sphere of protecting the environment, participation in establishing an all-encompassing international system for environmental protection;
- issues pertinent to migration policy;
- combating organized crime.

ARTICLE 8

The Parties recognize the global significance of the Chernobyl catastrophe and shall undertake to unite and coordinate their efforts to minimize and overcome the aftermath thereof.

To this end, the Parties have agreed to conclude a special agreement that will take into account the gravity of the catastrophe's consequences.

ARTICLE 9

Disputes with regard to the interpretation and application of the norms of this Agreement shall be subject to resolution through negotiations between the states involved, and, where necessary, at the level of Heads of Government and State.

ARTICLE 10

Each of the High Contracting Parties shall preserve the right to suspend the force of this Agreement or some of its Articles, provided it gives one year's notice of this to the parties to this Agreement.

The stipulations of this Agreement may be supplemented or amended by mutual agreement of the High Contracting Parties.

ARTICLE 11

From the time this Agreement is signed, the application in the territories of the signatories thereof of the norms of third states, including of the former USSR, shall not be permitted.

ARTICLE 12

The High Contracting Parties shall guarantee implementation of international obligations arising from the treaties and accords concluded by the former Union of Soviet Socialist Republics.

ARTICLE 13

This Agreement shall not affect the obligations of the High Contracting Parties towards third states. This Agreement is open to accession by all member states of the former USSR, as well as by other states that share the priorities and principles of this Agreement.

ARTICLE 14

The official location of the Commonwealth's coordinating bodies shall be the city of Minsk. The operation of the former USSR's bodies in the territories of the Commonwealth member states shall be terminated.

Done in Minsk on December 8, 1991 in triplicate, with each copy in the Belarussian, Russian and Ukrainian languages, and with the three texts having identical force.

For the Republic of Belarus	S. Shushkevich, V. Kebich
For the RSFSR	B. Yeltsin, G. Burbulis
For Ukraine	L. Kravchuk, V. Fokin

Originally published in *Sodruzhestvo [Commonwealth]*, Information Bulletin of the Council of Heads of State and Council of Heads of Government of the CIS, 1992, No. 1.

PROTOCOL to the Agreement on the Establishment of the Commonwealth of Independent States, signed on December 8, 1991 in the city of Minsk, by the Republic of Belarus, the Russian Federation (RSFSR) and Ukraine

The Republic of Azerbaijan, Republic of Armenia, Republic of Belarus, Republic of Kazakhstan, Republic of Kyrgyzstan, Republic of Moldova, Russian Federation (RSFSR), Republic of Tajikistan, Turkmenistan, Republic of Uzbekistan and Ukraine on equal grounds and as High Contracting Parties hereby shall form the Commonwealth of Independent States.

The Agreement on the Establishment of the Commonwealth of Independent States shall enter into force for each of the High Contracting Parties from the time of its ratification.

Based on the Agreement on the Establishment of the Commonwealth of Independent States and with consideration of the reservations made upon its ratification, documents will be drafted that will regulate cooperation under the framework of the Commonwealth of Independent States.

This Protocol shall be an integral part of the Agreement on the Establishment of the Commonwealth of Independent States.

Done in the city of Alma-Ata on December 21, 1991 in one original in the Azerbaijani, Belarussian, Kazakh, Kyrgyz, Moldovan, Russian, Tajik, Turkmen, Uzbek and Ukrainian languages. All the texts shall have equal force. The original copy is stored in the archive of the Government of the Republic of Belarus, which will send the High Contracting Parties a certified copy of this Protocol.

For the Republic of Azerbaijan	A. Mutalibov
For the Republic of Armenia	L. Ter-Petrosyan
For the Republic of Belarus	S. Shushkevich
For the Republic of Kazakhstan	N. Nazarbayev
For the Republic of Kyrgyzstan	A. Akayev
For the Republic of Moldova	M. Snegur
For the Russian Federation	B. Yeltsin
For the Republic of Tajikistan	R. Nabiyev
For Turkmenistan	S. Niyazov
For the Republic of Uzbekistan	I. Karimov
For Ukraine	L. Kravchuk

Alma-Ata, December 21, 1991.

Originally published in *Sodruzhestvo* [Commonwealth], Information Bulletin of the Council of Heads of State and Council of Heads of Government of the CIS, 1992, no. 1.

Collective Security Treaty [1]

(1992)

The states participating in this Treaty, hereinafter referred to as "participant states,"

observing the declarations of sovereignty of the Independent States,

taking into account the development by the participant states of their own armed forces,

undertaking coordinated actions in the interests of ensuring collective security,

acknowledging the need for strict observance of the agreements concluded with regard to the reductions of weapons and armed forces, and strengthening of the confidence-building measures, have agreed on the following:

ARTICLE 1

The participant states confirm their obligation to refrain from the use or threat of force in interstate relations. They shall undertake to resolve all disputes arising between themselves and with other states using peaceful means.

The participant states shall not accede to military alliances, or participate in any groups of states, or in actions directed against any other participant state.

In the case of the creation in Europe or Asia of a collective security system, and the conclusion with this purpose of collective security treaties, which the contracting parties will certainly strive for, the participant states will immediately start mutual consultations with a view to introducing relevant intentions into this Treaty.

---

1 Adopted under the framework of the Commonwealth of Independent States. The Treaty was signed by Azerbaijan, Armenia, Belarus, Georgia, Kazakhstan, Kyrgyzstan, the Russian Federation, Tajikistan, and Uzbekistan. Moldova and Turkmenistan did not sign the Treaty. Ukraine has acceded to the Treaty as an observer.

ARTICLE 2

The participant states will engage in consultations with one another on all important issues related to international security that affect their interests, and will coordinate their positions on these issues.

In the event of the emergence of a threat to the security, territorial integrity and sovereignty of one or several participant states, or a threat to international peace and security, the participant states will, without delay, bring into action the mechanism of joint consultations with the purpose of coordinating their positions and undertaking measures to eliminate the emergent threat.

ARTICLE 3

The participant states shall establish a Collective Security Council consisting of the Heads of participant states and the Commander-in-Chief of the United Armed Forces of the Commonwealth of Independent States.

ARTICLE 4

In the event of one participant state being subjected to aggression on the part of another state or group of states, this will be regarded as aggression against all the participant states of the present Treaty.

In the event of an act of aggression perpetrated against any one of the participant states, all other participant states shall render necessary assistance to it, including military support, and shall provide support for it using the means at their disposal, by way of exercising the right for collective defense as stipulated in Article 51 of the UN Charter.

The participant states shall without delay inform the United Nations Security Council of any measures undertaken on the basis of this article. When undertaking the measures in question, the participant states shall observe relevant provisions of the UN Charter.

ARTICLE 5

The coordination and support of joint activities by the participant states in accordance with this Treaty shall be undertaken by the Collective Security Council of the participant states and by the bodies established by the Council. Before the bodies in question are set up, coordination of the activities of the Armed Forces of the participant states shall be carried out by the High Command of the United Armed Forces of the Commonwealth.

ARTICLE 6

A decision to use the Armed Forces to meet aggression shall be adopted by the Heads of the participant states in accordance with Article 3 of this Treaty.

The use of the Armed Forces beyond the territory of the participant states may be exercised exclusively in the interests of international security and in strict conformity with the United Nations Charter and the legislation of the participant states of this Treaty.

ARTICLE 7

The deployment and operation of the facilities of the collective security system in the territory of the participant states shall be regulated by special agreements.

ARTICLE 8

This Treaty shall not affect the rights and obligations stipulated by other effective bilateral and multilateral treaties and agreements concluded by the participant states with other states, and is not directed against third countries.

This Treaty shall not affect the right of the participant states to individual and collective defense against aggression in compliance with the United Nations Charter.

The participant states shall undertake to conclude no treaties inconsistent with this Treaty.

ARTICLE 9

Any questions that might arise between the participant states with regard to interpretation or application of any provision of this Treaty shall be resolved jointly in the spirit of friendship, mutual respect and mutual understanding.

ARTICLE 10

This Treaty is open to accession by all interested states that share its goals and principles.

ARTICLE 11

This Treaty shall be concluded for a period of five years with a possibility of extension.

Any of the participant states shall have the right to withdraw from this Treaty, provided it gives notice to the other participants at least six months prior to withdrawal and fulfills the obligations connected to withdrawal from the Treaty.

This Treaty shall be subject to ratification by each signatory in accordance with its constitutional procedures. Ratification instruments shall be submitted to the Government of the Republic of Belarus, which is hereby appointed as a depositary.

This Treaty shall enter into force from the time of submission for storage of ratification instruments by all participant states that have signed it.

Done in the city of Tashkent on May 15, 1992 in one original copy in the Russian language. The original shall be stored in the Archive of the Government of the Republic of Belarus, which shall send certified copies of the Charter to all the signatories of this Treaty.

[Signatures]

Originally published in *Deystvuyushcheye mezhdunarodnoye pravo* [Contemporary international law], Moscow, Publishing House of the Moscow Independent Institute of International Law, 1997, vol. 2, pp. 269-272.

Charter of the Commonwealth of Independent States

(1993)

The States that have voluntarily united in the Commonwealth of Independent States (hereinafter, the Commonwealth)

based on the historical affinity of their peoples and the relations that have developed between them,

acting in accordance with generally accepted principles and norms of international law, the provisions of the Charter of the United Nations, the Helsinki Final Act and other documents of the Conference on Security and Cooperation in Europe,

seeking to secure through joint efforts the economic and social progress of their peoples,

firmly determined to observe the provisions of the Agreement on the Establishment of the Commonwealth of Independent States, the Protocol to that Agreement, and the provisions of the Alma-Ata Declaration,

developing cooperation with each other in order to ensure international peace and security, and also to promote civil peace and international harmony,

wishing to create conditions for the preservation and development of the cultures of all the peoples of the member states,

seeking to improve the mechanisms for cooperation in the Commonwealth and to increase their effectiveness,

have decided to adopt this Charter of the Commonwealth and have agreed upon the following:

Section I
Goals and Principles

ARTICLE 1

The Commonwealth is based on the foundations of the equality of all its members. The member states are independent and equal subjects of international law.

The Commonwealth serves the further development and strengthening of relations of friendship, good-neighborliness, international harmony, trust, mutual understanding and mutually beneficial cooperation between member states.

The Commonwealth is not a state and does not hold supranational powers.

ARTICLE 2

The purposes of the Commonwealth shall be:
- the realization of cooperation in political, economic, environmental, humanitarian, cultural and other spheres;
- universal and balanced economic and social development of member states within the framework of a common economic space, interstate cooperation and integration;
- the safeguarding of human rights and fundamental liberties in accordance with the commonly recognized principles and norms of international law and documents of the CSCE;
- cooperation of member states in ensuring international peace and security, undertaking effective steps to reduce arms and military expenditure, the elimination of nuclear and other types of weapons of mass destruction, and the achievement of universal and full disarmament;
- assisting citizens of member states in free interaction, contacts and movement within the Commonwealth;
- mutual legal assistance and cooperation in other spheres of legal relations;
- peaceful resolution of disputes and conflicts between the states of the Commonwealth.

ARTICLE 3

In order to achieve the goals of the Commonwealth, the member states, based on generally recognized norms of international law and the Helsinki Final Act, shall develop their relations in conformity with the following interrelated and equally indispensable principles:
- respect for the sovereignty of member states, for the inalienable rights of peoples to self-determination and the right to determine their fate without outside interference;
- the inviolability of state borders, the recognition of existing borders and the rejection of illegitimate territorial annexations;
- the territorial integrity of states and the rejection of any actions aimed at dismembering foreign territory;
- the non-use of force or threat of force against the political independence of member states;
- the resolution of disputes by peaceful means in such a way that international peace, security and fairness are not threatened;

- the supremacy of international law in interstate relations;
- non-interference in one another's internal and external affairs;
- ensuring human rights and fundamental liberties for all, without discrimination on the grounds of race, ethnicity, language, religion, political or other convictions;
- meticulous observance of the obligations undertaken pursuant to the documents of the Commonwealth, including this Charter;
- consideration of each other's interests and the interests of the Commonwealth as a whole, providing assistance on the basis of mutual consent in all spheres of their relations;
- uniting efforts and rendering assistance to each other for the purposes of creating peaceful conditions for the life of the peoples of the member states of the Commonwealth, ensuring their political, economic and social progress;
- development of mutually beneficial economic, and scientific and technological cooperation, broadening integration processes;
- spiritual unity of their peoples, which is based on respect for their originality, close cooperation in the preservation of cultural valuables, and in cultural exchange.

ARTICLE 4

The spheres of joint activity of the member states, realized on an equal basis through common coordinating institutions, and in accordance with the obligations undertaken by the member states within the framework of the Commonwealth, shall include:
- securing human rights and fundamental liberties;
- coordination of foreign policy activity;
- cooperation in the formation and development of a common economic space, common European and Eurasian markets, and customs policy;
- cooperation in the development of transport and communications systems;
- protection of health and environment;
- issues of social and migration policy;
- fighting organized crime;
- cooperation in the sphere of defense policy and the protection of external borders.

This list may be extended by mutual consent of the member states.

ARTICLE 5

The principal legal basis for interstate relations within the framework of the Commonwealth shall consist of multilateral and bilateral agreements in various spheres of interaction between member states. Agreements concluded within the framework of the Commonwealth must conform to the purposes and principles of the Commonwealth, and the obligations of the member states stipulated in this Charter.

ARTICLE 6

Member states shall facilitate the cooperation and development of relations between state bodies, public associations and economic structures.

Section II
Membership

ARTICLE 7

The founding states of the Commonwealth are those states that have signed and ratified the Agreement on the Establishment of the Commonwealth of Independent States of December 8, 1991, and the Protocol to that Agreement of December 21, 1991 at the time this Charter is adopted.

The member states of the Commonwealth are the same founding states that shall undertake obligations pursuant to this Charter within the course of one year after its adoption by the Council of Heads of State.

A state that shares the purposes and principles of the Commonwealth and accepts the obligations contained in this Charter may also become a member of the Commonwealth, by acceding to this Charter with the consent of all member states.

ARTICLE 8

On the basis of a decision by the Council of Heads of State, a state that wishes to participate in certain types of its activities may accede to the Commonwealth as an associate member, on the conditions stipulated by an agreement on associate membership.

Representatives of other states may be present at sessions of the bodies of the Commonwealth as observers, by decision of the Council of Member States.

Questions concerning the participation of associate members and observers in the work of the Commonwealth bodies shall be regulated by the rules of procedure of such bodies.

ARTICLE 9

A member state shall have the right to withdraw from the Commonwealth. The member state shall notify the depositary of this Charter of such an intention 12 months prior to withdrawal.

Obligations that have arisen during the period of participation in this Charter shall be binding upon the relevant states until complete fulfillment thereof.

ARTICLE 10

Violations by a member state of this Charter, systematic failure by a state to fulfill its obligations pursuant to agreements concluded within the framework of the Commonwealth, or decisions of the bodies of the Commonwealth, shall be examined by the Council of Heads of State.

Measures allowed under international law may be applied with regard to such a state.

Section III
Collective Security and Military-Political Cooperation

ARTICLE 11

Member states shall conduct coordinated policies in the spheres of international security, disarmament and arms control, and building of the armed forces, and shall ensure security in the Commonwealth, including with the assistance of groups of military observers and collective peacekeeping forces.

ARTICLE 12

If a threat arises to the sovereignty, security or territorial integrity of one or several member states, or to international peace and security, the member states shall, without delay, employ the mechanism for mutual consultations in order to coordinate their positions and undertake measures aimed at eliminating the threat, including peacekeeping operations and the use, when necessary, of armed forces by way of exercising the right to individual or collective self-defense under Article 51 of the UN Charter.

A decision on the collective use of armed forces shall be made by the Council of Heads of State of the Commonwealth or by interested member states of the Commonwealth in consideration of their national legislation.

ARTICLE 13

Each member state shall undertake appropriate measures to ensure a stable situation along the external borders of the Commonwealth member states. On the basis of mutual consent, member states shall coordinate the operation of border guards and other competent services that exercise control and bear responsibility for observance of the established procedure for crossing the member states' external borders.

ARTICLE 14

The Council of Heads of State shall be the supreme body of the Commonwealth for questions concerning defense and the protection of external borders of the member states. The coordination of the Commonwealth's military-economic activities shall be carried out by the Council of Heads of Government.

The interaction of member states in implementing international agreements and resolving other issues in the sphere of security and disarmament shall be organized through joint consultations.

ARTICLE 15

Specific questions concerning the military-political cooperation of member states shall be regulated by special agreements.

Section IV
Prevention of Conflicts and Resolution of Disputes

ARTICLE 16

Member states shall undertake all possible measures in order to prevent conflicts, primarily on interethnic and inter-confessional grounds, which may give rise to human rights violations.

On the basis of mutual consent, they shall provide to each other assistance in settling such conflicts, including within the framework of international organizations.

ARTICLE 17

Member states of the Commonwealth shall refrain from actions that could cause damage to other member states and lead to the escalation of possible disputes.

The member states shall meticulously, and in the spirit of cooperation, undertake efforts towards fair and peaceful resolution of their disputes through negotiations, or towards reaching an agreement on an appropriate alternative procedure for settling the dispute.

If the member states do not resolve a dispute by the means indicated in part two of this article, they may transfer it to the Council of Heads of State.

ARTICLE 18

At any stage of a dispute that may threaten peace or security in the Commonwealth, the Council of Heads of State shall have the authority to recommend to the parties a suitable procedure or methods for dispute resolution.

Section V
Cooperation in Economic, Social and Legal Spheres

ARTICLE 19

Member states shall cooperate in economic and social spheres along the following lines:

- creation of a common economic space based on market relations and free movement of goods, services, capital, and labor;
- regulation of social policy, development of joint social programs and measures to reduce social tensions connected with the implementation of economic reforms;
- development of transport and communications systems, as well as energy systems;
- coordination of the credit and financial policies;
- promotion of trade and economic relations between the member states;
- encouragement and mutual protection of investments;
- facilitation of standardization and certification of industrial products and goods;
- legal protection of intellectual property;
- assistance in developing a common information space;
- implementation of joint environmental protection measures, providing mutual assistance in mitigating the consequences of environmental catastrophes and other emergency situations;
- implementation of joint projects and programs in the sphere of science and technology, education, health care, culture and sport.

ARTICLE 20

Member states shall practice cooperation in the sphere of law, in particular, through making multilateral and bilateral agreements on rendering legal assistance, and shall seek mutual conformity of national legislation.

If there are inconsistencies between the norms of the member states' national legislation regulating relations in the spheres of joint activities, member states shall carry out consultations and negotiations for the purpose of drafting proposals in order to remove those inconsistencies.

Section VI
Bodies of the Commonwealth Council of Heads of State and Council of Heads of Government

ARTICLE 21

The Council of Heads of State shall be the supreme body of the Commonwealth. The Council of Heads of State, in which all member states shall be represented at the highest level, shall discuss and resolve fundamental questions pertinent to the activities of member states in the spheres of their common interests.

The Council of Heads of State shall gather for its sessions two times per year. Extraordinary sessions of the Council may be convened at the initiative of one of the member states.

ARTICLE 22

The Council of Heads of Government shall regulate the cooperation of executive authority bodies of member states in economic, social and other spheres of common interests.

The Council of Heads of Government shall convene four times per year. Extraordinary sessions of the Council may be convened at the initiative of the government of one of the member states.

ARTICLE 23

Decisions of the Council of Heads of State and Council of Heads of Government shall be adopted with common consent—by consensus. Any state may declare it is not interested in a particular issue, which must not be considered an obstacle for the adoption of a decision.

The Council of Heads of State and Council of Heads of Government can hold joint sessions.

The procedure for the operation of the Council of Heads of State and Council of Heads of Government shall be regulated by the Rules of Procedure.

ARTICLE 24

During sessions of the Council of Heads of State and Council of Heads of Government, heads of state and heads of government shall preside sequentially in the order of the Commonwealth member states' names, using the Russian alphabet.

Sessions of the Council of Heads of State and Council of Heads of Government shall be held, as a rule, in the city of Minsk.

ARTICLE 25

The Council of Heads of State and the Council of Heads of Government shall establish working and auxiliary bodies on both a permanent and temporary basis.

These bodies shall consist of representatives of the member states vested with the corresponding authorities.

Experts and consultants may be invited to participate in their sessions.

ARTICLE 26

For resolving issues pertinent to cooperation in specific spheres, or the development of recommendations for the Council of Heads of State and Council of Heads of Government, conferences of leaders of the corresponding state bodies shall be convened.

Council of Ministers of Foreign Affairs

ARTICLE 27

Based on decisions adopted by the Council of Heads of State and the Council of Heads of Government, the Council of Ministers of Foreign Affairs shall coordinate the foreign policy activities of member states, including their activities within international organizations, and shall organize consultations with regard to matters of world politics, in which they have a mutual interest.

The Council of Ministers of Foreign Affairs shall carry out its activities in accordance with a Statute adopted by the Council of Heads of State.

Coordinating Consultative Committee

ARTICLE 28

The Coordinating Consultative Committee shall represent a permanently functioning executive and coordinating body of the Commonwealth.

By way of executing decisions adopted by the Council of Heads of State and Council of Heads of Government the Committee shall:

- elaborate and submit proposals on issues concerning cooperation within the framework of the Commonwealth, and the development of socio-economic ties;
- facilitate implementation of agreements pursuant to specific spheres of economic relations;
- organize conferences of representatives and experts for the preparation of draft documents to be submitted to sessions of the Council of Heads of State and the Council of Heads of Government;
- ensure the conduct of sessions of the Council of Heads of State and the Council of Heads of Government;
- assist the operation of other bodies of the Commonwealth.

ARTICLE 29

The Coordinating Consultative Committee shall consist of permanent authorized representatives, two from each member state of the Commonwealth, and the Coordinator of the Committee, appointed by the Council of Heads of State.

To provide the organizational and technical support for the operation of the Council of Heads of State, the Council of Heads of Government and other bodies of the Commonwealth, under the Coordinating Consultative Committee a Secretariat shall be established, headed by the Coordinator of the Committee who is the Deputy Chairman of the Coordinating Consultative Committee.

The Committee shall operate in accordance with the Statute approved by the Council of Heads of State.

The location of the Committee shall be the city of Minsk.

Council of Ministers of Defense and the High Command of the United Armed Forces

ARTICLE 30

The Council of Ministers of Defense shall be the body of the Council of Heads of State that deals with issues concerning the military policy and military structures of member states.

The High Command of the United Armed Forces shall carry out control over the United Armed Forces, as well as over groups of military observers and collective forces for maintaining peace in the Commonwealth.

The Council of Ministers of Defense and the High Command of the United Armed Forces shall carry out their activities under relevant provisions approved by the Council of Heads of State.

Council of Commanders of Border Troops

ARTICLE 31

The Council of Commanders of Border Troops shall be the body of the Council of Heads of State that deals with issues concerning the protection of the external borders of member states and maintenance of a stable situation at them.

The Council of Commanders of Border Troops shall carry out its activities under a corresponding Statute approved by the Council of Heads of State.

Economic Court

ARTICLE 32

The Economic Court shall operate in order to ensure the fulfillment of economic obligations within the framework of the Commonwealth.

The jurisdiction of the Economic Court includes the resolution of disputes arising during the implementation of economic obligations. The Court may also resolve other disputes classified as being within its jurisdiction by agreement of member states.

The Economic Court shall have the right to interpret provisions of agreements and other acts of the Commonwealth for economic issues.

The Economic Court shall carry out its activities in conformity with an Agreement on the Status of the Economic Court and a Statute thereof, approved by the Council of Heads of State. The location of the Economic Court shall be the city of Minsk.

Commission for Human Rights

ARTICLE 33

The Commission for Human Rights shall represent a consultative body of the Commonwealth and shall ensure the fulfillment of human rights obligations undertaken by member states within the framework of the Commonwealth.

The Commission shall consist of representatives of member states of the Commonwealth and shall operate under a Statute approved by the Council of Heads of State.

The location of the Commission for Human Rights shall be the city of Minsk.

Sectoral Cooperation Bodies

ARTICLE 34

On the basis of agreements between member states on cooperation in economic, social and other spheres, sectoral cooperation bodies may be established, which shall elaborate agreed principles and rules for such cooperation and facilitate their practical implementation.

Sectoral cooperation bodies (councils, committees) shall fulfill the functions stipulated in this Charter and in statutes thereof, ensuring the consideration and resolution on a multilateral basis of questions concerning cooperation in relevant spheres.

The composition of the sectoral cooperation bodies shall include directors of the corresponding executive bodies of member states.

Within the bounds of their competence, the sectoral cooperation bodies shall develop recommendations, and will, when necessary, submit proposals for consideration by the Council of Heads of Government.

Working Language of the Commonwealth

ARTICLE 35

The working language of the Commonwealth shall be the Russian language.

Section VII
Inter-Parliamentary Cooperation

ARTICLE 36

The Inter-Parliamentary Assembly shall hold inter-parliamentary consultations, discuss issues of cooperation within the framework of the Commonwealth, and elaborate joint proposals in the spheres of activities of national parliaments.

ARTICLE 37

The Inter-Parliamentary Assembly shall consist of parliamentary delegations.

Operation of the Inter-Parliamentary Assembly shall be carried out by the Council of the Assembly, consisting of the leaders of the parliamentary delegations.

Procedural issues concerning the activities of the Inter-Parliamentary Assembly shall be regulated by its Regulations.

The location of the Inter-Parliamentary Assembly shall be the city of St Petersburg.

Section VIII
Financing

ARTICLE 38

The costs involved in financing the activity of the bodies of the Commonwealth shall be distributed in accordance with the member states' participatory shares, and shall be governed by special agreements on budgets of the bodies of the Commonwealth.

The budgets of the bodies of the Commonwealth shall be approved by the Council of Heads of State upon a submission by the Council of Heads of Government.

ARTICLE 39

Issues concerning the financial and administrative activities of the bodies of the Commonwealth shall be examined in accordance with the procedure established by the Council of Heads of Government.

ARTICLE 40

Member states shall independently bear the expenditure connected with the participation of their representatives, as well as their experts and consultants in conferences and bodies of the Commonwealth.

Section IX
Concluding Provisions

ARTICLE 41

This Charter shall be subject to ratification by the founding states in accordance with their constitutional procedures.

Ratification instruments shall be submitted to the Government of the Republic of Belarus, which will notify the other founding states of the submission for storage of each instrument.

For all of the member states, this Charter shall enter into effect from the time of submission for storage of ratification instruments by all founding states or, for the founding states who have submitted their ratification instruments, one year after the adoption of this Charter.

ARTICLE 42

Amendments to this Charter may be proposed by any member state. Proposed amendments shall be considered in conformity with the rules of procedure of the Council of Heads of State.

Amendments to this Charter shall be adopted by the Council of Heads of State. They shall enter into force after ratification by all member states in accordance with their constitutional procedures, from the date of receipt by the Government of the Republic of Belarus of the last ratification certificate.

ARTICLE 43

The founding states of the Commonwealth may, upon ratification of this Charter, make reservations and statements on sections III, IV and VII and Articles 28, 30, 31, 32 and 33.

ARTICLE 44

This Charter will be registered in accordance with Article 102 of the Charter of the United Nations.

ARTICLE 45

This Charter is done in one copy in the state languages of the founding states of the Commonwealth. The original shall be stored at the Archive of the Government of the Republic of Belarus, which shall send certified copies of the Charter to all the founding states.

This Charter was adopted on January 22, 1993 at a session of the Council of Heads of State in Minsk.

Originally published in *Deystvuyushcheye mezhdunarodnoye pravo* [Contemporary international law], Moscow: Publishing House of the Moscow Independent Institute of International Law, 1996, vol. 1, pp. 719–730.

Foreign Policy Conception of the Russian Federation[1]

(1993)

The essence of Russian foreign policy is predetermined by the following long-term tasks: to revive Russia as a democratic, free state; to provide favorable conditions for the formation of a modern efficient economy that will guarantee Russian citizens a worthy standard of living, and the country financial and economic independence; and to achieve the equal and natural incorporation of the Russian Federation into the world community as a great power that boasts a centuries-long history, unique geopolitical situation, considerable military might, and significant technological, intellectual and ethical capacities.

The most important foreign policy tasks requiring COORDINATED and consistent efforts on the part of all the country's state structures are: eradicating armed clashes, settling conflicts around Russia and preventing them from spilling over into our territory, and ensuring strict observance of individual human rights and minority rights in the countries of the near abroad, particularly the rights of ethnic Russians and Russian-speaking populations.

Another key goal we pursue is to preserve the unity and territorial integrity of the Russian Federation. In accordance with the Federal Treaty, Russia's foreign policy and international relations are under the jurisdiction of the federal bodies, while the entities of the Federation are independent in their pursuit of foreign economic exchanges, unless this contravenes the Constitution of the Russian Federation or federal laws. Russian foreign policy is based on consideration of the interests of both the Federation as a whole, and its individual entities. This unity of foreign policy is both a result of a mutual accommodation of interests and, at the same time, a firm guarantee of their complete security.

---

1 General provisions of the foreign policy concept of the Russian Federation were adopted under the Directive of President of the Russian Federation B. N. Yeltsin of April 23, 1993.

The Russian Federation in the Changing World

With one of the largest world powers embarking on a path of democratic development, there has been a need for a profound change in the global power balance. The end of the policy that saw the struggle of "two systems" projected onto all areas of international affairs has not only removed the threat of global war and rendered unnecessary most of the armaments accumulated during the era of confrontation, but it has also created new prerequisites for constructive international cooperation at both regional and global levels, as well as within the UN and other international organizations.

Russia acknowledges the significance of the concept of a "new political thinking," which represented the first attempt to overcome the deadlock of all-out confrontation. At the same time, Russia was prone to unjustified enthusiasm about the abstract notion of what may be called non-conflict (or non-confrontational) globalism, on the one hand, and, on the other hand, to striving to preserve as our foreign policy guideline outdated perceptions rooted in confrontation between the "two systems." For all the interim importance of the "new thinking," this ambiguity predetermined its inadequacies and weaknesses.

The democratic nature of the new Russian statehood allowed us to overcome that stage. The struggle of ideologies has come to an end. Now we have to take care to meet Russia's needs through economic, diplomatic, military, and other means. The foundations are being laid for equal partnerships with our neighbors and with the leading democratic and economically developed nations; partnerships in which we will promote our values and interests by way of real interaction, rather than veering between confrontation and utopias.

We have been accumulating experience in resolving disagreements and disputes between Russia and other countries. Opportunities are opening up for practical attention to be paid to the specifics of Russia's historical, geopolitical, and economic interests in the framework of civilized international relations.

What the world will be like by the end of the 20th century depends largely on the outcome of our reforms, on the strength and stability of Russia's civil society and its federal architecture, and on state foreign policy and other objective factors. In its turn, though, foreign policy cannot be efficient without a proper strengthening of the democratic Russian state and a thorough and realistic consideration of the processes going on abroad.

First and foremost, this refers to the former republics of the USSR, for the post-totalitarian crises that these states are undergoing directly affect Russia's security, as well as the speed of, and potential for, overcoming the economic and social crises within Russia itself. Even if the gravest forms of crisis, as well as the national and territorial conflicts they are fueling, are surmounted, transition to democracy and a healthy market economy is still going to be painful and protracted. In a number of CIS states, the formation of foreign policy is being affected by ostentatious dissociation from Russia, so typical of the initial stages of state-making, as well as by territorial disputes fueled by nationalist sentiments, including claims to Russia, and by an aversion to anything that is a reminder of their past dependence on the union structures. Some time will pass before these states realize that resolution of their national problems can be facilitated if they choose to rely on their ties with the renewed Russia. Moreover, in their search for their own place within the global community, some of these states, particularly those located in the Asian part of the former USSR, are seeking to rely on the nations close to them in ethno-social, religious and economic respects, including those that historically competed with Russia for influence in the region. Thus, we are faced with a complex process by which Russia's geopolitical environment is being formed. The outcome of this process will largely be determined by our ability to firmly assert the principles of international law, including respect for minority rights, and to establish good-neighborly relations through persuasion or even—in extreme cases— by using power methods.

Relying on their modern scientific and technological achievements, the leading industrialized western nations have been rapidly building up their economic and financial muscle, and their political influence in the world. With the end of the Cold War, there has been a dissipation of the "western solidarity" that prevailed in the conditions of confrontation, and this has led to more evident manifestations of geopolitical and economic controversies among the developed nations. However, as far as key issues of global development (the market economy and civil society) are concerned, the western powers maintain a considerable similarity of interests and are striving to develop common approaches to political, military, economic and other spheres, not only among themselves, but also with the democratic Russia.

The West is ceasing to be a military and political concept in the conventional power sense. It rather remains one of the major centers of the world economy and international affairs, as well as of the global civilizing process.

Though not without some difficulties, integration mechanisms are undergoing development, including in Western Europe, which is proving to be an increasingly independent global player. Another characteristic process will be the struggle between the polycentrism of world politics (the USA, Western Europe, Japan, and states claiming the roles of regional leaders) and the USA's ambition to maintain its dominance, even though the basis for this—the military potential designed for the confrontation with the USSR—is losing its relevance, given the end of the Cold War.

A group of Central and Eastern European nations that have overcome totalitarianism are faced with very complicated political, economic, and social problems. The difficulties of the transitional period have stimulated the revival of nationalism, and brought about social crises, the effects of which are felt beyond the borders of those states. The transition to democracy and the market economy is complicated by such phenomena, and it is likely that at least the next decade will be marked by instability and grave crises.

A complex search for a new political identity is going on. Along with the draw of the West that prevails in the region, and the attempts to gain security guarantees by joining the Western European integration structures as full or associate members, there is a tendency to seek to restore relations with Russia on a new basis, because the rupture of these ties, especially in the economic sphere, has aggravated the difficulties associated with overcoming the crisis, establishing the mechanisms of the market economy, and modernizing the economy.

The differentiation among the countries of the "Third World" has intensified. Some of them failed to embark on the path of economic development that would have ensured their internal stability and growing prestige in the global arena. The majority of them are increasingly falling behind the leading industrialized, developed powers. Given its grave social and economic, national and civilizational problems, the "Third World" is turning into the main locus of global and regional threat in the coming decades. Russia's interests and security will inevitably be affected by the danger of armed conflict with its destructive impact on international stability, by any arms race, including any attempts to gain access to weapons of mass destruction and means of their delivery, by outbursts of social and ethnic confrontation, by terrorism, drug trafficking, mass starvation and epidemics, all of which are global threats.

For all the multifaceted nature of the current developments, the coming decades will be marked by an increasing gap between the industrialized North and the backward South, by eruptions of hostilities along the South-South line, and by crises and conflicts brought about by social and economic, as well as ethnic issues experienced by the post-totalitarian regimes and poorest developing countries.

Therefore, the leading world powers or groups of powers will tend to rearrange the political structures of global affairs, and emerging regional powers will increasingly strive to secure their own spheres of influence, including by means of exerting power pressure.

The interaction of these factors will mandate a historically rapid change in the global situation that will be largely characterized by:
- dissipation of the global bipolar structure;
- multitrack international politics as a result of the dissolution of the global bipolar structure;
- the emergence of regionally centered power relations.

The end of the Cold War will not in itself bring about stabilization in the world arena. Military and power factors will continue to play a considerable role in the world. The devaluation of military might at the global level is accompanied by a tendency toward a gradual intensification of its importance at the regional and local levels. Power approaches remain crucial in provoking and escalating conflicts. Correspondingly, force will retain its consequential significance in resolving conflicts, as well as in the entire practice of regulating international relations. Russia takes all these realities into consideration both as a great power, responsible—along with other permanent members of the UN Security Council—for maintaining international peace and security, and as a state that bears the main burden of peacekeeping activities within the CIS.

As a matter of principle, Russia advocates exclusion of military force from the arsenal of world politics. When the security of a country and its citizens is in danger, or when it could prevent aggression or some other threat to international peace and security, Russia will accept the use of force in strict compliance with the UN Charter and other norms of international law, including within the framework of operations for peacekeeping and peacemaking.

The key aspects of future national and international development are increasingly determined by social and economic categories. Moreover, the place that states will occupy in the world will depend very largely on how readily their economies absorb scientific and technological achievements—something that is best attained in conditions of democracy and market economy. It is these factors that have a more decisive impact on the efficiency of the armed forces today than ever before.

It is vital that Russia's foreign policy be guided not by ideological stances or parties' needs, but by fundamental national interests. We must steer a decisive course towards developing relations with those nations whose cooperation with Russia may be instrumental in resolving the primary tasks of our national revival, i.e. above all with our neighbors, economically and technologically developed western states, and new industrialized countries in various regions.

Russia and this group of nations share the core values of world civilization and have the same interests in the key issues of global development, particularly peacekeeping and security, promotion of the Russian reforms, ensuring stability in the regions undergoing post-totalitarian social rearrangement, prevention of global destabilizing effects of existing problems, and the "Third World."

It is of prime importance that we can see the limits to any cooperation. Even with many interests that coincide, approaches to specific matters may differ and may even sometimes be opposite. The route of interaction must bring about a rise in our own standing; agreement on a particular issue cannot be an end in itself—still less can it represent a "payment" for help. Cooperation with anybody should develop to the extent, and in ways, that Russia's own long-term interests are met.

Relations with other states, freed from self-righteous ideological schemes, must evolve with consideration for the needs of our reforms, and for the significance of these reforms for the country's security in the new conditions. By retaining all that is rational in bilateral political, economic and cultural ties, and by filling them with new content that is relevant in the present-day realities, as well as by developing relations with those countries formerly outside our active policies, Russia is protecting its interests and gaining greater freedom to select foreign policy alternatives. Moreover, the prior conditions are thus being created for the country's growing stature in the world arena.

Foreign Policy Priorities and Principles

The goal of upholding the country's national interests is the conceptual core of Russia's foreign policy. It is within this fundamental task that the following key priorities can be formulated:

- use of political means to ensure Russia's security in all dimensions, including sovereignty, independence and territorial integrity, strengthening of stability along the Russian borders, in the regions closest to home, and in the world as a whole;
- protection of the rights, dignity and well-being of the Russian citizens;
- ensuring favorable external conditions for enhancing democratic reforms by way of promoting civil society;
- mobilization of financial and technological support to build an efficient market economy, develop the competitive strength of Russian manufacturers and secure their interests in the world markets, and assist in resolution of internal social problems;
- building fundamentally new, equal, and mutually beneficial relations between Russia, the CIS states, and other countries of the near abroad, maintaining the strategic course toward partnership and allied relations with those countries of the traditional far abroad that have most helped in resolving those problems that Russia is currently faced with;
- securing Russia's role as a great power within the global balance of influence, in such multilateral processes as regulation of the global economy and international affairs.

Russia rejects double standards and indiscriminateness in choosing the means of pursuing a policy. Russia's foreign policy activities are based strictly on the observance of international law, adherence to the principles of the UN Charter and the CSCE, including inviolability of borders and the territorial integrity of states. Borders can be changed in compliance with international law, in a peaceful way or by agreement.

Russia does not regard any state as *a priori* hostile or friendly. Instead it strives to build the most friendly and mutually beneficial relations with all states, and promotes resolution of disputes and conflicts by political means.

The Russian Federation believes that the best way of creating a belt of security and good-neighborly relations along its borders is to have comprehensive stabilization in the geopolitical space around Russia, and a zone of constructive regional cooperation. To this end, Russia intends—when pursuing its foreign policy—to make as much use as possible of the potential of those Russian regions that are linked with this space in the functional and geographic senses.

As a successor state of the former USSR, Russia exercises the rights and obligations it inherited in the world arena. In consultation with the CIS participants, Russia assists them in exercising the former USSR's rights and obligations insofar as these rights and obligations fall under their jurisdictions.

Key Areas of Foreign Policy Activities

Russia's geopolitical situation dictates the need to conduct an active, pragmatic, and balanced policy in many areas.

Therefore, it is not merely possible, but also necessary, to select priorities in accordance with the specifics of the current situation.

I. COUNTRIES OF THE COMMONWEALTH

The issue of Russia's relations with the Commonwealth states and other countries of the near abroad is directly linked with the fate of the Russian reforms, and the prospects for overcoming the crisis in the country and ensuring the well-being of Russia and Russian citizens. The establishment of economic and transport communications on a new footing, the resolution of conflicts and maintenance of stability along the perimeter of our territory are the most important conditions for the adequate development of Russia and the efficient implementation of its foreign policy in the far abroad.

Russia's links with this group of countries must be raised to the level of fully-fledged interstate relations that will ensure thriving, mutually beneficial cooperation with them in all spheres.

The resolution of conflicts and the creation of conditions that will help prevent the emergence of conflicts are our long-term mission. In order to carry out this mission, we have to employ bilateral forms of mediation and peacekeeping by Russia first of all, as well as multilateral mechanisms within the CIS, including with the support and—when needed—the sanctioning of these efforts by the UN, CSCE, EU, etc. The task to protect the outer CIS borders represents another urgent assignment. Without implementation of this task it is impossible either to insure the internal security of the CIS states, or to combat criminal activities, including drug trafficking, smuggling of weapons and other forms of crime that destabilize society.

Along with the other former USSR republics, Russia fully acknowledges its obligation towards our peoples and the world community to safeguard stability, human rights and freedoms within the former USSR, and to fulfill our international agreements.

While forming new relations with the countries of the near abroad, we must combine full-fledged development of bilateral ties with enhancement of diverse multilateral forms of interaction.

In order to achieve these purposes Russia will:

1. Seek transformation of the Commonwealth into an effective interstate formation of sovereign entities of international relations, based on the commonality of their interests and their voluntary participation in various forms of cooperation. It is in Russia's interests that the set of mutual obligations within the CIS should cover the greatest achievable number of various spheres of international affairs, and involve the broadest possible circle of participants. However, the principal criterion remains the voluntary nature of participation, which guarantees the durability and efficiency of the Commonwealth. A slower but steady progressive advance towards the chosen goal is more reliable than hastily reached accords that do not take account of realities, and therefore will not work.

2. Promote transformation of the Commonwealth and the forums created within its framework into mechanisms for political interaction between the participant states, and into a way to harmonize policies and identify common interests.

3. Seek improvement and expansion of the contractual and legal framework of the Commonwealth as a regional international organization, and particularly the final elaboration and adoption of the Charter, establishment of the Executive Secretariat, and resolution of the problems pertaining to the creation of a Collective Security Council, the promotion of the idea of a Council for Consulting and Coordination, and the formation of CIS peacekeeping forces.

    Russia advocates a flexible multi-speed approach to the forms of organization and operation of the Commonwealth that would allow, should some partners not be prepared to cooperate in certain spheres, for the development of enhanced interaction among only those CIS states interested in it.

    The level of efficiency of multilateral accords will increase if they are based on an adequate legal infrastructure for Russia's bilateral ties with each CIS member, and if they take into account specifics and priorities within particular areas of the European, Central Asian and Transcaucasian segments of the Commonwealth.

    Taking into consideration the significance of our relations with Ukraine, Belarus and Kazakhstan, we must seek to reach full-fledged political treaties with these states at the first opportunity.

4. Promote implementation of effective agreements on cooperation in the sphere of security.

    One urgent task is to strengthen our common military-strategic space. Russia believes that it is vital to ensure common centralized administrative and operational control over nuclear armaments. Since it regards any kind of division of the controlling functions as contravening the principles of the nonproliferation regime, and stability enhancement at both regional and global levels, Russia will seek to promote these tenets on the basis of the effective international accords concluded in this sphere.

Linked with this process, the issue of Russia's military presence must be resolved, including problems pertaining to withdrawal and deployment of the Russian military, and agreement on bilateral military cooperation or coordination of actions.

5. Seek preservation of a viable structure of economic relations, the resolution of problems pertaining to monetary exchanges, the legal regulation of economic ties between regions, as well as between Russian enterprises and their partners from other near-abroad states.

6. Seek to reach agreements and treaties with each former USSR republic with a view to safeguarding the rights of Russian citizens residing beyond the territory of the Federation, based on reciprocity and in full compliance with the norms of international law. Russia will seek to advance agreements on these issues on a multilateral basis within the CIS, and seek to involve the UN, CSCE and other international organizations in resolving these issues.

7. Assist in the maintenance and enhancement of scientific and technological cooperation, as well as cultural exchanges on a multilateral and bilateral basis. Given its mighty scientific and technological potential, Russia can and must become an attractive center for other CIS participants, on the understanding that the potentials in question are employed in civil spheres.

8. Develop interaction in the areas involving safeguarding law and order, fighting crime and drug trafficking, providing legal aid in criminal and civil legal cases as a prerequisite for overcoming the crises in Russia and the "near-abroad" countries.

Achieving these goals meets Russia's long-term interests. However, our partners must realize: it would be a mistake to believe that, by putting forward these suggestions, we mean to claim the role of a new Commonwealth "center" for Russia, or that the relevant Russian interests are so vital that we are prepared to pay any price in order to uphold them. The objective reality is this: reciprocal interests are involved here, and—while agreeing to compromises to resolve emerging problems—Russia will not make unilateral concessions in order to develop relations; it will not accept damage to its national interests, or encroachment on the rights of ethnic Russians abroad.

If any near-abroad states commit actions that infringe Russia's interests, or fail to fulfill the obligations they undertake, Russia will seek ways to protect its interests, of course in compliance with the norms of international law, using the capacities of the UN, CSCE and other international organizations, and—if need be—resorting to countermeasures of its own.

The success of the suggested policy will depend, in particular, on the approaches that third countries assume towards the Commonwealth. The world's leading democratic powers are interested in ensuring stability within the geopolitical space of the former USSR, and they acknowledge the importance of Russia and the policy it pursues in maintaining this stability. Moreover, they recognize the need to enhance this role. This does not mean they will not strive to gain advantages of their own, particularly in the economic sphere. However, the extent of the inherent commonality of the long-term interests allows Russian foreign policy sufficient room for maneuver.

The states in adjacent regions are pursuing their own policies conspicuously aimed at taking advantage of the disintegration of the USSR to reinforce their own positions, and in some cases to carry out their plans to form broad communities, under national or religious banners, that would include former Soviet republics. On the one hand, implementation of these plans may damage Russia's security and its economic interests. This process may bring about political and social conditions that would trigger mass emigration by ethnic Russians from the former Soviet republics into the territory of Russia per se.

On the other hand, the tendency in question appears to be inevitable, as it is a part of objective developments ongoing on a global scale. It is not an unambiguously negative tendency. Expansion of relations, and enhancement of the positions of third countries in cooperation with the former Soviet republics may assist economic development in these republics, which will, in turn, entail perceptible advantages for Russia, since our economies remain interdependent.

Therefore, in each individual case, the Russian Foreign Service should measure the potential damage to Russia against possible advantages the country may gain. However, if the disadvantages Russia will face are significant, political and diplomatic countermeasures may be undertaken, including in partnership with the West, especially if regional and global stability is shown to be under threat.

Relying on international law and employing its potential for partnership with the leading democratic countries of the world, Russia will actively oppose any attempts to enhance the military-political presence of third states in the countries adjacent to its territory.

II. Arms control and international security

The end of the East-West confrontation has virtually dispelled the prospect of any possible outburst of a full-fledged or premeditated military conflict. At the same time, there are still risks connected with the presence of powerful military infrastructures, as well as challenges engendered by the new global situation, particularly the danger of the uncontrolled escalation of regional conflicts in the zones of instability, and the threat of proliferation of weapons of mass destruction and means of their delivery.

With this in mind, the following tasks arise:

- to enhance the process of conversion of the international security system—at both regional and global scales—from being founded on the principles of stand-off between blocs, to relying on the tenets of cooperation involving joint efforts by different states to maintain stability by political means. Russia will seek relevant international legal accords on the issues of arms limitation and disarmament, as well on enhancing mutual understanding, trust and partnership with the leading world powers, and in particular interaction with the western defense authorities;

- to bring the military potential into line with the new conditions, remove from our arsenals those weapons that are not required by exigency (intercontinental weapons exceeding specific quantities, conventional arsenals exceeding quantities stipulated in the existing treaties and agreements) and whose very maintenance is a burden on our economy and poses a threat of accidental or unsanctioned use;

- to maintain the remaining armaments at a level that is sufficient for defense, and that will ensure the containment of potential threats, both along the perimeter of our territory and in the far abroad, especially taking into account the risk of the proliferation of weapons of mass destruction and means of their delivery. Russia's reformed military potential will remain a significant factor in protecting the country's vital interests in the foreseeable future.

The goals and the specific measures employed to achieve these goals, as contained in a formulated and agreed national security concept, must comply with the course of Russia's military reform and be congruent with the country's economic and social capacities.

In the nearest future, the key areas of the disarmament process will involve:

1. Implementation of the agreements achieved in the area of conventional and nuclear weapons reductions; at the same time, efforts will be undertaken to ease the financial burden associated with the reduction and monitoring.

2. Fulfillment of the provisions of the Russian–US START-2 Treaty once it is ratified: further elaboration of the President's initiative to build a global defense system against ballistic missiles and other means of delivery of weapons of mass destruction, including by involving other important military powers in the plan's implementation.

3. Appropriation by Russia of full control over the nuclear forces of the former USSR by withdrawing the means to its territory and subsequently destroying them. Practical implementation of the existing agreements on the nonnuclear status of Ukraine, Belarus, and Kazakhstan, their accession to the Nuclear Nonproliferation Treaty as non-nuclear states, and the establishment under the CIS framework of a system for control over nonproliferation.

4. Russia's joining the Missile Technology Control Regime as an equal participant.

5. Completing the work to enact the Chemical Weapons Convention; removing all concerns over the observance of the Biological Weapons Convention.

6. Continuing dialogue with the purpose of comparing the military doctrines of Russia and its main partners, above all the USA, by way of common acceptance at the functional level of the notion that they no longer regard each other as enemies.

7. Further efforts aimed at a considerable limitation of nuclear tests, with the final goal of their comprehensive and total ban.

8. Coordination of multilateral agreements on the principles governing arms exports, which would assist in safeguarding stability, while attending to Russia's legitimate commercial interests; elaboration of an internal legal basis providing for the control over arms deliveries in the new economic conditions; improvement of the system for export control and for licensing the trade in weapons.

9. Assisting elaboration and implementation of the program for conversion of the defense industry, including by launching relevant international interaction and attracting foreign investment.

10. Ensuring fulfillment of the intergovernment agreement "On coordination of export control of raw materials, equipment, technologies, and services that can be used for the development of weapons of mass destruction and their missile delivery systems" (signed by Russia, Armenia, Belarus, Kazakhstan, Kyrgyzstan, Tajikistan, Uzbekistan, Ukraine). Establishment of working bodies to conduct practical interaction between the CIS participants in this sphere.

11. Achieving greater transparency in the military sphere, including with regard to defense budgets, elaboration of further measures for stabilization, confidence-building and transparency within the CSCE framework.

12. Coordination and implementation of the plans for cooperation in 1993 with NATO and the North Atlantic Cooperation Council, intensification of contacts on a bilateral and multilateral basis; interaction with NATO agencies to address the issues of strengthening peace and security by means of developing political contacts, military ties, exchange visits, conducting joint maneuvers, sharing experience, and interacting in resolving crises.

III. PROMOTING ECONOMIC REFORM

Formation of an efficient and dynamically developing economy in Russia, an economy that would be organically integrated into the world economy, is the key condition for the survival of the country and the salvation of the nation. Without its economic revival, Russia cannot become an equal member of the great powers' club of the late 20th and early 21st centuries, and therefore it will be difficult for Russia to protect its own interests and the interests of its citizens in the international arena.

We need to act within three areas:

- First, the scientific and technological potential available in the military branches, which is comparable to that possessed by the western powers but, unlike the latter, is virtually isolated from the civilian sector of the economy, should be reoriented so as to be employed for civil needs.
- Second, broad international cooperation should be established to allow Russia access to foreign expertise, technology, and investments.
- Third, Russia will seek to establish favorable conditions for international trade, gain access to the world markets for its domestic products, and support Russian business.

All these should help the Russian economy integrate into world economic exchanges in an internationally competitive form that will ensure rational use of the country's industrial, and scientific and technological potentials.

Of crucial importance is a policy that supports scientific research and education, preserves the nation's intellectual potential and the intelligentsia, including those engaged in the technological production. This particular stratum has proven most vulnerable in the conditions of the emerging market economy. And it is this stratum that is of vital significance for the country's revival. If this nation loses its intellectuals, the market mechanism may acquire a conspicuous comprador nature, and the restoration and development of science-intensive production may take at least a whole generation.

Foreign policy should create the conditions necessary to resolve these tasks, by bringing about a dramatic easing of the country's military expenditure burden, carrying through conversion-related cooperation projects, attracting external support and foreign capital to carry out market reforms and resolve social problems, modernizing environmentally damaging enterprises, and eliminating barriers in the way of scientific and technological accomplishments, preferential loans and investments, and the search for practical ways to resolve the problems both of Russia's foreign indebtedness and the repayment of debts owing to it by foreign states.

Immediate attention should be paid to the following spheres:

1. Preservation and development of a single economic space on the former USSR territory, including the formation of a new contractual and legal framework for economic exchanges among the CIS states and other "near-abroad" states; progress in coordination of economic policy; creating stimuli for interaction of businesses in the former Soviet republics so that these states' economies might reintegrate on a new market-economy basis.
2. Implementation of existing accords—and conclusion of new ones—with international economic organizations and western governments concerning expert

assistance in carrying through our social and economic reforms, and providing consultancy and logistical support for Russian enterprises and associations at the stage they enter the market.

3. Working with the leadership of the International Monetary Fund and the World Bank in order to ensure timely and complete realization of declared programs for providing loans to Russia; interaction with the G-7 group, the EU, Organization for Economic Cooperation and Development, and other associations; mobilization of direct foreign investment in the Russian economy; use of foreign experience for the legislative and organizational provision of external investment.

4. The country's participation in the most significant programs of scientific and technological cooperation (Eureka, World Laboratory, International Scientific and Technological Center, International Thermonuclear Experimental Reactor, and others).

5. Political and diplomatic support for the entry by Russian manufacturers into world markets, and observance by our businesses of the rules operating in these markets.

6. Overcoming of the crisis in Russia's economic relations with Eastern European countries, and transition to a gradual enhancement of large-scale economic cooperation on a new footing (creation of a new contractual and legal framework addressing the development of new forms of trade, as well as entrepreneurship activities, including investment; formation of a market infrastructure for cooperation, involving international associations, stock exchanges, banks and other organizations).

7. Enhancement of Russia's relations with the most developed Asian, African, and Latin American countries; preservation of the existing potential for cooperation in the "Third World," including completing the construction, effective exploitation, modernization and expansion of the establishments launched by the former USSR as part of technological cooperation; active involvement of Russian business structures in market activities in developing countries, facilitation of Russian business structures' access to investment resources in developing countries by wiping out these countries' debts to Russia, if the debts cannot be paid in other ways.

8. Russia's participation in the existing and emerging regional economic associations, in particular within the frameworks of the Black Sea and Baltic economic cooperation pacts, as well as Asia Pacific Economic Cooperation (APEC), and others.

Whether the proposed goals are achieved or not will depend on the consistency with which the reforms are carried out in Russia itself. We can count on assistance in undertaking the above-mentioned measures from the leading western powers and our other foreign partners that are interested in Russia's stable development. This does not rule out possible disagreements with regard to specific issues in the areas where Russian manufacturers are competitive (space technologies, arms exports, etc.). In these spheres, Russia's interests require adequate political protection by diplomatic means on the basis of international legal norms.

Russia's status as a world leader in space technologies must be upheld. This task can be accomplished through adequately oriented international cooperation in the sphere of space exploration and its use for peaceful purposes, as well as by enhancing the commercial aspects of our activities in space.

Russia must become an active participant in international arms export treaties that would combine conventional commercial requirements with the needs of global stability. In particular, this requires agreements to be reached on limiting and banning arms exports to zones of instability, limiting the export of essentially offensive arms, the strict observance of embargoes imposed by a UN Security Council resolution, and so on.

On the whole, economic foreign policy must represent an inherent part of Russia's policy on the international scene. Therefore, economic foreign policy must be effectively coordinated within a general foreign policy that seeks to uphold the country's national interests and priorities in international affairs.

IV. THE USA

Our relations with the USA will, for the foreseeable future, remain a top priority for Russia's foreign policy, due to the status and weight of the United States in international affairs. Development of full-fledged relations with the USA can facilitate the creation of a favorable environment for conducting internal economic reforms in Russia.

Of course, there are forces in the USA that are skeptical of the prospects for the Russian–US partnership. However, the prevailing opinion supported by the two parties favors enhancement of cooperation with Russia.

This policy is determined by the US national interests, which are not susceptible to internal political fluctuations. However, there are constraining factors too: rather powerful neo-isolationist sentiments within American society, the inertia of suspicious attitudes to Russia, the US budget deficit, and the unfavorable investment climate in Russia.

In the strategic military sphere, the partnership that has started, and the establishment of common (rather than "counterpoised") security instruments, is likely to encounter attempts by the US rightist conservative forces to safeguard their unilateral advantages in the process of disarmament, and to have the ABM Treaty revised on their terms. Evidently, cooperation in the sphere of conversion of the military industry will not be easy, because preservation of Russia's military technological potential runs counter to the interests of the US military-industrial complex. When addressing international problems, our interaction with the USA is likely to focus primarily on the conflict situations along the Russian borders. We cannot rule out possible US attempts to turn to its advantage its mediation and peacekeeping efforts and to appropriate Russia's role in the countries of Russia's traditional influence.

Our active stance in strengthening the Russian–US ties, punctilious observance of the obligations we have undertaken, and effectiveness in implementing the coordinated plans will counteract these phenomena, and will build up a social basis in the USA that will provide support for constructive tendencies in relations between us, and reinforce the foundations for a long-term policy favoring partnership with Russia.

Based on our accords in the military and political, financial and economic spheres, Russia will promote steady development of relations with the USA, with a view to strategic partnership, and—eventually—to an alliance. At the same time, it is necessary to firmly resist the USA's possible relapses into a policy of imperial ambitions, or any attempt to embark on a policy of turning the USA into a "sole superpower."

Absence of antagonistic disagreements in our relations with the USA does not imply the complete absence of controversies. However, the existing disagreements will not lead to confrontation, if the sides consider the commonality of their long-term national interests and adhere to a realistic course.

It is crucial for us not to allow a pause in our relations when a new US administration enters office. It is important to avoid the impression that the Russian–US dialogue can progress "by default." We must immediately assume an active, assertive stance, and take the initiative if possible. We must start elaborating a "new agenda" for Russian–US interaction. And we have already done some work in this respect. What we have is a result of the positive outcome of our work with the previous US administration, and this has been strengthened, in particular, in the course of the first personal contacts between the President of the Russian Federation and the newly elected US President.

It is important that we enhance the policy we have embarked on. And yet, the expansion of our interaction and development of our partnership must not undermine Russia's independent role. Moreover, it must not damage Russia's interests, and it must be developed based on thorough consideration of our priorities.

The essence of the new agenda in the economic sphere lies in setting up a model for partnership that will aid the successful implementation of our reforms and promote the establishment of economic exchanges that will allow us broader scope for our foreign economic maneuver, without getting us involved in most of the critical controversies characteristic of the trade and economic "war" among the world's leading economic centers.

In particular, we mean to focus our efforts on the following areas to ensure

US support for economic transformations in Russia within the framework of existing accords.

We will encourage the Americans to lend us active support at the international negotiations on the USSR's foreign debts; we will seek the lifting of all remaining discriminatory restrictions, and will seek a cardinal turn in their attitude to relations with us in the scientific and technological sphere, with an emphasis on development of conversion technologies; we will endeavor to develop a joint strategy to open up our markets to one another and will strive to pursue this strategy in practice; we will seek the US government's unambiguous support for Russia within the G-7 group.

The main feature of the new partnership in the sphere of security is a transition to cooperation at the level of military planning and military construction. When resolving specific problems (e.g. the elimination of weapons of mass destruction, or peacekeeping operations), it is appropriate to integrate the efforts of the Russian and US defense sectors.

The following steps should be highlighted as of primary significance: to ensure conditions suitable for implementation of the START-1 and START-2 treaties; to enhance development of realistic parameters for a global defense system; to set out on a practical path the accords on cooperation for the safe elimination of nuclear and chemical weapons; to reach agreement on a mutual regime of strict limits on the number and yield of nuclear tests; to propose to the USA that a joint program should be developed for coordinated efforts, with a view to preventing proliferation of weapons of mass destruction, ballistic missiles and—especially—potentially hazardous technologies.

In the political sphere, launching partnership relations with the USA will allow us to be more decisive in claiming respect for our specific interests and concerns, including conducting joint actions for resolving international crises.

The top priority is to have America acknowledge Russia's leading role as the engine for market reform and guarantor of democratic transition within the post-Soviet space, to actively involve the USA in resolving conflicts and protecting human rights in the CIS and Baltic states.

V. EUROPE

Russia's relations with the European countries—both at the bilateral level and within various international organizations and forums—are of huge consequence for Russia's incorporation into the community of democratic states, and for ensuring security in the new environment.

Russia's practical policy with regard to European affairs should be built with an eye to the qualitatively new stage of development that the continent is entering at present.

This stage is characterized by two interwoven tendencies: towards the formation of a close European community, on the one hand, and—on the other hand—towards the emergence of a number of new challenges, with many of these representing serious threats to the traditionally high level of stability in European countries and to the general positive vector of development in the region. Among these challenges are: the increasing general conflict-proneness, the aggravation of ethno-political controversies, difficulties in the process of western European integration, a crisis of federalism, the lack of clarity in the shaping of a new power balance on the continent, the complications inherent in building a common Europe, the upholding of international regulatory legal instruments relevant to contemporary European developments.

These, alongside the remaining problems of Russian internal development, pose a danger of mutual alienation between Russia and Europe.

In the rapidly changing European context, it is of prime importance for us to build balanced stable relations with all European states, to maintain positive developments that enhance European integration. We should, as far as possible, stand aside from those controversies between individual countries that do not affect our own interests. Nevertheless, such controversies may be used to enhance Russia's status, provided this causes no damage to the sides or groups involved. Any attempt to gain advantage from those disagreements involving European affairs of fateful importance may prove counterproductive and could provoke anti-Russian sentiments that would impede the promotion of Russia's interests in Europe.

WESTERN EUROPE. Our key goal in this region is to safeguard the emerging partnership relations, fill these relations with specific content that would allow us to employ the new ties with Western Europe in order to strengthen Russia's security, resolve problems of internal development, incorporate Russia's economy on an equal basis into the European market and global economy. The constructive development of relations between the Russian Federation and Western European nations would create a positive atmosphere on the continent, which would enhance the formation of good-neighborly relations with Eastern European and Baltic states on a new footing. This approach is generating favorable feedback from Western European states, which logically regard Russia's development towards democracy as a guarantee of the continent's security and a crucial factor in overcoming crises in the entire post-Soviet geopolitical space.

Here are our priorities in Western European affairs:

1. Finalizing negotiations in order to agree and conclude a treaty with the European community concerning the development of relations in all spheres, including politics; formation of an efficient mechanism for cooperation (regular political consultations, establishment of joint commissions and parliamentary working groups, etc.); active application of European development experience in the interests of resolving the CIS's formative problems.

2. Establishment of permanent stable contacts with the Western European Union through political dialogue, exchanges of delegations, elaboration of conversion programs, studying possibilities for the WEU's participation in the system of global protection against ballistic missiles.

3. Further steps to ensure Russia's equal participation in the Council of Europe.

4. Deepening political interaction with Germany; carrying out the scheduled projects for cooperation in economic, scientific, and technological spheres; intensive expansion of bilateral ties; developing interaction under new geopolitical realities on the continent; resolving problems remaining in our bilateral relations.

5. Developing wide-ranging cooperation with France based on the existing Agreement, including through exchanges of experiences in economy regulation, conversion, price-formation, privatization, strengthening of the new legal foundations of our bilateral relations.

6. Transition from neutral partnership to a closer cooperation with the United Kingdom under the accords of the Russian–UK declaration "Partnership for the 1990s," the Agreement on principles of relations between the Russian Federation and the United Kingdom, and on the basis of practical fulfillment of the new contractual and legal basis pertinent to the relations between the two countries.

7. Enhancement of ties with the countries that command significant economic and technical potentials (Italy, Spain, Portugal, Turkey, Greece, and others) and boast levers of influence over the situation in the regions vital for us; full-fledged development of relations with the Baltic nations (Denmark, Norway, Sweden, and Finland), including within the framework of the Council of the Baltic Sea States and the Barents Region Council, and—for this purpose—promotion of joint projects with the northern countries in the spheres of the economy, environmental protection, radiation safety, housing of the military personnel withdrawn from the Baltic states, and development of infrastructures.

EASTERN EUROPE does not merely retain its significance for Russia as a historically predetermined sphere of interest. The importance of maintaining good relations with the countries of the region became incomparably greater when the belt of sovereign states was formed: Ukraine, Belarus, Moldova, Lithuania, Latvia, and Estonia, for our relations with these states will inevitably be affected by the nature of our ties with Eastern Europe.

Russia adheres to an essentially new strategy of interstate relations with the Eastern European nations, which is now fully freed from the elements of imperial arrogance and egocentrism that were typical of the former USSR, but is based rather on the principles of equality and mutual advantage. This does not rule out the necessity to make every possible use of those positive ties in practical spheres of cooperation that were formed in previous years.

Our strategic task at present is to prevent the transformation of Eastern Europe into a sort of buffer belt that would isolate us from the West. On the other hand, we must not allow the impending displacement of Russia from the East European region by western powers. This is a task that can be carried out, especially in view of the fact that—despite the way they have of late noticeably and rather ostentatiously distanced themselves politically from Russia— the Eastern European states remain economically, and, to a considerable extent, also culturally, oriented towards Russia and the other CIS states.

Our principal goal is to strengthen those positive achievements that have been made, particularly at the highest level, to restore mutual trust, and establish equal non-ideological relations with the Eastern European nations. Of especial importance are measures aimed at reviving our economic ties. We should conclude agreements concerning the procedures for regulating our payment interaction, and repayment of our accumulated debts, all of which would facilitate interaction between participants of economic relations, their exchanges of goods, capital, technologies, etc.

As far as particular countries of the region are concerned:

1. We should continue our efforts to restore our bilateral ties with Albania; complete the preparation of the Russian–Albanian political document.

2. We will undertake measures to strengthen the breakthrough in our relations with Bulgaria, to secure the implementation of the principal accords reached during B. Yeltsin's visit, in order to restore full-fledged cooperation; prepare an intergovernmental agreement on cooperation in the sphere of education, scientific and cultural exchanges.

3. We will seek utmost realization of the accords with Hungary that were reached during B. Yeltsin's visit, including those concerning mutual financial settlement connected with the withdrawal of our troops, regulation of the problem of mutual debts, property disputes, as well as of other agreements that open opportunities for reaching a qualitatively new stage in Russian–Hungarian relations.

4. We will seek to ensure implementation of the agreements with Poland that were reached in the course of Polish President L. Walesa's visit to Moscow, and will strive to sign new accords, including one on cross-border cooperation.

5. We will finalize the preparation of our agreement on cooperation, friendship and good-neighborliness with Romania; continue our systematic work with the Romanian government to convince the Romanian leaders to assume a constructive stance with regard to the issues connected with the settlement of the situation in Moldova.

6. Since the Czechoslovakian Federative Republic was divided into two sovereign states, we will employ ties with the republican bodies and make provisions for interstate agreements with the Czech Republic and Slovakia.

7. Through interaction with the UN, CSCE, EU and other interested parties, we will continue taking an active part in the peacekeeping efforts in Yugoslavia, based—while planning specific steps—on a realistic evaluation of the developments there; carry out practical measures conditioned by the establishment of diplomatic relations with Serbia, Croatia, Slovenia, Herzegovina, and Macedonia, and develop political, economic and other ties with these states; start preparing corresponding bilateral agreements, taking account of the development of the crisis settlement; maintain a permanent channel of contact with the Federal Republic of Yugoslavia regarding ways to overcome the crisis.

BALTIC STATES. Establishing good-neighborly, mutually beneficial relations with the Baltic states meets Russia's long-term interests.

There is both a solid background and sufficient objective opportunities to achieve this goal. At the same time, we will have to exert some effort to find mutually acceptable solutions to urgent problems, such as protection of the rights of Russians and withdrawal of Russian troops, to create the climate of trust, and to establish agreeable interstate cooperation.

In order to reach these goals, we will first of all:

1. Seek to form a contractual and legal basis to embrace the entire range of our relations, to develop cooperation in the area of political dialogue and consultations.

2. While conducting interstate negotiations, continue actively to search for mutually acceptable settlement of the issues pertinent to the legal status of the Russian troops, and the schedule for their withdrawal. We will strive to retain those facilities of strategic importance to Russia; continue exerting efforts to mobilize the capacities of foreign countries, and the Baltic states, to address the economic aspects of the redeployment of Russian troops.

3. Seek to have the state border and customs checkpoints duly established.

4. Endeavor, during the talks, to ensure reliable access to transport thoroughfares and port capacities of the Baltic states, above all transport communication with the Kaliningrad region.

5. Firmly adhere to the policy aimed at providing civil and social rights to the Russian-speaking population of the Baltic states, and having these rights stipulated in corresponding interstate agreements; undertake steps to mobilize international official and public support for Russia's stance that, if necessary, it should resort to mechanisms of inspections and observers, in order to ensure appropriate responses to any violations of the rights of the

Russian-speaking population; seek to conclude accords addressing regulation of citizenship issues, rights of national minorities, social security, recognition of educational degrees, and resolution of other humanitarian questions.

6. Continue efforts aimed at creating mechanisms for cooperation in the trade and economic, scientific and technological spheres based on principles of equality, mutual advantage and balance of interests of the sides involved, in order to resolve economic problems, including in the sphere of energy production, communications, fishery, environmental protection, as well as the issues related to interaction and cooperation in the Kaliningrad zone of free entrepreneurship.

7. Employ mechanisms and resources of the Council of the Baltic Sea States, and the Barents Region Council in order to exert adequate influence in the Baltic states.

CSCE. With the increasing instability in the countries of Eastern Europe and the near-abroad states, there has been a dramatic growth in the importance of the Helsinki process as an essential factor in maintaining peace and security, and as a mechanism for constructive interstate cooperation in various areas in the entire space "from Vancouver to Vladivostok." At present, development of this process is the central channel for ensuring Russia's broad involvement in European affairs, as well as in the formation of the "Euro-Atlantic" and "Euro-Asian" communities.

It is in Russia's interests to promote the steady development of the CSCE process, to assist its further institutionalization, and its transformation into a defining component of the new, formative international community architecture in all its dimensions.

Russia's participation in the CSCE helps the country's integration into the European community, elimination of the dangerous hotbeds of instability, translation of Russia's partnership ties in Europe into specific measures and accords. This facilitates the task of adjusting Russian legislation to conform to international standards in those areas that are critically important for the fate of democracy, particularly in the spheres of human rights and national minorities. Full-fledged participation of Russia's CIS partners in the CSCE and their fulfilling all corresponding obligations would also meet Russia's interests.

For these purposes, we should:

1. Focus our efforts on implementing the Helsinki summit resolutions, developing the established mechanisms for political consultations and interaction: the Council, the Committee of Senior Officials, the Conflict Prevention Center, and the "Troika".

2. Promote application of the CSCE potential for settling critical situations, for the "early prevention" of impending conflicts, including through interacting with the CSCE High Commissioner on National Minorities, and for

maintaining coordinated mechanisms for investigation, reconciliation, arbitration, and implementation of peacekeeping missions.

3. Employ the CSCE bodies and mechanisms, international legal norms and principles in order to encourage our CIS partners to reach the common European standards in the areas of protection of human rights and fundamental freedoms; when necessary we will resort to the CSCE human dimension mechanism, including the Office for Democratic Institutions and Human Rights, and the High Commissioner on National Minorities, in order to protect the rights of Russian citizens and Russian-speaking populations.

4. Practice, when necessary, involvement of the CSCE institutions and bodies with the purpose of settlement of conflict situations in the territory of the former Soviet Union.

5. Take advantage of the CSCE Economic Forum that will open in March 1993 to work out resolutions that would assist transformation of the Russian economy into a free market economy, and its integration into the European and world economy.

While seeking to maintain Russia's role as an important component of the Helsinki security system, we should also strive to interact with NATO, and other military-political mechanisms of the West, as well as with the UN in the spheres of crisis and conflict prevention and settlement, and establishment of a reliable system of preventive diplomacy. Moreover, it is of critical importance to ensure the closest possible links with the EU, NATO, WEU and the formative CSCE security system.

We will also need to pay serious attention to transforming sub-regional organizations into components of security and cooperation in Europe, and preventing the misuse of sub-regional cooperation for the formation of counterpoised alliances, including those involving the CIS states. We will seek to ensure that Russia is directly involved in sub-regional cooperation, provided it conforms to the existing conditions and our interests.

VI. ASIA-PACIFIC REGION

Acquiring a firm position in the Asia-Pacific Region (APR), which has been rapidly transforming itself into a center of world politics and economy, comparable to the Atlantic region, would promote Russia's domestic reforms, enhance Russia's influence over the general political and economic developments in the world, and help fulfill its unique Euro-Asian potential.

The confrontational policy conducted in the past by the USSR and marked by ideological narrow-mindedness gave priority to military rather than civilian industries and thus led to a certain isolation of the country from the principal tendencies in regional development, in particular the dominant tendency of economic growth. Russia's Far East regions remained outside the integration processes ongoing in the Asia-Pacific region. Subsequently, apart from the negative economic outcomes, one internal political problem emerged, namely that of preserving and strengthening the integrity of our state, for isolationist sentiments have emerged in Siberia and the Far East.

Russia commands the following political resources for its incorporation into the APR and adaptation to the regional political, economic and international-legal realities:

- first, Russia's rejection of the "messianic" communist ideology and expansionism;
- second, possession of a significant military might that—if adapted to new conditions (i.e. if its size is rationally reduced, its mobility is increased, and its goals and missions are reconsidered)—can transform itself from a general "bully" into a factor ensuring regional stability and an effective foreign policy instrument;
- third, the economic, and scientific and technological potentials that are hardly employed so far;
- finally, fourth, the positive experience we have accumulated interacting with a number of the countries of the region.

Our policy in the APR must be based on the necessity to ensure Russia's independent role in the polycentric system of regional international relations. Of prime importance are balanced, stable, and, where possible, mutually independent relations between Russia and the APR countries, especially with the key nations, such as the USA, China, and Japan.

It is long overdue for Russia to embark on close cooperation with the USA within the APR, for we are united today by our adherence to common democratic values, and unconditional striving for stability in the region. It would be appropriate for Russia and the USA to share responsibility for ensuring security in the APR, to become strategic partners in the region, which is of no less potential importance for us than partnership in Europe. For this purpose, our military potential should be reoriented so as to ensure regional stability, and to create—in cooperation with the USA—reliable guarantees of common security. It is possible, in particular, to develop our cooperation with the USA based on the principle of complementarity, broad information exchanges, and coordinated political activities. Among possible spheres for cooperation are development of monitoring of actions undertaken by ambitious and unpredictable regimes, prevention of local conflicts and crises, fighting organized crime and drug trafficking.

In order to carry out a realistic transformation of our relations with China, we must take account of the differences in the ideologies and socio-political systems of the two countries, as well as presume that Russia has no alternative but to establish good-neighborly, intensive and extensive ties with China. The past confrontation with China cost the USSR (and China) too dear, and was one of the key reasons for our alienation from the region. Besides, through practicing multifaceted ties with Beijing, we could draw on Chinese experience in conducting our own economic reforms.

On the whole, relations with CHINA must be built in such a way that no third countries might be tempted to use China to Russia's detriment, and nor must China play "the Russian card" in its relations with other countries. Russia should adhere to a balanced and cautious policy that would allow us room for maneuver as regards those foreign policy issues that we have disagreements on. In the spheres of military and technological cooperation we should measure our commercial interests against our missions to maintain security in the region and prevent a revival of the Cold War situation, when the USA was providing weapons to Taiwan, while we were doing the same for communist China.

Our relations with JAPAN should be rearranged and filled with independent content. This world power must not be regarded exclusively through the prism of our relations with the USA, despite the remaining close mutual dependence of the two countries. We can hardly expect full-fledged cooperation with Japan unless we settle the issue of the post-war legacy of Russian–Japanese relations. Unless this is done, the process of Russia's acquiring a respectable status in the APR will be hindered, and the formation of partnership relations with the USA and the entire G-7 group will be impeded.

As one of the world's largest technological and financial centers, Japan is capable of becoming a sole sponsor of any state's development process. Even now, Japan is leading a number of new industrial countries of the APR, thus influencing the economic orientation of the region. Unless Russian–Japanese relations assume a new course that will meet both parties' interests, Japanese capital may not eventually flow to Russia.

The KOREAN PENINSULA represents a special interest in the context of Russia's policy in the APR. We adhere to the assumption that unification of the two Korean states will be in Russia's interests. First of all, unification would eliminate a hotbed of tension in direct proximity to our borders. Besides, the appearance of a new geopolitical unit—a united Korea—on the map could diversify international relations in the region, and thus expand the room for Russia's diplomatic maneuvering.

It is important that the process of the unification of the two Korean states remain within the framework of peaceful evolution. The natural development should not be interfered with, so that no uncontrollable outburst might occur. Russia's inevitable distancing from North Korea should be combined with the use of our remaining levers of influence in Pyongyang, in particular with a view to containing possible negative manifestations on its part, and above all its plans to create its own weapons of mass destruction.

We should enhance full-fledged ties with South Korea, which shares with us the core values of world civilization. There are promising prospects for Russian–South Korean relations, above all in the spheres of trade and the economy.

Russia's partnership with the USA, cooperation with Japan and the Republic of Korea do not imply that Russia will "dissolve" in their common policy. Instead, Russia should become an influential, distinctive, partner among the countries of the region as they tackle both global and regional problems. We should proceed on a realization that the independence of our presence in the APR conforms to the interests of the overwhelming majority of the regional states, since it expands their freedom in conducting their own foreign policies.

There is considerable potential in cooperation with the member countries of the ASSOCIATION OF SOUTH EAST ASIAN NATIONS (ASEAN), which are increasingly involved in both economic processes in the region and formation of the APR's political climate.

Russia's independent policy would prove very appealing to these countries if reinforced with a manifestation of our moral and political support for these states' fight against ultra-left extremism and terrorism. In terms of trade and economic exchanges, they can be interested in Russia as an exporter of science-intensive products and advanced technologies. In their turn, these countries may become our reliable importers of food products and household equipment.

When reorienting our relations with Mongolia and Vietnam, which used to be close allies of the former USSR, we must preserve rational cooperation with them, using the accumulated experience to establish equal trade and economic ties. As regards our relations with the countries of Indo-China, practical new approaches are needed that could be based on the considerable funds invested in these countries' economies by the former USSR and on their striving to develop market economies and join ASEAN. Our important task is to develop business with them.

Active participation in settling conflicts in the APR is also in Russia's interests. This would enhance Russia's status not only in the region but also globally. It is important that the APR nations perceive us as an honest and suitable partner that is prepared to contribute all its efforts for the common cause of stability and development.

In revising its general views of the APR and the structure of its relations in it, Russia has to master some new political levers. Indeed, we should take into account that the Asians are tired of our old approaches that boiled down to a pathological striving for "epochal initiatives" and to attempts to transfer the European experience into the region. Firm disagreement with this approach, if it remains in place even partially, will continue to deepen the regional players' perception of Russia as a purely European state that treats the APR as "outskirts" and whose policy in the region is formed according to a leftover principle.

It is also of major importance to cultivate in the Russians a national feeling of belonging in the Asia-Pacific Region, and to rid Russian public consciousness of the stereotypical perceptions of the Asia-Pacific Region as psychologically alien countries and peoples.

Well-balanced, moderate diplomacy aimed at developing mutually advantageous relations with all APR countries, and ensuring freedom for maneuver and the opportunity to choose an optimal policy for different scenarios of regional developments, would appear to be the most productive course that Russia could adopt in the APR in the near future (up to the end of the 20th century), as well as in the more distant future.

VII. SOUTH AND WEST ASIA

Of all the countries of the far abroad, those in South and West Asia are most important for us in terms of the extent of the direct influence they exert on the situation within the CIS, particularly in the Muslim countries of the Commonwealth.

There are a number of states in the region that are important in terms of geopolitical location and that have not developed an established foreign policy orientation yet. This represents a source of dangerous unpredictability and instability in the region, rendering vague the prospects of its general political development. Iran can be cited as an example. Having ceased to be a US partner, yet coming no closer to us, Iran represents a tangible factor of uncertainty in regional international affairs.

The region in question is directly linked with some internal conflicts in the CIS, which is clearly visible in the way Tajikistan is being directly influenced by Iran and Afghanistan. There is a particular danger that the Afghan and Tajik conflicts might merge into a single one due to the ethnic affinity of the peoples inhabiting the countries.

In South and West Asia, the struggle between fundamentalist and secularist tendencies is particularly acute. This gives an additional impulse to the idea of Islamic fundamentalism. It is this region that represents its principal channel for spreading further over the Muslim regions of Russia and the CIS.

The situation is aggravated by the fact that South and West Asia is directly adjacent to the Commonwealth's southern frontiers and—importantly for us—to those republics that have the least experience in foreign political activities. This directly affects our interests, exerting as it does a largely destabilizing influence over interethnic and inter-confessional relations within the CIS, complicating the development of the southern states of the Commonwealth, as well as the nature of interstate relations and the prospects for developing such relations with them.

All these circumstances require that we conduct a well-weighted and balanced foreign policy in the region, which would allow diverse actions to be taken.

Unlike in the time of the Cold War, in today's conditions we do not have clear criteria for aligning ourselves with one state or another. While preserving positive cooperation with our traditional partners, we must develop relations with all the countries of the region, aiming to strengthen our standing in this region that is so vital for us, and to neutralize any negative influence that the processes ongoing there may produce on the situation in Russia and the CIS.

Economic and geopolitical considerations require close ties with INDIA. Russia must conduct its policy taking into account India's significance as a country that asserts itself as a regional power and is our biggest trading partner among the developing nations. At the same time, we must also take into consideration the factor of the Indo–Pakistani confrontation that has grown traditional, has been affecting the entire region, and has rather vague prospects for settlement.

Our policy must not cause others to view it as profoundly pro-Indian. It must not become an obstacle for us in developing other ties, particularly with Pakistan. We do not imply that our policy must be artificially moderated so that abstract balanced relations with the two countries might be established. Our task is to boost our ties with Pakistan up to the same level as our relations with India, i.e. to render the two countries equally close to us, rather than equally distant from us. In general, our policy with regard to the two states, as well as to other countries of the region, must be subject to consistent pragmatic reconsideration, prompted by the sides' actual capacities and legitimate interests, and resting on economic stimuli.

Our policy with respect to AFGHANISTAN should be elaborated with account taken of the fact that the country is likely to have to undergo a lengthy period of nation-making, that the prospects for stabilization of the situation and for national reconciliation are rather indefinite, and that the danger of a split due to national-ethnic disagreements remains. Since the USSR withdrew its troops from Afghanistan, the conflict has not narrowed to become one of internal political significance. Rather, it is still of great international import and involves the leading Islamic countries of the region. Therefore, this conflict will preserve its destabilizing influence over Russia, with consequences that are hardly predictable. We are interested in the stabilization of the situation in the country, which to this end presupposes active diplomatic work in cooperation with all interested countries, but without engaging in Afghanistan's internal developments.

To a considerable extent, it is worth defining Russia's policy towards this country and other states of the region bearing in mind the humanitarian aspect of the Afghan problem, which is of the utmost importance for us, and particularly the task of getting our POWs released. At the same time, we should strive to rid our relationship of the burden of the past by renewing and developing our trade and economic ties based on pragmatic needs.

Relations with the Islamic countries in South and West Asia cannot be developed without taking into consideration their policy towards those CIS states and Russian regions that are populated by Muslims; nor can the rivalry among these countries for influence in the states of the near abroad be ignored. Given this, it is especially important for Russia to seek ways of interacting and cooperating in different ways with the various individual countries of the region in order to prevent the spread of fundamentalist Islamic tendencies and establish the idea of secularism in our Muslim near abroad.

In this respect, TURKEY is a priority for Russia, for it is more susceptible to western values, particularly due to its membership in NATO.

Friendly relations with Turkey are important for us, both since there is every prospect that they will become mutually advantageous in terms of trade and the economy, and because of the possible positive impact they might have on Russia's southern neighbors within the Commonwealth as they develop their civil societies.

With those countries of the region whose foreign policy orientation has not yet become established, it is desirable for us to develop our relations on a pragmatic basis, so that the regional balance of power and ideas may not be disturbed. It is important that Russia assumes an independent stance in this respect, in order to become a sort of "flying bridge" between the West and the region and use its geopolitical situation both in its own interests, and in the interests of developing interaction and cooperation in the Euro-Asian space.

It is of prime importance that our policy in South and West Asia should involve joint efforts with the USA and other interested countries to prevent the entry of nuclear weapons into this region. Now that the Cold War has ended, and with it the "ring" of Soviet–American confrontation that restrained the nuclear ambitions of a number of states, those states' desire to possess nuclear weapons may grow.

Russia will actively cooperate with all civilized countries that seek to prevent such a development.

VIII. MIDDLE EAST

Russia's attitude to the region is determined above all by the region's geostrategic and geopolitical significance, by the role that the local oil reserves play for the global energy balance, by the presence of considerable financial resources, and by its territorial proximity to the frontiers of Russia and the CIS, which carries with it the danger that the destabilizing developments of the region may have a direct effect on the Caucasus and Central Asia. Russia's long-term interests in the region consist in safeguarding its national security on its southern frontiers, preventing the negative effects that the conflict situations that are persisting and emerging in the region may have on interethnic and inter-confessional relations within the CIS, creating the conditions necessary for the development of mutually profitable trade and economic exchanges, and using the regional states' potential to support Russia's economic revival. These are the reasons why Russia needs to assume an active foreign policy stance in the Middle East.

The costs associated with these policies are incomparably lower than the political and economic losses that may ensue if we distance ourselves unduly from the region's problems and assume the posture of an onlooker.

Among Russia's primary concerns in the region is the stabilization of the situation in the Middle East. Therefore, we should continue our active efforts aimed at settling the Arab–Israeli conflict, getting the sides to reach mutually acceptable agreements, by making full use of our status as a co-sponsor of the peace process and by retaining our own role as an initiator of the settlement. To this end, it is important, in particular, to enhance our dialogue with both the Arabs and the Israelis. In our contacts with the Arab side, particularly with the Palestine Liberation Organization, it is sensible to assume that the best formula to resolve the political problem must be worked out during the negotiation process.

As regards any instances of destabilization of the situation in the region, Russia must adhere to its firm and principled position of counteracting, together with the world community, any attempts to violate the commonly accepted norms of international law, to firmly stand upon the principle of the inadmissibility of international terrorism. By remaining an honest and impartial arbiter, and by using its status as a permanent member of the UN Security Council and its bilateral contacts with the interested states, Russia can help them find just and lawful resolutions to the complex knots of disagreements, and thus assist in the establishment of the supremacy of political means in settling disputes— means that rule out the use of force. It would be a contribution to regional stability and to preventing any more incidents like the war between Iran and Iraq or Iraq's aggression against Kuwait, if a security system could be created in the Persian Gulf zone that is based primarily on the capacities of the states of the sub-region, is of an exclusively defensive nature, and does not target any specific country. The search for this strategic goal must be combined with acknowledgement of those military and political structures that are actually operating in the region, and with active cooperation with all the states of the Persian Gulf. It is important that such a system should not be oriented towards individual states, but should embrace a sufficiently broad framework that is acceptable to everybody and that allows our interests to be adequately taken into account.

In this context, it is important to continue taking part in elaborating international agreements that will help forestall the proliferation of weapons of mass destruction, missiles and missile technologies in the entire Middle East, and regulate deliveries of conventional arms, while taking account of Russia's commercial interests and the interests of promoting stability in the region.

The new circumstances dictate the need for an essential transformation of Russia's ties with the countries of the region, for unburdening these ties of ideological layers, and adjusting them to contemporary realities. As we adjust our links with our traditional partners in line with the new conditions, we must also seek multifaceted, mutually beneficial cooperation with those states that had been beyond the framework of our active policy. With sober consideration of the legitimate interests of the world community in the region, we should seek to deepen the interaction that we have here with the USA, Western Europe and other countries, and seek further enhancement of our cooperation and partnership with them, with strict regard for Russia's national interests.

The trade, economic and investment capacities of the countries of the region are of great interest to Russia. We must endeavor to attract spare Arab capital into key branches of industry and scientific research, and to use this capital to develop contemporary energy-saving technologies. In this respect, particular attention should be paid to developing cooperation with the Arab countries of the Persian Gulf. While developing contacts at the state level, it would be desirable to create preferential regimes for trade and economic exchange in the spheres of both private entrepreneurship and interstate cooperation.

The priority role played by the export of fuel and energy in the economies of the Persian Gulf states and Russia must be given greater consideration when determining Russia's foreign policy principles in the region, as this is a factor that opens up additional opportunities for dialogue and interaction and may be more efficiently used in order to solve our own problems in the fuel and energy sphere.

Within the framework of its new Middle East policy, Russia no longer faces any restrictions in developing its relations with ISRAEL. As we endeavor to form normal comprehensive ties with Israel, including political dialogue and economic cooperation, we must simultaneously measure these ties against the task of strengthening Russia's position in the region as a whole.

A flexible approach is required when dealing with those states that the USSR had concluded political accords with, including agreements on friendship and cooperation. We face the task of reviewing these agreements or replacing them with new ones that will be adequate for the new realities. However, we should solve this task gradually, in order to minimize the likelihood of losing those political and economic positions that we had acquired earlier in our relations with the states in question.

Special attention should be paid to the issue of debt repayment, both in the form of direct payments—wherever possible on schedule—and by way of goods deliveries, reinvestment in joint projects, and—in some cases—transfer to third countries.

The Muslim aspect of the Russian foreign policy in the region must be built with a view to favoring the spiritual revival of Muslims in Russia and other countries of the Commonwealth, to enhancing their contacts with their foreign coreligionists, while simultaneously counteracting the spread of any form of religious extremism to our territory.

IX. AFRICA

Given the process of de-ideologization of interstate relations and moving from confrontation to interaction in resolving "Third World" problems, the emphasis of Russia's foreign policy in Africa has been shifting to the sphere of mutually beneficial cooperation, consistent with our national interests and freed from any military-political bias. There is a necessary basis for such cooperation. Decades of multifaceted ties with many states on the continent have built up Russia's position there.

We must seek not only to preserve, but also to expand, those ties we have developed, consistently and resolutely providing them with a new basis. We must endeavor to establish multidimensional forms of cooperation with those countries that have been beyond the scope of our attention so far. Above all, we should make use of the opportunities available to develop relations with those countries that represent promising markets for purchases of Russian products (the Republic of South Africa, Nigeria, Angola, Gabon, and others), as well as with exporters of the goods or raw materials we need (Guinea, Ghana, Zambia, Madagascar, Cote d'Ivoire, Zaire, Zambia, and others).

A prominent place in the establishment of a qualitatively new trade and economic cooperation must be given to efforts to create favorable conditions for the operation of Russia's state and private business structures in Africa.

Political, trade and economic interaction with African states should be used as a lever to encourage these states to pay back the debts they owed to the former USSR, including by way of reinvestment, resale of the debt liabilities, etc.

It is in Russia's interests to maintain stability on the African continent, develop democratic processes there, and involve African states (51 countries) in joint efforts to create a new world order.

Russia will promote conflict settlement in this region based on constructive partnership with other states, the UN, the Organization of African Unity, and other international and regional organizations.

Review of the nature of our relations with African states presupposes optimizing cooperation in the military sphere. We should strive to put the remaining ties on a commercial footing, with strict observance of international accords and regulations governing the supply of arms.

X. LATIN AMERICA

The democratic processes ongoing in Russia and on the continent create new premises for building up our relations with the group of countries in question, particularly with Argentina, Brazil, and Mexico, in political, trade and economic, scientific and technological, cultural and other spheres. This development has been confirmed by the visits a number of Russian leaders have paid to these states. Interaction with these countries may assist Russia's internal reforms, and become a considerable factor in strengthening both regional and international security, as well as our own status on the continent and in the global arena.

The mutual complementarity of our economic spaces, together with the significant export, import, scientific and technological potential of the continent's leading powers, can be utilized with a view to saturating the Russian market with food products, goods and services at relatively low costs, as well as gaining access to the advanced technologies that the leading countries of the continent possess.

Even today there is the opportunity for business partnerships to be formed in such fields as nuclear and space research, oil production and processing industries, automobile manufacture, information technology, and the construction industry. Russian businesses are springing up, and the ties involving them may become more effective, too. There are favorable prospects for military cooperation, including the supply of military equipment and armaments to a number of countries on the continent, and there is scope for cooperation in resolving conversion issues, etc.

The formation of a trade, economic and financial space in the western hemisphere, triggered by the creation of the North-American Free Trade Area, will enhance the significance of the "Latin American Channel" for us in terms of not only expanding trade and economic exchanges, but also acquiring loans and investments from the Latin American states.

In the political sphere, there are ready opportunities to engage in close cooperation with Latin American nations in a broad range of global and regional issues pertinent to peace maintenance, consolidation of democratic principles and law and order, respect for national sovereignty, and protection of human rights. It is perfectly feasible to establish practical cooperation to combat international terrorism and drug trafficking, as well as in the sphere of environmental protection.

Alongside conducting active political dialogue at the bilateral level, we should strive to deepen our cooperation with the Rio Group, use our status as a permanent observer in the Organization of American States more efficiently, seek the same status in the Latin American Integration Association, and endeavor to establish close contacts with other respectable regional organizations on the continent.

Among important areas for us to address, there remains the problem of Central American settlement (El Salvador, Guatemala, and—to some extent—Nicaragua), as well as reformation of our relations with Cuba.

In order to provide the necessary impulse to Russia's relations with the main countries of the region, it would be of great importance to organize, starting next year, a series of state visits by B. Yeltsin, preceded by preparatory contacts at ministerial level. At this stage, one of the crucial tasks will be elaboration (as required) of a new legal basis for our interaction with Latin America, above all in the economic sphere.

XI. THE UN AND OTHER INTERNATIONAL ORGANIZATIONS

Russia's foreign policy resources are currently limited by the exigencies of the moment, and this objectively increases the importance of the country's participation in international organizations. The opportunities the UN and regional organizations have in the sphere of security, the experience they have built up with regard to a broad range of international affairs, their wealth of expertise in forecasting, and certain financial resources represent important instruments that could be used to advance our national interests.

Through its participation in the UN, Russia acquires additional resources for more active involvement in international legal regulation of the current developments aimed at creating a new global order and strengthening Russia's own position in today's global strategic balance.

Our central goal is to make maximum use of the organization's mechanisms to promote international peace and security, particularly in those regions crucial to Russia's national interests, including the CIS. What matters to us in this respect are not merely the UN's own capacities, but also its experience of peacekeeping that can be successfully employed in the Commonwealth space to put in place the basic elements of the crisis regulation model that is taking shape in the CIS. Support by the UN and other organizations will confirm to the world the legitimacy of what Russia and its partners are undertaking in the countries of the near abroad to establish its responsibility for maintaining peace and security in the former USSR space.

It is in Russia's interests to expand the practice of interaction among the permanent members of the UN Security Council in order to assist crisis settlement, directly participate in international peacekeeping efforts when necessary, in every possible way enhance the potential of "preventive diplomacy" for early prevention of new conflicts and crises, including those emerging within states on ethnic, religious or other grounds, and improve the mechanisms for rapid response to emergency humanitarian situations, including large-scale or grave violations of human and minority rights. Russia advocates an enhanced role for the UN in peacekeeping, including by strengthening its capacity to counteract violence with the legitimate use of force, and its peace-enforcement potential.

An important sphere of Russia's activity within the structure of the UN includes employment of this structure's capacities to provide all-round support to Russia's internal reforms, and mobilization of international financial and technological resources, as well as expertise in forecasting.

Russia's participation in specialized international organizations within the UN system will make it easier to resolve the problems faced by the country, including those pertaining to cooperation within the CIS framework, particularly environmental protection, combating terrorism and illegal drug trafficking, etc. It will help Russian legislation reach international standards and overcome the current difficulties in developing the cultural sphere and education, etc.

Russia calls for rationalization and improvement in the efficiency of the UN agencies, including making best use of the money spent on supporting these agencies. At the same time, the measures undertaken to reform the international organizations must not undermine the UN's fundamental time-tested principles and its status as the leading multilateral forum. It is not in our interests to support attempts to revise the UN Charter, or the composition and operating principles of the UN Security Council. Russia advocates more efficient use of those mechanisms provided for in the UN Charter, including involvement of large regional states that do not participate in the Security Council in its decision-making.

XII. THE NON-ALIGNED MOVEMENT

Russia acknowledges the Non-Aligned Movement's constructive contribution to the formation of new law-based international relations, and to the settlement of regional conflicts, to disarmament, the provision of equal security for everybody, general observance of human rights, and the resolution of global problems. Russia is prepared to engage in constructive cooperation with the Movement and its participants, and to acknowledge their legitimate interests in the world arena.

XIII. HUMAN RIGHTS AND FUNDAMENTAL FREEDOMS

Fulfilling its obligations in the sphere of human rights and fundamental freedoms as laid down in the UN Charter, CSCE Final Act, the 1992 Helsinki Summit Declaration and other international documents and accords, Russia will develop HUMANITARIAN COOPERATION with other states on bilateral and multilateral levels. This will assist in the creation of a global commonwealth of constitutional states and the effective realization of human rights, which is one of the prerequisites for stable peace, international security, trust and justice.

Russia shares the widely accepted principle that obligations undertaken by states in the sphere of the human dimension represent everybody's legitimate interests and cannot be considered the exclusively internal affairs of one country or another. Russia will adhere to this approach in its relations with those states where there are violations of human and minority rights, or discrimination on ethnic or other grounds, and will actively support and participate in international efforts to prevent and stop such violations through the mechanisms of the UN, CSCE, and CIS.

It is a short- and long-term priority of ours to undertake efforts aimed at the formation of a single legal space under the CIS framework, which would help prevent the emergence and escalation of interethnic conflicts, and promote their peaceful resolution.

Among our most important tasks is concluding bilateral agreements with our CIS partners and other neighbors concerning a citizen's right to choose his nationality, the rights of ethnic, linguistic, cultural and religious minorities, the conditions governing the move of citizens into another state, legal assistance, mutual provision of pensions, migration and refugees, mutual recognition of educational diplomas and certificates, as well as degrees and titles, cultural exchanges and scientific cooperation, and signing consular conventions.

XIV. RELIGION AND RELIGIOUS ORGANIZATIONS

Acknowledging the role of religion and religious organizations in international affairs, Russia will, in every way, support the irenic potential of all religious communities and movements, which enriches the arsenal of the means serving mutual understanding and cooperation among peoples. Russia condemns any manifestation of religious fanaticism, extremism and intolerance, as well as any attempt to misuse religion as a means of political struggle, to destabilize a situation, incite hatred and unleash conflicts on ethnic and religious grounds.

XV. ENVIRONMENTAL PROBLEMS

Russia's renewed international ties must be employed in the interests of resolving environmental problems that are a legacy of the former USSR. Our top priority in this sphere is development of multilateral and bilateral interaction with the rest of the world to facilitate the mitigation of environmental disasters in Russia, adjusting the Russian environmental standards to meet international norms, elaborating and conducting a rational environmental policy, and mobilizing the material resources to resolve any problems. International cooperation is also necessary to prevent and remove cross-border environmental damage, which—unless properly addressed—may acquire a political dimension and complicate our relations with neighboring states. Large-scale cooperation in the sphere of environmental protection is becoming a component of international security and stability in general.

Russia will make use of the opportunities that opened up after the end of the Cold War, in particular to convert its military production, and establish cooperation with western states, including the USA, in carrying out the program for global environmental monitoring based on SDI and other corresponding systems.

Effective support from the international community for Russian environmental programs is inseparably linked to Russia's own contribution to the development of interstate cooperation in environmental protection, and first and foremost Russia's strict fulfillment of its international obligations.

Russia's preparedness to integrate into the community of civilized nations, not just in word but truly in deed, will be demonstrated inter alia by our ability to develop and implement a national program for implementation of the resolutions of the UN Conference on Environment and Development, as well as those of the CSCE Helsinki Summit of 1992.

Cooperation with the CIS member states in overcoming environmental disasters on the territory of the former USSR and preventing new environmental damage must be seen as one of the pillars of an efficient and lasting Commonwealth. These activities will consist in unfailing implementation of the measures stipulated in the Agreement "On Interaction in the Sphere of Environmental Protection and Improvement" signed by the CIS countries.

★ ★ ★

The main priorities of Russia's foreign policy shall be determined by the President of the Russian Federation, on the basis of the Constitution and legislation of the Russian Federation, as well as other acts issued by the country's Supreme Council.

Practical implementation of the foreign policy shall be conducted, under the supervision of the President and operative management of the Government, by the Ministry of Foreign Affairs, under effective control by the Supreme Council of the Russian Federation.

In accordance with Russian legislation, the Ministry of Foreign Affairs shall ensure coordination of international relations exercised by all entities of the Russian Federation, and shall engage in external contacts, to include agreeing Russia's policy with the policies of other CIS members states. The Ministry of Foreign Affairs shall coordinate the activities of the Russian agencies in international affairs, assist in the development of inter-parliamentary contacts, and support the activities of non-governmental international organizations and other forms of people's diplomacy.

The dynamic international situation typical of our time and the rapid developments within Russia itself dictate the need for regular review of foreign policy guidelines and practical goals. The immutability of the main goals and fundamental principles does not prevent flexibility in determining short-term tasks and specific measures. On the contrary, dogged pursuit of a policy that was formulated long ago, when reality dictates that it should be adjusted, is unnatural and may be hazardous. This is what conducting policy, not least foreign policy, means.

The proposed Foreign Policy Conception of the Russian Federation is subject to regular review and improvement. This is not a shortcoming, but a requirement dictated by reality.

It is the key matter—our strict commitment to the country's national interests—that remains immutable. Suggestions promoting compliance of the policy with the national interests will be adequately received and considered.

Ideally, it would be in the country's interests to reach as broad a consensus
as possible with regard to foreign policy options and principles.

MINISTRY OF FOREIGN AFFAIRS OF THE RUSSIAN FEDERATION
Originally published in *Diplomaticheskiy vestnik* [Diplomatic Review], 1993, no. 1–2,
Special Issue, pp. 3–23.

Agreement between the Russian Federation, the Republic of Kazakhstan, the Kyrgyz Republic, the Republic of Tajikistan and the People's Republic of China on Confidence-Building in the Military Field in the Border Area[1]

("Shanghai Declaration") (1996)

The Russian Federation, the Republic of Kazakhstan, the Kyrgyz Republic, the Republic of Tajikistan, making up a Joint Party, and the People's Republic of China, hereinafter referred to as the Parties,

believing that maintenance and development of long-term good-neighbour relations and friendship meet the fundamental interests of the five states and their peoples;

convinced that strengthening security, and maintaining peace and stability in the border area between Russia, Kazakhstan, Kyrgyzstan, Tajikistan, on the one side, and China, on the other (hereinafter referred to as the border area) is an important contribution to the maintenance of peace in the Asia-Pacific region,

affirming the mutual non-use of force or threat of force, the rejection of acquiring a unilateral military superiority;

guided by the Agreement between the Government of the Union of Soviet Socialist Republics and the Government of the People's Republic of China on the Guidelines for Mutual Reduction of Armed Forces and Confidence-Building in the Military Field in the Area of the Soviet–Chinese Border of April 24, 1990;

in conformity with the results attained by the Parties during the negotiations on mutual armed forces reduction and military confidence-building in the border area;

willing to build confidence and raise the level of transparency in the military field, have agreed on the following:

Article 1

The military forces of the Parties deployed in the border area, as an integral part of the military forces of the Parties, shall not be used to attack another

---

1 The document came into effect and is known as the "Shanghai Declaration."

Party, or conduct any military activity that threatens another Party and undermines peace and stability in the border area.

ARTICLE 2

1.   With a view to developing good-neighborly and friendly relations, maintaining long-term stability in the border area, strengthening mutual confidence in the military sphere in the border area, the Parties shall undertake the following measures:

1.1 exchange information on agreed components of military forces and border guard troops (border guard units);

1.2 refrain from conducting military exercises directed against the other Party;

1.3 restrict the scale, geographic area and number of troop exercises;

1.4 notify one another of large-scale military activities and troop movements caused by an emergency situation;

1.5 notify one another of any temporary entry of forces and armaments into the 100-kilometer geographic area on either side of the border line between Russia, Kazakhstan, Kyrgyzstan, Tajikistan, on the one side, and China, on the other (hereinafter referred to as the border line);

1.6 invite observers to troop exercises on a mutual basis;

1.7 notify one another of any temporary entry by river battle ships of the navy/naval forces into the 100-kilometer geographic area on either side of the line on the eastern part of the Russian–Chinese border;

1.8 take steps to prevent dangerous military activities;

1.9 make inquiries with regard to vague situations;

1.10 strengthen friendly contacts between service members of the armed forces and border guard troops (border guard units) in the border area and conduct other confidence-building measures agreed on by the Parties

2.   The application of the above-listed measures shall be specified in corresponding Articles of this Agreement.

ARTICLE 3

1.   The Parties shall exchange information on the personnel strength and the quantity of main types of armaments and military equipment of the ground forces, air force, air defense aviation, border guard troops (border guard units) deployed in the 100-kilometer geographic area on both sides of the border line.

The Parties shall exchange the above information in conformity with the Main Categories of Information Exchange, which is an integral part of this Agreement.

2.   The information will be provided in the following way:

2.1   sixty days after this Agreement enters into effect, the information as of the date of entry into effect of this Agreement;

2.2   before December 15 of each year, the information as of January 1 of the next year.

3.   The information that is exchanged by the Parties under the provisions of this Agreement and received during the implementation of this Agreement is confidential. Neither of the Parties shall disclose, publish or transmit to a third party this information without the consent of the other Party. In case of termination of this Agreement the Parties shall continue to respect the provisions of this paragraph of the Article.

ARTICLE 4

1.   The Parties shall not conduct military exercises directed against the other Party.

2.   In the 100-kilometer geographic area on both sides of the border line the Parties shall not conduct troop exercises with the number of participants exceeding: in the eastern part of the Russian–Chinese border, 40 thousand personnel; in the western part of the Russian–Chinese border and on China's border with Kazakhstan, Kyrgyzstan and Tajikistan, four thousand personnel or 50 battle tanks, separately or jointly.

3.   In the 100-kilometer geographic area on both sides of the line of the eastern part of the Russian–Chinese border, the Parties shall conduct troop exercises with the number of participants exceeding 25 thousand personnel no more than once a year.

4.   Within a 15-kilometer area on both sides of the border line, the Parties can conduct troop exercises with no more than one regiment participating in field firing exercises.

5.   Within a 10-kilometer area on both sides of the border line, the Parties shall not deploy new combat units, other than border guard troops (border guard units).

ARTICLE 5

1.   The Parties shall notify each other of their military activities in the 100-kilometer geographic area on both sides of the border line when:

1.1   a troop exercise is conducted with the number of participants exceeding 25 thousand personnel;

1.2   the troops deployed beyond the 100-kilometer geographic area on both sides of the border line are temporarily brought into the area in numbers of nine thousand personnel or more, or 250 battle tanks or more;

1.3   the strength of the military personnel drafted from the reserve into the 100-kilometer geographic area on both sides of the border line is nine thousand or more.

2. The Parties shall, on a voluntary basis, notify each other of troop exercises with the participation of nine thousand personnel or more, or 250 battle tanks or more, carried out at any time within the 100-kilometer geographic area on both sides of the border line and beyond this area.

3. Notification of such military activities shall be presented in writing through diplomatic channels no later than 10 days before their commencement.

    The notification shall contain information about the total number of the military personnel involved, the number of military units at the level of regiment and above, the number of battle tanks, armored combat vehicles, artillery systems of 122 mm caliber and above, combat aircraft, combat helicopters, tactical missile launchers, as well as about the tasks, duration, zone of military activities and levels of command.

4. If one of the Parties, due to any military activity, may cause damage to the other Party, or if an emergency situation requires the movement of nine thousand troops or more, or assistance from the other Party, this Party shall notify the other Party in due time.

ARTICLE 6

1. A Party conducting troop exercises within the 100-kilometer geographic area from the border line shall invite observers of the other Party, if the number of participating troops equals or exceeds 35 thousand personnel.

2. Parties conducting military exercises within the 100-kilometer geographic area on both sides of the border line shall, on a mutual basis, invite observers of the other Party, if the number of participating troops equals or exceeds 25 thousand personnel.

3. Parties conducting troop exercises within the 100-kilometer geographic area on both sides of the border line and beyond this area shall, on a voluntary and mutual basis, invite observers of the other Party, if the number of participating forces equals or exceeds 13 thousand personnel or 300 battle tanks.

4. The inviting Party shall send to the other Party through diplomatic channels at least 30 days before the beginning of such exercises a written invitation, which shall contain the following information:

4.1 beginning and duration of the exercises and planned duration of the program for observation;

4.2 the date, time, and the location of the arrival and departure of the observers;

4.3 means of observation available to the observers;

4.4 transportation and accommodation.

The invited Party shall reply to the invitation no later than 10 days before the indicated date of the observers' arrival. If the invited Party fails to reply in due time it will mean that the observers will not be sent.

5. The invited Party shall send to military exercises no more than six observers.
6. The invited Party shall cover the travel costs of its observers to the indicated location of arrival and from the location of departure. The receiving Party shall cover the costs associated with the observers' stay on its territory.
7. The inviting Party shall provide the observers with the observation program, relevant materials, and shall render them other assistance.
8. The observers shall comply with relevant rules of the receiving Party with regard to the location, itinerary and restrictions of observation.

ARTICLE 7

1. River battle ships of the navy/naval forces of the Parties (a ship, a boat designed for combat missions and equipped with battle armament systems) can temporarily enter the 100-kilometer geographic area on both sides of the border line for the following purposes:
1.1 mitigation of the consequences of natural disasters;
1.2 passage through the 100-kilometer geographic area on both sides of the border line without causing damage.
2. Russian navy river battle ships can temporarily enter the 100-kilometer geographic area from the eastern part of the Russian–Chinese border line for the following purposes:
2.1 repair, upgrading, disarming, dismantling, modifying for civil uses at ship-repair yards in Khabarovsk, Blagoveshchensk and other locations;
2.2 participation in celebrations in Khabarovsk and Blagoveshchensk on the occasion of national holidays.
3. Temporary entry by river battle ships of the navy/naval force into the 100-kilometer geographic area on both sides of the border line for purposes not indicated above, may be allowed only after a prior agreement has been reached by the Parties.
4. The total number of river battle ships of the navy/naval force of each Party simultaneously located within the 100-kilometer geographic area on both sides of the border line shall not exceed four.
5. Six months after this Agreement enters into force, the Parties shall, taking into account Paragraphs 1 and 2 of this Article, send each other, seven days in advance, through diplomatic channels or border guard representatives, written notification about temporary entry by river battle ships of the navy/naval force into the 100-kilometer geographic area on

both sides of the border line. In case of emergency, river battle ships of the navy/naval force shall temporarily enter the indicated area after prior notification to the other Party.

6.   The notification shall contain information on:

6.1   the purpose of the temporary entry;

6.2   types, hull numbers and number of entering river battle ships of the navy/naval force;

6.3   dates of the beginning and end of the entry;

6.4   precise temporary location (geographic name and coordinates).

ARTICLE 8

1.   The Parties shall take the following measures to prevent dangerous military activities and consequences these activities may bring about in the border area:

1.1   the personnel of the armed forces of the Parties shall exercise caution in conducting military activities in the border area;

1.2   during movement of forces, exercises, field firing, navigation and air flights, the Parties shall seek to prevent these operations from growing into dangerous military activities;

1.3   use of laser by one of the Parties shall not cause any damage to the personnel and materiel of the other Party as a result of the laser radiation emission;

1.4   radio interference used on its own control networks by one of the Parties shall not cause any damage to the personnel and materiel of the other Party;

1.5   during exercises involving field firing, measures shall be undertaken to prevent the territory of the other Party being hit accidentally by bullets, shells and missiles, or damage being caused to its personnel and materiel;

2.   In the event of incidents caused by dangerous military activities, the Parties shall undertake measures to terminate such activities, clarify the situation, and compensate the other Party for the damage. The damage caused by dangerous military activities by one of the states shall be compensated by that state in accordance with the generally recognized principles and rules of international law. The Parties shall settle their disputes by way of consultations.

3.   The Parties shall use all possible means to notify one another of dangerous military incidents.

ARTICLE 9

1.   In the event of an ambiguous situation in the border area, or if one Party has questions and doubts regarding compliance with the Agreement by

the other Party, each Party shall have the right to send a request to the other Party.

2. To settle questions and doubts, as they may arise:

2.1 the Party that receives an inquiry shall respond within seven days (in emergency situations, within two days) to the inquiry received from the other Party;

2.2 in the event that the inquiring Party, having received a response from the other Party, still has questions and doubts, it may demand additional clarifications from the other Party, or propose that a meeting be held in order to discuss the matter. A venue for the meeting shall be determined by agreement of the Parties.

3. To settle and resolve the questions and doubts that the other Party may have with regard to the ambiguous situation, the Party that receives the inquiry may, at its own discretion, invite the other Party to visit areas associated with the questions and doubts that have arisen.

Terms and conditions of such visits, including the number of invited representatives, shall be determined by the inviting Party. The inviting Party shall bear the costs of these visits on its territory.

4. Such inquiries and corresponding responses shall be transmitted through diplomatic channels.

ARTICLE 10

1. The Parties shall implement and develop the following forms of cooperation between their armed forces in neighboring military districts:

1.1 mutual official visits by military commanders;

1.2 mutual orientation tours by military delegations and groups of experts at different levels;

1.3 mutual invitations on a voluntary basis by observers to the army, and command and staff exercises;

1.4 exchange of experience in military construction, combat training, as well as of data and information on the way of life and activities of troops;

1.5 cooperation of logistical support units in construction, food and material supply of troops, and in other areas;

1.6 mutual invitations on a voluntary basis to national holidays, cultural events and sporting competitions;

1.7 other forms of cooperation as agreed by the Parties.

2. Specific plans for cooperation shall be agreed upon by the agencies for external relations of the Parties' armed forces.

ARTICLE 11

1. Border guard forces (border units) of the Parties shall develop cooperation in the following areas:

1.1   establishment and development of contacts between border guard units of all levels, discussion of issues concerning border cooperation and exchange of information with the purpose of facilitating border cooperation;

1.2   conducting consultations and undertaking agreed measures in order to prevent illegal activities and maintain order and stability on the state border;

1.3   prevention of possible incidents and conflict situations on the state border;

1.4   timely mutual notification and provision of mutual assistance in the event of natural disasters, epidemics, epizootics, etc. which could cause damage to the other Party;

1.5   exchange of experience in matters related to border guarding and training of border troops (border units);

1.6   exchange of delegations and promotion of cultural and sporting exchanges and other kinds of friendly contacts.

2.   Specific cooperation activities between border troops (border units) shall be agreed upon between the border guard departments of the Parties.

ARTICLE 12

Border troops (border units) of the Parties shall not use inhuman or cruel forms of treatment with regard to frontier violators. The use of arms by border personnel of the Parties shall be regulated under the internal legislation of the Parties and related agreements of Russia, Kazakhstan, Kyrgyzstan and Tajikistan with China.

ARTICLE 13

The Parties shall, based on mutual agreement, hold expert meetings to discuss progress in the implementation of this Agreement. The meetings shall be convened on an alternate basis in the capitals of the states party to this Agreement.

ARTICLE 14

This Agreement shall not affect obligations previously undertaken by the Parties with respect to other states and shall not be directed against third countries or their interests.

ARTICLE 15

1.   This Agreement is concluded for an indefinite period and may be amended or supplemented by agreement of the Parties.

2.   Each Party shall have the right to terminate the Agreement. A Party that intends to do so shall notify the other Party, in writing, of its decision at

least six months in advance. This Agreement shall cease to be in force after the expiration of six months upon such notification.

3.   Each state of the Joint Party shall have the right to withdraw from this Agreement. A state of the Joint Party that intends to withdraw from this Agreement shall notify the other Party, in writing, of its decision no later than six months in advance.

4.   This Agreement shall be valid as long as at least one state of the Joint Party and China remain party to it.

ARTICLE 16

The Parties shall notify each other of the completion by the Parties, including all states of the Joint Party, of internal procedures required for this Agreement to come into force.

This Agreement shall come into force on the date of the last written notification.

Done in Shanghai on April 26, 1996 in five copies, each in the Russian and Chinese languages, all texts in the Russian and Chinese languages being equally valid.

For the Russian Federation	B. Yeltsin
For the Republic of Kazakhstan	N. Nazarbayev
For the Kyrgyz Republic	A. Akayev
For the Republic of Tajikistan	E. Rakhmonov
For the People's Republic of China	Jiang Zemin

Originally published in *Politika i Diplomatiya stran Aziatsko-Tikhookeanskogo regiona* [Politics and diplomacy of countries of the Asia-Pacific region], Moscow, Nauchnaya kniga, 1998, pp. 222–230.

Founding Act on Mutual Relations, Cooperation and Security Between the Russian Federation and the North Atlantic Treaty Organization

(1997)

The Russian Federation on the one hand, and The North Atlantic Treaty Organization and its member States on the other hand, hereinafter referred to as Russia and NATO, based on an enduring political commitment undertaken at the highest political level, will build together a lasting and inclusive peace in the Euro-Atlantic area on the principles of democracy and cooperative security.

NATO and Russia do not consider each other as adversaries. They share the goal of overcoming the vestiges of earlier confrontation and competition and of strengthening mutual trust and cooperation. The present Act reaffirms the determination of NATO and Russia to give concrete substance to their shared commitment to build a stable, peaceful and undivided Europe, whole and free, to the benefit of all its peoples. Making this commitment at the highest political level marks the beginning of a fundamentally new relationship between NATO and Russia. They intend to develop, on the basis of common interest, reciprocity and transparency a strong, stable and enduring partnership.

This Act defines the goals and mechanism of consultation, cooperation, joint decision-making and joint action that will constitute the core of the mutual relations between NATO and Russia.

NATO has undertaken a historic transformation—a process that will continue. In 1991 the Alliance revised its strategic doctrine to take account of the new security environment in Europe. Accordingly, NATO has radically reduced, and continues the adaptation of, its conventional and nuclear forces. While preserving the capability to meet the commitments undertaken in the Washington Treaty, NATO has expanded, and will continue to expand, its political functions, and has taken on new missions of peacekeeping and crisis management in support of the United Nations (UN) and the Organization for Security and Cooperation in Europe (OSCE), such as in Bosnia and Herzegovina, to address new security challenges in close association with other countries and international organizations. NATO is in the process of developing the European Security and Defense Identity (ESDI) within the Alliance.

It will continue to develop a broad and dynamic pattern of cooperation with OSCE participating States, in particular through the Partnership for Peace, and is working with Partner countries on the initiative to establish a Euro-Atlantic Partnership Council. NATO member States have decided to examine NATO's Strategic Concept to ensure that it is fully consistent with Europe's new security situation and challenges.

Russia is continuing the building of a democratic society and the realization of its political and economic transformation. It is developing the concept of its national security and revising its military doctrine to ensure that they are fully consistent with new security realities. Russia has carried out deep reductions in its armed forces, has withdrawn its forces on an unprecedented scale from the countries of Central and Eastern Europe and the Baltic countries, and withdrawn all its nuclear weapons back to its own national territory. Russia is committed to further reducing its conventional and nuclear forces. It is actively participating in peacekeeping operations in support of the UN and the OSCE, as well as in crisis management in different areas of the world. Russia is contributing to the multinational forces in Bosnia and Herzegovina.

I. Principles

Proceeding from the principle that the security of all states in the Euro-Atlantic community is indivisible, NATO and Russia will work together to contribute to the establishment in Europe of common and comprehensive security based on the allegiance to shared values, commitments and norms of behavior in the interests of all states. NATO and Russia will help to strengthen the Organization for Security and Cooperation in Europe, including developing further its role as a primary instrument in preventive diplomacy, conflict prevention, crisis management, post-conflict rehabilitation and regional security cooperation, as well as in enhancing its operational capabilities to carry out these tasks. The OSCE, as the only pan-European security organization, has a key role in European peace and stability. In strengthening the OSCE, NATO and Russia will cooperate to prevent any possibility of returning to a Europe of division and confrontation, or the isolation of any state.

Consistent with the OSCE's work on a Common and Comprehensive Security Model for Europe for the twenty-first century, and taking into account the decisions of the Lisbon Summit concerning a Charter on European security, NATO and Russia will seek the widest possible cooperation among participating States of the OSCE, with the aim of creating in Europe a common space of security and stability, without dividing lines or spheres of influence limiting the sovereignty of any state.

NATO and Russia start from the premise that the shared objective of strengthening security and stability in the Euro-Atlantic area for the benefit of all countries requires a response to new risks and challenges, such as aggressive nationalism, proliferation of nuclear, biological and chemical weapons, terrorism, persistent abuse of human rights and of the rights of persons belonging to national minorities, and unresolved territorial disputes, which pose a threat to common peace, prosperity and stability.

This Act does not affect, and cannot be regarded as affecting, the primary responsibility of the UN Security Council for maintaining international peace and security, or the role of the OSCE as the inclusive and comprehensive organization for consultation, decision-making and cooperation in its area and as a regional arrangement under Chapter VIII of the United Nations Charter.

In implementing the provisions in this Act, NATO and Russia will observe in good faith their obligations under international law and international instruments, including the obligations of the United Nations Charter and the provisions of the Universal Declaration on Human Rights, as well as their commitments under the Helsinki Final Act and subsequent OSCE documents, including the Charter of Paris and the documents adopted at the Lisbon OSCE Summit.

To achieve the aims of this Act, NATO and Russia will base their relations on a shared commitment to the following principles:

- development, on the basis of transparency, of a strong, stable, enduring and equal partnership and of cooperation to strengthen security and stability in the Euro-Atlantic area;
- acknowledgement of the vital role that democracy, political pluralism, the rule of law, and respect for human rights and civil liberties and the development of free market economies play in the development of common prosperity and comprehensive security;
- refraining from the threat or use of force against each other, as well as against any other state, its sovereignty, territorial integrity or political independence in any manner inconsistent with the United Nations Charter and with the Declaration of Principles Guiding Relations Between Participating States contained in the Helsinki Final Act;
- respect for the sovereignty, independence and territorial integrity of all states and their inherent right to choose the means to ensure their own security, the inviolability of borders and peoples' right of self-determination as enshrined in the Helsinki Final Act and other OSCE documents;
- mutual transparency in creating and implementing defense policy and military doctrines;
- prevention of conflicts and settlement of disputes by peaceful means in accordance with UN and OSCE principles;
- support, on a case-by-case basis, of peacekeeping operations carried out under the authority of the UN Security Council or the responsibility of the OSCE.

II. Mechanism for Consultations and Cooperation, the Russia–NATO Permanent Joint Council

To carry out the activities and aims provided for by this Act, and to develop common approaches to European security and to political problems, NATO and Russia will create the NATO–Russia Permanent Joint Council. The central objective of this Permanent Joint Council will be to build increasing levels of trust, unity of purpose and habits of consultation and cooperation between NATO and Russia, in order to enhance each other's security and that of all nations in the Euro-Atlantic area and diminish the security of none. If disagreements arise, NATO and Russia will endeavor to settle them on the basis of goodwill and mutual respect within the framework of political consultations.

The Permanent Joint Council will provide a mechanism for consultations, coordination and, to the maximum extent possible, where appropriate, for joint decisions and joint action with respect to security issues of common concern. The consultations will not extend to internal matters of NATO, NATO member States, or Russia.

The shared objective of NATO and Russia is to identify and pursue as many opportunities for joint action as possible. As the relationship develops, they expect that additional opportunities for joint action will emerge.

The Permanent Joint Council will be the principal venue of consultation between NATO and Russia in times of crisis or for any other situation affecting peace and stability. Extraordinary meetings of the Council will take place in addition to its regular meetings, to allow for prompt consultations in case of emergencies. In this context, NATO and Russia will promptly consult within the Permanent Joint Council in case one of the Council members perceives a threat to its territorial integrity, political independence or security.

The activities of the Permanent Joint Council will be built upon the principles of reciprocity and transparency. In the course of their consultations and cooperation, NATO and Russia will inform each other regarding the respective security-related challenges they face and the measures that each intends to take to address them.

Provisions of this Act do not provide NATO or Russia, in any way, with a right of veto over the actions of the other, nor do they impinge upon or restrict the rights of NATO or Russia to independent decision-making and action. They cannot be used as a means to disadvantage the interests of other states.

The Permanent Joint Council will meet at various levels and in different forms, according to the subject matter and the wishes of NATO and Russia. The Permanent Joint Council will meet at the level of Foreign Ministers and at the level of Defense Ministers twice annually and also monthly at the level of ambassadors/permanent representatives to the North Atlantic Council.

The Permanent Joint Council may also meet, as appropriate, at the level of Heads of State and Government.

The Permanent Joint Council may establish committees or working groups for individual subjects or areas of cooperation on an ad hoc or permanent basis, as appropriate.

Under the auspices of the Permanent Joint Council, military representatives and Chiefs of Staff will also meet; meetings of Chiefs of Staff will take place no less than twice a year, and also monthly at military representatives level. Meetings of military experts may be convened, as appropriate.

The Permanent Joint Council will be chaired jointly by the Secretary General of NATO, a representative of one of the NATO member States on a rotation basis, and a representative of Russia.

To support the work of the Permanent Joint Council, NATO and Russia will establish the necessary administrative structures.

Russia will establish a Mission to NATO headed by a representative at the rank of Ambassador. A senior military representative and his staff will be part of this Mission for the purposes of military cooperation. NATO retains the possibility of establishing an appropriate presence in Moscow, the modalities of which remain to be determined.

The agenda for regular sessions will be established jointly. Organizational arrangements and rules of procedure for the Permanent Joint Council will be worked out. These arrangements will be in place for the inaugural meeting of the Permanent Joint Council, which will be held no later than four months after the signature of this Act.

The Permanent Joint Council will engage in three distinct activities:

- consulting on the topics in Section III of this Act and on any other political or security issue determined by mutual consent;
- on the basis of these consultations, developing joint initiatives on which NATO and Russia would agree to speak or act in parallel;
- once consensus has been reached in the course of consultation, making joint decisions and taking joint action on a case-by-case basis, including participation, on an equitable basis, in the planning and preparation of joint operations, including peacekeeping operations under the authority of the UN Security Council or the responsibility of the OSCE.

Any actions undertaken by NATO or Russia, together or separately, must be consistent with the United Nations Charter and the OSCE's governing principles.

Recognizing the importance of deepening contacts between the legislative bodies of the participating States to this Act, NATO and Russia will also encourage expanded dialogue and cooperation between the North Atlantic Assembly and the Federal Assembly of the Russian Federation.

III. Areas for Consultations and Cooperation

In building their relationship, NATO and Russia will focus on specific areas of mutual interest. They will consult and strive to cooperate to the broadest possible degree in the following areas:

- issues of common interest related to security and stability in the Euro-Atlantic area or to concrete crises, including the contribution of NATO and Russia to security and stability in this area;
- conflict prevention, including preventive diplomacy, crisis management and conflict resolution, taking into account the role and responsibility of the UN and the OSCE and the work of these organizations in these fields;
- joint operations, including peacekeeping operations, on a case-by-case basis, under the authority of the UN Security Council or the responsibility of the OSCE, and if Combined Joint Task Forces (CJTF) are used in such cases, participation in them at an early stage;
- participation of Russia in the Euro-Atlantic Partnership Council and the Partnership for Peace;
- exchange of information and consultation on strategy, defense policy, the military doctrines of NATO and Russia, and budgets and infrastructure development programs;
- arms control issues;
- nuclear safety issues, across their full spectrum;
- preventing the proliferation of nuclear, biological and chemical weapons, and their delivery means, combating nuclear trafficking and strengthening cooperation in specific arms control areas, including political and defense aspects of proliferation;
- possible cooperation in Theatre Missile Defense;
- enhanced regional air traffic safety, increased air traffic capacity and reciprocal exchanges, as appropriate, to promote confidence through increased measures of transparency and exchanges of information in relation to air defense and related aspects of airspace management/control. This will include exploring possible cooperation on appropriate air defense related matters;
- increasing transparency, predictability and mutual confidence regarding the size and roles of the conventional forces of member States of NATO and Russia;
- reciprocal exchanges, as appropriate, on nuclear weapons issues, including doctrines and strategy of NATO and Russia;
- coordinating a program of expanded cooperation between respective military establishments, as further detailed below;
- pursuing possible armaments-related cooperation through association of Russia with NATO's Conference of National Armaments Directors;
- conversion of defense industries;

- developing mutually agreed cooperative projects in defense-related economic, environmental and scientific fields;
- conducting joint initiatives and exercises in civil emergency preparedness and disaster relief;
- combating terrorism and drug trafficking;
- improving public understanding of evolving relations between NATO and Russia, including the establishment of a NATO documentation center or information office in Moscow.

Other areas can be added by mutual agreement.

IV. Political-Military Issues

NATO and Russia affirm their shared desire to achieve greater stability and security in the Euro-Atlantic area.

The member States of NATO reiterate that they have no intention, no plan and no reason to deploy nuclear weapons on the territory of new members, nor any need to change any aspect of NATO's nuclear posture or nuclear policy—and do not foresee any future need to do so. This subsumes the fact that NATO has decided that it has no intention, no plan, and no reason to establish nuclear weapon storage sites on the territory of those members, whether through the construction of new nuclear storage facilities or the adaptation of old nuclear storage facilities. Nuclear storage sites are understood to be facilities specifically designed for the stationing of nuclear weapons, and include all types of hardened above or below ground facilities (storage bunkers or vaults) designed for storing nuclear weapons.

Recognizing the importance of the adaptation of the Treaty on Conventional Armed Forces in Europe (CFE) for the broader context of security in the OSCE area and the work on a Common and Comprehensive Security Model for Europe for the twenty-first century, the member States of NATO and Russia will work together in Vienna with the other States Parties to adapt the CFE Treaty to enhance its viability and effectiveness, taking into account Europe's changing security environment and the legitimate security interests of all OSCE participating States. They share the objective of concluding an adaptation agreement as expeditiously as possible and, as a first step in this process, they will, together with other States Parties to the CFE Treaty, seek to conclude as soon as possible a framework agreement setting forth the basic elements of an adapted CFE Treaty, consistent with the objectives and principles of the Document on Scope and Parameters agreed at Lisbon in December 1996.

NATO and Russia believe that an important goal of CFE Treaty adaptation should be a significant lowering in the total amount of Treaty-Limited Equipment permitted in the Treaty's area of application compatible with the legitimate defense requirements of each State Party. NATO and Russia encourage all States Parties to the CFE Treaty to consider reductions in their CFE equipment entitlements, as part of an overall effort to achieve lower equipment levels that are consistent with the transformation of Europe's security environment.

The member States of NATO and Russia commit themselves to exercise restraint during the period of negotiations, as foreseen in the Document on Scope and Parameters, in relation to the current postures and capabilities of their conventional armed forces—in particular with respect to their levels of forces and deployments—in the Treaty's area of application, in order to avoid developments in the security situation in Europe diminishing the security of any State Party. This commitment is without prejudice to possible voluntary decisions by the individual States Parties to reduce their force levels or deployments, or to their legitimate security interests.

The member States of NATO and Russia proceed on the basis that adaptation of the CFE Treaty should help to ensure equal security for all States Parties, irrespective of their membership of a political-military alliance, both to preserve and strengthen stability and continue to prevent any destabilizing increase of forces in various regions of Europe and in Europe as a whole. An adapted CFE Treaty should also further enhance military transparency by extended information exchange and verification, and permit the possible accession by new States Parties.

The member States of NATO and Russia propose to other CFE States Parties to carry out such adaptation of the CFE Treaty so as to enable States Parties to reach, through a transparent and cooperative process, conclusions regarding reductions they might be prepared to make and resulting national Treaty-Limited Equipment ceilings. These will then be codified as binding limits in the adapted Treaty to be agreed by consensus of all States Parties, and reviewed in 2001 and at five-year intervals thereafter. In doing so, the States Parties will take into account all the levels of Treaty-Limited Equipment established for the Atlantic-to-the-Urals area by the original CFE Treaty, the substantial reductions that have been carried out since then, the changes to the situation in Europe, and the need to ensure that the security of no state is diminished.

The member States of NATO and Russia reaffirm that States Parties to the CFE Treaty should maintain only such military capabilities, individually or in conjunction with others, as are commensurate with individual or collective legitimate security needs, taking into account their international obligations, including the CFE Treaty.

Each State Party will base its agreement to the provisions of the adapted Treaty on all national ceilings of the States Parties, and on its projections of the current and future security situation in Europe.

In addition, in the negotiations on the adaptation of the CFE Treaty, the member States of NATO and Russia will, together with other States Parties, seek to strengthen stability by further developing measures to prevent any potentially threatening build-up of conventional forces in agreed regions of Europe, to include Central and Eastern Europe.

NATO and Russia have clarified their intentions with regard to their conventional force postures in Europe's new security environment, and are prepared to consult on the evolution of these postures in the framework of the Permanent Joint Council.

NATO reiterates that in the current and foreseeable security environment, the Alliance will carry out its collective defense and other missions by ensuring the necessary interoperability, integration, and capability for reinforcement, rather than by additional permanent stationing of substantial combat forces. Accordingly, it will have to rely on adequate infrastructure commensurate with the above tasks. In this context, reinforcement may take place, when necessary, in the event of defense against a threat of aggression and missions in support of peace consistent with the United Nations Charter and the OSCE governing principles, as well as for exercises consistent with the adapted CFE Treaty, the provisions of the 1994 Vienna Document and mutually agreed transparency measures. Russia will exercise similar restraint in its conventional force deployments in Europe.

The member States of NATO and Russia will strive for greater transparency, predictability and mutual confidence with regard to their armed forces. They will comply fully with their obligations under the 1994 Vienna Document and develop cooperation with the other OSCE participating States, including negotiations in the appropriate format, as well within the OSCE, to promote confidence and security.

The member States of NATO and Russia will use and improve existing arms control regimes and confidence-building measures to create security relations based on peaceful cooperation.

NATO and Russia, in order to develop cooperation between their military establishments, will expand political-military consultations and cooperation through the Permanent Joint Council, with an enhanced dialogue between the senior military authorities of NATO and its member States and of Russia. They will implement a program of significantly expanded military activities and practical cooperation between NATO and Russia at all levels. Consistent with the tenets of the Permanent Joint Council, this enhanced military-to-military dialogue will be built upon the principle that neither party views the other as a threat nor seeks to disadvantage the other's security. This enhanced military-to-military dialogue will include regularly scheduled reciprocal briefings on NATO and Russian military doctrine, strategy and resultant force posture, and will include the broad possibilities for joint exercises and training.

To support this enhanced dialogue and the military components of the Permanent Joint Council, NATO and Russia will establish military liaison missions at various levels on the basis of reciprocity and further mutual arrangements.

To enhance their partnership and ensure this partnership is grounded, to the greatest extent possible, in practical activities and direct cooperation, the respective military authorities of NATO and Russia will explore the further development of a concept for joint NATO–Russia peacekeeping operations. This initiative should build upon the positive experience of working together in Bosnia and Herzegovina, and the lessons learned there will be used in the establishment of Combined Joint Task Forces.

The present Act takes effect upon the date of its signature.

NATO and Russia will take the proper steps to ensure its implementation in accordance with their procedures.

The present Act is worked out in two original copies, each in Russian, French and English language.

The Government of the Russian Federation and the Secretary General of NATO will provide the Secretary General of the United Nations and the Secretary General of the OSCE with the text of this Act with the request to circulate it to all members of these Organizations.

Signed in Paris on May 27, 1997

On behalf of:

The Russian Federation	B. Yeltsin
Kingdom of Belgium	J.-L. Dehaene
Canada	R. Irwin
Kingdom of Denmark	P. Nyrup Rasmussen
French Republic	J. Chirac
Federal Republic of Germany	H. Kohl
Hellenic Republic	C. Simitis
Republic of Iceland	D. Oddsson
Italian Republic	R. Prodi
North Atlantic Treaty Organization	J. Solana
Grand Duchy of Luxembourg	J.-C. Juncker
Kingdom of the Netherlands	W. Kok
Kingdom of Norway	T. Jagland
Portuguese Republic	A. Guterres
Kingdom of Spain	J. M. Aznar
Republic of Turkey	S. Demirel
United Kingdom of Great Britain and Northern Ireland	A. Blair
United States of America	B. Clinton

Originally published in *Diplomaticheskiy vestnik* [Diplomatic Review], 1997, no. 6, pp. 4–10.

Union Treaty Between Belarus and Russia

(1997)

The Russian Federation and the Republic of Belarus,

proceeding on the basis of the spiritual affinity and commonality of the historic fates of their peoples, based on their will for closer unity, and seeking to effectively utilize the material and intellectual potentials of Russia and Belarus in the interests of their social and economic progress,

acting in compliance with the fundamental principles of the constitutional orders of the Parties and generally recognized principles and norms of international law,

based on the Treaty on the Formation of a Community of Russia and Belarus of April 2, 1996, and developing its provisions with a view to achieving effective integration within the economic and other spheres of social activities,

have agreed upon the following:

ARTICLE 1

The Community of Russia and Belarus shall be transformed into a Union with the terms of reference stemming from the Charter of the Union.

Each of the member states of the Union shall retain its state sovereignty, independence, territorial integrity, Constitution, national flag, coat of arms, and other attributes of statehood.

ARTICLE 2

The Union shall pursue the following goals:

- the strengthening of the relations of fraternity, friendship and all-round cooperation between the Russian Federation and the Republic of Belarus in the political, economic, social, military, scientific, cultural, and other spheres;
- the improvement of the living standards of the peoples, and the creation of favorable conditions for the all-round and harmonious development of the individual;

- ensuring the stable social and economic development of the member states of the Union on the basis of the unification of their material and intellectual potentialities and the use of market economic mechanisms;
- bringing closer together their national legal systems and forming the legal system of the Union;
- ensuring security, maintaining a high level of defense capacity, and jointly fighting crime;
- assisting in the maintenance of common European security, and in the development of mutually beneficial cooperation in Europe and the world as a whole.

ARTICLE 3

The Charter of the Union shall be an inalienable part of this Treaty.

ARTICLE 4

This Treaty and the Charter of the Union can be amended by mutual consent of the Parties. All amendments shall be ratified.

ARTICLE 5

This Treaty shall not affect the rights and obligations of the Parties under other international treaties signed by them, and shall not be directed against any third country.

ARTICLE 6

The Treaty on the Formation of a Community of Russia and Belarus, signed on April 2, 1996, and the normative legal acts adopted earlier by the bodies of that Community, shall remain effective in the parts not contravening this Treaty.

ARTICLE 7

This Treaty is open for accession by other states that are subject to international law, share the goals and principles of the Union, and fully undertake the obligations stemming from this Treaty and the Charter of the Union. Accession shall take place by approval of the member states.

ARTICLE 8

This Treaty and the Charter of the Union signed by the heads of state of the member states shall be ratified and shall enter into force on the day of the exchange of the ratification instruments.

This Treaty is of indefinite duration. Either of its Parties shall have the right to withdraw from this Treaty, provided it gives written notification to the other Party 12 months prior to withdrawal.

ARTICLE 9

This Treaty shall be registered in accordance with Article 102 of the United Nations Charter.

Done in Moscow on April 2, 1997, in two original copies in the Russian and Belarussian languages. Both copies shall have equal legal force.

For the Russian Federation   Boris Yeltsin
For the Republic of Belarus   Alexander Lukashenko

Originally published in *Diplomaticheskiy vestnik* [Diplomatic Review], 1997, no. 4, pp. 41–43.

Foreign Policy Conception of the Russian Federation[1]

(2000)

I. General Provisions

The Foreign Policy Conception of the Russian Federation represents a system of views on the content and principal areas of the foreign policy activities of the Russian Federation.

The legal basis of this Conception comprises the Constitution of the Russian Federation, Federal laws, other legislative acts of the Russian Federation that regulate the activities of the state federal bodies in the sphere of foreign policy, generally recognized principles and norms of international law, and international treaties concluded by the Russian Federation, and the Conception of National Security of the Russian Federation approved under Decree No. 24 of the President of the Russian Federation on January 10, 2000.

At the beginning of the 21st century the international situation demands rethinking of the overall situation surrounding the Russian Federation, the priorities of Russian foreign policy, and the resources available to support it. Alongside a certain strengthening of the international positions of the Russian Federation, there are some negative tendencies that have emerged. Some of the expectations for the emergence of new, equitable and mutually beneficial relations of partnership between Russia and the surrounding world, as set forth in the Basic Provisions of the Foreign Policy Conception of the Russian Federation, approved by Directive No. 284-rp of the President of the Russian Federation on April 23, 1993, and in other documents, have not materialized.

The topmost priority in the foreign policy of Russia is protection of the interests of the individual, society, and the state. Within the framework of this process, the main efforts should be directed towards attaining the following principal objectives:

- to ensure the reliable security of the country, preserve and strengthen its sovereignty, its territorial integrity, and its strong and respected position in the world community, which is what best meets the interests of the Rus-

---

1 Approved by the President of the Russian Federation V. V. Putin on June 28, 2000.

sian Federation as a great power and an influential center in the modern world, and is essential to the growth of its political, economic, intellectual and spiritual potential;

- to influence global processes with the aim of forming a stable, just, and democratic world order based on the generally recognized norms of international law, above all, the goals and principles of the UN Charter, and on equal partner relations among states;

- to create the external conditions favorable to the steady development of Russia, to building up its economy, improving the living standards of the population, successfully implementing democratic transformations, reinforcing the foundations of the constitutional system, and observing individual rights and freedoms;

- to form a belt of good-neighborliness along the perimeter of Russia's borders, to promote the elimination of existing hotbeds of tension and conflict, and prevent the emergence of any more, in the regions adjacent to the Russian Federation;

- to seek concord and common interests with foreign countries and interstate associations in the process of resolving the tasks determined by Russia's national priorities, and, on this basis, to build a system of relations involving partners and allies that will improve the conditions and characteristics of international cooperation;

- to uphold in every possible way the rights and interests of Russian citizens and fellow countrymen abroad; and

- to promote a positive perception of the Russian Federation in the world, to popularize the Russian language and cultures of the peoples of the Russian Federation abroad.

II. The Contemporary World and the Foreign Policy of the Russian Federation

The contemporary world is undergoing fundamental and dynamic changes that profoundly affect the interests of the Russian Federation and its citizens. Russia is an active participant in this process. As a permanent member of the UN Security Council, commanding a significant potential and resources in all spheres of human activity, and maintaining intensive relations with the world's leading nations, Russia exerts a considerable influence on the formation of a new world order.

The transformation of international relations, the end of confrontation, the steady elimination of the aftermath of the Cold War, and the advance of the Russian reforms have substantially broadened the scope for cooperation in the world arena. The threat of a global nuclear conflict has been minimized. While military power retains its significance in international affairs, an ever greater role is played by economic, political, scientific and technological, environmental, and information factors. Coming to the fore as the main components of the national might of the Russian Federation are its intellectual, information and communications capacities, its population's welfare and standard of education, the interaction of its scientific and production resources, concentration of financial capital, and diversification of economic ties. The overwhelming majority of states are firmly set on pursuing market methods of managing the economy and democratic values. The major breakthrough in a number of key scientific and technological fields that has led to a single, worldwide information environment, the enhancement and diversification of international economic ties—all this gives the interdependence of nations a global feel. The prerequisites are there for a more stable and crisis-proof global structure.

Simultaneously, new challenges and threats to the national interests of Russia are emerging in international affairs. There is a growing trend towards the establishment of a unipolar world order, with economic and power domination by the United States. Greater reliance is being placed on western institutions and forums of limited membership to resolve the cardinal issues of international security, and the role of the UN Security Council is being devalued.

The strategy of unilateral action could destabilize the international situation, provoke tension and an arms race, and aggravate interstate disagreements, national and religious strife. The use of force, in circumvention of the existing international legal mechanisms, cannot remove the deep socio-economic, interethnic and other discords that underlie conflicts; instead it only serves to undermine the foundations of legal order.

Russia will promote a multipolar system of international relations that will genuinely reflect the diversity of the contemporary world and its great variety of interests.

Mutual consideration of interests will guarantee the effectiveness and reliability of such a world order. The global order of the 21st century must be based on mechanisms for the collective resolution of key problems, and on the precedence of law and broad democratization of international affairs.

Russia's interests are directly linked to other tendencies, too, such as:

- globalization of the world economy. Apart from additional opportunities for socio-economic progress and the expansion of human contacts, this tendency gives rise to new dangers, especially for economically weak states, and increases the risk of the emergence of large-scale financial and economic crises. There is a growing risk that the economic system and the information environment of the Russian Federation may become dependent on outside influences;
- the enhanced role played by international institutions and mechanisms (the G-8 group, IMF, World Bank and others) in the world economy and politics, which has been brought about by an objective rise of the interdependence of nations, and by the need to promote the manageability of the

world financial-economic system in the current conditions. It is in Russia's interests to play a full and equal part in developing the fundamental principles of the operation of the global financial-economic system in the current conditions;

- development of regional and sub-regional integration in Europe, the Asia-Pacific region, Africa and Latin America. Integrated associations are acquiring an ever greater significance in the world economy and are becoming a considerable force in regional and sub-regional security and peacekeeping;
- military-political rivalry among regional powers, the growth of separatism, ethnic-national and religious extremism. Integration processes, in particular in the Euro-Atlantic region, are often pursued on a selective and limited basis. Attempts to decry the role of a sovereign state as the fundamental component in international relations generate a threat of arbitrary interference in internal affairs. The problem of the proliferation of weapons of mass destruction and means of their delivery is acquiring serious dimensions. Ongoing and potential regional and local armed conflicts pose a threat to international peace and security. The growth of international terrorism, transnational organized crime, and illegal trafficking in drugs and weapons are starting to have a significant impact on global and regional stability.

The threats brought about by these tendencies are aggravated by the limited resource support for Russian foreign policy implementation, making it difficult for Russia to uphold its foreign economic interests, and reducing the influence it commands abroad in information and cultural spheres.

And yet, the Russian Federation has the potential to attain a respectable place in the world. Further strengthening of Russia's statehood, consolidation of its civil society, and the rapid transition to a steady economic growth are of crucial importance in this respect.

In the past decade, Russia has been able to employ additional opportunities for international cooperation as a result of the radical transformations in the country; Russia has advanced significantly along the road of integration into the system of world economic ties; it has joined a number of influential international organizations and institutions. Through its intensive efforts, Russia has managed to strengthen its standing in a number of major areas in the world arena.

The Russian Federation is pursuing an independent and constructive foreign policy. The policy is based on consistency and predictability, on mutually beneficial pragmatism. This policy is as transparent as possible; it takes into consideration the legitimate interests of other states and is aimed at seeking joint solutions.

Russia is a reliable partner in international relations. Its constructive role in resolving acute international problems has been generally acknowledged.

A distinguishing feature of Russia's foreign policy is that it is balanced. This has been predetermined by Russia's geopolitical situation as one of the largest Eurasian powers, which requires an optimal combination of efforts along all vectors. Such an approach predetermines Russia's responsibility for maintaining security in the world at both the global and the regional level, and preconditions the development and mutual complementarity of its foreign policy activities at both the bilateral and the multilateral level.

III. Priorities of the Russian Federation in Addressing Global Problems

For Russia's foreign policy to be successful, it should be based on maintaining a reasonable balance between its goals and its potential to achieve these goals. Focusing political and diplomatic, military, economic, financial and other means on resolving foreign political tasks must be commensurate with their real importance to Russia's national interests, while the scope of participation in international affairs must be appropriate to strengthening the nation's standing. The diversity and complexity of international problems, and the existence of critical situations, mean that a timely assessment must be made of the priority each of them has in the Russian Federation's foreign policy activities. There is a need to enhance the effectiveness of political, legal, external economic and other instruments in protecting the state sovereignty of Russia and its national economy in conditions of globalization.

1. FORMING A NEW WORLD ARCHITECTURE

Russia is interested in a stable structure of international relations based on principles of justice, mutual respect and mutually beneficial cooperation. Such a structure should provide reliable security to each member of the world community in political, military, economic, humanitarian and other areas.

The United Nations must remain the key center for regulating international relations in the 21st century. The Russian Federation shall firmly resist attempts to downgrade the role of the United Nations and its Security Council in world affairs.

Building up the consolidating mission of the United Nations in the world implies:

- strict observance of the fundamental principles of the UN Charter, including preservation of the status of the UN Security Council permanent members;
- reasonable reform of the United Nations, with the aim of developing a mechanism for it to respond rapidly to world developments; this includes enhancing its potential to avert and resolve crises and conflicts;
- further enhancement of the effectiveness of the UN Security Council, which bears the main responsibility for maintaining international peace

and security; providing the body with broader representation by way of including new permanent members, and, primarily, notable developing countries. Reform of the United Nations must be based on the immutable right of veto by all permanent members of the UN Security Council.

Russia attaches great importance to its participation in the G-8 group of the most developed industrial states. Regarding the mechanism of consultations and coordination of positions on the most important problems of the day as an important means of upholding and advancing its foreign political interests, the Russian Federation intends to build up its cooperation with its partners in this forum.

2. STRENGTHENING INTERNATIONAL SECURITY

Russia supports a further decrease in the role of the power factor in international relations, along with the simultaneous enhancement of strategic and regional stability. To this end, the Russian Federation:
- shall steadily fulfill the commitments it has undertaken in compliance with treaties and agreements in the sphere of restricting and reducing armaments; it will participate in elaborating and concluding new accords consistent both with its national interests and the security interests of other states;
- is prepared to proceed with a further reduction of its nuclear potential, on the basis of bilateral agreements with the United States of America, and—on a multilateral basis—with other nuclear powers, provided strategic stability in the nuclear sphere is not undermined. Russia will seek the preservation and observance of the 1972 Treaty on the Limitation of Anti-Ballistic Missile Systems—the cornerstone of strategic stability. The implementation of the plans by the United States to create a national missile defense system will inevitably compel the Russian Federation to take appropriate steps to maintain its national security at a proper level;
- maintains its firm line of participating jointly with other states to prevent the proliferation of nuclear weapons, other weapons of mass destruction and means of their delivery, and corresponding materials and technologies. The Russian Federation is an ardent supporter of strengthening and developing relevant international regimes, including creating a global system for monitoring the nonproliferation of missiles and missile technologies. The Russian Federation firmly adheres to its commitments under the Comprehensive Nuclear Test Ban Treaty, and urges all nations of the world to join it;
- devotes special attention to ensuring information security as an aspect of consolidating strategic stability;

- intends to continue promoting the enhancement of regional stability by participating in the processes aimed at reducing and limiting conventional armed forces, and adopting confidence-building measures in the military sphere;
- regards international peacekeeping as an effective instrument for resolving armed conflicts, and calls for the strengthening of its legal foundation in strict accordance with the principles of the UN Charter. Supporting the measures to build up and modernize the potential of the United Nations Organization's anti-crisis rapid response, the Russian Federation intends to continue its active participation in peacekeeping operations mounted both under the aegis of the United Nations, and, in specific cases, by regional and sub-regional organizations. The need for, and the degree of, such participation shall be measured against the national interests and the international commitments of our country. Russia proceeds from the premise that only the UN Security Council has the authority to sanction use of force for the purpose of achieving peace;
- proceeds from the premise that the use of force in violation of the UN Charter is unlawful and poses a threat to the stabilization of the entire system of international relations. All attempts to introduce into international language such concepts as "humanitarian intervention" and "limited sovereignty" in order to justify unilateral force that bypasses the UN Security Council are unacceptable. While prepared for constructive dialogue on upgrading the legal aspects of employing force in international relations in conditions of globalization, the Russian Federation believes that the search for concrete forms of response on the part of the international community in various emergency situations, including humanitarian crises, must be conducted collectively, with strict observance of the norms of international law and the UN Charter;
- shall participate in activities conducted under the aegis of the United Nations and other international organizations to eliminate natural and man-made disasters, other emergency situations, as well as to render humanitarian aid to afflicted countries;
- regards as its most important foreign policy mission to fight international terrorism, which is capable of destabilizing the situation not only in individual states, but in entire regions. The Russian Federation calls for further measures to intensify cooperation among states in this area. It is the direct duty of every state to protect its citizens against terrorist encroachments, to prevent any activity on its territory aimed at organizing such acts against the citizens and interests of other countries, and not to provide asylum for terrorists;
- shall determinedly combat illegal drug trafficking and the growth of organized crime, in cooperation with other states on a multilateral basis, prima-

rily within the framework of specialized international agencies, and on a bilateral basis.

3. INTERNATIONAL ECONOMIC RELATIONS

The main goal of the Russian Federation's foreign policy in the sphere of international economic relations is to promote the development of the national economy, which, in conditions of globalization, is unthinkable without Russia's broad integration into the structure of world economic ties. In order to achieve these objectives, Russia shall:

- ensure favorable external conditions for forming a market-oriented economy in our country, and for establishing a renewed foreign economic specialization of the Russian Federation, one that will guarantee maximum economic returns on the country's participation in the international division of labor;
- seek to reduce to a minimum the risks connected with Russia's further integration into the world economy, with consideration of the need to maintain the country's economic security;
- assist in the formation of a just international trade system, with the Russian Federation's full participation in international economic organizations, provided the national interests of our country are safeguarded in those organizations;
- promote the expansion of domestic exports, and rationalization of imports; help Russian business ventures abroad, uphold their interests in foreign markets, oppose discrimination against Russian manufacturers and exporters, and ensure strict compliance by businesses engaged in foreign economic activity with the corresponding Russian legislation;
- encourage foreign investments, above all in the real sector and priority spheres of Russia's economy;
- seek to ensure the preservation and optimal use of Russian property abroad;
- strive to service its foreign debt in line with the country's actual capacities, and seek to maximize the recovery of credits granted to foreign states;
- form a comprehensive system of Russian legislation and international legal and treaty foundations in the economic sphere.

Russia must be prepared to utilize all available economic levers and resources to uphold its national interests.

Taking into account the growing threat of global natural and man-made disasters, the Russian Federation favors an expansion of international cooperation to ensure environmental security, including with the use of state-of-the-art technologies, in the interests of the entire global community.

4. HUMAN RIGHTS AND INTERNATIONAL RELATIONS

Committed to the values of democratic society, including respect for human rights and freedoms, Russia sees its goals as follows:

- to seek respect for human rights and freedoms all over the world, on the basis of respect for the norms of international law;
- to protect the rights and interests of Russian citizens and compatriots abroad on the basis of international law and effective bilateral agreements. The Russian Federation will seek to obtain adequate guarantees for the rights and freedoms of compatriots in states where they permanently reside, and to maintain and develop comprehensive ties with them and their associations;
- to develop international cooperation in the field of humanitarian exchange;
- to expand its participation in international conventions and agreements related to human rights;
- to proceed with bringing legislation of the Russian Federation into line with Russia's international obligations.

5. INFORMATION SUPPORT FOR FOREIGN POLICY ACTIVITIES

An important task pursued by the Russian Federation in its foreign policy activities is to communicate to the broad sections of the world public objective and accurate information about Russia's stance on key international problems, its foreign policy initiatives, and the actions undertaken by the Russian Federation, as well as about accomplishments of Russian culture, science, and intellectual creative pursuits. Foremost is the mission to shape a positive perception of Russia abroad and a friendly attitude towards it. An integral element of this work should be purposeful efforts aimed at explaining to the broad public abroad the essence of Russia's domestic policies and the processes inside the country. There is a pressing need for Russia rapidly to develop its own effective means of influencing public opinion abroad.

IV. Regional Priorities

It is a priority of Russia's foreign policy to ensure the suitability of multilateral and bilateral cooperation with the member states of the Commonwealth of Independent States (CIS) for the country's national security tasks.

Emphasis will be placed on the development of good-neighborly relations and strategic partnerships with all CIS member states. Practical relations with each of them should be developed with due consideration of their respective openness to cooperation and readiness to acknowledge, in a due manner, the interests of the Russian Federation, and in particular to guarantee the rights of Russian compatriots.

Proceeding from the principle of multi-speed and multi-level integration within the CIS framework, Russia will regulate the characteristics and nature of its interaction with CIS member states both within the CIS as a whole, and within smaller associations, primarily the Customs Union and the Collective Security Treaty. A priority task is to strengthen the Union of Belarus and Russia as the most advanced, at this stage, mode of integration of two sovereign states.

We attach prime importance to joint efforts toward settling conflicts in CIS member states, and to development of cooperation in the military-political sphere and in the sphere of security, particularly in fighting international terrorism and extremism.

Serious emphasis will be placed on development of economic cooperation, including the creation of a free trade zone and implementation of programs for joint rational use of natural resources. Specifically, Russia will work towards conferring such a status on the Caspian Sea, which will allow the littoral states to develop mutually beneficial cooperation in exploitation of the local resources on a just basis and with proper consideration of each other's legitimate interests.

The Russian Federation will undertake efforts to secure the observance of mutual obligations concerning the preservation and augmentation of the common cultural heritage in the CIS member states.

Relations with European states is a traditional priority of Russia's foreign policy. The main aim of Russian foreign policy in Europe is the creation of a stable and democratic system for European security and cooperation. Russia is interested in further balanced development of the multi-functional nature of the Organization for Security and Cooperation in Europe (OSCE) and will strive to achieve this end.

It is important that we make sure the legislative potential, which this organization has accumulated since the 1975 adoption of the Helsinki Final Act and which remains relevant, is applied as fully as possible. Russia will firmly oppose attempts to narrow down the OSCE's functions, and specifically any attempts to redirect its activities to the post-Soviet space and the Balkans.

Russia will seek to render the adapted Treaty on the Conventional Armed Forces in Europe an effective instrument for European security and for imparting an all-inclusive nature to the confidence-building measures, including, specifically, coalition activities and naval activities.

Based on its own need to build a civil society, Russia intends to continue its participation in the activities of the Council of Europe.

Of key importance are relations with the European Union (EU). The ongoing processes within the EU are increasingly impacting on developments within Europe. There is EU expansion, transition to a single currency, institutional reform, and the emergence of a common foreign policy and security policy, and the policy on EU defense identity. Russia regards these processes as an objective component of European development, and will seek due consideration of its interests, including in the sphere of bilateral relations with individual EU member states.

The Russian Federation regards the EU as one of its main political and economic partners, and will strive to develop with it an intensive, stable and long-term cooperation that is not susceptible to fluctuations governed by expediency.

The nature of relations with the EU is determined by the framework of the Agreement on partnership and cooperation of June 24, 1994, which establishes a partnership between the Russian Federation and the European communities and their member states, and which is yet to come into full effect. Specific issues, primarily that of adequate respect for the interests of the Russian side in the process of EU expansion and reform, will be dealt with on the basis of the Strategy for development of relations between the Russian Federation and the European Union, adopted in 1999. The EU's emerging military-political dimension should be a subject of particular attention.

Russia has a realistic appreciation of the role of the North Atlantic Treaty Organization (NATO), and, recognizing the importance of cooperation with the alliance in the interests of maintaining security and stability on the continent, is open to constructive interaction. The necessary foundation for such interaction was laid by the Founding Act on mutual relations, cooperation and security between the Russian Federation and the North Atlantic Treaty Organization of May 27, 1997. The intensity of Russia's cooperation with NATO will be determined by the latter's compliance with the key stipulations of the document, primarily those concerning non-use of force or threat of force, and non-deployment of conventional armed forces, nuclear weapons and means of their delivery in the new members' territories.

At the same time, in a number of areas, NATO's present-day political and military guidelines do not accord with the security interests of the Russian Federation and, in some instances, run counter to these interests. First and foremost, this relates to the provisions of NATO's new strategic concept, which do not rule out operations employing force beyond the zone of the application of the Washington Treaty and without the sanction of the UN Security Council.

Productive and constructive cooperation between Russia and NATO is possible only provided it is based on due respect for the interests of the sides and an unconditional fulfillment of mutual obligations assumed.

Interaction with Western European states, primarily with such influential ones as the UK, Germany, Italy and France, constitutes an important resource for Russia in upholding its national interests in European and world affairs, and for the stabilization and growth of the Russian economy.

In its relations with the states of Central and Eastern Europe, Russia's priority remains maintenance of existing human, economic, and cultural ties, overcoming ongoing crises, and giving further impetus to cooperation with consideration of the new conditions and Russia's interests.

There are good prospects for the development of the Russian Federation's relations with Lithuania, Latvia and Estonia. Russia wants these relations to develop as neighborly, mutually beneficial cooperation. In this respect, an indispensable condition is acknowledgement by the states in question of Russia's interests, including, most crucially, the rights of their Russian-speaking populations.

Russia will offer maximum assistance in reaching a settlement in the Balkans, which should be based on coordinated decisions by the world community. It is of fundamental importance to preserve the territorial integrity of the Federal Republic of Yugoslavia, and to oppose its disintegration, fraught as that would be with the threat of the emergence of a pan-Balkan conflict with unpredictable consequences.

The Russian Federation is prepared to overcome the considerable recent difficulties in its relations with the USA, and to preserve the infrastructure of the Russian-American cooperation, which has been in place for almost 10 years. Despite serious, and, in some instances, fundamental differences, Russian-American interaction is an essential prerequisite for improving the international situation and achieving global strategic stability.

Above all, this refers to the problems of disarmament, arms control and nonproliferation of weapons of mass destruction, as well as to prevention and settlement of the most dangerous regional conflicts. It is only through active dialogue with the USA that the issues of limiting and reducing strategic nuclear weapons can be resolved. It is in both our interests to maintain regular bilateral contacts at all levels, ruling out interruptions in relations and setbacks in negotiations on key political, military and economic matters.

Asia is a subject of steadily growing significance in the context of the entire foreign policy conducted by the Russian Federation, and this is preconditioned by Russia's direct affinity with this dynamically developing region and the need for an economic upturn in Siberia and the Far East. Emphasis will be placed on invigoration of Russia's participation in the main integrative structures of the Asia-Pacific Region, namely the Asia Pacific Economic Cooperation (APEC) Forum, the regional forum on security of the Association of South East Asian Nations (ASEAN), and the Shanghai Five (Russia, China, Kazakhstan, Kyrgyzstan, and Tajikistan), which was created with Russia's active involvement.

One of the crucial tasks of Russian foreign policy in Asia lies in developing friendly relations with the leading Asian powers, primarily China and India. The concurrence of the fundamental approaches of Russia and China to the key issues of world politics is one of the mainstays of regional and global stability. Russia seeks to develop mutually advantageous cooperation with China in all areas. The main task is, as before, to bring the range of economic interaction into line with the level of political relations.

Russia intends to strengthen its traditional partnership with India, including in international affairs, and to assist in overcoming problems persisting in South Asia and in strengthening stability in the region.

Russia regards the signing by India and Pakistan of the Comprehensive Nuclear Test Ban Treaty and their accession to the Treaty on the Nonproliferation of Nuclear Weapons as an important factor contributing to stability in the Asia-Pacific Region. Russia will advocate the establishment of nuclear nuclear-free zones in Asia.

The Russian Federation favors stable development of its relations with Japan and wants to achieve genuine good-neighborly relations that will accord with the interests of both countries. Within the framework of the existing negotiating mechanisms, Russia will continue to seek a mutually acceptable solution to the issue of formalizing an internationally recognized border between the two states.

Russian foreign policy is aimed at building up the positive dynamism of relations with the states of South East Asia.

It is important to develop further relations with Iran.

Of fundamental importance for Russia is overall improvement of the situation in Asia, which faces growing geopolitical ambitions on the part of a number of states, a mounting arms race, and persistence of hotbeds of tension and conflicts. Of greatest concern is the situation on the Korean Peninsula. Our efforts will be focused on ensuring Russia's equal participation in resolving the Korean problem, and on maintaining balanced relations with both Korean states.

The protracted conflict in Afghanistan poses a real threat to the security of the southern CIS borders, and directly affects Russian interests. Russia, in cooperation with other states concerned, will undertake consistent efforts to achieve a lasting and just political settlement of the Afghan problem and to prevent the export of terrorism and extremism from the country.

Russia will work to promote stabilization of the situation in the Middle East, including in the Persian Gulf zone and North Africa, in light of the impact that the situation in the region has on the whole world. As a co-sponsor of the peace process, Russia intends to pursue an active participation in the post-crisis mitigation of the situation in the region. Russia's priority here will be to restore and strengthen its status, particularly its economic status, in this region of the world that is so rich and important for our interests.

Russia views the Greater Mediterranean as a meeting point of a number of regions, namely the Middle East, the Black Sea region, the Caucasus, and the Caspian Sea basin, and intends to steer a purposeful course toward turning the area into a zone of peace, stability and good-neighborly relations, which will help advance Russian economic interests there, in particular in terms of defining routes for important energy flows.

Russia will expand interaction with African states and assist the earliest possible settlement of regional armed conflicts in Africa. It is also necessary to develop a political dialogue with the Organization of African Unity (OAU) and with sub-regional organizations, and to use their capabilities to enable Russia to join multilateral economic projects on the continent.

Russia strives for a higher level of political dialogue and economic cooperation with the countries of Central and South America, relying on the substantial progress achieved in its relations with this region in the 1990s. It will work, specifically, to expand interaction with the states of Central and South America in international organizations, to encourage Russian science-intensive industrial exports to Latin American countries, and to develop with them military and technical cooperation.

When determining the regional priorities of its foreign policy, the Russian Federation will take account of the rapidity and trends of the processes of formation of the key world centers and the degree of their members' readiness to expand their bilateral interaction with Russia.

V. Formation and Implementation of the Foreign Policy of the Russian Federation

The President of the Russian Federation, in conformity with his constitutional powers, provides guidance for the country's foreign policy and, as Head of State, represents the Russian Federation in international relations.

The Council of the Federation and the State Duma of the Federal Assembly of the Russian Federation, within the framework of their constitutional powers, pursue legislative work to support the foreign policy course of the Russian Federation and fulfillment of its international obligations.

The Security Council of the Russian Federation drafts decisions of the President of the Russian Federation in the area of international security and monitors their implementation.

The Ministry of Foreign Affairs of the Russian Federation carries out work on the direct implementation of the foreign policy course approved by the President of the Russian Federation. The Russian Foreign Ministry coordinates the foreign policy activities pursued by federal executive authorities and monitors them in accordance with Decree No. 375 of the President of the Russian Federation of March 12, 1996, "On the Coordinating Role of the Ministry of Foreign Affairs of the Russian Federation in the Conduct of the Unified Foreign Policy Line of the Russian Federation."

The constituent entities of the Russian Federation shall pursue their international ties in accordance with the Constitution of the Russian Federation, the Federal Law on coordination of international and external economic ties of the constituent entities of the Russian Federation and other legislative acts. The Foreign Ministry of Russia and other federal executive authorities render assistance to constituent entities of the Russian Federation in their international cooperation with strict respect for the sovereignty and territorial integrity of the Russian Federation.

While preparing decisions on the conduct of the state's foreign policy course, the federal executive authorities cooperate, if necessary, with non-governmental organizations of Russia. A more extensive involvement of non-governmental organizations in the country's foreign policy activities is consistent with the task of ensuring maximum support by civil society for state foreign policy and is capable of contributing to its effective implementation.

Consistent implementation of foreign policy will create favorable conditions for the fulfillment of the historic choice of the peoples of the Russian Federation in favor of a state based on the rule of law, democratic society, and a socially oriented market economy.

Originally published in *Diplomaticheskiy vestnik* [Diplomatic Review], 2000, no. 8, pp. 3–11.

Military Doctrine of the Russian Federation[1]

(2000)

The Military Doctrine of the Russian Federation (hereinafter referred to as the Military Doctrine) is a summary of the official views (guidelines) determining the military-political, military-strategic, and military-economic foundations for safeguarding the military security of the Russian Federation. The Military Doctrine is a document for a transitional period—the period of the formation of democratic statehood and a mixed economy, the transformation of the state's military organization, and the dynamic transformation of the system of international relations.

The Military Doctrine elaborates the Main Provisions for the Military Doctrine of the Russian Federation of 1993, and specifies, in respect of the military sphere, the guidelines of the National Security Concept of the Russian Federation. The provisions of the Military Doctrine are based on a comprehensive evaluation of the state of the military-political situation and a strategic forecast of its development, on a scientifically grounded definition of the current and long-term missions, objective requirements, and actual potential for safeguarding the military security of the Russian Federation, as well as on a systematic analysis of the content and nature of modern wars and armed conflicts, and Russian and foreign experience of military organizational development and the art of war.

The Military Doctrine is defensive in nature—something that is preconditioned by the organic combination within its stipulations of a consistent adherence to peace, together with a firm determination to protect national interests and guarantee the military security of the Russian Federation and its allies.

The legal basis for the Military Doctrine is provided by the Constitution of the Russian Federation, federal laws of the Russian Federation and other nor-

---

1 Approved by Decree No. 706 of the President of the Russian Federation on April 21, 2000.

mative legal acts, and the Russian Federation's international treaties on safeguarding military security.

The provisions of the Military Doctrine may be clarified and supplemented, taking account of changes in the military-political situation, the nature and content of military threats, and the conditions underlying the organizational development, advancement, and employment of the state's military organization, and may also be further spelt out in the Russian Federation President's annual messages to the Federal Assembly, in directives on planning for the use of the Armed Forces of the Russian Federation and other troops, military formations and bodies, and in other documents concerning the issues of ensuring the Russian Federation's military security.

Implementation of the Military Doctrine shall be achieved by means of the centralization of state and military command and control, and the implementation of a range of political, diplomatic, economic, social, information, legal, military, and other measures aimed at safeguarding the military security of the Russian Federation and its allies.

I. Military-Political Principles

MILITARY-POLITICAL SITUATION

1. The state of, and prospects for, the development of the current military-political situation are shaped by the qualitative improvement in the means, forms, and methods of military operation, by the increase in its expanse and the gravity of its consequences, and by its spread to new spheres. The possibility of achieving military-political goals through indirect, non-close-quarter operations determines the especial hazard that modern wars and armed conflicts represent for peoples and states and for preserving international stability and peace, and thus predetermines the vital necessity to take exhaustive measures to prevent them and to achieve a peaceful resolution to disputes at an early stage in their emergence and development.

2. The military-political situation is determined by the following key factors:
   • a reduction in the threat of the unleashing of a large-scale war, including a nuclear war;
   • the shaping and reinforcement of regional power centers;
   • the advance of national, ethnic, and religious extremism;
   • the rise of separatism;
   • the spread of local wars and armed conflicts;
   • an intensification of the regional arms race;
   • the proliferation of nuclear and other types of weapons of mass destruction and their means of delivery;
   • the exacerbation of information confrontation.

3. The following factors exert a destabilizing effect on the military-political situation:

- attempts to diminish (ignore) the existing mechanisms for ensuring international security (particularly the UN and OSCE);
- the use of military action by way of "humanitarian intervention" without the sanction of the UN Security Council, in circumvention of the generally accepted principles and norms of international law;
- the violation by certain states of international treaties and agreements in the sphere of arms limitation and disarmament; the use by the subjects of international relations of information and other (including non-conventional) means and technologies for aggressive (expansionist) purposes;
- the operation of extremist nationalist, religious, separatist, and terrorist movements, organizations, and structures;
- the expansion of the scale of organized crime, terrorism, and trafficking in weapons and drugs, and the transnational structure of these activities.

THE MAIN THREATS TO MILITARY SECURITY

4. Under today's conditions the threat of direct military aggression in traditional forms against the Russian Federation and its allies has been reduced, thanks to positive changes in international affairs, the pursuit of an active peaceful foreign policy course by Russia, and the maintenance of Russia's military potential—primarily its nuclear deterrent potential—at a sufficient level.

At the same time, the external and internal threats to the military security of the Russian Federation and its allies persist and, in certain spheres, are growing.

5. The main external threats are:

- territorial claims against the Russian Federation; interference in Russia's internal affairs;
- attempts to ignore (violate) the interests of the Russian Federation in resolving international security problems, and to oppose its strengthening as an influential center in a multipolar world;
- the existence of seats of armed conflict, particularly close to the state border of the Russian Federation and the borders of its allies;
- the formation (buildup) of groups of troops (forces), leading to the violation of the existing balance of forces, close to the Russian Federation's state border and the borders of its allies, or on the seas adjoining their territories;
- the expansion of military blocs and alliances to the detriment of the military security of the Russian Federation;
- the entry of foreign troops, in contravention of the UN Charter, onto the territory of friendly states adjoining the Russian Federation;

- the formation, equipping, and training on other states' territories of armed formations and groups, with a view to bringing them for operations on the territory of the Russian Federation and its allies;
- attacks (armed provocations) on Russian Federation military installations located on the territory of foreign states, as well as on installations and facilities on the Russian Federation's state border, the borders of its allies, or the high seas;
- actions aimed at undermining global and regional stability, in particular by inhibiting the work of the Russian structures of state and military control, or at disrupting the operation of strategic nuclear forces, missile attack early-warning, antimissile defense, and space monitoring systems and systems for ensuring their combat stability, facilities for nuclear munitions storage, and for nuclear power generation, facilities of the nuclear and chemical industries, and other potentially hazardous installations;
- hostile information (information-technological, information-psychological) operations that damage the military security of the Russian Federation and its allies;
- discrimination and the suppression of the rights, liberties, and legitimate interests of the citizens of the Russian Federation in foreign states;
- international terrorism.

6. The main internal threats are:
- attempts at the violent overthrow of the constitutional order;
- illegal activities by extremist nationalist, religious, separatist, and terrorist movements, organizations, and structures aimed at undermining the unity and territorial integrity of the Russian Federation and destabilizing the domestic political situation in the country;
- the planning, preparation, and conduct of operations aimed at disrupting the operation of federal bodies of state power, and attacking state, economic, or military facilities, or facilities related to vital services or the information infrastructure;
- the creation, equipping, training, and operation of illegal armed formations;
- illegal dissemination (trafficking) on Russian Federation territory of weapons, ammunition, explosives, and other means that may be used to carry out acts of sabotage, acts of terrorism, or other illegal actions;
- organized crime, terrorism, smuggling, and other illegal activities on a scale threatening the military security of the Russian Federation.

ENSURING MILITARY SECURITY

7. Ensuring the Russian Federation's military security is a crucial area of the state's activity.

The main goals of safeguarding military security are to prevent, localize, and neutralize military threats to the Russian Federation.

The Russian Federation is considering how to safeguard its military security within the context of developing a democratic state based on the rule of law, carrying out socio-economic reform, upholding the principles of equal partnership, mutually beneficial cooperation, and good-neighborliness in international affairs, consistently shaping an overall and comprehensive international security system, and preserving and strengthening peace throughout the world.

The Russian Federation:

- proceeds on the basis of the abiding importance of the fundamental principles and norms of international law, which are organically interconnected and supplement each other;
- retains the status of a nuclear power to contain (prevent) aggression against it and (or) its allies;
- implements a joint defense policy together with the Republic of Belarus, coordinates with it activities in the sphere of military organizational development, the development of the armed forces of the member states of the Union State, and the employment of military infrastructure, and takes other measures to maintain the defense capability of the Union State;
- attaches priority importance to enhancement of the collective security system within the CIS framework, on the basis of developing and strengthening the Collective Security Treaty;
- regards as partners all states whose policies do not damage its national interests and security, and do not contravene the UN Charter; gives preference to political, diplomatic, and other non-military means of preventing, containing, and neutralizing military threats at regional and global levels;
- strictly observes the international treaties concluded by the Russian Federation in the sphere of arms limitation, reduction, and elimination, and promotes implementation of these treaties and the safeguarding of the regimes they stipulate;
- scrupulously implements the Russian Federation's international treaties as regards strategic offensive arms and missile defense, and is ready for further reductions in its nuclear weapons, on a bilateral basis with the United States, as well as on a multilateral basis with other nuclear states, down to minimal levels that meet the requirements of strategic stability;
- seeks to make universal the regime of nonproliferation of nuclear weapons and their delivery systems, to resolutely enhance the effectiveness of that regime through a combination of prohibitive, monitoring, and technological measures, and to end and comprehensively ban nuclear testing;
- promotes the expansion of confidence-building measures between states in the military sphere, including reciprocal exchanges of information of a

military nature and the coordination of military doctrines, plans, measures for military organizational development, and military activities.

8. The military security of the Russian Federation is ensured by the sum total of the forces, means, and resources at its disposal. Under present-day conditions the Russian Federation proceeds on the basis of the need to possess a nuclear potential capable of delivering a particular level of damage to any aggressor (state or coalition of states) under any circumstances.

The Russian Federation views the nuclear weapons, with which the Armed Forces of the Russian Federation are equipped, as a factor in containing aggression, ensuring the military security of the Russian Federation and its allies, and maintaining international stability and peace. The Russian Federation reserves the right to use nuclear weapons in response to the use of nuclear and other types of weapons of mass destruction against it and (or) its allies, as well as in response to a large-scale aggression with the use of conventional weapons in situations critical to the national security of the Russian Federation.

The Russian Federation will not use nuclear weapons against states party to the Nonproliferation Treaty that do not possess nuclear weapons, except in the event of an attack on the Russian Federation, the Russian Federation's Armed Forces or other troops, its allies, or a state to which it has security commitments that is launched or supported by a non-nuclear state jointly, or under allied commitments, with a state possessing nuclear weapons.

9. The main principles for safeguarding military security are:
- the combination of firm centralized leadership of the state's military organization with civilian control over its activities;
- effective forecasting, the timely detection and classification of military threats, and adequate responses to them;
- sufficient forces, means, and resources to ensure military security, and their rational use;
- correspondence between the level of preparedness, training, and provision of the state's military organization and the requirements of military security;
- the rejection of damaging international security and the national security of other countries.

10. Following is the main content of safeguarding military security:
a) in peacetime:
- formation and implementation of a single state policy in the sphere of ensuring military security;
- maintenance of internal political stability and protection of the constitutional order, integrity, and inviolability of the territory of the Russian Federation;

- establishment and development of friendly (allied) relations with neighboring and other states;
- creation and improvement of the system of defense of the Russian Federation and its allies;
- comprehensive support for, and qualitative improvement of, the Armed Forces of the Russian Federation, and other troops, military formations, and bodies (hereinafter the Russian Federation Armed Forces and other troops) and maintenance of their readiness for coordinated actions to avert, contain, and eliminate external and internal threats;
- preparation of a package of measures for transferring the Russian Federation Armed Forces and other troops to a wartime footing (including their mobilization deployment);
- improvement of the economic, technological, and defense industrial basis; enhancement of the mobilization readiness of the economy; creation of conditions ensuring the timely switching of industrial enterprises, stipulated in the plan, to the production of military output; organization of the preparation of the bodies of state power, enterprises, institutions, and organizations, and the country's population for performing missions to safeguard military security and carry out territorial and civil defense;
- protection of the Russian Federation's facilities and installations on the high seas, in space, and on the territory of foreign states; protection of shipping, fishing, and other types of activities in the adjacent maritime zone and in distant regions of the ocean;
- protection and defense of the state border of the Russian Federation within the limits of border territory, airspace, and the underwater environment and of the exclusive economic zone and continental shelf of the Russian Federation and their natural resources;
- assisting (where necessary) political acts of the Russian Federation through implementing adequate measures of a military nature and by means of a naval presence;
- preparation for territorial and civil defense;
- development of the necessary military infrastructure;
- ensuring the security of citizens of the Russian Federation and protecting them from military threats;
- development of a conscious attitude among the population toward safeguarding the country's military security;
- monitoring of the mutual fulfillment of treaties in the sphere of arms limitation, reduction, and elimination, and the strengthening of confidence-building measures;
- ensuring readiness to participate (participating) in peacekeeping activities;

b) in a period of threat and on the commencement of a war (armed conflict):

- the timely declaration of a state of war; imposition of martial law or a state of emergency in the country or in particular regions within the country; full or partial strategic deployment of the Russian Federation Armed Forces and other troops, or units thereof; bringing them into readiness to perform their missions;
- coordination, in compliance with federal legislation, of the activities of the federal bodies of state power, the bodies of state power of the federal entities of the Russian Federation, local self-government bodies, non-governmental organizations, and citizens in the interests of repelling aggression;
- organization and coordinated implementation of armed, political, diplomatic, information, economic, and other forms of struggle;
- adoption and implementation of decisions on the preparation for, and conduct of, military operations;
- the switching of the country's economy, and of its individual sectors, enterprises and organizations, transportation, and communications, onto a footing of work in the conditions of a state of war;
- organization and implementation of territorial and civil defense measures;
- provision of aid to allies of the Russian Federation; engagement and fulfillment of their potential for achieving joint objectives in a war (armed conflict);
- prevention of the engagement of other states in the war (armed conflict) on the side of the aggressor;
- use of the potential of the United Nations and other international organizations to prevent aggression, force the aggressor to end the war (armed conflict) at an early stage, and restore international security and peace.

THE MILITARY ORGANIZATION OF THE STATE

11. The state's military organization serves the objectives of safeguarding the military security of the Russian Federation.

12. The military organization of the state includes the Russian Federation Armed Forces, which constitute its core and the basis of safeguarding military security; other troops, military formations, and organs assigned to perform military security missions by military methods; and their command and control bodies.

The state's military organization also includes that part of the country's industrial and scientific complexes that is designed for carrying out missions relating to military security.

13. The main goal of the development of the state's military organization is to ensure guaranteed protection of the national interests and military security of the Russian Federation and its allies.

14. Fundamental principles of development of the state's military organization are:

- adequate consideration of conclusions based on an analysis of the state of, and prospects for, the development of the military-political situation;
- centralization of leadership;
- unified command on a legal basis;
- achievable correspondence, within the bounds of the country's economic capacity, between, on the one hand, the level of combat and mobilization readiness, and the preparedness of bodies of military command and control and of the troops (forces), their structures, fighting strength and strength of the reserve, and reserves of material means and resources, and, on the other hand, the missions of safeguarding military security;
- unity of training and education;
- fulfillment of the rights and freedoms of service members and safeguarding their social protection and appropriate social status and living standards.

The development of all components of the state's military organization shall be carried out in accordance with normative labor acts regulating their activity, and on the basis of agreed and coordinated programs and plans.

15. The key priorities of development of the state's military organization are:
- creation of an integrated system of command and control of the state's military organization, and ensuring its effective operation;
- development and improvement of the troops (forces) ensuring strategic containment (including nuclear containment);
- creation and maintenance in sufficient readiness of structures for preparing mobilization resources, and for ensuring the mobilization deployment of the Russian Federation Armed Forces and other troops;
- manning, equipping, all-around support, and preparation of combined units and troop units for a state of permanent combat readiness of general-purpose forces for performing missions of containment and conducting combat operations in local wars and armed conflicts.

16. Basic principles of development of the state's military organization are:
- bringing the structure, composition, and strength of the components of the state's military organization into line with the missions of ensuring military security, taking into consideration the country's economic potential;
- enhancing the qualitative level, efficiency, and security of functioning of the technological basis of the system of state and military command and control;
- improving military-economic support for the state's military organization on the basis of the concentration and rational utilization of financial and material resources;

- improving strategic planning on the principle of joint use of the Russian Federation Armed Forces and other troops;
- increasing the effectiveness of the functioning of systems of personnel training, military education, operational and combat training, education of service members, all types of support, and military science;
- improving the system of manning (based on the contract and draft principle, with a gradual increase—as the necessary socio-economic conditions are created—in the proportion of service members performing military service under contract, first and foremost in the posts of junior commanding officers and specialists in the leading combat specialties);
- increasing the effectiveness of the system of operation and maintenance of arms and military equipment;
- improving special information support for the Russian Federation Armed Forces and other troops, and their command and control bodies;
- reinforcing the rule of law, order, and military discipline;
- implementing state policy to enhance the prestige of military service and to train Russian Federation citizens for it;
- assisting international military (military-political) and military-technical cooperation;
- improving the normative legal base for the construction, development, and utilization of the state's military organization and its relations with society.

17. An integral component and a priority task at the present stage in military organizational development is carrying out the comprehensive military reform required by the radical changes in the military-political situation and the tasks and conditions of safeguarding the military security of the Russian Federation.

Within the framework of military reform, there must be an interconnected, coordinated reform of all components of the state's military organization.

LEADERSHIP OF THE STATE'S MILITARY ORGANIZATION

18. The lead role in the organizational development, preparation, and use of the state's military organization, and in safeguarding the military security of the Russian Federation, shall be played by the President of the Russian Federation, who is supreme commander in chief of the Russian Federation Armed Forces.

19. The Russian Federation Government shall organize the equipping of the Russian Federation Armed Forces and other troops with arms and military and special equipment and their furnishing with material means, resources, and services; it shall take the overall lead in the operational equipping of the territory of the Russian Federation in the interests of defense; and it shall carry out other functions, as stipulated in the federal legislation, to ensure military security.

20. The federal bodies of state power, bodies of state power of the federal entities of the Russian Federation, and local self-government bodies shall exercise the powers vested in them by federal legislation in safeguarding military security.

Enterprises, institutions, organizations, public associations, and citizens of the Russian Federation take part in ensuring military security in conformity with the procedure specified by federal legislation.

21. Command and control of the Russian Federation Armed Forces and other troops shall be exercised by the leaders of the corresponding federal bodies of executive power.

22. The Russian Federation Defense Ministry shall coordinate the activity of federal bodies of executive power and organs of executive power of the federal entities of the Russian Federation on questions of defense, the formulation of concepts for the organizational development and the development of other troops, and procurement of arms and military equipment for them, and shall formulate—with the involvement of the corresponding federal bodies of executive power—the concept of the development of armaments, military and special equipment, and the federal state armaments program, as well as proposals for state defense procurement.

The General Staff of the Russian Federation Armed Forces is the main organ of operational command and control of the Russian Federation Armed Forces, coordinating the activities and organizing the collaboration of the Russian Federation Armed Forces with other troops in conducting missions in the sphere of defense.

The directorates of the commanders in chief (commanders) of branches (combat arms) of the Russian Federation Armed Forces (troops) shall carry out the formulation and implementation of plans for the organizational development and use of branches (arms) of the Russian Federation Armed Forces (troops) and their operational and mobilization training, technical equipment, and personnel training, and shall carry out command and control of the troops (forces) and their routine activities, and the development of the basing system and infrastructure.

The directorates of military districts (operational-strategic commands) shall implement command and control of inter-branch groups of general-purpose troops (forces) and the planning and organization of measures for joint training with other troops, military formations, and bodies for safeguarding military security within the established bounds of responsibility, taking into account their tasks and the integrated system of military-administrative division of the territory of the Russian Federation.

23. In order to carry out command and control of coalition groupings of troops (forces), corresponding joint bodies of military command and control shall be established by a coordinated decision of the bodies of state power of the countries participating in the coalition.

24. For the purpose of centralized leadership in safeguarding the military security of the Russian Federation, integrated strategic and operational planning shall be carried out with regard to the use of the Russian Federation Armed Forces and other troops in the interests of defense, as well as program-targeted planning of military organizational development envisaging the formulation of long-term (10–15 years), medium-term (4–5 years) and short-term (1–2 years) documents.

25. Organization of the lead role in safeguarding the military security of the Russian Federation in a period of threat, and the creation and operation of the relevant bodies of state power and organs of military command and control, shall be regulated by corresponding legislative and other normative legal acts of the Russian Federation.

II. Military-Strategic Principles

NATURE OF WARS AND ARMED CONFLICTS

1. The Russian Federation maintains its readiness to wage war and participate in armed conflicts exclusively with a view to preventing and repelling aggression, defending the integrity and inviolability of its territory, and ensuring the military security of the Russian Federation as well as that of its allies in conformity with international treaties.

2. The nature of modern wars (armed conflicts) is determined by the military-political goals they pursue, by the means of achieving those goals, and the scale of the military operations.

Accordingly, a modern war (armed conflict) may be:
- in terms of military-political goals—just (not contravening the UN Charter and the fundamental norms and principles of international law, and waged as self-defense by the side subjected to aggression); or unjust (contravening the UN Charter and the fundamental norms and principles of international law, falling within the definition of aggression, and waged by the party undertaking the armed attack);
- in terms of the means employed—using nuclear and other types of weapons of mass destruction; using only conventional weapons;
- in terms of scale—local, regional, or large-scale.

3. The main general features of contemporary warfare are:
- the impact it has on all spheres of human activity;
- its coalition nature;
- the broad use of indirect, non-close-quarter, and other (in particular non-traditional) forms and means of operation, and long-range fire and electronic destruction;
- a striving on the part of the sides to disrupt the system of state and military command and control;
- the utilization of highly efficient state-of-the-art systems of weapons and military hardware (including those developed on the basis of new physical principles);
- highly maneuverable operations by troops (forces) in disparate locations with the extensive use of air-mobile forces, airborne troops and special-purpose forces;
- attacks against troops (forces), rear-service and economic facilities, and communications throughout the territory of each of the parties engaged in the war;
- the conduct of air missions and operations; the catastrophic consequences of hitting (destroying) power-generation plants (primarily nuclear), chemical and other hazardous production facilities, infrastructure, communications, and sites of vital facilities;
- a high likelihood of new states becoming involved in the war, the escalation of warfare, and the expansion of the scale and range of the means used, including weapons of mass destruction;
- the participation in the war of irregular armed groups, as well as regular formations.

4. Armed conflict can emerge in the form of an armed incident, an armed action, and other armed clashes on a limited scale, and result from an attempt to resolve national, ethnic, religious, or other differences by means of military conflict.

Border conflict represents a special form of armed conflict.

Armed conflict can be international in nature (involving two or more states) or inter-ethnic and internal in nature (with armed confrontation waged inside an individual state).

5. Armed conflict is characterized by:
- a high degree of involvement and vulnerability of the local population;
- the engagement of irregular armed formations;
- the extensive use of disruptive and terrorist methods;
- the complicated moral and psychological atmosphere in which the troops operate;

- the enforced diversion of significant forces and assets to ensure the security of transportation routes or areas and locations where troops (forces) are deployed;
- the threat of the conflict's transformation into a local (international armed conflict) or civil (internal armed conflict) war.

6. With a view to performing missions in an internal armed conflict, unified (multi-departmental) groups of troops (forces) and command and control units may be established.

7. A local war may be waged by groups of troops (forces) deployed in a conflict zone, reinforced if necessary by transfers of troops, forces, and assets from other areas, and with the partial strategic deployment of armed forces.

In a local war the sides will operate within the borders of the warring states and pursue limited military-political goals.

8. A regional war may ensue from escalation of a local war or armed conflict and be waged with the engagement of two or several states (groups of states) in a single region, by national or coalition armed forces using both conventional and nuclear weapons.

The sides in a regional war will pursue important military-political goals.

9. A large-scale war may result from an escalation of an armed conflict, local or regional war, or from the involvement in them of a considerable number of countries from various parts of the world.

A large-scale war using only conventional weapons will be characterized by a high likelihood of growing into a nuclear war with catastrophic consequences for civilization and the foundations of human life and existence.

In a large-scale war the sides will pursue radical military-political goals. It will require the total mobilization of all the material and spiritual resources of the states involved.

10. A large-scale (regional) war may be preceded by a period of threat.

11. A large-scale (regional) war may have an initial period in which the main feature is intense armed action aimed at gaining the strategic initiative, preserving stable state and military command and control, achieving supremacy in the information sphere, and winning (maintaining) air superiority.

In the event of a prolonged large-scale (regional) war its goals will be achieved in the later stages and in the final period.

12. The Russian Federation consistently and firmly strives for the creation of an efficient system of political, legal, organizational, technological, and other international guarantees preventing armed conflicts and wars.

PRINCIPLES OF THE USE OF THE RUSSIAN FEDERATION ARMED FORCES AND OTHER TROOPS

13. The Russian Federation considers it lawful to use the Russian Federation Armed Forces and other troops to repel aggression directed against it.

The Russian Federation Armed Forces and other troops can also be used for protection against unconstitutional actions or illegal armed violence that threaten the integrity and inviolability of Russian Federation territory, as well as to perform missions in compliance with the Russian Federation's international treaties, and other missions in compliance with federal legislation.

14. The Russian Federation Armed Forces and other troops can be used in order to attain the following goals:
- in the event of a large-scale (regional) war unleashed by a state (group or coalition of states)—to protect the independence, sovereignty, and territorial integrity of the Russian Federation and its allies, to repel aggression, to effectively defeat the enemy, and to force the enemy to end its military operations on terms that meet the interests of the Russian Federation and its allies;
- in local wars and international armed conflicts—to contain the seat of tension, to create preconditions for terminating the war or armed conflict or for bringing it to an end at an early stage; to neutralize the aggressor and reach a settlement on terms meeting the interests of the Russian Federation and its allies;
- in internal armed conflicts—to defeat and liquidate illegal armed formations, to create the prerequisites for a full settlement of the conflict on the basis of the Russian Federation Constitution and federal legislation;
- in peacekeeping and peace restoration operations—to disengage the warring factions, to stabilize the situation, and secure the conditions for a just peace settlement.

15. The main forms of employing the Russian Federation Armed Forces and other troops are:
- strategic operations, operations, and combat operations—in large-scale and regional wars;
- operations and combat operations—in local wars and international armed conflicts;
- joint special operations—in internal armed conflicts;

- counter-terrorist operations—in fighting against terrorism under federal legislation;
- peacekeeping operations.

16. The Russian Federation Armed Forces and other troops shall be ready to repel aggression, effectively defeat an aggressor, and conduct active operations (both defensive and offensive), whatever the scenario under which a war or armed conflict is unleashed and waged, even in the event of the massive use by the enemy of modern and advanced combat weapons, including weapons of mass destruction of all types.

At the same time, the Russian Federation Armed Forces must ensure the implementation of peacekeeping activities by the Russian Federation, both independently and as part of international organizations.

17. The main missions of the Russian Federation Armed Forces and other troops are:

a) in safeguarding military security:

- the timely detection of a threatening development in the military-political situation or of preparations for an armed attack against the Russian Federation and (or) its allies;
- maintenance of the composition, condition, combat and mobilization preparedness, and training of the strategic nuclear forces, and of the forces and assets supporting their functioning and utilization, as well as of command and control systems, at a level that will ensure a given degree of damage to an aggressor, whatever the circumstances;
- maintenance of the combat potential, combat and mobilization readiness, and preparedness of peacetime general-purpose groups of troops (forces) at a level that ensures aggression on a local scale can be repelled;
- maintenance of arms and military (special) equipment and reserves of material resources in a state of readiness for combat use;
- ensuring designated (appointed) troops, forces, and resources are on duty (combat service);
- high-quality and full implementation of plans and programs for operational, combat, and mobilization training and education of troop personnel (forces);
- maintaining the readiness for strategic deployment within the framework of state measures for putting the country onto a wartime footing; protection and defense of the Russian Federation state border;
- development of the air defense of the Russian Federation as a unified system based on the centralized command and control of all air defense forces and means;

- creation of the conditions necessary for the security of economic activity and protection of the Russian Federation's national interests on the territorial seas, on the continental shelf, and in the exclusive economic zone of the Russian Federation, as well as on the high seas;
- defense of important state facilities;
- prevention and interception of acts of disruption and terrorism;
- prevention of ecological and other emergencies and mitigation of their consequences;
- organization of civil and territorial defense;
- ensuring the technical cover and restoration of communications systems;
- ensuring information security.

Carrying out missions in defense of the Russian Federation's national interests on the high seas shall take place in conformity with the Fundamentals of Russian Federation Policy in the Sphere of Naval Activity.

All missions to safeguard military security shall be conducted by the Russian Federation Armed Forces and other troops in coordination, in close collaboration, and in compliance with their functions as stipulated by the federal legislation.

b) in repelling an armed attack (aggression) on the Russian Federation and (or) its allies:
- partial or full strategic deployment;
- conducting strategic operations, operations, and combat actions (including jointly with allied states) to defeat the invaders and liquidate groups of troops (forces) that have been (are being) formed by the aggressor in regions where they are deployed or concentrated and on communication routes;
- maintaining in readiness for use, and use (in cases provided for by the Military Doctrine and in conformity with the established procedure) of the nuclear deterrent potential;
- containing and neutralizing border armed conflicts;
- maintenance of the regime of martial law (state of emergency);
- protection of the population, economic facilities, and the infrastructures against the enemy's weapons;
- fulfillment of the allied commitments of the Russian Federation in compliance with international treaties.

The conduct of missions to repel an armed attack (aggression) shall be organized and implemented in conformity with the Plan for Use of the Russian Federation Armed Forces, the Mobilization Plan of the Russian Federation Armed Forces, directives of the President of the Russian Federation on military security issues, orders and directives of the supreme commander in chief of the Russian Federation Armed Forces, and other normative legal acts, plans, and directive documents;

c) in domestic armed conflicts:
- the defeat and elimination of illegal armed formations, and bandit and terrorist groups and organizations, as well as the destruction of their bases, training centers, depots, and communications;
- restoration of the rule of law, and of law and order;
- ensuring public security and stability;
- maintaining the legal regime of a state of emergency in the conflict zone;
- containment and blockading of the conflict zone;
- putting an end to armed clashes, and disengagement of the warring parties;
- confiscation of weapons from the population in the conflict zone;
- strengthening public order and security in regions adjacent to the conflict zone.

The conduct of missions aimed at preventing and halting domestic armed conflicts, the containment and blockading of conflict zones, and the elimination of illegal armed formations, bands, and terrorist groups shall be entrusted to joint (multi-departmental) groups of troops (forces) created on a temporary basis and their bodies of command and control;

d) in operations to maintain and restore peace:
- disengagement of the armed groups belonging to the warring sides;
- ensuring conditions for the delivery of humanitarian aid to the civilian population and their evacuation from the conflict zone;
- blockading of the conflict zone in order to ensure the implementation of sanctions adopted by the international community;
- creation of the prerequisites for a political settlement.

Operations to maintain and restore peace shall be entrusted to the Russian Federation Armed Forces. In order to prepare for these missions, specially assigned combined units and troop units shall be identified. Alongside their preparation for use for their immediate purpose, they shall be trained according to a special program. The Russian Federation shall carry out rear and logistic support, training, and preparation of Russian contingents, the planning of their utilization, and operational command and control in line with the standards and procedures of the United Nations, the OSCE, and the Commonwealth of Independent States.

18. Forces and resources of the Russian Federation Armed Forces and other troops may be engaged with a view to providing support to the bodies of state power, bodies of local self-government, and the population in mitigating the consequences of accidents, disasters, and natural disasters.

19. In order to perform the missions that the Russian Federation Armed Forces and other troops face, groups of troops (forces) shall be formed on the territory of the Russian Federation, taking into consideration:

- the extent of the potential military threat in specific strategic sectors;
- the nature of the relations between the Russian Federation and adjacent states;
- the location of the Russian Federation's vitally important industrial regions and regions of strategic resources and particularly important facilities;
- the potential for strategic deployment in the threatened sectors in conjunction with the lowest possible volume of transport movements, as well as interregional maneuvers;
- the potential for timely withdrawal of troops (forces) and logistics reserves out of the range of possible missile and air strikes;
- the conditions for billeting troops and providing them with essential services, for resolving social and everyday issues; the availability and state of the mobilization deployment base;
- the socio-political situation in specific regions.

20. With a view to forming and maintaining stability and ensuring an adequate response to the emergence of external threats at an early stage, limited contingents of the Russian Federation Armed Forces and other troops may be deployed in strategically important regions outside the territory of the Russian Federation, in the form of joint or national groups and individual bases (facilities).

The provisions governing such deployment are stipulated in the relevant international legal documents.

21. When mixed military formations of the CIS are created, they shall be staffed by service members of the member states in compliance with their national legislation and the interstate treaties adopted. Service members who are citizens of the Russian Federation shall serve in such formations, as a rule, under contract.

Russian troop formations based on the territory of foreign states, regardless of the terms of deployment, shall form part of the Russian Federation Armed Forces and other troops and shall operate in accordance with the procedure there established, taking into consideration the provisions of the UN Charter, UN Security Council resolutions, and the Russian Federation's bilateral and multilateral treaties.

22. In order to create and develop the state's military infrastructure for supporting the strategic deployment of the Russian Federation Armed Forces and other troops, and their conduct of military operations, the operational equipping of the Russian Federation's territory from the point of view of defense shall be carried out under the leadership of the Russian Federation Government and in conformity with the federal state program.

23. The stockpiling and maintenance of reserves of material resources shall be organized by the Russian Federation Government under the plans for the creation of state and mobilization reserves approved by the Russian Federation President.

The Russian Federation Armed Forces and other troops and bodies of executive power, in compliance with federal legislation, shall carry out in peacetime the stockpiling, distribution, disposition, and maintenance of reserves of material resources to support the mobilization deployment of troops (forces) and their implementation of combat operations at the initial stage of a war (for certain types of material resources also for a longer period, based on the time scale for switching the economy of the country and its individual sectors and enterprises onto working according to the established plan), and the formation, preparation, regrouping, and utilization of strategic reserves.

The planning for the stockpiling, distribution, and disposition of operational reserves of material resources, and for maintaining them for other troops that are operationally subordinate for a given period to the Russian Federation Defense Ministry, shall be performed by the said ministry.

24. The planning of citizens' preparation for military service, military enlistment, and registration of means of transport made available to the Russian Federation Armed Forces and other troops shall be carried out under the general leadership of the General Staff of the Russian Federation Armed Forces.

25. In both peacetime and wartime, the country shall prepare for territorial and civil defense, and a number of measures shall be implemented to secure the stable functioning of economic facilities, transportation, and communications, and to ensure readiness for emergency rescue and other work in stricken areas and zones of accidents, disasters, and natural disasters.

III. Military-Economic Foundations

MILITARY-ECONOMIC PROVISION FOR MILITARY SECURITY

1. The main aim of military-economic provision is to meet the needs of the state's military organization for financial funds and material resources.

2. The main missions of military-economic provision are:
   • to ensure timely and complete financial provision for the missions performed by the state's military organization;
   • to optimize utilization of the material resources and funds channeled into safeguarding military security, and to assist the effectiveness of their use on the basis of the interconnected and coordinated reform of all components of the state's military organization;

- to develop the scientific, technical, technological, and industrial base of the country, of the Russian Federation Armed Forces and other troops, and of the military infrastructure in the interests of ensuring military security;
- to provide legal protection for the intellectual property contained in military products and in the techniques used to develop and produce them;
- to integrate the civil and military sectors of the country's economy and to coordinate the state's military-economic activities in the interests of ensuring military security;
- to create the state's infrastructure, taking into account the conduct of missions to safeguard military security;
- to enhance the level of social provision for service members and civilian personnel of the Russian Federation Armed Forces and other troops, and also for citizens working in the defense-industrial sector; to ensure the operation of, and to improve, systems of mobilization readiness and mobilization preparation of the country's economy and population; to build up and maintain stockpiles of material resources;
- to implement mutually beneficial international military (military-political) and military-technological cooperation;
- to fulfill the Russian Federation's international treaties in the military-economic sphere.

3. The priority missions of military-economic provision are:
   - to ensure timely and full (within the bounds of the state's current financial resources) financial support for plans for the organizational development, development, and combat and mobilization training of the Russian Federation Armed Forces and other troops, and of the requirements for all components of the state's military organization;
   - to ensure economic and financial provision for the improvement of strategic and conventional arms and military and specialized equipment;
   - to create the economic and financial prerequisites for the development and production of highly efficient standardized command and control of troops and control of weapons assets, communications, intelligence-gathering, strategic early-warning, and electronic warfare systems, and precision mobile non-nuclear weapons and the information support systems for them;
   - to enhance living standards, and implement the social guarantees envisaged by the federal legislation, for military personnel and their families.

4. The key principles of military-economic provision are:
   - to bring the level of financial and material provision for the state's military organization into correspondence with the requirements of military security and the resource potential of the state;

- to concentrate financial, material, technical, and intellectual resources on resolving the key missions of safeguarding military security;
- to provide state support for enterprises (industrial facilities) and institutions (organizations) shaping the military-technical and technological stability of the defense-industrial sector, city-infrastructure enterprises, and restricted administrative territorial entities;
- to ensure scientific, technical, technological, information, and resource independence in the development and production of the main types of military industrial output.

5. The basic guidelines for the mobilization preparation of the economy are:
   - the preparation of an economic management system to ensure stable operation during the period of transition to work under martial law conditions and during wartime;
   - the establishment, improvement, and effective operation of a system of mobilization preparation for bodies of state power, as well as for organizations and enterprises with mobilization assignments;
   - the optimization and development of the necessary mobilization capacity and facilities;
   - the creation, accumulation, maintenance, and renewal of stockpiles of material resources in mobilization and state reserves;
   - the creation and preservation of reserve stocks of design and technical documentation for wartime;
   - the preservation and development of the economic facilities needed for the stable operation of the economy and the population's survival during wartime; the preparation of the financial, credit, and tax systems and the money-supply system for a special system of functioning under martial law conditions; the development and improvement of the normative-legal base for mobilization preparation and the transition of the Russian Federation economy, the federal entities of the Russian Federation, and municipal formations to work in accordance with the established plans.

INTERNATIONAL MILITARY (MILITARY-POLITICAL) AND MILITARY-TECHNICAL COOPERATION

6. The Russian Federation carries out international military (military-political) and military-technical cooperation, proceeding on the basis of its own national interests and the need to secure the balanced performance of the missions of safeguarding military security.

International military (military-political) and military-technical cooperation is a prerogative of the state.

7. The Russian Federation implements international military (military-political) and military-technical cooperation based on foreign-policy and economic expediency and the missions of safeguarding the military security of the Russian Federation and its allies, in compliance with federal legislation and international treaties concluded by the Russian Federation, on the basis of the principles of equal rights, mutual advantage, and good-neighborliness, and observing the interests of international stability and national, regional, and global security.

8. The Russian Federation attaches priority importance to the development of military (military-political) and military-technical cooperation with the CIS Collective Security Treaty states on the basis of the need to unite their efforts to form a single defense area and safeguard collective military security.

★★★

The Russian Federation, reaffirming its underlying adherence to the aims of deterring aggression, preventing wars and armed conflicts, and maintaining international security and global peace, guarantees the consistent and firm implementation of the Military Doctrine.

Originally published in *Rossiyskaya gazeta*, no. 80, April 25, 2000.

National Security Conception of the Russian Federation

(2000)

The National Security Conception of the Russian Federation (hereinafter referred to as the Conception) is a system of views on providing security for the individual, society and the state, from external and internal threats, in every sphere of life in the Russian Federation. The Conception formulates the key guidelines of the state policy of the Russian Federation.

The national security of the Russian Federation is understood to mean the security of its multiethnic populace, as the subject of sovereignty and the only source of power in the Russian Federation.

I. Russia in the Global Community

The situation in the world is marked by a dynamic transformation of the system of international affairs. Since the end of the age of bipolar confrontation, two mutually exclusive trends have prevailed.

The first trend consists in increasingly strong economic and political positions of a considerable number of states and their integration associations, and in the improvement of the mechanisms of multilateral control over international affairs. Moreover, economic, political, scientific and technological, environmental and information factors are playing an ever greater part. On this basis, Russia will facilitate the development of an ideology aimed at the creation of a multipolar world.

The second trend is manifested in the attempt to establish a structure of international affairs based on the domination of the US-led developed western nations over the international community, and is designed to provide unilateral solutions to the key problems of global politics, above all through the use of military force, in circumvention of the fundamental norms of international law.

The development of international affairs is accompanied by competition and the striving of some states to enhance their influence over world politics, in particular through creating weapons of mass destruction. The significance of military force in international affairs remains considerable.

Russia is one of the world's largest nations, with a centuries-long history and rich cultural traditions. Despite the complex international situation and its own internal difficulties, Russia continues to play an important role in global processes by virtue of its great economic, scientific and technological, and military potential, as well as its unique strategic location on the Eurasian continent.

There are prospects for the Russian Federation's more extensive integration into the world economy and for expanded cooperation with international economic and financial institutions. The commonality of interests of Russia and other states is objectively preserved with regard to many issues pertinent to international security, including prevention of the proliferation of weapons of mass destruction, the resolution and prevention of regional conflicts, fighting international terrorism and drug trafficking, as well as the resolution of grave environmental problems on a global scale, including the problem of ensuring nuclear and radiation safety.

At the same time, a number of states have increasingly undertaken efforts to weaken Russia's position in political, economic, military and other spheres. Attempts to ignore Russia's interests when addressing major issues in international relations, including conflict situations, may undermine international security, stability, and the positive developments in international affairs.

In many countries, including Russia, the problem of terrorism has grown dramatically. The problem of terrorism is of a transnational nature and poses a threat to global stability, and this means the entire global community must pull together to enhance the effectiveness of the available ways to combat this threat, and to take emergency measures to neutralize it.

II. Russia's National Interests

Russia's national interests consist in a balanced combination of interests of the individual, society and the state in the economic, internal, social, international, information, military, border, environmental and other spheres. These are long-term interests, and they determine the fundamental goals, strategic and current tasks to be pursued by the government's domestic and foreign policy. Fulfillment of the national interests shall be ensured by state authority institutions, which function, in particular, in cooperation with non-governmental organizations operating in compliance with the Constitution and legislation of the Russian Federation.

The interests of the individual consist in the exercise of constitutional rights and liberties, in the assurance of personal security, in improved quality of life and standard of living, and in physical, spiritual and intellectual development.

The interests of society consist in strengthening democracy, establishing a social state based on the rule of law, in achieving and maintaining civil accord, and in the spiritual revival of Russia.

The interests of the state consist in the inviolability of the constitutional order, and Russia's sovereignty and territorial integrity; in political, economic and social stability; in unconditional ensuring of the rule of law and maintenance of legal order; and in the development of equal and mutually beneficial international cooperation.

Russia's national interests can be safeguarded only through stable economic development. Therefore, Russia's national interests in the economic sphere are crucial.

Within the domestic political sphere, Russia's national interests consist in stability of the constitutional order and state authority with its institutions; in ensuring civil peace and national accord, territorial integrity, unity of the legal space, and legal order; in completing the process of establishing a democratic society; as well as in eliminating the factors that bring about the emergence of political and religious extremism, ethnic separatism, and—as a consequence—social, ethnic and religious conflicts and terrorism.

In the social sphere, Russia's national interests consist in ensuring high standards of living for its people.

In the spiritual sphere, Russia's national interests consist in maintaining and developing the moral values of society, traditions of patriotism and humanism, as well the cultural and scientific capacities of the nation.

With regard to international affairs, Russia's national interests consist in ensuring the sovereignty and enhancement of Russia's position as a great power and one of the influential centers in a multipolar world, in developing equal and mutually beneficial interaction with all nations and integration associations, above all with the member states of the Commonwealth of Independent States and Russia's traditional partners, in general respect for human rights and liberties and inadmissibility of double standards in this sphere.

In the information sphere, Russia's national interests consist in observance of the constitutional civil rights and liberties, in acquiring and using information, in developing modern telecommunication technologies, in protecting state information resources from unwarranted access.

In the military sphere, Russia's national interests consist in protecting its independence, sovereignty, state and territorial integrity, and in preventing military aggression against Russia and its allies, as well as in creating conditions for a peaceful, democratic development of the state.

With regard to its borders, it is in Russia's interests to seek creation of political, legal, organizational and other conditions with a view to ensuring reliable protection of the state borders of the Russian Federation, and compliance with the procedure and rules of economic and other forms of operation in the border area of the Russian Federation as stipulated by the Russian legislation.

In the environmental sphere, Russia's national interests consist in the preservation and improvement of the environment.

The key components of Russia's national interests are safeguarding the individual, society and the state from terrorism, including international terrorism, and from technogenic and environmental emergencies and their consequences, as well as from the threats brought about by military actions or as a consequence of such actions.

III. Threats to Russia's National Security

The current state of the Russian economy, the imperfect organization of the system of state control and of civil society, the socio-political polarization of Russian society and the advance of crime in social relations, the growth of organized crime and terrorism, as well as the aggravation of interethnic relations, and the complication of international relations, pose a broad range of internal and external threats to the country's national security.

The threats arising in the economic sphere are of a complex nature and are predetermined first of all by a dramatic reduction in the gross domestic product, by a decline in investment and innovation activities and in the scientific and technological potential, by stagnation in the agrarian sector, by the unbalanced banking system, by growth of the state's internal and foreign debts, and by the domination of fuel, energy and raw materials in Russia's exports, and of foods products and consumer goods, including the basic necessities, in its imports.

The weakening of the nation's scientific and technological potential, decline in research in the strategic spheres of scientific and technological development, the exodus of experts and intellectual property to other countries may lead to the loss of Russia's advanced position in the world, the degradation of science-intensive industries, the growth of Russia's technological dependence on other countries, and the undermining of Russia's defensive capacity.

Negative economic processes trigger separatist aspirations in some federal entities of the Russian Federation. These developments, in turn, aggravate political instability, weaken Russia's common economic space and its crucial components, namely the industrial and technological ties, as well as transport, the financial-banking, credit and tax systems.

Economic disintegration, internal social differentiation and decay of spiritual values increase tension in the relations between the regions and the center, and threaten the federal system and socio-economic structure of the Russian Federation.

The ethnic arrogance, ethnic centrism and chauvinism manifested in the activities of some non-governmental organizations, as well as uncontrolled migration, enhance the growth of nationalism, political and religious extremism, and ethnic separatism, and may ignite conflicts.

The country's single legal space is being undermined by neglect for the principle of the superiority of the Constitutional norms of the Russian Federation over other legal norms, and of federal legal norms over the legal norms of the federal entities of the Russian Federation, as well as by the deficient exercise of state control at different levels.

The threat of criminalization of social relations that are taking shape in the process of the socio-political and economic transformation of the country is particularly acute. Major errors committed at the initial stage of reforms in the economic, military, law-enforcement and other spheres of state operation, the weakening of the system of state regulation and control, the inadequate legal base and the absence of a strong state policy in the social sphere, as well as the decline in society's spiritual and moral standards, are key factors in the growth of crime, especially organized crime, and corruption.

The consequences of the mistakes are also to be seen in the weakening of legal control over the situation in the country, the integration of some elements of the executive and legislative branches of power into criminal structures, the spread of crime to the management of banking and big business, major enterprises, trade establishments and distribution networks. Therefore, fighting organized crime and corruption is not just a legal, but a political task.

The scale of terrorism and organized crime is growing as a result of the frequently conflict-ridden changes in the form of property, and the growing power struggle incited by certain group and ethno-national interests. The absence of an efficient system for the social prevention of crime, the deficient legal and logistical support for efforts aimed at preventing terrorism and organized crime, legal nihilism, as well as the exodus of qualified human resources from the law-enforcement bodies increase possible effects that this threat may have on the individual, society and the state.

The current stratification of society into a small group of the rich and an overwhelming majority of low-income citizens, the growth of the number of citizens living below the poverty line, and growing unemployment pose a threat to Russia's national security in the social sphere.

The crisis in the health care and social welfare systems, the growth of alcohol consumption and drug addiction threaten the nation's physical health.

The deep social crisis has brought a dramatic reduction in the birth rate and life expectancy in the country, distortion of society's demographic and social structures, undermining of the labor force as the foundation for industrial development, weakening of the family as society's fundamental element, and a decline in the population's spiritual, moral and creative potentials.

Aggravation of the crisis in the domain of domestic policy, as well as in the social and spiritual spheres, may lead to the loss of our democratic achievements.

The main threats in the international sphere are conditioned by the following factors:

- a striving on the part of particular states and inter-state associations to devalue the role of the existing mechanisms for ensuring international security, above all those of the UN and the OSCE;
- the danger of the weakening of Russia's political, economic and military influence in the world;
- the strengthening of military-political blocs and unions, above all the eastward enlargement of NATO;
- possible emergence of foreign military bases and large military contingents in direct proximity to the Russian borders;
- proliferation of weapons of mass destruction and their means of delivery;
- decline of the integration processes within the Commonwealth of Independent States;
- emergence and escalation of conflicts in proximity to the state borders of the Russian Federation and external borders of member states of the Commonwealth of Independent States;
- territorial claims on the Russian Federation.

In the sphere of international affairs, threats to the national security of the Russian Federation can be seen in other states' attempts to impede the strengthening of Russia as a center of influence in a multipolar world, hinder the fulfillment of Russia's national interests, and undermine its position in Europe, the Middle East, Transcaucasus, Central Asia, and the Asia-Pacific region.

Terrorism poses a serious threat to the national security of the Russian Federation. International terrorism has launched an open campaign aimed at destabilization of the situation in Russia.

There are increasing threats to Russia's national security in the information sphere. Among major dangers are the endeavors of some states to dominate the world information space and oust Russia from the international and domestic information markets; development by some states of a concept of information wars, in particular, the creation of means designed to produce dangerous effects on other countries' information spheres; disruption of the routine operation of the information and telecommunications systems, and of the safety of the information resources, as well as attempts to gain unwarranted access to them.

The intensity and magnitude of military threats have been growing too.

NATO's assumption, as its strategic doctrine, of the practice of the use of (military) force beyond the alliance's area of responsibility and without the sanction of the UN Security Council may destabilize the strategic situation in the world.

The growing technological advantage of a number of the leading world powers and their growing capacities to create new-generation weapons and military technology are creating prerequisites for a qualitatively new stage in the arms race and a dramatic change in the forms and methods of waging military operations.

The operation of foreign special services and those organizations employed by them has been growing in scale on the territory of the Russian Federation.

The growth of negative trends in the military sphere is facilitated by the protracted reform of the military organization and defense industries of the Russian Federation, as well as by the insufficient funding of national defenses and an inadequate legal base. This can be seen now in the critically low standards of operational and combat training in the Armed Forces of the Russian Federation, other troops, military formations and bodies, the inadmissible fall in the provision of modern weapons, military and specialized equipment to the troops (forces), and the extreme aggravation of social problems. All these factors undermine the military security of the Russian Federation as a whole.

With regard to border protection, threats to the national security and interests of the Russian Federation are posed by:
- the economic, demographic and cultural-religious expansion of the adjacent states into Russian territory;
- the growing activity of cross-border organized crime and foreign terrorist organizations.

The threat of ecological deterioration in a country and depletion of that country's natural resources depend directly on the internal economic situation and on society's readiness to appreciate the global nature and significance of the problems. This threat is especially significant in Russia, because of the priority being given to the development of the fuel and energy industries, and because of its deficient environmental-protection legislation, the absence or limited use of low-impact technologies, and the low level of environmental awareness. There is a trend to use Russian territory as a site for the processing and burial of environmentally hazard materials and substances.

Given all this, the weakening of state control and the low effectiveness of legal and economic mechanisms to prevent and mitigate environmental emergencies increase the risk of technogenic catastrophes in all spheres of economic operation.

IV. Ensuring the National Security of the Russian Federation

Our fundamental tasks with regard to ensuring the national security of the Russian Federation are as follows:
- the timely forecasting and detection of external and internal threats to the national security of the Russian Federation;

- the implementation of operational and long-term measures designed to prevent and eliminate internal and external threats;
- securing the sovereignty and territorial integrity of the Russian Federation, as well as the safety of its border areas;
- the economic revival of the country and pursuit of an independent and socially-oriented economic policy;
- overcoming the Russian Federation's dependence on foreign sources in the scientific and technological spheres;
- providing individual security to citizens and guaranteeing their constitutional rights and liberties on the territory of the Russian Federation;
- improvement of the system of state control in the Russian Federation, of the federal relations, local self-government and legislation of the Russian Federation, development of harmonious interethnic relations, strengthening of legal order and maintenance of socio-political stability within society;
- ensuring unconditional compliance with the legislation of the Russian Federation on the part of all citizens, officials, state agencies, political parties, public associations and religious organizations;
- equal and mutually beneficial cooperation with other countries, particularly the leading world powers;
- reviving and maintaining, at a sufficiently high level, the country's military might;
- strengthening the regime of nonproliferation of weapons of mass destruction and their means of delivery;
- effective measures to detect, prevent and terminate foreign states' intelligence and subversive operations directed against the Russian Federation;
- fundamental improvement of the environmental situation in the country.

Ensuring national security and protecting Russia's interests in the economic sphere are our state policy priorities.

The key tasks of our foreign economic policy are the following:

- creating favorable conditions for international integration of the Russian economy;
- expanding the markets for Russian commodities;
- establishing a common economic space of the member states of the Commonwealth of Independent States.

With liberalization of Russia's foreign trade and growing competition in the world markets for goods and services, we should render greater protection to the interests of Russian producers.

It is of crucial importance for us to pursue a balanced credit-financial policy designed to gradually reduce Russia's dependence on foreign loans, and to strengthen its stand within the international financial-economic organizations.

The state must play a greater part in regulating the operation of foreign banks, insurance and investment companies, and should impose transparent and well-grounded restrictions on the transfer to foreign companies of deposits of strategic natural resources, telecommunications, transportation and distribution networks.

Effective measures must be undertaken in the sphere of currency regulation and control in order to create conditions for the termination of settlements in foreign currency in the domestic market and to prevent uncontrolled capital outflow from the country.

The basic guidelines for ensuring the national security of the Russian Federation in the domestic economic sphere are as follows:

- laying a legal groundwork for the reforms, and creating an efficient mechanism for ensuring observance of the legislation of the Russian Federation;
- strengthening state regulation in the economic sphere;
- adopting necessary measures in order to overcome the aftermath of the economic crisis, to maintain and develop the scientific and technological, as well as production potential of the country, to ensure economic growth while reducing the risk of technogenic catastrophes, to advance the competitiveness of domestic industrial goods, to enhance the well-being of the people.

Transition to a highly efficient, socially oriented market economy must be carried out by way of the gradual establishment of the best mechanisms for the organization of production, and distribution of goods and services with a view to achieving the highest possible growth of the prosperity of the entire society and each citizen.

Our primary tasks are to eliminate distortions in the structure of the Russian economy, encourage priority growth of the production of science-intensive and advanced goods, support those industries that constitute the basis of expanded production and guaranteed employment.

It is of major importance for us to build up state support for investment and innovation activities, undertake measures aimed at creating a stable banking system in the interests of the real economy, facilitating the access of business to long-term loans for capital investment, and provide appreciable state support to special programs for industrial restructuring.

The priorities include encouraging the development of competitive industries and enterprises, and expansion of the market for science-intensive products. In order to fulfill these tasks, we should undertake measures to assist the employment of advanced military technologies in civilian production, introduce a mechanism to identify and develop advanced technologies that could contribute to the competitiveness of Russian enterprises in the world market.

Fulfilling the tasks formulated above requires the concentration of financial and material resources in the priority areas of scientific and technological development, the provision of assistance to the leading research schools, the acceleration of research and technological achievements and the creation of a national technological base, the encouragement of private capital investment, including by way of establishing foundations and using grants, the implementation of development programs in territories with high scientific and technological potential, the state-sponsored establishment of an infrastructure that would promote commercial use of scientific and research achievements and ensure protection of intellectual property at home and abroad, and the development of a generally accessible network of scientific, technological, and commercial information.

The state should promote equal conditions for the development and enhancement of competitiveness of enterprises, irrespective of their form of ownership. In particular, this applies to the establishment and development of private businesses in all spheres where they may facilitate the growth of social prosperity, progress of science and education, society's spiritual and moral development, and protection of consumer rights.

There is a need for the rapid establishment of mechanisms to ensure sustainable and economic development of regions that are in a particularly bad way and those of the Far North. A new tariff policy that would ensure the unity of the country's economic space should also be elaborated.

The priority of economic factors in the social sphere is of fundamental significance for strengthening the state, for ensuring social guarantees by the state, for developing mechanisms of collective responsibility and democratic decision-making, and for social cohesion. Conducting a socially fair and economically efficient policy in the sphere of income distribution is of vital importance in this respect.

Organization of the efforts of the federal executive bodies and the executive bodies of the federal entities of the Russian Federation to implement practical measures to prevent and eliminate threats to Russia's national interests in the economic sphere also means Russian legislation in that sphere must be improved and its strict observance by all economic agents ensured.

The rapprochement of the interests of Russia's peoples, development of their all-round cooperation, pursuit of a responsible and balanced state national and regional policy will ensure internal political stability in Russia. A comprehensive approach in carrying out these tasks should form the core of the state's domestic policy, designed to ensure development of the Russian Federation as a multinational democratic federal state.

The strengthening of the Russian state and improvement in federal relations and local self-government will help assure the national security of the Russian Federation. We need to assume a comprehensive approach to resolving legal, economic, social and ethno-political problems, which would ensure a balanced observance of the interests of the Russian Federation and its federal entities.

The fulfillment of the constitutional principle of democratic government requires ensuring the coordinated operation and interaction of all bodies of state authorities, a strict vertical structure of executive authority, and the integrity of the Russian judicial system. These requirements can be fulfilled by way of observance of the constitutional principle of separation of powers, a more efficient functional distribution of responsibilities among state institutions, and strengthening of Russia's federal structure by way of improvement of its relations with federal subjects within the framework of their constitutional status.

The following are the principal guidelines for protecting Russia's constitutional system:

- ensuring supremacy of the federal legislation and improvement of the legislation of the federal entities based on this principle;
- developing organizational and legal mechanisms for protecting state integrity, ensuring the unity of the legal space and Russia's national interests;
- developing and conducting a regional policy aimed at ensuring an optimal balance between the federal and regional interests;
- improving the mechanism for preventing the establishment of political parties and public associations pursuing separatist and anti-constitutional goals, and suppression of their activities.

We must consolidate our efforts in the struggle against crime and corruption. Russia needs to eliminate the economic and socio-political basis of these socially dangerous phenomena, and elaborate a comprehensive system of measures for the effective protection of the individual, society and the state from any criminal infringements.

Of priority importance is the creation of a system of measures of effective social prevention of crime and education of law-abiding citizens. These measures should be designed to protect the rights and freedoms, morals, health and property of each citizen, irrespective of race, nationality, language, descent, property and official status, place of residence, religious beliefs, political convictions, membership of public associations, and other circumstances.

The following are our priority tasks in the sphere of fighting crime:

- to diagnose, eliminate and forestall the causes and conditions that engender crime;
- to strengthen the role of the state as the guarantor of security of the individual and society, and to form an adequate legal basis with a mechanism for its application;
- to strengthen the law-enforcement system, above all the bodies fighting organized crime and terrorism, and create conditions for this system's effective operation;
- to involve state bodies, within the framework of their jurisdiction, in actions aimed at prevention of illegal actions;

• to develop mutually beneficial international cooperation in the law-enforcement sphere, above all with member states of the Commonwealth of
Independent States.

The decisions and measures taken by the state authorities in the sphere of
fighting crime must be transparent, specific and perceivable to all citizens; they
should also be pre-emptive, ensure everybody's equality before law and
inevitable responsibility, and be supported by society.

In order to prevent and fight crime successfully, we must first of all develop
a legal basis as a foundation for reliable protection of the rights and legitimate
interests of citizens, and ensure compliance with the international legal obligations of the Russian Federation in the sphere of fighting crime and human rights
observance. It is of vital importance to deprive criminals of their "breeding
ground" created by shortcomings in legislation, and economic and social crises.

In order to forestall corruption and eliminate ways of legalizing capital that
has been accumulated in illegal ways, we must create an efficient system of
financial control, improve measures of administrative, civic and criminal-law
punishment, streamline a mechanism for controlling the property status and
sources of income of officials and staff members of organizations and establishments, irrespective of the form of ownership, as well as the balance of their
expenses and incomes.

The struggle against terrorism, drug trafficking and smuggling should proceed on the basis of a federal package of measures to prevent these forms of
criminal operation.

We must engage in productive collaboration with foreign states and their law-
enforcement and special services under effective international agreements, as
well as with international organizations whose purpose it is to fight terrorism.
We should also make broader use of international experience in fighting this
phenomenon, create a coordinated mechanism to counteract international terrorism, and to effectively stop all possible channels for illegal trafficking of
weapons and explosives inside the country and for their deliveries from abroad.

All over the country's territory, the federal state authorities shall pursue persons engaged in terrorist activities, irrespective of where the acts of terror damaging the Russian Federation were planned and carried out.

Among other prerequisites of the national security of the Russian Federation are the protection of the cultural, spiritual and moral heritage, historical
traditions and social norms, preservation of the cultural heritage of all Russia's
peoples, development of a state policy in the sphere of spiritual and moral
education, introduction of a ban on the use of media air time to show programs that promote violence and exploit base instincts, and resistance to the
negative influence of foreign religious organizations and missionaries.

The spiritual renewal of society is impossible without preserving the role of the Russian language as a factor of spiritual unity of all peoples of the multi-national Russian Federation and as the language of inter-state communication of the peoples of the CIS member states.

In order to preserve and develop our cultural and spiritual heritage, we must ensure adequate social and economic conditions for cultural institutions to conduct their creative activities and operation.

In the sphere of the protection and improvement of public health, public organizations and the bodies of state power in the Russian Federation must pay more attention to developing the state (federal and municipal) insurance and private health care, must pursue a protectionist state policy with regard to the national medical and pharmaceutical industries, implement federal programs in the sphere of hygiene, epidemiology, children's health care, first and emergency medical aid, and disaster medicine.

With regard to environmental protection, the state shall pursue the following priorities:

- to rationally use natural resources and raise the environmental awareness of the population;
- to prevent environmental pollution by way of introducing stricter safety standards for technologies dealing with the burial and utilization of toxic industrial and consumer wastes;
- to prevent radioactive pollution of the environment, and minimize the consequences of radiation accidents and catastrophes;
- to ensure environmentally safe storage and utilization of weapons removed from operational use, above all nuclear submarines, ships and vessels with nuclear power units, nuclear weapons, liquid missile fuel, and the fuel of nuclear power plants;
- to ensure the safe—from the point of view of both the environment and public health—storage and destruction of chemical weapons stockpiles;
- to develop and use safe technologies, search for ways to make practical use of environmentally safe energy sources, and undertake emergency measures for environmental protection in the environmentally hazardous regions of the Russian Federation.

We should take a new approach towards organizing and providing civil defense on the territory of the Russian Federation. We should strive to implement a fundamental improvement of the unified state system for the prevention and mitigation of emergencies, including continued integration of this system with similar systems of foreign states.

The foreign policy of the Russian Federation should be focused on:
- active engagement in foreign affairs;

- strengthening of the key mechanisms for multilateral control of global political and economic developments, above all under the aegis of the UN Security Council;
- creating favorable conditions for economic and social development of the country and maintenance of global and regional stability;
- upholding the legitimate rights and interests of Russian citizens abroad, including by way of undertaking political, economic and other measures;
- expanding relations with the member states of the Commonwealth of Independent States in compliance with the principles of international law, and enhancing integration processes within the framework of the Commonwealth of Independent States and in the interests of Russia;
- promoting Russia's full-fledged participation in global and regional economic and political structures;
- assisting the resolution of conflicts, including by way of undertaking peacekeeping efforts under the aegis of the UN and other international organizations;
- advancing progress in the sphere of nuclear arms control, and maintaining global strategic stability based on the fulfillment by states of their international obligations in this sphere;
- fulfilling mutual obligations in the sphere of reduction and elimination of weapons of mass destruction and conventional armaments, undertaking confidence- and stability-building measures, and ensuring international control over the export of commodities and technologies, as well as the provision of services of a military or dual nature;
- adjusting the existing agreements on arms control and disarmament to the new conditions in international affairs, as well as drafting, where needed, new agreements, above all with regard to confidence- and security-building measures;
- assisting in the creation of zones free from weapons of mass destruction;
- developing international cooperation in the sphere of combating transnational crime and terrorism.

Ensuring the military security of the Russian Federation is among the state's priority tasks. The main goal in this sphere is to develop the capacity to adequately deal with threats that may arise in the 21st century, with rational expenditure on national defenses.

The Russian Federation advocates political, diplomatic, economic and other non-military measures in the sphere of preventing wars and armed conflicts. However, the national interests of the Russian Federation require the presence of a sufficient military might. The Armed Forces of the Russian Federation play a key part in ensuring the nation's military security.

The main task of the Russian Federation is to pursue a containment policy to forestall aggression of any scale against the country and its allies, including with the use of nuclear weapons.

The Russian Federation must have at its disposal a nuclear arsenal sufficient to cause specified damage to any aggressor state or a coalition of states in any situation.

The peacetime operating strength of the Armed Forces of the Russian Federation must be sufficient to provide reliable protection for the country in case of possible air attack, to tackle, together with other troops, military formations and agencies, tasks of repelling aggression in a local war (armed conflict), and to ensure the strategic deployment of troops to deal with tasks that may arise in the course of a large-scale war. The Armed Forces of the Russian Federation shall undertake peacekeeping efforts on behalf of the Russian Federation.

One of the key strategic tasks related to ensuring the military security of the Russian Federation is to guarantee productive collaboration and cooperation with member states of the Commonwealth of Independent States.

The national security interests of the Russian Federation will, in certain conditions, require Russia's military presence in some strategically important regions of the world. The deployment of limited military contingents (military bases or naval forces) in such regions in compliance with agreements and international law, as well as on the principles of partnership, is designed to ensure Russia's ability to fulfill its obligations, facilitate the creation of a stable military-strategic balance of forces in these regions, enable Russia to react to crisis situations in their initial stage, and facilitate the achievement of the state's foreign policy goals.

The Russian Federation proceeds from the following principles with regard to the possibility of the use of military force to ensure Russia's national security:

- the use of all available means and forces, including nuclear weapons, if a need arises to repel an armed aggression, once all other ways to resolve the crisis have been exhausted or have proved ineffective;
- the use of military force within the country is possible only in strict compliance with the Constitution of the Russian Federation and federal laws and only in case of threat to the lives of citizens and to the country's territorial integrity, or in case of threat of a violent overthrow of the constitutional order.

The defense industries play a major part in ensuring the national interests of Russia. The restructuring and conversion of the defense industries should not come into conflict with the creation of new technologies and research and technological potentials, the modernization of weapons, military and specialized technologies, and the strengthening of the standing of the Russian producers in the world market of weapons.

We must create all necessary conditions for promoting priority fundamental, forecasting and exploratory research that would bring about promising, advanced achievements in the spheres of science and technology to be used in the interests of national defense and security.

With regard to border protection, the Russian Federation shall pursue the following priorities:

- developing the necessary normative legal basis;
- expanding international cooperation in this sphere;
- counteracting economic, demographic and cultural and religious expansion to the territory of the Russian Federation on the part of other states;
- suppression of transnational organized crime and prevention of illegal migration;
- undertaking collective measures to ensure the security of the border area of the member states of the Commonwealth of Independent States.

The priority tasks pertinent to the information security of the Russian Federation are the following:

- observance of the constitutional rights and liberties of the citizens of the Russian Federation in the sphere of information;
- improvement and protection of the national information infrastructure and Russia's integration into the global information space;
- addressing the threat of rivalry in the information sphere.

It is of especial importance for the national security of the Russian Federation to ensure effective use and all-round organizational development of the intelligence and counter-intelligence services with a view to prompt detection of threats and location of their sources.

The national security structure of the Russian Federation shall be established and developed in compliance with the Constitution of the Russian Federation, federal laws, decrees and directives by the President of the Russian Federation, resolutions and directives of the Government of the Russian Federation, and relevant federal programs.

The core of the national security structure of the Russian Federation includes the agencies, forces and means of ensuring national security that undertake political, legal, logistic, economic, military and other measures in order to safeguard the security of the individual, society and the state.

The functions of the bodies and forces that ensure the national security of the Russian Federation, their composition, principles of and procedures for their operation are stipulated in the relevant legal acts of the Russian Federation.

The policy of ensuring the national security of the Russian Federation shall be formulated and conducted by:

- the President of the Russian Federation, who acts within the framework of his constitutional powers to exercise control over the bodies and forces that ensure the national security of the Russian Federation; sanctions actions designed to ensure national security; acts in conformity with the legislation of the Russian Federation with a view to forming, reforming and dispersing the agencies and forces that ensure national security and are under his control; issues statements, addresses and directives with regard to problems of national security; amends individual provisions of the National Security Conception of the Russian Federation in his annual addresses to the Federal Assembly; and drafts guidelines for the country's current domestic and foreign policies;

- the Federal Assembly of the Russian Federation, which acts under the Constitution of the Russian Federation and upon recommendations of the President of the Russian Federation, and the Government of the Russian Federation to form the legislative base in the sphere of ensuring the national security of the Russian Federation;

- the Government of the Russian Federation, which operates within the framework of its jurisdiction, and with due consideration of the national security priorities formulated by the President of the Russian Federation in his annual addresses to the Federal Assembly of the Russian Federation, to coordinate the operation of federal executive bodies and executive bodies of the federal entities of the Russian Federation, and to formulate, in accordance with the established procedure, those items in the federal budget reserved for the implementation of practical targeted programs in this sphere;

- the Security Council of the Russian Federation, which acts to ensure pre-emptive detection and assessment of threats to the national security of the Russian Federation, to promptly draft decisions on threat prevention for submission to the President of the Russian Federation, to draft proposals in the sphere of ensuring the national security of the Russian Federation, as well as proposals on specifying individual provisions of the National Security Conception of the Russian Federation, to coordinate the operation of those agencies and forces that ensure national security, and to control the fulfillment of relevant decisions by the federal executive bodies and executive bodies of the federal entities of the Russian Federation;

- the federal bodies of executive power, which ensure implementation of the legislation of the Russian Federation, decisions of the President of the Russian Federation and of the Government of the Russian Federation in the sphere of national security of the Russian Federation; act within the framework of their jurisdiction to draft normative legal acts in this sphere and submit them to the President of the Russian Federation and the Government of the Russian Federation;

• state executive bodies of the federal entities of the Russian Federation, which act jointly with the federal executive bodies to address the issues associated with implementation of the legislation of the Russian Federation, decisions of the President of the Russian Federation and the Government of the Russian Federation in the sphere of the national security of the Russian Federation, as well as implementation of federal programs, plans and directives issued by the Commander in Chief of the Armed Forces of the Russian Federation in the sphere of military security of the Russian Federation; act jointly with local self-governments to undertake measures designed to involve citizens and public associations in resolving the problems associated with national security in conformity with the legislation of the Russian Federation; submit to the federal executive bodies proposals on improvement of the national security of the Russian Federation.

★ ★ ★

The Russian Federation intends to firmly and resolutely uphold its national security. The existing legal democratic institutions, the established structure of the state authorities of the Russian Federation, and broad participation of political parties and public associations in the implementation of the National Security Conception of the Russian Federation serve as a guarantee of Russia's dynamic development in the 21st century.

Originally published in *Diplomaticheskiy vestnik* [Diplomatic Review], 2000, no. 2, pp. 3–13.

Dushanbe Declaration by the Heads of State of the Republic of Kazakhstan, the People's Republic of China, the Kyrgyz Republic, the Russian Federation, and the Republic of Tajikistan

(2000)

The Republic of Kazakhstan, the People's Republic of China, the Kyrgyz Republic, the Russian Federation, and the Republic of Tajikistan, hereinafter referred to as the Parties,

convinced that further development of cooperation and close interaction, within the framework of the Shanghai Five and on the basis of friendship and good-neighbor relations corresponds to the fundamental interests of the peoples of the five countries, and to the present-day trends towards a multipolar world and the creation of a new, just, and rational international political and economic order,

proceeding from the common desire of the members of the Five to maintain relations of friendship that pass from generation to generation, and to resolve all issues by way of consultation, in a spirit of mutual understanding, equality and mutual benefit,

confirming their adherence to the spirit and goals of the documents signed during all the meetings of the Five, as well as to all the bilateral treaties and agreements concluded between them,

having discussed in an atmosphere of mutual understanding and constructiveness issues pertinent to the state of, and prospects for, multilateral interaction in the areas of common interest,

declare the following:

1. The Parties express deep satisfaction with the progress of relations between the member states of the Shanghai Five; they believe that considerable results have been achieved in strengthening mutual trust and cooperation, and that the Five play an increasingly important and active part in maintaining security and stability in the region and facilitate the common development of their member states.

The Parties will devote their efforts to making the Shanghai Five a regional entity of multilateral cooperation in various spheres.

2. The Parties confirm their interest in Central Asia being a zone of peace and good-neighborliness, stability and equal international cooperation, and they oppose any conflicts, threats and outside interference, which might lead to an aggravation of the situation in this region. Proceeding on this basis, and taking account of the geopolitical situation emerging in the region and around it, the Parties are fully resolved to deepen their interaction in the political, diplomatic, trade and economic, military, military-logistical, and other areas with the aim of strengthening regional security and stability.

3. The Parties note that the agreements reached by the five countries in the sphere of border settlement and military confidence-building embody a new concept of security, based on mutual confidence, equality, and cooperation, assist in strengthening mutual understanding and good-neighborliness, and make a constructive contribution towards ensuring stability across the region.

They express their firm commitment to implement all the provisions of the agreements of the five States on confidence-building in the military sphere and on the reciprocal reduction of armed forces in the border area, signed in Shanghai and Moscow, respectively, in 1996 and 1997, which create for the first time a zone of trust and transparency, predictability and verifiability of military activity in a border strip more than seven thousand kilometers long.

The Parties state with satisfaction the successful launching of the Joint Control Group of the states of the Five, which shall ensure the organization and coordination of inspection activities. They also consider that the capacities of this Group should be used to consider issues related to confidence-building in the military sphere. In line with this, the Parties support the enhancement of measures, including joint exercises and training aimed at forestalling dangerous military activity, the exchange of experience of coordinating peacekeeping operations, and joint conferences, seminars, symposia, and athletic competitions.

4. The Parties regard it as expedient, in further deepening the mutual confidence and friendly cooperation of the five states in the military area, and in consolidating their joint efforts to maintain peace and stability in the region, to hold meetings of the Defense Ministers, and have consultations between the defense agencies, of the member states of the Shanghai Five.

5. The Parties reaffirm their determination to wage a joint struggle against international terrorism, religious extremism, and national separatism, which together represent the main threat to regional security, stability and progress, as well as to combat such criminal activities as illegal drug and arms trafficking, and illegal migration. For these purposes, the members of the Five will shortly draw up an appropriate multilateral Program and sign the necessary multilateral treaties and agreements on cooperation, will hold regular meetings

of the heads of the law-enforcement, border, and customs bodies, and of the special services of the five countries, and, taking account of developments in the situation, will, within the framework of the Five, hold exercises to counter terrorist activities and violence.

The Parties express their resolve not to allow the use of the territories of their states for the organization of activities impairing the sovereignty, security and public order of any of the five States.

The Parties express their satisfaction with the development of cooperation of the law-enforcement bodies and the special services of the five countries within the framework of the Bishkek Group that they have created, support the initiative of the Kyrgyz Republic for the creation of a regional anti-terrorist structure based in the city of Bishkek, and authorize the competent agencies of their countries to start negotiations with the purpose of preparing specific proposals, and to continue consultations on this issue.

6. The Parties, firmly upholding the goals and principles of the UN Charter, and also confirming the right of each state to choose its own way of political, economic and social development in accordance with its own realities, oppose interference in the internal affairs of other states, including under the pretext of "humanitarian intervention" and "protection of human rights," and support each other's efforts to protect the independence, sovereignty, territorial integrity, and social stability of the states of the Five.

The Parties, confirming their adherence to the principle of respect for human rights, proceed on the basis of the conviction that the historical specifics of each state should be taken into account when applying this principle, and stress that the application of this principle should not contradict other generally recognized principles of international law.

The Parties declare their support for the aspirations and efforts of the People's Republic of China to maintain the unity of the country in keeping with the "one China" principle.

The Parties express support for the position of the Russian Federation with regard to the settlement of the situation in the Chechen Republic.

7. The Parties, taking account of the political and other challenges confronting the modern world, including attempts to change the established practice of solving international and regional problems, stress that they will steadily support the strengthening of the role of the UN as the only universal mechanism for the maintenance of international peace and stability. They oppose the use or threat of force not sanctioned by the UN Security Council in international affairs, and all attempts by any state or group of states to monopolize, in their own interests, decision-making with regard to global and regional problems.

8. The Parties emphasize the unconditional need for the preservation and strict observance of the 1972 ABM Treaty prohibiting the installation of anti-missile defense systems on the territories of countries. This Treaty is a cornerstone of strategic stability and a basis for further reduction of strategic offensive arms.

The Parties consider that the deployment of closed bloc-based ABM defense systems in the theater of operations in the Asia-Pacific Region may undermine stability and security in the region and bring about an escalation of the arms race, and they express support for the position of China in opposing plans to include Taiwan in the ABM defense system of a theater of war by any state and in any form.

9. The Parties declare that, having passed the test of time, the Treaty on the Nonproliferation of Nuclear Weapons, the 30th anniversary of which is marked this year, has confirmed its role as an effective instrument in containing the threat of nuclear arms proliferation and has decreased the risk of a nuclear conflict; the Treaty should now acquire a truly universal character.

10. The Parties support the initiative of the Republic of Uzbekistan to create a zone free from nuclear arms (ZFNA) in Central Asia and consider that a ZFNA treaty should correspond to the generally practiced principles and parameters of this kind of document.

11. The Parties express deep concern over the continuing military and political confrontation in Afghanistan, which poses a serious threat to regional and international security.

The Parties support the efforts of the UN and its leading role in achieving a political settlement of the Afghan conflict, and call upon all the forces involved to display restraint and to return to peace negotiations in the near future, taking into account the interests of all groups and strata of Afghan society.

12. The Parties welcome the completion of the process of a peaceful settlement and establishment of national accord in Tajikistan and support the course of the country's leadership towards the solution of problems of post-conflict rehabilitation and further economic growth, of the development of democratic institutions and of carrying out economic and social transformations, and call upon the international community to render necessary support in the development of the Republic of Tajikistan.

13. The Parties regard the Conference on Interaction and Confidence-Building Measures in Asia as a positive process on the Asian continent, ensuring, in parallel with the existing structures and mechanisms in Asia, additional possi-

bilities for political dialogue on matters of regional security, and enhancing the level of mutual trust and development of multilateral cooperation.

14. The Parties, proceeding from the principles of equality and mutually beneficial cooperation, will, in every possible way, encourage the development of trade and economic partnership within the framework of the Five, including issues of improving the investment climate and business activity in their countries, offering favorable conditions to the citizens and enterprises of the other states of the Five for conducting normal economic activities, and solving disputes in the process of their cooperation.

The Parties believe that carrying out Kazakhstan's initiative on holding a meeting of the heads of government of the five countries fully meets these goals, and support the setting up, when necessary, of joint expert groups by the corresponding departments of the five states to thoroughly carry out preparatory work.

The Parties support the interest of the People's Republic of China in the active participation of Russia and the Central Asian countries in developing the western regions of China.

The Parties believe that effective use of the energy potentials of the countries of the Shanghai Five and the strengthening of regional cooperation in power engineering on the basis of mutual benefit are an important factor in safeguarding stability and development in the region and will enable all the states of the Shanghai Five to reach a new level of multilateral cooperation.

15. The Parties will encourage the development of cooperation among the countries of the Five in the area of culture, including joint organization of various festivals, displays and tours, and consider it expedient to hold meetings of the Ministers of Culture of the member states of the Five at a convenient time.

16. The Parties, devoting serious attention to protection of the environment, including the use of water resources in the region, will cooperate in this area at bilateral and multilateral levels.

17. The Parties, paying great attention to the development of cooperation among the foreign-policy departments of the states of the Five, regard it as expedient to practice holding annual meetings of the Ministers of Foreign Affairs to consider questions of promoting interaction of the five countries in all spheres, discussing international and regional problems and working out common approaches to them.

18. For the purpose of increasing the coordinating element and efficiency in formulating questions of cooperation in the framework of the Five, the Parties

will render every assistance to national coordinators, appointed in each country of the Five, support the establishment of a Council of National Coordinators and the adoption of a corresponding five-sided regulating document aimed at increasing the efficiency of the work of the Council.

19. The Parties confirm that the interaction of the five states is not directed against other states and is of an open nature. They welcome the participation of other interested states in specific cooperation programs and projects of the Five on interstate and other levels.

20. President of the Republic of Kazakhstan N. A. Nazarbayev, Chairman of the People's Republic of China Jiang Zemin, President of the Kyrgyz Republic A. A. Akayev, President of the Russian Federation V. V. Putin, and President of the Republic of Tajikistan E. S. Rakhmonov welcome the participation of President of the Republic of Uzbekistan I. A. Karimov in the Shanghai Five summit in the city of Dushanbe.

President of the Republic of Kazakhstan	N. A. Nazarbayev
Chairman of the People's Republic of China	Jiang Zemin
President of the Kyrgyz Republic	A. A. Akayev
President of the Russian Federation	V. V. Putin
President of the Republic of Tajikistan	E. S. Rakhmonov

Originally published in *Diplomaticheskiy vestnik* [Diplomatic Review], 2000, no. 8, pp. 17–20.

Joint Statement by the Presidents of the Russian Federation and the United States of America on Principles of Strategic Stability

(2000)

1. The Presidents of the United States of America and the Russian Federation agree on the need to maintain strategic nuclear stability. Agreements between them help accomplish this objective.
2. They are dedicated to the cause of strengthening strategic stability and international security. They agree that capability for deterrence has been and remains a key aspect of stability and predictability in the international security environment.
3. The Presidents, welcoming the ratification of the START-2 Treaty and related documents by the Russian Federation, look forward to the completion of the ratification process in the United States.
4. They announce that discussions will intensify on further reductions in the strategic forces of the United States and Russia within the framework of a future START-3 Treaty, and on ABM issues, in accordance with the Presidents' Moscow Statement of 1998 and Cologne Statement of 1999.
5. They agree on the vital contribution of the ABM Treaty to reductions in offensive forces, and reaffirm their commitment to that Treaty as a cornerstone of strategic stability.
6. They agree that the international community faces a dangerous and growing threat of proliferation of weapons of mass destruction and their means of delivery, including missiles and missile technologies, and stress their desire to reverse that process, by means of existing and possible new international legal mechanisms. They agree that this new threat represents a potentially significant change in the strategic situation and international security environment.
7. They agree that this emerging threat to security should be addressed and resolved through mutual cooperation and mutual respect for each other's security interests.
8. They recall the existing provision of the ABM Treaty to consider possible changes in the strategic situation that could have a bearing on the provi-

sions of the Treaty, and, as appropriate, to consider possible proposals for further increasing the viability of the Treaty.

9. The Presidents reaffirm their commitment to the continuing efforts to strengthen the ABM Treaty and to enhance its viability and effectiveness in the future, taking account of any changes in the international security environment.

10. In reinforcing the effectiveness of the ABM Treaty in the present and possible future situations, the United States of America and the Russian Federation attach great importance to enhancing the viability of the Treaty by means of measures to promote greater cooperation, openness, and trust between the sides.

11. The Russian Federation and the United States of America the note the importance of the consultative process, and reaffirm their determination to continue consultations in the future to promote the objectives and implementation of the provisions of the ABM Treaty.

12. The key provisions recorded in our agreements and statements, including at the highest level, create a basis for the activities of both countries regarding strategic arms under present-day conditions.

13. Such an approach creates confidence that the further strengthening of strategic stability, and further reductions in nuclear forces, will be based on a foundation that has been tested over decades and that advances the interests and security of both countries.

14. The Presidents have given instructions for the development of concrete measures that will allow both sides to take the steps necessary to preserve strategic stability in the face of new threats, and have called on their Ministers and experts to prepare a report for review by the Presidents.

15. They agree that issues of strategic offensive arms cannot be considered in isolation from issues of strategic defensive arms, and vice versa—an interrelationship that is reflected in the ABM Treaty and that aims to ensure equally the security of the two countries.

16. The Russian Federation and the United States of America intend to base their activities in the area of strategic offensive and defensive arms on the principles set forth in this document.

President of the Russian Federation   V. V. Putin
President of the United States of America   W. D. Clinton
Moscow, June 4, 2000

Originally published in *Diplomaticheskiy vestnik* [Diplomatic Review], 2000, no. 7, pp. 15–16.

Treaty on the Establishment of the Eurasian Economic Community

(2000)

The Republic of Belarus, the Republic of Kazakhstan, the Kyrgyz Republic, the Russian Federation, and the Republic of Tajikistan, hereinafter referred to as the Contracting Parties,

propelled by their striving to ensure their dynamic development by coordinating their social-economic reforms, and making effective use of the economic potentials with a view to enhancing the living standards of their peoples;

full of determination to increase the efficiency of their interaction aimed at developing the integration processes between them and to deepen mutual cooperation in various spheres;

recognizing the necessity to coordinate their approaches while integrating into the world economy and international trade system;

expressing their preparedness to completely fulfill the obligations they undertook in accordance with the Agreement on Customs Union between the Russian Federation and the Republic of Belarus of January 6, 1995, the Agreement on Customs Union of January 20, 1995, the Treaty on Deepening Integration in Economic and Humanitarian Spheres of March 29, 1996, and the Agreement on Customs Union and Common Economic Space of February 26, 1999;

reaffirming their adherence to the principles of the United Nations Charter, and the generally recognized principles and norms of international law, have agreed on the following:

ARTICLE 1
ESTABLISHMENT OF AN INTERNATIONAL ORGANIZATION

The Contracting Parties hereby establish the international organization Eurasian Economic Community (hereinafter referred to as the EurAsEC or the community).

The EurAsEC shall command the powers that are voluntarily vested in it by the Contracting Parties in compliance with the provisions of this Agreement.

The Contracting Parties shall remain sovereign and equal subjects in international law.

ARTICLE 2
GOALS AND MISSIONS

The EurAsEC is established with the purpose of effectively promoting the process of the formation by the Contracting Parties of the Customs Union and Common Economic Space, as well as of fulfilling other goals and missions stipulated in the aforementioned Agreements on Customs Union, the Treaty on Deepening Integration in Economic and Humanitarian Spheres, and Agreement on Customs Union and Common Economic Space, and following the stages of this process as envisaged by the aforementioned documents.

The agreements and decisions of the bodies regulating the integration shall remain in force in the parts not contravening this Agreement.

ARTICLE 3
BODIES

Ensuring the continuity of the bodies earlier established by the Contracting Parties for regulating the integration, and with the purpose of fulfilling the goals and missions of this Agreement, the following bodies will operate within the framework of the EurAsEc:
- The Interstate Council;
- The Integration Committee;
- The Interparliamentary Assembly (IPA);
- The Community Court.

Any decision to terminate operation of the bodies regulating integration that were established under the Treaty on Deepening Integration in Economic and Humanitarian Spheres of March 29, 1996 and the Agreement on Customs Union and Common Economic Space of February 26, 1999, shall be made by the Interstate Council.

ARTICLE 4
CHAIRING

Chairmanship of the Interstate Council and Integration Committee shall be exercised, in rotation, by each member state of the Community for a period of one year, in the order of the Russian alphabet.

The order of chairing the other bodies of the Community shall be stipulated in corresponding provisions.

ARTICLE 5
INTERSTATE COUNCIL

The Interstate Council shall be the highest body of the EurAsEC. The Council will include the heads of state and government of the Contracting Parties.

The Interstate Council shall address the fundamental issues related to the Community and connected to the common interests of the member states, shall determine the strategy, guidelines and prospects for the development of integration, and adopt decisions aimed at fulfilling the goals and missions of the EurAsEC.

The Interstate Council shall issue commissions to the Integration Committee, make inquiries and recommendations to the Interparliamentary Assembly, and address inquiries to the Community Court.

The Interstate Council may adopt decisions with regard to the establishment of auxiliary bodies of the Community.

The Interstate Council shall convene at the level of heads of state at least once a year, and at the level of heads of government at least twice a year. A representative of the Contracting Party currently chairing the Interstate Council shall preside over the meetings.

The Interstate Council's functions and the order of procedure shall be stipulated in the Provision adopted by the Interstate Council at the level of heads of the EurAsEC member states.

ARTICLE 6
INTEGRATION COMMITTEE

The Integration Committee is a permanent body of the EurAsEc.
1. The main missions of the Integration Committee are the following:
  • making provisions for interaction between the EurAsEc bodies;
  • drafting proposals concerning the agenda of the Interstate Council meetings and the level of these meetings, and also drafting resolutions and documents;
  • drafting proposals with regard to the formulation of the EurAsEC budget and control over its implementation;
  • control over the implementation of decisions adopted by the Interstate Council.
In order to fulfill its tasks, the Integration Committee shall:
  • adopt decisions within its jurisdiction as stipulated by this Treaty, and vested in it by the Interstate Council;
  • submit annual reports to the Interstate Council on the situation in the Community and on the progress made in fulfilling its goals and missions, and annual reports on its own activities, as well as on the implementation of the EurAsEC budget;
  • consider measures aimed at achieving the goals pursued by the community, in particular concluding relevant agreements, conducting the common policy of the Contracting Parties with regard to particular issues, and drafting appropriate proposals;
  • have the right to submit recommendations to the Interstate Council, recommendations and inquiries to the Interparliamentary Assembly and to

the governments of the Contracting Parties, and inquiries to the Community Court.

2. The Integration Committee shall include the deputy heads of the governments of the Contracting Parties. The Chairperson of the Integration committee shall take part in the meetings of the Interstate Council.

The Integration Committee shall convene at least once every three months.

In the period between meetings of the Integration Committee, the routine operation of the Community shall be carried out by the Commission of Permanent Representatives of the Contracting Parties of the EurAsEC, appointed by the heads of the member states.

3. The job of providing organizational and information-logistic support for the Interstate Council and Integration Committee shall be entrusted to the Secretariat of the Integration Committee (hereinafter, the Secretariat).

The Secretariat shall be chaired by the Secretary General appointed by the Interstate Council, as advised by the Integration Committee, for a period of three years.

The Secretary General shall be the highest administrative official of the Community, and shall take part in the meetings of the Interstate Council and Integration Committee.

The Secretariat shall consist of citizens of the member states on a quota basis, and with account taken of the participatory contributions made by the Contracting Parties to the Community's budget, and of persons hired on a contract basis.

While performing their official duties, the Secretary General and secretariat staff members must not make inquiries to, or receive directions from, any Contracting Party or any authority outside the Community. They must refrain from any actions that might affect their position as international officials accountable exclusively to the EurAsEC.

The Contracting Parties shall undertake to respect the international nature of the official duties of the Secretary General and staff members of the Secretariat, and refrain from attempts to exert influence upon them while they perform their official duties.

The functions and the order of procedure of the Integration Committee shall be stipulated in a Provision adopted by the Interstate Council.

ARTICLE 7
INTERPARLIAMENTARY ASSEMBLY

The Interparliamentary Assembly is the body of parliamentary collaboration within the framework of the EurAsEC that shall address the issues of harmonization (rapprochement, unification) of the national legislation of the Contracting Parties and bringing it into line with the treaties concluded within the framework of the EurAsEC with a view to fulfilling the Community's missions.

The Interparliamentary Assembly shall include members of parliament delegated by the parliaments of the Contracting Parties.

Within its jurisdiction, the Interparliamentary Assembly shall:

- draft outline legislation in the fundamental spheres of legal relations, which shall be subject to consideration by the Interstate Council;
- adopt model patterns to be used as the basis for formulating acts of national legislation;
- have the authority to submit recommendations to the Interstate Council, inquiries and recommendations to the Integration Committee and to the parliaments of the Contracting Parties, and inquiries to the Community Court.

A Provision on the Interparliamentary Assembly shall be adopted by the Interstate Council.

ARTICLE 8
COMMUNITY COURT

The Community Court shall ensure uniform application by the Contracting Parties of this Agreement and other agreements in force within the framework of the Community, and also of decisions adopted by the bodies of the EurAsEC.

The Community Court shall arbitrate in disputes of an economic nature that arise between the Contracting Parties on issues concerning implementation of decisions of the EurAsEC bodies and provisions of the agreements in force within the framework of the Community, and shall provide appropriate clarifications thereof and conclusions.

The Community Court shall consist of representatives of the Contracting Parties in numbers not exceeding two representatives from each Contracting Party. The judges shall be appointed by the Interparliamentary Assembly, as advised by the Interstate Council, for a period of six years.

The organization and the operating procedure of the Community Court shall be stipulated in its Statute adopted by the Interstate Council.

ARTICLE 9
MEMBERSHIP

The EurAsEc is open to all states that accept the obligations stemming from this Agreement and other agreements in force within the framework of the Community, as listed by decision of the Interstate Council, and which, in the opinion of the EurAsEC members, are able and intend to fulfill these obligations.

Any Contracting Party is in a position to withdraw from the EurAsEC, after having fulfilled its obligations towards the Community and its members, and having submitted to the Integration Committee an official notice of its intention to withdraw from this Agreement at least twelve months before the date of withdrawal. The termination of membership shall be effected in the current budget year, should the notice be submitted before the adoption of the Community budget for the next budget year. In the event of the notice being submitted after the adoption of the budget for the next year, termination of membership shall be effected in the next year.

Participation in the operation of the EurAsEC bodies by any Contracting Party that violates the provisions of this Agreement and/or other agreements in force within the framework of the Community shall be subject to termination by decision of the Interstate Council. If the Contracting Party in question continues to violate its obligations, the Interstate Council may take a decision to exclude the Party from the Community, starting from a date determined by the Interstate Council.

ARTICLE 10
OBSERVERS

The status of a EurAsEC observer may be granted to any state or international interstate (intergovernmental) organization, if an appropriate request is submitted.

Decisions to grant, terminate or annul observer status shall be adopted by the Interstate Council.

ARTICLE 11
LEGAL COMPETENCE

The EurAsEC shall command, in the territory of each Contracting Party, the legal competence necessary to fulfill its goals and missions.

The EurAsEC may establish relations with states and international organizations and conclude treaties with them.

The EurAsEC shall have the rights of a legal entity and, with a view to fulfilling its goals and missions, shall, in particular, have the power to:
- conclude agreements;
- purchase assets and dispose of them;
- appear in court;
- open accounts and perform operations with monetary funds.

ARTICLE 12
LOCATION OF OFFICES

The Integration Committee shall be based in the city of Almaty (the Republic of Kazakhstan) and the city of Moscow (the Russian Federation).

The Interparliamentary Assembly shall be based in the city of Saint Petersburg (the Russian Federation).

The Community Court shall be based in the city of Minsk (the Republic of Belarus).

By decision of the Interstate Council, the Integration Committee may open missions in the member states of the Community.

ARTICLE 13
DECISION-MAKING PROCEDURE

The Interstate Council shall adopt all decisions by consensus, except in the case of decisions to terminate membership or exclude a Party from the Community, which are adopted based on the principle of "consensus minus the vote of the interested Contracting Party."

In the Integration Committee, the decisions shall be adopted by a majority of two-thirds of the votes. Should four Contracting Parties vote in favor of a decision, but this is short of a two-thirds majority, the issue shall be transferred for consideration by the Interstate Council. The number of votes of each Contracting Party shall correspond to its contribution to the Community's budget and shall constitute:

- The Republic of Belarus – 20 votes;
- The Republic of Kazakhstan – 20 votes;
- The Kyrgyz Republic – 10 votes;
- The Russian Federation – 40 votes;
- The Republic of Tajikistan – 10 votes.

ARTICLE 14
IMPLEMENTATION OF DECISIONS

Decisions of the EurAsEC bodies shall be implemented by the Contracting Parties by means of the adoption of necessary national normative legal acts, and in accordance with national legislation.

Control over the fulfillment by the Contracting Parties of their obligations with regard to implementation of this Treaty, other agreements in force within the framework of the Community, and decisions adopted by the EurAsEC bodies shall be exercised by the Community's bodies within the bounds of their jurisdictions.

ARTICLE 15
FUNDING

Funding of the activities of the EurAsEC bodies shall come from the Community budget.

The Community budget shall be administered for each year by the Integration Committee, as agreed upon with the member states and approved by the Interstate Council.

The Community budget cannot be in deficit.

The Community budget shall be made up of participatory contributions from the Contracting Parties in accordance with the following scale:

- The Republic of Belarus – 20 per cent;
- The Republic of Kazakhstan – 20 per cent;
- The Kyrgyz Republic – 10 per cent;
- The Russian Federation – 40 per cent;
- The Republic of Tajikistan – 10 per cent.

The budgetary funds shall be allocated for:
- funding the operation of the EurAsEC bodies;
- funding joint undertakings by the Contracting Parties, which are carried out within the Community framework;
- other purposes which do not conflict with the provisions of this Treaty.

In the event of one Contracting Party's budget liability exceeding the total amount of its annual participatory contribution, this Party may be deprived of the right to vote by decision of the Interstate Council, until its liability is fully redeemed. The votes that belonged to the Party in question shall be distributed among other Contracting Parties in proportion to their contributions to the Community budget.

ARTICLE 16
PRIVILEGES AND IMMUNITIES

The Community and its officials shall enjoy privileges and immunities, which are necessary to fulfill the functions and achieve the goals stipulated by this Treaty and other agreements in force within the EurAsEC framework.

The privileges and immunities of the Community and its officials, staff members of the Secretariat and Integration Committee missions, as well as Permanent Representatives of the Contracting Parties shall be specified in special documents.

ARTICLE 17
WORKING LANGUAGE

The Russian language shall be the working language of the EurAsEC.

ARTICLE 18
DURATION AND ENTRY INTO LEGAL FORCE

This Treaty is concluded for an indefinite period.

This Agreement shall be subject to ratification by the Contracting Parties and shall enter into force on the date of submission to the depositary, which is the Integration Committee, of the last confirmation of the fulfillment of the internal state procedures necessary for the agreement to enter in force.

Should the need arise, the Contracting Parties shall bring their national legislation into line with the provisions of this Treaty.

ARTICLE 19
AMENDMENTS AND APPENDICES

This Treaty is subject to amendments and appendices, which shall be drawn up by the Contracting Parties in the form of a separate protocol that shall constitute an integral part of this Treaty.

ARTICLE 20
REGISTRATION

This Treaty shall be registered pursuant to Article 102 of the Charter of the United Nations.

Done in the city of Astana on October 10, 2000 in one original copy in the Belorussian, Kazakh, Kyrgyz, Russian, and Tajik languages, all the texts being equally authentic. In the event of disagreements when interpreting the text of this Treaty, the Contracting Parties shall use the text in the Russian language.

The original shall be stored at the Integration Committee, which shall send a certified copy of the Treaty to each Contracting Party.

For the Republic of Belarus	A. G. Lukashenko
For the Republic of Kazakhstan	N. A. Nazarbayev
For the Republic of Kyrgyzstan	A. A. Akayev
For the Russian Federation	V. V. Putin
For the Republic of Tajikistan	E. Sh. Rakhmonov

Originally published in *Diplomaticheskiy vestnik* [Diplomatic Review], 2001, no. 7, pp. 63–67.

Strategy for Development of Relations Between the Russian Federation and the European Union 2000–2010

(2000)

This Strategy formulates objectives for the development of relations between Russia and the European Union over the next decade, as well as the means of their achievement, and represents a consistent elaboration of Russia's general foreign policy conception for Europe, which stem from the objective need to establish a multipolar world, the common histories of the peoples, the responsibility on the part of the European States for the future of the continent, and the complementarity of their economies. This Strategy is also directly linked with the conception of Russia's economic security.

This Strategy is primarily aimed at upholding national interests and enhancing the role and image of Russia in Europe and in the world through establishing a reliable pan-European collective security system, and at mobilizing the economic potential and managerial experience of the European Union to promote the development of a socially oriented market economy in Russia that is based on the principles of fair competition, and further development of a democratic state governed by the rule of law. In the transition period of reform, however, the protection of national production in particular sectors of economy is justified, subject to international law and experience.

The Strategy pursues the development and strengthening of strategic partnership between Russia and the EU in European and global affairs, and prevention and settlement, through joint efforts, of local conflicts in Europe, with an emphasis on supremacy of international law and non-use of force. It advocates the shaping of a united Europe without dividing lines, and the interrelated and balanced strengthening of the positions of Russia and the European Union within the world community of the 21st century.

With Europe currently undergoing a period of transition in its development (the need to stabilize the economy and continue the socially oriented reforms in Russia; expansion, institutional reform, establishment of a "defense identity," consolidation of a common foreign and security policy, and of EU economic and monetary union), the Strategy mainly focuses on achieving the short-

and medium-term goals of this stage and laying the foundation for advanced partnership relations between the Russian Federation and the European Union in the future. The Partnership and Cooperation Agreement of 1994 (hereinafter referred to as the Agreement), which established a partnership between the Russian Federation, on the one hand, and the European associations and their member states, on the other hand, remains its major legal and institutional basis.

The activities related to the development of cooperation with the EU, however, should be carried out in close coordination with the process of Russia's accession to the World Trade Organization, which will require a certain adjustment to be made to the Agreement after the process in question has been completed.

The Strategy, finally, reflects the main orientation and objectives of the European Union Collective Strategy with respect to Russia, adopted by the European Council in Cologne in June 1999. It is possible and desirable to pool the efforts of the parties to achieve the objectives of these documents through regular meetings of their leaders on the basis of dialogue, political consultations, joint programs for the Agreement implementation, adopted by the Cooperation Council, within the framework of the activities of the Agreement working bodies and through regular diplomatic channels.

The following areas shall be our priorities in developing and strengthening the relations of partnership and cooperation between Russian and the EU for the decade to come.

1. Establishing Strategic Nature of Russia–EU Partnership

1.1. During the period considered, partnership between Russia and the European Union will be developed based on the agreements concluded, i.e. without an officially stated objective of Russia's accession to, or "association" with, the EU. As a world power situated on two continents, Russia should retain its freedom to determine and implement its domestic and foreign policies, its status and advantages as a Eurasian state and the largest country of the CIS, the independence of its position and activities at international organizations. From this perspective, partnership with the EU can take the form of joint efforts to establish an effective system of collective security in Europe on the basis of equality without dividing lines, including through the development and implementation of the Charter on European Security, in progress towards the creation of the Russia–European Union free trade zone, as well as of a high level of mutual trust and cooperation in politics and the economy.

1.2. The development of strategic partnership between Russia and the European Union will be reflected in active interaction between the parties in resolving specific major collective issues of mutual interest, as well as European and global problems, and in enhancing the positive components of the European independence and identity in the economy and politics.

1.3. Such a partnership means that Russia does not only rely on the European Union's potential, but also supports the efforts made by the EU in the areas that are important for it and where the interests of the parties objectively coincide.

1.4. The Russia–EU partnership should be based on the utmost use of benefits offered by the Agreement, and the fullest possible implementation of its provisions and the objectives for further development agreed upon by the parties, and should take into account the expansion of the supranational powers of the EU bodies under the Amsterdam Treaty, which came into force on May 1, 1999.

1.5. Such partnership could include the following stages in the forthcoming decade:
- safeguarding pan-European security by the Europeans themselves without either isolation from the United States and NATO, or their dominance over the continent;
- formulating Russia's position on the "defense identity" of the European Union with the Western European Union (WEU) to be included in it, as well as developing political and military contacts with the WEU as an integral part of the EU, and promoting practical cooperation in the area of security (peacemaking, crisis settlement, various aspects of arms limitation and reduction, etc.) which could counterbalance, inter alia, the NATO-centrism in Europe;
- developing an advanced pan-European economic and legal infrastructure as a reliable basis for trade, investment, sectoral, sub-regional and cross-border cooperation (in particular, in the "Northern Dimension" format and in the European Mediterranean region); protecting the environment and establishing appropriate standards of living in Europe; making joint efforts in the spheres of science, education, and health; jointly fighting terrorism, illegal drug trafficking and transnational organized crime;
- consulting and, when appropriate, coordinating the positions of the parties in international organizations.

1.6. Efforts will continue to further open up the EU's market to Russian exports, eliminate the remaining discrimination in trade, encourage European investments, particularly in the real sector of the Russian economy, protect Russia's legitimate interests while the European Union expands further and the single currency (euro) is introduced, and oppose possible attempts to hamper economic integration in the CIS, in particular, by maintaining "special relations" with individual countries of the Commonwealth to the detriment of Russia's interests.

1.7. To use the positive experience of integration within the EU with a view to consolidating and enhancing integration processes in the CIS space. To strive for the coordination of activities with the member states of the Customs Union and other CIS member states in the spheres of trade, political, economic, financial, humanitarian and other relations with the European Union.

1.8. On the basis of reciprocity and the existing potential, Russia could contribute to the solution of a number of problems facing the European Union, and to the strengthening of Europe's general positions in the world: facilitation of economic growth and employment in Europe through trade and investment channels, the long-term and stable provision of energy resources and raw materials to the EU on a contractual basis (in particular, through product-sharing agreements and concessions); profound integration of scientific potentials of the parties and realization on the EU market of achievements made by Russian fundamental and defense researchers, networking of infrastructure (transport, pipelines, and electricity transmission lines) and information systems ("European information society"); facilitation of outer space research and exploration, including the creation of global navigation systems, communications and environmental monitoring systems; participation in the modernization and safeguarding of European nuclear power installations; facilitation of the strengthening of the euro as an international currency by officially including it in the foreign currency reserves of the Bank of Russia; military-logistic cooperation with due account for the prospects of establishing a European "defense identity"; joint prevention and eradication of local conflicts, and combating organized crime in Europe.

On the other hand, the development of partnership with the EU should contribute to consolidating Russia's role as a leading power in shaping a new system of interstate political and economic relations in the CIS space.

1.9. Interested regions of Russia should have an opportunity to actively participate in the development of partnership with the European Union in the economic and humanitarian fields, as well as in the implementation of cross-border cooperation programs (see also Chapter 8).

1.10. Since the implementation of the Strategy affects the relations of Russia with the United Nations, OSCE, the Council of Europe, NATO, OECD, the World Bank and EBRD, its operational realization will be linked to the policies of the country with regard to these organizations.

2. Expansion of the Format and Improving the Efficiency of Political Dialogue

2.1. It is necessary to establish working contacts and interaction with the EU bodies created in accordance with the Amsterdam Agreement, in the sphere of the EU common foreign and security policy, including the issue of the European Union's "defense identity." In order to develop a political dialogue it is necessary to institutionalize annual meetings within this format: the Chairman of the Government of the Russian Federation, the Chairman of the Commission of the European Communities, the Chairmen of the chambers of the Federal Assembly of the Russian Federation, and the Chairman of the European Parliament.

2.2. To work towards moving from reciprocal exchange of information about the parties' positions to holding advance consultations on the most acute issues in order to elaborate concerted decisions. To seek to draw up for summits and Cooperation Council meetings joint initiative packages of mutual interest. To ensure close business cooperation between the Russian federal entities of the Cooperation Council, the Cooperation Committee, and the Parliamentary Cooperation Committee.

2.3. To intensify cooperative work to preserve and strengthen the OSCE as a key basis of European security. In doing so, to elaborate a clear procedure for all OSCE bodies and institutions and unconditional preservation of consensus as a basis of decision-making. To continue the work related to the preparation and subsequent implementation of the Charter on European Security. To expand practical interaction with the EU in the prevention and peaceful settlement of conflicts in the OSCE area.

2.4. To continue the persistent search for possible forms of Russia's involvement in the ongoing dialogue between the EU and other world powers and economic groups. In this connection, to support Finland's proposal to hold a tripartite Russia–EU–US summit with a detailed agenda that takes into consideration Russia's interests.

3. Development of Mutual Trade and Investments

3.1. To continue the work on creating favorable conditions for access by Russian-made goods and services to the EU market and to eliminate elements of their discrimination; seek full recognition of the market status of Russia's economy.

3.2. To study the issue of adopting a package of measures to develop trade and economic cooperation with the European Union that provides for possible trade, financial, economic, tax and other exemptions to be offset by the inflow of investments to Russia's economy.

3.3. To develop, in the nearest future, jointly with the EU a package of reciprocal measures to promote foreign investments in the real sector of Russia's economy; on the Russian side, this means the adoption of favorable investment legislation and guarantee of the security of foreign investments and, on the side of the EU and its member states, financial instruments and programs to include the extension to Russia of the European Investment Bank operations. To expand the use of the TACIS program resources for the preparation of feasibility studies on foreign investments. To seek favorable conditions for Russian investments in the EU.

3.4. Taking into account the interrelation of trade and competition, to seek the EU's recognition of the progressive transformations in the Russian antitrust policy and develop active cooperation in this area.

3.5. To encourage the normalization of export to the EU of Russian nuclear cycle products, with the simultaneous preservation of the position of nuclear power plant equipment, fuel and services in the Central and Eastern European and Baltic markets, the provision of services related to commercial space launches, the positive review and phasing-out of applicable anti-dumping procedures, the preservation of existing trade preferences and granting of additional ones, and the prospective abolition of quotas on export to the EU of Russian steel products.

3.6. Cooperation in the nuclear field shall include:
- attraction of European capital to the construction in Russia of new generation nuclear stations (with credits to be repaid through energy supplies);
- Russia's participation in the development of the European power reactor and joint efforts to carry out an international pilot project to build a thermonuclear reactor;
- development of new nuclear energy technologies, including an environmentally sound fuel cycle;
- ensuring the safe transportation, storage and utilization of nuclear waste in the North-Western regions of Russia;
- efforts to join in the planned upgrading of the EU nuclear power engineering.

3.7. To work towards implementation, with the participation of companies of the EU countries, of major investment projects designed to develop promising oil and gas fields, establish energy transportation networks, which will make a substantial contribution to the process of the pan-European economic and energy integration. In this context higher energy efficiency in Russia and the European Union will be viewed as a major tool to diminish man-made pressure on the natural environment and to reduce greenhouse gas emissions in accordance with the decisions of the international Kyoto and Buenos Aires conferences. To seek development of a joint long-term energy policy to create a common European, and in the long run, Eurasian energy space.

3.8. To seek a realistic and positive approach by the European Union to the terms of Russia's accession to the World Trade Organization. Before the "millennium round" of the multilateral trade negotiations within the framework of the WTO, to press for Russia's full participation in the round by way of using the European Union's position on the issue.

3.9. Together with the experts of the European Union, to consider the availability of conditions for opening negotiations on the establishment of a free trade area under the provisions of the Partnership and Cooperation Agreement. To proceed based on the advisability of its gradual establishment after Russia's accession to the WTO on the basis of Article XXIV of GATT-94 and of the agreed interpretation of this article. Through the establishment of the area, to seek Russia's access to the entire European economic space; to insist that the corresponding obligations be balanced by the advantages gained, and not to allow contraventions between the arrangements and the CIS legal mechanisms of economic integration, including those of the member states of the Customs Union.

3.10. Taking into account the progress made in the development of a model of resource-saving production and the expected inflows of investments to Russia's production sector, to ensure growth in reciprocal trade by increasing the share of manufactured goods, machines, equipment, electric power and services.

3.11. To finalize as soon as possible, and to adopt jointly with the European Union, a plan of action in the area of copyrights, and to develop cooperation in this field, including exchanges of scientific information and personnel.

4. Cooperation in the Financial Sphere

4.1. To press for a broadened scope of the EU's programs of technical and other assistance to Russia. To channel a major portion of TACIS's resources to restructuring the Russian banking system and to attracting foreign investments into Russia.

4.2. To achieve arrangements on partial write-offs or restructuring of Russia's debts to the EU member states. To carry out negotiations with the CEC and the European Central Bank on the procedure for converting the interest payments and principal payments into euros, and to reach an agreement on interest rates for the loans granted to Russian debtors in national European currencies. To agree upon the terms and time scale for re-denominating a part of Russia's external debt currently denominated in national currencies of the EU member states.

4.3. To create conditions for the broader use of the euro in the external economic operations of Russian firms and banks, further increase the amount and range of the operations involving the euro in the Russian domestic financial market, primarily by improving the existing legislative basis. As the euro market develops in Russia, to undertake measures to enhance the role of the single European currency in the formulation and implementation of the exchange rate policy of the Central Bank of Russia. To expand and consolidate practical interaction with the European Central Bank, the European System of Central Banks and other bodies of the EU in order to coordinate actions in view of future reform of the international financial system.

4.4. In the context of increased inflows of European investments and assistance in restructuring Russia's banking system, to consider the possibilities of increasing the proportion of foreign capital, in particular, European capital, in the total assets of the Russian banking system, with the purpose of its improvement and re-capitalization.

4.5. To continue working towards further development of cooperation with the EU in other spheres, including those stated in the Agreement.

5. Safeguarding Russian Interests in an Expanded European Union

5.1. Taking into account the ambivalent impact of the European Union's expansion on the terms of its cooperation with Russia and on Russian interests, to seek to gain the best advantages of such expansion (decreasing the level of customs protectionism, civilized transit standards, etc.), while preventing, eliminating or setting off possible negative consequences.

5.2. Before the next expansion of the European Union, to hold consultations with it, its individual members and candidates with the purpose of securing Russia's interests as the rules of the EU agricultural, technological and anti-dumping policies, its visa and border regimes, or preferences to the developing countries which are competing with Russian exports are extended to the countries of Central and Eastern Europe and the Baltic states, as well as to ensure, in the interests of stability, security and cooperation in Europe, the rights of the Russian-speaking population in the Baltic states. To consider, as a reserve option, a rejection of the extension of the Agreement to cover those candidate states that, in spite of the existing agreements, do not ensure fulfillment of the generally recognized norms. To press for the EU's adherence to the high standards it established with regard to the accession of new members. In contacts with the EU, to pay special attention to securing protection, including under international law, of the interests of the Kaliningrad region as an entity of the Russian Federation, and of the territorial integrity of Russia (see also Chapter 8, item 4).

6. Development of the Pan-European Cooperation Infrastructure

6.1. To develop the state transportation policy in the western direction, taking into consideration the prospects of consistent growth of the volume of trade, passenger and cargo transportation between Russia and the European Union countries. To combine a search for a diplomatic solution to the problems of normalization of transit through the Baltic and the Central and Eastern European countries with the creation of our own alternative transportation routes and cargo handling points.

6.2. To start, once a corresponding agreement with the European Union is reached, connecting the gas and oil pipelines and the systems for distributing electric power in the European part of Russia to the respective systems of the European Union and the Central and Eastern European states. To insist on active participation of the European Union, including in settling financial issues, in implementation of the projects of a pan-European significance, in particular, in constructing the new gas pipeline Yamal-Western Europe and its laterals to Scandinavia, and the European transport corridors.

6.3. To seek participation in tenders for contracts and subcontracts in development and modernization of infrastructure projects of pan-European significance within the European Union. To modernize and enlarge the merchant fleet and the goods truck pool to ensure transportation in a western direction as financial and technical opportunities arise. To continue joint efforts with the countries of the European Union to create the railway rolling stock, including railway cars with expandable wheel pairs, that will allow the automatic transfer of railway cars, during their journey, from the European to Russian railway tracks.

6.4. To encourage share participation of Russian businesses in the European Union infrastructure projects, the creation of Russian or mixed transportation and shipping organizations, warehouses, storage tanks, port facilities, cargo handling terminals. To make the step-by-step access of European Union ships to the internal waters of Russia conditional on an adherence to the principle of reciprocity and on support by the European Union for modernization of those routes. To link this process to progress in Russia's joining the WTO.

6.5. To promote cooperation in elaborating a common transport policy, introduction of efficient transport process technologies on the basis of adjustment and harmonization of its legal framework, simplification of the border crossing procedures, subject to assuring the economic security of Russia.

6.6. To continue developing the pan-European transport corridors, first of all corridor No. 1 (in particular, its laterals to Riga-Kaliningrad-Gdansk), as well as Nos. 2 and 9. To improve the quality of transportation services and create more attractive conditions for users of the railway services in the aforementioned corridors. To promote active cooperation in development of the Eurasian transport connections via the territory of the Russian Federation, and in the first place, interaction between the European transport corridors and the Trans-Siberian trunk railway. To seek European Investment Bank funding for these and other infrastructure projects.

6.7. To promote the idea of joint design and development of new air transport means, to conduct negotiations in order to conclude an agreement on certification of Russian civil aircraft in the European Union, and to broaden access for the Russian air carrier companies to the airports of the European Union.

6.8. To encourage participation by Russian businesses in infrastructure projects in the territory of the European Union, the creation of Russian and mixed transportation and shipping organizations and cargo handling facilities.

6.9. In the process of implementation by the CIS countries of their projects for alternative gas and oil pipelines circumventing the territory of Russia, to endeavor to identify commercially advantageous forms of participation, sales of construction materials, technologies, work and services. To encourage Russian businesses to take part in such projects. To ensure that Russian interests are taken into account in the "Inogate" and "TRACECA" projects, carried out by the CIS and EU countries.

7. Cooperation in the Sphere of Science and Technology, Protection of Intellectual Property Rights

7.1. To strive for the earliest possible conclusion of the new Agreement on cooperation in the sphere of science and technology. Fully utilize the opportunities for participation by Russian scientists and scientific centers in the European Union's Framework programs on science and technology development and demonstration activities, as well as in its educational programs.

7.2. In accordance with the Declaration signed by the European Union, to take an active part in creating the "European information society" and to ensure that Russia is regarded as an integral part of it.

7.3. To take steps to implement large-scale joint projects in the area of the outer space exploration, in particular, by means of participation in the global navigation system that the European Union is now establishing, the new systems for satellite communication and remote sensing of the environment of Europe.

7.4. To examine, in cooperation with the European Union, the opportunities for drafting and launching a program on convergence and partial integration of the scientific and technological capacities of Russia and the European Union, enhancement of the international competitiveness of the European science and industry through the introduction of Russian advanced patents and developments, including conversion research and development, in exchange for the European Union's support for Russian science.

7.5. To take steps to use the technical assistance of the European Union for the programs aimed at the development of innovative activities and a deeper involvement of the EU in the programs of the International Science and Technology Center.

8. Cross-Border Cooperation

8.1. To take advantage of the common EU–Russian border and its possible extension with a view to raising the level of the cross-border interregional cooperation and regional development of both parties up to the standards established within the so-called Euroregions. To seek the extension by the European Union of the supranational and national incentive schemes operational within the EU to such activities, including the visa and border regimes. To encourage contacts between Russian and European Union regions, in particular by using the resources of the EU Committee of the Regions, with a view to strengthening the humanitarian and economic ties and sharing the experience of local self-government and business administration.

8.2. By joint efforts to fill with practical content the initiative of the Northern Dimension in European cooperation. To seek the European Union's financial support for it and attract investments from outside Europe. To ensure that implementation of the initiative is aimed not only at the promotion of exploration and exportation of raw materials, but also at the integrated development of Northern and North-Western Russia.

8.3. Given the special geographic and economic situation of the Kaliningrad region, to create the necessary external conditions for its functioning and development as an integral part of the Russian Federation and an active participant in cross-border and interregional cooperation. To determine the prospects for the optimal economic, energy and transportation specialization of the region, in order to ensure its efficient operation in the new environment. To establish reliable transportation links with the Russian mainland. To pursue a line to its conclusion, if appropriate, of a special agreement with the EU to safeguard the interests of the Kaliningrad region as an entity of the Russian Federation in the process of European Union expansion, as well as to effect its transformation into a Russian "pilot" region within the framework of Euro–Russian cooperation in the 21st century.

8.4. Pursuing the Mediterranean direction of interregional cooperation (the Barcelona Process), to follow a course towards Russia's selective involvement in its activities and upholding of Russian interests in the establishment of the Euro–Mediterranean free trade area.

9. Development of the Legal Basis for Cooperation. Adjustment of Economic Legislation and Technical Standards

9.1. To strive to support and develop the Agreement through specific agreements with the European Union in various areas of cooperation.

9.2. To pursue a line of making arrangements with the European Union for the joint elaboration and conclusion of a new framework agreement on the strategic partnership and cooperation in the 21st century that will succeed the Agreement. To advance to it progressively, depending on Agreement implementation, on the basis of practical achievements as well as general aspects of the strategies on development of partnership and cooperation between Russia and the European Union.

9.3. While preserving the independence of the Russian legislation and legal system, to pursue a line of adjusting and harmonizing it with European Union legislation in the areas where there is the most active EU–Russian cooperation, in particular, through the Parliamentary Cooperation Committee.

9.4. While preserving Russia's systems of standards and certification, to harmonize them with the respective systems in the areas of the most active trade and technical cooperation between Russia and the EU. To promote broader application of the ISO standards. To pursue a line of achieving mutual recognition of certificates, in particular, through establishing joint certification centers.

10. Cooperation in the Law-Enforcement Sphere

10.1. To establish operative cooperation with the existing and newly established bodies of the European Union and mechanisms competent in the field of combating international terrorism, illegal drug trafficking, transnational organized crime, including money laundering, tax evasion, illegal capital export, violations of customs regulations, human trafficking, unwarranted intrusions into databases, counterfeiting. To continue active work aimed at establishing and developing cooperation with Europol.

10.2. To use – to these ends and to the extent possible – participation in the European Union's programs and plans for fighting crime and training personnel, including technical assistance programs. To develop cooperation of judicial authorities in civilian and criminal cases, customs, tax and other law enforcement bodies of Russia and the EU and its member states, including through the exchange of liaison officers.

10.3. To work towards supplementing the Agreement with a special agreement in law enforcement.

10.4. To develop cooperation of competent bodies of Russia and the European Union in fighting illegal migration, including from outside Europe.

10.5. To seek assistance by the EU members in ensuring the inevitability of punishment for those violating Russian economic and currency legislation. To establish interaction in tracking and, if possible, returning capital illegally removed from Russia to the country of its origin, to study the possibility of its use in repaying part of Russia's debt to the European Union countries or for encouraging economic cooperation between the parties.

11. The Role of Business Circles in Cooperation Development

11.1. To promote in every possible way contacts between Russian and European Union enterprises and their associations, including for developing trading and investment cooperation, for sharing experience in market activities and preventing commercial disputes. To enhance the role of the Russia–EU Industrialists' Roundtable and - if necessary - to consult it on key issues and draft decisions, to focus its activity on attracting European investments to Russia, on expanding and industrializing Russian exports, scientific and technological cooperation.

11.2. To find forms of efficient consideration and representation of business circles' interests in the working bodies of Russian–EU cooperation.

12. Ensuring Implementation of the Strategy in Russia

12.1. To proceed on the assumption that, apart from the evolution within the European Union and development of the international situation, the successful implementation of this Strategy will, to a major extent, depend on the organizational and legal, as well as material support for the realization of its provisions in Russia.

12.2. To ensure and pursue a single state policy in relations with the European Union, primarily through the activities of the Governmental Commission of the Russian Federation on Cooperation with the European Union and the active coordinating role of the Russian Foreign Ministry. To perform a special assessment of draft legislative acts and other regulations as to their conformity with the Agreement, with the aim of preventing possible disputes.

12.3. For further development of cooperation and monitoring the implementation of the Agreement by the European Union and its member states:
- to work towards establishing, in all state authorities dealing with the issues of Russia–EU cooperation, teams of experts competent in the issues of the European Union's activities and its cooperation with Russia;
- to establish and update a comprehensive and accessible information system for Russian entrepreneurs about the European Union's activities and their advantages and obligations on the European Union market, pursuant to the Agreement and other bilateral documents;
- to organize, in the Permanent Mission of Russia to the European Union and Russian embassies in member states and prospective EU members, monitoring of the implementation by the European Union of the provisions of the Agreement and decisions of its working bodies, as well as of the search for new capacities to develop cooperation.

12.4. To work to ensure the operative development and adoption of legislative acts and other legal acts regulating the development of Russian–EU cooperation and implementation by the Russian side of obligations assumed. To actively expand interparliamentary cooperation by the parties to cover the priority areas of interaction between Russia and the European Union.

12.5. To take measures to intensify training in Russian higher educational establishments and business schools of professionals in various fields of activities of the European Union and Russia–EU cooperation, as well as to expand scientific research in these spheres. To encourage academic exchanges and training of highly qualified Russian personnel using the opportunities provided by the European Union and its member states.

12.6. To make the most efficient use of the TACIS program resources for the implementation of this Strategy.

Originally published in *Diplomaticheskiy vestnik* [Diplomatic Review], 1999, no. 11, pp. 20–28.

Declaration on the Creation of the Shanghai Cooperation Organization

(2001)

The heads of state of the Republic of Kazakhstan, the People's Republic of China, the Kyrgyz Republic, the Russian Federation, the Republic of Tajikistan, and the Republic of Uzbekistan,

highly appreciating the positive role of the "Shanghai Five" Agreement, during the five years of its existence, in promoting and deepening the relations of good-neighborliness, mutual trust and friendship among the member states, strengthening security and stability in the region, and facilitating common development,

unanimously believing that the establishment and development of the Shanghai Five has met the demands of humanity and the historic tendency toward peace and development in the conditions that came to prevail after the end of the Cold War, and has revealed an enormous potential for good-neighborliness, unity and cooperation via mutual respect and mutual trust between the states belonging to different civilizations and different cultural traditions,

especially appreciating the fact that the agreements on confidence-building in the military sphere and on mutual arms reduction in the border area, signed in Shanghai and Moscow in 1996 and 1997 by the heads of the Republic of Kazakhstan, the People's Republic of China, the Kyrgyz Republic, the Russian Federation and the Republic of Tajikistan, and also the final documents signed during the meetings in Alma-Ata (1998), Bishkek (1999) and Dushanbe (2000), have made an important contribution to peace, security and the maintenance of stability in the region and the world as a whole, have enriched the practice of modern diplomacy and regional cooperation, and have had a positive impact on the international community,

firmly convinced that, given the dynamic development of political multipolarity, and economic and information globalization in the twenty-first century, the transfer of the mechanism of the Shanghai Five to a higher level of cooperation will encourage a more efficient use of the original opportunities, and resistance to new threats and challenges,

declare the following:

1. The Republic of Kazakhstan, the People's Republic of China, the Kyrgyz Republic, the Russian Federation, the Republic of Tajikistan, and the Republic of Uzbekistan shall set up the Shanghai Cooperation Organization.

2. The goals of the Shanghai Cooperation Organization shall be: the strengthening of mutual trust, friendship and good-neighborliness between the member states; the encouragement of efficient cooperation between them in political, trade, economic, scientific and technological, cultural, educational, power generation, transportation, environmental, and other spheres; and the undertaking of joint efforts to maintain peace, security and stability in the region, and to build a new, democratic, just, and rational political and economic international order.

3. Annual formal meetings of the heads of state, and regular meetings of the heads of government, of the member states shall be hosted by each member state of the Shanghai Cooperation Organization. If it is deemed necessary, in order to expand and intensify cooperation in all spheres, new mechanisms may be created, in addition to the existing mechanisms, for the heads of appropriate offices to meet, and also permanent and temporarary expert groups may be established to consider plans and proposals for further development of cooperation.

4. Shaped during the development of the Shanghai Five, the "Shanghai spirit," which is characterized by mutual trust, mutual benefit, equity, mutual consultations, respect for the variety of cultures, and aspiration for joint development, is an invaluable asset accumulated by the countries of the region during the years of cooperation. It will be enhanced, so that it becomes the norm in relationships between member states of the Shanghai Cooperation Organization in the new century.

5. The member states of the Shanghai Cooperation Organization shall strictly pursue the goals and principles of the UN Charter, the principles of mutual respect for independence, sovereignty and territorial integrity, equality and mutual benefit, resolving all issues by means of joint consultations, non-interference in one another's internal affairs, non-use of military force and threat of force, and rejection of unilateral military superiority in the adjoining regions.

6. The Shanghai Cooperation Organization has been formed on the basis of the agreements on confidence-building in the military sphere and on mutual arms reductions signed in Shanghai and Moscow in 1996 and 1997. Today, cooperation within the Organization's framework covers political, trade, eco-

nomic, cultural, scientific and technological, and other spheres. The principles reflected in the aforementioned agreements shall provide the basis for relations between the member states of the Shanghai Cooperation Organization.

7. The Shanghai Cooperation Organization shall not be a union directed against other states or regions; it shall follow the principle of openness. It shall express its readiness to develop dialogue, contacts and cooperation in all forms with other states and appropriate international and regional organizations, and, on the basis of consensus, to admit as new members states that share the goals and missions of cooperation, and the principles formulated in Clause 6 and other provisions of this Declaration, and whose accession may promote such cooperation.

8. The Shanghai Cooperation Organization attaches primary importance to regional security, and shall make every effort necessary to safeguard it. The member states shall work closely to fulfill the Shanghai Convention on Combating Terrorism, Separatism and Extremism, including by establishing a regional counter-terrorism structure within the framework of the Shanghai Cooperation Organization, to be located in Bishkek. In addition, appropriate multilateral documents on cooperation to suppress the illegal trafficking of weapons and drugs, illegal migration, and other kinds of criminal activity shall be drafted.

9. The Shanghai Cooperation Organization shall deploy its huge potential and great opportunities for mutually beneficial cooperation between the member states in the sphere of trade and the economy, and shall seek to promote the further development of cooperation and diversification of its forms among the member states at the bilateral and multilateral level. To this end, a negotiation process on the issues pertinent to the creation of favorable conditions for trade and investment shall be started within the framework of the Shanghai Cooperation Organization, a long-term program for multilateral trade and economic cooperation shall be developed, and the appropriate documents shall be signed.

10. The member states of the Shanghai Cooperation Organization shall strengthen the consultation mechanism and coordinate action to address regional issues and the international agenda, render mutual assistance, and establish close cooperation on key international and regional affairs, and shall jointly promote the strengthening of peace and stability in the region and the world as a whole, proceeding on the basis of the especial importance of maintaining the global strategic balance and stability in the existing international situation.

11. In order to coordinate the cooperation and organize interaction between the competent ministries and agencies of the member states of the Shanghai Cooperation Organization, a Council of National Coordinators of member states of the Organization shall be established.

The operation of the Council shall be specified by a Temporary Provision to be approved by the ministers of foreign affairs of the member states.

The Council of National Coordinators shall be tasked with embarking, based on this Declaration and earlier documents adopted by the heads of state within the framework of the Shanghai Five, on the development of the draft Charter of the Shanghai Cooperation Organization, which shall include a clear statement of the provisions on the goals, the essence, missions, and areas of prospective cooperation within the Shanghai Cooperation Organization, the principles and procedure for the accession of new members, the legal force of decisions adopted by the Organization, as well as the ways of interacting with other international organizations, and shall submit it for signing during the meeting of the heads of state in 2002.

Summarizing the past experience and assessing the prospects, the heads of the member states firmly believe that the establishment of the Shanghai Cooperation Organization marks the start of a transition in cooperation between the member states to a radically new phase of development, and is in line with the present-day trends, realities of the region, and vital interests of the peoples of all the member states.

President of the Republic of Kazakhstan	N. Nazarbayev
Chairman of the People's Republic of China	Jiang Zemin
President of the Kyrgyz Republic	A. Akayev
President of the Russian Federation	V. Putin
President of the Republic of Tajikistan	E. Rakhmonov
President of the Republic of Uzbekistan	I. Karimov

Shanghai, June 15, 2001

Originally published in *Diplomaticheskiy vestnik* [Diplomatic Review], 2001, no. 7.

Treaty Between the Russian Federation and the United States of America on Strategic Offensive Reductions

(2002)

The United States of America and the Russian Federation, hereinafter referred to as the Parties,

embarking upon the path of new relations for a new century and committed to the goal of strengthening their relationship through cooperation and friendship,

believing that new global challenges and threats require the building of a qualitatively new foundation for strategic relations between the Parties,

desiring to establish a genuine partnership based on the principles of mutual security, cooperation, trust, openness, and predictability,

committed to implementing significant reductions in strategic offensive arms,

proceeding from the Joint Statements by the President of the United States of America and the President of the Russian Federation on Strategic Issues of July 22, 2001 in Genoa and on a New Relationship Between the United States and Russia of November 13, 2001 in Washington,

mindful of their obligations under the Treaty Between the United States of America and the Union of Soviet Socialist Republics on the Reduction and Limitation of Strategic Offensive Arms of July 31, 1991, hereinafter referred to as the START Treaty,

mindful of their obligations under Article VI of the Treaty on the Nonproliferation of Nuclear Weapons of July 1, 1968, and

convinced that this Treaty will help to establish more favorable conditions for actively promoting security and cooperation, and enhancing international stability,

have agreed as follows:

ARTICLE 1

Each Party shall reduce and limit strategic nuclear warheads, as stated by the President of the United States of America on November 13, 2001 and as stated by the President of the Russian Federation on November 13, 2001 and

December 13, 2001 respectively, so that by December 31, 2012 the aggregate number of such warheads will not exceed 1,700–2,200 for each Party. Each Party shall determine for itself the composition and structure of its strategic offensive arms, based on the established aggregate limit for the number of such warheads.

ARTICLE 2

The Parties agree that the START Treaty remains in force in accordance with its terms.

ARTICLE 3

For purposes of implementing this Treaty, the Parties shall hold meetings at least twice a year of a Bilateral Implementation Commission.

ARTICLE 4

1. This Treaty shall be subject to ratification in accordance with the constitutional procedures of each Party. This Treaty shall enter into force on the date of the exchange of the instruments of ratification.
2. This Treaty shall remain in force until December 31, 2012 and may be extended by agreement of the Parties or superseded earlier by a subsequent agreement.
3. Each Party, in exercising its national sovereignty, may withdraw from this Treaty upon three months' written notice to the other Party.

ARTICLE V

This Treaty shall be registered pursuant to Article 102 of the Charter of the United Nations.

Done at Moscow on May 24, 2002, in two copies, each in the English and Russian languages, both texts being equally authentic.

Originally published at *www.mid.ru.*

Declaration by Heads of State and Government of the Russian Federation and NATO Member States

(2002)

This is the full text of the Declaration on the new quality of the relations between the Russian Federation and the NATO member states, which was adopted on May 28, 2002 at the summit of the Russian Federation and 19 NATO member states at the air force base Pratica di Mare near Rome.

At the start of the 21st century we live in a new, closely interrelated world, in which unprecedented new threats and challenges demand increasingly united responses. Consequently, we, the member states of the North Atlantic Treaty Organization and the Russian Federation are today opening a new page in our relations, aimed at enhancing our ability to work together in areas of common interest and to stand together against common threats and risks to our security. As participants in the Founding Act on Mutual Relations, Cooperation and Security, we reaffirm the goals, principles and commitments set forth therein, in particular our determination to build together a lasting and inclusive peace in the Euro-Atlantic area on the principles of democracy and cooperative security and the principle that the security of all states in the Euro-Atlantic community is indivisible. We are convinced that a qualitatively new relationship between NATO and the Russian Federation will constitute an essential contribution to achieving this goal. In this context, we will observe in good faith our obligations under international law, including the UN Charter, provisions and principles contained in the Helsinki Final Act and the OSCE Charter for European Security.

Building on the Founding Act and taking into account the initiative taken by our Foreign Ministers, as reflected in their statement of December 7, 2001, to bring together NATO member states and Russia to identify and pursue opportunities for joint action by the "twenty," we hereby establish the Russia–NATO Council. In the framework of the Russia–NATO Council, NATO member states and Russia will work as equal partners in areas of common interest.

The Russia–NATO Council will provide a mechanism for consultation, consensus-building, cooperation, joint decision, and joint action for the member states of NATO and Russia on a wide spectrum of security issues in the Euro-Atlantic region.

The Russia–NATO Council will serve as the principal structure and venue for advancing the relationship between NATO and Russia. It will operate on the principle of consensus. It will work on the basis of a continuous political dialogue on security issues among its members with a view to early identification of emerging problems, determination of optimal common approaches and the conduct of joint actions, as appropriate. The members of the Russia–NATO Council, acting in their national capacities and in a manner consistent with their respective collective commitments and obligations, will take joint decisions and will bear equal responsibility, individually and jointly, for their implementation. In the Russia–NATO Council each member may raise issues related to the implementation of joint decisions.

The Russia–NATO Council will be chaired by the Secretary General of NATO. It will meet at the level of Foreign Ministers and at the level of Defense Ministers twice annually, and at the level of Heads of State and Government as appropriate. Meetings of the Council at ambassadorial level will be held at least once a month, with the possibility of more frequent meetings as needed, including extraordinary meetings, which will take place at the request of any Member or the NATO Secretary General.

To support and prepare the meetings of the Council, a Preparatory Committee is established, at the level of the NATO Political Committee, with Russian representation at the appropriate level. The Preparatory Committee will meet twice monthly, or more often if necessary. The Russia–NATO Council may also establish committees or working groups for individual subjects or areas of cooperation on an ad hoc or permanent basis, as appropriate. Such committees and working groups will draw upon the resources of existing NATO committees.

Under the auspices of the Council, military representatives and Chiefs of Staff will also meet. Meetings of Chiefs of Staff will take place no less than twice a year, meetings at military representative level at least once a month, with the possibility of more frequent meetings as needed. Meetings of military experts may be convened as appropriate.

The Russia–NATO Council, replacing the Russia–NATO Permanent Joint Council [PJC], will focus on all areas of mutual interest identified in Section III of the Founding Act, including the provision to add other areas by mutual agreement. The work programs for 2002 agreed in December 2001 for the PJC and its subordinate bodies will continue to be implemented under the auspices and rules of the Russia–NATO Council. NATO member states and Russia will continue to intensify their cooperation in areas including the struggle against terrorism, crisis management, nonproliferation, arms control and confidence-building measures, theater missile defense, search and rescue at sea, military-to-military cooperation, and civil emergencies. This cooperation may complement cooperation in other forums. As initial steps in this regard, we have today agreed to pursue the following cooperative efforts:

- STRUGGLE AGAINST TERRORISM: strengthen cooperation through a multifaceted approach, including joint assessments of the terrorist threat to the Euro-Atlantic area, focused on specific threats, for example, to Russian and NATO forces, to civilian aircraft, or to critical infrastructure; an initial step will be a joint assessment of the terrorist threat to NATO, Russian and Partner peacekeeping forces in the Balkans.
- CRISIS MANAGEMENT: strengthen cooperation, including through regular exchanges of views and information on peacekeeping operations, including continuing cooperation and consultations on the situation in the Balkans; promoting interoperability between national peacekeeping contingents, including through joint or coordinated training initiatives; and further development of a generic concept for joint NATO–Russian peacekeeping operations.
- NONPROLIFERATION: broaden and strengthen cooperation against the proliferation of weapons of mass destruction (WMD) and the means of their delivery, and contribute to strengthening existing nonproliferation arrangements through: a structured exchange of views, leading to a joint assessment of global trends in proliferation of nuclear, biological and chemical agents; and exchange of experience with the goal of exploring opportunities for intensified practical cooperation on protection from nuclear, biological and chemical agents.
- ARMS CONTROL AND CONFIDENCE-BUILDING MEASURES: recalling the contributions of arms control and confidence- and security-building measures (CSBMs) to stability in the Euro-Atlantic area and reaffirming adherence to the Treaty on Conventional Armed Forces in Europe (CFE) as a cornerstone of European security, work cooperatively toward ratification by all the States Parties and entry into force of the Agreement on Adaptation of the CFE Treaty, which would permit accession by non-CFE states; continue consultations on the CFE and Open Skies Treaties; and continue the NATO–Russian nuclear experts consultations.
- THEATER MISSILE DEFENSE: enhance consultations on theatre missile defense (TMD), in particular on TMD concepts, terminology, systems and system capabilities, to analyze and evaluate possible levels of interoperability among respective TMD systems, and explore opportunities for intensified practical cooperation, including joint training and exercises.
- SEARCH AND RESCUE AT SEA: monitor the implementation of the NATO–Russia Framework Document on Submarine Crew Rescue, and continue

to promote cooperation, transparency and confidence between NATO and Russia in the area of search and rescue at sea.

- MILITARY-TO-MILITARY COOPERATION AND DEFENSE REFORM: pursue enhanced military-to-military cooperation and interoperability through enhanced joint training and exercises and the conduct of joint demonstrations and tests; explore the possibility of establishing an integrated NATO–Russian military training center for missions to address the challenges of the 21st century; enhance cooperation on defense reform and its economic aspects, including conversion.
- CIVIL EMERGENCIES: pursue enhanced mechanisms for future NATO–Russian cooperation in responding to civil emergencies. Initial steps will include the exchange of information on recent disasters and the exchange of WMD consequence-management information.
- NEW THREATS AND CHALLENGES: In addition to the areas enumerated above, explore possibilities for confronting new challenges and threats to the Euro-Atlantic area in the framework of the activities of the NATO Committee on Challenges to Modern Society (CCMS); initiate cooperation in the field of civil and military airspace controls; and pursue enhanced scientific cooperation.

The members of the NATO–Russia Council will work with a view to identifying further areas of cooperation.

Originally published at *www.mid.ru*.

PART 2
Statements

Strategy for Partnership

Andrei Kozyrev

While addressing a mass rally of democracy supporters in Moscow in August 1991, I, the then Minister of Foreign Affairs of the RSFSR, officially stated something that I had already raised in print as a hypothesis: the United States and the other Western democracies are just as much the natural friends and potential allies of a democratic Russia as they were the foes of a totalitarian USSR. Generally speaking, this approach was widely hailed both in Russia and abroad.

There then followed a breakthrough in relations between Russia and the West. Virtually straight after the breakup of the USSR, the concept of a new relationship was formulated in the Russian–US Charter of Partnership and Friendship. The concept was subsequently further elaborated in the Declarations signed by Presidents Yeltsin and Clinton in Vancouver and Moscow, as well as in a number of pacts between Russia and leading Western European nations.

Doubts are today being voiced on both sides of the Atlantic concerning the feasibility of the partnership between Russia and the West generally, and between Russia and America specifically. Although there have been some achievements, such as the second Strategic Arms Reduction Treaty, the agreement to cease mutual targeting of nuclear weapons, and the joint efforts to resolve several regional conflicts, nevertheless, in some areas, partnership between Russia and the West either faces obstacles or falls well short of success. Personally, I am convinced that it is not on account of a wrong choice of strategy on our part that this is happening, but rather it is due to the very absence of any strategy at all. The need to cooperate, though, is recognized, above all by the leaders of our nations. There is already infrequent interaction in specific areas, but this interaction should develop into a strategic partnership, in which actions would live up to words.

Who is Unhappy about Building a Partnership?

I want to state my position clearly, right at the beginning: there is no alternative to the partnership. Rejection of it would likely mean the loss of a historic opportunity to resolve a twofold task: the formation of an open and democratic Russian state and the transformation of the insecure post-confrontational world into a stable and democratic one.

Achieving these goals is of crucial importance for both Russia and the West as they today promote common democratic values. Besides, the national interests of the two sets of democratic countries are not merely no longer in conflict, but even complement each other across a great number of international issues.

It is, above all, the cooperation between Russia and the USA that is crucial in this respect. Russia and the United States are now historically poised to influence the course of world affairs, but without imposing "condominium" principles or their own priorities on other nations. Russia and the United States have at their disposal everything they need to drive global partnership.

It is only certain military-industrial groups and factions within the government bureaucracies of both countries that oppose the partnership. These forces cannot reconcile themselves to the loss of the external "enemy," and seek to represent their narrow group interests as national. These forces, which built up considerable influence during the Cold War years, dig their heels in as they feel themselves losing a grip on things. They will persistently seek to exploit to their advantage the hostility and inertia of the past confrontation, and the inevitable difficulties associated with the efforts to build the new relationship.

Among the opponents of the new partnership are those "traditional" American Sovietologists who keep judging matters by their old Soviet-era yardstick. Hence their excessive suspicion, and their tendency to analyze the state of affairs in Russia using "gloomy scenario" logic. (Incidentally, a similar problem exists in Russia, for in the USSR it was often the case that professional "Americanists" were trained to be experts in "fighting American imperialism" rather than in US affairs.)

Some refer to the frightening complexity and unpredictability of Russia's internal processes, which do not fit into typical Western stereotypical expectations or judgments. Others cannot tolerate the idea of a powerful Russia, irrespective of whether it is an imperial or democratic state. Propositions are made that the West should either adopt a wait-and-see approach or develop a new containment strategy.

Opponents of the new partnership are active in Russia, too. These days, though, they rarely gather under the old communist red flags, but are increasingly attracted by the—occasionally overtly brown—banners of ultranationalism. They reject the idea of cooperation with the West as an inseparable constituent of Russia's transition to democracy. They regard an open civilized foreign policy as an obstacle to the revival of authoritarianism and the forcible establishment of "order" in the territory of the former Soviet Union. Internal nationalist and chauvinistic elements cherish the idea of restoring an imperial Russia, whose power would be based on its military might and the supremacy of an excessively centralized authoritarian state over its own and other peoples, as they drift into ever greater misery and deprivation. The speculation by some Russian diplomats over the "pro-American infantilism" typically stems from an inferiority complex, as well as from their unwillingness and inability to embark on sensible professional efforts to promote and protect our national interests.

All opponents of the partnership share the conviction that Russia is doomed to confrontation with the outside world and that the East and West are inherently antagonistic.

Russia is Facing a Historic Choice

Under its totalitarian regime, Soviet foreign policy was engineered in deepest secrecy by the Communist Party elite. No one in the Soviet Union had the right to discuss the policy openly, let alone to criticize it. The naive attempts by some Western "Kremlinologists" to locate the "doves" and "hawks" of the Politburo, and to build their policy towards the USSR by encouraging the former and isolating the latter, were always bound to end in failure.

Genuine public attitudes are becoming manifest in today's Russia. In a way, public opinion in Russia is as sensitive to foreign policy issues as in the West. It is precisely those popular public sentiments that are at stake in the struggle by supporters of democracy against those who promote the imperial choice. It is public opinion in Russia that is crucial at present, despite the fact that both Russia and the West perceived it to be of little consequence in past decades. It is the first time that Russian reformers and their foreign supporters must be aware of the public attitude to the policies that they devise.

It is crucial, though, that most political and public forces advocate a strong, independent and prosperous Russia. This means that the Kremlin's policy with regard to the West, and the policy pursued by the West with respect to Russia, can be efficient and reliable only if there is acknowledgement of the equality and mutual interests of both sides, and of Russia's status and significance as a great world power. In this context, Russia's foreign policy must, come what may, develop an independent stance and gain in self-confidence.

If Russian democrats, supported by their friends and sympathizers from abroad, fail to find the proper means to meet the above-mentioned requirements, they are bound to be swept away by a wave of aggressive nationalism that exploits the general demand for national self-assertiveness by the state. This is one of the lessons that should be drawn from the experience of Russia's first free parliamentary elections held in December of last year.

Some Western analysts hastily interpreted the election results as evidence of a supposed deep-rooted "imperial consciousness" among the Russian people, or even as their "national feature." And yet—as I happened to learn in the course of my own election campaign in the city of Murmansk—it was not for the restoration of the empire or a "breakthrough to the warm seas" that the electorate voted, although almost one third of them did cast their ballots for Zhirinovsky's party. Rather, they voted against the extremely high social cost of the economic reforms; against the crime and corruption flourishing on the rubble of the totalitarian state; against the inefficiency and arrogance of some democratic politicians. The ambiguity of the election results was confirmed, for example, by the fact that around one third of those electors who supported the democrat Kozyrev from the list of individual candidates, simultaneously voted for Zhirinovsky's party in the party list vote, even though the party had as a declared priority Kozyrev's dismissal and indictment.

As early as the beginning of last century, the famous Russian poet Vasiliy Zhukovskiy, appointed by the Tsar to educate the heir to the throne, the would-be reformer Alexander II, was instructing his pupil that "the genuine might of a monarch is not in the number of his soldiers but in the well-being of his people." It is our tragedy rather than our fault that this principle has until now been turned on its head. It was not the Russian people but the totalitarian communist regime that wasted the intellectual and spiritual power of the nation in the mindless arms race and in military escapades in Czechoslovakia, Hungary, and Afghanistan. In the same way, it was not the Russian people but the Communist system that was defeated in the Cold War. Moreover, it was the people themselves rather than a foreign liberator that eventually brought down the system. One should take full account of this specific feature of the collapse of Soviet Communism, which contrasts, in particular, with the fall of German Nazism or Japanese militarism.

In brief, Russia is facing a historic choice: either to continue the formidable task of reform, or to face the danger of sliding into one form of extremism or another. Only by conducting a policy that pursues her national and state interests through interaction and partnership with the West can Russia facilitate the reforms.

Choice of the West

Right now, as Russia is about to make her choice, it is of crucial importance for her to realize that the world needs the nation not as the "weakling" of Europe and Asia, but as a strong partner, a dignified member of the family of democratic legitimate states. A policy that meets these aspirations would be the best contribution the West could make to Russia's stability, and the most effective obstacle to any revival of "Russian imperialism." And vice versa, the West's alienation, its attempts to fence Russia off by new "iron curtains" or "sanitary cordons" would only provide "sustenance" for nationalist and imperial extremism.

It would be self-deception for anybody to believe that they could establish an unequal partnership of a paternalistic type with Russia, based on the principle that "since Russians have become good guys now, they must follow us in everything they do." First of all, Russia is destined to be a great power. It emerged as a great power from all the major historic cataclysms it has had to go through. And it will undoubtedly thus emerge again once the country overcomes its current crisis. Russia can be hostile and dangerous under nationalist chauvinists, or friendly and peaceable under democratic rule. However, one way or another it is going to remain a great nation.

It is a good sign that representatives of Western political thought are aware of this. Let me quote, for example, Stephen Sestanovich, the director of Russian and Eurasian Studies at the Washington Center for Strategic and International Studies: "Kozyrev's nationalistic rhetoric pursues the goal of not so much keeping his own parliamentary seat, as keeping Russia on its West-oriented foreign policy track. So far, the West has been lucky to have been dealing with a nationalism seeking international partnership. However, when we are faced with its alternative, we will immediately feel the difference."[1]

Second, partnership does not imply a rejection of a firm, even at times aggressive, policy of defending one's national interests. This can be demonstrated by the experience of the Western nations themselves. However, this same experience, for example the relationship between France and Germany, also shows that partner-type relations create the best conditions for promoting national interests, not through confrontation but by way of cooperation and compromise. It is even more naive to expect anything else, when such great and unique nations as Russia and the USA are involved.

We will study and use Western experience, as Russian reformers from Peter the Great onwards have always done. But we will remain aware of how counterproductive it is merely to copy mechanically. Each nation possesses its own specific features that cannot, and need not, be smoothed out.

Of course, the West has an alternative course it could take: to leave the matter where it is and act according to the principle that "we have done without Russia for 70 years, and we will survive for another 70 easily." A similar option is open to us, too. And yet we are not going to give up our reforms and our open foreign policy, since it has been a choice we have made for the sake of our own interests. However, without partnership the way to achieving these goals will be longer and harder for both Russia and the outside world. That is why it is in our common interests to accelerate the process through mutual adjustment and equal partnership.

---

1 *The New Republic*, April 11, 1994, p.27.

Partnership in a Multipolar World

There is the problem of how to adapt to the whole reality of the post-confrontational world.

Although the Cold War era is buried in the past, we do not have a clear conception of what kind of international system we will be faced with in the coming century. Today's world can be compared with a car driver who knows where he wants to drive from, but has no idea of his destination, no map, and no road signs.

On the one hand, there are undoubtedly great opportunities for the world to pursue democracy and economic progress. On the other hand, there is an equally obvious risk of unpredictability and chaos in the international domain, of new conflicts and splits within some countries, as well as between different states.

However, even now it is clear that the world of the future is not going to become either "Pax Americana," or any other version of a bipolar system. It is undoubtedly going to be a multipolar world. First, for all its power, the USA is not capable of controlling everything in the world, and anyway such a burden would definitely be detrimental to it. Second, although it is undergoing a difficult transitional period, Russia remains a great world power, not only because of its nuclear and conventional military potential, but also because of its new technologies, natural resources and geo-strategic location. Third, there are other influential centers that are striving to gain a more independent voice in world affairs. And finally, fourth, the very nature of today's international problems dictates that their solutions can only be found on a multilateral basis.

I want to be understood correctly: I am not talking about the USA, Russia or any other country ceasing to pursue its national goals in its foreign policies, or about letting any foreign or supranational agencies take care of these policies. Bill Clinton also objected to such a vision in his speech at the UN.

The international community is facing another dilemma. On the one hand, a narrow nationalistic, egotistic approach may prevail, which will turn the world into a site of competing national interests. This would throw the world back to another round of "balance" based on intimidation, or, even worse, to an international system similar to that of 1914. On the other hand, international life could rest on a stabilizing foundation shaped by partnership and cooperation between democratic powers sharing the same values. This would allow full advantage to be taken of a multipolar world, and would simultaneously prevent the negative consequences of uncontrollable competition between different centers of influence.

This is the reason why Russia persistently raises the question of the need for common resistance to aggressive nationalism, which has already ignited a number of bloody conflicts within the Eurasian space. Today it represents no less of a danger than a potential nuclear conflict did yesterday. Democratic societies must assume a firm moral stance and renounce any confrontation between different nations. The fight against totalitarianism in the 1970s also started with the postulation of certain moral principles. At that time, adherents of the *Realpolitik* also regarded such an approach as idealism and unnecessary rhetoric. Eventually, it was these principles, and unflagging loud restatement of these principles, that undermined totalitarianism to a far greater extent than the entire nuclear might of the West.

However, the establishment of democratic principles will remain just something on paper unless it is backed up by reliable mechanisms of cooperation. We may simply find ourselves overwhelmed by events, if we choose merely to respond to them and take appropriate decisions; if we proceed not from a long-term strategic vision, but rather from our immediate reactions to specific incidents or under the fleeting impression of a sensational episode shown by CNN.

After World War Two, the West managed to elaborate a holistic joint strategy to resolve the key problems of the time. The "Marshall Plan" played a crucial role in Europe's economic revival, while the containment concept proved an effective response to the challenge posed by totalitarianism.

Today's challenges could be tackled through a mature strategic partnership of democratic countries in both the West and the East. It would be strategic because we share core values. It would be mature because it is high time we moved from declarations of our intentions to their practical implementation.

Constituents of Strategic Partnership

First of all, one should make it clear what kind of partnership we are talking about: a really close and trusting interaction to address the world's problems, or just pressure exerted on one partner, while the other remains unburdened by any serious responsibilities.

As far as the form of partnership is concerned, we have no intention of imposing any rigid blueprints. I am in favor of a pragmatic approach. The partnership can definitely be "mission sensitive," i.e. can work within the scope and circumstances considered appropriate by the partners. In some situations, it would be reasonable to go for a rather close coordination of words and actions. In others, however, it would be better to allow each other more freedom of action while defining joint strategic goals. If the choice is made in favor of the full-scale partnership sought by Russia, then, in our opinion, the key components of such cooperation should be the following.

First, mutual recognition of each other as partner states that adhere to common values, and to the norms of the UN and OSCE. The need for such recognition is practically demonstrated by the existence of institutions that embody the values in question but still operate without Russia's participation, for example NATO and the G-7.

Although the G-7 is not a premier international agency, its members coordinate their political and economic approaches among themselves, and only subsequently with Russia. This practice to all intents and purposes perpetuates the "institutional" gap between Russia and the leading Western democracies.

The situation with NATO is similar. The North Atlantic alliance was set up to ward off Communist expansion. For present-day purposes, however, and despite its effectiveness, this institution is no longer adequate as such, since it has no military enemy, and does not number Russia among its members.

Second, partnership needs effective mechanisms. In the case of the "Big Seven," we can talk of its two-stage transformation into a "Big Eight." Political issues, where Russia is already an indispensable partner, should go first, while the inclusion of Russia into the world's economy would conclude the process.

As far as NATO is concerned, the Partnership for Peace program is sufficient to meet present-day needs for rapprochement between Russia and the alliance. But this program should not stimulate "NATO-centrism" in the alliance's policy, or "NATO-mania" among candidates impatient for membership of the alliance. In both cases, the interested parties are picking "evidence" that the Russian leadership is seeking to please the nationalist opposition in its foreign policy. In this way, they are playing into the hands of this very opposition, and—most importantly—avoiding both serious analysis of the problems of common European security and dialogue with Moscow on possible ways to resolve these problems.

Meanwhile, a united bloc-less Europe is not attainable through unjustifiable emphasis on limited-membership military and political structures, but can only be reached through reinforcement of the OSCE as a more inclusive organization. In the same way as it was the democratic principles of the OSCE, rather than the NATO military machine, that won through in the Cold War, it should be the OSCE that plays the leading role in rendering the post-confrontational Euro-Atlantic system of interaction a genuinely stable and democratic one.

In a multipolar world, the role of the UN, as a global structure, will grow; and above all cooperation between the permanent Security Council members will become closer.

Third, it is necessary to follow the "rules of partnership." The main rule is mutual trust. Nowadays, a baseless suspicion of Russia is in evidence. Now and then attempts are made to subject us to an "inspection approach," or to make us take "exams on good conduct." Western critics of Russia's foreign policy are sometimes a mirror-image throwback to the *Pravda* newspaper commentators of the past. *Pravda* used to see traces of "imperial policy" in every significant US foreign-affairs activity. The newspaper also depicted US allies—the states where American military bases were deployed—as "satellite" states that were seeing their independence slip away, and labeled the struggle for human rights, particularly in the Latin American countries, as a return to the "Monroe Doctrine."

What options are left to Russia? We have to listen to complaints about the United States quite often too. And there are abundant opportunities for us as well to "score points" for ourselves by utilizing the "historical" suspicion of the USA among the public of Russia and other countries. However, we will withstand such temptations. We are determined to resist all attempts to set Russia and the USA against each other or to misuse any existing disagreements between them, as was often done during the Cold War by certain forces that sought to profit at the expense of both Moscow and Washington.

We believe that trust can never be unilateral. We have the right to count on reciprocity on the part of the United States, and expect it to be more cautious in heeding those who offer "good advice" about being more vigilant when dealing with Russia.

Once partnership is based on mutual trust, it is only natural for the sides to follow another rule: that not only must each party inform the other about decisions taken, but they must also coordinate their approaches in advance. One can hardly accept a style of partnership which assumes that one party will coordinate each step it takes with the other, while that other party is given free rein. The partners should certainly be respectful of each other's interests and concerns.

Incidentally, this principle came as one of the key lessons learned from the Bosnian crisis. The NATO decisions to present the Bosnian Serbs with an ultimatum and to conduct subsequent air strikes against them were not agreed with Russia. And each time, the exclusion of Russia from the common conflict-resolution efforts in the Balkans, where we have our interests and are capable of contributing to a political settlement, would inevitably prove counterproductive. This was how both the effectiveness of the Russian–Western partnership, and its current absence and lag have become apparent. Instead of acting together and bringing our influence to bear on the conflict sides in order to bring them to reconciliation, we have been running the risk of returning to the formulaic "sponsor–client" relationship that was so detrimental in regional conflicts throughout the Cold War era.

Priority Areas

1. Global security

Russia and the United States have made considerable progress in this sphere, having resolved the problems that for decades were stumbling blocks for both the USSR and the USA. Disarmament issues have ceased to dominate the

Russian–American relationship. However, the nuclear potential of both countries, even after the reductions stipulated by the START-2 Treaty, will ensure that the nations play a leading role in maintaining strategic stability.

Now, attention is shifting to the need for cooperation in strengthening the impaired non-proliferation regime as regards nuclear arms, other weapons of mass destruction, and missile technologies. It is time we moved on from merely plugging the gaps in the non-proliferation regime to more integrative measures, including tightening control over the sale, particularly to conflict zones, of dual-purpose technologies, and of the most devastating types of conventional weapons.

Russia's policy in the weapons trade is no longer dictated by her motivation to support ideological "clients." And yet, Russia remains one of the biggest weapon producers. Arms exports are vital for Russia to stabilize its economy and proceed with the "arms conversion" program. Russian–US partnership should be oriented towards conventional competition in this domain, which would develop into a political rivalry.

2. PEACEKEEPING EFFORTS

The "new-generation" conflicts have posed an unprecedented challenge to both Russia and the West.

The example of Somalia is a rather telling one. The US-led peacekeeping mission, which had initially been perceived as very promising, came to face serious impediments. Eventually, Washington decided to leave the country. It is the easiest thing in the world to rub one's hands and speculate about the mistakes made by the military, as, for example, some western observers did with regard to Russia's mediation efforts in Abkhazia.

We have no intention of lecturing anyone on UN principles in connection with the failed Somali operation. It is obvious that one has to face entirely non-standard cases of civil wars or inter-ethnic conflicts in a number of regions. And we perceive problems encountered by others with empathy, for we ourselves have to tackle similar and even more complicated difficulties in conducting peacekeeping missions on the territory of the former USSR. And our efforts have also run into difficulties because of both lack of experience and the inertia of past Soviet habits. Matters are even more complicated, given that we are having to come up with ad hoc approaches now that the Soviet army is being transformed into a Russian one, and the diplomats are having to acquire new, as yet unfamiliar, techniques to replace the old methods.

This is why it is crucial that the West should show adequate understanding of our problems. The United States itself has had to deal with a number of complicated, multi-faceted situations in its relations with its European and Latin American partners. In some cases, allowances have had to be made for immature democratic processes and even overt violations of democracy. In other situations, one has had to take account of the national specificity of the processes in question, at times learning the regional realities, and use them as criteria to assess the desirable and the feasible.

The principal difference between Somalia, on the one hand, and Abkhazia and Tajikistan, on the other, is that we cannot merely pull out of the areas of conflict in the former USSR, as the Americans left Somalia. I do not believe that the USA, in its turn, would entertain such a course of action if the conflicts were raging right on their virtually open border.

We know that the West is neither able nor willing to solve our problems for us, and we do not ask the USA to take up peacekeeping operations in, say, Tajikistan or Georgia. But we would like our Western partners to respond to our request for them to support our efforts.

For example, when we voted at the UN Security Council for the "blue-helmet" peacekeeping operation, we did not demand an interim political settlement. Why, then, should the US representatives put forward such demands with regard to Abkhazia?

Russia does not seek carte blanche to proceed with its peacekeeping mission: it is acting in full accordance with the norms of international law and at the request of the states involved. What we are interested in is backing from the world community, not least in the sphere of international observation and material support. This is how the effectiveness of the peacekeeping as such, as well as the partnership between Russia and the West, could be greatly enhanced.

3. STABILITY IN THE TERRITORY OF THE FORMER SOVIET UNION

Up to very recently, the West opposed disintegration of the Soviet Union, even indicating its readiness to tolerate the Soviet leadership's persistence in clinging to the "socialist choice." It was no mere coincidence that Western support for Russia in 1991 came as a total surprise to the putchists. In the same indiscriminate manner, the West insisted on securing the unity of the former Yugoslavia. And the signal thus sent to Belgrade proved a false one: the Yugoslav army tried to reach the goal in question by means of force.

Russia did not fall into the same sort of trap as the Yugoslavs only because Russian democrats led by President Yeltsin happened to be in the Kremlin at the time. Instead of coercive measures to reintegrate the post-Soviet space, they opted for its reform on a new, voluntary basis by establishing the Commonwealth of Independent States. This very term contains two linked core components of our policy. First, there was recognition on the part of Russia of the sovereignty and independence of the former Soviet republics, which was reflected in particular in Russia's active support for their joining the UN and the OSCE—even the Central Asian republics. Second, another, no less important, need was recognized: that the CIS members had to cooperate closely, and taking account of their interdependence, in the economic, political, and cultural spheres, as well as at the personal level. Disregard for either of these policy components would inevitably have led to a repetition of the "Yugoslav scenario."

For a while after the collapse of the USSR, the West openly acknowledged Russia's role as a stabilizing factor and as the initiator of economic reforms in the post-Soviet space. And we never rejected this role, although it cost us billions of dollars. What is so bad about Russia proclaiming as its goal a gradual reintegration of the post-Soviet space, by and large in the economic sphere, and on a voluntary and equal basis? Is it not a similar situation to the European Union, with the accepted economic leadership of the largest nations, such as Germany and France? Incidentally, even large, developed countries of the CIS, such as the Ukraine, cannot dispense with their links with Russia. Is there any alternative? Is the West prepared, for example, to pay for the oil and gas delivered from Russia to Ukraine, Georgia and other CIS states, or to cover Ukraine's billion-dollar debts to Russia?

This is why Russia's special role and responsibility within the former USSR must be taken into account and supported by the Western partners.

4. Human Rights and the Rights of National Minorities

I suggest that Western researchers of Russia conduct the following thought experiment. If they had asked passers-by in a Moscow street ten years ago what the West wanted from the USSR, they would probably have heard from every other person: observance of human rights. And this would have happened in the time of the "iron curtain," the total lack of access to the Western press, "jamming" of Western radio stations, etc. Today, after the democratic revolution, with freedom of information in Moscow, and with any newspaper available to the public, I am sure nobody would give the same answer to the question. Meanwhile, every Russian citizen is well aware of the vital and genuine problem of human rights facing their compatriots living in other republics of the former Soviet Union. Almost every Russian has relatives or friends there, who either feel discriminated against or become refugees. And, despite that, today these people hear nothing in their defense from the West. In the meantime, ultra-nationalists are actively exploiting this silence.

One cannot fail to see a fundamental difference between the position of the Russian leadership and that adhered to by the proponents of the imperial policy. The latter regard the Russian-speaking population in the former Soviet republics as a kind of "fifth column" within the new independent nations, following, in fact, the same logic as Hitler did with regard to the Sudeten Germans. The goal of the Russian democrats is completely different. They do not want privileges for Russians in the regions in question. What they want for these people is standard citizenship and rights equal to those of the locals. It was only through great efforts that Russia succeeded in getting the OSCE

High Commissioner on National Minorities Office established. However, the Commissioner's recommendations are ignored by the Latvian and Estonian authorities, with "acquiescence" on the part of the West. We should be able to count on support in this respect too.

5. SUPPORT FOR RUSSIAN REFORMS AND RUSSIA'S INTEGRATION INTO THE GLOBAL ECONOMY

This issue merits a special discussion. I believe the fact that Russia is proceeding to the market economy in spite of all the obstacles to be of huge importance. One must take into consideration, however, that the old economic system, which was created through authoritarian control and frequent use of coercion, is incapable of self-renewal. Consequently, its replacement cannot be carried out except on the basis of political prescription.

Thus, properly organized political partnership between Russia and the West may give essential support for ensuring success of the economic reforms in Russia, and above all through the country's integration into the global economy.

Russia's enhanced rapprochement with the integration groups appears as the top priority. From the political perspective, it is important that support for economic reforms in Russia should be translated into efforts to allow the country access to the European and global markets of goods and technologies on an equal and non-discriminatory basis.

In presenting my views on the prospect for partnership between Russia and the West, the last thing I would want to do is draw a rosy image of Russia's foreign policy and the situation in the country. We are not trying to conceal our problems and do not expect the West to hail our every step. Equally, we do not intend to slavishly follow everything the West does. Divergence in the assessment of one another's actions is, naturally, acceptable. There is no doubt that in the future we may confront some problems that will require a frank and possibly disturbing discussion. What matters, though, is the approach we will take when such problems arise: whether we will be trusting or suspicious, and whether we will adopt a wait-and-see attitude or seek to resolve matters in the spirit of partnership.

Critics of the aspiration for partnership among democratic nations often see it as a product of "idealistic optimism." But that is our strength rather than our weakness. The magnitude and astuteness of our policy is largely dependent on our ability to see farther than short-term calculations, and to "look over the horizon" in order to achieve large-scale strategic goals. It is right now that partnership between Russia and the West may play the crucial role in transforming the Cold War into a lasting democratic peace.

Originally published in *Mezhdunarodnaya zhizn* [International affairs], 1994, no. 5, pp. 5–15.

International Relations on the Eve of the 21st Century: Problems and Prospects

Yevgeny Primakov

Approaching a Multipolar World

For all its historical significance, the cessation of confrontation between the blocs has not, as a matter of course, led to the triumph of democratic principles in international relations. Naturally, the end of the Cold War has become a starting point for progressing to a stable and predictable world on a global scale. However, at the same time there has been a dramatic expansion of regional conflicts, and the upsurge in terrorism has come as a shock to all. The threat of proliferation of weapons of mass destruction also remains a burning issue. Abandoning the ideological and military power confrontation brought about by the end of the Cold War proved insufficient to neutralize all the aforementioned threats and risks.

After the end of the Cold War we saw the emergence and evolution of a tendency in which the old bipolar confrontational world began to be transformed into a multipolar one. The centripetal forces that formerly drew most of what was left of the world to one or other of the two superpowers have suffered an abrupt decline. After the disintegration of the Warsaw Pact bloc, and the subsequent collapse of the USSR, the nations of Central and Eastern Europe gave up their orientation towards Russia, which had emerged as the heir to the USSR. There has likewise been a considerable weakening of the links between Russia and the new sovereign CIS countries, which used to be parts of the virtually unitary USSR.

At the same time, though not to the same degree or intensity, similar tendencies started to develop around the USA. The Western European nations showed more independence than before, once they abandoned their dependence on the American "nuclear umbrella." They found the gravitational pull to the European center prevailing over their transatlantic orientation. With Japan's vastly increased standing in the world, the bonds of its military and political dependence on the United States have slackened. It is interesting that one can even detect an increasingly independent stance among those nations that used to be at a distance from the epicenter of the bipolar confrontation, and were not directly linked to either of the superpowers. Above all, this applies to China, which is very rapidly increasing its economic potential.

Nevertheless, none of what has been said gives us grounds to conclude that a multipolar world has already acquired its final shape, or that—most importantly—equal partnership has come to replace the old power balance that used to form the foundation of the global order. In addition, the inertia of political thinking continues to produce the most negative effects. Unlike the dismantled strategic missiles and the thousands of destroyed tanks, the stereotypes that took firm root in the forty years of the Cold War continue to operate.

Therefore, it is, as yet, unclear what international relations will be like during the transition from the confrontational to the democratic world. Importantly, though, it is the nature of these relations that will determine the prospects and feasibility of overcoming new threats, dangers and challenges of the post-confrontational period.

Prerequisites for Transition to a New Global Order

First of all, no new lines of division must emerge in place of the old confrontation. This was the paramount problem, which Russian foreign policy has been seeking to resolve, that preconditioned our distinctly negative attitude towards NATO enlargement to include territory of the former Warsaw pact, and towards the attempts to transform the alliance into the axis of a new system of European security. We do not, of course, imagine for a moment that the expanding NATO is designed to attack Russia. However, political intentions are a variable value, while power potential is a constant one. It would not be an inappropriate reminder that in 1989–1990 the Western powers delivered explicit assurances to the Soviet Union that NATO would not expand its sphere of influence to the east, provided Germany reunified.

The archive materials we have at our disposal confirm the fact that assurances regarding NATO non-expansion were also given when the issue of winding up the Warsaw Treaty Organization started to be discussed at a practical level. In his conversation with Mikhail Gorbachev on May 6, 1991, French President Francois Mitterand said: "Each of the states I mentioned [Czechoslovakia and Poland] will strive to ensure their security by concluding separate treaties. With whom? Obviously, with NATO. This would enhance the USSR's impression of being isolated, or even besieged. I am convinced this way is not the right one for Europe."

Various assurances that NATO had no plans to draw the Eastern and Central European states into the North Atlantic alliance were given between 1990 and 1991 by US Secretary of State J. Baker, UK Foreign Secretary D. Hurd, and a number of other leaders of the alliance member states.

What is left of those assurances today? Yet scarcely anybody would claim that the situation in Europe is more menacing now than at the time when those assurances were made.

We do not claim the right to veto any country's accession to NATO. However, we are firmly convinced that any advance by the NATO military infrastructure towards Russia's territory will complicate our geopolitical situation, not least in the military sphere.

It is not just in Europe that indications of impending lines of division may be detected. The totally understandable intolerance of the extremism practiced by a number of Islamic groups and movements must not become a tendency to categorize virtually the entire Muslim world as hostile to contemporary civilization.

Russia is in favor of resolutely combating extremist and terrorist forces. These forces are particularly dangerous when they are state sponsored. Everything possible must be done to ensure that no state can provide totally unjustifiable support to them. Obviously, it is high time the UN used its framework to develop a universal convention that applies to all nations without exception, which would stipulate that individuals involved in terrorist activities must be deprived of the right to political asylum throughout the world. However, sanctions must not be used either as a mechanism to punish peoples, or as an instrument to depose governments. History has already demonstrated that the use of force to suppress troublesome regimes, irrespective of whether or not they support destructive tendencies in international affairs, is totally counterproductive. Far greater effects can be achieved by encouraging those who reject extremism and truly embrace the norms of conduct elaborated by the global community.

The second precondition for the new global order is rejection of the mentality of "leaders" and "followers." This mentality is fostered by the illusion that some countries emerged from the Cold War as the winners, and others as the losers. But this is not correct. The peoples on both sides of the "iron curtain" rid themselves of the policy of confrontation by their common efforts. The "leaders-and-followers" mentality will inevitably trigger a drift to a "unipolar world." The great majority of the world community will today not accept any such model of global order.

In addition, no state today enjoys sufficient power to cope with the multitude of problems on its own. All attempts to impose unilateral decisions on others merely provoke rivalry and will eventually trigger a chaotic and unpredictable drift in international relations. This is the worst possible scenario for the world, experiencing as it is a rapid growth in economic, environmental, and humanitarian interdependence.

The third condition is democratization of international economic relations, and above all a rejection of the use of economic means to achieve egotistic political ends. The US Helms–Burton Law, which provided for the "punishment" of any state involved in economic cooperation with Cuba, has been the subject of almost universal condemnation. Among other reasons, this telling response to the regulation can be explained by the risk of creating a precedent by attempting to extend domestic legislation to the extraterritorial sphere. A similar attitude towards those involved in economic partnership with Libya and Iran led to continuous attempts to stiffen the economic blockade against those countries. Implementation of UN Security Council Resolution 986 ("Oil for Food") with regard to Iraq is being artificially hampered.

Moreover, one cannot omit the fact that certain discriminatory trade restrictions are a remnant of Cold War times. For example, Russia is still regarded as a transitional-economy country; this allows the developed nations to apply the legal norms that pertain to states with a command-administrative system of economic regulation. Under the pretext of the alleged "non-market" nature of the Russian economy (which is no longer the case), the West is practicing anti-dumping measures with respect to Russian exports.

Finally, the fourth prerequisite for a successful progression to a stable global order lies in well-coordinated, cooperative steps by the international community for the purpose of resolving at least the following vital problems:

- settling conflicts;
- furthering weapons reduction and confidence building in the military sphere;
- strengthening humanitarian and legal security aspects;
- assisting and supporting those nations that, for various reasons, are experiencing difficulties in their development.

Process of Establishing a New Global Order

Considerable progress has been made recently in settling regional and local conflicts: peace agreements are being implemented in Bosnia; initial important accords have been achieved with regard to ways to a stable peace in the Middle East; ceasefires have been brokered in the Trans-Dniester region, Abkhazia, South Ossetia, and Nagorny Karabakh. The situation in the zones of conflict on the African continent has improved to some extent, too. There have been very positive developments in the effort to relieve the situation in Latin American "hot spots." However, nowhere has stable peace been achieved.

The situation surrounding the Middle East settlement raises serious concerns. Russia, a co-sponsor of the peace process, refuses to have the first results of the peace talks, attained through such great efforts, sacrificed to tactical considerations and internal political maneuvering. Implementation of the agreements reached is the only feasible way to secure the peace process. Taking into account the length of the process, and the lessons of past experience, it is important that all agreements—not just those already implemented, but also those only signed—must continue to be observed in practice. In this way, the "vertical" of the peace process must represent a continuous line.

As regards the "horizontal," it should run across all the "tracks" of negotiations. Attempts to move far ahead along one track, while ignoring the need for positive dynamics on another, will not bring about an advancement of the settlement process on the whole. In all the cases involved—i.e. in Palestine, Syria, and Lebanon—a recognizable success can be achieved at present, provided the measures taken are based on the principle of "peace for land," and on the UN Security Council resolutions 242, 338, and—in the case of Lebanon—425. Experience has already shown that the longer an artificial halt in the peace process—and there has been no advance since the new government came to power in Israel—the greater the risk of a retreat back to confrontation. When negotiating parties fall silent, that is when death-dealing weapons wake up. In many respects, the very opening of the notorious tunnel in Jerusalem, which so offended Muslim religious sentiments and led to fatal clashes, was the result of a four-month hiatus in the peace negotiations.

We appreciate the peace-supporting efforts made by the USA, the EU, France, Egypt and other members of the international community, and we advocate a further deepening of the partnership in peacekeeping. This is the most effective way to promote the peace process in the Middle East. On no account should any state try to monopolize the organization and mediation mission in the Middle East conflict settlement. On the contrary, coordinated efforts can produce the most effective results.

After the elections in Bosnia and Herzegovina on September 14, the settlement process in Bosnia moved into a new, extremely serious stage. There is a firmer prospect of stable peace now, and yet there remains some risk that there will be a slide back to a new circle of hostility and confrontation. Of course, the opportunity for a peaceful settlement created by the international community is, above all, for the conflict sides themselves to seize. However, it is vital now that the UN, OSCE, members of the Contact Group, and the High Representative assume a just and well-balanced approach to the problems that have not yet been resolved. There must be fresh, active efforts aimed at the social and economic restoration of Bosnia and Herzegovina, and at creating proper conditions for the refugees to return. It would seem there is a need for a rather lengthy and large-scale international presence by the military and police forces, in which Russia is one of the participants.

Once sanctions are lifted from Yugoslavia and the Bosnian Serbs, it is important to adhere to a consistent policy aimed at reintegrating Yugoslavia into international affairs as an equal participant. What is meant here is a renewal of Yugoslavia's participation in the proceedings of the UN General Assembly, the OSCE, and other international agencies.

It appears that the positive results of the end of the Cold War can be firmly established and made irreversible by adopting a *new program of disarmament, security and stability, intended for the 21st century*. The essential significance of the nuclear component of this program is unquestionable. Moreover, some fundamental progress has already been achieved in this respect. The Comprehensive Nuclear Test Ban Treaty (CTBT) has been elaborated and submitted for approval, inspired by our earlier unilateral nuclear test moratorium. It is no coincidence that Russia was among the first to sign the CTBT. In our opinion it is crucial that all countries that have the potential to create nuclear weapons should join the treaty. At the same time, it must be fully realized that a nuclear test conducted by any country before the treaty comes into effect would cause a cardinal shift in the international situation, will prove extremely detrimental to the treaty, and will make many parties change their attitude to the accord. It is a patent fact that the overwhelming majority of nations support the treaty, although there are some states that do not hide their negative attitude to it.

One might point out to the opponents of the treaty that the agreement will not merely promote the regime of nuclear nonproliferation, but will also give impetus to the process of a gradual transition to multilateral nuclear disarmament, i.e. to resolving the key task of the 21st century in this domain. This purpose is pursued by the proposal put forward by Russian President Boris Yeltsin that all nuclear powers should conclude a treaty on nuclear security and stability. During the 51st session of the UN General Assembly, we suggested that all interested states should start exchanging their visions of the issue. We continue to adhere to our suggestion that we should carry out a step-by-step transition to the deployment of nuclear arsenals only on states' own territories.

Reinforcement of the regime of nonproliferation of the weapons of mass destruction is also directly dependent on effective prevention of illegal trafficking in fissionable materials. A considerable contribution to resolving this problem was made by the Russian-initiated G-8 meeting on nuclear security, which was held in Moscow. The Comprehensive Nuclear Test Ban Treaty may give a serious boost to the implementation of the agreements reached in Moscow.

Naturally, we should continue to work towards cementing and implementing the existing treaties on nuclear reductions, as well as towards elaboration of new agreements of this sort. The effectiveness of cooperation among the nuclear states in this direction, and particularly between Russia and the United States, will depend largely on whether the footing for their equal and trusting partnership proves sufficiently sure. The same principles apply to the international treaties on other types of weapons of mass destruction.

Updating the Treaty on Conventional Armed Forces in Europe (CFE) appears to have a special significance in the pursuit of more stable relations in the post-confrontation world. After the end of bloc confrontation, which was taken into account when the CFE was elaborated, it became necessary to adapt the treaty to ensure equal security for all participant states, to prevent new dividing lines appearing in Europe, and to make sure that the treaty can effectively counteract the challenges posed to security in the contemporary world. Among other things, the updated version of the treaty must stipulate new, lower group ceilings, lower maximum levels for the strength of the armed forces in particular states, and the introduction of zone restrictions on the deployment of conventional armed forces in foreign territories. Reaching an agreement on dual-purpose aviation would be of particular importance.

The issues of human rights has been, and still is, a central component in the international security concept. At the same time, the legitimate striving to secure these rights must not be employed for political ends. This issue is too sensitive to be encroached on for political points-scoring.

The need to protect *national minorities* has intensified in many regions of the planet. The urgency of the problem is evident in today's world. However, the complexity of the present situation means that some way must be found to reconcile protection of the rights of national minorities with the principle of the territorial integrity of states. Russia is developing its policy so as to ensure such compromise. This concerns the Baltic states in full measure. While respecting the sovereignty of these nations and their territorial integrity, Russia cannot ignore the discriminatory policies that the Latvian and Estonian states practice with regard to the Russian-speaking population. While appreciating the measures that have already been taken to improve the situation, we believe that the UN and other international organizations should engage in more active and systematic work to ensure protection of national minorities, including in the Baltic states. The Declaration on the Rights of Persons Belonging to National or Ethnic, Religious and Linguistic Minorities must be a norm adhered to by all member states.

"Touchstone": the European Security System

In its most prominent form, the dilemma—whether to follow the path to a global democratic order or to slide back to blocs and coalitions—can be seen in the creation of a new security system in Europe.

During the Cold War, it was the power balance that—although without reliable guarantees—maintained stability in the main, European, theater of confrontation between the two blocs, and two superpowers. However, even in the final decades of the Cold War, all European nations, as well as the USA and Canada, came to realize the need to sign the Helsinki Final Act, primarily designed to secure the state borders formed as a result of World War II.

Today, the power balance engendered by the confrontation between the two blocs is no longer in place. Consequently, the Helsinki accords are not fully observed. The end of the Cold War brought about the disintegration of some European countries: the USSR, Czechoslovakia, and Yugoslavia. A number of new states were formed in the space formerly occupied by these, now disintegrated countries. The borders of the new states are not stipulated, and are not guaranteed by the Helsinki agreements.

Besides, the very events that have been taking place in the post-confrontation Europe dictate the need for a new mechanism to ensure its security. As we have already mentioned, new threats have replaced the old ones. Moreover, some of these threats take more dangerous forms than before, or have already reached a scale greater even than in the Cold War period. For the first time in the post-war period, i.e. the first time in 50 years, regional conflicts have become a reality in Europe. A truly menacing Yugoslavian crisis broke out right in the center of the continent. Grave conflicts have erupted along Europe's southern borders: the Armenian–Azerbaijani clash over Nagorny Karabakh, confrontation between Georgia and Abkhazia, on the one hand, and Georgia and Ossetia, on the other. The relations between Moldavia and the Trans-Dniester region are far from being settled either.

Many territorial and border disputes between states have emerged. Europe is confronted with the problem of refugees, which can be compared in scale only to the time of the world wars. In recent years, the OSCE member countries have received more than 4.5 million people fleeing from the conflict zones in Bosnia, Abkhazia, Nagorny Karabakh, and other "hot spots." A considerable proportion of the refugee flow, some 500 thousand persons, have been received by Russia.

Such were the circumstances when work commenced on elaborating the "architecture" of European security. One would presume that the work in question should include the following tasks, among others:

- defining categories of the threats and challenges that the European security system is to counteract;
- assigning functions (in terms of the threat categories) among the international organizations—both global and regional—designed to counteract such threats;
- specifying a mechanism to coordinate the activities of all the international organizations involved, and thus to incorporate them as constituents into the European security system;
- delineating principles, "rules of conduct," that would form the basis for the counteraction in question.

Tentatively speaking, one can isolate four groups of threats to Europe. The first is global, and, although it is rather hypothetical now that the Cold War has ended, it has not lost its significance completely. The second group is regional; it includes local conflicts and crises. The third group comprises "unconventional" threats: the spread of weapons of mass destruction, terrorism, organized crime, etc. The fourth embraces violations of the rights of national minorities.

The model for the European security system should, in one form or another, rely on all the international organizations involved in ensuring security in Europe: the UN, OSCE, Council of Europe, NATO in combination with the "Partnership for Peace," the EU, the WEU, and the CIS. And it should not merely rely on these organizations, but should amalgamate all these bodies into one composite structure. In order to achieve this end, the issues related to specific forms of interaction among the organizations must be thoroughly worked out.

Is there a need for any additional agencies? The Budapest OSCE summit came to the conclusion that it is this organization that should be assigned the central function within the new model of the European security system. There is a serious logic behind this conclusion. The OSCE has ample experience of establishing and developing a common European process, and it boasts great achievements in promoting a dialogue to strengthen mutual trust, to broaden communication between the states that belonged to the mutually hostile camps during the Cold War. The OSCE also acted as a stabilizing factor in Europe in the period of turbulent change in the USSR and Eastern Europe in the late 1980s and early 1990s, i.e. during the initial stage of the continent's drift away from bloc confrontation.

It is not, though, merely retrospective evaluation that matters. It is by virtue of their unique qualities that the CSCE and the OSCE have proved so essential to the peoples of the continent. First of all, the OSCE is the only European organization of universal membership. In addition, it addresses the profound interrelation of the interests of both the European and North American states. Furthermore, this is an organization that has proved capable of adapting, and of developing those functions that are essential to the European process at each stage of its progress. Although the organization does not always adapt fast enough to the changes, it still does so quicker than many other organizations operating in Europe. Finally, the OSCE is an organization based on the principle of consensus that guarantees the rights of all its member states, large and small.

Naturally, performing the role of the leading organization in the European security system has nothing in common with controlling or duplicating other agencies. At the same time, its coordinating role presupposes that the OSCE has to update its activities and structure.

Now let us turn to some principles that appear to be worth adhering to while creating the model.

Security of all OSCE member states without exception must be reinforced. Strictly speaking, it is not only European security that is implied here, since the system must address the interests of the United States of America and Canada as well. The model's Euro-Atlantic character will undoubtedly confer greater stability on the security system. And it is precisely this character that highlights the need to avoid the incorporation into the new system of any components that would ensure security of some participants at the expense of others.

The model must make provisions to counteract the entire range of the threats. With regard to the measures and mechanisms of conflict elimination, the security model must be designed to operate at all stages, i.e. to include a range of actions from preventive diplomacy up to "the imposition of peace." However, the model of European security must not "subsume" the functions of the UN. Today's world is faced not merely with attempts to employ, but with actual employment of, coercive methods that bypass the UN Security Council. Maintaining such practices may cause anarchy and chaos in the sphere of international relations. Quite naturally, in the cases of a conflict developing into an active phase of violence, collective peacekeeping operations, along with the introduction of sanctions, can and must be carried out. However, the decisions to take such actions must necessarily be made by the UN Security Council.

The model in question must be worked out so as to secure and guarantee the existing state borders in Europe. The recognition of border inviolability must be regarded as a criterion for states' accession to the collective security system.

Another such criterion would be the consent of the system members to adhere to the confidence-building measures, and their commitment to a number of duties in the spheres of transparency, control, military measures, including the relocation of armed forces and weapons across state borders, arms reduction, etc.

By no means does the collective security system exclude each member state's sovereign right to independent efforts to protect its individual security.

Certainly, the ideas presented here cannot be claimed to be complete and comprehensive. However, in my opinion, they may prove useful as a new architecture for security and cooperation is worked out.

I repeat: the architecture is bound to collapse if new dividing lines appear in Europe, or if another organization—not as universal as the OSCE—is selected as the foundation for the security model, e.g. NATO, even if it should establish "special relations with Russia."

NATO and Russia: "Special Relations"

Russia's approach to NATO is determined by two factors. On the one hand, it is affected by the fact that the organization was established during the Cold

War; it was initially intended to engage in military confrontation; and—even after the end of the Cold War—it is still far from having transformed itself. Second, it is evident for Moscow that NATO represents a significant power, while certain conditions are emerging for the nature of the alliance to change. Given these two factors, Russia will not simply adopt an extremely negative stance over NATO enlargement, but—instead—it is prepared to engage in a productive dialogue with the alliance's member states in order to work out Russian–NATO "rules of conduct" that would be acceptable to all parties involved.

Of course, a document could be drawn up that stipulates the relations between Russia and NATO. However, we do not see such a document as an end in itself. The document must be more than a mere declaration of, let us say, the parties' obligation of mutual non-aggression, their consent to the mutual transparency of the military construction, and to confidence-building measures aimed at easing relations.

All that is very important, but it has already been articulated in the documents that facilitated the end of the Cold War. Today, such an approach is no longer sufficient. A new document with regard to relations between Russia and NATO must be as specific as possible: an extended mandate for negotiations on updating the Conventional Armed Forces in Europe (CFE) Treaty to meet contemporary realities (aspects of such an update were discussed above); the nature, restrictions, obligations, and mechanisms for regulating mutual consultations and political decision-making, development areas pertinent to Russia's participation in the alliance's military infrastructure, etc.

There is no doubt that the document in question must not be used as a screen for NATO enlargement, on the one hand, while playing along with the idea of Russia's accession to the alliance as a member, on the other hand. We are fully aware of the "cunning" propagandistic nature of the discussion concerning the feasibility of Russia's membership of NATO. Should Russia apply for membership under the present circumstances, such a move would be used by the alliance for the purpose of its mass enlargement to the East, while Russia would be told (incidentally, we have already heard this): you are such a large and sophisticated power that you cannot become a member, since the alliance may not prove capable of ensuring your security.

It appears that the parties involved are gradually arriving at an awareness of the existence of three principal problems: NATO transformation, special relations between Russia and the alliance, and NATO enlargement. We believe that the problems in question should be addressed in sequence. At any rate, we are against simultaneity, which, we believe, would indicate that the content, schedule and conditions of NATO expansion have already been determined, which is something that is unacceptable to Russia.

The UN Mission in the New Conditions

For all the weight of the bilateral relations and regional agencies, the UN remains the principal mechanism that can ensure the transition from the bipolar confrontational world to a multipolar democratic one. While the multipolar system is being formed, the organization's task is to become a kind of "safety net" that will minimize the destructive aftermath of the changes, and channel the transition into an evolutionary democratic course.

Maintenance of global peace and security remains the UN's cardinal task. Moreover, the organization should, first and foremost, employ political and diplomatic means to settle conflicts in a peaceful way. It is worth recalling this principle, since a sort of "sanction syndrome" has become evident within the UN in recent years. Active attempts to use sanctions and other coercive measures on a wide scale have taken place, in some cases ignoring political and diplomatic opportunities. We are convinced: the UN is *to resort to such measures only in exceptional cases*, when all other means are truly exhausted.

Generally speaking, there is a need to update the UN sanction mechanisms. Today, for example, no sufficiently specific sanction-lifting procedure is stipulated, while—as experience shows—it is very important. The humanitarian damage caused by sanctions, as well as consequent losses suffered by third countries, must be minimized.

Importantly, the UN must remain the only organization that can authorize the use of strong-arm methods. Any use of force without sanction on the part of the UN Security Council must be ruled out completely.

We have no intention of suggesting that the UN should be transformed into a debating club. And yet, this organization should not hold back from formulating specific and conceptual proposals meant as the basis for settling post-Cold War conflicts, and developing a system of peaceful dispute resolution, with special emphasis on preventing the armed conflict phase, as well as on the diplomacy of national reconciliation. Improvement of legal norms and practices pertaining to peacekeeping, including the "peace enforcing" regulations, might make another issue for productive discussion.

Reality requires that the UN adhere to new approaches to peacekeeping operations. There is already the prototype of a pyramid-shaped structure embodying relations between the UN and regional organizations. Without developing such an interaction, the UN may not cope with the burden of peacekeeping activities. However, we are talking specifically of a pyramid, since it is of the utmost importance to avoid damaging the authority of the UN Security Council, which is principally responsible for global peace support.

Today, the global community is faced with the need to distribute the UN's limited peacekeeping resources so as to address the conflicts and their humanitarian consequences in accordance with the actual danger these conflicts pose. We count on the UN's much closer attention to the conflicts developing in the CIS space. So far, it has been mainly Russia and its Commonwealth partners that have played the major role here.

Russia calls on the UN to turn its attention to the Afghan conflict. A really critical situation has emerged in that long-suffering country. We must do our best to avoid its disintegration. The Afghan drama, as well as a number of ongoing conflicts in Rwanda and Liberia, is the most convincing argument in favor of the development of a new UN diplomacy of national reconciliation.

In order to tackle all these problems, the UN itself needs renewal and adaptation to new conditions. It is high time for reform; not the odd measure here and there, but a process involving the entire UN system. Certainly, while reforming the organization, one should take into account the need to ensure continuity. It is also obvious that it is not through hasty reorganization of the UN institutions, especially the UN Security Council, that the reform should be carried out.

Much is already being done in terms of implementing UN reform, including structural optimization and efficiency improvement. Russia favors continuation of this formidable and time-consuming work.

The twenty-first century is inheriting a complicated, turbulent world from the twentieth century. We are in no way fatalistic in our assessment of the chances of international relations straight away becoming stable and balanced in the new century. It may take decades and the efforts of many nations to achieve this. And yet, we remain optimists in our historical forecasts.

Originally published in *Mezhdunarodnaya zhizn* [International Affairs], 1996, no. 10.

Russia at the Turn of the Millennium

Vladimir Putin

The world today is marking two global events: the entry of humankind into the new millennium and the celebration of 2,000 years of Christianity. In my opinion, there is something greater and deeper behind the immense interest and attention to these events than simply the tradition of marking significant dates in a grand way.

New Opportunities—New Problems

Is it sheer accident that the turn of the millennium coincides chronologically with the profound global change of the past 20–30 years? *By that I mean the swift and fundamental changes in humankind's entire way of living, related to the formation of what is commonly called the post-industrial society.* I will recall some of the features typical of such a society.

It is characterized by a change in the economic structure of society: the weight of material production is decreasing, while the share of the secondary and tertiary sectors of the economy is growing. This means the introduction and constant updating of new state-of-the-art technologies, and the growth of science-intensive production. There is rapid development of information technology and telecommunications. There is preeminent attention to management, improvement of the organization and control of all branches of human activity. And finally, there is the dominance of the human being. It is people, their level of education, professional skill, business and social activities that constitute the major engine of development and progress.

The shaping of this new type of society has been going on long enough for observant politicians, statesmen, academics, and thinking people to notice *two aspects of the process that cause concern*. The first lies in the fact that the ongoing changes do bring fresh opportunities to improve human life, but they also produce new problems and dangers. These risks are evident above all in the environmental sphere. But not just there. Specific, quite acute problems have emerged in other domains of social life. Even the most economically advanced states are not free of organized crime, the growth of violence, alcoholism and drug addiction, decline in the role of the family in bringing up children, and so on.

Another concern is that only some nations can benefit from the modern economy, and the qualitatively new level of prosperity made possible by this economy. The dramatic development of science and technology and the progressive economic system have embraced only a small number of nations that make up the so-called "golden billion." A significant number of other countries have, this past century, also reached a new stage of economic and social development. However, one cannot say yet that they have become involved in the process of shaping post-industrial society. Most of them have not even as much as approached that phase. Moreover, there are grounds for believing that the current gap will persist for a very long time. Perhaps this is the reason why it is not only with hope, but also with concern, that on the eve of the new millennium humankind is looking to the coming age.

The Contemporary Situation in Russia

I do not think I am mistaken if I say that both these feelings—of hope and concern—are especially acute in our people. This is due to the fact that there are very few nations in the world that have been destined to go through as many ordeals in the 20th century as Russia was. Today, our nation is not among those embodying the world's highest economic and social accomplishments, on the one hand. And on the other hand our Motherland is facing formidable economic and social problems at present. Russia's GDP almost halved during the 1990s. The total value of our GDP is a tenth of that of the USA and a fifth of that of China. After the crisis of 1998, the GDP per capita dropped to $3,500. That is about one fifth the corresponding average value in the "Big Seven" countries.

The structure of the Russian economy has changed. Today, the key positions in the national economy belong to the fuel industry, power industry, and the ferrous and nonferrous metal industries. The share of these branches of industry constitutes 15 per cent of GDP, 50 per cent of total industrial output, and over 70 per cent of exports.

Labor efficiency in the real economy is extremely low. While in the raw materials and power industries it is close to the world's average values, it is much lower in the industries: 20–24 per cent of the corresponding rates for the US. The technical and technological standards of industrial products are largely determined by the proportion of equipment that has been in use for less than five years. In our country, this proportion dropped from 29 per cent in 1990 to 4.5 per cent in 1998. More than 70 per cent of all machinery and equipment has been in use for over 10 years. This figure is about twice as high as in economically developed countries.

Such a situation is above all a result of the steadily decreasing domestic investment in the real economy. Foreign investors are also slow to enter the Russian market. The total amount of accumulated direct foreign investment in Russia is a little over $11.5 billion. For the sake of comparison: the corresponding figure in China is $43 billion. While expenditure on research and development in Russia was decreasing until very recently, the 300 biggest transnational companies, for example, allocated $216 billion for this purpose in 1997, and around $240 billion in 1998. At best, only five per cent of Russian enterprises are engaged in innovative development. And the scale of this development is extremely narrow.

The lack of capital investment and the inadequate encouragement of research and development have brought about a dramatic reduction in the output of products that would meet the requirements of the global market in terms of their cost-quality ratio. It is especially in the markets of high-technology civilian production that our foreign competitors have outstripped us. Here, the share of Russian products is less than one per cent. For comparison, the corresponding US share in the markets in question is 36 per cent, and Japan's is 30 per cent.

The Russian population's actual monetary income has been steadily declining throughout the years of reform. Its most dramatic drop occurred as a result of the crisis of 1998. It will not be possible to restore the population's pre-crisis living standard this year. Today, the total monetary income of Russian citizens, as estimated using UN methodology, is less than 10 per cent of the corresponding indicator for a US resident. There has also been a decline in such crucial indicators of the nation's standard of living as the population's state of health and life expectancy.

The current hard economic and social situation in the country is largely the price we have to pay for the legacy of the Soviet-type economy. As a matter of fact, when the reforms were introduced, we had never had any other economy. Market mechanisms had to be introduced into a system founded on utterly different principles, and with an awkward, deformed structure. And this was bound to influence the course of the reform.

We have had to pay a price for the excessive promotion by the Soviet economic system of the raw material and military industries at the expense of civilian production and the service sector. It is also a result of the system's lack of attention to such crucial branches of the modern economy as information technology, electronics, and communications. It is a result of excluding competition among producers and industries, which hindered the technological progress and rendered the Russian economy unable to compete on the global market. It is a result of suppressing initiative and entrepreneurship on the part of both enterprises and staff. Today we have to face the bitter consequences of the past decades, in terms of both the material sphere and mentality.

Of course, certain expenditure was unavoidable in the course of the country's renewal. This was partly a result of our own mistakes and miscalculations, and our lack of experience. And yet, *the major problems that Russian society has had to face were inevitable.* The path leading to the market economy and democracy proved complicated for all states that opted for this course in the 1990s. All of them have gone through similar difficulties, although of varying degrees in different cases.

Russia is about to leave behind the period of economic and political transition. Notwithstanding all the problems and slip-ups, we have entered the main track of humanity. As global experience convincingly shows, it is this track that opens the real prospect for dynamic economic growth and improvement in the nation's standard of living. There is no alternative to this way.

Today, Russia faces an urgent question: what should be done next? What should be done to make the new market mechanisms work at full capacity? What should be done to overcome the profound ideological and political split within society, which is still manifest these days? What strategic goals can consolidate the Russian people? What is our vision of our nation's image in the global community of the 21st century? What level of economic, social and cultural development do we want to achieve in 10, and in 15 years from now? What are our strong points and our weak points? What material and spiritual resources do we have at our disposal today?

These are the questions posed by life itself. Without formulating an answer that is clear and understandable to the entire nation we simply cannot move ahead at an adequate pace to the goals worthy of our great nation.

Lessons to Learn for Russia

The answers to the above questions, as well as our future itself, are inseparably linked to what lessons we can draw from our past and present. This is a task that will require the efforts of the entire society and will take longer than one year. However, some clear lessons can be drawn even today.

1. For nearly three-quarters of a century, Russia's history was marked by implementation of the communist doctrine. It would be wrong to ignore, still less to deny, the apparent achievements of that time. However, it would be an even greater mistake to fail to acknowledge the immense price that society, the people, had to pay in the course of that experiment. *The most essential conclusion is, however, that Soviet rule failed to bring prosperity to the nation, prosperous, dynamic development to society, and freedom to the individual.* Moreover, the ideologically laden handling of the economy doomed our country to steadily lagging behind

the developed nations. However bitter it feels to admit the fact, we were moving along a path that was a dead-end and that ran clear of the highway of civilization.

2. *Russia has exhausted its "allowance" for political, social and economic cataclysms, and for radical reforms.* It is only fanatics or political forces that are profoundly indifferent to Russia and its people that are capable of calling for another revolution. Slogans like these—those of a communist, national-patriotic, or radical-liberal sort—could well bring about yet another bout of sweeping destruction, which would be impossible for the state and the people to survive. The nation's patience and endurance, as well as its creative potential, are close to depletion. Society would simply end up in total economic, political, psychological and moral disintegration.

Responsible social and political forces must offer the people a strategy for Russia's renaissance and success, a strategy that is based on all the positive achievements of the market and democratic reforms and that would be carried through by exclusively evolutionary, steady and balanced methods. It would also be implemented in conditions of political stability and without a drop in the standard of living of the Russian people, including all social strata and groups. This is an essential requirement that flows logically from the nation's current situation.

3. The experience of the 1990s clearly shows that genuinely successful renewal of our Motherland that avoids excessive costs cannot be achieved by a mere transfer of abstract patterns and schemes drawn from foreign textbooks. Mechanical copying of the experience of other nations will not lead to success.

Each nation, including Russia, must seek its own new way of development. So far, we have not achieved much in this respect. We have started to discern our own way, our own reform pattern, only in the past year or two. We can count on a worthy future only if we manage to naturally combine the principles of a market economy and democracy with Russia's realities.

This is the course that should be pursued within academic, analytic and expert activities, as well as by the state authorities at all levels and by political and non-governmental organizations.

Chances of a Worthy Future

Such are the key lessons of the century that is closing. *These lessons allow us to outline a long-term strategy aimed to overcome prolonged crisis prolonged crisis is overcome within a historically short period, and to create the preconditions for fast and sustained economic and social development of the nation.* I would like to underline that the development must be fast, since the country has no time for "warming up."

Here are some expert estimates. In order for Russia to achieve a GDP per capita comparable to the corresponding contemporary figures in Portugal and Spain—nations that are not among the leaders of the global economy—we will need some 15 years, provided the GDP grows at an annual rate of at least eight per cent. If we manage to achieve an annual GDP growth rate of 10 per cent, then we will be able to reach the level of GDP per capita of the UK and France today.

Let us suppose that the expert estimates are not completely correct, the current economic backlog is not that great and thus we will be able to catch up sooner. Even so, this work is going to take many long years. That is why we should start formulating and implementing the long-term strategy as soon as possible.

A first step in the right direction has already been made. At the end of December, a Center for Strategic Development started operating, which was founded on the initiative, and with the active participation, of the Russian government. The Center is designed to unite our country's best intellectual forces so that they might submit to the government recommendations, suggestions and projects of a theoretical and practical nature, aimed at developing the strategy itself, as well as at finding the most effective ways to solve the problems that will crop up in the course of strategy implementation. *I am convinced that achieving the necessary growth rate is not an exclusively economic issue. It is also a political problem, and—I will dare to say—in a certain sense it is an ideological one.* Or, rather, it is a conceptual, spiritual and ethical matter. And the latter aspect seems most essential at the current stage from the perspective of consolidation of Russian society.

(A) THE RUSSIAN IDEA

The kind of fruitful creative work that our Motherland needs is impossible in a society that is in a state of disruption and internally divided. It is impossible in a society where the key social strata and political forces adhere to different fundamental values and different basic ideological guidelines.

During the century that is coming to a close, Russia found itself in a similar situation on two occasions: following *October 1917* and in the 1990s. In the former case, the civil consent and social consolidation were achieved by coercive means rather than by what was commonly called ideological-awareness work. Those refusing to go along with the ideology and policies upheld by the authorities were subject to various kinds of persecution, including direct repression. Incidentally, this is one reason why I do not like the term "state ideology"— something that some politicians, journalists and academics believe must be established. This term has associations with the recent past. Once there is an ideology in place, as something officially favored and sponsored by the state, strictly speaking there will be no space for intellectual and spiritual freedom, pluralism of ideas, or freedom of the press. Or, in other words, there will be no political freedom.

I am against the restoration of official state ideology in Russia in whatever form. There must be no forced social consensus in the democratic Russia. Any social consensus here can only be voluntary. However, this is precisely the reason why it is so important to achieve consensus with regard to such vital issues as goals, values, and development prospects that would be desirable and attractive to the overwhelming majority of Russian citizens. One of the key reasons why the reforms are going slowly and with such difficulty lies in the lack of social consensus and consolidation. A lot of energy is invested in political strife, instead of in solving the specific problems of Russia's renewal. Nevertheless, some predisposition to a positive change in this sphere has become apparent in the past year or eighteen months. Most of the population manifests more wisdom and responsibility than many politicians. The people want stability, confidence, and opportunities to plan their future lives—both their own and their children's—for years and decades ahead, rather than for just a month. They want to work in the conditions of peace, security and firm legal order. They want to take advantage of those opportunities and prospects that involve a variety of property forms, freedom of enterprise, and market economy.

This has been the foundation, on which our people started to acquire and accept the supranational, universal human values that are above those of social and ethnic groups. People have accepted such values as the freedom of speech, the right to leave the country, and other fundamental political rights and individual liberties. People appreciate the fact that they can have private property, make business, and accumulate their fortune. This list can be extended.

Another basis for the consolidation of Russian society lies in what can be called the inherent, traditional Russian values. Today these values can be seen distinctly.

PATRIOTISM. This word is sometimes used in an ironic and even abusive sense. However, for the majority of Russian citizens it has preserved its original, totally positive meaning. This word refers to feeling proud of one's Motherland, of its history and achievements. It refers to the striving to make one's country more beautiful, more prosperous, stronger and happier. When these feelings are free from national arrogance and imperial ambitions, there is nothing obnoxious or conservative about them. They form the source of the nation's courage, endurance and strength. If we lose patriotism, and the national pride and dignity associated with it, we will lose ourselves as a nation capable of great exploits.

STATE AS A GREAT WORLD POWER [Derzhavnost]. Russia has been and will be a great power. This status is preconditioned by the inherent qualities of Russia's geopolitical, economic and cultural essence. These qualities have determined the attitudes of the Russian people and the state policy during the entire history of Russia. They cannot but determine them now as well. However, today these sentiments must acquire a new content. In the contemporary world, the power of national statehood is embodied not so much in its military might as in its ability to be at the forefront in the development and implementation of new technologies, to ensure the highest level of its people's well-being, to guarantee its stable security, and to defend its interests in the international arena.

STRONG STATE POWER [Gosudarsvennichestvo]. Russia will not soon, if ever, come to be a second version of, say, the USA or the UK, where liberal values spring from a deep-rooted historical tradition. In this country, the state, and its institutions and structures have always played a crucial role in the life of the nation. From the perspective of a Russian citizen, a strong state is not an anomaly; it is not something that one should fight against, but—on the contrary—it is rather a source and guarantor of order, the initiator and principal driving force behind any change.

Today's Russian society does not identify a powerful and efficient state with a totalitarian one. We have learned to appreciate the benefits of democracy, the rule of law, individual and political freedom. At the same time, people are concerned about the apparent weakening of state authority. Society wants a revival of the state's guiding and regulatory role, to the extent required by the traditions and current situation in the country.

SOCIAL SOLIDARITY. It is a fact of life that in Russia there has always been greater inclination for collective forms of life activities than for individualism. It is also a fact of life that paternalistic attitudes are deeply rooted in Russian society. Most Russian citizens tend to associate any improvement in their lives not so much with their own efforts, initiative and entrepreneurship as with the assistance and support of the state and community. This trend has been declining extremely slowly. Let us not try to answer the question of whether it is good or bad. What is important is that there are such sentiments. Moreover, they are still predominant. That is why they cannot be ignored. And they should be taken into account while developing social policy.

I believe that the idea of a new Russia will arise in the form of an alloy, an organic combination of universal, panhuman values with indigenous Russian virtues that have been tested by time, including by the turbulent 20th century. *It is important not to force, but also not to break and not to destroy, this vital process.* It is essential not to let the first shoots of social consensus be squelched in the vigor of political campaigns, or elections. In this sense, the outcomes of the recent State Duma elections inspire great optimism. They demonstrated that society has started turning to stability and social consensus. The overwhelming majority of Russian citizens rejected radicalism, extremism or any opposition of a revolutionary nature. It is the first occasion in the years of reform that such opportune conditions have arisen for constructive interaction between the executive and legislative branches of power.

Serious politicians, whose parties are represented in the new State Duma, are bound to draw the proper conclusions from this. I am convinced that responsibility for the fate of the people and the country will prevail, and the Russian parties, organizations, movements, and their leaders will not sacrifice Russia's collective interests and prospects—which require the consolidation of all healthy forces—for narrow party interests or political profits.

(B) STRONG STATE

Today, we are at a stage when even the most infallible economic and social policies will lapse now and then as they are being implemented, due to the weakness of the state authority and regulatory bodies. *Today, the clue to Russia's revival and rise lies in the sphere of state policy. Russia needs a strong state authority, and must have it.* This is not a call for the establishment of a totalitarian system. History presents convincing evidence that all dictatorships and systems with authoritarian rule are temporary. It is only democratic systems that last. For all their shortcomings, humanity has come up with nothing better so far. *A strong state power in Russia means a democratic, constitutional, competent federative state.*

I can outline the following guidelines for the formation of such a state:
- rationalizing the structure of the bodies of state authority and control, enhancing professionalism, discipline and responsibility of state employees, intensification of the fight against corruption;
- modifying the state personnel policy according to the principle of selection based on proficiency;
- creating conditions that would help promote establishment of a genuine civil society in the country, which would control and counterbalance the authorities;
- building up the role and authority of the judicial branch of power;
- improving federative relations, including in the budget and financial spheres;
- launching an active offensive against crime.

Changing the Constitution does not appear an urgent, top-priority task. What we have at present is a really good Constitution. Its chapter dealing with individual rights and liberties is regarded as the world's best constitutional act of its kind. Indeed, our key task today is not to draft another fundamental law of the country, but to make it a norm of life for the state, society and individual to adhere to the constitution we have and the laws that were adopted based on it.

An essential problem associated with this task is the constitutionality of the legislation adopted. Today, there are more than one thousand federal legislative acts, and several thousand laws of republics, territories, regions, and autonomous districts. Not all of these legislative acts meet the above-mentioned requirement. If the Ministry of Justice, Prosecutor's Office, and judicial authority keep up such a slow pace in resolving this problem as they have done up to now, the number of laws that are dubious or simply unworkable from the perspective of Russia's Constitution, may reach a critical mass in both judicial and political terms. As a result, the constitutional state security, the very authority of the federal Center and controllability of the country, and the integrity of Russia may be put at stake.

Another serious problem is associated with the branch of power that comprises the government. The world's experience shows that it is the executive authority that may pose the main danger to human rights and liberties and democracy on the whole. Of course, the legislature will also make its contribution if it adopts bad laws. And yet, the executive is of crucial significance. It organizes the life of the nation, applies the laws and—objectively speaking—can distort them by making considerable use of administrative procedures, although not always intentionally.

There is a global tendency towards a stronger executive authority. That is why the striving on the part of society to increase its supervision of this branch of power in order to forestall arbitrariness and abuse is no mere coincidence. This is why, personally, I attach primary importance to the establishment of partnership relations between the executive authorities and civil society, the development of the latter's institutions and structures, and the launch of an active and decisive struggle against corruption.

(C) EFFICIENT ECONOMY

As I have already said, the years of reform have resulted in a great number of formidable problems accumulated in Russia's economic and social spheres. The situation is hard indeed. *However, it is too early—to put it mildly—to write Russia off as a great power.* Notwithstanding all the difficulties, we have preserved our intellectual and human resource potential. Many promising research and development projects and advanced technologies are still at our disposal. We still have our natural resources. *That is why this nation has a worthy future.*

At the same time, we must draw lessons from the 1990s, and incorporate the experience of the market reforms.

1. I see one of the key lessons in the fact that during all these years we seem to have been groping about, in a hit and miss fashion, without any clear understanding of a general national idea and goal to ensure that Russia becomes a highly developed, prosperous and great world power. The lack of such a long-

term strategy, designed for 15–20 years or more, is most acutely discernible when it comes to the economy.

The government has a firm intention to build its activities based on the principles of unity of strategy and tactics. Without this approach, we are doomed to patching holes, and fire-fighting. Serious policy and big affairs ought not to be addressed in this way. *The country needs a long-term strategy for national development.* As I have already said, the government has commenced work to develop such a strategy.

2. *Another important lesson from the 1990s is that Russia needs an integrated system of state regulation in the economic and social spheres.* I do not mean a return to the system of command planning and control, when an omnipresent state used to regulate all aspects of operation of each enterprise from top to bottom. What is implied here is making the Russian state an efficient coordinator of economic and social forces in the country, which would balance these forces' interests, define the optimal goals and parameters of social development, and create the conditions for achieving these goals.

Of course, this goes beyond the boundaries of the popular formula that restricts the state's role in the economy to developing the rules of the game and making sure these rules are observed. With time, we are most likely to come to accept this formula. However, now the situation requires the state to make more of an impact on economic and social processes. Defining the scale and mechanisms of the system of state regulation, we must follow the principle: *there should be as much state intervention as there needs to be, and as much freedom as there needs to be.*

3. *The third lesson: transition to implementing a reform strategy that would be optimal for our country must be started.* It appears that the strategy should involve the following guidelines:

3.1 *To encourage dynamic economic growth.* Increasing investment activities must be given top priority in this sphere. So far, we have not managed to resolve this problem. During the 1990s, the total investment in the real sector of the Russian economy *declined by 80 per cent*, including investment in long-term assets (70 per cent decline). We have been witnessing a process by which the very material foundations of the Russian economy have been undermined. *We support implementation of an investment policy involving both purely market mechanisms and measures of state influence.* Simultaneously, we will continue working to create an investment climate that is favorable to foreign investors in this country. I will be frank: the nation's rise will be long and hard without foreign capital. We have no time for slow revival. That is why *everything must be done to get foreign capital into our country.*

3.2 To conduct an energetic industrial policy. The future of the nation, the quality of the Russian economy in the 21st century depends above all on progress in the high-technology industries producing science-intensive goods, for 90 per cent of economic growth in today's world is achieved by introducing new technology and know-how. *The government is prepared to pursue an industrial policy of priority development of those industries that lead in scientific and technological advance.* Among the necessary measures are:

- to encourage the development of extra-budgetary internal demand for advanced technologies and science-intensive products, and support export-oriented high-technology productions;
- to support non-primary industries oriented primarily at meeting domestic demand;
- to enhance export capacities of the fuel and power, and primary complexes.

In order to raise the funds needed to pursue this policy, we should apply the mechanisms that have long been used in global practice. They are based on target-oriented loan and tax incentives, and the provision of various types of state-guaranteed privileges.

3.3 To pursue a rational structural policy. The government believes that, as in other industrialized countries, there is a place in the Russian economy for the financial-industrial groups, corporations, on the one hand, and for small and medium-sized businesses, on the other. Any attempts to slow down the development of some, and artificially advance the development of other economic forms would only hamper the rise of the Russian economy. The government's policy will be aimed at creating a structure that will ensure an optimal balance of all economic forms.

Another major sphere is reasonable control of the operation of natural monopolies. This is a key issue, as it is these monopolies that largely determine the entire structure of production and consumer prices. And hence they influence both the economic and financial processes, and the dynamics of the population's incomes.

3.4 To create an effective financial system. This is a challenging task, which includes the following aspects:

- raising the effectiveness of the budget as a major instrument of state economic policy;
- implementing tax reform;
- eliminating non-payment, barter and other pseudo-monetary forms of settlement;

- maintaining a low inflation rate and stability of the rouble;
- forming civilized financial and stock markets, and making them an instrument for accumulating investment resources;
- restructuring the banking system.

3.5 *To suppress the shadow economy and organized crime in the economic and financial-credit sphere.* There is a shadow economy everywhere. However, whereas its share in the GDP does not exceed 15–20 per cent in most industrialized countries, in Russia the figure is 40 per cent. In order to resolve this acute problem, we should both improve the effectiveness of the law-enforcement agencies, and also strengthen the licensing, tax, hard-currency, and export regulations.

3.6 *To consistently integrate the Russian economy into world economic structures.* Otherwise we will not reach the level of economic and social advance that has been achieved in the industrialized countries. The main directions of this work are:
- active state support of the foreign economic operation of Russian enterprises, companies and corporations. In particular, the time is ripe for establishing a federal agency to support exports, which would provide guarantees for the export contracts of Russian producers;
- resolute resistance to the discrimination against Russia on the world markets of goods, services and investments. Adoption and application of national anti-dumping legislation;
- incorporation of Russia into the international system of regulation of foreign economic activity, above all into the WTO.

3.7 *To pursue a modern farming policy.* The revival of Russia will be impossible without the revival of the countryside and agriculture. We need a farm policy that will organically combine measures of state assistance and state regulation with market reforms in the countryside, and with regard to land property relations.

4. We must admit that virtually all changes and measures that may bring about a drop in people's living standards are inadmissible in Russia. We have approached a limit that we must not exceed.

Poverty is vast in Russia. In early 1998, the world's average income per capita amounted to some $5,000 a year, whereas it was less than half that in Russia, at only $2,200. Yet, the figure dropped still lower after the crisis of August 1998. The share of wages in the GDP has dropped from 50 per cent to 30 per cent since the start of the reforms.

This is the most acute social problem. The Government is developing a new incomes policy designed to ensure a steady growth of prosperity, based on the growth of the people's real disposable incomes.

Despite all the difficulties, the Government is determined to enhance measures to support science, education, culture and health care. For a country whose people are not healthy physically and psychologically, and who are poorly educated, will never rise to the summits of world civilization.

Russia is in the middle of one of the most difficult periods in its history. It appears to be the first time in the past 200–300 years when the nation is faced with the real threat of becoming a second-, and possibly even third-rate nation. In order to remove this threat, the nation must exert all its intellectual, physical and moral resources. We need coordinated creative work. Nobody will do it for us. Today, everything depends on our ability to realize the scale of the threat, to pool our forces and prepare ourselves for a long, hard work.

Originally published in *Nezavisimaya gazeta* [Independent newspaper], December 30, 1999.

Russian Foreign Policy on the Eve of the 21st Century: Problems of Formation, Development and Continuity

Igor Ivanov

Russia's entry into the new millennium has been marked by qualitative changes in both the country's domestic and its foreign policies. Following the stormy events of the 1990s, the gradual process of consolidating society around the idea of enhancing the democratic government took hold, as it came to be recognized as a prerequisite for the successful continuation of the political and socio-economic transformation of the country. The election of Vladimir Putin as President of the country, and the formation of a new State Duma after the December 1999 parliamentary elections laid the foundation for political stabilization and allowed us to undertake the elaboration of a long-term strategic development plan for the nation.

Given all this, defining the priorities of Russia's foreign policy, and the country's place within the global community is of major significance. Despite the immense difficulties the Russian Federation has experienced in recent years in the process of state-making, our nation has taken an active part in global affairs, and has played a central role in the efforts to shape a new system of international relations. Russian diplomacy has accumulated extensive practical experience of settling foreign policy issues, unprecedented in their complexity and novelty. It is important to recognize the significance of this experience in order to adequately define a role that the foreign policy should play at this difficult, and—in a certain sense—pivotal, point in the development of Russia's domestic affairs and the international situation.

1.

Until recently, the opinion prevalent in our domestic academic and political literature was that contemporary Russia had not yet fully charted its foreign policy strategy. The thesis that the "Russian foreign policy was still in its formative stage" seemed so indisputable that it even found its way into university textbooks dealing with international relations.[1]

However, today, for the first time in nine years, there appear to be grounds for asserting that the formative period of Russia's contemporary foreign policy is essentially complete. This conclusion is valid if by "formation" we mean the formulation of the fundamental principles guiding the country's foreign policy as determined by its national interests.

Naturally, no country's foreign policy starts with a blank slate. Despite the profound transformation Russia went through at the end of the 20th century, the very fact that the state is involved in the system of international relations presupposes the existence, for that state, of a certain set of key underlying foreign policy priorities that define the state's image and its long-term interests in the international political order.

The underlying priorities in question are more than a mere outcome of the will of a particular political leader. As a rule, they also spring from the objective features of a country's historical background, its economy, culture, and geopolitical situation. These factors thus constitute a kind of national foreign policy "constant," which is hardly affected by domestic political and international developments. In the history of diplomacy, the essence of continuity in foreign policy has been generalized in the formula "there are no permanent friends or allies, only permanent interests." This continuity, which is hardly subject to precise measurement, is typical not only of countries that are politically stable, but of all countries, including those, like Russia, that are undergoing a transition towards economic and socio-political modernization.

Contemporary Russia entered the global arena possessing a centuries-long experience in international relations and a broad network of multilateral and bilateral ties, as well as rich practice and a professional tradition based on the continuity of Imperial Russian and Soviet diplomacy. And yet, at the same time, it proved essential to formulate and systematize the state's general standpoints on a number of key issues pertinent to foreign policy, so as to come up with a more adequate reflection of the characteristics of the country's current stage of development and its place in the world.

On what basis, however, can we assert that this process is largely completed today?

First of all, it is demonstrated by the fact that the foreign-policy doctrine, which Russian diplomacy was for so long accused of lacking, today exists— and not merely on paper, but it also determines the state's day-to-day activities in the international arena. Russia's new Foreign Policy Concept, approved by President of the Russian Federation Vladimir Putin on June 28, 2000,

---

1 *Sovremennyye mezhdunarodnyye otnosheniya* [Contemporary international relations], Moscow, 2000, p. 484.

embodies the ideology of these activities. The Conception largely summarizes the extensive analysis provided by civil servants, politicians, prominent social figures, diplomats, and academics of what the role and place of our nation in the world community should be, and of possible ways for the country to achieve its long-term national interests in the global arena.

The fact that the Foreign Policy Concept should appear at this point is no accident, of course. It was elaborated as an integral part of the overall government strategy for national development, and was closely bound up with the strategy's other components: the economy, state making, federal relations, social welfare, defense, and security. At the beginning of 2000, Russia adopted a new National Security Conception, a primary document containing analysis of the external threats to the security of the Russian Federation. The Concept served as the basis for Russia's Military Doctrine, which further developed the Concept's positions on constructing defense. The Foreign Policy Concept is aimed at performing the same role for specific spheres of the government's foreign policy activities.

An important quality of the new Foreign Policy Concept is that it is not of a declarative character; instead, the aims it postulates are quite realistic and achievable. Nor does it reorient Russia's foreign policy course in a cardinal way. The Conception encompasses the principles and priorities constituting the key aspects of the foreign policy course, and which are largely familiar to the Russian public and our foreign partners, since these principles and priorities have determined the government's international activities in recent years and have proved most effective in protecting Russia's national interests. In short, this is a workable Conception based on the lessons of the past, and poised to last into the future. It thereby renders Russia's foreign policy more transparent and predictable. It gives the international community a clear indication of Russia's current actions and future steps in world affairs.

The way to this transparency was complicated, if not painful, and was accomplished in several stages. In agreement with the classic formula that foreign policy is an extension of domestic policy, the process by which Russia became an entity in global politics reflected the entire depth and breadth of the internal transformation that our state underwent in the last decade of the twentieth century.

In December 1991, Russia entered the global arena with a new image, absolutely different from all historical forms that the Russian state had previously had. This refers equally to the state's political order, to geographical boundaries, and to the adjacent geopolitical environment. The concept of "new Russia" acquired a quite specific, if not quite literal, sense for both the outer world and us.

At the same time, the fact that the Soviet Union was not removed from the historical stage by military defeat or violent social revolution largely predetermined the complicated intertwining of the elements of novelty and continuity in Russia's foreign policy. Russia broke with the Soviet ideology, but consciously succeeded to those positive components of Soviet foreign policy that met the country's national interests. It is remarkable that Russian diplomacy began its practical activities by ensuring that Russia would be internationally recognized as the state successor to the USSR. This, for example, allowed Russia to preserve its permanent membership of the UN Security Council. It also allowed Russia to resolve a number of complicated issues regarding relations with the former USSR republics. Hence Russia's foreign policy took the course of a sophisticated synthesis of the Soviet legacy, a revived Russian diplomatic tradition, and completely new approaches dictated by the cardinal changes within the country and in the global arena.

Right from the start, Russia's foreign policy activity was conducted in an essentially new legal and socio-political environment, which was characterized by the following features:

- radical change in the mechanism by which foreign policy was formed, which was brought about by the democratization of politics and society; the process was increasingly influenced by parliament, the mass media, and public opinion;
- weaker coordination in the development of international ties, which expanded considerably once Russian society became more open to the outside world;
- rapid and initially chaotic moves by Russian regions and the entities of the Russian Federation to establish direct ties with contiguous regions and local authorities abroad;
- an abrupt transition to transparency in information concerning foreign policy, combined with the total dismantling of the Soviet apparatus for foreign policy propaganda, and of other state mechanisms that managed the country's image abroad;
- transfer to the private sector of entire sectors related to international relations that were formerly under strict state control: trade, international investment, scientific and cultural exchanges, etc.

The initial formative stage of Russia's foreign policy reflected the stormy and largely chaotic process of establishing democracy and a free market economy in the country, with all the attendant contradictions and shortfalls.

The collapse of the Soviet political system was so sudden and complete that neither the government, nor—and even to a greater extent—the Russian people had—and could not possibly have had—a full understanding either of what further course the country would take, or of what its foreign policy priorities would be. The first President of the Russian Federation Boris Yeltsin discussed the matter openly and frankly in 1992, in a speech to the Supreme Soviet:

"Russia's painful transition does not allow us yet to appreciate its new or permanent character, nor does it allow us to gain clear answers to the questions: What are we abandoning? What do we wish to preserve? What do we wish to revive and create anew?" [2]

The euphoria of change overwhelmed the national consciousness. Many thought at the time that simply making an abrupt change in our ideological orientation would resolve most of the domestic and foreign affairs problems. For example, just as our economic strategy was founded on the belief that sudden price liberalization and the introduction of free-market mechanisms would, by themselves, create a favorable dynamic for development, so our foreign policy was predicated on the expectation that a radical shift from confrontation to rapprochement with the western nations would automatically change the West's attitude to Russia and mobilize mass political support and economic aid for us. These far-reaching expectations left their mark on the first version of Russia's Foreign Policy Conception, adopted in 1993.

One should admit that there were indeed considerable grounds for such hopes at the time. The international climate really had improved greatly in the late 1980s and early 1990s. The democratic changes in the USSR, and then in Russia, inspired an intense outpouring of sympathy for Russia and support from all over the world. Russia's public opinion largely applauded our policy of rapprochement with the USSR's former adversaries, and expected that it would bring concrete benefits to the country.

In actual fact, however, things proved to be much more complicated. As well as a serious aggravation of the socio-economic situation in the initial years of transformation, there was a severe intensification of the ideological and internal political struggle. Foreign policy emerged as an area of government activity where the debates about what kind of fundamental priority the country should pursue in its development came to the fore. Among other matters, the debates concerned the problem of Russia's relationships with the western nations. It is worth remembering that debates about the West as a particular socio-economic and political model date back to Russia's historic past. As was the case in the mid 19th century, attitudes to the West had once again come to signify a particular ideological orientation, embodied in either a virulent rejection of western civilization, or an equally passionate striving to integrate into that civilization, even if at the price of critical political and economic concessions.

Against this background, we gambled on integrating into the Euro-Atlantic structures as soon as possible, come what may. Unrealistic goals were set, such

---

2 Speech by President of the Russian Federation B. N. Yeltsin to the Supreme Council of the Russian Federation on October 6, 1992 in *Diplomaticheskiy vestnik* [Diplomatic Review], 1992, no. 19–20, p. 4.

as the virtually immediate establishment of a "strategic partnership" or even an alliance with the West, for which neither Russia, nor the Western nations themselves were prepared, since either side perceived the concepts in question in different ways. In addition, many in the USA and even Western Europe, unquestioningly believed that they had "beaten" Russia in the Cold War, and thus would not consider Russia an equal ally. At best, Russia was allowed the role of junior partner. Any manifestations of independence or attempts to stand its ground were regarded as a return to the Soviet "imperial" policy. The move by the US and NATO to extend their influence right up to Russia's borders, in overt disregard of Russia's national interests, prompted serious concern.

That is why the period of a straightforward, idealistic pro-Western orientation in Russia's foreign policy was short-lived and superficial. And Russian diplomacy quickly drew from it the proper lessons. These conclusions were impelled by actual developments: the making of Russia's foreign policy was carried out not in ideological debates, but while Russia was searching for solutions to real-life—and rather serious—problems in the international sphere. After the USSR's disintegration, we had to organize a new post-Soviet space, to create political mechanisms to regulate the conflicts that had flared up on the outer borders of the CIS. It was also necessary to protect the rights of Russians who now found themselves outside Russia's borders. Besides, we needed to lay a new political foundation for bilateral relations with other countries of the world. It was these painstaking efforts—largely unseen by the broad public—that dictated the logic of our foreign policy formation and helped to draw the first conceptual conclusions that later were crystallized into stable principles and a style for the Russian government's international activities.

One significant outcome of these efforts was the indubitable fact that Russia was able to undertake its unprecedented, complicated, and painful internal transformation in a largely favorable international environment. The Russian government was able to avoid chaos along its borders with its new neighbors, to maintain national security at a level that allowed for considerable cutbacks in military spending, and to mobilize broad international support for Russian reforms in word and in deed.

The very essence of the foreign policy problems that Russia faced induced our realistic evaluation of international conditions and a pragmatic, rather than an ideological, approach to formulating goals and tasks. The extremely volatile international situation strengthened Russia's conviction that protection of our national interests can be our only reliable foreign policy reference point. Only by protecting our national interests could we adequately address the contemporary threats and challenges, consciously formulate positions on international issues, and build purposeful relationships with other nations.

Foreign policy debates during the 1990s often raised a rather incisive question: what constituted Russia's specific national interests? Indeed, Russia's particular course of action in the international arena directly depended on the answer to this question.

One legacy passed on to us from the Soviet foreign policy was a "superpower mentality," and a subsequent striving to participate in any and all more or less significant international developments, which often bore a greater domestic cost than the country could afford. Given Russia's enormous burden of unresolved domestic problems, common sense dictated, however, that the country's foreign policy should first and foremost address the vital interests of domestic development. This meant providing reliable national security; creating the best possible conditions for sustained economic growth; boosting the living standard; strengthening the country's unity, integrity, and constitutional order; consolidating civil society, and defending the rights of citizens and compatriots abroad.

Our historical past also bore evidence that this was the correct approach. Indeed, the great liberation reforms of the second half of the 19th century were launched in Russia after the country's power had been undermined by defeat in the Crimean War. Russia was facing the real prospect of losing its Great Power status and turning into a second-rate country that would be pushed into the background of the European Concert of Powers. The then Foreign Minister A. M. Gorchakov defined the goals of Russia's foreign policy in his report to Emperor Alexander II as follows:

> Our political activity has to...pursue a twofold aim.
> First, Russia must avoid involvement in any and all external controversies that are likely to divert at least some of its resources from its own domestic development. Second, we must do all we can to forestall any territorial changes, or shifts in the power balance in Europe, which are likely to damage our interests or our political status.
> If these two conditions are met, we can hope that, after strengthening its potential and rebuilding its resources, Russia can restore its status, power, authority and influence among the great world powers.[3]

A. M. Gorchakov stressed that Russia would be able to attain such a status "only on the condition that it amplifies its domestic potential that is today's only real source for the political might of a state."[4]

For all the differences between Russia's situation in the mid 19th century and today, one can assert that the country's foreign policy had to address largely similar problems then as now. In particular it has to create conditions as favorable as possible for implementing domestic reforms, on the one hand, and—

---

3 *Kantsler A. M. Gorchakov. 200 let so dnya rozhdeniya* [Chancellor A. M. Gorchakov. 200th anniversary of his birth], Moscow, 1998, pp. 321–322.
4 Ibid. p. 334.

the other side of the coin—for forestalling possible undermining of the nation's status in the international arena.

From all of the above, another conclusion was drawn: the need for a "prudent" disbursement of foreign policy resources, and a rejection of superfluous diplomatic efforts in favor of an active, multi-vector foreign policy that took advantage of anything that might produce real returns for domestic development. Yevgeniy Primakov, Russia's minister of foreign affairs from 1996 to 1998, remarks:

> ...in the absence of an active foreign policy, it is difficult—if not impossible—for Russia to implement any fundamental domestic transformations or preserve the country's territorial integrity. Russia is far from being indifferent to the manner and capacity in which it will enter the world economy: as a mistreated appendage used as a source of raw materials, or as an equal participant. In many ways this constitutes the function of foreign policy.[5]

In other words, from the foreign policy perspective the need to focus on solving domestic problems is in no way an indication of "national egotism" or a retreat into isolationism. On the contrary, rational diplomacy on issues of vital importance to Russia and the global community can, in some cases, compensate for a lack of economic, military, and other domestic resources.

Concrete foreign policy experience has also cleared the issue of what is the best course to take in relations with the leading Western powers. Today, not only politicians and diplomats, but also the broad Russian public, are fully aware that unjustified concessions that are to the detriment of our national interests, on the one hand, and slipping into confrontation with the United States, Europe, and Japan, on the other, are equally unacceptable to Russia.

A foreign policy that aims at consistent and, where necessary, strict defense of our national interests in no way contradicts Russia's goal of further integration into the community of democratic nations and into the global economy. In particular, this is demonstrated by Russia's consistent efforts to integrate into the activities of the G-8. Within this authoritative forum, Russia has an opportunity to take an active part in discussions with the leading industrial powers on issues of key importance for both regional and global security and stability. No matter how complicated the problems that Russia faces in its relationship with the more developed countries, Russian diplomacy should strive for constructive cooperation and engage in a joint search for mutually acceptable solutions. It is in Russia's interests to broaden the circle of its friends and partners in the world. In pursuing this principle, Russia's foreign policy can only strengthen the state.

---

5 Primakov, Ye. M., "Rossiya v mirovoy politike" [Russia in world politics], in *God planety* [Year of the planet], Moscow, 1998, p. 52.

This way of formulating the problem gives a clue to resolving another long-standing debate: whether Russia is a European or an Asian power. Experience has shown the inadequacy of all attempts to juxtapose different possible orientations of Russia's foreign policy. The very unique geopolitical location of our country—apart from the realities of world politics and economy—dictates an equal need for Russia to cultivate its cooperation with the nations of West and East, as well as South and North. This is also in line with Russia's best traditions. While developing a long-term concept for Russia's industrial development at the end of the nineteenth century, the great Russian scientist Dmitry Mendeleev (1834–1907) stressed that the nation's interests required the cultivation of trade and economic relations with its neighbors both to the West and to the East. He had no doubt that "all Russia's politics would sooner or later take a course determined by this circumstance."[6]

Thus, fundamental principles and priorities have taken shape over time, and these have formed the basis for the updated Foreign Policy Conception. It was not, though, only the country's domestic goals and interests that determined the contents of the Conception. Another factor that required the earliest possible formation of Russia's foreign policy course was the need to formulate the government's essential position in the face of new global challenges, and to decide what system of international relations best meets the country's interests.

2.

On the threshold of the new century, struggle has escalated around the founding principles of the global order that is to replace the bipolar world structure of the second half of the twentieth century.

It seemed to many that the end of the Cold War would open new, unprecedented opportunities for reshaping the world order in accordance with just, democratic principles. By the beginning of the 1990s, the threat of a nuclear war had been virtually removed through the joint efforts of the USSR, the USA, and other nations. The strategic nuclear arsenals had been reduced, the atmosphere of trust in international relations had been strengthened, and military tension in Europe had abated. The knot of the German problem had also been unraveled. The world community had a unique chance to fundamentally reshape the global order on a democratic basis, and, as it entered the 21st century, to rid the world of the confrontational legacy of the past, while retaining the entire positive set of international agreements and treaties reached in previous years.

---

6 Mendeleev, D. I., *Granits poznaniyu predvidet' nevozmozhno* [There are no foreseeable limits to acquiring knowledge], Moscow, 1991, p. 101.

However, this historic opportunity was not fulfilled. Researchers from the USA's East-West Institute recognize:

> We missed a unique opportunity to take advantage of the end of the Cold War and the collapse of communism to promote a new world order that would be based on a concord of great powers, increased authority and efficiency of the United Nations, and a new architecture of European security, rather than on a counterbalance of two adversarial military alliances. This new order would also involve multilateral security regimes in the Far East, Central and Southern Asia and other regions. We missed an unprecedented opportunity for a breakthrough in nuclear disarmament, the disposal of the Cold War nuclear arsenals, nonproliferation of the weapons of mass destruction and means of their delivery, further cuts in conventional arms in Europe and the Far East, elaboration of effective mechanisms for peace enforcement and peacekeeping based on Russia and the West deciding jointly on when to use force, and on their joint implementation of the decisions made.[7]

We might ask: What are the reasons for this failure?

I believe there are several reasons. The end of the Cold War brought about the loss of something that formed the backbone of the world order throughout the previous half century: namely, the strict discipline imposed by two opposing camps that were equal in terms of military potential. In the absence of the fear of global self-annihilation that for so long served as a prop for the structure of international relations, this structure turned out to be vulnerable to many old and new plagues. Indeed, no new mechanisms were established to maintain international stability. In particular, according to A. Rotfeld, the director of the Stockholm International Peace Research Institute, "NO NEW ORGANIZING PRINCIPLE FOR INTERNATIONAL SECURITY HAS YET BEEN ELABORATED."[8]

There was—and still is—an opinion in the West that the broad spread of democratic values in the world and the transition of increasingly large numbers of nations to a free-market economy constitute in themselves powerful stabilizing factors in international affairs. A revealing example of this attitude is embodied in the concept of international relations that is held by US experts from the Institute for National Strategic Studies. The essence of the concept lies in the categorization of world states into four groups: core states, transition states, rogue states, and failed states.[9] By classifying them in this fashion, each

---

7 *Rossiya i mir: Novyi kurs. Politicheskiye rekomendatsii, osnovannyye na mezhdunarodnom proekte "Okruzhayushchaya Sreda rossiyskoy bezopasnosti"* [Russia and the world: the new course. Political recommendations based on the international project "Russian Security Environment"], Moscow, 1999, p. 11.

8 Adam Rotfeld, "Europe: In Search of Cooperative Security," in *SIPRI Yearbook 1997: Armaments, Disarmament and International Security*, Oxford: Oxford University Press, 1997, p. 35.

9 *Strategic Assessment, 1999*, Institute for National Strategic Studies, Washington 1999, p. 14.

state is given a kind of "conduct grade" depending on the level of development of democracy and free-market economy in this state, i.e. on the degree of the state's conformity with the "ideal" epitomized by the USA itself.

Meanwhile, it is becoming obvious that—for all its indubitable positive significance—the democratization process in itself cannot constitute the aforementioned "organizing principle for international security." This conclusion is confirmed by the nature of the threats and challenges faced by the world community in the 1990s, in particular by the development of contemporary local conflicts. Although almost all of them are exclusively internal, they are motivated not by confrontation between democracy and dictatorship, but—most often—by ethnic and religious hostilities, social degradation and militant separatism. Moreover, the risk of interethnic conflicts also exists in countries with an established democratic order, which is clearly demonstrated in the cases of some developed European states, such as the UK, Spain, France, and Belgium. At best, the presence of the democratic order can help prevent the spread of such problems and the search for civilized solutions to them. However, this order in itself will not remove the deeper causes of such conflicts.

Nor is democratization a proper response to a number of other serious challenges, such as international terrorism, organized crime, and the proliferation of weapons of mass destruction. It often happens that quite "respectable" democratic states get involved in regional confrontation and the arms race.

The transition of the overwhelming majority of nations and entire regions to open, free-market economy is an even more ambiguous issue. The consequent profound transformation of the global economic system, also preconditioned by the scientific and technological revolution, entailed globalization, which has become one of the major tendencies of global development. First affecting the sphere of international finance, the process went on to involve other constituents of modern-day civilization. At the beginning it appeared that the in-depth rapprochement of nations and regions induced by globalization would generate powerful stimuli to resolve global problems via international cooperation. However, the actual development proved more complicated. Globalization introduced significant new controversies and conflicts into international affairs. While it is a relatively small number of developed countries that have already experienced the positive returns that globalization can bring, its negative influence is felt by the entire global community, to varying degrees. Thus we are faced with a paradoxical situation: within such domains as international terrorism and organized crime, the advance of globalization is much faster than in areas where it could be truly beneficial for humanity, such as health care, education, scientific development, and cultural exchanges. Pino Arlacchi, UN Under-Secretary-General, rightly noted this tendency: "NEVER BEFORE HAVE THERE BEEN SO MANY OPPORTUNITIES FOR SO MANY PEOPLE.

HOWEVER, NEVER BEFORE HAVE THERE BEEN SO MANY OPPORTUNITIES FOR CRIMINAL ORGANIZATIONS EITHER."[10]

Russia's most painful experience in this context came with the Chechen crisis. As a matter of fact, it was the first overt armed aggression inflicted on a sovereign state by international terrorism. For all that, Chechnya was but one in a line of hotbeds of instability caused by international terrorism, which stretched from the Balkans, through the North Caucasus, into Afghanistan, the Central Asian states, and as far as the Philippines.

It is becoming more and more evident that globalization increases—rather than reduces—the gap between the poles of prosperity and poverty in individual countries and on a regional scale. Many nations are concerned about the excessive "economization" of international relations that results from globalization and that subjects these nations to the elements of a global market. The wave of mass crises that rolled across the globe in 1998 and affected Russia in so painful a way, is one of the most convincing manifestations of the phenomenon.

The French *Défense Nationale* magazine noted in this context that "unrestrained economic liberalism," which is what the USA calls for—even though it fails to practice what it preaches itself—only widens the abyss between the developed and developing nations. Hence the indignation at the inequality and injustice, which fuels upheavals and terrorism in developing countries. Besides, one of the main motives of human activity, namely the striving for profit, leads to the degradation of morals and sends humanity into a "suicidal drift."[11]

It is also obvious that globalization has not been efficient enough in resolving a number of long-standing global problems, for example in preventing environmental and technological disasters, fighting epidemic diseases, and dealing with mass migration. On the contrary, it appears that—for reasons mentioned above—globalization renders global processes less and less controllable by the world community.

To summarize, one can state that globalization in its present form has not only failed to bring about new mechanisms for regulating international affairs; it actually itself requires control and serious revision for the sake of all humanity.

As a result, the shaping of the new system of international relations has grown complicated and protracted. Foreign analysts find it difficult to come up with an exhaustive definition of the contemporary stage of global development. Some, like Henry Kissinger, label it "new international disorder," while others call it an "AMORPHOUS SECURITY SYSTEM DEPRIVED OF BIPOLAR STRUCTURE AND IDEOLOGICAL CLARITY OF THE WARTIME."[12] There are forecasts that

---

10 Tenth United Nations Congress on the Prevention of Crime and the Treatment of Offenders, UN DPI/2088/F-003219, p. 1.
11 Foiard de, P.A., "Liberalisme et humanisme," *Défense Nationale*, 1999, no. 11, pp. 10–11.
12 *Strategic Assessment, 1999*, p. 12.

the current "indefiniteness" in international development may last for many long decades. Suggested scenarios range from the beginning of an era of universal prosperity to complete chaos and anarchy in international affairs.[13]

And yet, one postulation appears indisputable: as in the previous historical periods following the end of major global conflicts and cataclysms, the international system is in a transitional state, and its "destiny" depends on the good political will of the world community. Thus, the world community has to determine the parameters of the future global order and develop reliable mechanisms for ensuring security and stability in international relations. In other words, humanity is faced with the situation when a new global order can be shaped only through conscious and purposeful efforts on the part of all nations. Otherwise, given passivity or national selfishness, or even a return to power rivalries and attempts to promote one's own interests at the expense of others, the "natural elements of globalization" will only inflict an aggravation of negative tendencies that will be increasingly difficult for the world community to keep under control.

Unfortunately, no universal conceptual unity has been reached yet with regard to this vital issue. Moreover, two essentially different approaches to the formation of a new world order have confronted each other of late. One approach seeks the formation of a unipolar model, where a group of the world's most developed countries would exercise global dominance based on the US and NATO military and economic power. The rest of the world is invited to follow the rules convenient for this "privileged club."

The roots of this conception are deep and lie, as has already been mentioned, in the wrong evaluation of the international situation in the late 1980s and early 1990s. As French Minister of Foreign Affairs Hubert Vedrine acknowledged, "thinking of itself as the winner of the third world war, i.e. the winner of the Cold War, the West came to believe in its own unrestricted powers, and—relying on its technological dominance—it failed to see why it could not impose its views everywhere."[14] As former UNESCO Director-General Federico Mayor shrewdly remarked, the USA and its allies "started using oligarchic ways in international affairs," in defiance of their own preaching.[15]

Such a one-sided approach naturally resulted in a gradual reconsideration of those democratic principles in international affairs, which started to be established after the fall of the Berlin wall. Consequently, the idea of building a united Europe started to be gradually replaced by that of "NATO-centrism,"

---

13 *New World Coming: American security in the 21st century*, Washington, 1999, p. 133.
14 Colloque de l'Institut de Relations Internationales et Strategiques sur «morale et relation internationales», 16 mai 2000. Intervention d'ouverture du Ministre des Affaire Etrangeres. p. 4.
15 *Izvestiya*, May 15, 1999.

i.e. by attempts to form a new system of European security based solely on one enclosed military and political alliance. Not satisfied with its territorial expansion to the East, NATO also assumed a new strategy that envisioned the expansion of the alliance's activities beyond the limits postulated by the North Atlantic Treaty, and allowed use of force without sanction by the UN Security Council, i.e. in violation of the UN Charter and the fundamental principles of international law.

The NATO aggression against Yugoslavia was a "trial" of the "NATO-centric" concept and caused the most aggravated international crisis since the end of the Cold War. The aftermath of the crisis is obvious. It deeply undermined the very foundations of the international legal order and stability. Military aspects of security came to the fore again. Many countries started considering rapid rearmament as the only way to avoid external aggression. As a result, there appeared an additional—and rather tangible—threat to the regimes of non-proliferation of weapons of mass destruction and means of delivery.

Under pressure from the facts, the West has now started reluctantly rethinking this unlawful action. Conclusions are being drawn that the operation cannot be used as a "model" for similar actions by the alliance in future.[16] Russia, however, foresaw the fallibility of the NATO line of action right from the very beginning. All the warnings of Russian diplomacy, issued while the struggle was underway to prevent aggression, unfortunately came to pass. The armed intervention not only failed to remove any of the Balkan problems. Instead, it brought them to a deadlock, which has to be disentangled now at the cost of tremendous diplomatic efforts.

By way of retrospective justification for the NATO military operation, new concepts of "humanitarian intervention" and "limited sovereignty" have been employed in the West. There have been attempts to force the world community to accept the thesis that the use of force against sovereign states without the UN Security Council's sanction is acceptable for the purpose of preventing humanitarian disasters.

There is no doubt that we cannot and must not remain indifferent to people's suffering caused by large-scale and gross violations of human rights. Furthermore, humanitarian crises may seriously threaten regional and international stability. However, using methods that undermine the very concept of law is inadmissible when dealing with human rights violations. Disregard for the principles of sovereignty and state territorial integrity postulated by the UN Charter may have far-reaching consequences, such as undermining the entire conventional security system and causing complete chaos in international affairs.

---

16 Kamp, K. H., "L'OTAN apres le Kosovo: ange de paix ou gendarme du monde," *Politique Etrangere*, 1999, no. 2, p. 255.

The concept of "humanitarian intervention" is based on an ill-judged notion that the role of the state as an entity in international relations will gradually become extinct in the conditions of globalization. However, the experience of Russia and some other nations that chose to undertake democratic reforms demonstrates the opposite: it is precisely the weakening of the state that leads to the spread of such phenomena as international terrorism, militant separatism, and organized crime. This is why Russia's move to strengthen its statehood, as well as its sovereignty and territorial integrity, proves beneficial not only to Russia's own national interests, but also—and essentially—to the interests of global stability and security.

Given the lessons of the Kosovo crisis, the multipolar world model suggested by Russia has crystallized more distinctly. The concept assigns the central role to collective mechanisms for maintaining peace and security; international law and equal security for all are regarded as the model's key features. These tenets were reflected in the "Concept for the World in the 21st Century" that Russia came up with in 1999. The Concept represents a collection of values and principles that would be applied in relations among the states and that would promote world order without wars or violence. So we in fact initiated the conceptual preparation for the UN Millennium Summit that was held in September 2000 in New York. The main provisions of the Concept were reflected in the final document of the Summit.

It should be stressed that the multipolarity concept is not a mere speculative slogan, but a philosophy for international affairs that is based on the realities of the age of globalization.

Many foreign experts admit that a multipolar world, in a sense, already does exist. No individual country is in a position today to mobilize sufficient resources for monopolistic implementation of its own will in a unipolar world with the other nations exercising their "limited sovereignty." In particular, neither the USA, on its own, nor NATO is able to ensure international security by way of taking up the role of a global policeman.

Apart from the USA and Western Europe, there are many other centers that command economic and political influence in the contemporary world. These are Russia, China, India, Japan, Muslim states, etc. Indeed, even when unipolarity is claimed, the reality will involve both partnership and competition (or even overt rivalry in a number of cases). Integration processes are developing in Europe, South East Asia, Latin America, and Africa. Remarkably, the higher the degree of economic integration, the more powerful the tendency to form collective positions with regard to international issues, and to conduct coordinated foreign policy. In particular, this is the case with the European Union, which has been striving to build its own "identity" lately in all spheres, including defense and security matters.

The well-known American political scientist S. Huntington believes that the

USA's present political stance in favor of a would-be unipolar system dominated by the US is counterproductive and will involve conflict with the interests of the world community. "The United States," writes the expert,

> would definitely prefer a unipolar system, where it would enjoy hegemony, and often
> acts as if such a system were already in place. Other large nations, on the contrary,
> would opt for a multipolar system, which would ensure that their interests be
> observed, both in bilateral and multilateral relations, without their being subject to
> restriction, coercion or pressure on the part of a stronger superpower. They are
> aware of the threat of what they perceive as the US's striving for global hegemony.[17]

Some Russian analysts think that the concept of multipolarity is not "econom-
ical," given Russia's limited resources, and will "deprive Russia of the free hand
to a certain extent, and will automatically involve it in confrontation with the
USA and, partly, with the West as a whole."[18]

I find it hard to agree with such an outlook.

Our choice in favor of the multipolar world order is dictated above all by
our national interests. At the current stage of its development, Russia would
be able to secure a worthwhile place for itself within the world community
only if the multipolar system operates.

It should be stressed that the multipolarity concept is promoted not by way
of abstract discussions, but in the course of the search for a joint solution to
the most pressing and complicated international problems that are directly
pertinent to Russia's vital interests: ensuring strategic stability, resolving
regional conflicts under the UN aegis, and building a comprehensive system
of European security without division lines.

We see the strengthening of major international institutions, first and foremost the UN, as of primary importance in resolving the issues listed above. The
multilateral format of international organizations and forums will open up broad
opportunities for promoting our position and forming a circle of supporters.

However, even from the perspective of bilateral relations, our struggle for a
multipolar world order by no means presupposes inevitable confrontation with
the West. Indeed, many industrially developed states, especially European
ones, do not themselves support the unipolar model. In this respect, as in others, Russia's position is dictated by the striving to find domains in which our
interests coincide, without slipping into confrontation. The facts demonstrate
that Russia's constructive approach towards the leading western powers has
combined both a firm resolve to protect Russia's own national interests and a

---

17 Huntington, S., "The Lonely Superpower," *Foreign Affairs*, 1999, March/April, p. 37.
18 *Strategiya dlya Rossii: povestka dnya dlya Prezidenta* [Strategy for Russia. Agenda for
   the President], Report of the Foreign and Defense Policy Council, Moscow, 2000, p. 91.

striving to seek mutually acceptable solutions, and is totally justifiable. In particular this strategy made it possible to get the Kosovo conflict resolved under the aegis of the UN and to retain what Russia sees as the important potential for bilateral relations with the USA and the EU countries. Despite the outburst of anti-Russian rhetoric at a sensitive period in Russia's anti-terrorist operation in Chechnya, the general position of the western nations was one of respect for Russia's territorial integrity and acceptance of the need to combat terrorism.

It is evident that Russia's stance with regard to the future global order appeals to many in the world, and the number of its supporters keeps growing. For example, when Russia, China, and India expressed their firm condemnation of NATO aggression against Yugoslavia in March 1999 and warned of the danger of extremely destructive consequences of the "humanitarian intervention," the voices of these nations, representing over one half of the world's population, were heard and affected the position taken by other UN member states. As a result, the united front of the nations that uphold the fundamental principles of the UN Charter is gradually expanding. The final documents of the 13th Ministerial Conference of the Non-Aligned Movement, held in Cartagena, Colombia on April 8–9 and of the G-77 summit held in Havana from April 10–14, 2000 read, in particular: "We reject the so-called 'right' of humanitarian intervention, which has no legal basis in the United Nations Charter or in the general principles of international law."[19] In Cartagena, the Non-Aligned Movement also unanimously reiterated "firm condemnation of all unilateral military actions including those made without proper authorization from the United Nations Security Council."[20]

That Russia's position on key issues pertinent to contemporary world order is gaining ever greater international support was clearly demonstrated by the results of the Millennium Summit and the documents it adopted. On behalf of the leaders of the UN member states and governments, the United Nations Millennium Declaration reaffirmed "faith in the Organization and its Charter as indispensable foundations of a more peaceful, prosperous and just world." It also reaffirmed its "commitment to the purposes and principles of the Charter of the United Nations, which have proved timeless and universal." Finally, it was stressed that the participants "are determined to establish a just and lasting peace all over the world in accordance with the purposes and prin-

---

19 The Final Document of the XIII Ministerial Conference of the Non-Aligned Countries, Cartagena, April 8–9, 2000, Paragraph 263; Declaration of the South Summit, Havana, April 10–14, 2000, Paragraph 54.

20 The Final Document of the XIII Ministerial Conference of the Non-Aligned Countries, Cartagena, April 8–9, 2000, Paragraph 11.

ciples of the Charter."[21] Russian diplomacy became actively involved in the practical work to carry out resolutions of the Millennium Summit.

Our vision of the future architecture of security in the multipolar world has been gradually gaining more specific content.

3.

One of the key issues related to the formation of the new global order lies in the need to elaborate collective responses to new challenges that face the global community in the 21st century. While the second half of the 20th century was marked by the struggle to prevent global nuclear catastrophe, today's task is far more complicated and multifaceted. The strategy for human survival needs to be replaced by a strategy for sustainable development and prosperity of mankind. This strategy must adhere to the following fundamental principles: acknowledgement of the indivisibility of international security, use of scientific achievements to benefit all humanity, a gradual bridging of the developmental gap between nations.

It is absolutely clear that these large-scale goals can be attained only if there is international stability and predictability, and trust in relations between different states. In other words, they can be achieved in the conditions of international strategic stability. The issues of strategic security became especially critical when the USA declared its intention of creating a missile security system banned under the ABM Treaty of 1972. This intention endangered not only the Treaty, globally recognized as the cornerstone of strategic security, but also virtually the entire system of international agreements that had been elaborated during the preceding 30 years in the sphere of arms control, disarmament, and nonproliferation of nuclear weapons. It would be no exaggeration to say that no international issue in the past decade has presented the global community with such a critical dilemma, a dilemma that is crucial for the architecture of international security in the 21st century.

Russian diplomacy found itself facing a serious choice, too. We had to define our position—the position that was most suited to our national interests and the realities of the international situation at the time. It was at this instant that the style, methods, and principles of the new Russian foreign policy that had been forming over previous years manifested themselves in the most distinctive form. Obviously, either going for another round of confrontation with the USA, as during the bitter USSR–USA dispute over the American "Strategic Defense Initiative," or taking up a passive and inert position in the face of plans that would affect Russia's security in a most serious way, would be equally damaging for Russia. In those circumstances, Russian diplomacy

---

21 UN Declaration of the Millennium (A/res/55/2), Paragraphs 1, 3, 4.

opted for an entirely new course. It initiated a constructive alternative to the demolition of the ABM Treaty and of global strategic stability. A number of measures were undertaken, aimed at further active pursuit of a reduction in strategic offensive weapons. The START-2 Treaty and the Comprehensive Nuclear Test Ban Treaty were ratified; and Russia indicated its readiness to start early negotiations on a START-3 Treaty aimed at a further reduction of strategic offensive arms. Russia introduced a number of specific proposals concerning weapons of mass destruction and the means of their delivery, as well as on the effective prevention of new threats to international security. Russia and the USA started active discussion of the proposals in question.

The disarmament aspects of strategic stability have gone beyond the framework of bilateral Russian–US relations. Nuclear disarmament and nonproliferation in the contemporary world has ceased to be a matter solely of interaction between nuclear states. The UN's multilateral mechanisms and the entire global community are becoming increasingly involved in the relevant processes at an operative level. This is a new phenomenon in international affairs, which is gaining greater significance in Russian foreign policy. The tendency has been eloquently manifested by the adoption at the UN General Assembly's 54th Session of a resolution, initiated by Russia, on the preservation of, and compliance with, the Anti-Ballistic Missile Treaty.

In the course of the UN Millennium Summit and Assembly, Russia brought forward a concept of comprehensive stability that organically combines all major approaches to a just and democratic global order. The concept implies promotion of strategic stability in its broadest sense in the conditions of globalization. Apart from the processes of disarmament and nonproliferation of weapons of mass destruction, this promotion will involve the following components: international information security; resolution of the ongoing regional conflicts and prevention of new ones; the fight against international terrorism and organized crime; protection of individual rights and freedoms; improvement and democratization of the international monetary and financial sphere, trade and economic relations, and environmental protection. All these components will constitute a comprehensive strategic stability based on the principles of multilateral participation, equality, and solidarity in resolving global problems.

It is absolutely clear that strategic security can be ensured only through specific efficient mechanisms for controlling global processes. In other words, a new architecture of international security has to be created to fit in with the multipolarity actually existing in the world. The "construction material" for this architecture is already available. It includes the ramified system of international organizations led by the UN, powerful regional relations, and the dense texture of bilateral relations. What remains to be done is to render these structures a holistic system and to create efficient mechanisms for coordinating common global and national interests.

The central position in the new system of international relations must belong to the UN, a unique and largely irreplaceable mechanism for regulating the entire realm of international affairs. Indeed, the UN is the only international structure capable of undertaking the role of guarantor of global strategic stability.

As a genuine global decision-making body, the UN is a true embodiment of the interdependence and sovereign equality of all members of the global community. The UN represents all nations, all—without exception—global and regional groups, whose joint efforts create the best conditions for elaborating balanced, generally acceptable approaches that are then followed in international affairs. The United Nations is the only institution that can provide a basis for joining the potential of all states and regions in order to respond to today's challenges, effectively combine national and international efforts, and achieve harmony of national interests with the cultural variety of nations. Only the United Nations can unite the entire global community in order to build a world without wars and based on the supremacy of law.

Despite the fundamental changes in the international situation that have taken place since 1945, when the UN was founded, this global organization continues to confirm its vitality on a daily basis. For over half a century, the UN Charter has been the main document of international law, the foundation for civilized interaction among nations. Yes, the UN has made mistakes and experienced failures. However, the global organization's overall balance on the threshold of the new millennium is definitely positive.

As UN Secretary General Kofi Annan rightly pointed out,

> The purposes and principles of the United Nations are set out clearly in the Charter, and in the Universal Declaration of Human Rights. Their relevance and capacity to inspire have in no way diminished. If anything they have increased, as peoples have become interconnected in new ways, and the need for collective responsibility at the global level has come to be more widely felt. The...values, which reflect the spirit of the Charter, are—I believe—shared by all nations, and are of particular importance for the age we are now entering.[22]

Persistently striving to remove the use of force as a method of resolving disputes between states, the UN developed peacekeeping theory and practice, which continues to evolve and to take account of the new realities. As was stated by the UN Secretary General in the UN Progress Report delivered at the 50th UN General Assembly session,

> there was a widespread belief that...the many regional conflicts flaring in different parts of the world could be quickly extinguished...Sadly, the record of world affairs

22 *"We the Peoples": The Role of the United Nations in the 21st Century*, Report by the UN Secretary General, Doc. A/54/2000, Paragraph 362.

over the past few years has largely belied those optimistic expectations. Many old conflicts continue to defy the efforts of the international community to bring about a settlement and new wars have continued to erupt, almost all of them within States.[23]

These words, pronounced more than five years ago, are just as relevant today. Since the moment the UN was created, 55 UN peacekeeping operations have been carried out, with 42 of them sanctioned just in the period since 1988. Many of the operations have, without exaggeration, played a historic role. UN peacekeeping operations have forestalled the disintegration of the Congo in the 1960s. They have made significant contributions to resolving the conflicts in Mozambique, Namibia, Cambodia, El Salvador, Nicaragua, and Guatemala. These activities have won the organization a reputation as a just and impartial arbiter. Warring sides increasingly seek UN mediation and its peace-promoting services.

The majority of the seventeen UN peacekeeping operations currently under way involve UN active engagement in the process of political resolution in the regions in question, including CIS territory. The experience of peaceful resolution in Tajikistan offers an example of successful and efficient cooperation between CIS peacekeepers and the UN mission. Joint efforts by Tajiks themselves and the global community set the country on course for national reconciliation, and helped bring back home over a million refugees. This is actually a unique example among ongoing regional and intrastate conflicts. It is also outstanding evidence of the peacekeeping potential of the Commonwealth of Independent States and Russia, which jointly had to bear the main burden of assisting the peace settlement in Tajikistan.

It is virtually impossible to name a sphere of international cooperation that the UN is not involved in, in one form or another. The UN framework comprises multilateral mechanisms that regulate almost all spheres of human activity and international interaction. Among these spheres are: problems of disarmament and nonproliferation of nuclear weapons, the fight against terrorism and illegal drug trafficking, issues pertaining to social and economic development, population, environmental problems, etc. In other words, the entire spectrum of issues that pose fresh challenges for humanity on the threshold of the third millennium. This is why the United Nations is designed, and is objectively able, to head efforts to regulate the globalization processes. Even long before the emergence of the term "globalization," the global organization initiated discussions on the need for packages of policies to regulate political, economic, environmental, social and other aspects of development of contemporary civilization, taking account of the interdependence of all nations. It was

---

23 Annual Report of the Secretary General on the work of the Organization (1995). Official Records, Fiftieth Session, Supplement No.1 (A/50/1), Paragraphs 2–3.

the UN that developed the universally recognized concept of sustainable development, which presumed an integrated approach to economic, social and environmental tasks. The UN Secretary General stressed: "[T]he central challenge we face today is to ensure that globalization becomes a positive force for all the world's people, instead of leaving billions of them behind in squalor."[24]

In short, as President of the Russian Federation V. Putin said at the UN Millennium Summit, "real prospects have opened up for all states and nations to progress to a worthwhile life in the conditions of socially oriented globalization."

Certainly, this presupposes that reform of the United Nations must be actively pursued, so that the organization can adapt itself to meet the new challenges. However, we should remember that it is not so much administrative improvements that can engender the UN's genuine efficiency, but rather the UN member states' political will. Just as—in the words of a saying—"the retinue makes the king," so the authority of an international organization is critically determined by the readiness of its member states to abide by the organization's decisions and strive for complete accomplishment of its charter mission. In the presence of political will on the part of all its members, and based on the UN Charter and its extensive experience, we can and must conduct healthy reforms in order to strengthen the UN's leading role in international affairs. The UN Charter provides for the organization's potential to come up with efficient global responses to the global challenges of the time. However, this potential can be effectively deployed only collectively, without anyone claiming unconditional global leadership or attempting to impose their vision of world order on others. The future depends on the UN's capacity to combine the new ideas and tendencies of global development with the tried and tested fundamental principles of international law and justice.

Thus, the UN can be seen as the key link in the future system of a multipolar global order. However, for its holistic essence to be secured, another component must play a significant role: the UN's interaction with the broad network of regional organizations and movements.

The expansion and strengthening of such organizations is one of the major universal tendencies of recent decades, which is closely connected to the process of a multipolar world formation. The assessment made by France's President Jacques Chirac is revealing in this sense:

In order to organize the system of international relations of the 21st century in the best way, it is necessary, first of all, to chart a course for a multipolar world. In response to the globalization process and striving to become masters of their fate,

---

24 *"We the Peoples": The Role of the United Nations in the 21st Century*, Report by the UN Secretary General, Doc. A/54/2000, Paragraph 14.

most nations opt to unite at the regional level. The European Union is the most accomplished example of addressing this need for regional integration."[25]

However, the problem of creating a new European architecture has a broader significance in reality. For centuries, Europe was the main center for world politics and the major "enactor" of the principles and norms of international law. It was here that military and political coalitions and alliances would be shaped and destroyed. It was here that they were involved in the bloodiest conflicts in human history. Today's Europe can be seen as a miniature model of the actual global variety and multipolarity. This is why there is no need to prove that the future of the whole of international affairs will be largely determined by the security system that is shaped within Europe.

Today, the continent experiences those difficulties and contradictions typical of the global process of formation of a new order. The fall of the Berlin Wall opened opportunities for forming a new Europe as a single democratic space of equal and indivisible security. A unique historic chance emerged to build a comprehensive European security system that would have a worthy place for each state of the continent. An adequate regional structure to undertake this role is already in existence, namely the Organization for Security and Cooperation in Europe. For all its imperfections, the organization was, and remains, the central pan-European structure that unites all nations of the continent for the sake of peace and stability in Europe.

Attempts to dispute the OSCE's role as the foundation for the future European security architecture, in favor of other structures with limited circles of parties are counterproductive, for such attempts *a priori* exclude other states from participation in the security architecture altogether, or assign them secondary roles in it. The architecture in question can be firm and reliable only if it is genuinely pan-European. Indeed, any striving to ensure one's own security by cutting the neighbors off with new military and political boundaries is not merely a delusion, but it will also distract from the actual problems of the continent.

None of this is meant to belittle the significance of other European organizations and associations, such as the European Union and NATO. Multipolarity, both on the European and the global scale, presumes interdependence and partnership among individual "building blocks" of the future global order, rather than their competition. At any rate, it is essential that the interrelations of these structures with other participants in the pan-European process should be based on the principles of equality and democracy, and should conform to the norms of international law. In recent years, the prerequisites for such rela-

---

25 Chirac, J., "La France Dans un monde multipolair," *Politique Etrangere*, 1999, no. 4, p. 85.

tions have been created, largely due to Russia's diplomatic efforts. In particular, the principles in question were postulated in the Charter for European Security adopted at the OSCE Istanbul summit in 1999, a document that became a kind of "conduct code" for European states and organizations. The document specifies the readiness of the OSCE member states to build their relations in the spirit of partnership and mutual assistance, and directs that the continent's international organizations should strictly observe the UN Charter, and adhere to the principles of transparency and predictability of action.

Important stipulations of an essential nature are also included in the Founding Act on Mutual Relations, Cooperation and Security signed by Russia and NATO in 1997. Suffice it to point to its postulation of refraining from the threat or use of force against each other, as well as against any other state, its sovereignty, territorial integrity, or political independence, in any manner inconsistent with the United Nations Charter. There is no doubt that, should NATO adhere to this postulation, Europe could avoid many problems that emerged as a result of the alliance's involvement in the Balkans.

Economic integration processes have taken place on an unprecedented scale in Asia of late. These processes have been accompanied by an active search for mechanisms to safeguard security and strengthen the balance among different power centers. Among the developments are: the creation of the Asia Pacific Economic Cooperation (APEC) Forum, a major economic integration structure formed by the countries of the Pacific region, the establishment of mechanisms for regular Asia Europe Meetings (ASEM), etc. Another idea currently under consideration is to form a genuinely pan-Asian—from the Middle to the Far East—system for dialogue, based on the Kazakhstan-initiated Conference on Interaction and Confidence-Building Measures in Asia. Sub-regional organizations are gaining more consequence. Among these are: the Shanghai Forum, with Russia, China, Kazakhstan, Kyrgyzstan, Tajikistan, and Uzbekistan as participants; a mechanism for consultations ASEAN+3 (including China, Japan, and Korea); the Indian Ocean Rim Association for Regional Cooperation (IOR-ARC); and the Bangladesh–India–Myanmar–Sri Lanka–Thailand Economic Cooperation (BIMST-EC).

The desire of the majority of states in the region to jointly counteract any threat to security led to an expansion of the authority and influence of multilateral structures involved in political dialogue. The most important such structure is the ASEAN Regional Forum (ARF), which unites all the leading powers of the Asia-Pacific region (APR): Russia, the USA, China, Japan, India, and also the European Union. We advocate a further increase in the ARF's role as the key regional mechanism for policy and security dialogue, and attach major significance to the work in progress within the Forum's framework on a concept and principles for preventive diplomacy in the APR. The draft Pacific Concord, which was proposed by Russia and which contains guiding principles for relations within the APR, could—as a regional "code of conduct"—form a constituent element of the concept. Simultaneously, the ARF is expanding its efforts to coordinate current, and develop new, confidence-building measures in the military-political sphere. A dialogue is also in progress on other aspects of interaction that are also designed to strengthen regional security. All these are components of the ARF's common endeavor to shape a multipolar global order.

Of course, the picture of a rapidly developing network of regional organizations and integration-oriented associations will not be complete without mentioning corresponding structures that unite Arab nations, as well as the countries of Latin America and Africa. Our political dialogue with these countries is of increasing importance in Russia's foreign policy.

And finally, bilateral relations between states are to become the third basic element of the new world order. Certainly, these relations can perform this role only if all bilateral relations strictly conform to the norms of international law. In this respect, European legislation can also be cited as a positive example. In particular, the OSCE summit in Istanbul proved the commitment on the part of participating states to the fundamental principles of the UN Charter and the Helsinki Final Act. Therefore, relations among European nations will remain based on respect for the sovereign equality of states, their territorial integrity, inviolability of borders, non-use of force or threat of force, peaceful resolution of disputes, non-interference in each other's internal affairs, and observance of human rights.

Accordingly, the future global architecture appears to us a kind of "pyramid," with the UN, as the main instrument for maintaining peace and security, on the top, and the base formed by cooperation within frameworks of regional organizations and at the bilateral level. Universal and meticulous observance of international law will serve as the "mortar" keeping the pyramid together.

There is no doubt that the evolution of global processes requires adapting the norms of international law to the new realities. This refers, in particular, to the need to react to humanitarian crises in a more efficient and coordinated fashion, or—better still—to preclude their emergence altogether. However, this work must be performed by joint efforts and in compliance with the UN Charter. It should not be forgotten that all the instruments of international humanitarian law provide a mechanism for dealing with possible infractions, including the right to pass corresponding issues to the UN Security Council for consideration. Set out in numerous multilateral conventions and treaties, the procedure in question is mandatory when enforcement measures are being considered as a response to humanitarian crises. Russia submitted an initiative to the UN concerning collective upgrading of the legal aspects of employing force in international relations in conditions of globalization. Serious attention should also be paid to specific ways of developing preventive diplomacy and peacekeeping, improving systems of sanctions, and the principles and practice of post-conflict peace-building. Russia came up with a number of specific suggestions on these matters in the aforementioned "Concept for the World in the 21st Century."

The USA's attitude to those states regarded as "problematic" has recently become a serious source of international and regional tension. It also poses a grave problem in terms of international law. In fact, an apparently undeclared war has been launched against such states. In particular, these states are subjected to a variety of sanctions and trade embargoes, as well as political and military pressure, including the direct use of military force, as in the cases of Iraq and Yugoslavia.

The counterproductivity of such a course of action is obvious. In no case so far has the USA been able to have the unwanted regimes deposed, while it is these states' populations that are the true victims of the sanctions and military interventions. A serious issue emerging in this context is that of the attitude the world community should assume with regard to those countries allegedly abusing human rights and other norms of international law. Russia believes that strong-arm measures, even if sanctioned by the global community, should be resorted to only after thorough consideration and with great caution, lest the cure prove to be worse than the illness. It is important that none of the so-called "problematic" countries should feel driven into a corner and perceive its security to be threatened. Such situations will merely provoke confrontation. Meanwhile, the art of politics, according to the French philosopher Adrien Helvetius is "to make it so that it is in each person's best interests to be virtuous." The "problematic" countries must be given a tangible alternative for positive participation in the global and regional security systems. This approach is exemplified by Russia's efforts for national reconciliation of the two Korean states.

Another practice that needs to be reconsidered is that of the use of sanctions by the world community. The UN experience in this sphere is ambiguous. Since the 1970s, when persistent sanctions employed by the global community against the Republic of South Africa and Rhodesia finally undermined the apartheid regimes there, there have been no other instances of sanctions achieving just ends. In the final analysis, the enthusiastic application of indefinite and indiscriminate blanket sanctions in the early 1990s (13 of the 15 regimes that the UN ever applied sanctions against were subjected to this measure after 1991) merely caused suffering to the populations both of the sanctioned countries and their neighbors. For Iraq, the aftermath of sanctions was especially critical in humanitarian and economic terms, and in terms of the fate of civil society in general.

It is important that the United Nations proved capable of learning the right lessons from this sad experience. Initiated by Russia, China, France and many of the non-aligned states, there has been a rejection of the detrimental practice of indiscriminate sanctions. New policies are being undertaken to affect specifically those persons guilty of violations of international laws and of ignoring the Security Council's resolutions. It was such sanctions, well-balanced and targeted, that were applied against the Afghan Talibs in order to make them stop supporting international terrorism. This is especially topical in the light of the recent disclosure that the Talibs are sponsoring the Chechen militant groups. In addition, Russia and its associates are calling for the UN Security Council sanctions to be applied for both strictly specified periods and indefinite terms. Moreover, mandatory evaluation of possible humanitarian consequences of such measures is needed, and suffering of the civilian population must be precluded. Neither should the sanctions have a negative effect on third countries. This is a way to carry out the recommendations of the UN General Assembly, which stipulated that the Security Council should use such an approach to sanction regimes. This expanding new approach to sanction application reflects the aspirations of the non-aligned states, which used the Non-Aligned Movement's ministerial conference in Cartagena on April 8–9, 2000 to reiterate that sanctions must be applied for strictly defined purposes, based on the law, for limited periods, and that they must not be used as an instrument of political pressure.[26]

On the whole, it must become one of the fundamental principles of the new world order that there should be the broadest possible involvement of all nations in joint efforts to strengthen security and stability. Only thus can international affairs be rendered a predictable sphere. Only thus can sufficiently powerful joint multilateral diplomatic efforts be undertaken to achieve political resolution of current conflicts and to prevent new ones.

4.

At present there is a link between Russia's foreign policy and the process of reinforcing the nation's internal potential, i.e. above all the Russian state *per se*. Presenting the essence of the new political course in his annual address to the Federal Assembly, President of the Russian Federation Vladimir Putin remarked: "only a strong and efficient democratic state is able to protect civil, political and economic freedoms, and to create the conditions necessary for the people's well-being and prosperity of our Motherland." He stressed that external challenges cannot be properly addressed unless the state is strengthened.[27]

26 The Final Document of the XIII Ministerial Conference of the Non-Aligned Countries, Cartagena, April 8–9, 2000, Paragraphs 29–30.
27 Address by President of the Russian Federation to the Federal Assembly of the Russian Federation "The State of Russia. The Way to an Effective State," Moscow, 2000, p. 8.

There is no need to prove that our foreign policy's efficiency is directly determined by the smooth and well coordinated operation of the entire state mechanism. Successful foreign policy and diplomacy can only be based on consensus, and must reflect the interests of the main political parties and civil movements representing our country and entire nation.

In this context one cannot fail to see positive changes in the social and political environment of Russian foreign policy. Whereas during its initial period, and especially in 1992–1993, international affairs would often be a site of intensive ideological and political struggle, now, starting from around the mid 1990s, our society is gradually coming together on fundamental foreign policy principles. This tendency can be traced in the way relations between the executive and legislative branches of power have evolved. The process has developed from bitter confrontation to constructive cooperation (after the parliamentary elections of December 1999). Symbolically, the new style of relations between the newly elected President and the State Duma first manifested itself in the sphere of foreign policy: on the President's initiative, the State Duma took the serious decision to ratify the START-2 Treaty by a majority of votes.

The tendency for political stability to be strengthened in Russia allows Russian diplomacy to pursue a confident policy in international affairs, looking to the long-term future. The new version of the Foreign Policy Concept adopted by the President provides our diplomacy with reliable guidelines for promoting our national interests in a complicated and rather unpredictable international situation.

Of course, we will still have to keep adjusting and improving our course in the light of specific foreign policy issues, and in order to properly address new problems and challenges of our time. More than any other function of the state, foreign policy must remain flexible and adaptable. Even now, we can clearly discern the key domains that will require development and expansion of diplomatic efforts, both at the global level and in our relations with Russia's high-priority partner groups.

It is quite natural that our relations with member states of the Commonwealth of Independent States will be one such priority for us. Our experience of the last decade has dispelled any illusions of a rapid and problem-free integration within the CIS. And yet, it has also disproved the forecasts that the role of the Commonwealth would be reduced to "civilized divorce" of the former USSR republics. Russia is acting on a firm conviction that the CIS can become an influential regional association that will stimulate prosperity, cooperation and good-neighborly relations in the entire post-Soviet space. However, it is necessary to assume a realistic stance here and consider the degree of openness our CIS partners will demonstrate in return, and their readiness to attend to our interests.

Integration is not an end in itself for Russia. What matters to us are the positive outcomes integration could bring to Russia itself and to other member states. The establishment of effective interaction in the economic sphere is a top-priority task for us. While we support cooperation at different levels of intensity and in various forms, Russia readily promotes higher forms of integration within the CIS. An example of this is the Collective Security Treaty and Customs Union comprising Russia, Belarus, Kazakhstan, Kyrgyzstan, and Tajikistan. Strengthening of the Union of Russia and Belarus is a supreme task for us too, for it embodies the highest possible form of integration of two sovereign states at the present stage.

Relations with Europe remain Russia's traditional foreign policy priority. In this sphere, we can see two major tasks for the immediate future. The first is to maintain the course of creating a stable democratic system of European security. The second is to add new momentum to multifaceted cooperation with the European Union. Even now, the EU is one of our key partners in world politics and the world economy. There is every reason to expect that the significance of these relations will keep expanding for both sides. Our goal is a stable long-term partnership with the EU, free of politically motivated fluctuations. In the short term, we should focus our efforts on conducting mutual strategies to enrich our relations.

New opportunities for our interaction in the international arena are offered by the formation of the "European defense identity." The development of this process will require special attention, since it may lead to a considerable change in the entire European structure. There is no way that Russia would wish to remain outside this transformation. Moreover, our participation in the process can become one of the most important stabilizing factors that will expand the continent's security and cooperation potential.

Our approach to relations with NATO will be determined by realistic and pragmatic criteria. Russian–NATO interaction has the potential to become an essential factor that can safeguard security and stability on the continent. Russian–NATO relations, which suffered in the wake of events in the Balkans, are gradually warming again. However, the effectiveness of this cooperation and the level of its intensity will depend on the two sides' readiness to thoroughly fulfill the obligations they undertook, above all under the Founding Act.

We will continue to try to persuade our NATO partners that the policy of further expanding the alliance is counterproductive and will lead to the formation of new dividing lines on the continents, and thus bring about the establishment of zones with varying degrees of security in Europe. This is an erroneous course, which goes against both Russia's interests and general considerations of unity and stability in Europe.

Russia is striving for further active dialogue with the USA. Irrespective of who, Democrats or Republicans, will run the White House after the presidential elections, we do not believe there is any alternative to constructive interaction between the two nations. There are many spheres in which our interests objectively coincide and create a basis for productive cooperation. Our nations bear a special responsibility for maintaining strategic stability, and promoting nuclear disarmament. The period ahead is going to be of especial consequence in this respect. Those decisions that are to be made in this sphere will determine the long-term general development of global processes.

Relations with Asia will be increasingly significant in Russia's foreign policy. Not only is Russia an integral part of this dynamically developing region, but the task of securing the economic advance of Russia's Siberia and Far East demands increased international cooperation.

Motivated by our national interests, Russia's diplomacy in Asia will be aimed first and foremost at ensuring the security of Russia's frontiers and creating favorable conditions for the country's social and economic progress. In tackling these tasks, Russia will, firstly, play an active part in multilateral and bilateral international efforts to maintain peace and military-political stability in the region, and to form a regional security community based chiefly on community of interests and economic interdependence. Secondly, Russia will intensify its involvement in the rapidly evolving processes of regional political and economic integration, and in the search for new forms of broad, mutually beneficial cooperation with Asian states. This striving is welcomed by our partners, who perceive Russia as a natural participant in the ongoing processes in the region.

Our policy in Asia is focused primarily on expanding relations with the largest Asian nations: China, India, and Japan.

Even today, Russia and China are entering a new stage of development of their political relations, which will be set out in our Treaty of Friendship and Cooperation. Work on this important document is already under way. The Treaty is meant to define the key lines of our long-term strategic cooperation. The partnership has already become a weighty factor of global security. However, much is yet to be done for this high level of political relations to be augmented by more solid trade and economic ties. The cooperation can and must be set in motion through large-scale joint projects. There is a huge potential for interaction in the power industry, including the nuclear power industry, construction, fuel and transport infrastructures, as well as related research and development projects and the introduction of new technologies. The significance of direct economic ties at a regional level is constantly increasing too.

A similar issue of strengthening the economic component of bilateral partnership is present in relations between Russia and India. This would boost the importance of Russian–Indian interaction in the international arena, based on the community of the two sides' key interests and their approaches to global political issues.

Qualitative changes are taking place in our relationship with Japan. The process is conditioned by rapprochement between us on such key international issues as establishing the rule of law, enhancing the UN's role in international affairs, reinforcing stability in Asia and the entire world, and the joint search for responses to global challenges, such as international terrorism. These developments form the basis for Russia's continuing pursuit of intensification of all aspects of its relations with Japan, including proceeding with peace treaty negotiations.

Participation in the search for a comprehensive settlement in the Middle East and in the Persian Gulf zone, and expanding cooperation with all states of the region will remain one of the priorities of Russian foreign policy. For Russia, the region is close in the geopolitical, historical, and many other respects. That is why establishment of lasting peace and stability in the region, full settlement of the protracted Arab–Israeli conflict, stabilization of the situation around Iraq, and guaranteed security in the Persian Gulf zone chime with Russia's national interests.

Sometimes, both in our country and in the Arab world, one can hear speculation about Russia's likely "withdrawal" from the Middle East and loss of the influence it used to have there. Not only are such ideas superficial, but they are very far from the truth. It is true that in the early 1990s, in the early stages of Russian foreign policy formation, when the new principles were being shaped—including those to be applied in the Middle East—our role in the region's affairs was not as distinct as it had been. What was happening then can be explained not merely by a review of our foreign policy conceptions, but also by the cardinal changes in the Middle East itself. It appeared that a historic breakthrough was about to occur in what had seemed a deadly confrontation between Israel and the Arab states. Russia's new policy in the Middle East had thus to be elaborated taking this into account. We shifted our strategy from supporting one conflict side towards cooperation with all states of the region, which opened the way for Russia to contribute its share to settling the Arab–Israeli conflict.

As a co-sponsor—along with the USA—of the peace process in the Middle East, Russia actively assists in settling critical situations that keep emerging during the peace process. We put serious effort into searching for resolutions acceptable both to the Israelis and the Palestinians, not least with regard to the problem of Jerusalem. Moreover, in doing so, Russia is working in its own interests, too: the spiritual renaissance going on in our country and our attraction to the Holy Land do not allow us to display indifference to the fate of the Jerusalem shrines.

Russia has done much to assist in the resolution of the Syrian–Israeli and Lebanese–Israeli conflicts.

Russia's capacity to influence the situation in the Persian Gulf zone has, on many occasions, helped forestall a further escalation of tensions around Iraq. Russia has been consistent in its efforts to promote stabilization of the situation and elimination of weapons of mass destruction by the Iraqi government in compliance with the UN Security Council's resolutions. At the same time, Russia is firmly in favor of stopping the bombing of Iraqi territory, and—as Baghdad proceeds with fulfilling its obligations—of lifting the sanctions that are bearing heavily on the Iraqi people and threatening a humanitarian disaster.

In short, we are firmly convinced that it is high time the Middle East and the Persian Gulf zone were converted from a source of instability into a zone of peace, cooperation and prosperity, with no place for mutual alienation or weapons of mass destruction.

Russia is open to the establishment of mutually profitable relations with all states of Africa, Latin America, and their integrated formations. All sides involved are seriously interested in economic cooperation, political dialogue and developing lots of room for interaction in the interests of a just and democratic world order.

It is an important feature of contemporary foreign policy that there are a number of issues that used to fall outside "classical" diplomacy.

We can state with confidence that the share of economic diplomacy will be increasing in Russian foreign policy in the very near future. In this respect the following tasks are coming to the fore: promoting the market economy in Russia, ensuring equal participation in international economic organizations, protecting the interests of Russian business abroad, creating favorable conditions for foreign investments, resolving the problems of foreign debts.

Russian diplomacy will persist in promoting an international financial architecture that will ensure the best possible conditions for a stable and smooth development of Russia's economy, its organic incorporation into the world's network of economic ties, while at the same time giving due consideration to the factors that affect Russia's economic security.

Another essential criterion that will be increasingly applied when evaluating the efficiency of Russia's foreign policy is our ability to ensure the security of rights and interests of Russian citizens and our compatriots abroad, wherever they might stay or reside. This issue will be seriously addressed by Russian diplomacy on a concrete basis, both within the framework of international organizations, and within our bilateral relations, in a manner proportionate to the acuteness of the problem in each country.

As Vladimir Putin pointed out, "neither do we have a right to 'sleep through' the information technology revolution that is in progress in the world."[28] Russian diplomacy has two tasks: to enhance the state's information security, and to employ contemporary information technologies in order to create an objective picture of Russia in the world.

That the work has been started in both these domains is clear, in particular, from the adoption by the UN General Assembly of Russia's resolution "Devel-

---

28 Ibid. p. 7.

opments in the field of information and telecommunications in the context of international security." Incidentally, there is work for the future to remove the existing and potential threats in the sphere of information security at the multilateral, bilateral and unilateral levels.

Another inalienable component of foreign policy lies within the domains of cultural and scientific exchanges. The Russian state's role and authority in the world are determined not only by its political weight and economic resources, but also by the cultural and scientific resources of the peoples of the Russian Federation, and their spiritual and intellectual potentials. The development of cultural and scientific exchanges must contribute to strengthening our mutual understanding and trust with other nations and help the further advance of Russian culture into the global intellectual and cultural space. A Russian cultural presence abroad should help Russia acquire a position and role in the world arena that is worthy of our nation's great history and cultural heritage.

* * *

For Russia, the main outcomes of the past decade have been that it has established itself as one of the contemporary world's influential centers, whose relations with other nations are based on the principles of equality and mutual advantage, and that it has acquired a confidence in its powers. We know what kind of system of international relations we want. We also know what can and what cannot be expected from foreign policy. Russia's foreign policy concept rejects national egotism and blind worship of military power, on the one hand, and, on the other, romantic idealism in international affairs, the inappropriateness of which has been confirmed by real-life experience. Our concept embodies sound pragmatism. One of its key components is the idea that it is the task of foreign policy to effectively assist the state in resolving its internal problems at this, in many respects critical, period of Russia's development. Our foreign policy resources are objectively limited today. Therefore, they will be employed, first and foremost, within those spheres that are crucial for us now. The primary goal that Russian foreign policy will pursue is to create the necessary external conditions for the country to completely overcome the economic crisis and embark on the path of confident economic growth and prosperity.

Russia has the resources and capacities it needs to take a respectable place in the new world order at the outset of the third millennium. Given its inherent qualities—its geopolitical situation, demography, history and cultural heritage, economic and military potentials—Russia objectively was, is and will remain an important center of global politics.

Originally published in Ivanov, I. S., *Vneshnyaya politika Rossii i mir* [Russian foreign policy and the world], Moscow: ROSSPEN, 2000.

On the New Version of the National Security Conception of the Russian Federation

Sergei Ivanov

The National Security Conception is, in essence, a *political document that formulates the most important guidelines of Russia's state policy*. Based on this document, the ministries, official organs, government and non-governmental organizations will formulate and adjust their conceptual foundations, as well as the part of normative legal acts that relates to their activities of safeguarding Russia's national security (for example, in February the Security Council reviewed the Military Doctrine of the Russian Federation at its sitting, while the Russian Federation's Foreign Policy Conception will be discussed at the next meeting, both documents representing, in fact, the provisions of the National Security Concept as they apply to the respective spheres of operation of the agencies of state power).

As far as the current situation is concerned, the Concept serves as the basis for the *annual report by the Presidential Administration to the President of the Russian Federation* with regard to the internal and international state of affairs, and also for the *annual address by the President of the Russian Federation to the Federal Assembly*. The Report and Address specify the government's current goals and missions, as well as the plans of those ministries, state agencies and organizations that constitute the system to safeguard Russia's security.

Therefore, the Concept in principle determines *two fields of operation for state structures: first, in fulfilling their routine functions they should uphold the national interests and goals; and, second, they should safeguard national security by identifying and neutralizing internal and external threats using instruments and means designed to safeguard security. It is obvious, though, that the two areas of activities mentioned are interconnected and interdependent.*

One of the FUNDAMENTAL DIFFERENCES between our Concept and similar documents in other countries (incidentally these operate in a large number of states: from the UK to Ukraine, where they bear various titles, such as "doctrine," "strategy," etc., and address exclusively external aspects of interests and security) is that, in our Concept, national interests and security are considered in the internal and external spheres jointly and as they affect one another. Consideration of internal factors prevails.

In May 1999, the President of the Russian Federation issued a decision on the adoption of amendments and additions to the Concept that was passed in December 1997.

In view of the media speculation that the new version of the Concept was timed to coincide with V. Putin's accession to the presidency, I would like to state straight away that it was Putin who, as the then Secretary of the Security Council, started developing the amendments and additions to the Concept on the instructions of the President of the Russian Federation. He then continued this work in his capacity as Chairman of the Government, and approved it as the acting President of the Russian Federation on January 10, 2000.

What has been the impetus for introducing the changes to the Conception?

It is a long time since the original Conception was issued. During this time, the *economic state of the Russian Federation* has not only failed to improve, but has deteriorated still further, largely because of the financial crisis that took place in Russia in August 1998.

The state of our economy has led to a dramatic decline in the state's capacity to influence certain international developments by economic methods, and to participate fully in the international labor distribution. The weakening of the country's military might and its defensive potential is also evident. Moreover, all this has been happening just as some states are coming to regard military force as the cornerstone of their policy and its key instrument.

A situation has emerged with *Russia being increasingly forced out of the world economy and, therefore, out of world politics.*

The complex economic situation has, in our opinion, engendered a *dramatic growth in the scale of terrorism and crime*, organized crime above all. This also forces us to conclude that the *situation with federal relations in the multinational Russia has been deteriorating too.*

Nor is our assessment of the foreign policy situation very optimistic.

First, we have to point to a significant escalation of the threat to Russia's national security in the sphere of international relations. This is primarily manifested in the fact that particular countries and coalitions have created conditions that hinder Russia from properly protecting its natural and legitimate national interests in international affairs. I will elaborate on this below.

Second, there has been a considerable intensification of the threat to the security of Russia and the entire world community, with terrorist organizations selecting Russia as a test site for their far-reaching global ambitions.

Third, there is concern over the prospects for global strategic stability, which, although much weakened, is still in place, and over the state of the disarmament process.

Naturally, this will not be the last update of the National Security Conception. As the situation inside the country and in the world changes, so the apparatus of the Security Council will, in cooperation with all interested authorities, proceed with the development of corresponding supplements.

I will elaborate on the DOMESTIC POLITICAL ISSUES reflected in the Conception.

The economic policy that is being pursued at present has allowed us to go a long way towards eliminating the negative consequences of the financial crisis of August 1998.

We are succeeding in maintaining a relatively low inflation rate. The budget deficit has been cut. Last year, we received 25 per cent more revenue than planned. We have decreased our foreign borrowings and are fully servicing our internal and foreign debts. There has been a positive shift in the dynamics of industrial development. Unemployment is on the decline, and the marketability of the goods produced is growing.

At the same time, we need solid international support for our reforms. Unfortunately, we have often received "support" in the negative sense. Suffice it to say that at present there are 99 anti-dumping and other restrictive procedures enforced in the world, which target Russian exporters (rolled metal, scrap iron, textiles, nitrogen fertilizers, etc.). As a result, Russia annually receives US$1.5-2 billion less than its due. Russia has not been recognized as a market-economy country yet. Russia's accession to the World Trade Organization has been hedged around by discriminatory restrictions. The issue of granting Russia loans has been increasingly linked to political questions.

Consequently, Russia has had to focus on the domestic, rather than the international market, even though it possesses huge natural resources, advanced scientific and technological potentials, qualified human resources that could be effectively utilized by the world community.

It is no accident that the *alleviation of Russia's foreign economic dependence* is a fundamental factor in the formation of Russia's economic policy. Moreover, our goal is neither to create a closed-type economy and isolate ourselves from the outer world, nor to rely on a "kind uncle" to solve our problems for us.

Another important condition is *improvement of our financial-economic policy.* To this end, we have developed what appears to us efficient measures to strengthen state support for investment and innovation, concentrating resources within the priority areas of scientific, technological and industrial advancement, as well as creating a stable state banking system. At present, we are developing a state program for promoting Russia's securities market in order to restore investor confidence.

We will pay greater attention to *fostering links between research and production, state regulation in the market economy, ensuring environmental safety, and the population's health.*

In order to achieve industrial and technological parity with the leading world powers in the areas of strategic significance for Russia, we are elaborating steps to restructure and convert the *defense-industrial complex.* The complex in question still contains research and technological potential that is immense and largely unique, as well as capacities to create competitive science-intensive military-purpose, dual-purpose and civilian-purpose goods. We must use this potential to the full. I am not going to conceal the fact that the development of this field, so vitally important for Russia, is also necessary for our armed forces. For that reason, defense funding is going to be 1.5 times more this year than last year.

Taking into account the current situation, the Conception devotes special attention to such important economic tasks as the *international integration of the Russian economy and the formation of a single economic space together with the CIS member states, legal support for the economic reforms, strengthening of state regulation in the economy, creation of a stable banking system, preservation and development of the research and technological potential, etc.*

The woeful state of the economy, deficient coordination of state control at all levels, the weak normative and legal basis, mistakes committed in many areas in the past, not least with regard to changes in the forms of property—all these have proved to be key causes of the deterioration in relations between the center and the regions, and in the social sphere, as well as of the escalation of terrorism and organized crime, and the dissolution of the country's single legal space.

The Conception offers an assessment of the degree of threat to Russia's federal order and socio-economic system. It points to a remaining danger of emerging conflicts.

Great attention is devoted to combating crime. For the first time ever, 1999 saw over three million criminal acts recorded in the country, as well as the growth of organized crime, and serious damage caused to economic relations by the spread of criminality. We believe that in this transitional period the growth of crime is engendered not by the essence of the reforms, but by their shortcomings, their dark side. And *we are going to fight these phenomena, not the reforms.*

That is why our intention is to embark on a *decisive attack against the criminal world*, restore the system of social prevention of criminal acts, and undertake other measures, including of an economic nature.

This is why the new version of the Conception makes it a priority, in fighting crime and corruption, to restrict the economic and socio-political basis of these socially dangerous phenomena, and to establish the preventive nature of the corresponding countermeasures.

The new version of the Conception spells out the need to improve the *system for prevention of emergencies and elimination of their consequences*. It provides for the integration of the system with similar systems in the CIS member states, and even in other countries. The need for such an approach is conditioned by the growing danger of emergencies, the potentially greater scale of natural and industrial, as well as environmental catastrophes, and the considerable experience of international cooperation.

The tasks related to *safeguarding information security* have also been specified. We believe that there is an increasing competition for influence over the development of the world information sphere, and for the leading position in the information markets in both individual countries and the entire world. There have been attempts by some states to turn the information sphere into a conflict site, and this in itself revives a phantom of the Cold War.

These are the reasons why Russia proposed adopting UN General Assembly Resolution 53/70 "Developments in the Field of Information and Telecommunications in the Context of International Security" of December 1998. We believe that it is possible and sensible to successfully reduce threats in this sphere by having the entire world community exert itself, and by creating an international system of information security.

Now I will explain our position with regard to international relations.

Over the past few years, and especially in 1999, there have been attempts to *exclude Russia from the zone of its traditional interests*.

Above all, I mean the *Yugoslavian events*, when the North Atlantic alliance undertook to simultaneously perform the roles of prosecutor, judge, and executor of punishment in respect of the peoples of Yugoslavia, having ignored the UN and all its agencies, as well as the OSCE, not to mention Russia. As a result, an acute crisis emerged in relations between Russia, on the one hand, and the USA and NATO, on the other.

It appears that the main goal pursued by NATO is *to safeguard its own security and indisputable leadership, based on its military dominance*. This is confirmed by the strategic doctrine adopted by the alliance, which envisages a considerable expansion of the so-called area of responsibility, and declares its right to adopt decisions in circumvention of the existing UN structures. This was tested first in Iraq, and then, to the full, in the Balkans.

Therefore, the tendency of international relations to develop in the direction of a multipolar world may be derailed, and a unipolar world order may emerge, based on unrestricted military force without a counterbalance. In this case, a group of states will enjoy special rights to safeguard their own national interests and their own security, while ignoring the interests of other nations in this sphere. We are fully aware of their intentions in this field, and yet we adhere to the position that the dependence of a majority of nations on the will of one state or group of states—particularly when based on military force—is dangerous and counterproductive. Was not the past experience of the Cold War sufficient? In this connection we realize that the creation of a unipolar world, although possible in principle, can only be based on temporary and extremely unstable and dangerous foundations. We do not believe that, on the threshold of the 21st century, there should be a return to the year 1815.

In addition, NATO's jubilee celebrations highlighted the alliance's intentions of *expanding further to the East,* this time to the territories of the former USSR republics. This will hardly put Russia's mind at rest as to its own security. However many placatory words may be uttered on this matter, we will remain pragmatic and base our assessments on actual deeds rather than declared intentions.

Here is another very important issue. The US administration is reconsidering its views on *safeguarding global strategic stability.* While declaratively *recognizing the 1972 ABM Treaty* as the cornerstone of this stability, the USA has taken the decision to create a strategic ballistic missile defense of their national territory, which is by definition ruled out under the framework of the above-mentioned Treaty. Moreover, the American side suggests that we should take part in amending the ABM Treaty to "rule out violations of its essence and mission." In other words, what is proposed is a transformation of the ABM Treaty from a treaty banning the creation of national missile defense systems into a treaty envisaging the creation of such systems, i.e. the complete opposite.

We are prepared to tackle the most difficult problems round the negotiating table on an equal and honest basis. However, we are not going to get involved in destroying the global strategic stability, which will be inevitable if the ABM Treaty collapses. This is the reason for our firm stance on this, rather than any belief we have that the USA's creation of a National Missile Defense is engendered by the dramatic decline in Russia's nuclear potential, as some mass media allege. As far as the matter in question is concerned, the overwhelming majority of the world's nations support Russia, Belorussia and China, while only three states offer their backing to the US administration. Is this not conclusive?

What is this destruction of global strategic security, which could, we believe, follow from the creation of National Missile Defense (NMD) by the Americans?

The creation of NMD is linked to the *military reclamation of outer space, i.e. to its militarization.* It is also connected with a considerable breakthrough in the sphere of advanced, and exceptionally expensive, military technologies, which is bound to lead to *a new arms race of unprecedented scale.* Indeed, those targeted by the national and regional missile defense system will seek and finally find ways to overcome it. Eventually, the sword will always prevail against the shield. However, there is more to it than that. The creation of NMD by our partners will trigger *the complete derailment of the processes of limitation and reduc-*

tion of armed forces and armaments. This could lead to abandonment of the treaties on banning nuclear tests, on nonproliferation of nuclear weapons, regimes of international control over arms proliferation, and maybe, who knows, renunciation of the UN Conventions on chemical, biological, and toxicological weapons. Is not this a catastrophe?

What has been happening recently in the sphere of strategic stability and in the relations between Russia and the West is a *signal for Russia,* and not only for Russia. Does not what I have described constitute a dramatic turn in global politics? Therefore, our national policy must take these things into account. Adequate conclusions have been drawn in the new version of the Conception.

The question of when the State Duma will ratify the START-2 Treaty— signed by the US and Russian presidents as far back as January 3, 1993— remains a rather troublesome issue in the context of Russian–US relations, and one that is being exploited by the supporters of NMD. Inside Russia attitudes towards ratification are ambivalent. More than one generation of short-lived politicians have tried to build their careers by criticizing the basic provisions of the Treaty. Quite honestly, I would like to assure you that the earliest possible ratification of the START-2 Treaty is undoubtedly in the interests of Russia's national security, and the government will do its utmost to resolve this problem as soon as is feasible. The first hearings on ratification of the START-2 Treaty will begin in the State Duma in just a week's time, i.e. on March 21, 2000.

I will now briefly discuss the problem of TERRORISM.

As our own experience has shown, underestimating the threat posed by terrorism has resulted in the threat becoming an act of international terrorism against Russia and on Russia's territory, and in a particularly large-scale and vicious form.

We have to admit with regret that the global community has failed to adequately recognize the scale and international nature of the threat posed today by global terrorism, which has taken hold of a part of Russian territory and has been absorbing international criminals from all over the world. Think about it: where would the hundreds of terrorists who have tasted blood head if they were simply forced from Russian territory? Our society has not forgotten the acts of terror carried out by the criminals in Dagestan, Moscow, Volgodonsk, and nor will it forget the thousands of Russian and foreign citizens captured and enslaved by the bandits. The government's actions in Chechnya are supported by the overwhelming majority of Russian citizens, who truly feel the pain caused by the bandits.

The anti-terrorist operation in Chechnya will be brought to its logical conclusion. Three interconnected tasks are being resolved in the course of the operation. First, Russia's territorial integrity is being protected. Second, the state is exercising its responsibility for safeguarding the rights and freedoms of its citizens, and restoring the civilized norms of life. Third, we are fighting one of the mightiest enclaves of international terrorism, and therefore defending the interests of the peoples of Europe and of the entire world.

However, the operation in question requires more than mere military measures. It involves political, economic, informational and other measures. It requires every possible assistance and support on the part of the world community.

Nevertheless, the most commonly expressed opinion is that Russia is engaged in inappropriate use of military force in Chechnya. I would like to ask: what would be appropriate use of force with respect to bandit formations consisting of tens of thousands of mercenaries, well trained and armed to the teeth, who have built defensive lines all over the republic?

So far, Russia's immediate goal is the *physical eradication of the means of existence of the terrorists, as well as of the terrorists themselves, on Russian territory* by using all available means, as well as the creation of normal human conditions for living in the multinational Chechnya, and safeguarding the right of Russian citizens to a secure existence. It was the problems of restoring the state institutions and socio-economic life in the Chechen republic that the latest sitting of the Security Council of the Russian Federation addressed.

Neither these, nor any further actions are conceivable without *consolidation of the efforts of the world community in fighting terrorism*. We have already taken some important steps. As you know, in January 2000, a decision was taken at a meeting of the heads of state of the CIS to set up an International Anti-Terrorist Center.

This issue is also reflected in the new version of the Conception.

I will address the military aspects of the Conception, which have raised such a lively discussion in the mass media, especially in the West.

The Conception points out that the level and scale of the threats in the military sphere are growing. There are both external and internal reasons of an economic nature behind this development.

On the whole, Russia's military policy is based on unconditional adherence to the norms of international law, and to the UN and OSCE principles, and is of an exclusively defensive nature. It organically combines a commitment to peace and a firm resolve to protect the national interests and security of Russia and its allies. *Priority is given, however, to preventing wars and military conflicts by using political, diplomatic, economic, legal, and other non-military methods, as well as by using the world community collectively to forestall threats to peace, violations of peace, and acts of aggression.*

Given the great significance that is attached to non-military means in safeguarding the state's peaceful development, Russia's current most important task—a task for the entire state, rather than just the military, as the previous version of the Conception had it—is *to contain aggression on any scale, including nuclear.*

In order to carry out this mission, Russia must possess contemporary means of armed struggle, including nuclear weapons, which we continue to regard as a political means for containing aggression. The Conception stipulates what Russia's conventional and nuclear forces should be like.

All that is planned and implemented in the military sphere is subordinated to the task of containment. This is the key to understanding the issue.

Russia has never said—and is not saying now—that it could be the first to use nuclear weapons. At the same time, *Russia will not undertake never to be the first to use nuclear weapons.* This is the essence of the most profound dialectics of containment.

To elaborate on the aforementioned dialectics, Russia *does not link the possibility of using nuclear weapons with some theoretical classification of armed conflicts* by scale, intensity, etc. Rather Russia associates this possibility with the emergence of specific circumstances, namely:

- when there has been a failure to achieve the goals of containment, having used the entire available set of non-military means;
- when aggression has been launched against Russia;
- when the use of non-nuclear weapons and means, in combination with non-military means, has proved ineffective and incapable of repelling the aggression.

Therefore, a close consideration of the conditions and the order in which the range of means and methods of preventing and repelling aggression is used demonstrates that *the use of nuclear weapons by Russia would be mandated by the emergence of a situation critical for the state.*

Incidentally, I would point out that suggestions made by certain mass media that Russia has lowered its nuclear threshold do not reflect the essence of the matter clearly described in the Conception. It is important to understand that *Russia attaches the utmost priority to the achievement of the containment goals,* and will employ all its powers to adequately rebuff an aggressor in a resolute and firm way. Russia, on the other hand, will never become an aggressor, something that is guaranteed by its legislation, as well as by its current National Security Conception.

It should also be pointed out that, unlike western politicians, NATO's military experts take a more pragmatic view of the new version of the National Security Conception; they are less inclined to dramatize, or to regard as somehow extreme, the stated aim of maintaining nuclear forces capable of "inflicting guaranteed severe damage on any aggressor state." They realize that, at its core, nuclear containment means employing nuclear weapons exclusively "as a last resort." According to the assessments of the military, given the well-documented decline in its conventional armed forces, it is "logically justified" for Russia to maintain a stake in nuclear weapons, and to seek to use them as a guarantee of the country's security and to maintain its status as a great power. I had the chance to see for myself that this approach to the Conception is shared by most American politicians during a visit I made to the USA at the invitation of the US President's National Security Adviser Samuel Berger, and also during a meeting I had with US Vice Presidential aide Leon Fuerth. The rumpus in the USA surrounding the provisions of the Conception has clearly been dictated by the needs of the upcoming election.

Originally published as Ivanov, S.B., *O novoy redaktsii Koncepcii natsionalnoy bezopasnosti Rossiyskoy Federatsii* [On the new version of the National Security Conception of the Russian Federation], Moscow MGIMO–RAMI, 2000, pp. 3–14.

PART 3
Analysis

International Relations after the Kosovo crisis

Anatoly Torkunov

The Kosovo crisis with its—still not fully predictable and foreseeable—consequences has obviously had a considerable effect on the entire system of international relations, the general situation in the world, and the relations between many powers of key importance within today's world order. Today, the new Kosovo factor and the problems and trends it has bred are of particular significance, because the system of international relations itself is still in the process of formation and transition from the previous bipolar system that was successfully overcome at the turn of the nineties, to a different world architecture that is not yet fully shaped.

This inevitably gives rise to a series of questions, the answers to which are of crucial importance for the theory and practice of international relations. Above all, which of the Kosovo crisis elements will be of short-lived political importance, and which of them will cause irrevocable shifts in foreign policy or long-term political consequences? What will be its aftermath in the sphere of international law, and which of the problems pertaining to international law require a constructive answer from the world community? Should the actions of the United States and NATO be taken to imply that Kosovo was the first step toward a new division of the world? Would they be able to carry it through? What political alternatives confront Russia and the other great powers (China primarily) that have their own perception of the world and its problems, which they are prepared to defend? What are the general dynamics and contours of the world order that is in the process of formation?

The Kosovo Crisis and Its International Consequences

We believe that one can clearly diagnose what the United States and NATO did in Yugoslavia as *an attempt to revive "the politics of force" and to undermine the entire system of international law* embodied, inter alia, in the Pax Europeana idea. The Pax NATO model that relies on force rather than law stands opposed to it. The efforts of the world community during the UN-sponsored International Law Decade (1989–1999), and the very foundations of 2000 as the UN International Year of the Culture of the World, have received a body blow, too.

What we are dealing with is a vivid manifestation of a regional defense organization's ambitions to usurp the UN's powers and arbitrarily assume the role of a sort of pivot of "global responsibility" in the European Atlantic area and the entire world. These ambitions were confirmed by NATO's departure, in its new doctrine, from its defensive strategy and its simultaneous assumption of the right to conduct military operations outside the alliance's area of competence. This undermines the very foundations of the UN Charter, which rests on respect for sovereignty and on the non-use of force or threat of force. The OSCE has also suffered severe political damage: its future role in the European security system has, to all intents and purposes, been called into question.

The publicly declared goal of transforming NATO from a military into a fundamentally political organization has been obviously abandoned. The Russia–NATO Founding Act has been discredited or, at the very least, its ineffectiveness has been clearly revealed. And finally, moral damage has been done to the idea of peacekeeping.

Judging from the outward signs, the USA and NATO have managed to score definite military and political points. In particular, they have demonstrated to the world a model of a new type of high-tech war that places virtually no significant economic strain on those who launch it. Besides, notwithstanding some doubts that have been expressed, the United States and NATO have managed to rally a considerable part of the western community around them, and to prevent any breaches of discipline among their allies.

However, a true assessment of the international impact of the Kosovo crisis is *not that unambiguous*.

First of all, one might question the key point: did the US and NATO actions really demonstrate a triumph of military force as an effective foreign policy instrument to be applied in the world today? The answer to this question is far from simple, if one objectively compares the stated goals and the sum total of worldwide repercussions brought about by NATO's act of aggression.

Indeed, the Kosovo events made it more likely that there will be *another spiral of proliferation of nuclear weapons* or other weapons of mass destruction, as a guarantee against foreign armed intervention, no matter whose or under what pretext. This puts the international system of control over nonproliferation to a serious test, which it might fail if the worst comes to the worst.

Furthermore, another negative consequence for international security and stability (to which, paradoxically, NATO itself may fall victim along with the others!) lies in the *reduced predictability and manageability of international relations*. This may first of all be brought about by the likely formation of anti-

NATO (or even anti-West) coalitions of states that otherwise have little in common. By acting in the way it did, NATO appears to be creating *new regional (or even global) opponents*. The *increased threat of terrorism*, above all international terrorism, supported from abroad but employed to deal with domestic problems, is another negative result. (This is illustrated by the recent events in Dagestan, Buynaksk, Moscow, and Volgodonsk.)

It seems that the worst fears of Russian opponents of NATO's enlargement to the East have been confirmed. Incidentally this creates a new domestic political situation in Russia, provoking not only anti-NATO, but also anti-American and anti-Western political sentiments in Moscow, especially among those seeking to exploit the Kosovo developments to resolve their own domestic issues. What NATO did in Kosovo has developed into a DOMESTIC POLITICAL FACTOR in Russia that is used as an argument by the most aggressive and nationalist forces of the Russian political spectrum. In fact, then, this has dealt a blow not only to the first, still vulnerable shoots of democracy in Russia, but has also, *de facto*, created new threats to international security. Indeed, in the worst case scenario (which should never be excluded from political argumentation) an economically and politically weak and unstable Russia might become an unprecedented source of destabilization in Europe, Eurasia, and across the world.

In this new international and domestic situation, Russia is faced with the need to considerably revise its foreign political and general strategic priorities. The Russian military doctrine is likely to undergo certain changes, especially in the sections dealing with nuclear deterrence (including with respect to non-nuclear threats). In any case, for a whole raft of foreign and domestic reasons, Russia will not be able, or willing, to pursue its old foreign policy line; and particularly not in relation to NATO.

To rehash an adage from a Greek philosopher, you cannot step twice into the same foreign political river. This, together with the ancient Chinese character denoting crisis, implies that the crisis can be overcome. Today Russia is presented with *fresh opportunities to develop relations* with powers of key regional and global consequence, above all with *China and India*. This does not imply any attempt to create an anti-NATO "axis" or "triangle." There are no objective or subjective prerequisites for establishing such constructs. Even in the post-Kosovo era, Russia will not regard NATO through dark-colored lenses. This is not a search for allies against NATO (that could lead to blocs of traditionally anti-Western forces, which are themselves anti-democratic, aggressive and, not infrequently, terrorist regimes that have isolated themselves from the global community). Instead, Russia needs to form a balanced foreign policy based on properly identified and upheld national interests, rather than on some romantic expectations. Incidentally, in this respect Russia might draw on the *foreign policy experience China has accumulated in recent years*.

Contemporary International Law and "Humanitarian Crises"

The international legal aspects of the "humanitarian problems" (so-called *"humanitarian crises"*) constitute, in a sense, an independent problem area, though one now closely connected with the Kosovo crisis. In his time, Max Weber described the main attribute of a national sovereign state as its legitimate right to exercise violence on its own territory. Indeed, national politics pursued this line (which would also be legally registered) ever since the Treaty of Westphalia. Today, however, there are many new circumstances that should be taken into account.

As the new century approaches, there is less cohesion about the old consensus, which used to exist within the world community and was registered in international law, on how and when interference in the domestic affairs of a sovereign state is possible. This has been brought about by the ongoing processes of *globalization and democratization*. These processes are breeding justified doubts as to the assumption that it is foreign sources, i.e. interstate violence, that constitute the main, if not the only, threat to international security and stability. Today, *organized large-scale violence carried out within a state* (such as was the case in Haiti, Somalia, Rwanda, etc.) has emerged as a real international security issue, rather than a mere domestic political problem. Neither the world community nor international law can come up with a fully satisfactory response to it.

This problem should be considered at different levels: from a clear international legal assessment of NATO's actions in Yugoslavia, to a conceptual re-evaluation of the significance of the humanitarian factor in international affairs today.

There is no doubt that the Kosovo crisis, which, as fate would have it, coincided with the centenary of the First Hague Peace Conference and the last year of the UN International Law Decade, requires an adequate legal assessment, which, in its turn, needs a discussion of how it may affect international law or, at least, its development trends.

Today, international law includes a *principle banning the use of force or threat of force*, which is reflected in the UN Charter. This is a universal principle that is incumbent equally on UN members and all other states. It means that armed force may be used against a state only is that state's actions threaten international peace or security. The UN Charter directly stipulates that a state may utilize armed force as a means of self-defense, in case of foreign aggression or by way of implementing a decision of the UN Security Council. International practice has shown that the UN Security Council can be an efficient body of high prestige whose decisions uphold international peace and security.

At the same time, conflicts that represent a potential threat to peace and security in the world have, of late, often developed not only between states but also within states (the so-called *domestic conflicts*). It is clear that not all such conflicts endanger international peace and security. The threat arises in the case of those conflicts in which human rights and freedoms are violated on a massive scale, i.e. in the cases of so-called *domicide* (as distinct from genocide), ethnic violence, etc. They create a new—and as yet unresolved—international legal problem: *may force be used in cases other than self-defense?* In particular, can force be used in "humanitarian crises"?

The UN Charter *de jure* does not envisage armed intervention for humanitarian reasons, that is, when human rights and freedoms are violated. From the strict legal standpoint, any Security Council decision to send armed forces into any state on humanitarian grounds can be regarded under Article 2 (7) of the UN Charter as an intervention in that state's domestic affairs. This can be confirmed by precedent of the UN International Court of Justice, which in 1986 stated with regard to the Nicaragua case that "THE USE OF FORCE CANNOT BE ACCEPTED AS THE RIGHT METHOD...TO ENSURE... RESPECT" of human rights.

And yet, notwithstanding the lack of theoretical substantiation, the legal complexity, and the political sensitivity of all these issues, we are witnessing a certain *lag of international law behind actual developments in the political and moral spheres*. Today, there is an urgent need for a new, and far more detailed and unambiguous, *definition of the legal aspects of the use of force in international affairs in the conditions of globalization and democratization*. There is a need for additional criteria for the use of force in compliance with the UN Charter, including in extraordinary humanitarian situations. A *clear international legal interpretation of humanitarian crises* must receive special attention.

In addition, *precedent* for interference by the world community in the domestic affairs of states for humanitarian reasons should be taken into account. In practice, the Security Council considers humanitarian aspects and arguments when contemplating the use of force against any state. For example, by its Resolution 688 (1990) the UN Security Council authorized a multinational force to carry out an armed intervention in Iraq to protect the Kurds. Resolutions 794 (1992) and 929 (1994) empowered a group of states to establish a multinational force for use in Somalia and Rwanda in order to secure the delivery of humanitarian aid and carry out other humanitarian operations.

One might recall that the 1991 Moscow meeting of the CSCE Human Dimension Conference agreed that "issues relating to human rights, fundamental freedoms, democracy and the rule of law are of international concern, as respect for these rights and freedoms constitutes one of the foundations of the international order." The states that participated in the meeting emphasized that they "categorically and irrevocably declare that the commitments undertaken in the field of the human dimension of the CSCE are matters of direct and legitimate concern to all participating States and do not belong exclusively to the internal affairs of the State concerned."

The globalization and democratization taking place in the world today dictate that *humanitarian problems and human rights issues extend beyond the exclusive competence of individual states.* The world community has a justified right to respond to human rights violations by any state. At the same time, it is fundamentally important that, in each case, the world community's responses and actions (including the use of force) should be *appropriate and proportionate, and authorized by the UN Security Council.*

All of the above would indicate that the time has come to place on the agenda the elaboration and adoption of an international treaty that would be based on current international law and take account of new realities. Such a treaty would determine in what cases, and to what ends, it might be possible (or even necessary) to intervene on humanitarian grounds. In particular, it would stipulate the violation of which human rights and the infringement of which freedoms may be regarded as justification for such intervention. We probably need an international body (possibly under the UN Security Council) to pursue the goals of such a treaty.

"Asymmetric Multipolarity" and Russia

I would like to touch on another issue that is, in a way, connected with the Kosovo crisis, but is also of global consequence. What can be said about the general dynamics and contours of the world system that is taking shape, and contemporary international affairs in the context of the "Kosovo factor" and its broader perspective?

President Clinton has said recently: "WE [THE USA AND NATO—A. TORKUNOV] ARE TRYING TO SET UP A MODEL FOR THE ENTIRE WORLD." He also formulated the task of "INVOLVING OUR RECENT ADVERSARIES, RUSSIA AND CHINA, IN THE INTERNATIONAL SYSTEM AS OPEN, FLOURISHING AND STABLE NATIONS."

A logical question may arise: how—given the Kosovo crisis—does this task fit into the real-life context and global political developments in the contemporary world?

Obviously, *Russia and China,* two strong and independent powers that consistently uphold political positions of their own, *fail to fit into the Pax NATO scheme with its unipolarity* (sometimes described as a pyramidal international system). We are aware of the fundamental flaws in this unipolar ("pyramidal") world order model. It is not simply that Russia, China, or any other power will never agree to play the role of weak, yet "open", third-rate NATO satellites.

Equally important is the fact that the strategists of unipolarity underestimate these countries on a number of important criteria related to their aggregate national might (the nuclear potential, territories, population, etc.). The USA does occupy a special place in the world today, and does possess special foreign political and other resources. And yet, this is not enough to carry out its policy single-handedly, independently of other powers that belong either to a limited circle of great powers (with large and comparable potentials and combined resources, which, even taken individually, may considerably exceed the resources of other countries), or even to influential regional power centers. *No world power*—not even the United States, which is regarded by some as the only remaining superpower—*has sufficient resources to perform the role of a "global policeman" in a unipolar world.*

It should be added that *the unipolar pattern runs counter to many key and long-term trends* in world development, especially those that are independent of short-term political considerations. What we are talking about here are the radical changes that have been taking place in the world over the past decade, including *democratization and globalization*; in principle, these *open up the prospect of a global transformation of the entire system of international relations* towards a world without violence, in which the centuries-old ideals of peace and humane international relations will be realized.

It is clear that globalization is not developing along a straight line, but is accompanied by the world's fragmentation, relapses of religious and ethnic fundamentalism, etc. *The world has not yet arrived at genuine multipolarity; it is just taking shape.* Today's situation is often described as a bizarre hybrid: a "uni-multipolar system" (or even "pluralistic unipolarity"). It seems, however, that *"asymmetric multipolarity"* is an apt term for today's world order. It implies a sort of transition period that reflects a specific (and therefore inevitably transient) distribution of power and resources in a common "force field" of the long-term global trends outlined above.

The transitional nature of the current period consists also in the fact that the bipolarity, unipolarity and multipolarity of today's world are nothing more than specific and largely *formal denotations of the ways in which the totality of power and national might is distributed in the world, rather than descriptions of the content of the present-day international affairs.* For example, in a multipolar world several powers that are approximately equal in strength may oppose each other. On the other hand, they may cooperate within the same pattern of the distribution of national might. In other words, the *formal structure of the emerging world order has yet to acquire adequate content.*

To a large extent, this process will be determined by *subjective factors*, including particular strategies and tactics of foreign policy, and conceptions and doctrines adopted by the key actors on the world stage, Russia in particular. This explains why the Russian foreign political community of experts and analysts attaches special importance to developing the conceptual aspects of our strategic idea of international relations: that is, to developing *a conception of the world in the twenty-first century.*

Discussion of this problem, which is today of major theoretical and practical importance, has been initiated by the Ministry of Foreign Affairs of the

Russian Federation. It is anticipated that all the leading Russian experts in foreign policy—practical experts and analysts, researchers and lecturers—will unite their efforts in resolving this problem.

Incidentally I would like to add that a *Russian International Studies Association* is being established to pool the efforts of Russian foreign policy experts. We hope that the Association will bring together prominent representatives of the research institutes and higher educational establishments of Russia's capital and regions. The Association will provide a firmer scientific substantiation of the country's foreign political activity and will promote practical applications of scholarly efforts. It will also help formulate and support the most promising trends in international research, etc.

Returning to the conception of the world in the twenty-first century that is being developed in Russia, it should be emphasized that it is based on an acknowledgement of the need to create an adequate and cooperative mechanism to regulate the current globalization processes. The effectiveness of this regulation will depend on a combination of national and international efforts, and the special role of the UN as the sole universal mechanism for safeguarding global peace and security. While recognizing that qualitatively new threats to the multipolar world order are emerging (proliferation of weapons of mass destruction, new-generation regional conflicts, a threat of another spiral in the arms race, the widening gap between rich and poor countries, the spread of international terrorism, grave demographic problems, etc.), we are proceeding on the basis of our strategic long-term goals that *reflect our interpretation of the dominant, rather than the short-lived, trends in global political development in the context of globalization.*

Taking account of all that has been said, Russia's foreign policy regards *democratization and humanization* of international relations as its strategic goals. We know that, in the political situation that has taken shape, our progress toward these goals can be neither rapid nor simple. No matter, though, what obstacles we might encounter, our progress requires:
- the rejection of any claims to unilateral domination, and an acknowledgement of the need for multipolarity, and the promotion of it;
- the establishment of effective international and national mechanisms and procedures to safeguard the rights of ethnic minorities within sovereign states;
- the active involvement of civil society's potential in dealing with international problems;
- ensuring the minimum of coercion allowed under international law;
- the establishment of clear humanitarian limits to international sanctions;
- ensuring national and international guarantees of human rights and freedoms, etc.

Finally, a genuinely multipolar world order of the twenty-first century is possible only if the larger part of the world community, and all actual and potential centers of influence, pool their efforts to support it. It is of crucial importance that Russia should develop and improve her partnership relations with all other participants in international affairs that share its interpretation of the newly emerging architecture of world policy in the twenty-first century.

Originally published in *Mezhdunarodnaya zhizn* [International affairs], 1999, no. 12, pp. 45–52.

The Syndrome of "Absorption" in International Politics

Aleksei Bogaturov

The first decade after the deplorable demise of bipolarity in 1991 is coming to a close. After a short crisis in the regulation of world order, when states were no longer able to rule the world by the old methods and were still incapable of running it in a new way, there emerged pluralistic unipolarity. The USA and the "old" G-7 members that joined in, namely the West European nations, Japan, and Canada, have set the pace. Skillfully interacting with the UN and exploiting the "NATO card," these countries carried out a sort of bloodless revolution in international relations in the period between the Dayton Agreements (December 1995) and the Kosovo operation (May 1999). A new route for decision-making and action (the G-7 and NATO) started operating alongside the former structure for global regulation (where the UN was the center). In less than ten years, this parallel informal mechanism for international regulation has established itself so firmly that it has proved more effective than the formal, UN, mechanism.

Despite lamentations on the part of Beijing and its calls for building a multipolar world, which have been echoed in Moscow, the community of peoples and nations has become even more hierarchical. The USA and their closest allies have assumed the place at the top of the pyramid, projecting their dominance all over the planet and using force in a rather off-hand manner. Having overcome their hesitations, the most developed countries have rushed for the historic chance to rapidly transform the "international system" and "international society" (to use the terms of Hedley Bull, a classic author of the British school of international relations).

I

Hedley Bull coined and introduced into international intellectual discourse the term "world society," believing that the *international system* embracing all world states has always included a sort of proto-nucleus that he termed *international society*. The difference between the former and the latter notions consisted in the fact that the members of international society would adhere not only to their current pragmatic interests in their interrelations, but also to a more or less commonly acknowledged code of conduct, which, in turn, was based on the moral values shared by these states. Bull regarded the aggregate of the Greek *poleis* as an example of an ancient international society, emphasizing that the international system of the time included also non-Greek states, namely Persia and Carthage.[1] Having analyzed different types of international societies (Christian, European, etc.), Bull finally formulated the idea of *world international society*, still distinctly separate from the totality of "the rest" constituting the international system.

In this article, I will use the term *world society* to denote what Bull termed "world international society," and the term *international community* instead of the "international system." The former substitution has been adopted to facilitate the Russian-speaking reader's perception. The latter, though, addresses the substance. Bull saw international relations as a system, a typical and innovative notion of the period from the 1960s to the 1980s. However, by the 1990s, this approach had ceased to appear the only one that fitted the methodological level achieved. This change was largely caused by the fact that the study of international relations had by then incorporated the concepts and logic of synergetics, with its approaches going beyond the study of systems. That is why I will refrain from applying the term "system" in its broad sense, all the more so since the study of international relations as a system will be incomplete, to say the least, unless they are regarded as a global conglomerate.[2]

Bull's concept, which was introduced to the reading public in 1977 but received the appreciation it deserved only as late as in the *perestroika* period, by no means represents an official "dogma" for Western politicians. However, the scholar's ideas, and—even to a greater degree—their subsequent reinterpretations remain almost fundamental in understanding the essence of today's world politics and the basic disagreements in international relations.

There is no doubt that Bull himself was preoccupied not so much with the structure of the world, contemporary to him, but foremost with the maxims that determine the states' conduct in the world arena and the ways in which these

1 Bull, H., *The Anarchical Society: A Study of Order in World Politics*, N.Y.: Columbia University Press, 1995. Ch. 1, 2: 3–50, 36, 39.

2 Among the Russian journals specializing in humanities, the *Voprosy filosofii* [Problems of philosophy] occupies the leading position in the discussion of the problems of synergetics (e.g. see a series of articles in issue no. 3, 1997). Among Russian scholars, Marat Cheshkov is the pioneer in practical application of the analytical capacities of synergetics (see Cheshkov, M. A., *Globalnyi kontekst postsovetskoy Rossii: Ocherki teorii i metodologii mirotselnosti* [Global context of post-Soviet Russia: an outline of theory and methodology of world unity], Moscow: MONF, 1999). Leonid Borodkin should also be mentioned. He, however, works mainly with historical material.

maxims operate (providing they do operate). Bull perceived interrelations of the world society and international community as secondary. He was even less interested in the prospects and methods of "educating" in those maxims the states that, for one reason or another, had not (yet?) become members of the group of industrialized democratic countries. Bull saw these latter countries as a somewhat idealized prototype of world society, its nucleus in the international community that radiates benevolent influence over the rest of the world, including by spreading the norms of international law.

In this image of the world, the countries that embodied the consciousness of the world society constituted a minority. However, they belonged to the democratic tradition and therefore represented the advanced group of international community enjoying moral supremacy, along with dominance in military technology and the economy. Naturally, the value of this tradition was self-sufficient and could not be called into question from the perspective of an intellectual belonging to the liberal school. Such an intellectual stance may be common for the Western consciousness brought up on decades of the triumphant advance of liberalism. However, such an approach may prove somewhat perplexing in Russia, where sound analytical consciousness is used to preserving some skepticism and is allergic to any maxims, unless they are confirmed by historical and country experience. Some of the logical analogies suggested by Bull's concept, unimpeachably elegant in its reasoning and absolutely anti-totalitarian, will discourage the Russian reader. The world society will typically be perceived as an "avant-garde of the international community," which, to a tragicomic extent, resembles the representation of the unforgettable communist party as the proletarian avant-garde in the works of Lenin.[3] Just as Lenin did not think it necessary to raise the entire working class to the level of its avant-garde, Bull—to his credit—did not insist on the expansion of the world society to embrace the entire international community.

Bull rightly assumed that the countries in the international community may have much in common, for example their striving to minimize the danger of war so as to avoid casualties. However, it is only members of the world society that are united by deep commitment to their common ethical and moral standards. In such a situation, Bull argued, there is no point in waging wars at all: they contravene the very disposition typical of the member states of the world society to base their relations on respect for freedom, democracy and peace— the values shared by each, and the conditions necessary for all to thrive. Hence the famous romantic conclusion: democracies (by definition) will not fight against each other (they are not able to; they are not designed to fight).

Indeed, Bull could not conceive of the "export of the world society," i.e. of its explosive spread all over the world, although in principle he did not rule out such a development. Apparently, the idea of the worldwide proletarian revolution

---

3 Lenin, V. I., *Chto delat?* [What is to be done?], Complete Works, vol. 6.

was too repulsive to the scholar, and he tried to refrain from vulgar proselytizing while developing his concept. Moreover, the very spirit of his work was essentially defensive: while postulating the selectiveness of the democratic countries, even though this was the selectiveness of minority, as a value, the author endeavored to separate the "advance guard" from the "rear guard."[4]

Bull's self-defensive pathos was in line with the spirit of the first half of the 1970s, when western society was, quite naturally, experiencing a shock caused by the US defeat in Vietnam (1973), on the one hand, and the daring "oil attack" against the West launched by the Arab countries, on the other. In that context, the idea of the world society emphasized the value of consolidation among the developed countries: democracies that do not fight against each other and are born for cooperation appeared as a prerequisite of well-being, foremost for the "world society," but also for all other nations.

Although Bull himself did not live to see *perestroika*, his ideas seem to have inspired an entire generation of authors theorizing about globalization. Since the situation had changed, their interpretations lost the defensive and mobilizing attitude of the original. Various theories of globalization acquired such a distinctive, expansive nature that they can be associated today not so much with the "ghetto of the chosen" [*getto izbrannichestv*], as with a specter of the "worldwide liberal revolution," which appears as a mirror image of the Comintern's chimera of the worldwide proletarian revolution, transformed, though, in line with the realities of the late 20th century.

After the USSR collapsed and the post-socialist states reoriented themselves towards the West, the world society that was originally conceived as a privileged club of civilized countries started to be regarded as the only possible prospect for all humankind, unless—to its own detriment—it intends to remain outside the paradise embodied in the industrial and post-industrial benefits of culture and well-being. There emerged sincere voices suggesting that the countries belonging to the international community "grow up" to achieve the level of the world society. Meanwhile, these countries were promised assistance and support, on the one hand, and on the other hand were dismayed with the inevitable prospect of globalization leading to the "inevitable" absorption of these nations by the super-powerful economic machine of the West. The international community came to be reminiscent of an outer shell surrounding the expanding nucleus of the world society, which was bound to gradually fill the entire space within.

---

4 Subconsciously one may recall Marina Tsvetayeva's poetically tragic "ghetto of the chosen" [*getto izbrannichestv*] (see: Tsvetayeva, M., *Poema kontsa: Stikhotvoreniya. Poemy. Dramaticheskiye proizvedeniya.* [Poem of the end: Verses. Poems. Dramatics.], Collected Works, vol. 1. Moscow: Khudozhestvennaya literatura, 1980, 393), and simultaneously the "humbling" early Soviet "it is better to have less, but of better quality."

As a result, the initial concept of the world society, supplemented by the globalization theories, gave birth to a new intellectual paradigm and an ethical-theoretical platform of international relations. The concept of "expanding democracy" formulated by Anthony Lake, National Security Advisor to the US President, in the spring of 1993 played the role of a political-ideological framework designed to help actualize the platform. The beginning of the negotiations on NATO enlargement in 1997 and the simultaneous expansion of the European integration structures eastwards became milestones: what the theoreticians had prefigured started to materialize. The expansion[5] of the world society over the planet became the key tendency in the international affairs of the 1990s. In Eastern Europe, in the post-Soviet space, in some Asian countries, and everywhere else where it was possible, weak and unstable post-totalitarian pluralistic market-oriented regimes started to be cultivated. Each of them would claim to be democratic.

II

Of course, the expansion of the world society into the sphere of international community was not a mere fruit of theoreticians' speculations and politicians' short-lived designs. It was founded on both material and virtual innovations summarized by the vague and inaccurate term "globalization" in the everyday theoretical political discourse.[6] The literature of the 1990s associated at least

---

5 I am using this term not in any evaluative sense, but rather as a synonym for "spread" and "enlargement."

6 The Russian academic literature started dealing with the issue of globalization at least two to four years later than corresponding Western publications. Today, there are at least three types of publications present in the Russian academic discourse: translated articles by foreign authors (in fact, adapted versions of the originals), works by authors of Russian origin who permanently reside abroad, and publications by Russian authors proper who are trying to examine globalization from the perspective of the Russian economic and political realities. Virtually no-one among Russian researchers dares to come up with negative evaluations of globalization. However, the publications clearly imply some concern over the exaggeration of globalization's positive outcomes for international relations and development of particular countries (see: Volodin, A. G., Shirokov, G. K., "Globalizatsiya: istoki, tendentsii, perspektivy" [Globalization: origins, tendencies, prospects], *Polis*, 1999, no.5; Kolontay, V., "O neoliberalnoy modeli globalizatsii" [On the neo-liberal model of globalization], *Mirovaya ekonomika i mezhdunarodnyye otnosheniya* [World economy and international relations], 1999, no. 10). However, a sober and critical attitude in the analyses of globalization and research of its contradictory outcomes is also present in Western sources available to the Russian reader (see, e.g.: Cox, R.W., "A Perspective on Globalization," in *Globalization: Critical Reflections,* ed. J.H. Mittelman, Boulder, Colo. and London: Lynne Rienner, 1997, 21–32; Mittelman, J.H., "The Dynamics of Globalization," in *ibid.* pp. 1–20).

eight main tendencies and phenomena with the notion of globalization used in various contexts:

1. objective increase in the permeability of the state boundaries (phenomena of "overcoming borders" and "economic citizenship"[7]);
2. dramatic increase in the amount and intensity of the trans-state and transnational flows of capital, information, services and human resources;
3. massive global spread of Western standards of consumption, lifestyle, perception of self and the world;
4. strengthening of the extra-, supra-, trans- and simply non-state regulators of the world economy and international relations;[8]
5. rapid export and "implantation" into other countries' political "tissue" of the model of democratic state order in its multiple varieties;
6. formation of a virtual space of electronic communication, which preconditions a dramatic growth of opportunities for an individual's socialization, i.e. for their direct initiation—whether in a passive or interactive way, and irrespective of their physical location—into the worldwide information processes;
7. emergence and promotion within the global information networks of the idea of the responsibility of each and every individual for the fate, problems and conflicts of others, as well as for the environment, and also for political and other developments in all, even unfamiliar, parts of the world;
8. emergence of the "globalization ideology" as a set of mutually linked postulates designed to justify both the benefits and the inevitability of the tendencies towards global unification under the guidance of the world's civilized center, which invariably implies the USA and G-7.

A mere review of the globalization manifestations enables one to classify them into the material (objective) and the virtual (manipulative). The former category includes everything related to the actual movement of financial flows and the mechanisms that ensure this flow, transfer of technologies, goods and services, mass migrations, the creation of global information networks, etc. The latter category embraces the substantial content of the networks in question, the spread of particular values and standards of assessment, formation and promotion of psychological and political-psychological attitudes in international public perception. Obviously, globalization is not merely what is happening in reality, but also what people are supposed to believe, and what they do believe, with regard to current developments and future prospects.

---

7 Sassen, S., *Losing Control?: Sovereignty in the Age of Globalization*. N.Y.: Columbia University Press, 1996. pp. 31–33.
8 Julius, D., "Globalization and Stakeholder Conflict: a Corporate Perspective," *International Affairs*, 1997, no. 3, 453–455.

The previous remark is important. Indeed, while the material manifestations of globalization raise no doubts, since they are constantly confirmed by reality, a number of "conclusions" formally associated with the material part of globalization appear neither unimpeachable, nor the only possible interpretations of reality. At least it is the case as far as the experience and analysis of the situation in the new post-Soviet states, particularly in Russia, is concerned. Moreover, if one proceeds from reflecting on the need to analyze international relations by going beyond the framework of the vision of reality as a system, one will arrive at the same conclusion.

In the Russian political intellectual perception, three postulates of the globalization theory appear most controversial, namely:

- crisis of the state, and its becoming obsolete;
- modernization and Westernization as a natural outcome of globalization;
- "democratic unipolarity" as the preferable way for self-organization of the international system.

III

In the Russian intellectual tradition, the idea of gradual decline of the state system is well known from the works of communists and left social democrats, who borrowed from western European sources the notion that the old state may be replaced by "self-ruled" communities of citizens. However, after Soviet power was established and the "real socialism" emerged, the idea of the fatality of the state system was put off until the indefinite future. The strengthening of the socialist state started to be regarded as a national mission of major importance, in the same way as it was during Romanov rule with respect to the empire. The situation did not change much until the late 1980s, when Mikhail Gorbachev had to start his timid attempts to reform the state system, that is, to change the relations between the communist party and the state and to modify the foundations of the Soviet federation.

The attempt to reject the presumption of the value of a firm state system had a deplorable outcome for the USSR. However, Boris Yeltsin personally gained success by playing on the anti-state wave. As a result, he was able to acquire supreme power, as the Russian Federation "separated" from the USSR. The restless years of general "sovereignization" and self-determination crises (including the Chechen war of 1994–1996) and instability of the old state institutions were, by inertia, marked by rejection of the "old" state order. This would turn into the rejection of state as such, and unified state in particular, until in September 1998 a government under the leadership of Yevgeniy Primakov was established, which made a U-turn back to the ideology of a firm state system, although changed in form. The second Chechen war gave a militant-restorative character to the state system. Once again the country started to rely on a strong state as the main, although not the only or exclusive, instrument to protect the national interests.

The developments of 1998–1999 in Russia led to the organizational formation of a tendency that had even earlier distinguished the country against the European background. In the 1980s and 1990s, European intellectuals and politicians would consistently and voluntarily, if not somewhat masochistically, tend to reject the national-state principles, while idealizing supranational, integration and pan-regional foundations. By incorporating Central Europe (above all, the GDR), Western Europe was prepared to sacrifice the separate German, French, Italian or British states for the sake of consolidation of the European Union's common being. Together (and eventually along) with the historical EU states, i.e. France, Germany, Spain, and the United Kingdom, the Union might have incorporated historically established regions of these countries (Corsica, Savoy, Bavaria, the Basque Country, Scotland) or maybe even new entities ("cross-border" European regions, such as the Ukrainian–Ruthenian–Hungarian Carpathians, the Austro–Italian Tyrol region, Polish–German Pomerania, and—who knows—Russian–Lithuanian–Polish–German Prussia-Kaliningrad).[9]

Europe, which went through the revolution of self-determination in the 19th century to turn into the contemporary world center, reached the 20th century through the world wars, engendered by nationalism, to face the same threat again at the turn of the century in the conditions of peace, well-being, and even prosperity. As a reaction to the revival of the nationalist threat "from within," the western intellect and political will started to elaborate their own recipe that would take into account regional specifics and help prevent the threat, and control the emerging conflict. There emerged an almost agitated interest among liberal intellectuals with regard to the problem of the "obsolescence" of the national state. This "induced" neurosis spread all over the world, including the USA.[10] The European project is indeed bold and grandiose. The attempts to carry it through make observers' hearts sink: what will be the lesson for Russia, if they fail or succeed?

The European recipe suggests that the problem of self-determination of particular ethnic groups will be "dissolved" in the integration of all European peoples. The worse Scottish and Northern Irish threats are felt in London, Corsican in Paris, Catalonian and Basque in Madrid, and South Tyrolean and Lombardic in Rome, the more persistently the politicians press for speeding up the integration. By strengthening the supranational foundations, the West-

9 Zonova, T. V., "Ot Yevropy gosudarstv k Yevrope regionov?" [From the Europe of states to the Europe of regions?], *Polis*, 1999, no. 5.

10 Lauterpacht, E. "Sovereignty : Myth or Reality?" *International Affairs*, 1997, no 1, 137–139.

ern European countries are creating an instrument for restraining radical self-determination. This striving is quite understandable while the Western Europeans are solving their own problems. It is threatening, though, when the methods of supranational regulation are exported beyond the boundaries of the "integrated Europe," in particular to the Balkans or to the territory of the former USSR.

The globalization theories come up with a peremptory emphasis on the world tendency towards modernization and overcoming "backwardness" according to the known patterns. Particular solution templates, which were elaborated based on the grandiose, and yet specific, Western experience, are put forward as universal. While this attractive experience continues to impress, there are no grounds for objection. However, when the standards of the "world society" are imposed by force, things should be called by their proper names. Persistent attempts to act on the basis of the "secondary importance" and irrelevance of state sovereignty in precisely those situations where objectively the main task should be to reinforce it, will lead to bloody conflicts. The situation in the Balkans represents an example of enforced projecting of the world society's standards to the "boundary" zones.

It is clear that European leaders are aware of the burgeoning self-determination problem in that part of the world: from the West European capitals it appears a natural sphere of the "Great Europe's" influence, almost in the same way as the CIS space is perceived by most of the Russian elite. However, the typologically "non-integrated" Europe differs greatly from the "integrated" Europe. Moreover, this has nothing to do with the leaders' stances. Although he disavowed communism, the late Croat president Franjo Tudjman differed in neither theory nor practice from the "relatively communist" Serbian president Slobodan Milosevic. However, Croatia was arbitrarily admitted by the West as a partner, while Serbia was treated as a rogue, because it attempted to do the same thing in Kosovo, as Croatia had done in the Serbian Krajina. Both Croatia and Serbia were fighting for what they considered most important, i.e. for their state identity. They perceived the liberal treatises about the general global tendency towards the dissolution of the state system as a pretentious construct begotten by an intellect weary with satiation.

From the Western European perspective, striving for the "super-Europe" and preparing theoretical and political-ideological grounds for the coming integration is a reasonable way to act. First, Western Europeans face a real threat from the fragmentation of the Old World states and have to address this threat. Second, in the period from 1870 to 1945 Western Europe went through three exhausting wars (the Franco–Prussian war, and two world wars), which were fought precisely over the final establishment of the system of European nation-states. This part of Europe is ready now to "overcome" the traditional state system.

However, the majority of the new states in Southeast and East Europe, as well as in the former USSR, do not regard nationalism as a threat to the same degree, but are rather appreciative of it as a force that made possible their very appearance on the world map. None of these countries, including Russia, has had a chance to become "fed up" with statehood and "get tired" of it. The Western European recommendations to "overcome" statehood by way of integration and regionalization are perceived in Russia as analogues of the failed Soviet-era attempts to transform backward "medieval" societies without any experience in market relations or initial industrial production straight into "socialist" and "communist" states. Even in the new Russia, which has risen from the wreckage of the Soviet Union, there is a fear of a further escalation of the territorial disintegration. It is to this threat that the Russian elite reacted in 1999 by trying to revive (probably for the time being) the idea of strengthening the state system.

As a matter of fact, theoreticians rightfully reproach statehood. First of all, they have doubts whether there is a need for it, when every citizen can protect his or her rights by directly appealing to international human rights agencies, judicial and other bodies, including Amnesty International and the International Court. Second, in the stability of Western Europe calls to protect the omnipotent state against individuals are rather less persuasive than calls to protect the individual against the state. Third, supranational and transnational entities (international financial institutions and multinational enterprises) indeed possess resources that exceed those of many states. That is why the sovereignty of states, at least as far as the economy is concerned, turns into fiction. And finally, researchers note that a "conventional" state may not be able to regulate interethnic relations, which are easier to address within the framework of supranational communities.

There is hardly anyone who would undertake to seriously debate any of the above statements. These and other weaknesses of the state system are obvious to Russians, too. However, in Russia there is a different correlation between the need to protect citizens from the state and protecting them with the help of the state. It is possible, although not easy, for a citizen to find protection from a Russian bureaucrat in the Hague (an entire network of agents has grown up in Moscow to offer adequate assistance to citizens). And yet, how can any sanctions from abroad help protect residents of the Stavropol and Rostov regions, or even people in Moscow, from expulsion from their own homes, kidnapping, explosions, terror and racketeering?

Wherever the situation is unstable and dangerous, there is no firm ground for the idea of the extinction of statehood. Weakening of the state order in Russia may bring about disintegration of the country. Even firmly convinced radical democrats do not dare to ignore this danger today. It is no coincidence that last fall the pro-western Union of Rightist Forces—the heir to the democratic movement of the early 1990s—resolutely adopted a position in favor of the state system in the political sphere, while continuing to advocate the idea of a free market.

The experience of the CIS states, as well as the majority of Eastern European countries, is also telling. There is a tendency generally to strengthen the state system, rather than "overcome" it. In the cases in question, the state system is designed to provide, first of all, the forcible settlement of internal civil relations (Croatia, Serbia, Romania, Latvia, Estonia, Belarus, Georgia, Kazakhstan, the new states of Central Asia), to withstand hypothetical or real external threats (Albania, Macedonia, Armenia, Azerbaijan), and to resolve problems of a social and economic nature (Ukraine). Finally, when conducting their policies, all these states use the assertive statehood philosophy as an instrument for establishing their (often excessive) new identities. I should remark that, even in that part of the North American continent that is occupied by the United States, the principal globalization postulate, i.e. "overcoming" the state system by supranational principles, raises more doubt than understanding.

IV

The failure of globalization theories to logically embrace all international realities is often ascribed to the effects produced by the factor of historical asynchronism, namely the backwardness of Russia and the Central Eurasian belt connected with Russia, compared to the countries of Western Europe or North America. But this explanation is unsatisfactory. That is why I dare to question the validity of the globalization constructs, as far as their methodology is concerned.

Globalization theories are based on a single interpretation of global development: the linear progressive one. If we proceed from this interpretation, we should indeed expect "backward" countries to "catch up" in a while, to become enlightened, get rid of the unnecessary burden of archaic traditions, and modernize themselves following the pattern set by the progressive West. This will prepare these countries for their integration into the world society. If we adhered to this approach, there could hardly be any doubt that the entire world is "naturally bound" to become "the West" sooner or later, while the international community is to transform into the world society. The current unipolar structure of international relations would raise no doubts either, for it best able to transmit impulses sent by the westernizing version of globalization.

Any theory is apt to simplify matters. The globalization theory is no exception. Its cornerstone postulate, concerning the prospect of the general assimilation to the post-industrial western society, is based on the vision of rigid and radial channels linking together different entities. It is implied that these channels permeate everywhere and change everything on their way. They are assigned the role of an instrument of global unification, and of the formation of uniform layers of social, international and other realities all over the world (universal standards of consumption, conduct and lifestyle, common values, similar political practices and behavioral patterns, comparable artistic tastes, etc.).

However, the radial impulse transmission is not the only transmission possible in the social and international environment. The channels may not be rigid, pervasive, and of the radial type. They may also be soft, flexible and encircling. Therefore, the influence that is transmitted via such channels does not have to "penetrate deeply" but can instead flow over the surface, along external membrane-shells of the object, which is indeed happening. Of course, the transforming impulses may penetrate inside through the membranes, but only gradually, by doses, and as far as the membranes' permeability allows. External impulses are capable of changing the internal structure of objects, but not necessarily in a radical way, i.e. by assimilating them to the source of the original impulse.

If we accept this logic, the countries that are not members of the "ghetto of the chosen" (including Russia) may not necessarily be affected by the external world to the degree that would change their essence, determined by their geopolitical situation, cultural tradition and history. Moreover, these societies may avoid assimilation by way of pragmatically using favorable components of external impulses, i.e. admitting them into some spheres of their internal operation, and not admitting them into others. So, having adopted western business standards, Japan and Korea have not allowed external influences to destroy their traditional behavioral patterns employed in production (treating work as a sacred duty; the correlation between consumption and leisure, on the one hand, and saving and work activities, on the other, where the latter are considered more important, etc.). In addition, having found the optimal combination of the innovative and the archaic, these countries have acquired a new feel and have transformed themselves into a template to be followed by western societies themselves.

Societies relatively remote from the center of the world society, which have become objects to be modernized (civilized, and globalized), have developed a special internal structure, a *conglomerate,* that allows the new and the archaic to be successfully combined so that they do not destroy each other, but instead form separate enclaves.[11]

The enclaves are co-situated and influence each other, but do not transform

11 The enclave-conglomerate structure of societies is dealt with in a special work written by Andrey Vinogradov and myself (see: Bogaturov, A. D. and Vinogradov, A. V., "Model ravnopolozhennogo razvitiya: Varianty sberegayushchego obnovleniya" [Model of equally-situated development: variants of preserving renewal], *Polis,* 1999, no. 4.

into a joint homogeneous entity by undergoing the traditional succession of changes: destruction of initial qualities—amalgamation-alloy—synthesis and formation of a new substance. Enclaves are stable because they are invariably demanded by society over extended periods of time, each of them just as it is. That is why three centuries of modernization failed to make Russia "modern" in the western sense of the word. However, it did form an internal large enclave of the "modern," which continues to coexist with an even larger enclave of the traditional (informal social relations, lifestyles, patterns of economic and political behavior).

The conglomerate structure is typical of Russia, as well as of most other "transitional societies" in the East European and post-Soviet spaces, China, India, Japan and a number of other non-western states. This structure by itself does not doom society to backwardness or stagnation. Instead it can be perfectly adjusted and adopt innovations. Thus, each enclave will simply incorporate the innovations in its specific way by undergoing some transformation within its own structure. The total potential of innovations accumulated in the society will grow, while the enclave structure will remain intact and the correlation between the enclaves (no matter whether there are two or more of them) will remain more or less stable.

For example, the current relations between the Russian governors and members of the federal government are naturally different from those that existed between mandate clerks and the public in the times of Tsar Alexei Mikhailovich. However, the relations in both cases were regulated by informal connections and sympathies or antipathies (appealing to the common native land, blood relation, acquaintance, school comradeship in the past, the same club membership, formal or informal associations based on interests, etc.) rather than by formal laws.

In the same way, the bureaucratic methods of control of the early 18th century, employed in the time of Peter the Great, differed from the procedures used today, but the solidarity of officials in dealing with the public, as deprived of rights as before, has hardly undergone any major change. Just as three hundred years before, the actual mechanisms by which bureaucratic deadlocks can be overcome depend on whether or not the individual has access to channels of informal influence over the decision-making agency. It is beneficial for an official to emerge as a carrier of "the modern." That is why he will behave in the spirit of the time by campaigning for "his" deputy to be elected to the legislative assembly. However, it is not in his interests to ensure transparency in the way papers pass through his office. That is why, in other cases, the official will act in a "traditional" way (for example, he will extort bribes from the public).

Many relevant examples can be cited. For the sake of my analysis, it is more important to show that both society and the elite equally need the modern and the archaic. And while this motivation remains in place, the complex conglomerate structure of society will not change, as it has not changed over the last three centuries. One may lament or celebrate the fact, but one must not believe that everything will change "soon." In my opinion, one of the fundamental shortcomings of contemporary Russian political science consists in its reliance on foreign works, at the same time as it ignores the need to supplement these studies with a thorough examination of the actual Russian developments. This would allow general conclusions to be reached based on the accumulated data, and would allow clarification and further elaboration of the foreign theories.

Can one assert that contemporary international relations have the enclave-conglomerate structure? There is no reason to reject this thesis, merely because the educated mind is used to thinking otherwise. Nor is there sufficient reason to believe that the unity of the world can be regarded as the unity of a system based on a rigid interconnection of the system's components that affect the system itself so that it gradually becomes homogeneous.

The world is not going to lose its integrity on either a practical or a theoretical level if it rejects its linear-progressive *credo*. It is well known (particularly from the works on synergetics) that movement-progress can follow various trajectories: oscillatory, spiral-shaped, and even more complicated ones. For example, by using the spiral-cyclic perspective, it is easy to explain the growth of illiteracy among particular population categories in the post-industrial USA and post-totalitarian Russia.

I believe that the vision of the world as a conglomerate of enclaves that interact but are not doomed to mutual assimilation (through the virtual absorption of the non-West by the West) fits the actual reality. There are three aspects by which this approach differs from the globalization–westernization vision of the world.

First, the enclave-conglomerate vision organically goes in line with the actual world's diversity, by offering a natural structural location and functions to both its western and non-western components. The world ceases to be divided, as it is today, into the West and the "under-West," which is to become the West, but has not done so yet owing to its lack of reason, its "backwardness" and malicious (communist) obstinacy.

Ideally, the conglomerate world can be seen as consisting of several constitutive enclaves that are dissimilar and will not strive for similarity, but wield mutual influence and are mutually adaptive. Moreover, a layer of values shared by everybody (for example, peace) will be gradually taking shape on the "surface" of the conglomerate. However, each enclave's internal structure will not degenerate merely because particular economic, environmental and resource considerations engender a more developed enclave's interest (that of the world society in our case) in taking over the space of neighboring enclaves, even at the cost of the destruction of the latter.

Second, the enclave-conglomerate vision of the world has an advantage in its peaceful, reconciliatory nature that contrasts with the militant globalization theories, their unhidden orientation towards the absorption of the "backward" by the "progressive," and struggle among different civilization entities for survival. The proposed approach makes a new global antagonism avoidable. Ways open up to prevent its emergence: rejection of persistent modernization attempts, even those engendered by the benevolent motivation to share the best standards of political order, management of the economy, consumption and lifestyle.

Third, the proposed approach essentially represents a version of environmentally friendly (and, in this respect, ecologically mindful) rationalization. It contrasts with the instrumental-transforming treatment by the world society of its environment, i.e. of the international community. The suggested approach calls for treating the environment as an equal component of international relations, rather than as an impotent object of the "global social" tendencies. Perhaps the world ought to slow down and think where it may be carried by post-industrialism, with its steadily growing consumption of resources and impoverishment of the cultural and spiritual diversity of the planet.

In a way, the enclave-conglomerate approach embodies the idea of the world's integrity. It implies that there are common regularities operating in the planetary system and governing the natural and material aspects that determine the main characteristics of social human behavior. On the other hand, this approach runs counter to attempts to represent one possible way (the one attractive from the perspective of contemporary consumption) of rationalizing behavior as the highest achievement of the human intellect.

The contemporary rationality and corresponding interpretations of good and evil are inseparably linked to a consumerist attitude to the environment— whether social, national, international or some other. This vector of development, engendered by material interests and the very powerful driving forces of multinational corporations, is likely to continue to operate in the future. Taking this into account, the globalization theories perform an applicative role by substantiating the least costly methods for a non-conflict expansion of the natural basis for this model of development. However, the resource-consuming type of development is becoming obsolete. Moreover, this process may be unexpectedly accelerated by a global natural resource (chiefly environmental) crisis.

V

Western politicians may perceive such a turn as more likely than they are prepared to admit. In any case, the West has jumped at the opportunity to take advantage of the current situation that had taken shape in the sphere of international relations by the turn of the century, in order to usurp the most favorable positions in the world for at least twenty-fifty years. A review of the foreign literature will show that the West is largely satisfied with the international situation and is not fearful of the impending "Fronde" that may be formed by China, Russia, India, as well as, possibly, some smaller countries. As one of my American colleagues pointed out with captivating frankness, the USA achieved decisive supremacy over all its rivals and is currently conducting "the same strategy for attaining dominance, which they followed from 1945 to 1991."[12] As for the Western Europeans and Japan, they are quite satisfied with the "enlightened authoritarianism" of the US leader, and are merely somewhat apprehensive of the USA getting "carried away" and starting to ignore the opinions of Washington's weaker, but loyal, partners.[13] At the same time, the picture seen from outside the world society appears less soothing. The harmony is disturbed first of all by the discrepancy between the objective nature of the regulation of contemporary international relations and the corresponding methods and procedures.

The reality of the 1990s revealed a number of important regularities. First, the structural configuration of the world has changed and continues to change. After 1991, the world can tentatively be regarded as bipolar only so far as military power is concerned, and then only with a proviso regarding the asymmetric capacities of the USA and Russia. The USA emerged as a single complex leader, but the world has not become essentially unipolar. The USA and the "old" G-7 members assumed the functions of the new pole. However, the USA is, of course, the "most equal" member of the group. These states have formed a kind of organ for political regulation within the world society, and—to the extent the latter determines the affairs in the international community—within the entire world.

Second, having hardly established itself, the pluralistic unipolar structure started to experience significant pressure exerted by China and India, which emerged as global actors in the 1990s. Beijing dramatically advanced its economic and military potential, while Delhi, despite resistance from the "old" great powers, made a breakthrough in possessing nuclear weapons, which significantly changed the military-strategic balance in Central Eurasia.

Both India and China are especially concerned with the USA's implicit endeavor to create conditions for the possible future expansion of the NATO

---

12 Layne, C., "Rethinking American Grand Strategy: Hegemony and Balance of Power in the Twenty-First Century?," *World Policy Journal*, Summer 1998, 8.

13 A work by the French author J. M. Guehenno is rather telling in this respect. Offering quite an objective analysis of the contradictions present in the contemporary development, he seems to be most concerned about what he sees as Washington's increasing reluctance to share the burden of leadership with Europe (see: Guehenno, J.M., "Globalization and the International System," *Journal of Democracy*, 1996, no. 4, 30).

zone of influence deep into Eurasia, i.e. selective accession of Central Asian states and Russia to the systems of paramilitary cooperation with the alliance. In response, Beijing undertook to forestall Moscow's pro-western drift, and concluded a declarative "anti-unipolar act" with Russia, namely the Declaration on a Multipolar World (1996), which is perceived by both parties as anti-western.

The real meaning of the Russian–Chinese rapprochement and some invigoration in Russian–Indian relations does not provide sufficient grounds for concluding that a multipolar structure has come into being. However, the unipolarity of today makes decision-making less centralized than it was under the bipolarity of 1945–1991. The decentralization tendency is supported by the "dispersed anti-western Fronde" of the Arab-Islamic world, as well as by the Latin American states that emphasize the sub-regional essence of their policies. There are grounds for suggesting that—while remaining pluralistically unipolar as far as means of regulation are concerned—the world will simultaneously grow increasingly decentralized and fragmentary.

Third, the West has been conducting a stricter policy since 1996 in response to the decentralization that the "old" G-7 states perceived as a challenge to their influence. There was a certain change in the motivation for the US presence in Europe and in the logistical basis of this presence (the military contingents were reduced, and the nuclear weapons were removed). NATO enlarged its boundaries eastwards (to Hungary, Poland, and the Czech Republic). On two occasions, the alliance tested mechanisms for military decision-making in the conditions of crisis, and for direct use of the alliance's armed forces for offensive purposes outside the member states' national territories.

The actions of NATO sparked off corresponding reactions on the part of other states. In the fall of 1999, Russia launched persistent regular military operations against the Chechen insurgents that it had treated with tolerance for some time. The threshold of the use of force has declined in the world, which has led to a situation whereby armed conflicts have ceased to be regarded as extraordinary events.

Fourth, there has been a serious conceptual shift in the perception of the world order components. After the crises in Bosnia and Kosovo, the world society virtually dismissed the principle of non-interference (*laissez faire*), which was considered a fundamental one since the times of the Treaty of Westphalia (1648) that postulated unlimited freedom for sovereign states in conducting their internal policies, unless the latter directly threatened other states' security.

During the war in Kosovo, the NATO countries interfered in the internal affairs of Serbia, though it had no common borders with any of the alliance members. It became clear that the G-7 follows a new international order doctrine in its actions, the doctrine of "selective legitimacy." Following this doctrine, NATO usurped the right not only to assess the degree of legitimacy of the actions taken by sovereign governments, but also to determine the limits of state sovereignty. NATO's demonstration of its military supremacy over potential objects of the "selective legitimacy" policy allowed the alliance to depart from the established principle of regulation in international affairs. This caused escalation of the potential for conflicts and mistrust in international politics.

Despite all the contradictions, the 1990s can be regarded as the time when a new international order was established.

1. There emerged—no matter whether for good or ill—the principle of "selective legitimacy." Under pressure from the G-7, the international community is starting to adhere to this principle *de facto*. The UN and other international organizations increasingly often consider the issues related to the "legitimacy" of the policies pursued by the governments in particular states. These discussions lead to a broader and more confident practice of introducing sanctions and a variety of strong-arm and coercive interference. There are more and more precedents of the classic principle of non-interference in the internal affairs of sovereign states being violated. Undoubtedly, this is one of the key characteristics of today's international order.

2. There emerged a particular balance of capacities and potentials that determines a distinct hierarchy of countries in world politics. It is clear to everyone today which states and groupings occupy the higher levels of the pyramid, and which are crowding around its base.

3. The majority of the world's countries, irrespective of whether they accept the existing situation, take it into account when pursuing their foreign policies.

4. For all its weakness and imperfection, there exists a conciliating mechanism in the world. When the world society's attempts to rule the international community bring about acute conflicts, the actual "demiurges" of the main international decisions can—if they so choose—settle these conflicts relying on UN assistance.

5. The agencies of the real (informal) regulation in international affairs (the G-7) remain, at least to an extent, open. Formally speaking, Russia and—in the future—China as well can participate in these agencies. Although the new members of the group can hardly expect to catch up with the old ones soon, any interaction within the G-7 is better than the absence of dialogue or overt disunity. Bad control over the world is not worse than an entire absence of any control. This is a weak consolation for the following reason. As compared to the chimeras of a multipolar world with its inevitable inclination to big wars, unipolarity may be preferable. And yet unipolarity is not organic, since it does not match the objective structure of the world. This may prove one of the reasons for the short life of the new world order.

The new world order does not appear reliable. Too many countries are alienated from participating in the regulation. Besides, its proponents rely on force too much. In this sense, the concept of "selective legitimacy" does not inspire optimism, for changing the rules in the course of the game rarely leads to general satisfaction. The West's endeavors to establish the rules based on its own interests is risky in today's circumstances. It is tolerable only insofar as the members of the international community led by the world society do not have resources sufficient for resistance, or they simply believe that the inconvenient role of a junior partner is still better than any conceivable alternatives. This situation, however, does not fit into the conglomerate world structure. It is artificial, vulnerable and inevitably implies opposition between the world society and international community.

Today's situation is not favorable from Moscow's perspective. Russia has had to play a passive and limited role while the contemporary world order has been formed and regulated. Russia is taken into account in the world power balance because of the country's huge geopolitical potential and remaining military might. However, its partners also take into consideration Russia's inability to efficiently dispose of its resources or formulate goals corresponding to its real needs and capacities, in particular the government's inability to concentrate available means in the priority areas when needed.

As far as its geopolitical status is concerned, Russia represents a fragile formation, with its economy relying on expansion and resource exploitation rather than on the principle of instrumental transformation. The formula of the admission of Russia into the world society's economic and industrial sphere may raise the living standards of the country's population in a short time. Even today it enables Russian citizens to live better than citizens of Bulgaria, Georgia and Armenia, which are poor in resources. It is Russia's role as an appendage to the world's more developed part that is embarrassing. It is bad that the state is not in a position to decide whether it wants to play this role while accumulating riches in foreign banks, or whether it prefers to spend less, keep the money inside the country, and live better than during the Soviet time but more modestly than the average western country.

Squeezed into today's world order, Russia is not only deprived of the opportunity to make choices, but it cannot even conceive of the possible disadvantages and benefits of the alternatives it is facing. The phenomenon of the "inherited presidency" demonstrated that Russia's freedom of choice in contemporary conditions is rather tentative. Is the situation different in the international community?

★ ★ ★

The last decade of the 20th century turned out to be the most successful one from the perspective of the world society's expansion to the remote parts of the planet that were closed to external influence. When bipolarity collapsed, the internally welded democratic nucleus of the international community seized the epochal chance to break through to the formation of a world society on a planetary scale.

At the same time, it turns out that the initial expectations have been largely exhausted. For years, the West relied on a simplified vision of the world. According to that vision, it was the political and ideological opposition between the East and West that engendered the "wrong" development. Now the image has proved deficient. While retaining its unity, the world has emerged as a system that may develop on the basis of principles other than linear ascent. Having got rid of the fear of being dragged into a fight between two nuclear giants, countries started making out their own realities and emphasizing their domestic traditional cultural, social and other resources. Many see these resources today as a means to resist the increasing temptation to become "a part of the West."

If this tendency continues to grow, it may hinder globalization to a degree, or at least its superficial and short-lived forms, namely some standards of culture, lifestyle and conduct. And yet, without being conceptualized and institutionalized in the organizational-political sense, the tendency in question is unlikely to stop globalization altogether. However, it seems to me that it may restrict the influence of the globalization impulses. For the impulses to preserve their weight, it will be necessary to search for not simply more sophisticated, but also more appropriate forms, above all for forms that are compatible with the state's interests that were previously subject to international influence only.

How long might the development keep to this vector? That is a breathtakingly huge question that it is up to contemporary analysts of international reality to answer.

Originally published in *Pro et Contra*, 1999, no. 4, pp. 28–48.

Russia's National Security in a Multipolar World

Aleksei Arbatov

Global security and its constituents, i.e. national security of individual states, have traditionally been interpreted as a complex of military-political relations among states and alliances. In this sphere of international relations, new, non-traditional aspects have acquired greater weight in recent years and will continue to gain significance in the foreseeable future. Among these aspects are economy and finances, modern communications and information systems, state-of-the-art breakthroughs in research and technology, transnational crime, trafficking in drugs and weapons, illegal migration and environmental issues.

The explosions of September 11, which shocked the world, have demonstrated with horrendous persuasiveness that traditional concepts of national and global security have grown out-dated and require profound and comprehensive revision. The new realities call for reconsideration of the entire system of interrelations between Russia and the West in the context of a revision of the totality of issues concerning international security in general and the national security of the Russian Federation, as its inalienable component. Moscow has already proposed that traditional priorities pertinent to security and means of its safeguarding should be revised. Moreover, it has suggested that this revision should be done in cooperation with the USA and its allies. The events of September 11 have shown that the adoption of this approach is indeed long due and overdue, and that there is a need for even more radical initiatives and measures in this sphere than seemed adequate before September 11.

The tragedy offers a chance that the suggestions will be attended to in the West and will invoke constructive response. In this case, at least in a certain sense, it will be possible to state that all the deaths and destruction will not have been in vain, that the civilized world is capable of learning lessons no matter how bitter they might be, and that the casualties suffered will help avoid new, maybe even more disastrous, catastrophes in the future.

The new security strategy based on cooperation of all civilized countries, primarily Russia and the West, involves a new integrated approach to social-political instability in a number of the world's regions, to local conflicts, religious and ethnic extremism and separatism, international terrorism, the proliferation of weapons of mass destruction and their means of delivery. Furthermore, the approach in question requires the integration of conventional military coercion and special operations, action undertaken by the special services, the use of diplomatic, contractual and legal means, as well as financial, economic, political and information measures. Finally, the strategy envisages the optimal combination of the measures ensuring internal and external security, profound reform of national defense and civil defense, and also security systems. Of course, China, India and all other states that share the goals and priorities of the new strategy are welcome to join in the anti-terrorist coalition.

With the 21st century in prospect, at the same time as giving due consideration to these new phenomena, we must not forget more traditional issues related to the dynamics of the world power centers, correlation of their might and influence, and their common and conflicting interests. These centers will continue operating as the framework that supports the system of international relations, and will also serve as a foundation to principally new security aspects. It is this system-forming domain of world politics that involves quite a few aspects that are far from being clearly outlined and unambiguous.

As a counter to the US claims to global monopoly, the concept of a multipolar world has gained broad support in Russia, since this concept is more in keeping with the state's national goals. However, when considered closely this concept also has serious difficulties.

For all the variability of the domestic and foreign policies of many countries, the economic and military development of states is still subject to long-term forecasting with an admissible range of error. According to the forecasting research by the IMEMO [Institute of World Economy and International Relations] of the Russian Academy of Sciences, as of the late 1990s the shares of the world's leading powers in the world's GDP were distributed in the following way: the USA—21 per cent; the European Union—20 per cent; Japan—7.5 per cent; China—12.5 per cent; Russia—only 2.4 per cent. Calculations show that—with deepening economic integration at the regional level—by 2015 the USA along with Canada and Mexico (NAFTA) will produce 19 per cent of the world's GDP; the European Union—16 per cent; China—16.5 per cent; Japan—5.5 per cent; the ASEAN countries—7.0 per cent; and the group of East-Asian "tigers" (South Korea, Taiwan, Hong Kong)—5.0 per cent. According to this research, Russia will, at best (i.e. providing its annual economic growth amounts to between five and six per cent), increase its share in the world's GDP to three per cent. Economic integration within the CIS framework, given the same growth rate on the part of our neighbors, will bring the Commonwealth's share in the world's GDP to a maximum of 4.5 per cent.

With a maximum of three per cent of the world's GDP fifteen years from now, Russia will have problems claiming for itself the role of an independent pole in the multipolar world. Moreover, this refers both directly to its political influence based on the role it will perform in the global trade and finance sphere, and to its political weight determined by its military power, which, in the long run, will be critically shaped by the country's economic potential.

1. Nuclear Deterrence after the Cold War

In terms of military expenditure, Russia falls not only behind the largest NATO powers, but also behind China, India, and Japan. Provided the optimistic scenario of rapid economic growth (five to six per cent annually) works out, and 3.5 per cent of Russia's GDP is allocated for defense (today's figure is 2.8 per cent), Moscow will be capable of retaining its status as one of the two nuclear superpowers over the next 10 to 15 years. This means maintaining Russia's strategic nuclear forces (SNF) at the START-2 level (i.e. 3,000 warheads) while keeping to today's level of limitations pursuant to the ABM Treaty of 1972. However, in order for this scheme to work, Russia would have to allocate between 40 per cent and 50 per cent of its total military budget to maintaining its SNF (today's figure is 15 per cent), which would minimize the level of its conventional armed forces (CAF). At the same time, as was clearly demonstrated by the NATO aggression against Yugoslavia in 1999 and the new Chechen campaign of 1999–2000, as well as the new war in Afghanistan, we can expect a comparative growth in the role of the CAF in safeguarding Russia's national security, which is reflected in the present version of Russia's military doctrine.

Most likely, the share of expenditure for the maintenance and modernization of the SNF will not exceed 20 per cent of Russia's military budget, which will suffice to maintain the SNF at a level of 1,500 warheads in 10 to 15 years from now, provided the military budget amounts to 3.5 per cent of GDP. Under START-2, this will mean an almost three-fold US superiority, and under the agreed framework of START-3 of 1997—an almost two-fold supremacy on the part of the Americans. The only way to preserve the balance by modifying START-3 (envisaging 1,500 warheads for each side) is by agreeing to the US suggestion that the ABM Treaty be revised. However, in this case, with the offensive SNF potential of the sides equal, the USA will acquire some superiority owing to the deployment of the National Missile Defense System.

In this context, a reasonable and fundamental question arises: will nuclear deterrence be preserved as the essence of strategic relations between Russia and the USA after the Cold War, and particularly with closer cooperation of the great powers in fighting terrorism? If so, how important will this deterrence be for bilateral and multilateral relations after the Cold War?

The sudden cessation of the Cold War in the early 1990s brought about great optimism concerning the opportunity to overcome the nuclear confrontation and build international security based on fundamentally different relations, instruments, and institutions. Many hoped that the end of the bipolar confrontation would entail a radical reduction in nuclear weapons (there were propositions that the remaining nuclear stockpiles should be transferred to UN control), and that the "nuclear factor" would be ultimately removed from the agenda of world politics, and national and international security.

However, things turned out differently. A little over one decade later, the public perception of the problem was seized by deep disappointment and growing concern, while the "nuclear factor" came to the fore of world politics again, although in a significantly changed form. The development can be explained by both objective and subjective reasons.

In the period of the encouraging upswing in relations, when Russia and the USA were talking about partnership, integration, and even possible alliance in the future, in practice the 1990s saw the reduction by both sides of SNF under START-1 to 6,000 warheads (by the rules of reckoning). The sides had had almost the same number of warheads in the late 1970s, when a new round of the Cold War started after the Brezhnev–Nixon détente.

The missile-nuclear "fabric" proved far more resilient than political relations between states, and even the viability of social systems, as well as the imperial might of some of these states that crumbled apart with the end of the Cold War. Moreover, if the warheads, designed primarily to hit the targets of each other, are retained by the two powers for the foreseeable future, the situation can hardly be said to have changed.

Symptomatically, for all its official declarations that Russia and the USA are no longer enemies, Washington's operational plans and its lists of targets for nuclear strikes remained virtually unchanged during the 1990s—something that severely limits the prospect of weapons reduction.

As far as Moscow was concerned, unlike in the times of the Cold War, when Soviet propaganda called for the elimination of nuclear weapons, in a democratic Russia that is building a market economy following western standards and that expects large foreign investments, the maintenance of a considerable nuclear potential aimed primarily at the West (simply because there are not enough other targets) enjoys the unequivocal support on the part of the government, the political and strategic elite, and the entire nation. Moreover, counter to the 1982 Soviet declaration of no first use of nuclear weapons, the Military Doctrine of the Russian Federation incorporates as its cornerstone rejection of the no-first-use posture in extraordinary situations.

Another paradox of the 1990s is connected with the negotiation process on nuclear disarmament. The point is that during these years—an apparently golden time for disarmament—the actual achievements of Russia, the USA and other countries in this sphere proved rather modest, and even quite counterproductive in a sense. The maximum consensus that the leaders of the two powers were able to reach envisaged the reduction of the nuclear arsenals from 6,000 warheads under START-1 to 3,000–3,500 warheads under START-2. This slightly exceeds what the USSR and USA had in their strategic forces at the beginning of the Brezhnev–Nixon détente, almost thirty years ago (subsequently the nuclear arsenals of both sides grew to 11,000–12,000 warheads by the end of the 1980s). Neither embraces during summits, nor friendly declarations made in the 1990s helped even to conceive of ceilings lower than 2,000 warheads (under the 1997 Helsinki and New York framework agreements on START-3).

To make things worse, the START-2 Treaty signed in 1993 remained "frozen." The US Senate ratified the treaty at the end of 1996, while the Russian Parliament did so only in spring 2000. Besides, it turned out that the two sides ratified two different treaties: Russia ratified the treaty of 1993, along with the protocols to this treaty, while the USA—the same treaty without the protocols. As a result, the treaty did not come into force after all. After the Republican administration took office, the US intention to abandon the ABM Treaty and formal treaties and agreements on START rendered the prospects of START-2 and START-3 hopeless, and they were "stillborn" once the USA left the ABM Treaty in 2002.

The situation regarding agreements on other types of weapons of mass destruction (WMD) is no better. The Chemical Weapons Convention was signed in 1993 and ratified by all major countries. However, for financial reasons, Russia has experienced serious problems ensuring timely implementation of the agreement. The USA, in its turn, came up with certain qualifications that undermine the regime of control over the fulfillment of the Convention. The effectiveness of the Biological and Toxin Weapons Convention of 1972 is increasingly in doubt too, since there is no system of control over its fulfillment. In 1996, the Comprehensive Nuclear Test Ban Treaty (CTBT) was also concluded. This treaty was ratified by Russia in 2000, but was voted down in the US Senate, and thus did not come into force. Moreover, the new Republican government took the decision to prepare the Nevada test ground for possible recommencement of nuclear weapons tests.

The applause on the renewal for an indefinite term in 1995 of the Nuclear Non-Proliferation Treaty (NPT), which had by then been signed by 187 states, was interrupted by nuclear explosions in India and Pakistan in 1998. At present, the situation with the proliferation of nuclear weapons looks more worrying than ever and even continues to deteriorate. The world seems to be entering a new nuclear age, when the use of nuclear weapons may become probable, at least on the regional scale, while the information revolution makes the threat of their use—or their actual use—more effective, including on the level of psychological perception.

It is not hard to surmise that nuclear weapons and other types of weapons of mass destruction, as well as their missile and other delivery systems of ever longer range, will be created by an increasing number of new countries in the conflict-prone regions, while the likelihood of the combat use of these arms will be growing, along with their unsanctioned utilization and accidents with catastrophic environmental consequences. With development of corresponding technologies, the production of nuclear weapons and their long-range delivery means may become affordable and profitable for a growing number of countries. Today, many of these countries are falling behind in the process of globalization and are displaced into the category of the "poor" or the backward for good, at least psychologically. It is these states that may pose the greatest threat to the regime of nonproliferation in the future.

For the sake of objectivity, it should be pointed out that the 1990s saw some achievements apart from the reduction by half of the warheads belonging to the SNF of both the Russian Federation and the USA. Both countries have considerably reduced their arsenals of tactical nuclear means and removed them from most foreign bases (Russia—from everywhere). There has been a noticeable cut in expenditure on the modernization of nuclear weapons. The list of the programs of scientific research and development projects has been radically narrowed. Purchases of new nuclear weapons systems have been curtailed. The UK, France, and China have shown a good deal of moderation in building up their nuclear forces. Ukraine, Kazakhstan, and Belarus have agreed to the withdrawal of all nuclear arms from their territories and have rejected the nuclear status. South Africa has liquidated its secretly produced nuclear potential. Brazil and Argentina have unambiguously assumed the nuclear nonproliferation posture, and are determined to adhere to it for the time being.

A genuine breakthrough has occurred in the sphere of the cooperative threat-reduction program, which stipulated that the USA and a number of other countries should provide Russia with financial and logistical assistance to ensure the safety and elimination of those nuclear weapons that are not deployed, including their transportation, as well as to decommission nuclear submarines, and dismantle missiles and chemical weapons. However, despite this valuable assistance that has facilitated Russia's burden, Russia is still facing financial and logistical problems on a large scale.

Strategic problems in the relations between the great powers, their relations with third nuclear states and the threshold nuclear states, as well as relations among the latter, are closely linked to the issues of nuclear deterrence. Indeed, the Cold War is in the past, although a relapse cannot be ruled out (let us recall simply the outburst of hostility between Russia and the USA during the

NATO air strikes against Yugoslavia in 1999 and the US-led war against Iraq in 2003). As for deterrence, just like nuclear weapons, it is not going to retire into the past along with the global rivalry between the USSR and USA.

Practically speaking, the concept is not that bad. First of all, it implies that nuclear weapons are not regarded any longer as a powerful or effective means of waging war that enables one to achieve a reliable victory in an armed conflict. (This precise position prevailed in the US military doctrine until the end of the 1950s and lasted somewhat longer in the USSR's military doctrine. Even now, a similar approach is still preserved with regard to the operational and tactical nuclear means of both sides.) According to the philosophy of deterrence, the immense destructive power of these weapons is regarded as a factor that renders a war mutually unacceptable. The main function of nuclear weapons is to forestall the use of nuclear weapons by the other side, by virtue of having the ability to deliver unacceptable damage to any possible aggressor.

The possession of such destructive weapons by a state is, in itself, the greatest inherent threat to another state's national security. The only thing that can reliably guarantee its security is that state's own nuclear deterrence potential, even if the countries involved do not regard each other as enemies at a given point in time. Indeed, political interrelations may change rather rapidly, while a significant change in the strategic deterrence balance requires a prolonged period—decades—due to the high complexity, costs, and overall dimensions of missile-nuclear weapons and their infrastructure.

In this context, we can formulate the principle that nuclear powers are destined to conduct the policy of mutual deterrence, as the essence of their strategic interrelations. The deterrence may come to the fore in a crisis, or retreat into the shade when the relationships improve. However, it remains an objective reality and is always present, even if in its latent form. While nuclear weapons exist, mutual deterrence is the best variant of relations between nuclear powers (especially if it is regulated by a system of treaties). Nothing more attractive has been invented to replace the policy of deterrence after all, despite the ample rhetoric of the 1990s.

Unlike various utopian and unfeasible schemes, the actual alternative to the policy of deterrence is much worse and far more dangerous. This alternative consists in treating nuclear weapons as practically useable and effective means for achieving ends in armed conflicts. Incidentally, even today this approach is ingrained in the great powers' strategic concepts and plans, in the form of the principle of the first use of nuclear weapons under specific conditions at both tactical and strategic levels.

Deterrence strategy admits a broad range of models in the case of both equal and unequal positions of the sides. Deterrence of nuclear aggression may be based on the capacity to deliver unacceptable damage to the enemy with a retaliatory strike ("minimal nuclear deterrence"), which was the core of the policies pursued by the UK, France and China with regard to the USSR. Deterrence may also consist in the potential for the guaranteed annihilation of the other side with a retaliatory strike (former US Secretary of Defense Robert McNamara defined it in the 1960s as one affecting 30 per cent of population and 70 per cent of industry). This type of mutual potential has been possessed by the USA and USSR/Russia since the late 1960s.

There is a variant of deterrence strategy based on the nuclear supremacy of one side and its ability to reduce its own damage by means of knocking out a considerable part of the enemy's forces with the first strike (the USA had such a potential against the USSR until the mid 1960s). In this case, deterrence can be regarded not merely as a guarantee against a nuclear attack, but also as a potential to prevent large-scale non-nuclear aggression. This strategy envisages the possible first use of nuclear weapons at the level of both tactical and strategic nuclear weapons. It is termed "extended deterrence."

The USA was using this strategy against the USSR until the end of the 1950s and was to continuously try to renew it in the 1970s and early 1980s; and against China until now. The USSR was to adhere to the same strategy with regard to China in the 1970s and 1980s, as well as Israel with regard to its Arab neighbors. The Russian Federation has kept to a strategy of a type similar to "extended deterrence" since 1993 as part of its official military doctrine. However, Russia does not possess an adequate material basis for pursuing such a strategy in terms of either SNF or tactical nuclear weapons.

In addition, deterrence is also considered to be a guarantee against the other side's abandonment of a regime established under a treaty and against a renewal of an offensive or defensive nuclear arms race. It is this aspect of deterrence that has become increasingly important since the end of the Cold War and into the foreseeable future.

Any rule is confirmed by its exceptions. In particular, nuclear states may not pursue the policy of mutual deterrence if they are military and political allies (as the USA, UK, and France); if they are beyond the range of their nuclear delivery means (as the UK and China); if their nuclear means are targeted against a third side (France and Israel, Pakistan and China, Russia and India); if one of them has overwhelming nuclear supremacy and potential for a disarming strike against the other (the USA and USSR until the end of the 1950s, or the USA and China until recently). Mutual deterrence may exist but be extremely shaky if the nuclear forces of both sides have a low survivability level and/or if the control and warning systems are vulnerable and deficient (the USA and USSR in the late 1950s, probably India and Pakistan now).

Finally, the traditional model of nuclear deterrence may be abolished if one side or the other creates efficient missile defense systems and systems for defense against other means of delivering nuclear weapons. However, the availability of defense systems (above all, air and ballistic missile defense) in itself does not necessarily rule out nuclear deterrence. Since no defense can be 100 per cent efficient and reliable, an arsenal of offensive retaliatory weapons will always be preserved as an additional guarantee against aggression. Most probably, the emphasis in the deterrence strategy may shift from the potential for nuclear retaliation to systems that directly ward off a strike by a possible enemy.

If this is happening on a mutual basis and within the framework of corresponding regulating agreements, deterrence stability grows, thus ruling out the prospect of a first nuclear strike or accidental, limited or selective use of nuclear weapons (including for disarming, "decapitating" or demonstrative purposes). If, however, the strategy is pursued by one side, deterrence will be destabilized, there will be intensification of the offensive and defensive arms race, and there will be a growth in uncertainty with regard to the enemy's capacities and intentions. The side that has created the most efficient defense systems may face no restrictions on the use of offensive nuclear means, for it will rely on its defense systems against the enemy's weakened retaliatory strike. Thus, mutual deterrence will be undermined.

Today's strategic interaction between Russia and the USA does not fit into any of the exceptions described. Therefore, there is still mutual nuclear deterrence in place. The strategic nuclear forces of either side have between five and six thousand nuclear warheads at their disposal. As long as there are weapons, there are operational plans for their use, as well as lists of targets for nuclear strikes. The weapons in question are largely aimed at each other, since there are not as many targets as there are nuclear weapons. The lowering of the level of alert and the non-targeting of the SNF will not change the essence of the relations, but will merely allow some delay before launch of missiles and bombers.

Mutual nuclear deterrence, although not equal, is also a component in strategic relations between Russia and the UK and France, and between Russia and China. In the near future, such relations may also take shape between the USA and China, India and Pakistan, India and China, as well as between a number of other threshold nuclear states, or between them and great powers.

The inconsistency and low effectiveness of the policies that were conducted in the 1990s by the Russia Federation and the USA in the sphere of reduction and limitation of nuclear arms can largely be explained by the lack of understanding on the part of the two countries' leaders of the essence and role of nuclear deterrence, their striving for premature abandonment of deterrence, and vain attempts to come up with some replacement for deterrence. Instead, they should have made use of the partnership relations in order to undertake decisive measures to stabilize mutual deterrence through the radical reduction and limitation of nuclear arms and establishing total transparency of these processes, ensuring predictability of operational plans and modernization programs, verifiable lowering of the level of alert, integration of the early-warning systems and also subsequent integration of particular components of the SNF control systems, and monitored agreements on operational and tactical nuclear weapons.

Had all this been done in the 1990s, perhaps today we would be in a position to start the serious joint search for an attractive alternative to mutual nuclear deterrence for the next 10 to 15 years. However, owing to the generally lamentable outcomes of the policies in the previous decade, our central task today is not to search for alternatives, but rather to preserve stability of nuclear deterrence in the foreseeable future at both the global and regional/trans-regional level.

Meanwhile, growing threats to stability arise from—on the one hand—the likelihood of disintegration of the entire regime of nuclear disarmament, unilateral development of a ballistic missile defense (BMD) system by the USA, reluctance on the part of the USA to cut its SNF beyond the level envisaged under the framework agreements of 1997 (1,700–2,200 warheads), and—on the other hand—Russia's plans to carry out deep reductions and restructuring of its SNF (which will entail a dramatic decline in the viability and effectiveness of Russia's SNF). More threats are posed by the probable further building-up of nuclear forces by other great powers, by further missile and nuclear proliferation in the world's conflict zones, possible access to nuclear weapons and other weapons of mass destruction by extremist and terrorist organizations. Moreover, destabilizing tendencies in the very sphere of nuclear weapons may be aggravated by ongoing transformations affecting the global power balance, established alliances and coalitions, lines of rivalry and boundaries of conflicts and confrontations.

In the conditions described, the role of nuclear weapons for Russia may be different depending on the country's position in each of the possible architectures of the future world order, the development of the processes of proliferation of nuclear weapons, other weapons of mass destruction, their means of delivery, and also on the nuclear policies adhered to by the official members of the nuclear club. We should not only take these processes into consideration, but also influence them where possible. For this purpose we need to develop a consistent and well coordinated strategic policy for Russia to keep to for the next 10 to 15 years.

2. Nuclear Multipolarity—A New Dimension of Deterrence

In the years of the Cold War and bipolarity, the nuclear potentials of the USSR and USA were so much superior to the forces possessed by third countries (the UK, France, and China, as well as Israel's clandestine potential) that the influence these latter countries could exert on the strategic balance was a matter of secondary importance for the two superpowers. China's nuclear weapons carried by strategic-class delivery means would not reach US territory; British and French weapons were not aimed at the USA, and made up in total no more than 10 per cent of the Soviet SNF. The key attribute of multipolarity, namely proliferation of missile-nuclear and other weapons of mass destruction, will bring about a drastic change in this picture. If there is further proliferation of missile and nuclear weapons, the reduction in their nuclear forces by the Russian Federation and the USA may render the aggregate arsenals of third countries comparable to (or even greater than) Russia's SNF. Apart from the UK, France, and China, new members of the nuclear club have emerged—India, Pakistan and Israel (secretly), which may soon be joined by Iran, North Korea, Taiwan, and Japan.

For a number of reasons, Russia's security will consequently suffer greater losses than the USA's. Unlike in the case of the USA, the forces of all third countries may be aimed at Russia (which does not have nuclear allies), and they will be deployed much closer to Russian territory. The USA is likely to start developing its strategic BMD to protect itself against third countries, which will objectively affect Russia's potential for nuclear deterrence. Russia's economic capacity to modernize and expand its BMD is far more restricted. It is possible that the classical type of mutual nuclear deterrence will not work out with the new member states of the nuclear club. Moreover, their weapons may be more prone to the danger of unsanctioned or accidental launch, theft or environmental catastrophe.

As far as conventional armed forces are concerned, the multipolar world may create additional dangers and problems in this sphere too. Today, Russia's army is still third in personnel strength in the world (following China and the USA), despite its triple reduction during the 1990s to 1.2 million. However, taking into account Russia's economic prospects over the next 10 to 15 years, the maintenance of such a large army is only possible at the expense of further degradation of the army's technological equipment (the share of new armaments and equipment has already declined to 20 per cent, and will fall to three to five per cent five years from now, while the figure is between 50 and 60 per cent in the developed countries), and ultimate disintegration of the military industrial production, or a slide down to the level of third-ranking countries in terms of nuclear and space potential. In order to avoid such a scenario, Russia will have to cut its army by a further 30 per cent and reallocate the maintenance expenses to scientific research and development projects and purchases of arms and military equipment (at present, the maintenance expenses amount to 70 per cent of funds).

Simultaneously, the forces of the countries to the West, East and even South of Russia will be growing in relation to the Russian armed forces. In the West, NATO will acquire a three- or four-fold superiority over Russia in the next 10 to 15 years. In the East, China will also gain considerable superiority thanks to its military budget, twice as big as Russia's, and the massive purchase of

Russian weapons. Even the Japanese army and navy will be superior to the Russian Far East grouping of armed forces. In the South, Turkey has armed forces whose strength amounts to 50 per cent of the Russian forces; the aggregate forces of Turkey and Iran are equal in strength to those of Russia; and, taken together with Pakistan, these countries are half as strong again as Russia.

In a multipolar world, unlike in a bipolar one, apart from the objective correlation of economic and military potential, it is the essence of mutual relations and the degree of cooperation among the key power centers that will have huge significance. These relations predetermine the likelihood of an alliance formed by several power centers against one. In this respect, Russia is in a very unfavorable situation.

At the global level, Russia's relations with the USA are worsening over the problems of nuclear and missile proliferation in the world and US plans to create the national BMD. In the West, the Russian Federation is getting involved in increasingly acute controversy with NATO over the question of the alliance's further expansion to the East, its unilateral use of force outside the bloc territory, and Russia's internal policy of the use of force. Aggravation of the economic and political disagreements with a larger European Union is also possible. In the South, Russia's engagement in local conflicts in the North Caucasus, Transcaucasia and Central Asia sets the Muslim world against it, with the West maintaining a stance that is far from friendly to Russia. In the East, the unresolved territorial dispute hinders the growth of cooperation with Japan.

One cannot rule out a possible escalation of tension in Russia's relations with China over the resources and territories of the Far East, as well as in connection with demographic problems.

Given that it has more tense relations with other power centers than they have among themselves, and given that it is lagging behind these centers in terms of economic and military potential, Russia may find itself in an extremely vulnerable position in the multipolar world.

Judging from the assessments of tendencies in economic and military development, a US-led unipolarity is unlikely in the 21st century. However, multipolarity is not the only alternative. There may emerge a new bipolarity with the USA and China as the key poles of confrontation, and with the main scene of rivalry shifted from Europe to the Asia-Pacific super-region. There is a possibility that Japan might move to the foreground of confrontation with China with the support of the USA, Taiwan and South Korea.

In such conditions, Russia may find itself between the upper and the lower millstone of this confrontation. Joining the USA (along with Japan, Taiwan, and South Korea) would doom Russia to confronting China, with Russia's Far East extremely vulnerable and China having a large military superiority in the region. A full-fledged alliance with China against the West—a trend that is discernible today—would be an even more dangerous option. While struggling against the US-led unipolarity, Russia would come under China's dominance. However, China is a country with a far more alien civilization and authoritarian state system, huge demand for resources and living space, and the tradition of cruel suppression of ethnic minorities (the role that Russian in the Far East may come to play). Total subordination to China or separation of the Asian part of Russia's territory would be the most ruinous outcome for Russia of the new bipolarity.

3. Conclusions

This analysis enables us to come up with a number of fundamental conclusions. First of all, leaving aside the US-led unipolar world, there is no less, and possibly much more, danger for Russia in the possible new bipolarity and confrontation between the USA and China, in which Moscow would hardly be able to retain either its neutrality and equidistance from the power poles, or its sovereignty over Siberia and the Far East.

Today, the likelihood of such bipolarity appears greater than the likelihood of both a unipolarity that Russia opposes in every possible way and the multipolarity that Russia struggles to promote. To make things worse, by counteracting the US unipolarity, Moscow is conducting its policy in a way that actually pushes international relations towards a new bipolarity rather than towards multipolarity, although the West also bears considerable responsibility for this tendency.

However, even if the first two unfavorable models of an international system (unipolarity and bipolarity) could be avoided, the multipolar international configuration would not in itself guarantee protection of Russia's national interests and security if the current tendencies described above persist. These tendencies have to be changed. And for this, Russia needs to develop a consistent and accurately coordinated strategic policy for the next 10 to 15 years.

It is obvious that Russia's primary mission must be to ensure its economic growth, and to create a favorable investment climate for domestic and foreign investors.

In its foreign policy, the Russian Federation must prioritize relations with those countries that may influence the prospects of Russia's economic growth and affect the process of attraction of big foreign investments to Russia, and the expansion of Russia's participation in international trade and financial organizations, i.e. relations with the countries of Western Europe and Japan.

The same countries will play a crucial role for Russia from the perspective of its long-term political interest and security concerns. It is Moscow's relations with these states that will determine the prospects for avoiding a new bipolarity in the world or the type of multipolarity that would bring Russia into confrontation "in all dimensions," and with weak economic and military positions at that.

Relations within the CIS, as well as with the USA, China, India, and Iran are, of course, also important for Russia. However, these relations in themselves are not going to safeguard Russia's security in the multipolar world. Certainly, trade, mutually beneficial investments, and transit in the post-Soviet space are of great significance to Russia, but they are negligible as compared to the investments that need to be made in Russia's economy to ensure that it grows steadily and that its primary deformation is overcome. Russia can receive such investments only from the EU and Japan. Russia's most important concern in the post-Soviet space is its security in the light of new threats: social and political consequences of local conflicts, terrorism, transnational crime, trafficking in weapons and drugs, and illegal migration. Russia cannot build a "wall of China" to separate itself from these threats. Nor can it control these phenomena by conducting a neo-imperial policy of subjugating the "near-abroad" states. The best way to act in this situation is to assume a strategy of economic and political stabilization, which requires Russia's cooperation first of all with the USA, Western Europe, Japan and China.

Russia's interests also include the greatest possible expansion of the role, and enhancement of the effectiveness, of international security structures, such as the UN and OSCE, in settling conflicts and conducting peacekeeping operations. There is a large space for Russia's more active participation in the CIS space, as well as in Europe, the Persian Gulf zone, South Asia and the Far East. In addition, development of Russia's economic, political and military cooperation with the European Union is the only alternative to NATO's further expansion to the East and to the alliance's attempts to supersede the UN and OSCE.

In view of the unfavorable tendencies in the economic and military power balance in the world, Russia is more interested than other countries in expanding and strengthening the regime and system of limitations on arms and military activities, as well as of disarmament and nonproliferation of weapons of mass destruction and their means of delivery. In this sphere, Russia's role will remain a crucial one, and we should make the best use of this "trump card." The considerable danger that proliferation of nuclear missiles poses for Russia is clearly underestimated in favor of commercial and ministerial interests. In the multipolar world, the task of involving third countries in the system of arms limitation and nonproliferation must become a priority in Russia's policy (tightening of the regimes under the NPT, CTBT, and of the Missile Technology Control Regime (MTCR)).

In the defense sphere, the military budget must be increased to 3.5 per cent, even in the current complicated financial situation. In addition, army strength must be reduced by approximately a further 30 per cent (down to 0.8 million service members); and the ratio of maintenance–investment expenditure must be changed from 70:30 to 55:45. This will allow the advanced branches of the military-industrial production complex to be preserved, as well as schools and groups dealing in the fundamental and applied sciences, which—once lost— are extremely difficult to restore. Besides, this would allow the SNF to be maintained at the level of at least 1,500 warheads (and—even more importantly—with an emphasis on highly reliable mobile land-based missiles); the stable balance with the USA to be retained for 10 to 15 years; more compact but much better trained and equipped special forces to be kept for selective local operations and to contain threats such as the NATO action in the Balkans; and the army to be transformed into a totally voluntary contract-based service within five years.

The importance of the Russian initiative to create a joint non-strategic Russian–NATO BMD system is clearly underestimated. First of all, this is an indirect application by Russia to join NATO, since it is impossible to have a joint BMD system without joint air defense. And a common system of defense facilities presupposes nothing less than alliance.

Moreover, Russia will not be in a position to create its BMD for the European part of its territory without extending this system to the Asian part of the country. Similarly, if BMD is deployed to protect the European NATO members, it is impossible not to create a similar defense for the US's Asian allies: Japan and South Korea. Such developments are undesirable from China's perspective. Therefore, Russia and China will move apart in their relations. Moreover, Russia will have to curtail its cooperation with Iran, North Korea and other countries, whose missiles the joint Russian–NATO BMD will be intended to counteract.

Originally published in *Mirovaya Ekonomika i Mezhdunarodnie Otnoshenia* [World economy and international relations], 2000, no. 10, pp. 21–28.

The Phenomenon of Globalization and National Security Interests

Andrei Kokoshin

1. Key Features of Globalization in the Economy and Politics. Russia's Interests and Capacities

Today, the phenomenon of globalization covers not only the sphere of the economy and business, but also the political and social spheres.

Globalization is not merely one of the main trends in global development. Today, this term refers chiefly to the establishment of a new system in international economic and political relations, which replaced the system that operated between 1945 and the early 1990s and was marked by the all-out confrontation between two ideologically antagonistic superpowers. The new system of international relations described by the term "globalization" is governed by the market economy, rather than by transnational relations or political ideological solutions.

In its turn, the development of a world market becomes more dependent on the trends dominating the global consumer psychology, primarily of those consumers that make up the so-called "golden billion" of the human race. It is their consumer behavior that determines the tastes of all other people, including in countries that have their own wealth of cultural traditions different from the western ones (China, India, Indonesia and others, to say nothing of Japan).

Globalization in the economy becomes apparent in the following:

- an uneven increase in the scope and rates of capital transfer;
- growth in international trade outstripping global GDP growth;
- establishment of international production chains with rapid deployment of production facilities for manufacturing standardized and unified products;
- formation of world financial markets where most transactions are conducted almost round the clock;
- the financial sphere becomes a self-sufficient force that determines any possible development of industry, agriculture, infrastructure, or services. Today the financial sphere has become a "real economy" in itself;
- owing to the development of telecommunications systems and software, information on any changes in the financial and other markets spreads almost instantly, which engenders real-time, often reflex-driven, decision-

making where transferring capital, selling or buying foreign currency, securities, bonds, etc. are concerned;

- world financial markets become independent from the jurisdiction of individual states – even the largest;
- there is an emergence of new powerful entities of the world economy due to mergers and takeovers by transnational corporations.[1]

Globalization involves many negative consequences, including a growth in the gap in living standards between the "golden billion" and the rest of the world, including Russia.

Under the conditions of globalization there is a progressive accumulation of environmental problems, especially in developing countries. The shortage of clean water is becoming one of the severest problems.

Moreover, an increasing gap in development levels between various population strata and regions is typical of many countries, including the most developed ones. Under the conditions of the recent eight-year economic growth, the gap in income between those who have higher education and those who do not has, according to a number of different assessments, increased in the USA by between 25 and 30 per cent.

Consequently, globalization faces opposition not only in those countries that are on the margins of this process, but also inside the most developed countries that are the "locomotives" of globalization. These phenomena deserve the closest attention from the perspective of Russia's national security interests. In order for the gap between the "golden billion" and Russia to start narrowing, even slowly, rather than increasing, Russia needs to achieve an annual GDP growth of 10 per cent, which is quite feasible, judging by the experience of a number of other countries. The prerequisites exist for such a growth in the Russian economy, especially if the potential competitive advantages of our country and our people in the global economy are fully taken into account.

These advantages are based on more than just Russia's natural resources and enormous power sources. They are related primarily to our human resources, to what is called HUMAN CAPITAL—science, education and culture. Above all, it is this capital that makes Russia different from the developing countries.

Exploitation of the human capital potential at the current stage in technological, industrial, financial and economic development requires political freedom

---

1 See more on globalization in: Kokoshin, A. A., *Put Rossii v globalnuyu ekonomiku* [Russia's way to the global economy], Moscow, Moscow State University Press, pp. 10–16; Martynov, V. A., Dynkin, A. A., *Innovatsionnyye kontury mirovoy ekonomiki. Prognoz razvitiya na 2000–2015* [Innovation outline of world economy. Forecast of development for 2000–2015], Institute of World Economy and Foreign Relations, Russian Academy of Sciences, Moscow, 1999, pp. 6–7.

in the country, and the formation of a stable democratic system based, first and foremost, on the middle class that has achieved a certain level of self-awareness.

It is worth noting that the fastest rates of development in the USA are characteristic of high-end technologies and the knowledge-based economy, and are generally in the states and regions known for their democratic traditions, cultural and religious tolerance (California and New England). The recent boom of high-end technologies in the UK has been related to the activity of hundreds of companies, above all those grouped around Oxford and Cambridge Universities.

It is science, education, culture and public health care that form the basis for a knowledge-based economy; an economy that determines the real power of the nation, its ability to protect its national security interests. Thus, it is quite reasonable that today a number of Russian authors keep speaking about the value of education and science for protecting national security.[2]

This is a long-lasting tendency, which will determine the main features of the world economy and politics for the whole of the 21st century and beyond. It is also absolutely typical of the political and military area, and of military affairs, where no national defense system that meets the current requirements and true interests of Russian national security can be developed without an essential intellectualization of the military sphere and our officer corps.

When counting on human capital and high-end technologies, of course, one should not forget about Russia's natural resources, which are perhaps among the most impressive in the world. As a matter of fact, natural resources and human capital are the two supports, and two basic elements, that will ensure Russia's breakthrough to become a member of the group of the most developed countries in the next 30 40 years.

Our potential in natural resources can be described by Russia's shares in the world mineral and energy resources:

- oil   13 per cent
- natural gas   35 per cent
- coal   12 per cent
- iron and tin   over 27 per cent
- copper   11 per cent
- lead   12 per cent
- zinc   10 per cent
- nickel   30 per cent
- cobalt   20 per cent
- metals of the platinum group   40 per cent

2 For example, see Yusupov, R. M., *Nauka i natsionalnaya bezopasnost Rossii* [Science and Russia's national security], St Petersburg, St Petersburg Institute of History, Russian Academy of Sciences, 2000.

About two million people are employed in mining and mineral prospecting, which accounts for at least 25 per cent of the GDP, and provides about 50 per cent of the exchange profit from foreign commerce.

Russia accounts for three per cent of the world's population; it possesses 12.5 per cent of the whole dry land area in the world, and has 22 per cent of the world's forest resources, 20 per cent of the world's fresh water resources (surface and subsurface waters) and 30 per cent of the world's shelf area.[3]

In particular, fresh water is gaining in value as one of the world's resources under the current conditions of growing human population and increasing human impact on the environment.

The value of this resource remains underestimated in the Russian economic development policy, as well as in our national security policy. There is an urgent need for the federal government to make (jointly with the Federation's entities) a thorough inventory of this resource and to develop a national policy in this sphere, both in terms of domestic consumption and with regard to its use in our export policy. The policy in this field can have a direct effect on the health of the population in our multinational country. Promotion of public health must finally become one of the priorities in the national security policy.

2. Special Role of the Information Sphere in the Globalization Process

The main element in the world information infrastructure is the Internet, which emerged on the basis of network developments made, primarily, at the request of the US Department of Defense (DARPA). One of the major indices confirming the impact of the Internet on the world economy (apart from its purely information function) is the average reduction in product costs of between 10 and 12 per cent owing to e-marketing and e-management.[4]

We are now witnesses to the fourth "information revolution," characterized mainly by the maximum introduction of multimedia technologies and services in networks and, accordingly, the establishment of new corporate multimedia giants and companies specializing in e-trade. The USA is the indisputable leader in the "fourth information revolution."

In the 1990s, the structure of US business underwent a tectonic shift in favor of companies specializing in the information sphere. As a result, judging by their financial and economic power reflected in their rankings on the US stock exchanges (above all, on the New York Stock Exchange), information companies have secured dominant positions, compared not only to automobile companies but also to those aerospace business giants that became a symbol of US

---

3 See Rundkvist, D. V., *Prirodnyye natsionalnyye bogatstva Rossii i ikh ispolzovaniye* [National natural resources of Russia and their use], Report in the Ministry of Science, February 8, 2000, Moscow, Ministry of Science, Appendix, pp. 1, 2.

4 Information Society—Europe: Progress Report. Annex 2. 2000. p. 8.

power in the 1970s and 1980s, and a major support of the knowledge-intensive industry.

Lawrence Summers, the current US Secretary to the Treasury, keeps saying at different forums over and over again that, as early as in 1998, the capitalization volume of Microsoft alone exceeded the total capitalization of the entire US aerospace, automobile and steel industries.[5]

Having elaborated a development strategy for the European Information Community at the end of 1999, the European Union has made vigorous efforts to bridge the gap between the EU and the USA in this sphere. Japan is pursuing a similar policy. China and India are following their own national policies in the information sphere.

In particular, in the past eight to ten years, India has received active state assistance and has built an impressive national software industry primarily oriented towards export and interaction with the largest western telecommunications companies (especially in the USA). According to a number of assessments, by 2000 the capitalization of major Indian companies in this sphere exceeded US$25 billion, and the software export volume made up US$3 billion.

As for the role of Russia in the world information space, it remains vanishingly insignificant and is neither up to our otherwise justified claims to "great power" status, nor up to our scientific and technological potential or the general cultural level of the Russian people.

As far as its achievements in the information sphere are concerned, Russia is somewhere between the second and third information revolutions, though a number of technologies and developments meeting the requirements and level of the fourth information revolution have been developed in Russia lately.

These fresh shoots need careful treatment, stimulation and protection against any bureaucratic interference.

In its information policy Russia cannot imitate either India, or the European Union, or any other country, or any international union. It must develop its own formula, its own strategy for building the "Russian information community" that would, in some format, embrace all former republics of the Soviet Union, as well as, probably, some other countries. This model strategy must be totally compatible with the concept of the "European information community" and must be developed taking into account relevant policies pursued by China, India, and Japan, so that the "Russian information community" might also serve as a bridge between Europe and Asia.

The development of such a strategy is one of our priority missions that are directly related to the protection of Russia's national security interests.

---

5 In the first half of 2000, the Microsoft capitalization (before the anti-trust law decision was made with regard to this company) made up some US$400 billion. The largest US telecommunications company, Cisco, which ranked first in the world at some point in spring 2000, had similar capitalization.

3. Onset of New Long and New Superlong Cycles in World Politics

We are now witnessing the completion of not merely a long cycle in world history, which began in 1945, but also a superlong centuries-long cycle.

One can say that the previous superlong cycle in the development of the system of international relations began in 1648, when the Treaty of Westphalia was concluded, putting an end to the Thirty Years' War in Europe.

The Peace of Westphalia actually laid the international contractual foundation for international relations, which remained largely unchanging, despite such cataclysms as the Great French Revolution, Franco–Prussian war and Bismarck's establishment of the German Empire, World War I, and World War II. It is obvious that the French hegemony was not only eroded during this superlong cycle but was practically lost, when in certain periods France suffered crushing defeats (1812–1814, the Franco–Prussian war of 1870–1871). This is all about the duration of the period of one superpower's domination within the framework of a new superlong cycle of world politics.

As for the development of the system of international relations, the superlong cycle that began in the middle of the 17th century coincided in Western Europe with the formation of the foundations of current scholarly concepts pertinent to nature and human beings, and with the establishment of the fundamentals of modern science and its methods, which is associated with such names as Francis Bacon, Rene Descartes, and Isaac Newton.

In the new superlong cycle commencing today, revolutionary achievements in fundamental sciences and technology, as well as in research methods (above all, related to mathematical simulation and avalanche-like construction of virtual worlds) are proceeding side by side with major changes in world politics.

Giant achievements in the development of physics and chemistry in the 20th century are now followed by developments in information science, molecular biology and genetics.

The concept of national sovereignty is becoming dissolved today both from above, owing to the world market dictate, and from below, owing to separatism, racial, ethnic and religious conflicts, etc.

Today, the principle of national self-determination more and more often opposes the principles of territorial integrity and inviolability of borders, while the principle of humanitarian intervention contravenes the principle of national sovereignty. Unless the process going on "from below" encounters any resistance, then in 10–12 years, according to a number of different assessments, another 100 formally independent and sovereign states will emerge in the world, including those segregated from some CIS states, e.g. Georgia or Moldova.

The same problem is faced by Russia, too, and not only in connection with Chechnya. Given the absence of rapid economic growth, of appropriate efforts in the field of public construction, and of a corresponding target-oriented cultural policy, the threat of separation of certain territories from Russia may grow.

Unfortunately, this fits in with a current trend in international relations that is opposed by a great number of other states (apart from Russia), including such Asian giants as China and India, and we have more and more parallel and concurrent interests with them.

In Europe, similar problems are typical of the United Kingdom of Great Britain and Northern Ireland (Ulster), Spain (the Basque Country), Belgium (the Walloons), etc.

Promotion of the idea of humanitarian interventionism and superiority of humanitarian law over traditional international law is actually encouraging radical groups within religious and ethnic minorities to aggravate conflicts, right up to using armed force with a view to winning with the help of peace-making forces. This process may affect not only the peripheral system of international relations but also its "core" countries. In this respect, it is not accidental that we can observe a revival of separatist activities in the Basque Country in Spain or of Christian minorities in some Indonesian islands after the NATO operations in Kosovo or UN operations in East Timor.[6]

The emergence of new hotbeds of conflict is not accompanied by an adequate strengthening of conflict-resolution tools. Instead, we can observe a crisis in the institutions safeguarding international security. At the global level, the international security system is seeing a weakening of the role of the UN and the UN Security Council; at the regional level—a weakening of the newer OSCE.

The UN crisis is closely related to the nuclear factor. During the entire post-war period, only permanent members of the UN Security Council were official nuclear powers, and the exclusive nature of the nuclear club was emphasized by this fact. It was forgotten that the organization itself had been initially established as a union of the anti-Hitler coalition countries, and that the term "United Nations" had been applied to these countries long before the end of World War II, while permanent members of the Security Council were the countries that won the war.

Now we can observe increasingly active efforts being undertaken by some western states, mainly the USA, to have the case law principle accepted by the UN General Assembly. It is not unlikely that Russia's new President V. V. Putin will have to face this problem in all its magnitude at the New York session of the UN General Assembly in the fall of 2000. Thus, he must get prop-

---

6 See Sergeyev, V. M., *Mnogopolyarnost i perspektivy regionalnogo politsentrizma* [Multipolarity and prospects of regional polycentrism], Moscow, Moscow State Institute of Foreign Relations, Ministry of Foreign Affairs of the Russian Federation, March 6, 2000, p. 9.

erly prepared by mobilizing support of all likely allies, both among UN members and among the international public, including among lawyers.

If the UN General Assembly does accept the case law principle, this will be an event historically comparable to the 1648 Treaty of Westphalia. By introducing international legal norms that ensured Germany's fragmentation, France, an emerging European superpower of that time, safeguarded its interests for almost 250 years. By introducing corresponding international legal norms today, the USA may nail down what was done by NATO in Yugoslavia in 1999 and legalize the right to humanitarian intervention for centuries ahead.

It must not be ruled out either that this right may cease to be the USA's exclusive right by the middle of the 21st century, for by that time the USA may have lost its status as the single superpower.

4. Possible Changes among the Key Actors of International Relations in the First Half of the 21st Century

With regard to possible changes in the statuses of participants in the system of international relations, the following long-term trends (for the next 40–50 years) may be discerned:

- emergence of China as a "second-rank superpower" capable of pursuing an active policy not only in the Asia-Pacific region but also on the global scale, by approximately 2025–2030;[7]
- transformation of the European Union into a confederate entity, an entity in international relations, surpassing in its prerogatives and activity all traditional European entities of world politics, including the great powers, the United Kingdom and France;
- growth of India's population by 2025 to reach the Chinese population figure for the same period, with India's middle class comparable with that of China in terms of size, while the degree of India's integration into the global economy will surpass that of China thanks to the traditional Indian ties with the Anglo-Saxon world and the proficiency in English of almost the entire Indian middle class;
- emergence of Iran as a "regional great power" possessing nuclear weapons (with intercontinental delivery systems that will be able to reach US territory, by approximately 2012, which will bring Iran up to the global level).[8]

---

7 Of course, this forecast about China (as well as any further forecasts) is based on certain assumptions; the main assumption is that China will remain a centralized state, that the separatism crises will not develop immediately after the incumbent party and government leaders have left their positions, that there will be no collapse of the political and state system brought about by the democratization of the political system.

8 The implementation of this program is not predetermined. The problem of non-conversion of Iran into a "regional nuclear superpower" can be solved at a political level.

It should also be mentioned that, even given the great economic might of an integrated Europe, and the availability of a united military organization with its own strategic intelligence facilities, rapid deployment forces, European transport vehicles (possibly, including the Russian–Ukrainian AN-70 transport aircraft), the European Union has virtually no chance of becoming an independent center of world economy, such as the US, China, India, or, under certain conditions, Russia.

Nevertheless, the enlargement of the European Union must be taken into account by Russia in its national security policy and, where possible, employed to Russia's advantage.[9]

5. Possible Armed Conflicts and Wars of the 21st Century

Among the most likely large armed conflicts that might occur in 2000–2025, it is necessary to mention the threat that the Kashmir conflict might develop into a full-scale war between India and Pakistan, possibly with the use of nuclear or other weapons of mass destruction, e.g. biological or genetic.

Russia must not keep aloof from this process. It is necessary to ensure that Indian–Pakistani relations do not develop into a war. Russia's foreign policy must contribute to the peaceful resolution of this conflict in every possible way.

One cannot rule out the possible emergence of an armed conflict brought about by the growing separatist sentiments in Taiwan either. Not only official statements made by the Chinese leaders in 1999–2000 but also actual preparations by China testify to the fact that our great Asian neighbor may not refrain from the use of military force on a large scale when exercising its internationally recognized rights with respect to Taiwan.

However, it is most likely that Beijing will vigorously use methods of military and psychological pressure, without any direct application of military force, in the manner of the ancient Chinese treatises on war policy and the art of war, which were reflected in the military-political thinking of Mao Zedong and Deng Xiaoping.

There are many indications that, once the Taiwan issue is resolved, the Chinese leaders may put on the agenda the problem of Chinese sovereignty over the Spratley Islands, Senkaku Islands and a number of other disputed territories.

A conflict may also emerge on the Korean peninsula, in the immediate prox-

---

9 As a part of this process, the European Union experiences apparent deprivation of its members of their sovereign status. These are traditional nation-states that have been the main elements and entities of international relations for centuries. In particular, the Central and Eastern European states, which used to belong to the Warsaw Treaty Organization led by the USSR, are now becoming quasi-sovereign entities of international relations, just as they used to be as members of the Warsaw Treaty Organization.

imity to Russia's territory, between the Democratic People's Republic of Korea and the Republic of Korea. The Democratic People's Republic of Korea has already demonstrated its capacity for developing intercontinental ballistic missiles and nuclear weapons.

However, the above-mentioned scenarios do not rule out other possible conflict and crisis situations involving the use of armed force, including nuclear as well as biological or radiological weapons.

Each such conflict can entail a huge medical, biological and environmental aftermath in various parts of the world, including on Russian territory, and can lead to the collapse of the modern global economy, which would be comparable to the Great Depression of the late 1920s–early 1930s, in view of the high interdependency.

6. "Second Nuclear Age" and Strategic Stability

With regard to the nuclear dimension of the system of international relations, it seems obvious that we have entered "the second nuclear age," which is going to be considerably different from the first one that began in 1945. It is in the nuclear sphere that multipolarity will be developed, although with significant limitations.

By the end of this decade China will have a far more significant (five to six times more) intercontinental potential than today. In the next eight to ten years, India will also have intercontinental facilities for delivering nuclear weapons. At least, it is clear to anyone who has studied carefully all the statements made by the scientists working for the National Security Council of India that this task has already been set. And the idea is to achieve for India a status at least equal to that of China in the nuclear sphere. Of course, in the immediate future India will, in the first instance, be developing a nuclear potential as military-space deterrent against China and Pakistan.

Israel, which, for several decades, has pursued the policy of nuclear deterrence called "bombs in the basement," has come to the fore of the stage of world politics in the nuclear sphere after the well-reported recent debates in the Knesset. It could not remain unnoticed in the Arab world, where a number of countries are still discussing the possibility of developing their domestic facilities and forces of nuclear deterrence.

The behavioral pattern of new nuclear powers in conditions of conflict or crisis could be significantly different from the one formed between the USSR and USA, and Russia and the USA after decades of their cold war confrontation.[10]

Thus, there is a completely new strategic stability equation that differs substantially from the one we used to have when there was absolute domination

---

10 For more information see: Kokoshin, A. A., *Yadernoye sderzhivaniye i natsionalnaya bezopasnost Rossii* [Nuclear deterrence and Russia's national security], Moscow, Institute of International Security Problems, Russian Academy of Sciences, 2000.

The components of the nuclear control system of various countries can be shown as follows

Component	Russia	US	UK	France	China	India	Pakistan
Strategic nuclear triad component:							
Intercontinental ballistic missiles	+	+	−	−	+	−	−
Combat control systems	+	+	−	−	+	−	−
Submarine-launched ballistic missile	+	+	+	+	+	−	−
Combat control systems	+	+	+	+	+	−	−
Heavy bombers with cruise missiles and nuclear warheads	+	+	−	−	−	−	−
Combat control systems	+	+	−	−	−	−	−
Medium range resources:							
Medium-range ballistic missiles	−	−	−	−	+	+	+
Bombers	+	−	−	−	+	−	−
Operational-tactical and tactical nuclear weapons	+	+	−	+	+	+	+
Anti-missile defense systems	+	−	−	−	−	−	−
Missile early-warning systems:							
Earth-based array	+	+	−	−	−	−	−
Space-based array	+	+	−	−	−	−	−
Space control systems	+	+	−	−	−	−	−

by two superpowers, and from the one we have today. China, unnoticed by many, has worked out a very distinct and persistently demonstrated policy of threatening the use of military force, including the possible use of nuclear weapons. Every conflict or crisis situation around, say, Taiwan, is settled by resolving the dispute at a relatively low level of escalation; yet, each time the resolution involves some economic concessions by the USA to China. Of course, this linkage is reflected in no official documents, and yet it does exist. This model of using one's military power to uphold one's pragmatic and well-regulated economic interests is highly instructive.

Speaking of other attributes of "the second nuclear age," the USA's recurring attempt to develop a "limited" national missile defense system should be mentioned. The previous attempt in the early 1980s, when US President Ronald Reagan put forward a "strategic defense initiative" – the idea of developing large-scale missile defense for the territory of the entire country with the use of a significant space component – had virtually no success. At that time, though, it was a question of significantly greater developments and far more unusual technologies, including nuclear particle accelerators, various surface- and space-based lasers (excimer laser, free-electron laser, gamma-laser, etc.), mass electrodynamics accelerators and other exotics.

Then, through the efforts of Soviet scientists, experts from the Ministry of Defense and defense industry, a concept and specific policy of "asymmetric response" to the SDI program was developed. This program brought fruit that is still reaped today by the domestic developers of arms, weapons and military technology, and the Russian Armed Forces.[11]

Today's agenda emphasizes the use of traditional surface-based interceptor missiles, the same as in the 1950s and 1960s, when such systems were developed in the Soviet Union and the USA, but based on the latest achievements in missile technologies.

7. Biological Weapons Proliferation as a Threat to Russia's National Security

Any discussion of the issues of international security directly related to Russia's national security must emphasize the problem of biological weapons proliferation. The danger of such proliferation is greatly increased today because of the imminent boom in general-purpose biotechnologies.

The current regimes of nonproliferation of biological weapons have not been up to the magnitude of the threat at all. Virtually no nonproliferation regimes have been established with regard to the new types of bacteriological weapons.

Biological weapons are natural pathogens of special hazardous infections, such as bacteria, viruses, fungi, toxins, poisons of biological origin, deliberately used to debilitate and cause death or serious disability. The threat posed by BIOLOGICAL TERRORISM to Russia's security must be perceived as seriously as the threat of nuclear war, and must be reflected in the legislative base and budgets for the development of adequate means for protection.[12]

8. Lagging behind Most Developed Countries is a Major Long-Term Threat to Russia's National Security

A major problem, and the main complex factor in the threat to our sovereignty, territorial integrity and cultural civilization identity, is the way RUSSIA IS INCREASINGLY LAGGING BEHIND THE MOST DEVELOPED COUNTRIES OF THE

---

11 For example, see: Arbatov, A. G., Vasiliyev, V. V., Gerasev, M. I., Kokoshin, A. A., Rodionov, S. N., *et al.*, *Udarnyye kosmicheskiye vooruzheniya i mezhdunarodnaya bezopasnost* [Offensive space weapons and international security].

12 For Russia the problem of vulnerability in the face of biological terrorism is doubled by the low immune status of a considerable part of the population, absence of an efficient system of public health protection and sanitary epidemic control, dependence on food imports, collapse of the national pharmaceutical industry and high level of dependence on drugs imports, endless migration flows, existence of a significant marginal layer of the population, etc.

Large-scale non-conventional acts of war with the use of new types of biological weapons (biological war) directed against a significant part of the population can-

Dynamics of energy and power intensity of the world economy and individual countries

	2000	2010	2020
World energy consumption, kg of fuel equivalent per capita	2200	2240	2290
Power intensity of the world economy, tonnes of fuel equivalent / million ECU (1985), *including:*	540	470	410
CIS states	1770	1425	1180
US	410	370	340
European Union	390	330	290
Japan	250	220	200
China	1290	800	540

WORLD. IN SOME RESPECTS, IT EVEN LAGS BEHIND CERTAIN COUNTRIES THAT ARE NOT ON THE LIST OF MOST DEVELOPED COUNTRIES. Even if, in the very near future, Russia's GDP growth amounts to five or six per cent per year, instead of the three to four per cent forecast by the Russian Ministry of Economic Development, Russia will continue progressively to lag behind not only the

---

not be ruled out. They can be carried out, in particular, by using pathogenic organisms (first of all, viruses) with a considerable latent period, thus allowing for a long-term proliferation before the first signs of alarm can be noticed.

For the same purpose, artificial genetic structures containing the genes of toxins of the peptide or protein nature (toxins of cobra, ricin, botulotoxin, death-cap toxins, etc.) can be applied. At present 430 types of amino acid sequences of only snake poisons and, consequently, 430 coding genes have been decoded. Scrutinizing the body cells (for example, human bowel epithelium or symbiotic microflora of the intestinal tract) they can launch the synthesis of death toxins by these cells. Besides, the genes coding toxins of insects, plants, fungi or marine invertebrates can be used.

Genetic structures capable of starting a perverted immune response of the human body through the accumulation of superantigens, cytokines, protein antigens causing autoimmune diseases can also be used.

The impossibility of identifying the source of infection due to the long latent period, quite often coupled with the impossibility of proving the reasons behind the violation of the body's normal functions, is sufficient to forecast fast development of the methods of clandestine destruction of this type aimed at individual enemies, as it has been practiced for centuries.

As is well known, wide use of poisons ended only because of the development of methods for detection of their traces in the organism and methods for proving their criminal use. A non-toxic genetic structure is practically undetectable (without prior information) among 100,000 similar structures of the host's body, and the similarity of the symptoms of diseases induced by different causes complicates identification of the death causes even further. See: *O sozdanii sistemy zashchity strany ot biologicheskogo terrorizma* [On the development of a national defense system against biological terrorism], Pushchino Research Center, Russian Academy of Sciences, Pushchino, Moscow region, 1999.

world's most developed countries, but also China and a number of Asian countries, and this will also negatively affect the sphere of military security and Russia's national defensive capacity.

This situation is reflected not only in the aggregated economic indices but also in the indices of social development. No less – and in several cases even more – important is the fact that there are ALMOST NO RUSSIAN STATE OR PRIVATE COMPANIES OR RUSSIAN BUSINESS ASSOCIATIONS THAT CAN BE REGARDED AS MAJOR PLAYERS IN THE GLOBAL ECONOMY. Moreover, this is the case even in the spheres where Russia's share in the product output is significant, as, for example, in the production and export of crude oil.

Today our power industry looks even worse in this respect than, for example, the power industry of the People's Republic of China, which has recently started developing energy-saving technologies, and increasing the efficiency of the industry.

When discussing the gap between Russia and the most developed countries, one should mention the problem of a woeful shortfall in the efficiency of the use of energy supplies (according to many ratings, the average efficiency factor in most of our energy facilities is half that of Western Europe) – while the power intensity of Russian industries and public energy consumption under northern climatic conditions are much higher.

The capital outflow from Russia is also a very important factor. We often say: let's take back all the money that has flowed out of Russia, and this amount will make sufficient investment resources for us. According to most assessments, the capital outflow over the past five years totals $120–130 billion. The required capital is estimated at hundreds of billions of US dollars – about $500–600 billion up to 2110. That is approximately as much as China received during the years of reforms. Such a comparison testifies to the fact that, even if we take back all our capital, we will not be able to modernize our economy. This is a major problem for our external and internal policy. In many respects, this problem is similar to those that China has already solved and is solving today.

One of the key problems in attracting both domestic and foreign capital into the Russian economy is ensuring proprietary rights.

At present, from the perspective of the attractiveness of investment, Russia is still falling behind countries with comparable economic potential per capita.

Remarkably, political and, especially, political-psychological factors are of no less consequence than economic factors or the legal situation. Now, at the beginning of the 21st century, Russia's international image has grown significantly worse; negative stereotypes with regard to Russia have started dominating the western mass media, mass and elite consciousness. Given the prevalent share of the western mass media in the world telecommunication system, it means that Russia's image is deteriorating throughout the world. To improve

Russia's image is a major national mission, which has to be carried out by combined efforts on the part of the state and the public. Even if the problem is approached in the best way, it will take several years to be resolved. By a number of parameters, the situation has started to improve since the presidential elections of 2000. However, this tendency needs to be consistently enhanced.

★★★

RUSSIA'S FUNDAMENTAL PRIORITY CONSISTS IN MODERNIZING ITS ECONOMY, ESTABLISHING A POST-INDUSTRIAL MARKET ECONOMY, A STABLE SYSTEM OF POLITICAL DEMOCRACY, A GENUINE CIVIL SOCIETY, THE PRESERVATION AND ENHANCEMENT OF RUSSIA'S BEST CULTURAL AND CIVILIZATION HERITAGE. THIS IS THE ONLY WAY TO SECURE OUR REAL SOVEREIGNTY AND TERRITORIAL INTEGRITY. IT IS A CORNERSTONE THAT SPECIFIC POLICY MUST BE BASED ON.

9. Russia's Self-Identification in Contemporary World

The problem of Russia's self-identification in the contemporary world is acute. I want to support the thesis formulated by my colleagues from the Russian Academy of Sciences, who claim that Russia is not a multinational state, but a multi-ethnic one, in which the Russian people constitute the super-ethnos. If we accept this postulate, we will be able to see the concept of federalism in this country, as well as many other issues, in a completely different light. Hypothetically speaking, had we, in good time, accepted a concept different from that formulated by Lenin and stipulating the building of the Soviet Union as a conglomeration of sovereign national states, we might have avoided the subsequent adoption of all USSR Constitutions, which largely predetermined the collapse of the Soviet Union.

I presume, in order to resolve the problem of Russia's self-identification, we should, among other things, make use of the formula accepted by the United Nations. The formula postulates that the notions of state and nation are identical in many respects. The idea is reflected in the very name of this most consequential international organization, which plays a crucial role in international relations despite all its faults and problems.

10. On Some Principles and Specific Guidelines in Russia's National Security Policy in the International Arena

The idea of enlightened national egoism, as well as maximum economization of RUSSIAN POLICY, must be fundamental. Among other things, this means that in the foreseeable future (i.e. in the next 30–40 years) Russia – regrettably – will have to abandon its claims to be a power of global consequence, as was the Soviet Union.

At the same time, it is necessary to secure Russia's interests both close to its borders and in some quite remote regions. For example, we should have established closer cooperation with Mexico in working out the oil pricing policies.

We must refrain from close long-term allied relations that could lead to the formation of a single federal state with other countries, with the exception of Belarus and two or three other CIS countries. Today, Russia's alliances with anyone – with the exception of the CIS countries I have mentioned – would either mean becoming subordinate to a powerful state (in case of alliance with a powerful country), or constant subsidizing of a weaker partner (in case of alliance with a weak country).

Nevertheless, we must be able to rapidly form coalitions and quasi-alliances with various partners and for specific, primarily economic, purposes. Today, struggle for a better position in the world markets means fighting by using strategic partnerships and various alliances, both state, non-state, and mixed.

If we recognize the paramount importance of modernization and formation of a dynamic modern post-industrial market economy in Russia, we must promote Russian goods and services in the broadest and richest markets, above all in the US and Western European markets.[13]

Russia must pursue aggressive export policies by making use of its competitive advantages in a number of new high-tech fields. The Defense Ministry used a very simple way to find out in which areas we hold competitive advantage. They simply examined which of our technologies are being stolen or bought legally.

In particular, Russia's competitive advantage lies in the following fields of high-end technologies:
- development and production of fundamental types of space systems;
- a number of biotechnologies; genetic engineering;
- a number of sectors in the field of nuclear engineering and nuclear safety;
- microwave electronics;
- civil airplanes;
- applied mathematics; production of computer and network software;
- complex computer architecture.

---

13 When visiting China, I heard that Chinese leader Deng Xiaoping in his time had set the task of penetrating the US market above all things and securing the Chinese positions on the market at all costs. Such missions have not been formulated in Russia as yet. I am sure that this must be one of the most important objectives in our strategy of Russian national security and our national policy.

It is clear that this is not a complete list of all fields where we can supply competitive products on the world market.

It would also be possible to give a more detailed description of the technologies that are in demand not only in Asian states but also in the world's most developed countries. Incidentally, we have achieved tangible results in a number of fields. And yet, we do not have a functioning specific policy in this area and still fail to make use of our competitive advantages.

11. Importance of Government Policy with Regard to the Russian Language

This issue is, without any exaggeration, directly related to the national security policy. Today, Spain can make an economic and political return to Latin America primarily owing to its cultural association with Latin America and its long-term support for the Spanish language in the region. Language is a powerful tool to safeguard many of Russia's interests. From this point of view, there are great opportunities to be used in many regions of the world, apart from the near-abroad countries. In particular, this applies to Israel, roughly one sixth of whose population is made up of Russian-speaking people. They even have their own dynamic political parties.

Elaborating on the foreign policy component of the Russian national security policy from the regional point of view, we can emphasize the following in the first place:

- maintaining equal and mutually beneficial relations with the United States, with the principal purposes of advancing civil high-tech products made by Russian businesses in the US and world markets, ensuring strategic stability, and achieving a greater degree of certainty in the international military-political sphere;
- forming new relations with the European Union as Russia's closest counterpart in the civilization and cultural respect; implementation of Russian-initiated large-scale projects targeting the EU in the field of power engineering, telecommunications, transcontinental Eurasian transport systems, etc.;
- securing concurrent strategic partnership relations with China and India, with simultaneous development of cooperation in resolving a number of coincident or parallel problems in international security within the framework of the flexible Russia–China–India "triangle"; maintaining and enhancing cooperation with these countries in the military-technological sphere, on the one hand, and promoting collaboration in the field of civil industry and economy, on the other hand;
- pursuing a long-term power engineering policy in the Far East, above all within the Russia–China–Japan "triangle" (Russian energy supplies, includ-

ing natural gas and electric power, Japanese investments, and Chinese market);[14]

- naturally, relations with the near-abroad countries, including the CIS countries, Baltic states and Finland, must be a top priority of the Russian national security policy. It is necessary to promote mutually beneficial and in-depth economic, social and cultural relations in a number of the CIS countries, and ensure the dominant influence of the CIS transnational companies (first of all, with a Russian core) over other companies.

The CIS Collective Security Agreement must remain valid in the foreseeable future. We must develop and intensify cooperation among the CIS countries in fighting terrorism, organized crime and drug traffickers.

Another fundamental goal is maintaining and building up the common information space in the territory of the former Soviet Union, by pursuing a coordinated target-oriented policy relying on the television and other mass media, by developing telecommunications systems, and by intensifying scientific collaboration and cultural exchanges, etc.

12. On the Military Component of the Russian National Security Policy

The military component of the Russian national security policy will continue to play a very important, if not fundamental, role in the foreseeable future, especially if we achieve a new level of development of the Armed Forces and the defense research and production potential that would meet contemporary standards. Russia's military power must be made more compact within the next eight to ten years. However, in the long run, it must also become much more efficient. The same applies to the entire complex of forces and means of nuclear deterrence at the heart of Russian military power, for there is no alternative to nuclear deterrence in the next 50 years, albeit in a modernized form that takes into account the specific nature of "the second nuclear age."[15]

---

14 Implementation of this policy can become a very important component in ensuring the stabilization of economic and political relations, including in the military-political sphere, as well as in securing the inviolability of Russia's frontiers. This is a vital interest of Russia's national security. Japan and many other countries of the region are also interested in such development. Provided China receives Russian electric power and natural gas at stable and moderate prices, the future Chinese leaders could abandon their claims to the oil-rich continental shelf in the area of the Spratley Islands. Moreover, the use of the energy sources in question would lead to significant improvement in the environmental condition both in China and Japan, which suffers from acid rains originating in China where coal is used on a large scale.

15 For more information please refer to: Kokoshin, A. A., *Yadernoye sderzhivaniye i natsionalnaya bezopasnost Rossii.*

We can formulate the following components of the Russian nuclear deterrence policy, in addition to what is stipulated in the National Security Concept of the Russian Federation, and in the Military Doctrine of the Russian Federation:

- We must elaborate flexible and multiple strategies for putting into play a threat to use nuclear weapons, in case Russia's vital interests are threatened. On the one hand, this will increase the degree of uncertainty for our potential enemies. On the other hand, it will enable us to demonstrate our determination to resort to nuclear weapons in case of a critical situation, which will deter the enemy from further escalation. We must develop the art of "strategic gesture" and build up an "escalation procedure" consisting of a greater number of stages with regard to exercising the nuclear deterrence effect in case of conflicts and critical situations endangering Russia's vital interests.
- We must preserve the complete independence of Russia's entire nuclear deterrence potential, including the missile attack warning system (MAWS), space control system (SCS) and strategic reconnaissance means.
- The deterrence means must enable us to deliver unacceptable damage to the potential enemy, regardless of the type of response we can resort to. The level of possible damage must be calculated based on consideration of the primary, secondary and tertiary consequences of the nuclear attack, as well as on ecological, medical, biological and other factors.
- Qualitative improvement in nuclear ammunition and its delivery means must be regarded as a priority in developing our deterrence capacity. This would enable us to ensure the deterrence effect with regard to any potential aggressor given far lower ceilings for strategic nuclear weapons and lower reserves of pre-strategic and tactical nuclear weapons. We must also enhance our ability to overcome the enemy's ballistic missile defense, including space-based defense.
- We must achieve a new level of integrity and compactness of the entire nuclear deterrence system. In both the strategic and the conceptual respect, Russia's nuclear deterrence potential must involve all nuclear means: strategic, pre-strategic, tactical, and also MAWS, SCS, strategic reconnaissance means, etc. The issues pertinent to operational control shall be in the hands of chief decision-makers from the Defense Ministry and Central Command. The Security Council of the Russian Federation shall have supervising authority.

Ratification of the START-2 agreement serves the interests of Russian national security, although the treaty falls short in some respects. It is necessary to begin START-3 negotiations as soon as possible. Within the framework of this treaty, Russia and the United States must reduce their absolute limits down to

1,500 nuclear warheads and even less. Only radical (bilateral, on a contractual basis) reduction in strategic nuclear forces can enable Russia adequately to develop its conventional forces and facilities, for in this sphere we have been lagging behind the West since as early as the 1970s.

In general, without accelerated development of conventional forces—Ground Forces, Air Forces (including anti-aircraft defense facilities) and the Navy—it will be impossible to ensure reliable and convincing deterrence against any aggression against Russia at a level much lower than that of the threshold of potential use of nuclear weapons.

A modular approach must dominate in the formation of new units and forces. It will enable us to form corresponding complex units, complying with specific targets, in a flexible and task-oriented way.

The Russian military reform program must include accurate figures of long-term budget allocations and numbers of units and forces, as well as a description of their technical equipment. A dramatic increase in expenditure on research and development, including fundamental scientific research, for military purposes must be a key aspect of military reform. We must lay the foundations for the radical re-equipping of the Army with brand new weapons, by supporting and developing Russia's defense research and technologies. It may not be possible to begin such a large-scale re-equipping exercise any sooner than the end of the first decade of the 21st century, even if we ensure a 10 per cent annual increase in GDP. Until then, and even beyond, we must preserve the most valuable and efficient weapons and military equipment by ensuring their proper maintenance and modernization.

Military reform in Russia means, in the first place, the formation of units and forces of new types, as well as the development and practicing of new forms and methods of utilizing the Armed Forces in combat operations and in peacetime. New forms and ways of waging wars, designed to be used over at least 25–30 years, must be stipulated in the training regulations and in the instructions for operations and strategy.

Russia's military power must be totally independent. It must not be a constituent of any coalitions, except alliances within the framework of the CIS Collective Security Treaty. First and foremost, the forces and facilities of nuclear deterrence – both means of destruction themselves and MAWS, as well as the activities in the field of ballistic missile defense – must as far as possible be independent. Any activities aimed at the creation of joint ballistic missile defense or MAWS outside the bounds of the CIS do not appear productive, at least in the next decade. Such actions would limit Russia's sovereignty, as far as its military aspect is concerned.

At the same time, Russia must uphold its interests by maintaining and strengthening the policy aimed at the limitation and reduction of arms on an equitable basis, as well as the policy of nonproliferation of weapons of mass destruction and missile technologies. Russia will have to employ creativity and initiative in pursuing these interests, in order to compensate – as in some other cases – for the weakness of its economic, military and political positions by exerting intellectual efforts and exercising dynamism.

13. Fundamental Science as a Crucial Factor for Maintaining Russia's National Security

The broad development of fundamental science in all its main fields is a far rarer phenomenon than many people believe. Russia is one of the few countries that can boast such development. Unfortunately, both fundamental and applied sciences have been in a critical state in the past years of reforms. This situation came chiefly as a result of the drastic reduction in funds allocated to science, a drop in the prestige of research activities, and lower demand for science on the part of the top authorities.

Consequently, we are facing a substantial drain of highly skilled human resources to the most developed countries and the most prestigious universities and other research institutions. This is just another piece of evidence confirming the high prestige and level of Soviet and Russian science.

We should welcome the actions of the new government, as it has begun paying more attention to Russian science. However, state policy must be backed up with large-scale measures to support research activities and education.

In speaking about the importance of science for the national economic and post-industrial development, we must emphasize that today's fundamental sciences—physics, chemistry, biology, and mathematics—mean the most competitive civil and military technologies and products of tomorrow. However, neither businessmen, nor public officials must look upon fundamental science from a utilitarian perspective. It is the mighty spurt in the development of fundamental science within the first post-war decades that enabled the United States to meet the challenge of Japan and Western Europe in the 1970s and 1980s, and to shoot ahead again in the 1990s.

Huge government investment in the research activities of NASA, the US Department of Defense and the National Science Foundation, as well as the establishment of an efficient mechanism for relocating scientific achievements from the military to the civil sector have achieved their purpose.

A mechanism like this was virtually non-existent in the Soviet Union owing to an excessive level of secrecy typical of states and societies of this type, as well as to a lack of understanding of the regularities of technological evolution and innovation processes.

In order to safeguard Russia's national security, we must resolve one of the most urgent problems faced by Russia's economy today, namely to develop a reliable mechanism of interaction between defense and civil research and development, and between research and production.

Fundamental science is among the most important means for the timely identification of threats and problems in the sphere of national security, as well as for the elaboration of measures to address these threats and problems. Alongside the natural sciences, the previous statement refers equally to the humanities, for they, too, must be developed to ensure management at all levels of government and society, including in the sphere of corporate management, that is adequate for the contemporary standards of global economic entities.

The loss of fundamental science in most of the fields, which is a possibility in the next three to five years, would likely prove even more disastrous for us than the loss of many industrial productions. History has shown that, unlike many industrial spheres, fundamental science—once lost—cannot possibly be rehabilitated, even with ample support over several generations. Germany after World War II can serve as an example.

Another very valuable asset possessed by Russia is its capacity to develop and put into operation extremely intricate engineering systems (civil and military missile and space systems, nuclear power plants, big surface and submarine battleships, civil and military airplanes, strategic nuclear forces control systems, missile attack warning systems, nuclear fusion plants, etc.) based on achievements in the sphere of the exact sciences. Apart from Russia and the United States, only two or three countries in the world have such capacities. This wealth must be preserved and amplified. We must also promote its application in the civil economy.

Originally published in *Mir i Rossiya na poroge XXI veka* [The world and Russia on the threshold of the 21st century], Moscow: MGIMO-Rosspen, 2001, pp. 10–34.

A New Turn in Russian–American Relations

Sergei Rogov

The events of September 11 brought momentous consequences for Russian–American relations.

Ten years after the end of the Cold War, the status of the relations between the two former adversaries remained vague. The ideological conflict and the geopolitical confrontation between Moscow and Washington became things of the past. However, the strategic partnership proclaimed by Clinton and Yeltsin in 1993 was never conducted. And this was not merely a result of subjective mistakes committed by the leaders of the two nations.

On the one hand, it was the lack of affinity of their principal interests, which is usually generated by the existence of a common enemy, that meant the USA and Russia failed to become strategic partners. During World War I and World War II, it was the presence of a common enemy in the international arena that led to the union of the two nations, notwithstanding fundamental ideological and political differences between the USA and Russia.

On the other hand, the 1990s became a period of unprecedented growth in the USA and a most severe crisis in Russia, which did not have a well thought-out strategy of economic and political reform. Consequently, a huge gap emerged between the power potentials of the two nations, and a clear asymmetry of their positions within the new system of international relations.

With its pretension to the role of the world's sole superpower, the USA was not prepared to regard Moscow as an equal partner. It tried to dictate the conditions for Russia's integration into the global market; it banked on NATO expansion to the former Soviet allies; it was to ignore Russia's interests in resolving regional conflicts; and it adopted a policy of reviewing the strategic military balance in its advantage.

By the late 1990s, Russia and the USA had accumulated a number of serious disagreements on a raft of economic, political and military issues. The NATO-led war against Yugoslavia in 1999 provoked the most acute crisis in Russian–American relations since the Cold War. The change of leadership in both the USA and Russia in the year 2000 allowed the crisis to be relieved, and yet the controversies between the two powers were not completely resolved.

At the summits that were held in Ljubljana and Genoa in the summer of 2001, presidents G. W. Bush and V. V. Putin agreed to resume the dialogue on all aspects of US–Russian interaction. However, the consultations that started at the level of higher state officials failed to lead to any serious shifts in the parties' positions. The Bush administration declared that it did not regard Russia as an "enemy," and intended to set up a new "strategic framework" for US–Russian relations. The USA, however, is not eager to reveal the contents of this "framework," while it continues to press for the earliest possible demolition of the previous model based on the concept of mutual nuclear containment. Washington called on Moscow to join in a common declaration of the termination of the ABM Treaty, without offering anything in return. Such an approach proved unacceptable for Russia.

In spite of apparent warming of the tone of the dialogue, Russian–American consultations had failed to bring tangible results by the fall of 2001. The USA continued to insist on the termination of the ABM Treaty, threatening to repudiate it by the end of the year. The Bush administration backed the second wave of NATO enlargement, including the possible inclusion of the Baltic nations in the alliance. There was no advance in the economic sphere either, in particular on restructuring Russia's foreign debts.

Following the terrorist attack on the USA there was an abrupt turn in US–Russian relations. Russia had long emphasized the danger of international terrorism, above all with regard to the Chechen war that started in 1999 after the raid launched by Chechen fighters into Dagestan's territory and explosions in residential buildings in Moscow and several other Russian cities. Fighting terrorism was proclaimed the priority in the Concept of National Security and doctrinal documents on foreign and military policy, which were adopted after V. V. Putin came to office. The USA and other western powers rejected the anti-terrorism interpretation of the Chechen war and condemned the methods used by the Russian military against Chechen civilians, while recognizing Russia's right to protect its sovereignty and territorial integrity.

At this point, however, the Bush administration proclaimed fighting global terrorism to be the main priority in its foreign policy. There are grounds to believe that this thesis will be reflected in the doctrinal documents, including the US National Security Strategy, which the President is due to pass to Congress in early 2002, as well as in other documents determining US foreign and military policy. Although it is far too early to come up with final conclusions, one cannot rule out that fighting terrorism will become the crucial constituent of the US international strategy, as was anti-communism in the Cold War years.

The reaction of the Russian public and authorities to the acts of terror of September 11 was appreciated in the USA. President Putin expressed his condolences to the American people and called for a minute's silence to be held in Russia to remember the victims of the anti-US terror.

A survey conducted by the Russian Public Opinion and Market Research Monitoring Agency (ROMIR) showed that 89 per cent of respondents objected to involvement by the Russian armed forces in the Afghan campaign (seven per cent were "for" the Russian army participation); 64 per cent were against providing military bases on the territory of the CIS to the United States (vs. 27 per cent); 51 per cent were against the use of Russia's air space by the USA (vs. 40 per cent). Only sharing intelligence data with the USA was supported by the majority: 51 per cent in favor vs. 39 per cent against.[1] According to the results of a survey by the All-Russian Center for Public Opinion Research (VTSIOM), 62 per cent of Russian citizens (vs. 14 per cent) believed that the US military operation would lead to destabilization of the situation in Tajikistan and Uzbekistan, while 80 per cent (vs. nine per cent) thought that it would provoke Islamic extremists to commit new acts of terror, including against Russia.[2] Nevertheless, according to the VTsIOM data, the majority of Russian citizens (57 per cent vs. 26 per cent) wanted the US military operation against terrorists to achieve success.[3]

At the same time, 71 per cent expressed their "good attitude" to the USA, while only 20 per cent said they had a "bad" attitude. Remarkably, during the NATO operation in Kosovo in spring 1999, the respective ratio was 39 per cent to 49 per cent. A survey on September 12 revealed that 80 per cent of Russian citizens believed that the September 11 terror acts were a matter "for all humankind," while only 15 per cent thought them a "US internal affair." Some 70 per cent of respondents believed the West treated Russia "as an ally in fighting international terrorism."[4]

It is noteworthy that, at the same time, conflicting attitudes to Russia are present in the USA. According to a survey conducted by the Gallup organization in spring 2001, 52 per cent of Americans expressed a "favorable" opinion about Russia, while 42 per cent said their attitude was "unfavorable." In 2000, only nine per cent regarded Russia as an "ally," and 34 per cent said it was a "friendly nation" for the United States.

The Bush administration's position was also rather ambivalent. The *Quadrennial Defense Review*, the administration's first doctrinal document, which was published on October 1, 2001 but prepared mainly before the events of September 11, runs:

An opportunity for cooperation exists with Russia. It does not pose a large-

---

1 Interfax, November 5, 2001.
2 Interfax, November 6, 2001.
3 *Ibid.*
4 www.wciom.ru/vciom/new/press120927_27.htm

scale conventional military threat to NATO. It shares some important security concerns with the United States, including the problem of vulnerability to attack by ballistic missiles from regional aggressors, the danger of accidental or unauthorized launches of strategic weapons, and the threat of international terrorism. Yet, at the same time, Russia pursues a number of policy objectives contrary to US interests.[5]

In the new conditions, the US leadership started reconsidering Russia's possible role. Earlier it had been widely believed in Washington that Russia had already lost its influence on the international scene, and Moscow's opinion could easily be ignored. However, the declaration of war on international terrorism as the key goal of US policy and the launch of military operations against Bin Laden and the Taliban regime in Afghanistan made the Bush administration redefine the priority of its relations with Russia.

First, the USA is interested in Russia's support, and even participation, in forming an international anti-terrorist coalition. As a permanent member of the UN Security Council, Russia has the right of veto, which it can use with regard to the resolutions lobbied for by US diplomats. If Russia adopts a negative stance, this may affect China's position and those of some other countries. This is the reason why the Bush administration is interested in winning Russia's support, which would create a picture of unanimous endorsement of US actions by the international community.

Second, Russia is undoubtedly the key player on the Central Asian scene of military operations. Moscow's political and military support is of considerable—and in some cases crucial—significance for the former Soviet Central Asian republics, which gained independence ten years ago. In recent years, Russia has also backed the forces of the Northern Alliance, which confronts the Taliban in Afghanistan itself. Besides, Russia maintains good relations with Iran, another influential player in Central Asia.

Third, the political problems that hinder the use of Pakistan's territory as a foothold for operations in Afghanistan drew Washington's attention to former Soviet military bases in Central Asia, which could be used for the deployment of US armed forces. The use of the bases would not be feasible without Russia's consent.

In the first days after the acts of terror, the Russian leadership was in no rush to make any decisions. As the *Wall Street Journal* put it, "President Putin has to make the most difficult choice since he has been in the presidential office: he must decide how far Russia can go in its support of America's war against terrorism."[6]

---

5 *Quadrennial Defense Review Report.* Department of Defense, September 30, 2001, pp. 4–5.
6 *The Wall Street Journal*, September 25, 2001.

In Moscow, Deputy Secretary of State Armitage and Deputy Foreign Minister Trubnikov held negotiations on the issues of cooperation in fighting terrorism. Intensive contacts took place at a higher level too. Presidents G. W. Bush and V. V. Putin had several telephone conversations. Russian Security Council Secretary Rushailo and Chief of General Staff Kvashnin visited the Central Asian states. On September 22, V. V. Putin held a six-hour talk with the chiefs of power-wielding ministries and law-enforcement bodies. The President also met with the leaders of the Russian Duma and the Federation Council.

On September 24, President Putin delivered a TV address to Russian citizens. He said that Russia's participation in the anti-terrorist operation will comprise several parts. V. V. Putin said that "the Russian Federation has been fighting international terrorism on its own for a long time, and has on many occasions called on the international community to join in the efforts." He confirmed Russia's readiness to contribute to fighting terror, and pointed to the growing role of the UN and the UN Security Council, as international institutions that had been designed to ensure international security, and to the need to improve international legal foundations, which would allow an effective and efficient response to acts of terror.

The President outlined five points for Russia's course of action:

- First, Russia will develop active international cooperation in intelligence service sphere. Moscow intends to share the information at its disposal concerning the places of deployment of international terrorists and fighters' training bases.
- Second, Russia is prepared to open its air space to aircraft carrying humanitarian cargoes to the area of the ongoing anti-terrorist operation.
- Third, Russia has coordinated its position with its allies among the Central Asian states. In particular, this concerns the possibility of using these states' airfields for operations against terrorists.
- Fourth, Russia is also prepared, if necessary, to take part in international search-and-rescue operations.
- Fifth, Russia will expand its cooperation with the internationally recognized Afghan government (the Northern Alliance) and provide its armed forces with additional aid in the form of deliveries of arms and combat vehicles.

Other, more extended, forms of cooperation between Russia and the USA are also possible, however the "extent and essence of such cooperation will directly depend on the general level and nature of our relations" as well as on "mutual understanding as far as fighting international terrorism is concerned."

To help in coordinating activities in all the above-mentioned spheres, the President established a group chaired by Defense Minister Ivanov. The group's task is to gather and analyze all new information and to carry out practical interaction with the operation participants.

Putin stressed that the events in Chechnya cannot be viewed out of the context of the struggle against international terrorism. He suggested that "all members of illegal armed groups and those claiming to be political activists should without delay abandon their contacts with international terrorists and their organizations." The federal authorities are prepared to discuss issues related to disarmament of illegal armed groups and integration of their members into Chechnya's peaceful life.

President Bush welcomed Moscow's decision. Secretary of State Colin Powell said that the USA was "pleased" with Putin's statement, underscoring the fact that Russia's backing of the Northern Alliance would "help" combat terrorism.

US National Security Adviser Condoleezza Rice said that "in a new strategic framework, Russia promptly joined the war against terrorism." According to her, Russia had made its "strategic choice...in favor of the alliance and cooperation with the West instead of dallying with 'third world' countries."[7]

The US press started a lively discussion of the new turn in Russian–US relations. The *Washington Post* wrote in its editorial:

Russian President Vladimir Putin's announcement of Russian support for US military operations against Afghanistan this week represented a significant step by his government toward cooperation with the West—larger, even, than it might appear at first to many Americans...The Russian leader moved farther than he ever has before toward accepting what, in Moscow, is still a controversial notion: that Russia's best future lies in integrating with the liberal democracies and open economies of the West, and sharing in their wealth and security cooperation rather than trying to establish a competing center of power.[8]

The *New York Times* drew the following conclusion:

[C]ombined with the Russian effort to rally Central Asian countries to the American side, Putin's pledge provides crucial support to the international coalition that the White House is seeking to build in the wake of the terrorist attacks. It seems that after long reflection and some doubt, Russia has finally tied its fate to the western anti-terrorist camp.[9]

According to the *Christian Science Monitor* "of all the nations that the United States would like to see as members of its global anti-terrorism coalition,

---

7 *The Washington Post*, October 18, 2001.
8 *The Washington Post*, September 27, 2001.
9 *The New York Times*, September 25, 2001.

strategically none may prove as essential to achieving success as Russia."[10] The fact that

> the USA and Russia are once again friends confirms the truth of the saying that there are neither permanent friends, nor permanent enemies, but only permanent interests…A common adversary helps clear the mind. All those issues that US President G. Bush and Russian President Vladimir Putin discussed in the recent past—the US national anti-missile system, denunciation of the ABM treaty of 1972, NATO expansion, Russia's joining of the World Trade Organization—have fallen into the background for the time being.[11]

These assessments show that an essentially new period may start in relations between Russia and the USA, which will be based on the commonality of the principal priorities of the national security of the two powers. For the first time since 1945 Russia and the USA have a common enemy. It is common because Bin Laden's organization used to provide support to Chechen fighters, while the Talibs pose a great danger to the current regimes in the former Soviet republics of Central Asia. Should these regimes fall, any new power will adhere to more pro-Islamic and anti-Russian positions.

Russia and the USA have often been allies throughout the two centuries and more of American history. It was the presence of a common enemy that united the two nations, which had different political and economic systems. The Cold War was the only exception to this.

Naturally, the US–Russian asymmetry that emerged after the Cold War hinders the formation of equal-partner relations between the nations. However, a political alliance does not require the parties to be equally powerful. It is sufficient that they share their principal national interests. To illustrate this with an example, one may refer to the far more asymmetric, but very efficient, US–Israeli alliance, which has not been instituted by any formal treaties, and yet is no less firm than officially sealed alliances between the USA and South Africa or even the USA and NATO.

While speaking at a meeting of the leaders of Russia's Armed Forces on November 12, 2001, V. V. Putin stressed:

The content of the program documents concerning defense, and the analysis of the recent months' rapidly changing situation in the world, demonstrate that we have rightly identified the nature of new threats to Russia's national security. It is not merely particular nations that are threatened by terrorism, but the entire system of strategic stability.

Bin Laden's organization or the Taliban pose a threat to our national interests. Once the USA and Russia come to the conclusion that they have a com-

---

10 *The Christian Science Monitor*, September 27, 2001.
11 *Ibid.*

mon enemy, an opportunity—and even a necessity—emerges for them to form mechanisms for cooperation and determine the conditions for mutual assistance. However, the transition to this new model will depend on Moscow and Washington being able to agree on their approaches to solving specific problems that have, until recently, been addressed by the two nations from different perspectives.

In recent years, one might have formed the impression that the USA was playing a zero-sum game against Russia in the former Soviet republics, i.e. that Washington was striving to reinforce its position in the new independent states at the expense of Moscow. It was the US activities in Central Asia—particularly the Americans' attempts to establish control over the Caspian basin energy resources—that caused especial concern in Moscow political circles. In its turn, the USA interpreted the support that Russia rendered to the Central Asian regimes in their fight against radical Islamist movements as a striving to "restore the Russian Empire."

Many American observers believe that Russia, whose troops are deployed in Tajikistan, adjacent to the Afghan border, and virtually control the bases close to the territories held by the Talibs, plays the key part in the US-led military operation. The USA wanted Russia to allow it to use its air force bases in Central Asia to conduct the planned campaign against Osama Bin Laden.[12]

In the new conditions, Russia rendered political support and logistical assistance to the deployment of the US armed forces at a number of former Soviet military bases in Central Asia. This required not only participation of Russian military and technology experts, but also agreement on the issues related to the use of the former Soviet bases by US special forces. As a result, US forces have been deployed on the territory of the former Soviet Union for the first time. However, the cooperation is unlikely to involve joint military operations.

"Mr Putin's support for George Bush marks the closest military cooperation since the end of the Cold War"[13]—pointed out the British *Guardian* newspaper, while the *Los Angeles Times* wrote:

> Russia can prove to be a valuable ally, supplying assistance to a military effort and intelligence on Islamic extremists such as Osama bin Laden and guerrilla networks in Afghanistan and Central Asia. By gaining access to bases in the republics that were part of the Soviet Union and where Russia still has great influence, such as Tajikistan and Uzbekistan, the United States gets what may prove the key region for the concentration of its forces. Russia also maintains close ties with the guerrillas of the Northern Alliance fighting against the Talibs' government in Afghanistan, which provides shelter to Bin Laden and his Al-Qaeda network.[14]

---

12 *The Wall Street Journal*, September 25, 2001.
13 *The Guardian*, September 26, 2001.
14 *The Los Angeles Times*, September 26, 2001.

In his interview published soon after the acts of terror in Washington and New York, V. V. Putin said that Russia was prepared to cooperate with the USA in the "broadest sense," but would not directly participate in military operations, for it was already engaged in fighting terrorism in Chechnya, and could not afford to open a second front. Besides, Putin said that Russia was concerned over the possible inflow of refugees into Tajikistan and other former Soviet republics once the conflict started, which may "destabilize the political situation there."

During his visit to Germany at the end of September, Putin ruled out the possibility of Russia's direct involvement in military operations on Afghan territory. "For us, direct involvement in the military operations in Afghanistan would be the same as the USA's return to Vietnam," said Russia's leader during his meeting with the editors-in-chief of the key German mass media. V. V. Putin pointed out that Russia's partners "are aware of and recognize" the inappropriateness of the use of the Russian armed forces in Afghanistan.

Defense Minister S. Ivanov said that "Russia is virtually fighting terrorism on two fronts today: directly in Chechnya, and by lending its support to the Northern Alliance in Afghanistan." Ivanov stated at the same time: "we are not planning to participate in the anti-terrorist operation on the territory of Afghanistan in any form—either with fire, or people, or sword."

There is a certain concern in Russia that, once the USA finds a foothold in the Central Asian states, these states will leave Moscow's sphere of influence, as did the countries of Central Europe, when the US military arrived to conduct its operations in the Balkans. Even more importantly, the Russian military are afraid that the Americans might try to impose a puppet government in Afghanistan and—as soon as a pro-western government is installed there—start building a long-distance pipeline to pump Uzbek and Turkmen oil and gas to Pakistan. If such a development takes place without Moscow's consent, Moscow will virtually lose its influence in the region.

A considerable part of the Russian political elite still treats the USA with suspicion, being quite aware of the risks involved in providing the United States with permission to conduct its military operations from territory that fall within Russia's sphere of influence. Besides, there is concern that Russia may become a target for Islamic extremists, should it get involved in another war similar to the one in Chechnya.[15]

The Bush administration tried to dispel apprehensions with regard to American intentions in Central Asia. In her interview to the *Izvestiya* newspaper, Condoleezza Rice maintained that the USA was motivated by "the spirit of Ljubljana and Geneva," and did not intend to force Russia out of Central

---

15 *The Guardian*, September 26, 2001.

Asia, recognizing that Russia had its interests in the region.[16] In early November, Defense Secretary Rumsfeld visited Moscow in order to gain Russia's consent for US military expansion to the former Soviet republics.

According to the *Guardian* newspaper,

> the Americans did promise not to establish permanent military bases in Central Asia, and have undertaken to cooperate with the Russians in support of the Northern Alliance. There is also an informal agreement between Washington and Moscow that neither would seek to impose a regime in Afghanistan without further consultations, and that no oil and gas pipelines would be contemplated without a further mutual agreement. For the moment, therefore, Moscow and Washington are in step.[17]

Although Russian public opinion is still apprehensive of the possible intentions of the USA, opinion surveys reflect support for President Putin's actions on the part of the majority of Russian citizens. In a survey conducted on October 13, 54 per cent of respondents favored the President's stance on cooperation with the USA, while 25 per cent expressed their disapproval.[18] A survey of October 27 showed that 69 per cent of the population advocated an improvement in US–Russian relations. This point of view was expressed not only by 73 per cent of the President's supporters, but by 62 per cent of Zyuganov's followers.[19]

Among the respondents of a 1997 survey 48 per cent regarded the USA as an enemy, but this number had dropped to only 13 per cent by November 2001.[20] Surveys documented that 71 per cent of Russian citizens favored the creation of Russia's alliance with the USA to fight international terrorism.[21] On the eve of Putin's visit to the USA, a survey conducted by the ROMIR agency demonstrated that Russian citizens deem fighting international terrorism (33 per cent), adhering to the ABM Treaty (16 per cent), economic problems (16 per cent), the situation in Chechnya (14 per cent), and the limitation of strategic offensive arms to be the most crucial issues pertinent to Russian–US relations.[22]

It should be pointed out that the new turn in relations between Russia and the USA produced a dramatic effect on American public attitudes. A CBS survey conducted on November 13–14, i.e. during Putin's visit to the USA, revealed that 25 per cent of respondents considered Russia an ally, and 55 per

16 *Izvestiya*, October 15, 2001.
17 *The Guardian*, September 26, 2001.
18 Interfax, October 18, 2001.
19 Interfax, November 1, 2001.
20 Interfax, November 9, 2001.
21 Interfax, November 18, 2001.
22 www.romir.ru/sociopolit/actual/11_2001/us-russia-relations.htm.

cent considered it a friendly nation. Only five per cent regarded Russia as an unfriendly country, and another five per cent as an enemy.[23] There has been no precedent for such a positive attitude to Russia in the USA since World War II.

Cooperation between the two nations will encompass political—rather than military and technical—aspects of interaction. Will Russia and the USA eventually come up with a joint strategy that has prospects? At the current stage, the parties' stances regarding a political settlement in Afghanistan are rather close. Both Russia and the USA believe that decisions that are made concerning the post-conflict settlement must be implemented under the UN's aegis. The future Afghan leadership in Kabul must represent all ethnic groups living in Afghanistan, and must command broad international support. For all that, both Russia and Afghanistan oppose the Taliban's participation in the new Afghan government, although the American side does not rule out the inclusion of "moderate" Talibs in the government. And yet, the USA has failed to divide the Taliban from within.

After the meeting of the US–Russian workgroup in Moscow in late October, the sides agreed that "the Taliban movement must not be represented in the future state authorities of the country." Apparently, the role of Russia as a US ally will continue to expand.

Germany's Chancellor Gerhard Schroeder stated without delay that the West should "reassess" the situation in Chechnya, thus making it clear that it is worthwhile examining the possibilities for Russia's membership of NATO. Replying to a question concerning the UK's attitude to Putin's assertion that fighting international terrorism includes fighting terrorists in Chechnya, a UK Foreign Ministry spokesman said that "owing to the acts of terror in the USA, attention is presently focused on the terrorism originating in Afghanistan." He did not think the situation should be associated with events in Chechnya or Northern Ireland.

The Bush administration called on separatist Chechen rebels "to cut their ties with international terrorist groups" that provide them with weapons to fight for their independence, and advised the Chechens to comply with the Kremlin's proposals for peace negotiations.[24] "To the extent that there are terrorists in Chechnya, Arab terrorists associated with the al-Qaeda organization, I believe they ought to be brought to justice," Bush said. "We do believe there are some al-Qaeda folks in Chechnya."[25]

Answering a question concerning the 72-hour ultimatum to begin peace talks, delivered by President Putin to the Chechen rebels, White House spokesman Ari Fleischer said: "we welcome the steps by the Russians to engage the

23 CBS News Poll, November 13–14, 2001.
24 *The Washington Post*, September 27, 2001.
25 *Ibid.*

Chechen leadership." Fleischer also denied any suggestion of a link between the US support for Russia and Russia's assistance in the US anti-terrorist efforts.[26]

The US administration's expressions of support for the position of Russia, which has on many occasions blamed the war in Chechnya on international Islamic extremists, mark a considerable shift in the US attitude to the issue.[27] Previously, over several years, the USA had harshly criticized Russia for "violating human rights in the separatist republic." The change in tack came directly after Moscow proposed that the United States use Russian military bases and air space to wage its war on terrorism.

According to *The Times* newspaper,

> the West's anger roused by the terrorist attacks on America may have determined the fate of the Chechen Islamists fighting against Russia, after US President George W. Bush took the side of Russia's President Vladimir Putin in order to unite in a single front against the separatists. At present, this is the most convincing sign of the strengthening cooperation between Washington and Moscow in fighting terrorism. The White House called on the Chechens to cut all contacts with international terrorist groups such as Osama bin Laden "immediately and unconditionally."[28]

The prospect of allied relations will be very consequential with regard to those issues that have caused the greatest controversies between Russia and the USA in recent years.

First of all, it pertains to the problem of missile defense and the proclaimed intention of the Bush administration to abandon the ABM Treaty. According to *Newsweek* data, after the terror attacks only 18 per cent of Americans believed that more money should be spent on missile defense, while 71 per cent thought it appropriate to finance other security measures.[29]

Of particular significance was the refusal of Democrats to try to forestall funding of the further planning of the NMD, which ran counter to the ABM Treaty. Shortly before the terrorist operation, by 13 votes (Democrats) to 12 votes (Republicans), the Senate Committee on Armed Services had voted to cut the budget for missile defense by $1.3 billion, which was now to be divided up and spent on fighting terrorism and purchasing conventional weapons. To avoid bitter debate on the issue in Congress, the Committee Chairman Carl Levin agreed to change the language, making a compromise with the Republicans, and thus helping to pass the National Defense Authorization Act for the fiscal year 2002.[30] "We are focusing on those issues that we agree upon,"[31] said Mr Levin.

---

26 *Ibid.*
27 *Ibid.*
28 *The Times*, September 28, 2001.
29 www.pollingreport.com/terror/htm, 19.09.2001.
30 *The Washington Post*, September 19, 2001.
31 AP, September 19, 2001.

Apparently, the USA intends to continue large-scale development of the missile defense system. The preparation of the Alaska base (felling of the forest) for deployment there of five strategic interceptor missiles has been under way since August, which may be in contravention of the ABM Treaty, which provides exclusively for an area in North Dakota to be used as a US interceptor base. In theory, the issue could still be resolved by signing an additional protocol to the ABM Treaty, as was done in 1974. However, the Bush administration is aiming to remove any restrictions on anti-ballistic missile defense and repudiate the treaty itself. The Pentagon intends to complete the deployment in 2004, although the majority of experts believe it may happen a few years later, since the project to develop an interceptor has not been completed yet. Some representatives of the Bush administration continue to insist that the US should unilaterally back out of the ABM Treaty unless a compromise is reached with Russia, suggesting that the USA should withdraw from the treaty even before the end of 2001. However, President Bush has not so far set a particular deadline.

There are hopes in Moscow that the threat of new terrorist attacks will make Washington abandon its program of developing the National Missile Defense (NMD) system, which—should it be deployed—would in 10–15 years call into question Russia's potential for nuclear containment.[32]

In October, Russia declared its intention of scrapping its military bases in Cuba and Vietnam. The closure of the bases was motivated by strategic military and economic considerations. "This decision is another indication that the Cold War is over. President Putin understands that Russia and America are no longer adversaries,"[33] said George Bush.

During the summit of the ASEAN countries in Shanghai, the American side suggested for the first time that it might abandon its strict approach to the ABM Treaty. While earlier the Bush administration had insisted that Russia accept the abolition of the treaty, now the US leaders started talking about possible adoption of coordinated amendments. In this case the ABM Treaty would remain in force, although in a modified form.

At the end of October, the Pentagon announced that a preliminary test of the anti-missile technologies was being postponed for an indefinite period, so that no accusations of ABM Treaty violations might arise. The decision, declared by US Defense Secretary Donald Rumsfeld, demonstrated at least a symbolic departure from the administration's earlier assertions that the ABM Treaty of 1972, which bans national anti-ballistic missile systems, must not prevent the USA from developing such a system. "We will not violate the ABM treaty while it is in force," said Mr. Rumsfeld. "...to keep from having it suggested

---

32 *The Guardian*, September 26, 2001.
33 Reuters, October 18, 2001.

that we might not be keeping that commitment, we have voluntarily restrained our ballistic missile defense test program."[34]

Newsday wrote: "it looks like nobody in the Bush administration wants to risk relations with Russia for the sake of observing the BMD test schedule."[35] According to the *New York Times*, President Bush's "declaration of war on global terror after Sept. 11 now requires that he stay on good terms with Mr Putin, and with European allies that largely share Russia's view that the ABM treaty should be preserved." However, the administration is trying to present "the latest development not as a pragmatic *quid pro quo* with the Russians, but as an American breakthrough in the administration's constant efforts to change the Kremlin's mind about the plans for missile defense."[36]

At the end of October, the Pentagon also announced a shift in the missile defense schedule and a postponement of three missile defense tests under the NMD program. Furthermore, another test kinetic intercept of an ICBM has been postponed until the end of November (i.e. after Putin's visit to the USA), while the terms for the tests of sea-based radars were not defined.[37]

Remarkably, the US President's National Security Adviser Condoleezza Rice said that an evolution is evident in Russia's approach to the ABM Treaty: "I think the Russians are beginning to see that what we have said all along is true: that the near-term program for missile defense, which is really a testing and evaluation program, is not actually a threat to them."[38] This served as grounds to assume that Russia may agree to permit the tests — and that the USA, in turn, will give up its intention of immediately abandoning the Antiballistic Missile Treaty.

Soon after the USA announced the postponement of the tests, there appeared suggestions in the press that an agreement in principle had been reached on strategic arms. It was reported that the Bush administration was prepared to abandon its intention of pulling out of the ABM Treaty, if in turn it received a free hand to test various NMD components. At the same time, the Pentagon allegedly agreed to a "gradual reduction by both nations of the number of strategic warheads to between 1,750 and 2,250 each."[39]

However, Russia's Foreign Minister I. Ivanov's visit to Washington for talks with US Secretary of State Colin Powell showed that the sides have not been able to overcome their disagreements. After the talks, Mr Ivanov said that it was "premature" to speak of any accords with the USA regarding missile defense.

34 *The International Herald Tribune*, October 26, 2001.
35 *The Newsday*, November 16, 2001.
36 *The New York Times*, October 28, 2001.
37 *The International Herald Tribune*, October 26, 2001.
38 *The New York Times*, October 28, 2001.
39 *The Washington Post*, November 1, 2001.

He expressed his satisfaction with the manner in which "the American side responded to our proposals concerning deep strategic offensive reductions."

At a briefing in Washington prior to his departure for a visit to Russia, Defense Secretary Rumsfeld refused to confirm allegations that an agreement concerning the NMD issue had been reached. Mr. Rumsfeld said that neither an agreement on missile defense, nor any further development with regard to the 1972 ABM Treaty would be achieved until the presidents of the two countries met and sorted through the remaining important issues.

During his meeting with Mr. Rumsfeld on November 3, President Putin referred to the cooperation between the two countries' "power structures" as an important aspect of the bilateral dialogue, since "it creates an essential atmosphere of trust in all other spheres." One may judge the nature of the military cooperation between the relevant services of the two powers by the talks that were held by the defense ministers of the USA and Russia with the participation of Deputy Chief of Strategic Planning and Policy of the Joint Chiefs of Staff General Keith Dayton, First Deputy Chief of the General Staff, head of the Main Operations Directorate Colonel General Yury Baluyevsky, and Chief of the Main Intelligence Directorate of the General Staff V. Korabelnikov. Above all the composition of the US and Russian delegations points to the fact that the sides are continuing their active exchange of intelligence information. In addition, as US Ambassador to Russia Alexander Vershbow admitted when speaking to journalists, the exchange "is now reciprocal." The Ambassador stressed the importance of the development of the process.

The problem of strategic arms reduction was also discussed during Mr. Rumsfeld's visit. This was the reason why the Chief of Strategic Missile Forces, Colonel General N. Solovtsov was also a member of the Russian delegation. Evidently, so far the sides have not been able to come up with a resolution formula that would satisfy both Moscow and Washington, but S. Ivanov pointed out that both parties were prepared to "follow the road of cutting strategic offensive weapons with absolutely open and transparent verification." He also stressed that there was an opportunity to enhance the process. With regard to the NMD problem, Mr. Rumsfeld said that it should be left to the presidents to resolve.

Thus, the apparently imminent confrontation on the NMD issue at least seems to have been put off for the time being. Moreover, there is the prospect of a serious compromise with regard to arms control.

On the one hand, it seems feasible to negotiate a new agreement to halt offensive strategic arms (START-3). Russia and the USA can agree to impose a quantitative restriction on the strategic arsenal at a level of 1,500–2,000 warheads, with either party having the authority to decide on the composition and structure of its strategic forces within the common limits established. Simultaneously, many previous restrictions would be canceled, including the ban on installing divided warheads with individual targeting on intercontinental ballistic missiles. As far as verification is concerned, the parties may agree to introduce minor amendments, but otherwise preserve the verification procedures envisaged by the START-1 Treaty.

On the other hand, there is an opportunity to maintain the principal provisions of the ABM pact while amending those articles of the treaty that are concerned with restrictions on the testing of new systems. Besides, certain amendments are to be introduced into the Protocol of 1974 regarding the number and deployment areas of the ground-based interceptor missiles.

Consequently, the strategic offensive and defensive arsenal can remain subject to verification for at least another several years, and possibly until the end of the current decade. Furthermore, if the Bush administration consents to sign new legally binding treaties that are ratified by the Senate, the general situation in the sphere of arms control will improve dramatically. If, instead of "burying" the current verification regime, the Republican administration agrees to draw up new accords, one may assume that arms control mechanism will remain effective in the foreseeable future.

A question arises in the USA: what is the point of spending billions of dollars on sophisticated missile defenses, if the actual threat to the United States emanates from a mere handful of criminals? "[W]e could not have put together a viable coalition if President Bush had already walked away from the ABM treaty,"[40] stressed President of the US Senate Committee on Foreign Relations Joseph R. Biden. While speaking to the American Jewish Congress Convention, President of the US Senate Committee on Armed Services Carl Levin said that the war on international terrorism did not serve to justify the US withdrawal from the ABM Treaty. Levin supported amending the ABM Treaty in a manner that would preserve the principal restrictions on the NMD program.[41]

As the *Washington Post* noted in its editorial, US unilateral withdrawal from the ABM Treaty would undermine the global strategic balance:

> It would be an even greater mistake now, when what is at stake is not just the testing of missile defenses...but preservation of US-Russian cooperation in a military campaign in Central Asia, and encouragement of a fragile and uncertain but potentially historic move by Russia toward partnership with the West.[42]

Even the extremely right-wing *Washington Times* drew the conclusion in an editorial that "today's geopolitics may render a decision to postpone the inevitable withdrawal from the ABM treaty an advantageous concession."[43]

---

40 Remarks By Joseph R. Biden Jr., United States Senator, Delaware. Council on Foreign Relations, New York City, October 22, 2001.

41 "Missile Defense and the Terrorist Threat." Speech by Senator Carl Levin to the American Jewish Congress Convention, October 22, 2001.

42 *The Washington Post*, October 24, 2001.

43 *The Washington Times*, November 2, 2001.

Russia and the USA may agree to postpone resolving the issue of missile defense, because the existing balance will anyway be preserved in the next few years, even if large-scale research and development work continues. The deployment of five interceptor missiles in Alaska is not going to pose a serious threat to the Russian strategic forces. While the development goes on, the sides can proceed with consultations to seek a compromise solution.

In addition, Washington may not pursue intensified NMD deployments, while focusing its efforts on new military development priorities linked to plausible changes in the US defense policy as a result of the US–Russian cooperation in fighting international terrorism. For all that, the USA is not going to reject operational TMD deployment, but that is not going to be a major concern in Russia.

Another issue that arouses acute controversies between Russia and the USA is NATO expansion. Moscow is known to have a rather negative attitude to the process, especially if it involves former Soviet republics. Serious problems may also arise due to the European Union enlargement. Russia is not a member of the key organizations, such as the EU and NATO, that determine the structure of the new Europe today. The very notions of "Europe" and "European Union" have already become synonymous. That is why, if Russia has no opportunity to become a member of the EU, in effect it implies the prospect of the country's exclusion from Europe. Thus, the "window" that Peter the Great "cut through to Europe" was threatening to slam shut.

Of course, the question of Russia's joining the EU or NATO is not on the agenda today. It should not be discussed among the top-priority matters. Before the issue advances to a more practical level though, some time may be needed for Russia to gain factual experience of interaction with the West. Ultimately, the renewed Russian–American partnership might simply render pointless the next stage of NATO expansion in Central Europe, a move that is also largely opposed by the Russians.[44]

At present, new forms of interaction between Russia and the USA, Russia and NATO, as well as Russia and the EU are taking shape. Some efforts in this line have already been undertaken. Let us recall, for example, the NATO–Russia Permanent Joint Council (PJC) set up in 1997 and obstructed by the West later. Now, there is an opportunity to revive the PJC and conduct under its aegis joint Russian and NATO activities to fight terrorism. Similar affiliations can also be created between Russia and the EU to allow Russia's integration into new European defense and foreign policy. There are new openings in Russian–American relations too, including the possible signing of a mutual security agreement by the two states.

Russia is prepared to cooperate with NATO "to the extent of political inter-

---

44 *The Guardian*, September 26, 2001.

action," Russia's President Vladimir Putin stated when speaking at the Russia–European Union summit on October 3. As for the prospects for cooperation between Russia and the North Atlantic alliance, the Russian President said that NATO was undergoing transformation at present, "taking on a different shade and becoming more of a political organization." According to Mr. Putin, Russia is prepared to cooperate further. Mr. Putin also referred to his meetings with US President George Bush, "who welcomes closer ties between Russia and NATO."

Of particular significance was the Brussels meeting between President Putin and NATO Secretary General George Robertson, when the parties discussed problems related to the reinforcement of international stability and security, including joint actions in fighting terrorism. Mr. Putin stressed that Russia "is prepared for a qualitative change in its relations with NATO, as well as to enhance the European security structure." On behalf of the alliance, Lord Robertson expressed appreciation of Russia's prompt response in the wake of the acts of terror in the USA. "The recent tragic events that happened in the USA confirmed that there is much more to our relations that unites us than divides us," he said, underscoring Russia's status as a special partner of the North Atlantic alliance.

The Russian President suggested that the parties should give consideration to at least two courses of possible development in their relations: enlarging their cooperation in the political domain, and broadening cooperation in fighting terrorism. Mr. Putin said that, on the initiative of the North Atlantic alliance, a decision had been made to establish a working body that would assess the possibility of "broadening, deepening, and changing the quality of the relations between Russia and NATO."

The President of the Russian Federation also spoke of the possible expansion of NATO and a shift in the quality of the dialogue between Russia and NATO. Russia believes that NATO expansion will not guarantee the security of the member states' citizens; it is necessary to reject the old logic, when the question of the Alliance's expansion will incite destructive debates. V. V. Putin pointed out that cooperation with NATO and improvement of the European security structures are "among the principal issues today." "Within our cooperation with Europe, we must give consideration to the set-up of permanent effective structures in the sphere of security." Nevertheless, as Lord Robertson stressed, "no suggestions concerning Russia's joining NATO were put forward."

It is necessary to draw up new approaches that would help mitigate the negative consequences for Russia that would result from NATO expansion, and would allow Russia to play the part of an equal partner as far as security in Europe is concerned. In order for Russia and the North Atlantic alliance to establish genuine partnership relations, Moscow must be given access to the NATO decision-making process. This could raise cooperation to a level that would allow fulfillment of the "principle of joint responsibility for joint decisions and their joint implementation," as Russia's Foreign Minister I. Ivanov put it.

Discussions have started in the western capitals concerning a transformation of the routine mechanisms of the NATO–Russia PJC with a view to rejecting its current "19 + 1" principle, and making it a decision-making body with Russia's equal participation.[45] An alternative form of relations between Russia and the North Atlantic alliance was proposed by British Prime Minister Tony Blair in his letter to the leaders of the NATO member states and Russia. Among the proposals was the creation of a new Russia–North Atlantic Council, in which 20 governments would discuss a variety of issues of common security as equals. The issues in question would include nonproliferation of nuclear arms and peace support operations. The council would replace the Permanent Joint Council set up in 1997, which, according to Mr. Blair, no longer conforms to the relations established among the nations after the terror acts of September 11. The suggestion is to set up the new council before the NATO summit in Prague in November 2002.[46] Such a scenario would virtually imply the Russian Federation's membership of NATO, although without Moscow's signing the Washington Treaty of 1949, which established the principle of collective defense, and without Russia's participation in the NATO military organization.

To conclude the 8th European Union–Russia summit, the summit participants issued a joint statement on October 3. The statement pledges active joint efforts by Russia and the EU to combat international terrorism. In their joint statement, the sides also gave consideration to an entire range of issues related to cooperation between Russia and the European Union. For the first time, the EU expressed its support for the Russian leadership's efforts aimed at political settlement in the Chechen republic. It was decided that joint bodies of Russia and the European Union would hold meetings at least twice a year in order to discuss the issues pertaining to their cooperation.

Economic questions are of great consequence in Russia's relations with the West. The conditions of Russia's integration into the global market cannot be regarded as satisfactory.

Foreign debt repayment is an extremely heavy burden on the Russian economy. Around one third of Russia's total federal budget is allocated to this. The situation may grow still more complicated in the coming years. In 2003, the servicing of the foreign debt will require around $20 billion. Meanwhile, the western creditors are very slow to resolve the problem of restructuring Russia's foreign debts.

---

45 *The Washington Post*, November 15, 2001.
46 *The Times*, November 17, 2001.

Serious problems also arise in connection with Russia's accession to the WTO. If no favorable entry conditions are provided for the transition period, the Russian economy will prove uncompetitive if customs barriers are removed, which may provoke another economic crisis. There has been a certain advance in the negotiations on the matter lately. Russia's accession to the WTO, which had been perceived as a distant prospect, was scheduled for early 2002 after negotiations between US Trade Representative Robert Zoellick and Russian official representatives at the end of September. And yet, a number of controversies concerning the specific conditions of Russia's entry remain unresolved.

US Commerce Secretary Donald Evans visited Moscow too. After expressing his high opinion of Russia's economic success in recent years, Mr. Evans said: "We are considering whether or not the Russian economy can be deemed a market-based economy and that is an answer we will not have for months."[47]

However, at the end of October the White House started consultations with Congress concerning the ending of application to Russia of the Jackson–Vanik Amendment, which limits trade between the two countries, as was envisaged by the agreements achieved by the presidents of the two nations at the Shanghai summit.[48] US Congressman Tom Lantos, the leader of the Democrats on the House of Representatives International Relations Committee, said there was a high probability that the operation of the Jackson–Vanik Amendment would be terminated in spring 2002.[49] Mr. I. Ivanov called the beginning of the procedure for the termination of "the most obnoxious relic of the Cold War in Russian–American relations" an "encouraging sign."

Influential senators Richard Lugar (a Republican from Indiana) and Joseph Biden (a Democrat from the state of Delaware) brought forward an initiative envisaging writing off a part of the Soviet debts. The suggestion is being considered by the Bush administration, which has not decided on this yet.[50] And yet, the US Senate Committee on Foreign Relations voted to write off $3.5 billion, if Russia agrees to spend the money on destruction of nuclear and chemical weapons, as well as other purposes agreed with the USA.[51]

The new sentiment in Congress was reflected in the statement of November 7 titled "US–Russia Partnership: New Time, New Beginning" which was prepared by Republican Congressman Curt Weldon with the participation of 85 House and Senate members from both parties.

Our bilateral relations have too often been focused on military issues that have often aroused a conflict of interests. It will be advisable for the American policy with

---

47 *The Wall Street Journal*, October 17, 2001.
48 Reuters, October 26, 2001.
49 Reuters, November 2, 2001.
50 *The Washington Post*, November 4, 2001.
51 AP, November 14, 2001.

respect to Russia in the 21st century to be integrated, and include a variety of other interests of the USA and Russia.[52]

However, there are many obstacles in the way of new relations, i.e. of cooperation and position interaction. The inertia of confrontation and distrust remains considerable, in spite of the ongoing changes. Some circles in the West have an inappropriate perception of Russian initiatives. According to the *Los Angeles Times*, "Russia's assistance will have a price, but Washington should try to reduce the cost as much as possible."[53]

"Putin's vision of a Russian–Western partnership is still far from what the United States could consider acceptable...In short, Mr. Putin would like to move his country toward the West, but do so in a way that constrains or rolls back US leadership,"[54] wrote the influential *Washington Post*. Sometimes calls for increased pressure on Russia can be heard: "The Bush administration cannot afford to yield to Mr. Putin so easily. Instead, it should push him toward a further change in Russian policy."[55]

"In fact, both Mr. Putin and Mr. Bush face opposition to a broad Russian–American alliance within their governments," pointed out the *New York Times*. The newspaper believes:

> The White House must contend with deep suspicion of Russian intentions on its political right and with resistance to an alliance in the Pentagon and the intelligence establishment. Mr. Putin faces the same problems. Cold war sentiments dominate the Russian military and intelligence bureaucracies, and anti-Americanism courses broadly, if not deeply, through the average Russian's political outlook.[56]

In this respect, George Bush's Texas statement is remarkable, when Mr. Bush told American journalists:

It is essential that both of us convinced some parties in our countries that we must not suspect each other of anything any longer. I will continue to prove that our nation is interested in various kinds of agreements between Russia and the United States, to reduce the amount of offensive weapons, to continue negotiations on the NMD, to cooperate in the sphere of weapons nonproliferation, and to develop counter-terrorism measures. Incidentally, he [Putin] rendered us great help in our efforts in Afghanistan. A new day has dawned in our relations, which were based on hostility, distrust and irritation, when I was growing up, when both of us were growing up. Now, on the contrary, we find ways to reveal a sphere in which we can cooperate for the sake of our nations.

---

52 *The Washington Post,* November 8, 2001.
53 *The Los Angeles Times*, September 26, 2001.
54 *The Washington Post*, September 27, 2001.
55 *Ibid.*
56 *The New York Times*, October 21, 2001.

★ ★ ★

The drastic aggravation of the threat of terrorism has thus motivated a search for new forms of cooperation between Russia and the West. The global change that followed the acts of terror in the USA proved so significant that apparently it brought about a new period in international relations. Arguably, in its scale and aftermath, the current shift is comparable to that engendered by the fall of the Berlin Wall or by the Pearl Harbor attack.

The *Financial Times* wrote:

> Russia's President Putin's decision to take part in the US-led campaign against global terrorism confirms the extraordinary rearrangement of the world's political geography. The old confrontation is gone. And this is a positive effect of the tragic 11 September events. However, the consequences of this step are no less important for the USA and its allies than for Russia itself.[57]

President Putin's visit to the USA on November 12–15, 2001 secured positive shifts in Russian–American relations, and demonstrated that "they should be based on common interests, common values and mutual respect." According to Mr. Putin, "today's Russia is a country whose integration into the community of free democratic nations has already become irreversible." Six bilateral agreements were signed in the course of the talks between Putin and Bush, the "Joint Statement on a New Relationship Between Russia and the USA" being the most important.

In this document, the sides virtually stated the absence of essential differences between the two nations in ideological, and the social and economic spheres. Mr. Vladimir Putin and Mr. George Bush confirmed their "commitment to advance common values," such as protection of human rights, tolerance, religious freedom, free speech and independent media, economic opportunity, and the rule of law. The presidents emphasized that "a market economy, the freedom of economic choice and an open democratic society [are] the most effective means to provide for the welfare of our citizens." The statement also reads: "Our countries are embarked on a new relationship for the 21st century, founded on a commitment to the values of democracy, the free market, and the rule of law. Russia and the USA have overcome the legacy of the Cold War."

The presidents stated that neither of the parties "regards the other as an enemy or threat." Simultaneously, they confirmed their "determination to meet the threats to peace in the 21st century." Among the common threats are terrorism, proliferation of weapons of mass destruction, militant nationalism, ethnic and religious intolerance, and regional instability. As Vladimir V. Putin and George W. Bush said:

---

57 *The Financial Times*, September 27, 2001.

These threats endanger the security of both countries and the world at large. Dealing with these challenges calls for the creation of a new strategic framework to ensure the mutual security of Russia and the USA, and the world community.

The document formulated the task of every possible promotion of cooperation, as well as relations of partnership and alliance between the two powers.

Aware of our responsibility to contribute to international security, we are determined to work together, and with other nations and international organizations, including the United Nations, to promote security, economic well-being, and a peaceful, prosperous, free world.

The statement in fact recognizes Russia's place in the community of western countries.

> We support the building of a European–Atlantic community whole, free, and at peace, excluding no one, and respecting the independence, sovereignty and territorial integrity of all nations. To this end, Russia and the USA will work, together with NATO and other NATO members, to improve, strengthen, and enhance the relationship between Russia and NATO, with a view to developing new, effective mechanisms for consultation, cooperation, joint decision, and coordinated/joint action. We believe that these mechanisms should reflect the fact that the members of Russia and NATO are increasingly allied in the struggle against terrorism, regional instability and other contemporary threats, and that the relationship between them should therefore evolve accordingly.

Russia is determined to follow the path toward equal cooperation with NATO "as far as the North Atlantic Alliance itself is prepared for it, and is capable of appreciating Russia's legitimate interests," Mr. Putin said in Washington.

During the summit, the presidents came to the conclusion that the existing nuclear arms levels do not reflect the contemporary strategic realities. For that matter, the mutual readiness to embark on major reductions in strategic offensive arms was confirmed. With respect to strategic defense and the ABM treaty, the presidents agreed to continue consultations in a broad framework of the new strategic relationship. The US administration thus virtually abandoned its intention of repudiating the ABM Treaty until the end of 2001, although no compromise solution has been worked out yet.

As Condoleezza Rice underlined at a press briefing at Crawford, the American side is striving to move forward with an extensive test program in order "to evaluate the potential for missile defenses." At present, large-scale deployment of the missile defenses is not on the agenda; probably this issue will come up later. At the same time, Ms Rice said that the USA was still open to the final form of "the new strategic framework," and "nobody has ruled out codification" of the new relationship.[58]

---

58 Transcript: Afghanistan Dominates Bush–Putin Talks, Rice Says. November 15, 2001.

A separate presidential "Joint Statement on a New Russian–American Economic Relationship" posits the need "to foster a new dynamic in Russian–American economic interaction." The presidents agreed on cooperation with a view to further strengthening Russia's integration into the world economy:

> We are committed to creating conditions that will enhance our trade and investment relations and help Russia reach its economic potential as a fully integrated and leading member of the world economy. Russia has a role to play in this century as an engine of world growth and a center of innovative thinking.

It was also decided to accelerate Russia's WTO accession negotiations "based on standard conditions."

An agreement was reached concerning

> renewed efforts of the Export-Import Bank, the Overseas Private Investment Corporation, and the Trade and Development Agency of the United States to promote bilateral trade and investment opportunities through project finance, risk insurance, and project assessment, as well as their readiness to expand financing in support of our growing economic relationship.

Besides, the US administration and Congress promised to end the application of the notorious Jackson–Vanik amendment to Russia, i.e. to recognize the Russian Federation's market-economy status.

The "Joint Statement by President Vladimir Putin of Russia and President of the United States George Bush on Afghanistan" is of great consequence, too. Speaking about a post-war arrangement in the country, the presidents stated:

> Russia and the United States do not intend to, and cannot, create the future government of Afghanistan. It is up to the Afghans themselves to determine their future. We believe that, in order for any future government to bring peace to the people of Afghanistan and promote stability in the region, it must be broad-based, represent all Afghans, men and women, and be drawn from all ethnic groups. We agree that the Taliban as a movement should have no place in future bodies of state power in Afghanistan.

Another "Joint Statement" stresses Russia and the USA's role as co-sponsors of the Middle East peace process. The presidents called upon "the leadership of Israel and the Palestinian Authority to take urgent steps to ease tension, as well as to refrain from actions that are harmful to the other side and to resume the dialogue at a high political level." In addition, the Russian Federation and the United States, "acting in concert with other key parties," intend to facilitate "resuming negotiations on all tracks—Palestinian, Syrian, and Lebanese—in the interests of making progress toward a comprehensive settlement in the Middle East, based on the Madrid principles, UN Security Council Resolutions 242 and 338, and existing agreements and accords."

Finally, the remaining two statement reflected the sides' intention of cooperating against bioterrorism and in combating illegal narcotics trafficking.

Presidents Vladimir Putin and George Bush thus found common ground on the issues seen as vital to both Russia and the United States, as well as all around the world. The presidents have done much for Russia and America to develop relations based on mutual consideration of each other's interests. Today, Russia and the USA do not only have to meet the challenge thrown down by international terrorism, but also to assess the history and logic of the relations between the two nations anew, and conceive of ways to continue building the interaction, as well as suggest what it should be based on and aimed at.

Although the Russian–American relationship should not be considered exclusively in the context of the events associated with the terror attack and its aftermath, it was this new historic turn that rendered the bilateral ties long-term relations of genuine partnership and alliance.

The Cold War stereotypes, double standards and needless suspicions must be eradicated completely. "Russia has changed fundamentally,"[59] George Bush said during Vladimir Putin's visit to Washington. Now, the potential for Russian–American constructive interaction ought to be embodied in actual mechanisms for cooperation, partnership and alliance. Russia and the USA, as well as Russia and the West, have acquired an obvious new common interest, based on the existence of a common adversary. Therefore, the entire complex of relations in the economic, political, and military spheres can be developed in a new way. Although it is certainly premature to draw ultimate conclusions, the Russian initiatives in the wake of the September 11 attack have engendered a realistic prospect of cardinal transformation of Russian–American relations. In fact, a new international security system is in the process of formation. Thus, a great opportunity has arisen for Russia to strengthen its position in the international arena; and favorable conditions may be created for conducting and renewing Russia's economic might.

Originally published as "Noviy povorot v rossiysko-amerikanskikh otnosheniyakh" [A new turn in Russian-American relations], excerpt from *11 sentiabria 2001 g.: reaktsia CSA i posledstvia dlya rossiysko-amerikanskikh otnoshenii* [September 11, 2001: Reaction of the United States and Russian-American relations], Moscow: The Institute for the USA and Canadian Studies, 2001, pp. 46–68.

---

59 AP, November 13, 2001.

The Russian Bridge Over the Atlantic

Vladimir Lukin

How Can We Unite Europe and America?

What role will be played in this century by Russia, a country that had on the eve of the 21st century lost nearly all its positions on the international stage? Does it have a chance to become a leading power on which the vector of world development will depend to a large extent?

Don't hasten to include me among the dreamers possessed by the mania for insane suppositions. Let us first think about what, in the coming decades, will shape the drama of world politics, primarily the system of relationships along its leading axis—the Eurasian–Atlantic one.

Some scholars believe that the main international political problem of this century will be a clash of civilizations. There have always been frictions between civilizations and one cannot rule out an intensified confrontation in the future. But in the first decade of this century, one of the most substantial political problems is not so much a conflict between civilizations as inside them. At issue are increasingly serious and deep differences between the two great democratic poles on either side of the Atlantic—American and European.

One can, of course, reduce the US–European conflict to a set of political discrepancies, such as the differing interpretation of international law as a whole, and as applied to the situation with Iraq; the attitude to the Kyoto Protocol; Europe's objections to the US withdrawal from the ABM Treaty; the differences concerning the destruction of biological weapons; and the clearly negative US attitude to the European idea of establishing an International Criminal Court. This is to say nothing about the usual competitive struggles, accompanied by regular trade wars between the Old and the New Worlds.

One gets the feeling that it is not only a matter of political and economic competition but also a question of dissimilar basic notions of contemporary life and future paths of its evolution. Over the past quarter-century, having overcome the complex of a "former European province," the US became an increasingly less "European" country in the economic, cultural, national and ethnic respects.

Europe and the US do indeed have a common system of values (democracy, market economy, priority of human rights and so on) and this is constantly stressed on both sides of the Atlantic. On the other hand, the US and the European views on ways of the state's self-realization differ greatly. Old and wise Europe is becoming aware that the Westphalian principle of national sovereignty, dominant in international relations, is becoming increasingly less applicable. In Europe, they believe that the time has come to make more resolute steps toward establishing a comprehensive world legal order, one where it will be possible to accommodate both Europe's own interests and the interests of other serious world players. The traditional European view of the world relies on the Cartesian principle of doubt and thus generates the propensity for compromise and permanent self-adjustment.

Being relatively young, unprecedentedly powerful and thus self-confident, the US reduces international relations to the following simple principle: "What is mine is mine, and what belongs to somebody else is also potentially mine." This view of the world is based on the notion instilled by the Founding Fathers of US democracy, of America being somehow "chosen" and of its special mission in the world as the "country closest to God."

Very much depends on how the relations between Europe and America will develop. If they manage to overcome their differences (which is quite possible), the situation in the world will become more predictable and the threat of conflicts will be reduced in many regions, including where there are elements of competition between civilizations.

Conversely, if the "intra-species" struggle between the US and Europe increases, the confrontation will sharpen the world over: in the Asia-Pacific region, in South Asia, and in Latin America.

Russia and America

Over the long term, Russia may substantially influence the political climate on both sides of the Atlantic. Historically and culturally, Russia is a European country *par excellence* and an Eurasian culture in geopolitical terms. At the same time, the very specificity, so to say, the "chemistry" of Russia's relations with the US is unique by virtue of many historical, psychological and strategic circumstances.

A number of parameters suggest the Russian mass consciousness is substantially closer to the American than to West European. Both countries have vast territories populated by many peoples of different religions. The Russians and the Americans have always had the sense of superpower status. The long period of confrontation along the fronts of the Cold War has, in a way, brought them closer together: the two have grown accustomed not only to fear but also to respect each other.

It appears that these psychological circumstances hide a paradox: at the height of the Cold War in the Soviet Union there was almost no clear feeling of anti-Americanism at the level of everyday consciousness. It arose, rather, precisely in the years of reforms and upheavals as a feeling of frustration over the perceived US failure to fulfill the promise to turn us into a "second America." But the feeling of proximity, a "connectivity," remained. This manifested itself immediately in the wake of the September 11 events of 2001, when Russia's president was the first to express solidarity with the US.

Russia and Europe

In Europe, two tendencies are now in conflict in regard to its Eastern neighbor. One proceeds from the assumption that Russia should remain an "external factor" in regard to the integrated Europe, a mineral resource and energy "underbelly" and do the "dirty work" (discuss disputable strategic issues with the US, the EU being assigned to a "number two" role acting behind Moscow's back; participate in the settlement of local conflicts, supplying human resources, ordinary military equipment and so on). For the rest, the EU must clearly regulate the degree of Russia's involvement in Europe, confining itself to decorative, external forms of cooperation.

Adherents to the other trend are aware that the role in a global world rather belongs to a Europe which unites all states—from Lisbon to Vladivostok. To maintain its leading positions in the international arena until the middle of the current century, the Old World will need to concentrate all its economic, technological, geopolitical and cultural resources. This second current tends to regard the Russian–European situation in less practical terms, without rejecting outright the strategic perspective of Russia turning into an "internal factor" of European integration.

In any event, there is a growing realization in Europe that any intelligible European policy is impossible without accommodating the factor of Russia. The recent developments (Iraq, Middle East) demonstrate that the US has tended to heed the Russia–EU duet while the soloist — the EU without Russia or Russia without the EU — is immeasurably less significant for it.

An "Inter-Atlantic Integrator"

And so, Russia at the turn of the century is returning to Europe with its baggage of perfectly special relations with the United States. This provides Russia with an historic chance to take the niche of an "inter-Atlantic integrator"—a country positioned in the inter-Atlantic space between the two Atlantic poles, assuming the mission of eliminating the political gaps and striving to be the catalyst and initiator of concerted tripartite political actions.

This foreign policy line and the related diplomatic strategy and tactics are the best way of a stage-by-stage, long-term return of Russia into Europe with the consent and support of the United States. This is the most effective way of establishing favorable international political conditions for modernizing the country and turning it into a "subject," not an "object" of the world economy, politics and culture of the 21st century. If Russia does not miss this chance, it will, even with its limited possibilities, already in the near future become an active political force in the world and exert serious influence on the destinies of the world.

One ought to point out that, in the foreseeable future, no other country can realistically claim the role of an "inter-Atlantic integrator." The desire to take such a niche is sometimes observed in British foreign policy. However, today's Britain is hardly prepared to fulfill the uniting mission. On the European continent, London is sometimes perceived as a US Trojan Horse rather than an "honest broker." In addition, being an EU member, Britain cannot play for one team while being the referee of the game.

In the last quarter of the 20th century, many analysts believed that a global political role in the early 21st century could be played by Japan rapidly moving to take the position of the third world center after the US and the EU. It soon turned out, however, that its political possibilities were clearly inadequate. And in the economic sense Japan entered a stage of structural stagnation, and one has difficulty seeing prospects for it emerging from the stagnation in the foreseeable future.

Within the context of Russia acquiring a long-term inter-Atlantic status, the position definitively expressed by Russia's president in the first hours following the September 11 terrorist attack undoubtedly played a positive role. Another indispensable prerequisite was another initiative of Russia's president—proclaiming Russia's European course as a strategic priority. The Kremlin then made it clear enough that the course of rapprochement with Europe was not a political maneuver, albeit of a long-term character. It marked the return of the "prodigal son" to his organic civilized environment, abandoned after the stormy and tragic cataclysms of the early 20th century.

Earlier, Russia had also tried to wedge itself in-between the two Atlantic coasts, playing on the specific relations between Washington and the European capitals. For half a century the US regarded itself as the guarantor of the security of Europe experiencing pressure from the East. The Europeans, however, were not completely confident in the reliability of US guarantees (including nuclear) in the event of a conflict between the North-Atlantic Alliance and the Warsaw Pact.

In periods when relations between Moscow and Washington became exacerbated, the European capitals did not rule out that Washington could sacrifice Europe for its own salvation. To avoid this eventuality, the Old World strove to get increasingly closer to the US. Moscow would be told that, to engage Europe in a successful dialogue, it ought to establish constructive relations with Washington. When the USSR strove to relax tensions in its relations with the US, the European leaders would seriously begin to suspect Moscow and Washington of wishing to come to a separate agreement and to relegate Europe to the periphery of world politics.

Incidentally, there was some ground for suspicion, especially when the Republicans were in power, a party that traditionally has more respect for force than for law. Those were usually the peak periods of detente in US–Soviet relations.

In the post-Soviet time, one still feels the inertia of the old approach making itself felt from time to time, but the counterpoint message, characteristic of Russia's European policy, lost any sense. When Russia turned out to be weakened militarily and politically and the US–EU confrontation grew sharper, Europe cautiously but insistently began to seek its own foreign-policy and defense identity. Today the US is needed increasingly less by the European Union as the "strategic guarantor" in the old sense. There is no need for a guarantor if there is no threat. Moreover, Russia is increasingly regarded as a possible new guarantor in equalizing the threatening pressure from the traditional "guarantor."

Indeed, on quite a number of significant political issues Russia occupies "European" rather than "American" positions. It is most important that Europe should not get the impression that Moscow strives in a purely Soviet style to use the contradictions between the two Atlantic poles. Russia must "inscribe itself" into this space and become its internal factor. Only then will it be able to manifest its originality to the maximum extent.

Unity in Diversity

It goes without saying that Russia very much differs from other subjects of the common Atlantic space which, incidentally, is not fully homogeneous itself. Spain and Greece are very different from, for instance, Sweden and Norway, although they are also members of one civilized family of nations. As frequently happened in Russian history, now, at the turn of the century, it is time to decide whether Russia is the most Eastern country of the West or it is the most Western country of the East. Where, in what macrostructure, is the Russian originality materialized? Where is Russia's creative potential fulfilled most fully and where is the destructive potential contained? In my opinion, the answer is clear: Russia's specificity, which has already exerted a most benefical impact on world civilization, is capable in the 21st century of manifesting itself in the optimum way inside the common Atlantic space rather than outside it.

This determines the basic parameters of Russia's foreign-policy strategy for the coming decades—to remain in the Euro-Atlantic "habitat" and, in the process, stay the political and diplomatic integrator of the two Atlantic poles so as, on the one hand, to avoid an open domination of one of them and, on the other, to prevent overly acute conflicts among them.

It is my conviction that such a position holds out the greatest promise for Russia in terms of the cardinal interests of its security and prospects of socio-economic growth. It can only be implemented if the line is not crossed, beyond which we will no longer be regarded as a kindred community, albeit complex and specific.

Contemporary history has repeatedly demonstrated how important it is to follow these principles. Thus, Greece during the times of the "black colonels" fell out of the field of Euro-Atlantic civilization, despite successes in the social and economic fields. The country paid dearly for the years of isolation. On the contrary, de Gaulle's France, very much testing the nerves of the US, Canada and European partners, never permitted itself to abandon the common Euro-Atlantic space. Despite all his arrogance, globalist ambitions and a certain nationalism, Charles de Gaulle was clearly aware of the line dividing civilizations and never crossed it.

Neither should the present and future politicians of Russia forget in any circumstances the need to combine the specific interests of expediency, on the one hand, and the long-term interests, on the other. Russia has its interests in the East and in the South and in different overseas regions. It is important not to confuse the means and objectives and not to lose sight of the basic priorities.

If we hold on to this strategic line, stick to it by not becoming a victim of morbid imagination and nostalgia, we will accomplish the main thing—relatively calm, sustainable development over the next two or three decades. In addition, this goal can be accomplished not through refusal to participate in international relations but rather through revitalizing foreign policy in a really pivotal direction. In this way, Russia will use a unique chance to become a factor leading to a balance of interests and positions inside a kindred (and in this sense "unipolar") Atlantic space, united in its diversity.

On the whole, Russia did not make a mistake taking the course of integrating into Europe: the nation's importance in the world increased, its economic and political potential has grown, and the political situation at home has improved. Of course, far from all of Russia's political and diplomatic steps, taken from the time the European course was proclaimed two years ago, corresponded to the course chosen. Sometimes one had the impression that the routine of official diplomacy, like a quagmire, swallowed up all long-term strategic planning and each time the "strategic choice" was the country where another summit was planned. (It shall be noted for the sake of justice that European bureaucracy is not always up to the mark either.) It will be possible to maintain a correct line only if the Russian leadership proves capable of pursuing on a systematic basis a home policy based on state interests, i.e. a policy that does not boil down to a timid maneuvering between various interest groups seeking goals that by far do not coincide with the interests of the state.

One should not forget the main thing: Russia's strong foreign-policy strategy, aimed at assuming a new global role and emphasizing the Euro-Atlantic factor, is only possible on the basis of a strong and purposeful home policy, a gradual and consistent expansion of democratic principles and institutions. This is an objective difficulty and, at the same time, a great historical challenge.

Originally published in *Russia in Global Affairs,* 2002, no. 1.

Back to the Concert

Vyacheslav Nikonov

Global This Time

Megascenarios for world development in the 21st century are not terribly diverse. The first among them, held to be the mainstream in present-day political thought, is reduced to forecasting American domination for the foreseeable future. US preponderance over all other powers, certainly as concerns the main components of might, is unprecedented. The United States can cope with anything. Arguments to prove American omnipotence become even more convincing when presented with the kind of emotion that always underlies lofty patriotic upsurges, like the one that has swept the United States following the 9/11 tragedy.

In American political quarters any other country is usually discussed not so much from the point of view of potential cooperation, as with regard to its ability to challenge US might or to throw doubt upon the possibility of unilateral action. The rest of the world has perceived the concept of US hegemony as something quite convincing, though not always as a cause for elation.

It is, in many ways, within this framework that the second scenario emerged; a scenario that is associated with anticipation of chaos in international relations and one which has become especially widespread among the left and anti-globalist circles. Humankind faces the prospect of environmental calamities, proliferation of weapons of mass destruction and a deadly clash of civilizations, of the North and the South. But there will be no one to grapple with these global challenges, for the only superpower that can provide world leadership will be preoccupied with its own egotistic interests that will have little or nothing in common with those of the rest of humankind.

It would seem, however, that there is a third scenario in prospect, too. The world is moving, and will keep moving, towards greater consolidation and governability, rather than increasing unilateral trends and chaos. That is, to the rather forgotten Concert of Powers that provided a century-long peace for Europe from 1815 to 1914.

It will be recalled that the European Concert (let me call it the First Concert here) was born of joint efforts of Russia and Great Britain. The Russian Czar Alexander I, in a benevolent move, suggested that application of force should be relinquished and any conflicts arising should be resolved through arbitration by the great powers. The British Prime Minister, William Pitt the Younger, however, transformed the idea of the Russian Emperor into a more pragmatic concept based on a balance of power.[1] At the Congress of Vienna, following the downfall of Napoleon's empire, a sort of diplomatic oligarchy of the victorious powers emerged, in which Russia, Britain, Austria and Prussia undertook to pool their efforts to maintain international stability and the status quo. With France soon returning to the "European club" (it was France that had been the target when the Concert was formed), the quartet turned into a "pentarchy," and, with accession of the Kingdom of Italy, into a "hexarchy," "the big six" (G-6) of the time. In the late 19th century, the French historian Antoine Debidour described the Concert of the period:

These states have not always lived in full accord. Bitter conflicts have erupted at times between some of them. Some of these states gained in strength and acquired greater influence than before, while others suffered a decline in one way or another and lost their former authority. But not one of them lost its strength to such an extent that the others could destroy it or expel it from the community. All of them continue to exist, time and again ensuring tranquility, equally, by their rivalry and their accord.[2]

In the period of the First Concert, the main strategies of the victor countries were cooperation in the area of security and economic engagement.[3]

In my opinion, today, in the conditions of globalization, the Concert will be performed on the global stage with participation, at least, of the USA, Europe, Russia, Japan, India, most probably China, and some other countries.

Naturally, this assumption will evoke plenty of criticisms, chiefly associated with the fact that the First Concert was built on a balance of forces. There can hardly be any talk of balance in a situation where, as they say, "the United States has no rival in any critical dimension of power. There has never been a system of sovereign states that contained one state with this degree of dominance."[4] How can powers with different clout get along in a Concert? And what can Russia, weakened and thrown back to its boundaries of the 16th century, have to do with a Concert?

---

1 Kissinger, Henry, *Diplomacy*, New York, 1994, pp. 75–76.

2 Debidour, Antoine, *The Diplomatic History of Europe: From the Congress of Vienna to Berlin (1814–1878)*, vol. 1, Moscow, Foreign Literature Publishers, 1947, p. 25 (Russian edition).

3 Kurth, J., "The American Way of Victory," *The National Interest*, Summer 2000.

4 Books, S. and Wohlforth, W.,"American Primacy in Perspective," *Foreign Affairs*, July–August, 2002, p. 23.

Meanwhile, there are reasons to believe that creation of a new Concert is possible. First: even though America is the only superpower today, a certain balance of forces does exist in the world. The USA is not capable of exercising global regulation unilaterally and will *de facto* be moving towards more cooperative approaches.

Second: Russia, discarded as it is by many today, remains an important factor in the world system, and can and will, therefore, play a significant and independent role in it.

Third: conditions for a "century-long peace" among great powers are in no way worse than they were in Europe in the 19th century. And the world has already started its long-term movement towards Global Concert, the composition and format of which are yet to be identified.

The USA, the Sole Superpower, but not the Only Power

The key significance for a hegemonic power is, of course, its economic resources. As a result of the economic boom of the 1990s, the USA has increased its share in the world economy to 30 per cent. This is a very big share. But the figure is less impressive for a more adequate indicator—purchasing power parity, which is put at 21 per cent. To be sure, there were countries in world history at a higher or comparable level. In the mid 18th century, China accounted for 32.8 per cent of the world production volume, and India in its boundaries of the time (that is, together with Pakistan), for 24.5 per cent. Britain held leadership, with 22.9 per cent, in 1880, and the United States moved to first place, with 23.6 per cent, by 1900.[5] It isn't today, but right after World War II that the United States reached its high point in terms of economic might (up to 40 per cent) relative to other countries. Today, apart from America, there are other major economic players in the world. The European Union has almost caught up with the USA in aggregate GDP, while some of the EU countries are ahead of America in standard of living indicators. No doubt, after the expansion of the EU, with countries in Central and Eastern Europe joining, the Union will move to the fore. China's GDP has trebled in the past 20 years and continues to grow at a rate of 10 per cent, surpassing Japan's indicator. Fast growth has also resumed in post-Soviet countries.

Meanwhile, the situation in the American economy is not very impressive. Continual prosperity has not materialized. Over the past decade, American society has been consuming too much, importing and borrowing too much, and saving too little. Within the two-and-a-half years of stock exchange crises, recessions, and unprecedented corporate scandals and bankruptcies, the US

5 Kennedy, Paul, *The Rise and Fall of Great Powers*, New York, Vintage Books, 1989, p. 149.

stock markets have lost up to $7 trillion in capital drain. Foreign investments in the US economy in the second quarter of 2002 fell to an all-time low since 1995.[6] When in New York, in July 2002, after a long interval, they switched on the clock recording the size of American public debts it showed a sum of $6.1 trillion which, moreover, was climbing at a rate of $30 a second.[7] The dollar suffers from fevers, and its exchange rate depends on joint currency interventions by the European Central Bank and the Bank of Japan. Of course, no economic difficulties have ever (at least in the post-World War II period) forced the USA to give up any of its principal plans in foreign policy. But it is equally clear that the US share in the world economy will be shrinking rather than growing.

America's military machine is unprecedented. Possessing as it does a giant striking force and unparalleled target precision, it has no equals either at sea, in the air, or in space. But the American ground force (1,384,000 men) is not the most numerous. It is noticeably smaller than that of China (2,470,000) or the aggregate European forces, and only a little bigger than those of India (1,303,000), North Korea (1,082,000) and Russia (1,004,000). In the nuclear arms component, the USA, at least quantitatively (with tactical nuclear warheads counted), lags behind Russia.[8] It is quite possible that the plans of European policies in the area of defense and security, which at present are viewed rather with tongue in cheek, may develop into something more serious. This is the more probable considering the return of the European Union's main driving force, Germany, to the international military arena in Kosovo and Afghanistan.

But even dominant defense might does not ensure quick achievement of desired political and military results. Can Desert Storm be said to have been that victorious if a new tornado threatens to break out a decade later? After Kosovo, one of the leading Republican Congressmen inquired, "If this is victory, then what in this case is defeat?" It was Russia (and Victor Chernomyrdin personally) that relieved the USA and NATO from the deadlocked Yugoslav situation, which put into question the ability of the superpower and the alliance it led to act as sole European arbiter. After the quick victory over the Taliban and Al-Qaeda in Eastern Afghanistan came a long period of hostilities in other parts of the country, the terrorists' flight into Pakistan, the shaky situation of the central and local Afghan authorities, an upswing in drug trafficking, mass migration, and humanitarian catastrophe. Meanwhile, bin Laden is

---

6 Overchenko, Mikhail, "The USA Losing Attractiveness," *Vedomosti*, September 16, 2002 (Russian edition).

7 Sysoyev, Vladimir and Skogoreva, Anastasia, "Terrorists Hit at America Again," *Gazeta*, July 15, 2002 (Russian edition).

8 *Military Almanac 2001–2002: Handbook on US Armed Forces.* Center for Defense Information, Moscow, Gendalf Publishers, 2002, pp. 14–16 (Russian edition).

apparently alive and kicking. On top of this, in order to achieve military success, the USA should move in ground forces (something it avoids doing for fear of heavy casualties). The USA should also be prepared to assume responsibility for restoring the country. However, the money to help Yugoslavia and Afghanistan is allocated chiefly by other countries.

America's military superiority today is akin to that of Britain in the 19th century. Britain at that time dominated the seas (the then sea, air and space) but was weak on the ground, feared "mass retaliation" by any other great power, and cared for its own financial interests. This, however, was no handicap for Britain to play solo in the First Concert.

A hegemonic power that doesn't want to be at war with all and everyone has to bribe, persuade, use financial, diplomatic and other means. The USA, however, has for many years delayed its payments to international organizations. America is at the bottom of the OECD list in allocating resources, per capita of population, for aid to developing countries (and most of this money is sent directly to the Middle East). In the 1990s, the USA was closing its embassies and consulates in many countries. The sole superpower proved unable to prevent the emergence of two new nuclear powers, India and Pakistan. It lacks the resources to bring peace between Israelis and Palestinians, or to protect its own territory from strikes, the most destructive in all US history.

Aspiration for world hegemony in the USA today is stronger than ever. America has changed considerably, but not to such an extent as it can change its own nature. It was and remains a rather self-centered country, not particularly outward looking to the world around. American political culture has a considerable isolationist stratum within it. This society can hardly maintain for a long time, for decades, an internationalist spirit that is not inherent in it. A new 9/11 would be required to keep up the fighting morale in the USA public opinion would not go along with a unilateral drive. In September 2002, 64 per cent of Americans supported efforts to oust Saddam Hussein, but only 30 per cent favored going in without allies.[9] Besides, it should be kept in mind that the American two-party system is a real factor. As long as the inertia of "rallying around the flag" keeps its momentum and George Bush's popularity ratings stay high, the Democrats will tone down their opposition, but this situation cannot last indefinitely.

The strategy of world hegemony implies performing the role of not only world policeman, but also world manager. However, the essence of the present-day US policy does not involve assuming above all responsibility for global management. The core of it is to ensure its own freedom of action, freedom from responsibility for anything that represents no immediate interest from the point of view of security or electoral support. But most of the world problems

9 *Time*, September 16, 2002, p. 40.

have no connection to any direct threats to US security or interests of the American electorate. The concept of "humanitarian intervention" has and will be applied selectively: not at the points of worst violations of human rights but in the regions where the USA has some other interests at stake. America's aspiration is not so much to be the orchestra conductor as to ensure the opportunity for solo parts.

As for the role of the USA as moral leader, this is something that has obviously not shown any growth recently. "The leader loses in aspirations for moral superiority if he ignores major international agreements,"[10] and this is often the case with the United States. Amnesty International last year noted that the record of the USA was top of the list "of the greatest disappointments in human rights in the past 40 years."[11] That same year, the USA lost its seat in the UN Human Rights Commission. Furthermore, domestic security measures taken in the past months by America have evoked numerous doubts.

America's information domination is vast, but an interesting paradox arises amidst conditions where information flows are increasing exponentially. With information overflowing, perception is blunted. English is increasingly becoming the lingua franca of the power elite today, but remains only a second world language, with three times more people speaking Chinese (1.2 billion) than English (479 million). Some time in the future, it may even become a third language, since the numbers of those speaking Hindi are growing rapidly (437 million in 2001).[12] And it is by no means certain that it is the American lifestyle which is winning over the world and not the European.

The present strategy of the American leadership renders doubtful the US ability to lead even its allies. The United States and Europe cannot reach accord on a number of issues. The USA has not signed or has not ratified such documents as the Kyoto Protocol or agreements to ban nuclear testing, biological weapons and anti-personnel mines. There is no unity in views on the National Anti-Ballistic Defense and the Middle East. The USA and Europe have differences in their views regarding the situation of the Afghan POWs in Guantanamo, the International Criminal Court, and the issue of the death penalty. There are also differences in the areas of trade relations, European defense and security policies, and the problem of Iraq. All of a sudden, anti-American sentiments have intensified in Japan. It looks like contradictions between the USA and its closest allies today are in no way less than between the USA and Russia, India and even China. This, apart from everything else, indicates a

---

10 Nuscheler, Franz, "New World Politics," *Internationale Politik*, 1998, 11, p. 45 (Russian edition).

11 Kempster, Norman, "US Sharply Criticized on Human Rights," *International Herald Tribune*, May 31, 2001.

12 Washington online, September 9, 2001.

possibility that allied and bloc systems may not necessarily become a really serious impediment to Concert.

There is awareness in the United States that a policy of unilateral actions may be detrimental to the country's own interests. Joseph Nye, in his book on the subject, *The Paradox of American Power*, regarded almost as a classic, justly noted, "The danger posed by the outright champions of hegemony is that their foreign policy is all accelerator and no brakes. Their focus on unipolarity and hegemony exaggerates the degree to which the United States is able to get the outcomes it wants in a changing world."[13] There is also an understanding based on historical experience that overloading and overexpansion of an empire may lead to internal anemia, to creation of "turbulent frontiers,"[14] "self-encirclement,"[15] and demise from "its own hubris."[16]

For all the obvious indications of a unilateralist trend in the rhetoric and actions of the Bush Administration, there are quite concert-inclined elements discernible in the US policies. For the first time in many years, the USA has fulfilled its obligations to the UN and repaid all its debts. Eighteen years after America left UNESCO, President Bush announced resumption of membership. Anti-Chinese moods have noticeably cooled in Washington. Revolutionary positive changes have occurred in Russian–American relations. The United States has for the first time recognized the Palestinians' right to their own independent state—much to the satisfaction of Europeans. In the run-up to the G-8 summit in Kananaskis, the Bush Administration lifted anti-dumping duties from 116 metal products that are mostly manufactured in the European Union.[17] Contrary to its earlier intention, the USA did not withdraw from the international peacekeeping force in the Balkans and agreed to a certain compromise regarding the International Criminal Court. The United States no longer sponsors Al-Qaeda, no longer helps the Taliban, no longer considers the Chechen terrorists as freedom fighters, and does not provide arms for the Kosovo Liberation Army. The very nature of newly emerging threats to America's security, coupled with scandals flaring up around major corporations, has required a new portion of government regulation that subverts the libertarian "Washington consensus," the cause of allergy for many countries, with a greater degree of regulation and social orientation of the economy.

13 Nye, Joseph S. Jr., The Paradox of American Power: Why the World's Only Superpower Can't Go It Alone, New York: Oxford University Press, 2002, p. 140.
14 See, for example Kurth, James, "The American Way of Victory," *The National Interest*, Summer 2000.
15 Ikenberry, G. John, "America's Imperial Ambition," *Foreign Affairs*, September–October 2002, p. 58.
16 Hirsh, Michael, "Bush and the World", *idem*, p. 43.
17 Skogoreva, Anastasia, "Bush Turns Over Metal," *Gazeta*, June 26, 2002 (Russian edition).

The United States is probably not the worst example in the ranks of major countries which Charles de Gaulle once called "egotistic monsters." It would be interesting to see how other nations would behave had they been as powerful as America is today.

America is the sole superpower, but not the only power. It cannot cope with everything, the less so all at once. A certain balance of forces does exist in the modern international system. Henry Kissinger wrote in his *Diplomacy*, "Of course, in the end a balance of power always comes about de facto when several states interact. The question is whether the maintenance of the international system can turn into a conscious design, or whether it will grow out of a series of tests of strength."[18]

A Concert in which one of the instruments is louder than the others is quite possible. At the time of the Congress of Vienna, Russia was Europe's military superpower: in Debidour's words, "Alexander I was at that time all-powerful."[19] The European Concert survived quite successfully throughout the 19th century, with Britain's overwhelming superiority in most components of strength. Moreover, as follows from the theory of hegemonic stability, developed above all by Robert O. Kohane, the international system may only function efficiently if it is maintained in a workable condition by hegemonic powers. At the same time, in Kohane's opinion, domination by one great power was neither a necessary nor a sufficient condition for preserving world stability.[20]

A Global Concert is in the interests of the USA itself. It provides the right to be heard and a sense of protection for other countries, which means it makes it possible to regard America not as a threat to stability, but as guarantor of the world order.

Russia as an Indispensable Power

Russia paid a high price for stopping the Cold War, pulling down the Berlin Wall, and stepping down from the imperial plane. We have received economic catastrophe and, instead of assistance as had been expected, condescending smiles from the "victors." The attitude of the West towards Russia was rather in the manner of that of the victorious great powers towards post-Napoleonic France. As Talleyrand wrote, "The Allies wished to leave France with only a passive role; it had to be not so much a participant in events as a mere spectator. The fear of it had not yet disappeared, its strength was still causing alarm, and they all hoped to achieve security only if Europe would be incorporated in

---

18 Kissinger, *Diplomacy*, p. 77.
19 Debidour, *The Diplomatic History of Europe,* p. 40.
20 Kohane, Robert O., *After Hegemony: Cooperation and Discord in the World Political Economy,* Princeton, N.J., Princeton University Press, 1984, p. 46.

a system directed solely against France".[21] In the 1990s, the West went about arranging and expanding its system acting mainly either in disregard of Russia or against its interests. And Russia, following the euphoria caused by prospects of cooperation with the West, started, from the mid-decade, paying back in kind. But this happened not out of any inexhaustible "imperial nostalgia,"[22] as Zbigniew Brzezinski would have it, but due to the not unfounded impression that the motive force of the West's policy was doctrinal Russophobia, a desire to encircle and isolate Russia. There have been ample indications of this, from expansion of NATO to the bombing of Yugoslavia in spite of Russia's desperate protests. Besides, the Russians themselves throughout the past decade indulged in self-humiliation, became all nostalgic about the country lost, and exaggerated the weaknesses of the country newly acquired.

Russia is not the USSR. It is smaller and weaker in many parameters. But it still retains its positions, and is even strengthening them in some areas.

Disintegration of the USSR set in motion a process of formation of nation states, which has obviously been underrated in the West. Never before 1991, had there been on this planet such ethnically based sovereign countries as Ukraine, Belarus, Azerbaijan, Kazakhstan, Uzbekistan, Kyrgyzstan, Tajikistan, Turkmenia, and—the Russian Federation. Always a multiethnic community (or empire, whatever you prefer), Russia (the USSR) was a country where Russians were the lesser part of the population, and which was governed mostly by non-Russians (the Romanov dynasty, starting with Catherine II, was in essence German, Stalin was a Georgian, and Khrushchev and Brezhnev came from Ukraine). Now, for the first time, the Russians constitute not just the majority, but the overwhelming majority (up to 85 per cent) of the population. This phenomenon has required not only a painful (and yet to be completed) quest for national identity, but also set the stage for the formation of a qualitatively new national consciousness. The resulting growth in national awareness may consolidate society more strongly than the Communist dogma or the old formula: "Autocracy, Orthodoxy, Popular Spirit" of Russia under the czars.

Russia does not possess one-sixth of the world's land, the way it was with the USSR, but even with its one-eighth it remains the world's largest country. Population-wise, it occupies sixth place on the planet (145 million), and the Russian language is fifth in terms of number of users (284 million).[23] Russia's cultural, economic and political influence are factors to contend with across

---

21 Talleyrand, *Memoirs,* Yekaterinburg, Urals University Press, 1997, pp. 307–309 (Russian edition).
22 Brzezinski, Zbigniew, "NATO Should Remain Wary of Russia," *The Wall Street Journal Europe*, November 29, 2001.
23 Washington online, September 9, 2001.

the post-Soviet space. Russia is not one of the two superpowers. But it has retained the status of one of the great powers, a permanent member of the UN Security Council with the right of veto, and is decisive in legitimizing whatever actions are to be taken by the world community or individual countries.

The situation in Russia's economy is far from perfect, but in recent years its rate of growth has been clearly higher than the world's average. In five years, according to estimates by the Brunswick UBS Warburg's directors, labor productivity in Russia has increased by 38 per cent, while America's 13 per cent, by comparison, looks rather unimpressive.[24] The GDP, which is mainly estimated according to the ruble/dollar exchange rate and therefore looks comparable to that of the Netherlands, when calculated by the parity purchasing capacity of the ruble, amounted to $1,085 billion for the year 2000. This brings Russia to ninth place in the world, ahead of Brazil and Canada. The forecasts are that by the size of its economy in 2015, Russia will outstrip Britain, Italy and France, and move to sixth place in the world.[25]

In Soviet times, not one of this country's enterprises featured on the Fortune-500 list of the world's largest companies. There are several of them on this list today, even though the capitalization level of all Russian companies is underrated. In the Soviet period, the country's foreign debt was growing, while in 2001 alone it went down by $13.2 billion and now amounts to a comfortably payable sum of $130.1 billion.[26] Russia has noticeably improved its credit history. The USSR was importing grain, while the Russian Federation this year has exported grain to Brazil, Germany, Canada, and Bulgaria. The market environment, even if imperfect, does work.

Russia possesses the world's largest mineral resources and is a major player on the world energy market. In 2001–2002 (April to April), Russia produced 15 per cent of all crude oil from exporting countries, lagging only a little behind Saudi Arabia (16.1 per cent) and twice the level of third-placed Iran (7.4 per cent).[27] With exports of natural gas added, Russia has become the largest supplier of energy resources in the world. On top of this, it is the only country that can play on the side of OPEC or against it, participating officially at conferences of both exporters of liquid fuel and consumers as well (G-8), and playing the role of "petroleum referee."[28] The West is increasingly con-

---

24 Boon, Peter and Rodionov, Denis, "How Russia Can Get Rich," *Vedomosti*, September 5, 2002 (Russian edition).

25 *The World at the Turn of the Millennium*, p. 555.

26 Bekker, Alexander, "Amendment for $8 Billion," *Vedomosti*, March 1, 2001 (Russian edition).

27 Tyumenev, R. and Tankaev, R., "Russia and Prices on the World Oil Market," *World Energy Politics*, no. 5–6, 2002, p. 37 (Russian edition).

28 Konoplyanik, Andrei, "The Oil Referee," *Expert*, November 13, 2000, p. 12 (Russian edition).

scious that Russia is a lot more stable and reliable partner in energy matters than Arab producers. And after the USA refused to ratify the Kyoto Protocol, it now depends on Russia whether this document will come into force.

Russia retains a vast, even though largely residual, military potential. Russia is a nuclear superpower, one of the two countries that can blow up the whole world in a twinkling. Throughout recent years, the Russian Federation has been the world's second largest arms exporter and the main supplier of modern arms to two great powers, China and India. Russia's stocks of tanks and armored vehicles are considerably greater than those of the USA. In the components of military might where America dominates, air force, navy and space, Russia is in second place.[29] Former Soviet superiority in space is a thing of the past, but even so, there are 43 Russian military satellites in space today. This is more than the total number of satellites orbited in all history by any country, except for the USA and also Japan (72 space satellites).[30] The international space station built and maintained with Russia's most active participation represents a good symbol of Concert.

It transpired at the turn of the century that solution of a whole number of regional problems depends on Russia. By way of trial and error, the West has already established that democratization in Belarus or stabilization of the situation in Central Asia and the southern Caucasus cannot be achieved without Russia, the less so contrary to its interests. The transport lines in Eurasia in one way or another depend on Russia. Incessant attempts to create alternative channels, bypassing Russia, to transport energy resources in actual fact reflect Russia's already existing decisive role in this area. Russia is a most important element in the European security system, which is emphasized by the special format of the Russia–EU and Russia–NATO relationships. Russia is regarded as the only "fair broker" in inter-Korean relations, and hardly any resumption of North–South dialogue or the launching of economic reforms in North Korea would be possible without Russia's efforts.

Moscow's role is just as unique in the Middle East, where it enjoys the trust of both the old friends, the Palestinians, and the new ones, the Israelis. The obvious improvement of Russian–Israeli relations has changed the nature of Russia's ties with the West. The Jewish lobby in Washington, once traditionally harshly anti-Russian, is now pressing for repeal of the Jackson–Vanik Amendment and defends Moscow's policy in Chechnya. For its part, Russia takes a more pro-Israeli stance than the European Union or even the USA.

Russia plays a paramount role in the world community. At the same time, it is objectively destined to come out as an independent player, a separate center of force not to be dissolved in any international amalgamations. In the fore-

---

29 *Military Almanac 2001–2002*, pp. 14–15.
30 Washington Profile, Aug. 5, 2002 at www.washprofile.org/SUBJECTS-3/space3.mtml

seeable future Russia will not be integrated in the main Euro-Atlantic structures, while in Asia it simply has nowhere to integrate. Unlike numerous countries, the Russian Federation will preserve its sovereignty. And, even if by force of its geographic situation, it is destined to be a global player.

The tendency to treat Russia as a defeated third-rate country began to subside already before the 9/11 tragedy. And after this day, a feeling has been mounting in the West that Russia is in many respects an "indispensable power." Thomas E. Graham, chief expert on Russia in the US National Security Council, points out that "ignoring Russia is not a viable option. Even in its much reduced circumstances, Russia remains critical to the United States' own security and prosperity and will continue to do so well into the future."[31] Moscow has proved to be a highly valuable participant in the anti-terrorist coalition. Its stakes and experience in the region of Afghanistan are greater than anyone else's, and it rendered substantial help to the USA, supplying intelligence information and arranging air passages for US combat aircraft and access to bases in the former Soviet republics.

A number of US foreign policy priorities have been revised, which set off what I would call a revolution in Russian–American relations. Andrew C. Kuchins, director of the Russian and Eurasian Program at the Carnegie Endowment, writes on the subject, "On the US side, the basis for a new US–Russian partnership rests on reconfiguring US foreign and security policy goals, which include (1) successfully conducting the war on terrorism, (2) a new urgency to preventing the proliferation of weapons of mass destruction and their means of delivery, (3) peacefully managing the rise of China as a great power, and (4) achieving a stable, global energy supply…No one would seriously question the weight of these items or that they can be pursued effectively without Russian cooperation. In fact, no country except Russia could possibly bring as much to the table on these goals."[32]

On the Russian side, the conceptual basis for rapprochement was provided by the pragmatic Putin Doctrine aimed at the country's revival through integration into the global system, which, in turn, depends above all on cooperation with the West. As Vladimir Putin has stated, the core of a "trusting partnership" with the USA is "a new interpretation of national interests of the two countries and also a similar perception of the very nature of present-time threats."[33]

---

31 Graham, Thomas E., *Russia's Decline and Uncertain Recovery*, Wash.: Carnegie Endowment for International Peace, 2002, p. 74.

32 Kuchins, Andrew C., "Summit with Substance: Creating Payoffs in an Unequal Partnership," *Policy Brief* (Carnegie Endowment for International Peace), no. 16, May 2002, p. 3.

33 Statement by President of the Russian Federation V.V. Putin at an Enlarged Conference with Participation of Russia's Ambassadors in the Foreign Ministry of Russia, July 12, 2002, (in Russian).

As a result, Russian–American relations have in recent months reached, I am sure, the highest point in their history, since the time of the US Declaration of Independence. Proclaiming a cessation of rivalry, presidents Putin and Bush have expressed their "commitment to promoting common values," among which they mentioned human rights, tolerance, freedom of religion, freedom of speech, economic opportunity, and supremacy of law.[34] The Russian–American Anti-Terrorist Group is no longer confined to Afghan problems only. It has expanded its mandate and is now tackling problems associated with Central Asia, the Indian–Pakistani conflict, South-East Asia and Yemen. It also takes measures to prevent nuclear, chemical and biological terrorism, and fights drug trafficking.[35] The Strategic Arms Reduction Treaty was signed, even though the Bush Administration at the outset had no intention of making any commitments in the nuclear field. And on June 6, 2002, the USA recognized Russia as a market economy, much earlier than this recognition came from our main trade partners in the EU.

There are still many differences between Russia and the USA. Both have officially excluded each other from the list of potential military adversaries, yet both have kept the old lists of nuclear targets. But this is no sign of aggressive spirit, rather it calls for further reductions of strategic offensive arms: indeed, the remaining warheads (1,700 to 2,250) have to be targeted somewhere! There is no one else to be contained with such an enormous stock. Russia does not agree with America's destabilizing decision to withdraw from the ABM Treaty, but it seems this decision would sooner have an impact on American–Chinese relations. Any national missile defense (NMD) that the United States may set up in the coming decades will constitute a serious obstacle for Chinese strategic weapons, not Russian. Many of Russia's steps in its relations with Iran and Iraq, and also Russian supplies of missile technology to China cause disputes. However, Russia coordinates its actions in these directions with Washington and would never step over the line where confrontation with the USA may start. I suppose, America would act the same way. The still remaining issues are steel imports (although American sanctions affected Russia less than other steel producing countries), chicken legs, and the Jackson–Vanik Amendment. But try finding someone who does not have some contradictions or other today. The main thing is willingness to discuss differences constructively and move ahead.

The USA and Russia no longer play against each other using major third countries as trump cards, as was the case before, when Russia sought to aggra-

34 Official Visit of President of the Russian Federation V.V. Putin to the USA, (in Russian) at www.kremlin.ru/
35 Orlov, Arkadiy and Volkhonsky, Boris, "Secret Collusion at the Level of Deputy Ministers," *Kommersant*, July 29, 2002 (Russian edition).

vate, for example, American–European contradictions, while Washington had the same aims with regard to Soviet–Chinese relations. Partnership is easily discernible—even by the fact that during the European tour of President Bush in May 2002 the numbers of anti-American protesters in Moscow were considerably smaller than the crowds in Germany and France.

Observer Jim Hoagland has remarked that the American and Russian leaders are moving towards an era of Global Entente, which will diminish the strategic influence of Europe, China and Japan on Washington and Moscow. And this is something that is already causing concern in the capitals of other great powers.[36] I am in no way against the Entente that was born in the era of the First Concert. But I see no formal reasons why it should not be global and aimed not at restricting the strategic influence of Europe, China and Japan but at joint action.

After all, Russian–American partnership is no impediment to development of Russia's relations with NATO. Alliance's Secretary-General George Robertson is confident, "We are on the threshold of qualitatively new relations between Russia and NATO...What unites us is, in many ways, greater than what disunites."[37] Nor does partnership between Russia and the United States represent any handicap to G-8 cooperation: at the latest summit in Canada, Russia acquired the status of a full-fledged G-8 participant in the entire range of issues discussed. For the first time, Western countries empowered the Russian leader to carry out a collective assignment, bridging relations between India and Pakistan. Russia had not been entrusted with such a serious mediatory mission before.

The media in the West still tend to treat Russia with prejudice, but to a lesser extent than before. The country's image is today better than ever. It is also better than in pre-Bolshevist times of the First Concert. A stereotyped opinion of an American journalist of that period was of "a Jew-hating czar and the Jew-hating oligarchy [who] had so long perpetuated atrocities among the peasants" that it was hard to imagine if Christ ever turned up in a Russian village.[38] Russia's image is especially attractive against the background of the West's other allies in the grand anti-terrorist coalition where the central role is assigned to a number of Islamic countries. Compared to these countries, Russia may with every reason be considered a prosperous democracy of a Western type. In addition, Russia's image has also improved with the Western public coming to

36 Hoagland, Jim, "US, Russia and Global Entente," *The Washington Post*, July 25, 2002.
37 Robertson, George, "Russia and NATO: Time to Implement a Joint Scheme," *Izvestia*, April 2, 2002 (Russian edition).
38 Davis, Ronald E. and Trani, Eugene P., *The First Cold War: The Legacy of Woodrow Wilson in US–Soviet Relations*, Columbia, Mo., University of Missouri Press, 2002, p. 8.

know better their future NATO allies. In all the countries, except Slovenia, to be admitted to NATO following the Prague summit, the governments only managed to stay in office for one term; everywhere it is the left, the former Communists, who are in power. In some of these countries, anti-West and anti-American moods are spreading, and corruption is way bigger than in Russia.[39] Incidentally, 60 per cent of Europeans and 68 per cent of Americans favor Russia's accession to NATO.[40]

Moscow has turned into a potential strategic partner of the West with no harm caused to its earlier formed strategic partnership with China and India. The Russian–Chinese Comprehensive Treaty is more binding than any other agreement signed by Beijing. A lull in Russian–Indian relations, caused by Boris Yeltsin's physical inability to get to Delhi in the course of eight years, has long ended, and both countries are now engaged in active cooperation. Russian–Japanese relations are on the rise, although over the decades they were wholly concentrated on the issue of Russia's South Kurile Islands, alias Japan's Northern Territories. At any rate, there are now signals coming from Tokyo indicating Japan's willingness to set the territorial issue aside and get busy with others, less entangled. These may include, for example, development of energy resources in Sakhalin Island, which involves construction of the first ever pipeline to take natural gas from the Sakhalin shelf to the Japanese Islands.[41]

Meanwhile, the question arising time and again is: how lasting is Moscow's turn towards partnership, and would it not return to the former, Soviet, confrontational paradigm? I see no reasons for that. Russia has neither strength, nor desire for confrontation. Putin is going to press ahead with his course, even despite the resistance by part of the elite and bureaucracy, which the president may just as well ignore in a country with a millennium-old czarist political culture. But Putin is by no means a lonely figure. Rallied behind him is the advanced part of the intellectual elite, the more successful members of the financial and political community, and the petroleum, metallurgical, high-tech and other giants that have already broken out of the national shell and turned into transnationals.

From the First to the Second Concert

The main prerequisite for resumption of Concert is that it (and the "century of peace" it provides for) represents a mode of relationships natural for civi-

---

39 See: Gati, Charles, "All that NATO Can Be: To Prague and Beyond," *The National Interest*, Summer 2002.

40 Kemp, Frederik, "The West Consolidates in the East," *Vedomosti*, September 10, 2002 (Russian edition).

41 Golovnin, Vasili, "Japan Wants to Forget Old Times," *Izvestia*, August 20, 2002 (Russian edition).

lized states. It is natural for normal people to seek peace and tranquility. The purpose of the First Concert was confirmed if only by its long history, a record for all international systems (except, of course, the longevity of the Westphalia Treaty system of 1648, which is only just about to die out). World War I was a result of a fatal miscalculation by several European governments—Kaiser Wilhelm's, in the first place—rather than irreversible malfunctioning in the mechanism of the First Concert. When the war ended, the Concert could have been restored, had it not lost two great powers for quite a while. One of these was Germany, which was given much harsher treatment in Versailles than had been meted out to post-Napoleonic France in Vienna. The second was Russia where the Bolsheviks, seizing power in the 1917 Revolution, challenged directly the system of values and the way of life of all other great powers, which resulted in the country's isolation and self-isolation lasting for decades. The least governable system, that of Versailles–Washington, that found its expression in the impotent League of Nations, came to its end amid the flames of the bloodiest world war. Recreation of Concert after World War II, now on a global scale, not just European, had prospects for being quite a practicable endeavor, considering the experience of the anti-Hitler coalition and the establishment of the United Nations, with the USA turning into a global player, and Germany, Italy and Japan successfully integrated in the international system. But again, for reasons that are a separate theme, this system left outside the Soviet Union, a country that was already controlling a good half of the world's population. This made the world bipolar, divided by a big curtain. As the experience of the 20th century indicates, no Concert is possible without Russia, and, moreover, by the end of the century it became obvious that no Concert was possible without the reviving new-old great powers, China and India.

By the late 1990s, Russia had carried out a revolution most important in its history: it created a world that was no longer divided by impassable lines. This facilitated the process of globalization, which has now reached almost all places on the planet. The fall of the "iron curtain" became decisive for emergence (or, recreation?) of a system of non-confrontational interaction of major powers.

September 11, 2001 and the events that followed provided additional arguments in favor of not so much unilateral action, as actions in the spirit of a new, Second Concert. US Secretary of State Colin Powell, characterizing the incipient anti-terrorist coalition, stated, "What is unique about the coalition... is that, except for about three or four countries, every other country on the face of the Earth has signed up."[42] Of course, one should not overestimate either cohesion of the coalition, or the sincerity of its participants, or the contribution of some of them to the success of the common cause, but the coali-

---

42 Colin Powell, The Campaign Against Terrorism (as delivered), October 25, 2001, at www.state.gov/secretary/rm/2001/5751.htm

tion is a fact. For the first time since the era of the First Concert, all great powers with no exception, each proceeding from its own interest, have rallied to fight a common enemy, international terrorism. Certainly, we can in the future expect differences in interpretations of such notions as "terrorism" and supporting it." But for the first time in decades, those who are regarded as terrorists by a group of great powers have not become "freedom fighters" for another group of powers. For the first time we hear chords of the Concert, or Concerto, in global performance.

Coalitions "pro" are more viable than coalitions "contra." This, however, does not mean that the latter are not viable. There's nothing like a common enemy to consolidate. The First Concert was directed against a former enemy, Napoleonic France. However, the powers that can form a Second Concert have different former enemies. The common enemy, terrorism, has come from the outside and has been on a global scale from the outset; the global fight against it as the joint mission of the orchestra has become an imperative. The enemy is very strong, and its strength is linked with Islam in its most radical forms. Although pointing out this linkage is considered as lacking in political correctness,

> Islamic leaders who aver that Islam has no relation to terrorism engage in wishful thinking. The linkage is there and discernible, above all, in the ideological substantiation of terrorism and extremism. For this purpose, they employ the long known Islamic concepts that concern jihad, attitude to the unfaithful, suppression of all that is forbidden by the Shariah, and relationships with the powers that be.[43]

Of course, creation of a Second Concert is a development that is far from certain and one that provokes numerous questions. Anticipating them, I'd like to point out that the First Concert should not be idealized either. And the world today is not any worse than the one where our ancestors lived in the 19th century.

At first glance, Concert may look impossible in the conditions when the powers differ in opinions on major issues, are divided into blocs, and have different basic values and cultural codes. But there was never unanimity in the First Concert; all major and even minor issues evoked bitter disputes. Members of the 19th century Big Six also participated in various blocs. Already during the Congress of Vienna, not without the assistance of the cunning Talleyrand, Austria, Britain and France formed a temporary secret alliance against Russia and Prussia.[44] Britain, a member of the Quadruple Alliance, never joined the Holy Alliance of the monarchs of Russia, Austria and Prussia. And later, the countries broke into the Entente and the Triple Alliance. It is

---

43 Syukiyanen, Leonid, "International Terrorism and Islam: Allies or Enemies?" *Constitutional Law: East European Review*, no. 4, 2001, p. 81 (Russian edition).
44 Talleyrand, *Memoirs*, p. 299.

rather doubtful that members of the First Concert shared all the values. The difference between constitutional monarchy in Britain and Russia's autocratic monarchy was a lot more significant than between today's representative democracy in the USA and socialist democracy in China. On the contrary, the values associated with peaceful coexistence and the rights of the individual, as well as market principles in the economy, have in recent decades become practically universal. As for cultural values, these, whether it is good or bad, are being leveled out. Martin Heidegger once remarked that there were two downfalls in the history of humanity: the first time in sin, and the second—in banality. Modernism and post-modernism, representing, in essence, simplification of culture, are becoming a universal asset as a result of the information revolution and broad international exchanges. The only cultural entity that denies the Western system of values is based on Islam. In any case, China, India, Japan and Russia do not set themselves in confrontation to the process of globalization, to Western mondialism.

How can we talk of any concert if we have no agreement on how we read the music and everyone interprets international law in his own way? Can "century-long peace" be really possible with wars flaring up all around and the United States planning a series of armed interventions? However, international law in the 19th century was an even more ephemeral matter than today. And European Concert in no way meant absence of any wars and aggression. Great powers waged numerous colonial wars and conducted military operations on the European periphery. Russia in the 19th century fought two wars with Persia and three wars with Turkey, it annexed Central Asia by force, etc. It was not a matter of no war as such, but, rather, a situation where major clashes were prevented between great powers. And the Concert performed this mission successfully, with only two hitches that led to the Crimean war in the 1850s and the Franco–Prussian war in the 1870s. In our day it is just as difficult to imagine a situation causing a military conflict between major countries. Not the least because almost all of them are nuclear powers. A potential hot spot is Taiwan, which may be destined to play the role akin to that of the Black Sea straits in the 19th century. That is, it may become a source of endless tension in relations between leading powers (in this case, between the USA and China). And although quite possibly the planned American interventions will not meet with universal approval, they, nevertheless, will not necessarily cause an end to concert activities. Tectonic shifts in the world system have in the 21st century formed a situation where the strategy of territorial divisions and military containment is giving way to a strategy of the times of the First Concert, viz., cooperation in the area of security and economic engagement. These are obvious prerequisites for a new Concert, and the performers and the organizational format still remain unclear. However, the final answers will take a long time to come.

Concert without US participation will either be senseless or turn into a counterproductive anti-American scheme. The main question is whether the USA will be prepared to join in. In the long run and, maybe, in a mid-term prospect, undoubtedly yes. In a short-term prospect, more probably yes. Even that ode to America's unilateral stance, the recently adopted National Security Strategy of the United States of America carries the following statement: "America will implement its strategies by organizing coalitions—as broad as practicable—of states able and willing to promote a balance of power that favors freedom."[45]

Russia is actually already engaged in a global game of concert. So is the European Union; the question is only what kind of participation in the Concert this is going to be—collective or individual. All depends on whether the EU becomes an independent major player in the area of international and defense policy and how soon this may happen. If not, it will be represented by heirs to the performers in the First Concert.

Today, impediments are diminishing to overall global integration of India, which for decades was alienated from world affairs and culturally detached from the West. A decisive role in this matter was played by the deliberate policy pursued by Washington, which even before 9/11 had embarked on the course of partnership with Delhi. Now, after a period of sharp Indian–US contradictions over India's nuclear programs, the two countries, as their leaders assert, are "natural allies."[46] It should be noted in this context that the chronically complicated Indian–Chinese relations are improving, albeit slowly, which means that one more obstacle is coming down on the way to global Concert.

China's participation in the Concert is the hardest to forecast: the USA is wary lest Beijing should claim the status of a second superpower and defy America. Indeed, China is capable of becoming an Asia-Pacific superpower in the coming twenty or thirty years, but it will have no potential to threaten American security. No desire either. "The further China moves along the way of modernization...the more important for it is partnership with America."[47] Today, the USA is China's leading trade partner, so why threaten the goose that lays golden eggs? It is hard to predict the consequences of American troops' arrival in Central Asia, just as those of the creation of NMD. There is a possibility of a new hotbed of tension emerging and nuclear missile stocks being built up. Or else, it is possible, on the contrary, that Beijing will revise its strategy in favor of greater moderation. I would agree with Henry Kissinger who maintains that Washington should let China understand that the USA,

---

45 The National Security Strategy of the United States of America, Washington. 2002, p. 25.
46 Blackwill, Robert D., "Natural Allies," *The Times of India*, November 2, 2001.
47 Xsuewu Gu, "China and the USA: Partnership in the Search for Strategic Foundation," *Internationale Politik*, no. 2, 2002, p. 13 (Russian edition).

while countering its hegemonic aspirations, still prefers constructive relations and will promote China's participation in a stable world order.[48]

The organizational format of the Second Concert does not look like a crucial problem. The First Concert was rather loose organizationally, having no clearly defined objective and setting no legal obligations. There was no entity like a European government, and there were only sporadic European congresses, most of all reminiscent of what we know today as G-8 summits.

The Second Congress may be more formalized — for example, it may function on the basis of the UN Security Council. But this requires expansion of the Council, with more countries represented in it, while the USA has to get rid of its prejudice against this body, which, as a matter of fact, is not easy. G-8 could also serve as the basis for the Concert, growing into G-9, G-10 and so forth. NATO could also offer a platform for the global Concert. By accepting ever more and weaker members and setting up the Russia–NATO Council, it has been turning from a serious military organization into a political association. In this new status the Alliance could opt for similar councils formed with other countries (it is already stepping up its partnership with Uzbekistan and Mongolia), or use Russian channels to establish contact with them. There are already forums functioning in the manner of Concert—the World Trade Organization and the Organization of Economic Cooperation and Development that Russia is planning to join in the near future. It is quite possible that some entirely new format may be required.

The world is moving and will arrive at an actual global Concert, despite all efforts at unipolar hegemony. It is on a concert basis that problems of survival on Earth can be resolved, with the second, chaotic megascenario thereby forestalled. Whether it is a matter of nonproliferation of mass destruction weapons, or preservation of habitat, or poverty, or epidemics, it has all got to be a matter of concern for all countries with influence, for, indeed, none of them can fly away to live on another planet.

The word "concert" derives not only from the Italian "concerto," but also from the Latin "concerto" (compete). A concerto in music is a composition written for one or, more seldom, for several instruments and an orchestra. What is typical of a concerto is virtuoso solo performance and competition of the soloist with the orchestra. A symphony in which one instrument acquires a solo role on its own has ever since the 18th century been called *symphonique concertante* or *konzertierende Symphonie*.

I have nothing against symphony concerts, the supreme form, make note of it, of instrumental music.

Originally published in *Russia in Global Affairs*, 2002, no. 1.

---

48 Kissinger, Henry, *Does America Need a Foreign Policy. Toward a Diplomacy for the 21st Century*, Simon & Schuster, New York–London–Toronto–Sydney–Singapore.

The Backside of Foreign Policy: Internal Factors in the System of International Ties, Obligations and Projects of the Russian Federation

Aleksei Salmin

> Neither the former Minister of Foreign Affairs Ye. Primakov, nor the former Ambassador to Israel A. Bovin was able to say what kind of mechanism was used for making foreign policy decisions in Russia. [Referring to Russia's nonparticipation in the negotiations in Sharm el-Sheikh].
>
> TV Program *Itogi*, October 22, 2000

> The Ministry of Foreign Affairs has no strategy whatsoever…When it came to serious matters, decisions would be made by either Berezovsky, or—later—by way of usual last-resort assistance, by the Russian President.
>
> Newspaper *Moskovskiy komsomolets*, April 9, 2001

> The previous structure [from Yeltsin's time] for conducting foreign policy was functioning in a sound way.
>
> Newspaper *Kommersant*, April 12, 2001

…Located in the basement of the Ministry of Foreign Affairs of a European country, where an international seminar is being held, is a room, possibly lower than the level of the famous river flowing nearby. Suddenly, a scarcely discernible door opens and swings shut again. Through the door can briefly be glimpsed the building's foundation structure, bunches of colored wires and a seemingly chaotic tangle of tubes. Somebody comes up with a joke: "One seldom witnesses the inner workings of foreign policy with one's own eyes…"

Indeed, whatever the country, far less research is conducted into the mechanisms governing the development of foreign policy than into the policy's actual contents. Foreign policy content is an area that is best compared to a "black box," where the input is made up of virtually everything and the output represents the foreign policy *per se*. To an extent, this is predetermined by the inherent protection of foreign policy issues from outsiders. Incidentally, this protection is always notional, if not indeed ritual to some degree. It is one of the conditions of the foreign policy game. "People's diplomacy" is always eagerly encouraged, but is rarely admitted further than the entrance to the "black box." In part, though, the lack of transparency in the making of foreign policy can be explained by the great public interest in foreign policy issues. Foreign policy, just like medicine, is a sphere in which everybody claims to be an expert; and many people sincerely believe they can influence it, which makes it more difficult than it may seem to discern the voices—or silence—of the true actors in this chorus. Yet, in some measure, the singularity of foreign policy can be explained by the conventionalism, and lack of dramatism that represent a condition for the successful functioning of a mechanism inherently protected against daily domestic political collisions and allowing for almost no improvisations or reforms that could be of interest to a researcher. Those who speak of changes in the mechanisms of foreign policy decision-making sometimes merely mean style shifts predetermined by the actors' personalities or the political cultures these actors belong to. Situations in which the mechanisms themselves are transformed (or at least seem to be bound to be transformed) are a completely different matter. However, such changes are rare phenomena that may be brought about by historical cataclysms, such as the breakup of the USSR and the emergence of a new political reality, a new foreign policy among other things, from the wreckage.

In any case, analysis of the domestic "inner workings" of Russian foreign policy is a new enterprise, which has so far raised greater interest among researchers abroad than at home.[1] Practical concern about this subject matter prevails over academic interest, which at least partly determines the content of most of the relevant works published so far. A historical descriptive—or one may say "ideographic"—approach is apparently given preference over a systemic diachronic, or "nomothetic," one. This is hardly the result of some general philosophical stance; rather it is a consequence of the lack of very basic information, combined with an urgent need to provide answers to rather specific questions of substance within relatively short time spans. As a result, any research in the sphere will boil down to a case study or a political-historical chronology, with both involving particular foreign policy connotations. Various *agents* or *actors* operating in the foreign policy domain appear as forces that affect a certain political and administrative process that is unstructured, possibly since its structure is *a priori* denied or questioned. In slightly crude terms, one may say that the approach contains either the implicit or explicit suggestion that every actor involved will consistently seek to subordinate "foreign policy" to their own "agenda" (that is to their rationally interpreted interests) and can be restrained only by other actors operating in the same field in accor-

---

1 In our opinion, the following is the best published collection dealing mainly with the activities of particular actors, i.e. state agencies and societal institutions: Godzimirski, J. M. (ed.), *New and Old Actors in Russian Foreign Policy*. Conference Proceedings. Norwegian Institute of International Affairs, Oslo, 1998. In Russia *per se* to date nothing has been published that could be compared to the above-mentioned collection in its scope, although individual articles (including by the Russian authors of the collection) dealing with particular facets and aspects of the operation of the foreign policy mechanism do appear sometimes.

dance with the same logic. Consequently, what we call "foreign policy" will emerge as the resulting vector of the interaction of these actors ensuing from their striving to maximize their gains while minimizing their losses. Naturally, if one chooses to adhere to this approach, the vector in question is likely to appear rather bizarre. Indeed, this may suggest that the actors behave irrationally, for they will not consider the factor of foreign policy consistency as contributing to their gains. The irrationality in question is bound to make itself felt in the absence of personnel continuity and responsibility, in institutional instability and other such consequences—that is, in what, for the sake of simplicity, we might call deficient policy consolidation, in particular in the foreign policy sphere.

We will not deny the merits—and in some instances the inevitability—of the approach in question. However, we will lean towards another perspective that focuses on the most important, though frequently changing, functions of various subsystems within the general system responsible for the operation of the state, i.e. of the Russian Federation, nationally, globally and regionally, rather than on individual manifestations or violations of these functions, however significant they might be in understanding the actual history. In other words, one does not have to proceed from the presumption that the "black box" is the same for all, like a mass grave. Even at the moment when an objective is identified, there may already be a number of "black boxes." An essential presumption from this perspective is that—as they operate within different subsystems—the same actors (state institutions, agencies, NGOs, etc.) may behave in different ways in accordance with different rationales. For these actors retain their status as institutions that have emerged within dissimilar paradigms and are relatively inertial in their operation, and they do not possess exclusive rights to the rationales in question. The rationales themselves may be more or less obviously in conflict, and this can reveal itself in the apparent, and sometimes even typically scandalous, inconsistency of the actors' actions.[2] The point is that—apart from having to compete and make reasonable accommodations with other parties involved—the actors simultaneously have to meet a kind of "schizophrenic" objective of reconciling the initially heterogeneous rationales governing their own behaviour. Such conflicts not merely may, but are bound to, lose at least their apparent intensity, when affected by the high degree of internal institutional fragmentation, constant reforming of the institutional structures, chaotic shifts in personnel appointments, or by all these factors together in different combinations and sequences.

The approach in question requires account to be taken of a number of specific features—not only of the mechanism that shapes foreign policy, but also

---

2 Examples could be the "clarification of the position" in connection with NATO enlargement in the first half of the 1990s, and the diplomatic maneuvering around the BMD problem more recently.

of the political system as a whole, which will make it more difficult to directly compare the experience of the Russian Federation in 1991–2001 with the practice either of other countries, or of Russia's own ancestor in geographic, demographic, and institutional terms, or from the perspective of international law. The following are three factors that primarily influence the principal basis upon which foreign policy decisions are made:

- First, foreign policy challenges and involvement, both new and inherited by the Russian Federation from the USSR, and also the emerging—in connection with the challenges in question or irrespectively—elements of a new world order and new regional order.
- Second, general characteristics of the political regime that is taking shape in post-soviet Russia under the influence of, but not necessarily in conformity with, specific ideological perceptions. This has so far been insufficiently researched, which hampers analysis of the foreign policy decision-making process.
- Third, the impulses originating from society and its elite; the conceptualization of the state's foreign policy by society, which may arguably be called "civil society" and which forms, or fails to form, an integrated notion of foreign policy objectives.

The Challenges and Historical "Anchors" of Foreign Policy

There is an assertion (which has become commonplace) that it was the absence of consolidated power that was the principal feature of the regime in 1991 that hampered not only its confident development towards democracy (the regime's declared goal) but also its ability to build its relations with the outside world in a way that would not be humiliating for the country. However, the "absence of consolidated power" is a very general and abstract notion. As one Russian observer remarks,

> while campaigning in electoral races, representatives of nearly all sectors of the Russian political spectrum make broad use of the idea of decline of the strong state order in Russia and the loss of the country's worthy position in the world order. They repeatedly propose a multitude of simple recipes of how to strengthen the state, how to find a way out of various crises, and how to effectively protect Russia's state interests in the international arena. All these propositions, however, are but mere slogans. No successful attempts to analyze the deeper roots of the emergence of a truly new type of state, i.e. the "weak" state that we had a chance to observe in the 1990s, have been undertaken by either Russian political scientists, or active politicians.[3]

---

3 Baluyev, D. G., "Vneshnepoliticheskaya rol Rossiyskogo gosudarstva v perekhodnyi period [The role of the Russian state in the foreign policy sphere in the transitional period], http://www.kis.ru/~dbalu, p. 1.

Whether this is a new type of state or not (it is rather one of the old, long-forgotten ones), the lamentable lack of coordination of its actions both within the country and in relation to the outside world can by no means be ascribed solely to the apparent shortcomings or contradictions of lawmaking perceived as "canonical" by jurists and seen as technologically uncomplicated by political scientists specializing in institutionalism, nor to the apparent inability of the branches of power, the ministries and other state agencies to conduct consistent state policy. The main reason for the poor coordination consists in a conflict between the command logic that still forms the basis of the expectations of all institutions of state power, and the actual behavior of those new and old actors that either must be the state's instruments—either *ex officio* or *dum officio*—or claim the right to this status.

There were a few important factors that influenced the state authorities' operation in the 1990s, in particular the ambiguous behavior by the bureaucracy, which almost openly demonstrated that it was not merely an obedient agent of the state authorities,[4] the covert and overt struggle among monopolists, "oligarchs" and other figures that would at times usurp particular functions of state power and use their lobbies in the state power bodies, and, last but not least, the decade-long *war of all against all* at the level of regional clans. These factors would now and then paralyze more or less rational moves by the state authorities, or bring (stimulate) the authorities to act irrationally as far as the national interests were concerned, or—even more importantly—would often simply reduce the authorities' actions to absurdity. One can suggest an analogy with the classic scene of a croquet game described in *Alice's Adventures in Wonderland*. The spectacular absurdity of the game depicted by Lewis Carroll is not merely a result of the players breaking the rules of the game, their lack of skill, or unfair and helpless refereeing, but is above all associated with the fact that the conventional "instruments" and "means"—the balls, mallets, and hoops—suddenly turn out to be living creatures acting as they choose. They intentionally, or unconsciously, undermine the players' plans until the latter, together with the referees, manage to replace them again with inanimate objects, or establish a new living, complicated, yet predictable, system that can incorporate the new creatures and develop an internal balance and self-regulation.

The state power of the 1990s did not always have a chance to act as an actual state power, that is as a strong player, let alone as an arbiter in resolving conflicts of internal bureaucratic, economic, and regional (located both within and between regions) interests, or as a successful promoter of optimized promising policies, particularly in the economic and social spheres. No attempts to *con-*

---

4 For details see: Salmin, A., "Nepobezhdennyi nepobeditel [Undefeated non-winner]. In lieu of an introduction." In: *Epokha Yeltsina. Ocherki politicheskoy istorii* [Yeltsin's epoch. Essays in political history], Moscow, Vagrius, 2001.

solidate such power by "improving" the legislative process, by ordering coordination of its different branches and agencies, or by subordinating their components to a single coordination center were successful in removing the main
cause of the state power infirmity. The living "balls" and "mallets" did not
overtly counteract the laws, but nor would they follow orders. The authorities,
of course, were aware of the situation, but continued to keep up appearances
so as to avoid further loss of face, behaving in extraordinary circumstances as
any authority would behave in a conventional situation. A simple analysis of
the presidential decrees and regulations issued by the government shows that
virtually no officials lost their positions during the decade, notwithstanding the
anecdotal precedent when A. Illarionov was dismissed for "poor performance"
and "misconduct" (remarkably, when such terms were used they would actually imply other motives).

As for domestic policy of the 1990s, i.e. the system of relations between
national actors exclusively, the decision-making mechanism—including in the
spheres directly or indirectly associated with foreign policy—appeared to result
from arbitrary interaction among the actors in question, which was to an
extent regulated by rather flexible norms, largely determined by the interaction
itself. However, the situation in those spheres that are not absolutely dependent on internal factors is somewhat different. For the sake of simplification,
one might say that influential actors were able to "make deals" within the internal political domain, even behind the backs of the state authorities, thus facilitating—or complicating—their existence. However, in the sphere of foreign
policy, it is not really possible to do this, since the authority is the only legitimate subject in international relations. In this case the "lack of consolidation"
of state policy has a different meaning as compared to the sphere of domestic
policy. In this sphere, several "strata" and "subsystems" that formed and adopted
foreign policy decisions can be singled out. The specialization of these subsystems was determined by world history itself, with its inertia and consequent
long-lasting systemic inconsistency, rather than by the reversible—given sufficient concentration of will and resources—resultant of anybody's individual
planned or random actions. Let us refer to the subsystems formed at different
times by different foreign policy challenges as follows: the subsystem of maintaining the superpower paradigm, the energy and raw materials export subsystem, the foreign debt service subsystem, the post-communist space disinte-
gration/reintegration subsystem, and the global/European integration subsystem.

SUPERPOWER PARADIGM SUBSYSTEM. After the collapse of the Soviet Union, the
Russian Federation preserved its jurisdiction over two-thirds of the territory of
the former USSR and a little over half of what used to be the Soviet population. Russia's share in the global GDP dropped by nearly an order of magni-

tude, i.e. from eight to 1.5 per cent.[5] The country's armed forces were cut by more than two-thirds. In the cases of all countries that in the 20th century experienced cataclysms (of any political origin) comparable in scale, the essence of their foreign policy always underwent rapid change. This was true of the Russian Empire, as well as of the Austro-Hungarian, Ottoman, German and Japanese empires, and also of the colonial empires, namely the British, French, Portuguese, and Dutch empires. Obviously, the foreign policy horizons of the USSR, the Austrian Republic, Turkish Republic, post-war Japan, Germany in various periods of its post-Versailles history, and post-colonial Great Britain, France, Belgium, Portugal, and the Netherlands were essentially different to those of their predecessors. One cannot, however, make (at least so far) the same unconditional statement with regard to the Russian Federation. The Foreign Policy Concept of the Russian Federation that was approved by President of the Russian Federation V. Putin in 2000 places the section "Priorities of the Russian Federation in addressing global problems" prior to the section "Regional priorities," the latter containing what is intended as a formulation of Russia's interests and goals in the post-Soviet space.[6] Despite the ideological mutation, institutional reformation and geopolitical cataclysms that Russia underwent, the country's foreign policy has been characterized by essential structural continuity, at least in articulating problems, if not in suggesting solutions, which can be explained by specific reasons.

One of the reasons is that—for all that has been happening—Russia lost only a "cold"—i.e. primarily economic—war, and not a real one. Russia's withdrawal from the regions that had belonged to the Russian Empire and the USSR did not result from lost battles. Russia retained all its sovereignty, or at least did not lose any against its will. Russia does, and will remain, a nuclear power in the medium term. For this reason it continues to be closely connected with the principal of its former rivals, the USA, as well as with other nuclear powers, through the system of mutual obligations within the framework of the disarmament process, mechanisms of mutual deterrence, control over the nonproliferation of nuclear weapons, etc. The Russian Federation inherited the status of one of the five permanent members of the UN Security Council with the power of veto. This is a strategic position that allows Russia to play a considerable role in safeguarding its national security and global stability based on the "Yalta" decision-making paradigm, insomuch as this system is still preserved, despite the disintegration of the Yalta system of domination, despite the decline of the UN's role in taking important decisions in the various

5 The calculation is based on: Bolotin, B., *Sotsialno-ekonomicheskiye pokazateli Zapada i Rossii*, MeiMO, 1999, no. 8, pp. 114–128.
6 *Nezavisimaya gazeta, Nezavisimoye voyennoye obozreniye*, July 14, 2000; see also this volume.

spheres, despite the possible reform of the UN Security Council, etc. It was in the post-Soviet period that Russia joined the G-7 of the leading world powers that eventually, arguably, became the G-8. And it was as a military, rather than as an economic, superpower that Russia joined. Obviously, the institutional and procedural continuity of Russia's foreign policy was largely preconditioned, since Russia had assumed all the international legal obligations of the USSR after its formal disintegration and—most importantly—had to carry the burden of the actual superpower-status legacy that cannot be rapidly shaken off, even if the will is there.[7] Had Russia been a state similar to any of the Eastern European post-communist countries, its institutions and agencies concerned with the country's foreign policy would likely have undergone entirely different transformations.

The Ministry of Foreign Affairs of the Russian Federation, its Defense Ministry and the General Staff together have constituted a "strategic institutional bloc" supported by influential intelligence and analytical services in the same form they took during each stage of Russia's recent history. Behind the Ministry of Foreign Affairs there has been a global network of embassies, while the bloc's military component has been supported by the Strategic Missile Forces, Space Forces, the Navy deployed on the high seas, Strategic Air Forces, and the entire military-industrial complex. According to some sources, the Russian Federation retained some 60 per cent of the USSR's industrial potential, with 80 per cent of its military-industrial and scientific capacities.[8] This externally oriented bloc can probably be regarded as the key institutional, as well as conceptual, "anchor" that—at least hypothetically—provides foundation for Russian foreign policy as the successor to Soviet foreign policy.

The priority status of the global geo-strategic complex in Russia's foreign policy has been reinforced by one more factor, namely by the preservation of the essence of the global geopolitical position of Russia as a great Eurasian power, or—one may say—by a relative immutability of the world itself. Indeed, the main actors involved in world politics remained in place throughout the 1990s, a relatively peaceful period from their perspective. The geopolitical "landscape" around the Russian Federation has changed enormously since the Soviet times. Nevertheless, Russia's "main" neighbors and some associated knots of problems remain unchanged, even though the latter have been ideologically reinterpreted in the new conditions. Moving clockwise, there remains the USA, not only as Russia's global partner and rival, but also as a simple

---

7 In a sense, the same can be said of the USA, which has also been experiencing a kind of "abstinence syndrome" owing to the loss of its role as a "fighting superpower," and is also, to an extent, burdened by the foreign policy legacy of the Cold War, détente, and *perestroika*.

8 Fyodorov, Y. Ye., "Russian New Industrialists and Foreign Policy." In: Godzimirski J. M. (ed.), *New and Old Actors in Russian Foreign Policy*. Conference Proceedings. Norwegian Institute of International Affairs, 1998, p. 208.

geographic neighbor. There is Japan with its territorial claims on the South Kurile Islands. China has emerged as a new strategic partner, involved, in particular, in the formation of the security system within the framework of the Shanghai Cooperation Organization (SCO). However, it has not yet settled its territorial dispute with the Russian Federation. The knot of problems associated with Afghanistan has not disappeared, even though it has undergone numerous ideological reinterpretations. Iran and Turkey also remain among the traditional concerns of Russia's foreign policy. In so far as their national governments' powers have not been transferred to EU jurisdiction, the countries of Western and Central Europe maintain their traditional relations with their eastern neighbor, irrespective of the changes in the political order of the latter. There remain various international organizations, such as the European Union, NATO, OSCE and others, each performing its function, while continuing to develop. The former USSR Ministry of Foreign Affairs became the Ministry of Foreign Affairs of the Russian Federation and upheld the continuity of the established routine foreign policy activities in all traditional areas. At the same time, Russia's presence in the world arena has declined (especially in the regions that were less promising to the state, for example in Africa and Latin America). Interestingly, though, there was an "interface" that, to an extent, promoted continuity of the foreign policy process: namely, the key political figures of the world who remained in their positions and only gradually, and at different times, were replaced by other figures who still tended to have had experience of interaction with Soviet/Russian partners.

There is no need to make any special comment on the fact that the "global geo-strategic subsystem" was operating under new conditions in a completely different context. Indeed, instead of the Communist Party Central Committee Politburo, presided over by the party's general secretary, or by the president of the USSR who was simultaneously acting as the general secretary of the Party Central Committee, the political system was now managed by a nationally elected president of the Russian Federation, along with the Presidential Administration and Security Council (i.e. constitutional bodies), which inherited both the institutional and the actual power "niches" founded by the previous system.

The decline in the inertia described above is likely to cause a shift in the significance of the key "institutional and conceptual anchor" of Russian foreign policy, which had secured the continuity of this policy. Probably, the "center of gravity" of foreign policy will shift towards other subsystems, which will probably lead to its essential (rather than immediate formal) restructuring. There is another possible scenario that could develop alongside this one. There is a body of opinion that believes the military-industrial complex, which is extremely interested in both selling its products within the country and exporting them, will persistently lobby for a policy of "controlled confrontation" with regard to the traditional "sparring partners" that the USSR had within the framework of

the Yalta peace process. This will imply selling arms to these powers' rivals
and enemies, for example to the People's Republic of China and the so-called
rogue states.[9] The revival of the "Yalta paradigm" confrontational component
will require serious efforts in order to mobilize institutional and popular support within the country, as well as an equally serious correction of the foreign
policy emphasis. Remarkably, a second version of the old paradigm is likely to
turn out to be a mere pseudomorph, for its actual content, with the exception
of the scenario of a revolutionary change of the entire political system, will be
radically different from the original.

However, there are no serious grounds for demonizing the military-industrial complex as a possible consistent lobbyist for this political course. First of
all, the military-industrial complex is by no means an internally unified entity.
There are various interests in play, which may not be easily reconcilable or
may not even be close enough to be integrated at all. Second, the impulses
generated by the military-industrial complex are not necessarily a reflection of
a purely egotistic posture, incompatible with the national interests. It is not the
perceived "egotism" on the part of the military-industrial complex that poses
an essential problem for the state and society in this case. In fact, an absolute
absence of this kind of "egotism" would appear odd, if not unnatural. The "egotism" will persist, as long as there is the military-industrial complex or any
other established economic and political complex. Neither is it an admissible
degree of conformity—or nonconformity—between the corporate and national
interests that matters the most. It is hard to say who can specify this degree
today, or indeed whenever and wherever, and what criteria they should use to
do so. It is a misconception that national interests can be formulated as an
abstract idea, irrespective of the political process. Such ideas can, at best, be
used as outlines or draft editorial amendments to the political interpretation
of national interests. Ultimately, the process of political interpretation of these
ideas will produce not academic schools, but rather nations, i.e. nation states
with a dominant "civic culture" and subordinated "subject political" and
"parochial political" cultures.[10] What poses a really significant problem is the
fact that the Russian Federation, a state that—to use constitutional terms—
adheres to the democratic principle of decision-making, or—broader—to the
political decision-making process, has not yet formed a mechanism that would
serve for political conceptualization of national interests and be integral to the
process in question. In speaking of national interests here and later, we mean

---

9 *Ibid.*, pp. 209–211.
10 Almond, G., Verba, S., *The Civic Culture.* Princeton (N.J.), Princeton University
   Press, 1963. Of course, it would be another extreme to suggest that nation states
   may emerge only in the process of working out national interests that will single
   these states out from the otherwise homogeneous world. As E. Renan said, the
   nation is also a "daily plebiscite"; "Qu'est-ce qu'une nation?" Conference faite
   en Sorbonne, le 11 mars 1882, p. 27.

a mediated consensus, stimulated and articulated by the elites (with the foreign policy elite actively involved), between the main societal groups that are capable of political expression and assertion of their positions, with regard to the foreign policy goals and missions.

Of course, the above-mentioned mechanism will not guarantee success in all cases. It is possible to imagine a consensus that lacks flexibility, or representativeness, or durability, or that is deprived of political imaginativeness or historiosophic depth, etc. Virtually the same arguments that are usually used to support the market economy or political democracy can be put forward in favor of the mechanism in question. Namely, the principle of self-regulation, which is the foundational principle in all three cases, involves stimulated reflection and, therefore, will rarely produce dangerous situations while in the routine operating mode, unlike other principles that do not provide for the emergence of competitive political and economic ideas in the course of debates, disputes, rivalries and political struggle.

As long as there is no such mechanism, the discrepancy between the institutional and procedural foreign-policy-making patterns will produce the danger (which may be either real or perceived, but—most importantly—politically unverifiable) of monopoly over the policy being gained by the military-industrial complex within the subsystem in question, or by other agencies in other cases. Another associated danger will consist either in the underestimation of real threats and challenges, or in a constant perceived underestimation of these threats and challenges. It is hard to estimate which of the three scenarios is worst, but it is obvious that any of them may prove very bad in certain contexts.

ENERGY AND RAW MATERIALS EXPORT SUBSYSTEM. Russia's economic ties with the rest of the world today are rather specific in nature. Russia is mainly involved in exporting energy sources, raw materials, and arms, and plays the role of a chronic and rather irresponsible loan recipient and debtor. This reality has changed the conventional Soviet notion of foreign policy to a considerable extent and has led many authors to describe the future of this policy in terms typical of the "globalization paradigm," the latter perceived as prioritizing the economic over the political, and in a sense dissolving the borderline between domestic and foreign policies.[11] Today, Russia's fuel and energy complex appears to have been playing an outstanding role in securing the eco-

---

11 The range of possible scenarios is very broad in this sense: from those countries in which economic and political interests can, in principle, be integrated, with the "national interests" as the dominant factor, to those states where, for some reason, there is no national economic complex at all, and the state also ceases to be the key governing entity on the territory that is formally under its control (the so-called failed states). One special case is the remaining totalitarian regimes, where the border between the economy and politics, as well as between the internal and external is, in a sense, rather tenuous.

nomic and political stability of the country. This complex represents the most profitable and significant subsystem of the Russian national economy for both exporters and importers, as far as the interaction between the Russian and world economies is concerned. In 1994–2000, the fuel and energy complex supplied from 42 to 56 per cent of currency inflow into the Russian budget, including 40–55 per cent from exports to the countries of the "far abroad," and 52–69 per cent from trade with the CIS countries, with a continuous growth trend.[12]

We consider the fuel and energy complex to be a second "institutional anchor" of Russian foreign policy that connects it with the past, on the one hand, and, on the other hand, forms a future-oriented foundation for a special subsystem in the sphere of foreign policy decision-making.

The problem associated with the country's dependence on the fuel and energy complex emerged long before the 1990s—in 1958, when the Communist Party and USSR leadership made the fundamental decision to supply increasing quantities of oil (and—as from the 1970s—natural gas) to the West for the sake of maintaining the political and economic stability of a system whose efficiency was clearly declining. While implementing what they perceived as a rather subtle scheme (supporting the Arab world in order to undermine the West politically and economically, attempting to achieve the same goal by keeping Western Europe dependent on Soviet energy supplies, increasing the dependence of the Eastern European economies on the USSR, and investing in the Soviet economy), "the Soviet leaders actually weakened their own country and reduced it to the role of a raw-material supplier governed by all kinds of uncertainties of the world economy. The results proved quite lamentable for the USSR: the oil dollars[13] were largely spent on the production of tanks, missiles, nuclear warheads and chemical weapons that had to be destroyed later [within the framework of the first foreign policy decision-making subsystem—author]. This is what the last Soviet Minister of Foreign Economic Relations K. F. Katushev said in this regard: 'Indeed, our country received large funds in those years. However, we, the government, failed to make effective use of the money. I would say that, to some degree, the money distracted us, or even corrupted both our leaders and us.'"[14]

---

12 *Tamozhennaya statistika vneshney torgovli Rossiyskoy Federatsii* [The customs statistics of the foreign trade of the Russian Federation], Moscow, 1995, pp. 10, 14, 18; Moscow, 1999, pp. 17, 21, 25; Mikhailov, V. G., Khlebina, Yu. A., "Izmeneniya v strukture vneshneekonomicheskoy torgovli posle 17 avgusta 1998 goda [Changes in the structure of foreign trade after August 17, 1998], www.rio.ru/rus/Economic/199909ImportExport/default.htm

13 In 1973–1985 alone, some 200 billion oil dollars were received. See *Expert*, 1998, no. 42, p. 41.

14 Denchev, K., "Neftegazovyi faktor v mezhdunarodnykh otnosheniyakh [The factor of oil and natural gas in international relations]," *Politiya*, 1999, Fall, no.3, p. 133.

In the Soviet period, the ever increasing—or, one may say, accumulating—dependence of the superpower on the dollars gained from the oil and gas sales remained a latent and potential factor, as far as the country's foreign policy was concerned. This dependence did not lead to the emergence of an autonomous decision-making system in the sphere of foreign policy, or even the practice of systematic lobbying for the fuel and energy complex's interests within the power structures. The dissolution of COMECON and the subsequent disintegration of the USSR caused a collapse of the previously united fuel and energy complex. After the functional components of the fuel and energy complex were privatized, the situation changed. The export complex, in a broad sense, became a most important independent decision-making subsystem in the spheres of the economy and politics, including the foreign policy sphere. This complex comprises an immense domestic Russian component and impressive foreign constituents. The administrative entities in the border regions of the Russian Federation "produce no more than 15 per cent of the country's exports. The predominant location of the export production in the heart of the country implies that the regions in which such production is concentrated will depend on the federal trans-regional communications and other infrastructures necessary for opening gateways to foreign markets, as well as on the transit territories. In their turn, the transit territories, lacking in their own resources, will depend on budget transfers, largely formed at the expense of the inflow from exports. The banking centers in ports and capitals will play a more active role as mediators between exporter regions and foreign markets, domestic and foreign investors, etc."[15] To be more precise, some authors believe a key factor in Russia's economy in the 1990s, and also indirectly in its politics, is "the oil-finance trunk route Tyumen–Moscow."[16] Indeed, 60 per cent of the export production of the Russian Federation is concentrated in Siberia. Almost 100 per cent of the exported Russian natural gas, some 90 per cent of the oil exports, and 60 per cent of the coal exports are produced in Western Siberia. Eastern Siberia supplies 85 per cent of Russia's aluminum exports, 70 per cent of copper exports, and 50 per cent of nickel exports.[17]

The nature of the dependence on what is termed in political-economic jargon "the pipe," and all the hustle around it determine the most important economic, social and political (including in the sphere of foreign policy) characteristics of the current regime. The following factors in their inseparable, although often chaotic, unity largely determine the Russian domestic and foreign policies: the struggle for investments in the energy sector of the economy,

---

15 Vardomskiy, L., Treyvish, A., "Strategicheskaya ustoychivost ekonomicheskogo prostranstva Rossii [Strategic stability of Russia's economic space]," www.ccsis.msk.ru/RUSSIA/1/vardom.htm

16 *Ibid.*

17 *Ibid.*

on the one hand, and, on the other, the struggle for control over its resources, for the right to export oil, gas, and other resources, for the opportunity to participate in the privatization of the energy facilities and systems in Russia and other countries, for the opportunity to establish domestic prices and tariffs, and to benefit from, if not influence, oscillations in the world prices. The fuel and energy complex, as a political entity (or, rather, an assemblage of entities constituting an internally conflict-prone system for decision-making and lobbying), comprises a variety of components: the largest corporations, the regions specializing in either production and/or transportation of energy resources, the associated ministries, State Duma committees, so-called "invisible factions" and pressure groups lobbying for particular interests over the inter-factional and inter-ministerial barriers. In the 1990s, the practice of exchanging managers and executives became common among the most important state institutions and export complex components.

Nevertheless, there is some direct and indirect evidence of considerable structural tensions in the relations within the "subsystem number two" of Russian foreign policy in the 1990s. In particular, the tensions were caused by the competition within the complex, and "frontal" collisions of interests—at times merely declared ones—of representatives of the energy complex, "bureaucracy," and "politicians." According to the opinion expressed by P. Kandel in 1998, "the Ministry of Foreign Affairs does not really lay the road for the Gazprom, Lukoil, Rosvooruzheniye [arms exporting organization], or Ministry of Atomic Energy, but rather follows or checks them *post factum*."[18] The situation has supposedly undergone systemic changes in recent years. At any rate, there are data and estimations showing that such a suggestion may be well grounded. For example, V. Zlatev, the General Director and Chairman of the Managing Board of Lukoil Bulgaria, believes that:

Russia has abandoned the stance it adhered to from 1992 to 1994, when it apparently tried to isolate the states of the Caspian region and Central Asia from the world market. Russia's position today looks entirely different, not least owing to the influence exerted by Gazprom, Lukoil and other energy companies that affect the Russian economy today to a far greater extent than they did three or four years ago. In general, despite the seeming disagreements between the largest Russian energy-producing corporations and the state, the corporations have, in reality, become one of the most efficient instruments of Russian foreign policy."[19]

---

18 Kandel, P., "Rossiyskaya vneshnyaya politika: diagnoz i sostoyaniye [Russian foreign policy: diagnosis and condition]," *Vlast*, 1998, no. 6, p. 23.

19 Zlatev, V., Rol i mesto energeticheskogo faktora v politicheskikh protsessakh [Role and place of the energy factor in political processes]. A comparative analysis of the Caspian and Balkan knots. The author's summary of a dissertation for the Candidate of Political Science degree, Moscow, 2001, p. 19.

It is obviously implied here that the largest companies of the export complex, which eventually constituted the fuel industrial complex, have gained rather firm positions in a number of foreign countries in recent times and are actively pursuing their interests in others.[20] According to Director of Public Relations at the Siberian Aluminum group Ye. Ivanov, the largest corporations involved in international business activities "may become instruments of the state's foreign policy. For example, Lukoil represents such an instrument in the Near East, while Gazprom—virtually all over the world. Incidentally, their involvement in the world markets makes patriots of big businesses, even against their will. If a corporation is new in the market, it will be interested in support by a strong state pursuing an active foreign policy doctrine. Any corporation needs state protection. For example, when the Russian steel producers were faced with the anti-dumping process, a strong state was what they were dreaming about."[21]

In these conditions, the state, embodied in the Ministry of Foreign Affairs and the government, gained—at least theoretically—an opportunity to influence the courses pursued by the energy producers to the best advantage of the national interest, instead of having to try to impose its idealistic political and economic projects in the face of similar idealistic projects lobbied for by the energy producers. There is a chance that "strategic partnership" between the state and some corporations in the sphere of foreign policy may enhance consolidation of the domestic decision-making process under the aegis of the state authorities.

If one ventured to forecast the possible development of relations in all "export" subsystems of the foreign policy decision-making (i.e. in the fuel and energy complex, the Unified Energy System of Russia, the atomic energy industry, military-industrial complex, etc.), one might suggest that this development will, *mutatis mutandis*, follow the scenario that is already evident in the case of the "advanced" part of the fuel and energy complex. The logic of a zero game that the "complexes" and the state are playing against each other will eventually be replaced by the logic of reconciliation of the existing private and national interests (represented in "conventional" situations by the ministries managing relevant industries, the Ministry of Foreign Affairs, the government in general). Ideally, the state should have the final say. However, such a development cannot be guaranteed. That is why much has to be done in order to rule out the scenario in which the state may approach the point where the big corporate interests may, even if not deliberately, bring the state to play somebody else's games, dangerous for everybody.

---

20 For instance, Lukoil Bulgaria provides over one quarter of the country's budget and controls some six per cent of its GDP.
21 Gotova, N., "'Novaya zhizn' oligarkhov [The 'New Life' of the oligarchs]," http://cherchez.try.md/kompr012.html

FOREIGN DEBT SERVICE SUBSYSTEM. The third essential foreign policy "anchor" is also partly (or, to be precise, half) associated with Russia's role as legal "executor" of the USSR. This subsystem comprises the totality of issues related to the country's foreign debts. In April 2001, the amount of the foreign debt (including the USSR's debts assumed by the Russian Federation) made up 144.4 billion USD, which exceeds the country's three-year budget and amounts to some two-thirds (65 per cent) of its GDP.[22] The political process in this vital sphere, inherited from the recent past, was remarkable for the high level at which the main decisions were made (e.g. whether to contract new state debts in principle), on the one hand, and for the rather dispersed process of decision-making in other cases (e.g. who and at what level can receive loans, how they should be used, what conditions for debt restructuring should be bargained for, etc.), on the other hand. Today, it appears that the key decision making chain looks as follows: President—Government—Foreign Trade Bank—Ministry of Finance—State Duma of the Russian Federation. Besides, at every stage, there is always a special link in the chain that serves as an "interface" whose task is to conduct negotiations with creditors. Naturally, the new elite was not satisfied with the old flexible and largely improvised scheme for servicing the foreign debt (or indeed with the debtor life-style as such). It was President Putin who first came up with the idea of reforming the existing routine. It was suggested that a unified mechanism should be created to manage the foreign debt, which would comprise a special agency and a reformed Foreign Trade Bank.[23]

POST-COMMUNIST SPACE DISINTEGRATION/REINTEGRATION SUBSYSTEM. This institutional "anchor" of Russian foreign policy refers to Russia's relations with the newly independent states that used to be part of the Russian Empire and the USSR, as well as with the countries of the former "socialist community." The oxymoron "disintegration subsystem" embraces the more or less lengthy process of "divorce" from the former parts of the single ideological system that used to be managed from one center (the USSR and its periphery: the "socialist community") and related issues.

There were several circumstances in the first post-communist decade—and even today—that suggested Russia's relations with the majority of former USSR republics should be considered in a context different from the context of interaction between the Russian Federation and any other states.

First, in Russia's relations with the former Soviet republics, the law does not play exactly the same role as it plays in its relations with the countries of the "far abroad." At any rate, it does not do so as far as the principle of "*pacta sunt*

22 *Rossiyskaya gazeta*, April 17, 2001.
23 *Ibid.*

servanda" is concerned. As Belarussian President A. Lukashenko said, "you would hardly conclude an agreement with Germany or the USA, only to fail to keep it, would you?"[24] Between 1991 and 2001, some 1,200 judicial acts were signed within the CIS framework at various levels (i.e. international, inter-governmental, inter-ministerial). The majority of these documents are not operating in reality. The reason why the agreements will not work is not only that the CIS was, as many believe, still-born (or, as former Ukrainian President L. Kravchuk put it, an organization that at best fulfilled the function of "divorce proceedings" for the former USSR republics), whereas it should have been bilateral ties that were developed in the first place. Experience shows that the situation is nearly the same in the sphere of bilateral relations. For example, by mid-2001 Russia and its biggest CIS partner Ukraine had concluded more than 160 interstate and inter-governmental agreements. However, most of the contents of these documents have remained merely on paper. All this applies equally to other legal realities (or fictions) of multilateral cooperation, such as the activities of the CIS Council of Defense Ministers, founded in 1992, the CIS Collective Security Treaty, which envisaged the establishment of a Collective Security Council,[25] the Union of Belarus and Russia, the Customs Union.[26]

One gets the impression that most of the international legal acts that were

---

24 *Vesti*, June 5, 2001.
25 Referring to the activities of the Collective Security Council and the need for its renewal and specification of its mission, former Security Council Secretary S. Ivanov emphasized the factors of the "traditional bureaucratic red-tape" (*Interfax*, October 8, 2000), while B. Khakimov, a member of the Collegium of the Ministry of Foreign Affairs and director of the first CIS Department of the Ministry of Foreign Affairs, admitted that the "first stage of the treaty operation (1992–1999) proved scarcely productive. The process of development of cooperation lacked dynamism. The proclaimed plans for the formation of the security system were not implemented. The Collective Security Council, the highest authority of the Collective Security Treaty, did not convene on a regular basis, its sittings having been held on what may be called the 'leftover principle,' i.e. after the CIS summits, and would boil down to the mere signing of documents." See Khakimov, B., "Kollektivnaya bezopasnost v SNG [Collective Security in the CIS]," *Mezhdunarodnaya zhizn*, 2001, no. 7, p. 16.
26 Referring to the Customs Union, N. Isingarin (Kazakhstan), Chairman of the Integration Committee of the Customs Union, said: "Let us clear up the matter right away: the Customs Union has never existed as a legally formalized organization with this title. In 1995, agreements on the Customs Union were concluded, which rather defined the goal of the interstate cooperation, but did not stipulate the formation of an international organization that would implement the postulated missions. In February 1999, the Agreement on a Customs Union and Single Economic Space was signed, which, however, did not contain any decision on the organization either." See *Nezavisimaya gazeta*, October 14, 2000.

concluded on CIS territory, irrespective of their status, are largely meant as protocols of intention, for there are no mechanisms that would ensure their unconditional execution, while the parties involved are, by and large, hardly interested in creating or mobilizing such mechanisms, despite the official rhetoric they employ. One might suggest that there are three important circumstances affecting the situation:

- The existence in the recent past of a unified and well integrated economy, which largely disintegrated and was reorganized based on new foundations during the 1990s, and yet retained its unity in some very important spheres of cooperation, and in terms of operation principles and style.
- Those hardly definable "contacts" of various kinds and at different levels among people and communities, including organizations and power bodies, which had been developing over centuries and cannot fade away in the course of a mere decade. In order to perceive the depth and—simultaneously—indefiniteness of the matter, it would suffice to carry out a simple mind experiment, namely to try to think of how (by whom, with what kind of resources involved, and in what kind of style) any political or economic issue is dealt with in relations between two post-Soviet countries, on the one hand, and in relations between any of them and a country of the "far abroad," on the other.
- Lack of a strong political and economic alternative to the Russian Federation, from the perspective of most of the post-Soviet states. This is the case even though the post-Soviet states apparently were striving to distance themselves from Russia, or at least to diversify their foreign ties, throughout the 1990s (which almost all of them managed to achieve to varying degrees).[27]

Second, there is the problem of the former administrative borders, which suddenly turned into state borders in 1991. It is not simply a question of the involvement of those state agencies responsible for maintaining the border

27 There is even a supposition that the "ideas, such as the Eurasian Union…are in fact employed as a smokescreen to hide the reluctance to allow integration to take place in reality. This is confirmed by some frank statements made, confidentially, by high-ranking officials of the Republic of Kazakhstan. For instance, one of them confessed recently in a private conversation with the author: 'We had a strategic goal to disengage from Russia and reduce the significance of the Russian ethnic factor. And we succeeded. As for the economy, it is not the key matter. There is oil, and that is enough. We will pump the oil. And then we will sort things out. The most important thing is the power.'" See Todua, Z., "Yeshche raz o postsovetskoy integratsii. Nekotoryye tendentsii razvitiya Tamozhennogo soyuza i pozitsiya Kazakhstana [Again on post-Soviet integration. Some tendencies in the development of the Customs Union and Kazakhstan's position.]," *Nezavisimaya gazeta*, December 21, 1999.

regime, including the visa regime (where it has been established), such as the Federal Border Guard Service and the State Customs Committee, in elaborating particular policies in relation to the new neighboring countries in the period of delimitation, demarcation (where it is being carried out) and organizing the state border, as well as subsequently overseeing the border regime. These practices are conventional in relations between independent states and may appear extraordinary only in the period of the introduction and "adjustment" of the border regime. The main issue is the emergence of real state borders where, historically, there were none, while those established during the Soviet period were set up in arbitrary ways, or rather, according to a logic completely different from the one normally governing the process of separating ethno-religious communities, and political and/or cultural groups. In this case, both sides, although not always with equal persistence, will press for the abolition of the borders, or at least the "liberalization" of their status. The considerable complication, if not breach, of ties between neighboring regions, first of all between Russia and Ukraine, Russia and Belarus, and Russia and Kazakhstan, naturally brings about dissatisfaction and the emergence of lobbies and/or political forces striving to rectify the situation. At least, this is what is happening where the interest groups still have opportunities for political self-expression. It is equally natural, though, that the emergence of a new border will lead to the formation of a corporation "profiting from the border," which may be more or less politically active and/or capable of lobbying for its interests. It is the competition of the two lobbies—the one interested in maintaining and stiffening the border regime and the one acting to "liberalize" it—that influences the political decision-making process. As far as Russian–Ukrainian relations are concerned, the Council of the leaders of border regions of Russia and Ukraine, which was founded in 1994, has been playing a significant role as a political lobbyist for the interests of the border regions of the two countries. In particular, the Council has been interacting with the ministries of foreign affairs and other agencies involved in developing foreign policy.[28]

Last but not least, there is the problem of compatriots that have remained beyond the borders of "their" national state. From Russia's perspective, this is mainly the problem of Russians beyond the borders of the Russian Federation. The collapse of the USSR left some 30 million Russians outside Russia. According to the 1989 census, the Russian population made up 38 per cent in Kazakhstan and Latvia, 32 per cent in Estonia, 22 per cent in Ukraine and Kyrgyzstan, 13 per cent in Belarus and Moldova, 10 per cent in Turkmenistan, 9 per cent in Lithuania, some 8 per cent in Uzbekistan, Tajikistan, and Georgia,

---

28 For details of the Council's activities see: Kolosov, V. A., Kiryukhin, A. M., "Prigranichnoye sotrudnichestvo v rossiysko-ukrainskikh otnosheniyakh [Cooperation in border regions in Russian–Ukrainian relations]," *Politiya,* no. 1, 2001, pp. 157–160.

1.5 per cent in Azerbaijan, and 1 per cent in Armenia. The collapse of the USSR engendered one of Russia's internal problems caused by the developments in the newly independent countries, namely the problem of refugees and migrants. In total, some 4.5 million persons, including 0.5 million with the status of Russian nationals, moved to the Russian Federation from the CIS countries and the new Baltic states after 1992, according to data cited at the parliamentary hearings in the State Duma in January 1998. Apart from ethnic Russians, people of other ethnic backgrounds have been immigrating to Russia. It is estimated that hundreds of thousands of ethnic Georgians, and almost as many Armenians and Azerbaijanis, have left Georgia, Armenia and Azerbaijan and settled in Russia.[29] In other words, Russia has become a shelter for people from the entire post-Soviet space.

After the USSR disintegrated, there was neither an unequivocal notion of a policy that should be pursued with regard to those compatriots who found themselves abroad (whether to encourage them to move to the Russian Federation, or assist them to adapt to the local conditions), nor even an established understanding of who these "compatriots" *are*: nationals of the Russian Federation, ethnic Russians by passport and members of other ethnic groups that are administratively and territorially represented within the Russian Federation, or all citizens of the USSR and/or subjects of the Russian Empire who choose to become Russian citizens.

The role of the Federal Migration Service in elaborating a policy in this sphere is a history yet to be written. (Initially, in 1992–1994, this agency existed in the form of a federal committee; in 2000, its functions came under the jurisdiction of the Ministry for Federal Affairs and Nationalities and Migration Policy.) What we can observe today is probably a transition from the general political—declarative in nature—to a more instrumental protection of compatriots abroad with the use of international law and international organizations. On April 23, 2001, the first case concerned with violations of the rights of ethnic Russians in Latvia and supported by the government of the Russian Federation came before the European Court of Human Rights. At any rate, if the problem of compatriots has ceased to be as urgent as it initially was, this has come about thanks to the "natural" processes of migration, adaptation and assimilation, rather than as a result of a relatively well thought-through and funded state policy.

Throughout the 1990s and early 2000s, the leadership of the Russian Federation was apparently hesitating as to what bodies should be authorized to develop and/or coordinate a state policy concerning the countries of the "near abroad," and at what level. The Appendix to Decree of President of the Russian Federation No. 1148 "On the structure of central bodies of the fed-

29 *Rossiyskaya gazeta*, November 5, 1997; *Novyye Izvestiya*, January 15, 1998.

eral executive authorities" issued on September 30, 1992 envisaged that a State Committee of the Russian Federation on Economic Cooperation with Member Countries of the Commonwealth of Independent States should be introduced as a component into the central bodies of the federal executive authorities. The Regulation on a State Committee of the Russian Federation for Economic Cooperation with Member Countries of the Commonwealth of Independent States [*Goskomsotrudnichestvo Rossii*] was approved by Resolution of the Government of the Russian Federation No. 27 of January 15, 1993. One and a half years later, the status of the body was raised. Decree of President of the Russian Federation No. 66 of January 10, 1994 provided for the State Committee of the Russian Federation on Economic Cooperation with Member Countries of the CIS to be transformed into a Ministry for Cooperation with Member Countries of the Commonwealth of Independent States [*Minsotrudnichestvo*].

Three years later, another decision was made which registered a change in attitude. The *Minsotrudnichestvo* was abolished by Decree of President of the Russian Federation No. 483 of April 30, 1998 "On the structure of the bodies of executive power." The Ministry's functions were delegated to the Ministry of Foreign Affairs of the Russian Federation and Ministry of Industry and Trade of the Russian Federation. There was some opposition to this measure. On May 22, 1998, the State Duma of the Federal Assembly of the Russian Federation issued Resolution No. 2488-11 GD "In regard to the decision to dissolve the Ministry for Cooperation with Member Countries of the Commonwealth of Independent States" which contained a request to the President and Chairman of the Government of the Russian Federation to preserve the Ministry "taking into account the need to enhance the role of the legislative, executive and judicial authorities of the Russian Federation in the development of integration processes within the CIS framework." Half a year later, President Yeltsin reconsidered his decision. A Ministry of the Russian Federation on Affairs of the Commonwealth of Independent States [*Minsodruzhestvo*] was founded by Decree No. 1142 "On the structure of the federal bodies of executive power" issued on September 22, 1998.

Another half a year later, President Putin, on entering office, restored virtually the same model as the one envisaged by Decree No. 483 of April 30, 1998. As its predecessor, the Ministry of the Russian Federation of CIS Affairs was dissolved in accordance with Decree No. 867 "On the structure of the federal bodies of executive power" of May 17, 2000; and the Ministry's functions were once more delegated to the Ministry of Foreign Affairs of the Russian Federation and a new Ministry of Economic Development and Trade of the Russian Federation, which was set up by the same Decree.

Generally speaking, the state's posture with regard to the "disintegration subsystem" and—especially—to the "new foreign" countries is remarkable for its multifaceted nature. The Foreign Policy Concept stipulates: "It is a priority of Russia's foreign policy to ensure the suitability of multilateral and bilateral cooperation with the member states of the Commonwealth of Independent States (CIS) for the country's national security tasks." Furthermore, the section "Regional priorities," which provides an—albeit short—account of relations with post-Soviet political formations, is placed after the section "Priorities of the Russian Federation in addressing global problems."

The "Regional priorities" section of the Concept's version approved in 2000 is marked by its pragmatic spirit and reasonable minimalism, emphasizing as it does the interests of the Russian Federation and Russian compatriots, rather than abstract interests of "everybody in everything," which can only be welcomed:[30]

> Emphasis will be placed on the development of good-neighborly relations and strategic partnerships with all CIS member states. Practical relations with each of them should be developed with due consideration of their respective openness to cooperation and readiness to acknowledge, in a due manner, the interests of the Russian Federation, in particular to guarantee the rights of Russian compatriots.
>
> Proceeding from the principle of multi-speed and multi-level integration within the CIS framework, Russia will regulate the characteristics and nature of its interaction with CIS member states both within the CIS as a whole, and within smaller associations, primarily the Customs Union and the Collective Security Treaty. A priority task is to strengthen the Union of Belarus and Russia as the most advanced, at this stage, mode of integration of two sovereign states.
>
> We attach prime importance to joint efforts toward settling conflicts in CIS member states, and to development of cooperation in the military-political sphere and in the sphere of security, particularly in fighting international terrorism and extremism.
>
> Serious emphasis will be placed on development of economic cooperation, including the creation of a free trade zone and implementation of programs for joint rational use of natural resources. Specifically, Russia will work towards conferring such a status on the Caspian Sea, which will allow the littoral states to develop mutually beneficial cooperation in exploitation of the local resources on a just basis and with proper consideration of each other's legitimate interests.
>
> The Russian Federation will undertake efforts to secure the observance of mutual obligations concerning the preservation and augmentation of the common cultural heritage in the CIS member states.[31]

Clearly, the idea of a "multi-speed and multi-level integration within the CIS framework" is interpreted in a rather broad and flexible sense in the Concept

---

30 Salmin, A., "Soyuz posle Soyuza [The Union after the Union]," *Polis*, 1992; Salmin, A., "Rossiya, Yevropa i novyi mirovoy poryadok [Russia, Europe and the new world order]," *Polis*, 1999, pp. 10–31.

31 *Nezavisimaya gazeta, Nezavisimoye voyennoye obozreniye*, July 14, 2000; see also this volume.

and, more importantly, in practice. Every new turn in the history of Russia's relations with one or other new entity of international law may require—unique in a sense—political and organizational approaches and even some protocol and procedural abatements. Manifestly, the mechanism for developing and conducting policies with regard to the former USSR Baltic republics is considerably different from the practice of interaction with other post-Soviet states and—at least in appearance—is almost identical to what appears a conventional approach in relations with the "old foreign" countries. Indeed, international organizations are actively involved with Russia's attempts to "sort out" issues of dispute with the Baltic republics, and particular Russian regions (e.g. Kaliningrad Region and Moscow) also try to interfere in the matter, which is not the case with the policies Russia pursues in other post-Soviet regions (with the arguable exception of Ukraine). Naturally enough, the role of the "power" ministries and state agencies in forming the system of relations between the Russian Federation and its partners under the Tashkent and Bishkek Treaties (not to mention the special case of Tajikistan) is more significant than in the system of Russia's relations with other post-Soviet countries. The same may be said of Russian–Georgian relations for clear—although completely different—reasons. The logic of the Russian–Armenian and Russian–Azerbaijani relations is strongly affected by the conflict surrounding Karabakh, which has not been settled yet, and the entire system of diplomatic "operations" related to it.

Today, there is a unique and hardly reproducible mechanism for Russian–Belarussian interaction. In April 1996, a treaty to establish a Community of Sovereign Republics was signed. The authors of a report by the Council for Foreign and Defense Policy [SVOP] believe that B. Yeltsin resorted to concluding the Treaty "merely in an attempt to change his prevailing notorious image as a signatory to the Belovezhskoye accords, and without any real intention of developing the new association, which still has a negative effect on the progress of integration."[32] In May 1997, the Charter of the Union of Russia and Belarus was adopted; and in December 1998, the Declaration of the Establishment in 1999 of the Union State of Russia and Belarus was passed. Since December 8, 1999, relations between Russia and Belarus have been formally regulated by the Treaty on the Establishment of the Union State of Russia and Belarus. According to this document, the countries will retain their state sovereignty, their constitutions and national legislation will remain in effect, their systems of national state bodies will remain in place, and all vital political issues, including those under common jurisdiction, will remain within national purview. The legislative acts of the "Union State" must not contravene the constitutions and national legislation of the two countries. Thus,

---

32 "Rossiya i Belorussia—2001 [Russia and Belarus—2001]." Theses of the Council for Foreign and Defense Policy, p. 2.

despite the formal progress in the integration of the two countries and their systems of political decision-making, it is, in reality, a case of merely "running on the spot."

Plainly, the fundamental reason why the diplomatic mechanism is coasting in neutral is overt and covert disagreement in the parties' positions, the lack of manifest willingness to go for what is termed in American decision-making theory "logrolling," that is cooperation and trading of concessions along the entire "front line" of negotiations. At the same time, the "hard line" adhered to by each side may result from the lack of concurrence in the positions of both states engendered in each case not only by chance factors and circumstances, but also by the different fundamental political and ideological orientations of the parties. In the case of Russia and Belarus, the disagreements in the orientation of the sides do not merely—as it may seem—divide and polarize the society, or a part of society and the government, but also the very state institutions that have traditionally performed the role of quasi-parties in Russia.[33] According to the above-cited SVOP report,

> Russia's government, in which it is liberal economists that are setting the pace, is still at the stage of elaborating a long-term strategy for integration with Belarus. The liberals' latent apprehension with regard to a negative effect that the integration may have on the market reforms in the Russian economy is notorious. The administration of the President of the Russian Federation has preserved some stereotypes typical of the Yeltsin epoch, when Lukashenko was commonly disliked for his authoritarian tendencies and suspected of harboring an ambition to "take over the Kremlin." Russia's "power agencies" are clearly interested in rapprochement with Belarus for geopolitical and security considerations. The President of Russia is acting as a "resultant force" of these three groups. Outside of the executive state bodies, it is only the Union of Rightist Forces and the "Yabloko" grouping that oppose integration with Belarus on a political level. However, the liberals command considerable influence in the non-state mass media, which seriously hinders the idea of Russian–Belarussian rapprochement in the information space.[34]

The prospect of real, rather than merely formal, integration may be associated with particular bilateral agreements and with activities of the union executive bodies (the State Council and the Council of Ministers), which have the potential to become "lobbyists" for a genuine union of Russia and Belarus. For example, one highly binding agreement, which is likely to change some mechanisms of the two systems' interaction in principle, has been concluded. The agreement stipulates the introduction of a common

---

33 As V. O. Klyuchevsky would say, there is no contest among parties in Russia; there is only contest among institutions.

34 "Rossiya i Belorussia—2001 [Russia and Belarus—2001]." Theses of the Council for Foreign and Defense Policy, p. 2.

currency in the form of the Russian ruble from January 1, 2005, and a new common currency from January 1, 2008. If this agreement is implemented, then some functions of the current Russian authorities that elaborate the policy with regard to Belarus (as well as the other way round) may be taken over by economic decision-making agencies, on the one hand, and by super-state (or new state) bodies, on the other hand. Today, however, the prospects for Russian–Belarussian relations are hardly any more definable in this sense than five years ago.

Efforts have been undertaken to create another unique, although completely different, mechanism of interaction with Ukraine. Remarkably, the presidents of Russia and Ukraine have had eight (!) meetings in the last year alone. At any rate, one cannot consider it conventional practice when one side appoints its former deputy prime minister to the post of ambassador to the other country, while the other side makes its former prime minister the ambassador (as well as a special presidential envoy) to the partner country. Naturally, in such a situation the decision-making process in the foreign policy sphere will be marked by its non-trivial nature. The newly appointed Ambassador Extraordinary and Plenipotentiary of the Russian Federation to Ukraine, Viktor Chernomyrdin said: "Before my departure for Kiev, I was closely examining all issues, including in the sphere under the control of the Ministry of Foreign Affairs..."[35]

Traditionalism and inertia in the perception of the role of the former USSR republics in Russian foreign policy is indirectly manifested in one circumstance related to the academic establishment. Namely, while the Institute of USA and Canada Studies of the Russian Academy of Sciences, the Institute of Far Eastern Studies of the Russian Academy of Sciences, and the Institute of European Studies of the Russian Academy of Sciences preserve their influence and rank (although less significant than before), there are no academic institutions engaged in dealing with various "territorial problem blocs" on the territory of the former USSR, i.e. the Baltic states, European CIS members, states of the Transcaucasus, and the Central Asian states...

There has been a change in the post-Soviet space in the past couple of years. Hypothetically, the Agreement on the Establishment of the Eurasian Economic Community (EurAsEC, October 10, 2000)[36] that was signed in Astana by the members of the Customs Union offers the chance of the organization becoming a full-fledged international free-trade organization, although it is still

---

35 *Kommersant,* May 31, 2001, p. 2.
36 "The draft treaty on the establishment of the Eurasian Economic Community was prepared by the Ministry for Economic Development and Trade and agreed upon with the ministry for Foreign Affairs and other federal executive state bodies." See *Nezavisimaya gazeta,* October 14, 2000.

too early to speculate about its likely prospects.[37] The same can be said of the
Bishkek Agreement on the status of formations of forces and means of the collective security system, and the plan of basic measures to establish a system of
collective security for the period 2001–2005 (signed on October 11, 2000 by
the Collective Security Treaty signatories, i.e. the same countries that signed
the EurAsEC agreement plus Armenia). The same can also be said of the
Yerevan protocols reached by the members of the Collective Security Council
on the creation and formation of a Collective Rapid Deployment Force in the
Central Asian region, directly involving Russia, Kazakhstan, Tajikistan and
Kyrgyzstan (the Yerevan summit of the Collective Security Council members
was held on May 24–25, 2001). It is, therefore, obvious that a more definite
"nucleus" of defense and economic cooperation, which does not exclude, but
rather includes, Russia, has started taking shape on the territory of the former
USSR. This time it is a "nucleus" that presupposes collective decisions and
collective responsibility based on mutual obligations, instead of a mere "network" relations that were largely bilateral, if they ever worked at all. The nucleus
is reminiscent of a "binary star," i.e. it represents a system of mutually comple-
mentary (at least from Russia's perspective) blocs: an economic bloc, including a military-economic one, around the axis Belarus—Russia—Kazakhstan,
and a military bloc *per se*, which is oriented (as a bloc, and not merely as the
totality of all forms of multilateral and bilateral cooperation of the member
states) first of all towards cooperation in the Central Asian region.

The prospect of a genuine—albeit modest in its missions and scale—and
not merely declarative integration, which was based mainly on what had not
disintegrated yet, will raise the question of the prospects for changing the foreign policy decision-making mechanisms within the subsystem in question,
and may entail far-reaching consequences in other subsystems too. In fact,
changes of the kind have already started happening. For instance, the agreements signed by the member states of the Collective Security Council stipulate that decisions on the use of the Rapid Deployment Force be taken by the
heads of the states upon the consent of the party that requested assistance and
without mandatory approval by the parliaments of the member states. So far,
one cannot see in what ways the established political and legal realities may be
reconciled with the emerging realities. However, current developments in the
post-Soviet space can obviously be characterized as raising serious interest for
the first time.

---

37 According to N. Isingarin, "the thorough work resulted in the appearance of a constituent document, which dotted all the i's. The casual title was discarded and there
   emerged the official one that reflected the essence of the association—the Eurasian
   Economic Community." *Ibid.*

By comparison with its ties with the former USSR republics, Russia's relations with the former member states of COMECON and the Warsaw Treaty are less significant as a "post-Soviet institutional anchor" of the country's foreign policy. This is a result of both the abrupt and unequivocal reorientation of these countries away from the USSR and towards the West in the 1990s, and a no less abrupt decline in their share of Russia's foreign trade, as well as in their significance for the Russian economy as a whole. Remarkably, the causal connections between both the former and latter circumstances are complicated and hardly definable. At any rate, this sphere also contains fewer mechanisms that affect it and are characteristic of this sphere exclusively. And yet, there are some. First of all, there is a special lobby: an organized "coalition" of those in the Ministry of Foreign Affairs of the Russian Federation, the Presidential Administration, and other state agencies who are in some way associated with the process of elaborating and conducting foreign policy and—owing to inertia or established personal ties and/or ideological preferences—oriented towards cooperation with those political forces in the countries of the former "socialist community" that are the successors to local communist parties. The above-mentioned group of officials and diplomats, mainly a fragment of the former Soviet bureaucracy, in principle recognize the principle of noninterference in the domestic affairs of the former allies and freedom of choice of their peoples, and are prepared to interact with any legitimately elected leadership of the countries in question. However, in practice members of this group—often almost subconsciously—reckon on a better mutual understanding with those governments that are either formed by, or comprise, former communists. Evidently, though, these expectations are not always fulfilled. But the orientation of the former "comrades" from former "fraternal parties" is preserved. In all likelihood, it is based both on a sincere delusion of both sides, and on disinformation—whether intentional or unintended—put about by the post-socialist "left" forces and addressed to both Russia and the traditionalist post-communist part of the electorate in these countries. Such an attitude on the part of a fragment of the foreign policy apparatus is psychologically reinforced by a corresponding, overtly formulated, position of the Russian Communist party and other CPSU successor parties represented in the State Duma and operating outside. Today, there is no adequate structure (including in the ideological sense) that can act as a counterbalance to this position. There are three reasons why.

The first reason lies in the genuinely anti-Soviet and/or anti-Russian rhetoric—if not policy—typically promoted by non-communist sectors in the post-socialist countries, where some forces are unwilling to differentiate between the USSR and Russia.

The second reason lies in the unpopularity among members of the Ministry of Foreign Affairs of the Russian Federation of the scarcely balanced pro-western policy that was pursued in the period when A. Kozyrev held office, and their consequent specific psychological reaction to that policy.

The third reason is the relatively weak influence that Russian "rightist" parties and factions can exert on the state foreign policy establishment, especially taking into account that these forces do not prioritize relations with the former USSR partners in COMECON and the Warsaw Treaty, and many non-communist politicians have no special immunity to, or prejudice against, the eastern European "neo-socialism."

In any case, even if there really is some "leftist nostalgic culture" that may to an extent (that should by no means be exaggerated) facilitate mutual understanding among those politicians and officials of the former COMECON member states that come from the former nomenclature, today there is nothing as yet that might be seen as a liberal or conservative "international" that could embrace Russia, and such an entity is unlikely to emerge in the near future.

On the whole, the economic systems and security systems in both the "post-communist" space (the COMECON and Warsaw Treaty states, and the USSR) and in other zones of Russian interests were, until recently, shaped within the frameworks formed by the standard and retrospective paradigms, such as those of "post-Soviet space reintegration" (either complete, or fragmentary), "military opposition to NATO," "prevention of the former allies' conversion to the potential enemies' camp," etc. The paradigms in question were preserved, largely thanks to the stable—in the case of each inertial subsystem—group of actors involved, while particular combinations of the actors were able to make all individual decisions at the institutional or personnel level. Opposing this inertial logic were not so much any alternative logic and strategy, as other equally inertial subsystems of the foreign policy development and coordination, which were acting along different vectors and involved different combinations of actors. Among these subsystems were the energy and the foreign debt service subsystems that enjoyed relative autonomy, and even independence at times, after the collapse of the Soviet decision-making system in the foreign policy sphere.

GLOBAL AND EUROPEAN INTEGRATION SUBSYSTEM. Today, one of the necessary conditions for Russia to be a member of the club of countries that wish to remain active subjects, rather than passive objects, of the policy of the so-called "civilized world community," which is what Russia has striven for in the past three centuries, would be its active role in the global community of developed states within the system of corresponding international organizations. In the 1990s, by joining the Council of Europe and establishing "special" relations with the EU and NATO, by striving for full-fledged membership of the G-7 and the WTO, Russia indicated its wish to renew its membership of the "club," which was terminated in 1917. The problem that Russian politics is facing today is how to square the country's national interests with the international obligations it has already undertaken and may have to undertake in the future. On the one hand, this will require maximum use of the opportunities offered by the membership of international organizations and partner associations for the benefit of the rightly perceived national interests. On the other hand, there will be a need to constantly influence the organizations and associations in question with the same purpose, since they are inclined to impose their own, largely universal norms and their perceptions of the ends and means of world politics in rather tough and straightforward ways. For the most part, the norms and perceptions in question were formulated during the period when Russia took a seventy-year "timeout" and are, therefore, perceived as something alien, if not hostile, to the country's historical tradition.

One of the most important circumstances that have changed Russia's identity recently is the qualitative enhancement of its economic integration with the outside world, i.e. its deeper dependence on foreign economic ties. The Russian economy is now integrated into the world economy to a far greater extent than the Soviet economy ever was. Importantly, the integration has taken place on different levels that do not always require the sanction of the state authorities. While in the 1980s the share of exported goods made up five per cent of the industrial production in the Russian regions (according to the data of the Foreign Ministry's Department on ties with the federation constituents, parliaments and non-governmental and political organizations), in the 1990s this figure exceeded 20 per cent, according to some estimates. The figure covers more than cooperation in border regions. Over 50 per cent of exported goods are produced in ten regions, of which only one is a border region. As far as imported goods are concerned, twenty regions, mainly central ones, import some 40 per cent of all imported goods. There are estimates that its current economic ties with foreign countries are already having a direct effect on the economic and social status of at least one third of Russia's population, and indirectly they may influence the lives of the vast majority of the country's population. The issue of integration of the Russian economy into the world economy has already been largely resolved in a natural way, having thus ceased to be a strategy-choice issue, as some still perceive it through force of habit. Nonetheless, some other problems keep emerging.

First, there is the danger of marginalization of the economic system that ensures citizens' well-being and security, as well as the country's political weight. The haphazard inclusion of fragments of the Russian economy in the world economy may lead to Russia's lasting—if not permanent—status as a "primary-production periphery" of the developed world and a rather big consumer market, which will nevertheless have no real impact.

Second, there is a danger of disintegration of what has historically taken the shape of an integrated territorial political-economic complex. Uncontrolled economic integration may contribute to a "softening up" of Russia, and even to its territorial disintegration. First and foremost, this refers to the potential problem of preserving the unity of European Russia, which is becoming increasingly drawn to the European Union, with the Far East and a part of Siberia, which are getting increasingly engaged in the Asia-Pacific region. The emergence of the European Union, a new attractive economic center in the West, on the one hand, and the opening of our underpopulated and relatively underdeveloped Far East towards the Asia-Pacific region that has been undergoing rapid economic and demographic development, on the other hand, may turn into a "rupture test" for Russia in the very near future, at least in economic terms, rather than lead to the immediate building of a gigantic "bridge," let alone integration, between the European Union and the Asia-Pacific region through—and including—Russia. However, this sort of development may even provoke political "weakening" of the state.

Today, the controversial complex of problems related to modernization, economic growth and internal integration has to be considered in the context of Russia's inclusion in the world economy. The contemporary world market represents a rigorous hierarchical system, oriented towards the preservation of the dominant status of the most developed nations by means of manipulating financial markets, artificial overvaluation of innovation products, etc. If it is not integration into the world market (that is already happening anyway, as is mentioned above) *per se* that is our goal, but rather integration with the developed nucleus of the world economy, then a special federal policy should be applied to support the economic expansion of Russian producers (apart from those operating within the fuel and energy complex), and a long-term strategy should be elaborated for cooperation with economic organizations that are important for Russia. The close coordination of domestic policy decisions and foreign policy decisions must become a key component in the national strategy for the survival and development of the country as it enters the 21st century. To resolve this task will require both taking special economic measures and formulating a more mature concept of federalism, envisaging a distinctive and efficient distribution of powers between the country's center and regions.

Third, there is the problem of Russia's interaction—and integration—with structures that historically emerged as incompatible with the internal logic and rules of the "communist world" in principle, if not as overtly hostile to it. A search for ways of such interaction is becoming symbolic in the new, post-Soviet reality in the international relations of the 1990s. As long ago as May 1992, the Russian Federation joined the IMF. In June 1992, it became a member of the World Bank. In this way, it demonstrated that it was now a "normal" state, prepared to get involved in the system of institutions established by the western community, although foremost, of necessity and lamentably, as a recipient of loans, humanitarian aid, and technical assistance. Russia became a member of the Paris and London "clubs," first of all as a major debtor. In the early 1990s, the search began for ways to join the Council of Europe, the WTO, and to start interacting with the European Union, NATO and other originally western associations. On February 28, 1996, Russia was admitted to the Council of Europe. On May 27, 1997, the Founding Act on Mutual Relations, Cooperation and Security between NATO and the Russian Federation was signed. On December 1, 1997, lengthy negotiations resulted in the Agreement on Partnership and Cooperation signed by Russia and the countries of the European Union. The issues related to Russia's cooperation with the European Union, joining the World Trade Organization, and interaction with other economic organizations are considered and resolved foremost within the triangle of the Ministry of Foreign Affairs—Ministry of Economics and Trade—specialized committees of the State Duma. This process is also agreed upon with the Ministry for Antimonopoly Policy and Support for Entrepreneurship and other ministries and state agencies. However, one gets the impression that the "weak link" in this sphere today is not so much the lack of coordination of Russia's foreign policy or poor expertise as such, but rather the total absence of a long-term strategy for Russia to integrate into the established economic structures in an optimal way, while securing its national interests. This cannot be regarded as resulting from exclusively personal or other chance factors, no matter how significant their role might have been.[38] It is known that the reality of the EEC was largely ignored in the USSR. Unlike some individual European countries, not to mention the USA, China and others, the EEC was an object dealt with by large research institutions or academic communities. By and large, it was studied by a handful of individual enthusiastic academics, often at their own risk. As a result, both the period of the 1950s to the 1980s and the post-Soviet period failed to produce a vivid developing culture of relations with the EU or attitudes to the EU, or an "interface" between political cultures of Russia and the new supra-national Europe. The same—*mutatis mutandis*—can be said of other geo-economic realities of today's world.

Originally published in *Politeia*, 2002, no. 3.

---

38 The head of one of the leading economic ministries said, after the death of former Minister of Foreign Trade G. Gabunia: "the country has neither a strategy of cooperation with international economic organizations, nor even an idea of the multiple variety of these organizations and their powers."

Foreign Policy Therapy "a la Dr Putin"
Andrei Melville

Over 100 years ago, Dr Freud, the famous therapist from Vienna, developed a psychotherapeutic method that enabled psychological traumas and problems that had been displaced into the unconscious, and therefore hidden, to be revealed and analyzed. Such traumas represent syndromes that are not admitted and that subsequently manifest themselves as neurotic symptoms that complicate people's lives to a considerable extent. Whatever the fate of psychoanalysis proper, or Freudianism on the whole, it is clear that at least some of the analytical procedures developed within these fields (for example, externalization of displaced, and therefore unarticulated, problems) still have heuristic value, moreover in a much broader topical context.

Dramatic in its scale and potential consequences, the pro-western turn in Russian foreign policy (already labeled "the Russian diplomatic revolution") that was carried out by President Putin after the events of September 11, has radically transformed the general configuration of contemporary international relations, chiefly those between Russia and the USA (and the West on the whole). At the same time, many foreign policy problems—isolated, and yet potentially destructive for this new international configuration, and capable of badly complicating the existence of the international community—still remain "displaced" and "unarticulated" (at both national and international levels). Equally, so far there is no sign of a new conceptual framework, a "big picture of the new world," the absence of which will complicate the search for solutions to these "isolated" problems.

Consciously allowing for some amplification of the thesis, I will dare to suggest that, given such serious reorientations, today's Russian foreign policy (as well as that of the USA and other western countries, for that matter) needs to undergo a kind of psychotherapeutic procedure—"a la Dr Putin"—including raising those problems, still hidden but possibly fraught with serious international traumas, to the conscious level. Such procedures may deliver us from the mutual illusions and disappointments that so often haunted us in the past, (which is what Mr. Haass, the Director of the Policy Planning Staff at the Department of State, recently wrote about in the *Moscow News* newspaper) and fix the foundations for a new system of international partnership.

What changed after September 11: the world or our concept of the world?

Almost immediately after the terrorist attacks in the USA, this question started to be discussed. The discussion is continuing, and the opinions expressed differ greatly. This has been talked about lately on more than one occasion: the scale and nature of the threat posed by international terrorism have clearly changed. Indeed, a new type of territorially non-localized, network terrorism has emerged; international terrorist networks have acquired structural flexibility; high military technologies are not always, to say the least, efficient in preventing terrorism; it appears that international terrorists do not have specific political or other goals: their activities are rather a general fundamentalist reaction to Modernity and Globalization (in the western sense of the terms); the large scale and dispersed character of the new international threats diminish the role of direct military methods in counteracting these threats; the liberal democracies must ultimately internally adapt themselves to resist international terrorism; etc. However, does the emergence of the new threat of international terrorism in the foreground mean that the entire world, as some say, has indeed been transformed beyond recognition?

The general dynamics of the globalization forces and tendencies seem to remain the same, despite the increasing split of the world into disproportionately different "poles" and the anti-globalist reaction that feeds on this split. One pole of the global system is getting increasingly entrenched in its hypertrophied state, and is striving to "build" the rest of world relying on the principle of force (in different meanings, including economic and technological). Other—"smaller"—poles largely remain nonintegrated into the new international order. As for the threats to international security, the focus here is shifting to new—increasingly indirect and non-military—forms. The very notion of "weapons" is changing. Finally, new geo-economic factors are coming to unambiguously prevail over traditional, geo-political factors in determining the role and place of countries in the world.

It is not the world itself that has changed, but rather the internal and external context in which the key global actors will have to implement decisions and make choices. They will have to make multiple decisions and choices in the conditions of changing international rules. Among others, this concerns both Russia and the West (as well as individual components of the latter). Despite the obvious common interest—fighting international terrorism—the decisions and choices largely lie in different areas from the perspectives of different participants, and often go beyond the common interest in question.

In the changed internal context, the USA, and the West as a whole, will have to transform many traditional notions, in particular sort out the new dilemma between individual freedom (including in the financial sphere) and public security: to what extent can the former be subordinated to the latter? To what degree can this change lead to the reconsideration of the very concept of democracy, and how far is it safe to move in this direction? As for the new external context, the USA, and the West as a whole, will have to decide on the basis, framework, conditions and limits of their integration with Russia. What kind of specific attitude to Russia as a really equal partner must and can be assumed (where geo-politics, geo-economics, trade, labor division, participation in international organizations, etc. are concerned)?

The key decisions Russia has to make are located in another domain: first of all, are the Russian political elite and Russian public prepared to "choose the West" (to use L. Shevtsova's term) based on shared values, rather than merely on specific common interests (even resistance to international terrorism)? In addition, the common enemy may prove to be a short-lived and shaky foundation for the new international relations, and the anti-terrorist motivation for Russia's rapprochement with the West may turn out to be insufficient for a really radical change in the entire global construction. In this case, what should be done with regard to other (traditionally strategic) interests that Russia has in Asia, the CIS, the Baltic states, as well as in its relations with China, India, Iran, etc.? In what ways could these interests be reformulated and incorporated in the new context? What would be a new outline of the "Russian project" proper?

These and other problems, not merely unresolved so far but largely not even articulately included on the agenda of strategic discussions, may generate serious national and international traumas. Incidentally, even some "sacred cows" of international law—this most conservative but crucial legitimizing component in the global system—will also have to undergo difficult reconsideration and transformation. This concerns the norms and the very concepts of national sovereignty, the right to self-determination, territorial integrity, correlation between individual human rights and the missions related to the safeguarding of national and international security, humanitarian intervention, etc. The new international configuration that is emerging today, in particular owing to the new partnership between Russia and the West, will require a normative basis among other things. The mere slogan postulating the "rapprochement" of Russia and the West, used as a substitute for an all-inclusive strategic concept of the "big global picture," is nothing more than a naïve construct, a dangerous one at that, since it may bring about new and even graver mutual disappointments unless there is agreement (or clearly articulated disagreements) with regard to other issues involving dissimilar interests and expectations of the parties.

Contours of the new "Putin doctrine"

At least until the events of September 11, Russian foreign policy involved some ambivalence and uncertainty, although at the very beginning President Putin assumed a moderately pro-western orientation and laid an absolutely distinct emphasis on a pragmatic and "economized" approach in foreign affairs (which was described as "Putin's initial doctrine" by V. Nikonov in the *NG* newspaper as early as two years ago). Among relevant examples are Bosnia and Kosovo, Abkhazia and the Trans-Dniester region, Iraq and North Korea, NATO enlargement and debates surrounding the ABM Treaty. Putin's distinctly personalized "gesture to the West" after the terrorist attacks on the USA was more than a mere gesture of sympathy. It also engendered a chain of new decisions in the sphere of foreign policy, which could—in their trend or their actual strategic entrenchment—be regarded as the embodiment of "Putin's new doctrine."

Of course, in discussing this issue, one should take into consideration important components of conceptual and diplomatic continuity. For example, the Foreign Policy Conception that was adopted by the President of the Russian Federation in summer 2000 contained an altogether adequate formulation of the assessment of the new dangers to security, which still appears applicable today, above all with regard to international terrorism. On the other hand, many practical approaches assumed by Russian diplomacy, especially after the Ljubljana summit, created a generally favorable background for constructive development of relations between Russia and the USA (as well as the entire West). At the same time, it would be a mistake to emphasize exclusively those policy components marked by continuity, and overlook at least such aspects of conceptual novelty and foreign policy reorientation as (in no particular order of importance):

- a far more radical pro-western slant in Russia's foreign policy, even as compared to the moderate and generally balanced "westernism" of Putin's "world picture," which was first represented in the well-known keynote "Internet article" in December 1999;
- a shift in foreign policy priorities: first, partnership with the USA, foremost in the interests of a new and extended interpretation of the problems pertinent to national and international security; second, Russia's direct involvement in the European economic space; third, relations with the CIS countries on the basis of a pragmatic and "economized" approach, which would—once again—emphasize security issues;
- a more active promotion of the course towards Russia's integration into the western society's institutional system, chiefly into international economic organizations (for example, the WTO);
- de facto acceptance and support of the USA's using military force on the Russian border in Afghanistan;

- similar recognition of the US right to project their military force in the regions that have traditionally been considered zones of Russia's exclusive interests (Central Asia and Transcaucasus);
- reorientation in Russian policy with regard to at least several CIS states, including recognition of their far greater freedom of maneuver internally (in particular in their treatment of their separatist forces and movements) and externally (chiefly, with respect to their choice of new foreign partners and allies);
- a shift of emphasis in Russia's Middle East policy, particularly under the influence of the common anti-terrorist modus;
- the unthinkable—even a short time ago—unprecedented softening of the Russian Federation's stance with regard to some issues in the sphere of arms control (the ABM Treaty) and Euro-Atlantic policy (NATO enlargement); the shifting of these issues into a category of the problems of subordinate importance, which became possible owing to the change in Russian policy priorities: from concern over the traditionally perceived security, influence and prestige to orientation towards integration with the West and acquiring external resources to carry out internal economic and socio-political modernization.

The list can easily be extended. Indeed, there is a hope that it will be considerably extended in the future, including by way of, at least, "articulating" (ideally finding compromise solutions) those actual problems that still remain "displaced" in the "unconscious" of the foreign policy but may hinder and even undermine the new tendencies taking shape.

Obviously, the pragmatic approach and general ideological flexibility, the absence of a "party line" or any other "program response" in the aforementioned Putin "world picture" have facilitated reorientation and confirmed the apparent continuity. Nevertheless, if this is more than mere pragmatism or a tactical course (which is our hope, for, after all, we are not agnostics), i.e. if the shifts in question develop further to turn into an all-embracing strategy, we may eventually not simply observe a significant U-turn in foreign policy, but also see a fundamental political—and, in a sense, even existential—choice being made that may prove crucial for the nation.

It is not quite clear, though, how much freedom the actor who is making this kind of choice has. What is the actual "corridor of choice"? Or, to use the language of sociology, what is the extent of the agent's dependence on structure? Yet, the consistent course towards rapprochement with the West, given adherence to the current profound reconsideration of many key national interests, goals and priorities, may prove a way out of the earlier vague and ambivalent situation mentioned above. Moreover, the significance of the reconsideration in question goes well beyond the framework of pure foreign policy (for all its importance) and may acquire the character of a civilization choice of a new national and state identity.

New identity? Multiple identities?

To make my argument stronger, I will dare to formulate a rather straightforward thesis: national and state identity is not so much "objective," i.e. determined by the geo-political situation and history, culture and traditions, as "subjective," that is a specific form of the elites' awareness of their key interests. Simultaneously, geo-politics, history and culture represent absolutely tangible factors (or rather the context) that form the identity, crystallize it in a variety of ideological forms including the foreign policy doctrines.

However, within the framework formed by these factors, the national and state identity represents—*par excellence*—a subjective choice and appreciation by power elites of their long-term goals and interests, along with the means of their acquisition. The choice made by the elites is translated to the mass level and becomes embodied in a certain cultural and ideological form. Therefore, identity is a concentrated, stable national and state self-awareness, which is normally passed through generations, based on a certain consensus, exists as a super-political phenomenon, and—in its contemporary sense—emerges in the epoch of formation of nation-states. In other words, national and state identity is a historical phenomenon, and, as such, is transitory and transitional, that is evolutionary, and may transform at the points of historic bifurcation.

When and how do identities get destroyed? Apparently, this happens precisely at the key bifurcation points, when internal and external environments undergo a radical transformation, and the power elites become aware of their new goals and interests. In the past, such developments would take place in various ways, for example as a result of foreign occupation, internal disintegration, revolution, or in the course of a gradual emergence of a new self-consciousness. To use a widespread cliché, Russia turned out to be right there at a historical bifurcation point. After the disintegration of the USSR and the collapse of communism as both an idea and an international reality, the nation is still undergoing a deep identity crisis. Indeed, what is Russia today? Is it the only successor to the USSR? Is it merely one of the fifteen "fragments" of the Soviet Union? The "skeleton" of the world's last great empire? A conquered metropolis? A new independent state in transition?

Whatever the case, we are not an exception. There have been other peoples and societies that have "abandoned empire"—*ab imperio*. They would be either conquered, or would disintegrate under the burden of their own bulk. However, in accordance with the regularities determining the imperial geo-political architecture, even after the collapse and disintegration there would remain the nucleus of the metropolis, which could evolve to become a nation-state.

There would also remain post-imperial continuity of the cultural and civilization traditions belonging to the pre-imperial and imperial past. However, owing to a number of reasons the *ab imperio* Russia found itself in a far more difficult situation than its post-imperial predecessors.

Russia has not been, and is unlikely to become, a nation-state, as, for example, other new independent states. Owing to its ethnic composition, Russia will not be able to exploit any sort of Russian national idea for ideological and political consolidation, if we compare it again with other post-communist countries. There are no signs of continuity in today's Russia, and therefore, there is no synthesis of the pre-Soviet, Soviet and post-Soviet conceptual traditions or, for that matter, identities. Crucial internal factors that determine the choice of self-identification are still rather vague in today's Russia. Russia has made no definite internal selection of political, economic and value systems yet. The state and society retain a "hybrid" condition. At last, for all the radical innovations undertaken by the President in the sphere of foreign policy after September 11, it seems one can hardly assert that Russia has made—and (NB!) implemented—its final foreign policy choice. There is a tangible mighty tendency; there are factual results and broad prospects. And yet, there are also problems displaced into the political unconscious, which so far have deprived the foreign policy system of not so much harmony, as of a comprehensive holistic character.

Another important issue is the departure (confirmed by quantitative and qualitative research of the mass and elite attitudes) by—so far "Teflon-coated"— President Putin from the foreign policy priorities habitual for the influential groups of the Russian political class and for public opinion. Potentially, this represents a very serious matter, since the "way to the West" is Russia's internal problem first and foremost. Incidentally, the vast majority of the problems, challenges and threats Russia faces today originate from inside the country. The problem in question can be resolved primarily through political, social and economic modernization. Today this modernization can only be achieved (alas!) at the expense, and on the basis, of a favorable external environment and external resources. Unlike many other members of the Russian elite, not to mention the public, President Putin is aware of this. In such circumstances foreign policy may become an "engine" for domestic policy.

There may be many ways to address and overcome the "departure" mentioned above. However, there is one obvious, effective—though probably rather idealistic—way to deal with it: to declare the "Putin doctrine" (which has not been done yet), to "articulate" the displaced foreign policy problems, and to achieve a basic consensus through discussion on a broad nation-wide basis (which was proposed by A. Yanov) and frank consultation with foreign partners (who, in their turn, should sort out their differences with their own domestic opposition with regard to the new international tendencies).

But how feasible is this scenario? In fact, there is powerful inertia, and both internal and external opposition to such a development in Russia. Besides, this scenario cannot be interpreted exclusively from a one-dimensional pro-western perspective. Russian foreign policy has its own multidimensional priorities (although of a different degree of importance), which is absolutely normal, not least for the western countries themselves. Finally, for the foreseeable future, Russian diplomacy will have to navigate by the multiple interests of the country, and find dynamic solutions in the conditions of limited resources and the transitional state. This could lead to the establishment of multiple identities: the European (or even western European) state and the Eurasian bridge; integration into the "mainstream" of civilization and cultivation of a specific distinctive character; acceptance of the common rules of the game and insistence on special conditions.

However, multiple identities can coexist only for a while. Sooner or later, a choice will have to be made, and the state of "identity schizophrenia" will have to be overcome. Dr Freud showed that it is unbearably hard to live with grave psychological syndromes and proposed an adequate therapy. In order to redefine its place and role in the world in an appropriate way, the Russian political class should fully articulate the problems that still remain displaced into the unconscious, including by applying the foreign policy therapy "a la Dr Putin."

Originally published in *Cosmopolis*, Fall 2002, no. 1.

Putin's "New Course" is Now Firmly Set: What Next?

Dmitri Trenin

May and June 2002 saw a burst of diplomatic activity on the part of the Russian president. The G8 meeting; summits held with the leaders of the United States, the European Union, and NATO; meetings took place within the framework of the Shanghai Organization for Cooperation and on the margins of the regional conference on security in Central and Southern Asia as well as of the Baltic Sea States Cooperation Council. Even earlier, the President held consultations with the participants of the Euro-Asian Economic Union, with the members of the CIS Collective Security Treaty, and with the presidents of Ukraine and Belarus individually. Finally, President Vladimir Putin made a number of important statements on foreign policy while addressing regional governors in the Presidium of the State Council, and concerning military policy at a session of the Security Council. Ten months after Mr Putin's decision to actively support the United States in the fight against terrorism, there is sufficient material to compose a rather broad picture of the vectors and dynamics of Russia's foreign policy.

Foreign Policy is Turned Upside Down—But Keeps its Balance

The main conclusion to be drawn is that figuratively speaking, Putin's "Atlantic Somersault"—in theory diametrically opposed to the well-known "Primakov loop"—has been politically fixed. To accomplish this was not easy. From the White House's decision in December to withdraw from the ABM Treaty, to the US Congress's refusal in May to rescind the Jackson–Vanik Amendment, the durability of this new course has been tested. President Putin, however, has not budged from his decision and the semi-authoritarian system of rule that has been maintained in this country has provided him with the support he needs to stand firm. The political elite have come out in favor of their formal leader. In the State Duma, only the Communist faction has sharply criticized the president's diplomacy, and it has already formally become an opposition party. The Federation Council has demonstrated even greater loyalty to the Kremlin's foreign policy course than that of the Duma. The state bureaucracy, as is its custom, has met the new needs of the powers that be, mastering their new phraseology, and so on. The military leadership, albeit without enthusiasm, has given its approval to the Strategic Offensive Reductions Treaty and has agreed to the stationing in Moscow of a permanent military mission from NATO. Meanwhile, Russia's regions remain absorbed in their own problems.

In this sense, the behavior of the recent critics and skeptics among Russia's up-and-coming political figures and TV journalists has been noteworthy and instructive. The former—Dmitri Rozogin, for example—have taken positions (for instance with regard to NATO) which they themselves were criticizing not long ago. Similarly, the latter—on the state-owned ORT and RTR television channels in particular—have gone from public doubts about the wisdom of *rapprochement* with the West to gushingly positive coverage of the "historic" summits. Incidentally, such metamorphoses allow one to conclude that television's strange political "opposition" of this year's late winter and early spring was probably just one part of a game being played by the Kremlin administration to win concessions from the United States on the eve of the Moscow–St. Petersburg summit.

Thus, in the last ten months, Putin has succeeded in turning Russian foreign policy upside down. The demands of the country's modernization—above all, its economic needs—and not the elite's outdated and clearly inflated ideas of super-power status, determine the Kremlin's deeds in practice. Such concepts as parity, a multipolar world, CIS integration, the image of the OSCE as a central element of the European security system, union with Belarus and many others that were in wide parlance not so long ago, have all become things of the past. Putin was not afraid to assume the role of a leader, and he has won.

The Fulcrums of the New Course's Stability

Today, in spite of the fears sometimes expressed, Putin is hardly threatened by Gorbachev's fate of being overthrown by high government officials. As before, he is marching way ahead of the absolute majority of the political elite. While doing so, however, he nevertheless continues to rely on a number of important factors that have so far operated in his favor.

Mr Putin remains phenomenally popular. His constantly high approval rating (70%) is especially striking when seen against the backdrop of growing criticism of the government. This "Teflon effect" means that Putin's high marks are not being given for concrete achievements, but rather for his guarantee of overall political predictability. Putin's rating is a rating of hope, demonstrating that among the public at least, hope is a resource that is far from exhausted.

Public opinion on foreign policy issues is ambivalent; it responds to both positive and negative "teletherapy". Thus, despite the outburst of anti-American emotion provoked both by sports functionaries and by the directors of state-controlled mass media during the Winter Olympics in Salt Lake City, and by the propaganda campaign during the recent so-called "steel" and "chicken" wars, the public has reacted favorably on the whole to the US president's arrival in Russia. Street protests were rare and not very well-attended. As a result, the public atmosphere during the Russian–American summit turned out to be more positive than that of the either the German or French phases of Bush's European tour. This testifies to the fact that anti-Western outbursts in Russia are often the result of the public consciousness being manipulated. For the overwhelming majority of Russian citizens, foreign policy remains something distant and abstract. Its connection with domestic affairs is usually poorly understood. Under conditions such as these, any change in what is shown and said on television produces startling results. Since the year 2000, the Kremlin has continued to strengthen its influence over television and other mass media.

Putin may be out in front of the political elite, but he is far from being alone. His "new course" is finding support among the richest and most successful segments of Russia's economic and financial circles. The United States' recognition of the Russian economy as a market economy, along with similar promises from the European Union, have not only brought Russia's membership in the WTO closer, but have raised the status of its economic players as well. In particular, the country's oil and gas companies, which long to be accepted into the world business community, are vitally interested in the practical development of the announced energy partnership with the US and the EU. Alongside Russia's entrepreneurial class, the economic wing of the government and the section of the bureaucracy linked with business also support Putin.

There is simply no more attractive alternative. It is telling that Putin's critics have not offered their own version of a foreign policy strategy. By virtue of this silence, the "Primakov line" is the only obvious alternative. This line was, however, already used throughout the second half of the 1990s, causing great damage and compelling Putin to replace "Primakovism" with pragmatism. One might say that Putin's pragmatism results from having lived through that bad experience. Although the political elite is still ready today to revert to the "Primakov line", a more radical reaction is not likely. The elite can be reproached for its narrow and archaic way of thinking, but one cannot deny its sense of self-preservation. Accordingly, any discussion on the topic of Moscow reorienting itself toward Beijing remains a fantasy, while calls for Russia to join the "Axis of Evil" are nothing more than malicious rants.

In addition, one must keep in mind that Putin's "new course" does not yet threaten the *interests* of most of the elite as much as it threatens the *ideas* they hold. Interests are concrete; ideas are functional. In the last decade and a half, the country's political upper echelons have invariably demonstrated the correctness of this formula. When those at the top believe that the time has come to display flexibility, they will settle the new frontier without any fuss. They can tell those who insist on an explanation that, for example, it is not their views that have changed, but the position of their opponents, etc.

Factors of Vulnerability

Some of the strong aspects of the "new course" listed above are, simultaneously, its most vulnerable points.

The lack of resistance to Putin's course from both the elite and the public does not mean that it is widely accepted. For the elite, the most natural position is the "Primakov line", while the public largely clings to the stereotypes of a bygone era. Lip service to the "new course" from one public figure or another does not prove that such figures, like Putin, have performed the required internal restructuring.

The bureaucracy, on which the president is forced to rely as the conduit of his intended course, is in fact a hindrance to reform in the field of foreign and defense policy—those areas least affected by the changes that have taken place since 1991.

The most serious problems are: the lack of reform inside the Foreign Ministry, the *impossibility* of reform within the Defense Ministry, and the already chronic uncertainty over the status and functions of the Security Council. Igor Ivanov's activism and personal loyalty to the president do not compensate for the fact that the Foreign Ministry, which has seen the exodus of many of its most talented staffers over the past decade, has been transformed into a bastion of neo-Soviet conservatism. The "insertion" of Sergei Ivanov and his small band into the Defense Ministry in 2001 did not create the critical mass required to effect the radical changes that have long been urgently needed there, and therefore did not signal the beginning of military reform. Admitting this, the minister refrained from even mentioning the term "reform", preferring the phrase "military reconstruction" instead. With the appointment of Vladimir Rushaylo as Secretary of the Russian Security Council, this organ too "went astray" once again. The Council lost the positions of coordinator and brain center of political security to which it had been appointed under the previous leadership.

Will We Take Advantage of the New Opportunities in the West?

As a result of this, the danger of just marking time and inevitably sliding backwards is quite real. The "new course" might end up being discredited: not by its opponents but by its own adherents, if they turn out to be incapable of seizing the new opportunities that have opened up.

The first of these opportunities is the prospect of demilitarizing Russia's relations with the West. The new content of the country's relationship with the US (an end to rivalry, recognition of the two nations' asymmetry, and the beginnings of a partnership) demands that new conclusions be drawn regarding many aspects of Russian policy. These aspects include not only foreign, defense, and security policy, but also questions of military doctrine, the structure of the armed forces, military planning, the instruction and training of troops, and the handling of their weapons and equipment, to name a few. What we are talking about here is official and *de facto* excluding the United States from Russia's list of potential military foes in the twenty-first century. Such a decision, adopted unilaterally, would allow Russia to free itself from the death-grip of Cold War tradition (and from those groups and private interests that thrive upon it), and to turn finally to the security problems that exist in the real world.

On the other hand, the price of Russia's inability or unwillingness to proceed with this self-liberation will be the further decay of its armed forces—resulting in a situation which increasingly reminds one of the Kremlin palace guards at the end of the seventeenth century.

The next opportunity that has opened up is Russia's new relationship with NATO. The creation of the Russia–NATO Council is forcing Moscow to determine what it really wants from its new relationship with the alliance. The required clarity still does not exist. The idea of membership has been set aside, which testifies to the Kremlin's realism. However no functional substitute has yet been suggested. If Moscow's aim is to "take the pulse" of what is happening within NATO, it has given itself a much too narrow, essentially mundane task: for what does it need to know? If its goal is to block NATO "from within" via the formation of different interest-based coalitions, this is hardly feasible and not even worth trying. Even if Moscow's aim is to join with NATO countries in creating a universal security system in Europe and to work generally to strengthen security and stability in other regions of the world, then an integration strategy must first be devised.

Ideally, new people should be a key factor in realizing this strategy—people who would be governed in their actions by a new set of instructions and by new rules of behavior. The president might "borrow" many of these people from the Russian business community for however long it takes to train modern civilian and military diplomats.

Finally, concrete results from the work of the Russia–NATO Council will be needed in the foreseeable future—results that would give an impetus to the new forum.

Despite traditional opposition, Russia's relations with the European Union supplement its relationship with NATO, and *vice versa*. In both cases, we are talking about the single process of Russia drawing closer to Western institutions. By the spring and summer of 2002, the main dilemma of Russia's Europe-oriented policy became clear. It can be reduced to this: either limit the damage caused by the EU's expansion, or maximize the opportunities that expansion is opening up. Kaliningrad is a clear illustration of this dilemma.

The President and his government have consistently tried to get the European Union to grant exceptions to the Schengen Rules in the case of Kaliningrad. This has been dictated by a desire not to let the position of the inhabitants of Kaliningrad Region get any worse, especially in respect to their ties with the rest of Russia are concerned. This is clearly a damage-control policy. It would be more farsighted to promote and implement a special *Kaliningrad project*, which would not only permit the region to be placed in a new economic, political, and social context, but which would also facilitate "Mainland" Russia's drawing closer to the EU.

For a number of obvious reasons, Kaliningrad is of course not the most convenient springboard for developing transnational Russian–European cooperation. In this sense, the role played by St. Petersburg is unique and indispensable. Under Putin, the northern metropolis has become Russia's alternate diplomatic capital. This is a good start. The facades of St. Petersburg's buildings are being transformed, and images of them are now being beamed to television screens around the world. Preparations for the 300th anniversary of the city's founding next year are underway. Much more is needed however: St. Petersburg should be endowed with modern material and intellectual content, and turned into a locomotive of Russia's progress toward an ever closer integration with the European Union. The first condition required for such success is a city administration that is up to this truly national task.

The Eastern Direction

Having outlined the main thrusts of his new "Western policy," Putin has yet to define his strategy toward the East, having so far not placed it within the general scheme of the Russian foreign policy he has created.

The President has of course sensed the need for a serious dialogue with the Chinese leadership. As early as autumn of last year, Moscow's drawing closer to Washington provoked many questions in Beijing. It was, after all, not long before that the last hurrah of the multipolar world had been heard: the joint declaration by the RF and the PRC on the missile defense issue, which Russia soon *de facto* disavowed. The signing of the declaration was clearly a mistake, but Moscow's reluctance to speak frankly with Beijing about the fundamentals of its policy could be another. One needs to come up with a serious concept of bilateral relations—now that hints about creating an anti-American entente of sorts (which earlier were often made by the Russian side) are being been expunged (again by Moscow) from the notion of Sino–Russian strategic partnership.

It is in Russia's interests to convince China where the transfer of power to a new generation of leaders has already begun, that Russia's comprehensive moves toward Europe and its incipient partnership with America should not be construed as a threat to China's security. Russia, as a European country with enormous territories in Asia, has a fundamental interest in stable, neighborly relations with China. For the purposes of its own internal development, Russia needs close economic ties with the fast-growing giant across the border. Political collaboration with China is important both for the stabilization of the situation in Central Asia, and for ensuring the security of the Korean Peninsula.

The missile defense issue is primarily a problem of China's nuclear strategy and of US–Chinese relations. Russia can only hope that Beijing and Washington will come to an understanding on this issue and that they will avoid any confrontation. Moscow would hardly be happy to see either a sharp increase in the Beijing's nuclear missile capability, or any major qualitative improvement of it. Nevertheless, Russia will eventually be forced to recognize the legitimacy of China's desire to bring its military arsenal into line both with the nation's expanded political role, and with its increased economic power. Like the US, Russia is interested in China's smoothest possible integration into existing international institutions, and in the future predictability and moderation of Beijing's foreign and defense policies.

To this end, one prospective field of cooperation is Central Asia where— through the Shanghai process—China linked up first with Russia and then (*de facto*, as a result of its anti-terrorist operation in Afghanistan) with the United States as well. Moscow will be able to strengthen its position if it practices openness and transparency in relation to both the US and China. Its political and military partnership with the US together with its political collaboration with China might create a balance of cooperation that is acceptable to all, including other countries of the region.

For all the obvious importance of Moscow's relations with Beijing, China— if only by virtue of the sheer scale of its aggregate national might—cannot assume the role of main prop for Russian policy in East Asia: it is simply too big. On the contrary, Japan is best suited for this part. Over time, Tokyo could become to Moscow in Asia what Berlin is to it in Europe, i.e. a truly strategic partner and the principal pillar of its regional policy. This policy "East of the Urals," even more so than to the West of them, is guided by Russia's modernization requirements. Japan is not being asked to be friends against China, but to help Russia make Siberia and the Far East economically and socially viable. In spite of its already decade-long economic stagnation, Japan remains the world's second (after the US) source of capital and modern technology. After a promising debut in 2000–2001, an unforeseen pause (which occurred due to Japanese domestic political reasons) took place in Russian–Japanese relations. It is not in the interests of either Moscow or Tokyo to prolong this break. These interests are so much more important than the old territorial dispute. In the century which has just started, Japan and Russia are natural, though currently estranged partners and should work to overcome that estrangement. Putin's meetings with Prime Minister Koizumi, begun at the G-8 summit in Canada, could pave the way to a new breakthrough.

If one considers China a giant neighbor comparable in size only to America, and Japan the primary modernization resource for the Russian Far East and Siberia, then South Korea must be regarded as an important regional partner, and one whose significance in the long term (taking into account the eventual demise of the North Korean regime, hopefully in a soft landing mode, and the resultant reunification of Korea) will continue to grow. As any viable development strategy for the Russian Far East and Siberia can rest only on the principle of openness to the surrounding world (especially in the Asia-Pacific region), Russia must maintain the optimal balance of cooperation in its relations with those partners and contractors to whom it must open up in the future. Alongside the Asian countries, the nations of North America and Australia must be included in the list of Russia's leading partners. Just as Russia continues to draw closer to the EU in Europe, it would make sense in the Far East to build similar bridges to the North American free trade zone (NAFTA). In sum, it would make much more sense for Russia to position itself as a European/Pacific country rather than a European/Asian one.

The Southern Flank

The periodic flaring up of tensions between India and Pakistan over Kashmir demonstrates the new character of today's nuclear threat. Strategic stability at the beginning of the twenty-first century depends not (as before) on the size and condition of the nuclear arsenals of the US and Russia, but primarily on how such Asian crisis situations develop. Cooperation between the US (which is objectively performing the role of a leading peacemaker) and the major regional powers (including Russia) is needed to maintain and strengthen this stability. Moscow's unsuccessful bid in Almaty to play the role of intermediary between Delhi and Islamabad shows how much things have changed in the 36 years that have passed since the countries' trilateral peace summit in Tashkent. Similar coordination of peace-seeking actions is needed to limit and gradually settle the Israeli–Palestinian conflict.

The world's strategic stability is also being undermined by the proliferation of weapons of mass destruction and long-range missiles. In this area, the issue of Iran has long been a stumbling-block in Russian–American relations.

Obviously, the US administration's pressure on the Kremlin over Iran will continue to grow in the future. To remove what is an increasingly serious source of irritation, a genuinely harsh tightening of export controls is needed from Russia, and essentially for its own sake, along with a readiness to compromise on issues of nuclear cooperation with Teheran. From the United States, a willingness to provide compensation for the financial losses of Russian firms will be in order. Additionally, considering the influence exerted by Israel on the American position on this issue, it might make sense for Moscow to hold serious discussions on Iran-related issues with the Israeli authorities.

Moscow has made another attempt to renew the Collective Security Treaty, and to revive the Euro-Asian economic union. However such renewal and revival are possible only if Russia and its partners orient themselves toward new strategic and economic realties. In the area of security, this means partnership both with one another and with the US in the fight against terrorism, the proliferation of weapons of mass destruction, and regional instability. In the economic sphere, it means the development of an energy partnership between the interested parties and the West, and the gradual building up of a common economic area with the European Union. The stress placed by Moscow in this area on bilateral economic ties with Belarus, Kazakhstan, Ukraine, as well as Azerbaijan and Turkmenistan, demonstrates the growing pragmatism of the Russian approach to the nations of the CIS. The debunking by Putin of the Belarusian "union mythology" is another proof of that.

The stated desire to refrain from imitating the "Great game" in the Caspian also testifies to a greater sense of realism. Abandoning the stereotypes of behavior in the region will not be easy, as was demonstrated by the pressuring of the LUKOIL Company to refrain from taking part in the Baku–Ceyhan project. Nevertheless, the decision to display solidarity with oil consumers on the international market and the announcement of an energy partnership with the West, demand a shift to a completely different *modus operandi*.

Postscript—Almost

Finally, one last item. As military reform is not a subject of this article we shall limit ourselves to the following position: the combat capability of the Russian armed forces today is so low, and the level of corruption within the military establishment so high, that the reform of the military machine in its current condition is unfeasible. This not only makes the army and navy dangerous to society in peacetime and of limited use in time of conflict, but it also sharply limits the possibilities for international military cooperation. Joint operations with the armed forces of the US and West European countries—for which the need is growing—demand the creation of adequate Russian forces. Their formation within already-existing organizations (as was attempted experimentally in the 76th Pskov airborne division for example) is hardly capable of yielding positive results: the existing system emasculates the best of plans. The only way out of the current intolerable situation is probably the gradual creation of elements of a new army *separately* from the one that now exists. Such a new force would include among other features autonomous systems of command and control, of training and equipping personnel, and of supplying and provisioning troops, etc. Such a "new army"—or more accurately, twenty-first century-style mobile force units—might be oriented toward carrying out missions primarily along the southern strategic axis (Central Asia and the Caucasus).

In order to become part of the contemporary European and global communities, Russia will have to undergo thorough reform in all aspects of life. This necessarily includes social values. Until the rule of law, a democratic regime, and a market economy are all firmly established, and human rights and basic liberties are guaranteed, Russia's relations with the West will be of a limited and pragmatic (not integrated or value-based) nature. Nevertheless, Russia's interaction with the outside world could be a powerful factor in its internal transformation. The country's imminent membership in the WTO is the greatest economic event since the collapse of the Soviet planned economy. The asymmetric partnership with the US is helping Russia free itself from the crushing burden of superpower status. Drawing closer to NATO and to the military structure of the European Union might provide the impetus for a revolution in Russia's armed forces. It is possible that much of the above lies beyond the station to which Vladimir Putin is now prepared to steer (and haul) the country. The main thing, however, is not reaching the "promised land" in one or two presidential terms, but the direction in which the tracks are being laid.

Originally published in *Carnegie Endowment for International Peace Briefing Papers*, vol. 4, issue 6, June 2002.

The Chances and Challenges of the New World

Sergei Karaganov

The 300th anniversary of St. Petersburg provides a wonderful opportunity for reviewing Russia's record of interaction with Europe and the rest of the world. History is unlikely to play the role as the guiding star of modern policymaking, however beneficial it may be for people to draw correct lessons from it; but mapping out approaches to the future is definitely impossible without an acute knowledge of the past. We also depend upon a pragmatic assessment of the world we live in.

Europeanization Of The World

Russia's northwest became one of the early cradles of the Russian state at the end of the first millennium AD. It served as a channel of communication between the Russian mainland and the rest of Europe. The old town of Ladoga, located not far from the site of St. Petersburg, and Novgorod stood on the junctions of the trading routes between Russia and the Baltic area. These were the crossroads of civilizations. Russia was a bridge through which the cultural influences of the Great Byzantium and the Moslem Orient were reaching a less developed Europe at the time.

Although St. Petersburg is a relatively young city, its historical record embodies the history of the country which has been a melting pot of different ethnic groups, cultures and creeds for over a thousand years. Nationalities with different cultural and religious backgrounds enriched each other and melted into a unique civilization, known for its cultural openness and tolerance of other nations and religions. Academician Dmitry Likhachev, a great scholar and a refined representative of the St. Petersburg intelligentsia, made an acute observation that Nevski Prospect, the city's major avenue, was Europe's only main street where an Eastern Orthodox cathedral (Our Lady of Kazan) could stand side-by-side with a Lutheran Petrikirche, an Armenian church and a Roman Catholic cathedral (St. Catherine's). The city also boasts a magnificent mosque which is recognized as one of the most beautiful in Europe; it also plays host to a splendid Buddhist datsan.

For 300 years, the Russian mentality has been firmly associating St. Petersburg with the road which leads to Europe. The city has come to symbolize Russia's continual modernization, as well as its desire to catch up with the more advanced western parts of Europe after centuries of tormenting wars and conquests. Although the modernization was often a forced one, not to mention a heavy burden on the populace, it was responsible for opening up many new vistas. Two hundred years of relentless development eventually produced a culture which enriched the entire European continent.

St. Petersburg also gave birth to a modernization experience of another sort—the socialist one. It was here that Marxism, a Western social and political theory, first took root. The Soviet era produced remarkable achievements, above all, universal general education and an explosion within the diverse fields of science. The modernization program, Soviet-style, proved to be too expensive, however; it kept the nation's creative potential restrained, and eventually overtaxed the nation's total strength. The Soviet path turned out to be a blind alley and the country, which sought to catch up with the industrialized nations of the West, only fell far behind them. The cultural self-isolation the nation had imposed on itself proved deleterious: it contravened the very spirit and genetic memory of Russia.

Russia's military and political confrontation with the wealthy and advanced countries had a predictably lamentable result. Russia paid a dear price in order to emerge victorious from World War II, but it was unable to win in peacetime, postwar settlement and development.

Now Russia has entered a new stage of modernization, the third since the early 18th century. The public consciousness views this process as a natural return to Europe, a continent where Russia originated, having imbibed the rejuvenating strength of Asian civilizations.

The present integration into Europe possesses a different color than decades or centuries ago. European values—human rights, democracy, personal freedom, inviolability of private property, and a market economy—have reached out to all corners of the world, embracing America and large parts of Asia. Of course, each nation and each region chooses a road of development of their own, yet today these roads eventually lead to a common civilization. An increasing number of countries, while retaining their national traits, now orient themselves to a pattern of development that has proven to be efficacious.

This "Europeanization" of the world puts an end to the 300-year-old dispute between Russia's *zapadniki* (proponents of sweeping Westernization) and Slavophiles, between liberals and *pochvenniki* (people asserting the unique value of native culture), and—in the last few decades—between Westernizers and adepts of the Eurasian integrity. Debates between those various groups of intellectuals were occasionally fruitful and helped the Russians to decide upon their course of development. But usually these debates simply distracted public attention away from the more pressing need for reforms. The disputes were mostly between people who aspired for integration into the West, as well as for the opportunity to engage in competition with it, and those who did not trust any associations with the West. The situation has since changed, and an orientation with Asia no longer implies a yearning for a traditionalist, collectivist or authoritarian rule. Both to its east and to its west, Russia now borders on fast-developing and competitive cultures with open societies.

Many nations have been unable to integrate into the new successful cultures. They are mostly located to the south of Russia's borders—in Central and South Asia, Africa, and the Middle East. Russia is facing a simple alternative—either it orients itself with the wealthy and dynamic democracies, or it leans toward the poor, degrading or authoritarian regimes. For true patriots, the dilemma of what option to choose does not exist: it would be difficult to find one citizen who wants his country categorized in the second group. The Russians have made their choice—they have renounced the confrontation that depleted their state, and the social and economic system that repressed individual freedom and initiative. Russia has parted with the system that was increasingly disadvantageous for the weak, that baffled the strong and proved its historical inefficiency. History showed Russia where it should move— toward progress, wealth and freedom.

The Challenges Of The New Times

It was originally believed that the path to Europeanism and Westernization would be a smooth and easy transition; that transition would be encouraging and peaceful.

The reality turned out to be different in many ways. There were glaring divisions in economic development, inefficient economic structures and the demoralization of the elite. Furthermore, society's general fatigue after seven decades of Soviet rule, and the new government's erroneous policies brought about a horrendous economic slump and a protracted systemic crisis. The results of the reforms were mixed and insignificant. The first perceptible effects were felt only after Russia had achieved a relative political stability, and people became accustomed to the new economic conditions.

The Russians placed their hope for effective reform initiatives on financial aid and the business acumen from the West; this support fell short of its expectations. Actually, the support that was provided very often produced adverse results and simply made for poor strategies. Russia was given formal signs of respect, for example, with its official membership in the Group of Eight industrialized nations; Russia found its status being gradually enhanced. However, in many other areas, Russia's opinion was simply ignored on many important issues, such as the question of NATO enlargement. Yet, the most important thing was that the outside world remained friendly all the time, and there was no need to divert resources for a potential confrontation.

Russia's renunciation of socialism, together with the ensuing collapse of the old international system based on ideological, political and military confrontation, ushered in profound changes around the world. At the same time, dangerous new threats and challenges arose alongside the new opportunities; the new threats took some time to identify themselves.

A range of rapidly unfolding processes, highlighted by the general term "globalization," boosted development in the advanced countries. These countries were able to make use of the new tendencies, such as an increasing share of foreign trade in the world's Gross Domestic Product, the growing amounts and faster pace of international financial flows, and a multilevel revolution in information technology. The higher level of economic development within these countries, largely attributable to their higher quality of human assets, aggravated the gap between them and the rest of the world; the role of human knowledge and information as a productive force became greater than ever before.

This period of change occurred at a time when Russia was struggling to transform its social and economic systems, and it missed the new wave of development. Russia has been unable to use the most precious asset that it inherited from the Soviet times—the creative potential of its highly educated population. The delay in carrying out a reform in the general and vocational training systems—perhaps the main source of Russia's modernization—may result in their ultimate collapse. Globalization is a positive challenge which Russia must meet. Russia must not fence itself off from globalization, but devise a comprehensive strategy for adapting to the new processes and trends for the absolute benefits of its society.

As globalization gains momentum, a degradation of the international security system is following dangerously in its footsteps. Conflicts formerly kept in check by the two confronting military blocs, and by the Cold War discipline in general, are beginning to flare up again. New standoffs, this time being propelled by social and economic disparities between or inside countries, have emerged.

In light of this situation, a politically incorrect and even provocative idea comes to mind. The national liberation movements that have swept the world between the 1940s and the 1990s quadrupled the number of independent states. Yet, many of them remain unviable and unable to achieve economic growth or to ensure elementary human rights. There are large regions on the planet where countries are unstable, degrading, and dangerous for their own populations, as well as for the entire international community. The experiment with the "self-determination of nations" has obviously proven unsuccessful.

Social and economic imbalance sparks off public and religious discord which gives rise to terrorism. Naturally, the international community's duty is to consider initiatives to wipe out the in-depth economic and social causes of terrorism, but the sense of realism suggests that many social ills have been overly neglected and are practically irremovable now. That is why radical methods are required to eliminate them, including the use of force against terrorist organizations and even countries that sponsor terrorism or proliferate weapons of mass destruction.

Russia has been hit by terrorism—the plague of the 21st century—much harder than many other countries. At some point, the Chechen seat of international terrorism began to spill over into the neighboring regions and posed a threat to the entire Russian Federation, as well as the international community. Russia stopped its spread by force, incurring heavy human losses and high costs. The Russians realize the importance of decisive struggle against terrorism much better than people in many other countries; we hope that the international antiterrorist coalition will be preserved and further developed.

A possibility that terrorists may gain access to increasingly destructive technologies makes the danger of terrorism much more ominous. Technological progress makes weapons of mass destruction more easily accessible, and the risk of a bad marriage between international terrorism and WMD proliferation calls for a special strategy and resolute action on the part of the global community. No country, however powerful it may be, can solve this problem alone. Solitary efforts will only give rise to new problems and provoke overt and covert standoffs.

A desire to obtain weapons of mass destruction is whipped up by political and military instability in many parts of the globe and the frequent use of, or threats to use, force, especially outside the framework of international law. The Yugoslavian and present Iraqi syndromes may prompt many countries to obtain WMD, thus provoking a new arms race.

Following a period when military force seemed to have given way to economic and humanitarian instruments, it is now moving to the forefront of international politics once again. The world is becoming less predictable and more dangerous. In view of this, Russia requires an urgent reform of its general-purpose forces. It must continue to rely on a rapidly renewable, albeit downsized, nuclear arsenal as a guarantee of its national security. This is necessary in order to thwart the possibility of uncivilized conduct in international politics.

Another source of concern are the persistent imbalances in the world trade and the consequential growth of protectionist attitudes, as major countries are striving to solve their economic problems unilaterally and against the interests of other nations. These factors jeopardize economic and political stability around the world.

The situation is further aggravated by a crisis in international relations management. Many organizations that were set up in a different epoch and for different purposes have fallen victim to institutional inertness and are becoming inadequate to the new challenges. Meanwhile, the world community does not display the determination and readiness to radically reform old international institutions or create new ones, thus we are witnessing a "governance vacuum."

The only institution capable of countering this process is the G-8. To eliminate the "governance vacuum," it must be vested with formal functions and have a permanent secretariat so as to make maximum use of its potential. The secretariat would facilitate preparations for meetings and verify implementation of the decisions made.

The European Union, an engine for economic and social development of the entire European continent and a source of its unprecedented political stability, has been successfully developing over several decades. The EU now has a greater say in world economic issues than before. But its adaptation to the changing world is not an easy matter. The EU's common foreign and security policies are falling short of modern requirements. They are often formed to provide for the elementary common interests, while practical solutions melt away amidst bureaucratic inertia. As a result, the combined efforts of European countries paradoxically diminish their potential instead of augmenting it. The EU is taking steps to rectify the situation and Russia has a genuine interest in Europe playing a crucial role on the international stage, since Russia and the EU share many of the same goals.

Russia made a historic decision a few years ago when it declared rapprochement with the EU a top priority of its foreign policy. Since then, the two parties have developed a mutual understanding and intensified regular contacts. However, decisions on individual issues occasionally come too late or never at all. Partly, this is due to the lack of initiative on the part of the Russian policymakers in Europe, the inefficiency of Russia's bureaucratic machine in managing relations with the EU, and the lack of dedicated institutions of cooperation.

The EU must also assume a share of the blame. The EU is an overly bureaucratized mechanism which often strips European policies of their dynamism and resolve. The Union's political decisions get drowned in red tape. The practical results of dialogue between Russia and the EU are occasionally unproductive, especially on issues of vital importance to Russia: the lifting of trade restrictions on Russian goods, the easing of visa-issuing procedures and eventual abolition of visas, and the reduction of the former Soviet Union's foreign debt. A breakthrough on these topics requires an innovative approach to our common prospects. Lack of flexibility in European regulations often impedes relations that are critical to both sides.

As an influential force, the EU is a necessary institution to fill in the "governance vacuum" and to add stability to international relations. It is also important to prevent a situation where only one NATO member-state, the US, would have a capability and willingness to counter new threats and choose to act of its own accord. Such a turn of events would be highly undesirable—and eventually run counter to America's own interests. It is one thing when power rightly serves in a leadership position amongst a coalition of allies, but it is something totally different when the "leader" has nobody else to rely on, and when its power is perceived as a threat of hegemony, as well as a direct challenge to the world's security. The latter case would only augment the "governance vacuum" and bring about new confrontations and mistakes that may have irreparable consequences.

Such a situation actually manifested itself during the war on Iraq. The unilateral actions of the US and the participation of its "coalition of the willing," have outraged a majority of the world community, including Russia. It also aggravated the "governance vacuum" and further destabilized the world political environment. The US, compelled to wage a war amidst strong international protests, is undermining its moral and political repute as a world leader, and undermining the coalition of countries which have united to confront the new challenges. The "unnecessary war" in Iraq has entailed a huge loss of human lives and only served to increase the mistrust and hatred within the Moslem world.

NATO, a traditional security organization, has found itself in a rather difficult situation. As its historical mission was fully completed by the early 1990s, there were calls for reform; the organization needed to be remade as a viable tool for countering new threats. If NATO had wisely followed that line and established a solid alliance with Russia, it would have given birth to an entirely new security system. But inertia and old habits prevailed, and NATO chose to simply expand and initiate useless cosmetic reforms. Numerous problems eventually emerged in its relations with Russia, and much energy was spent in unfruitful discussions.

In the long run, NATO came to a position where it is now—overlooking the backwater of world politics. Russia is prepared to cooperate with the bloc in a new format which both sides are now constructing. Unlike in the past few years, the Russia–NATO dialogue is becoming more constructive and useful for both sides. Yet many in Russia have doubts as to whether NATO, which has missed a good opportunity for development, will be able to become an efficient instrument of international security in the new environment.

Russia is also watching with alarm the rise of controversies within the traditional North Atlantic community. Their causes are well known. To list just a few, the member states have developed contradictory values after their common enemy disappeared; the divisions between the defensive and political capabilities of different NATO countries have been growing; and the US has been demonstrating a propensity for unilateral military actions. An aggravation of these tendencies presents many dangers for the world. Today, unity of all responsible countries and their continued efforts to combat international terrorism are of crucial importance. Thus, there have been growing suggestions in Russia that it should assume the role of a "political bridge" connecting the two continents.

Europe has a range of other organizations contributing to the general European process. Eventually, the Europeans will have to revise the inventory of those institutions and to estimate their expedience with regard to meeting current and future challenges.

The United Nations, as the world's central body monitoring international law and order, also stands in need of modernization. Many analysts justly point to the deficiencies of that institution. True, the UN was established in a different epoch, but it remains the sole all-embracing institution for maintaining peace. Russia believes one of its priorities is to help strengthen this institution, specifically, the vital decision-making arm of the UN Security Council. Undermining the UN is inadmissible now that many other international organizations are losing strength and are suffering deep divisions. A divorce from the UN structures and political procedures is tantamount to plunging into chaos.

This does not mean, however, that the UN system is immune to change. The Security Council needs to be reformed to markedly increase its efficiency, specifically by admitting new major powers and, presumably, by introducing the principle of a qualified veto, in which case decisions will not be endorsed if two countries use their veto power.

The Iraq crisis, which triggered heated disputes among the Security Council's permanent members, calls for certain conclusions. We cannot accept a situation where the UN obeys one country or a minority of countries, while acting against the opinion of a majority of states, including Russia. Nor is it admissible to ignore decisions of the Security Council. Russia and other members of the international community should have been more insistent that Iraq unconditionally fulfill its commitments for disarmament, eliminate all banned weapons, stop mass violations of human rights, and genocide (use of chemical weapons against Kurds). The painful crisis could have been avoided in that case.

Upkeep of the antiterrorist coalition is critical for consistent efforts to prevent and counter new challenges that mankind may face in the next few decades. In the early 1990s, the international community lost the chance to build a union that would maintain peace and stability. Such a union could have been built around the coalition set up to repel the Iraqi invasion of Kuwait, but it simply failed due to the short-sightedness and insignificant discords among its members. It would be irresponsible to lose such a chance again.

The antiterrorist coalition that emerged after September 11 must lay the foundation for a new union to avert threats and to build a stable and just world order. Initially, it may comprise the G-8 countries, and later include other key nations, such as China and India. The alliance may become an executive body of the UN Security Council.

Russia must insist that international problems be addressed on a multilateral basis. Unilateral actions are acceptable only in real emergencies when there is a direct threat to a country's vital interests.

Russia's Policy In The 21st Century

The reality calls for adoption of new principles in Russia's foreign policy to ensure a favorable environment for the country's modernization. Russia should not squander its political and, most importantly, economic resources, and should focus them on top priority tasks. It implies a pragmatic policy that would avoid confrontation, unless vital national interests are concerned. These include territorial integrity, security for Russian nationals, and maximum sovereignty. In all other cases, Russia should remain above conflicts or get involved only as a mediator or peacekeeper.

Russia's other top priorities include maintenance of peace and stability in the former Soviet republics and mutually advantageous reintegration with some of them.

Russia's foreign policy must be oriented toward an integration into the world economy that would bring her maximum benefit, boost domestic social and economic reforms and will help raise the living standards. This policy implies broad cooperation with other developed countries in the knowledge sphere, which is essential for developing human assets—the main factor of Russia's future successes.

Efforts to build an alliance with advanced democratic nations do not mean that Russia will neglect cooperation with other countries or stand in the rear of the more powerful nations. We must be active where we can benefit. Variegated approach guarantees flexibility in foreign relations in the fast-changing modern world.

Gaining economic benefits must become a major guideline of our foreign policy. Upholding national interests, as well as the interests of Russian businesses and major groups of the population, has a clear priority over many geopolitical ambitions or other such elements of prestige. Unlike the 19th or 20th centuries, the two latter principles cannot govern foreign policy in the 21st century. By making the global community respect Russia's economic interests, we will make much headway toward becoming a modern power. Russia's preparation to act within the new conditions will be demonstrated by its capability to reserve a place for itself in the postwar peacekeeping efforts in Iraq and the rebuilding of that country.

Over the last 300 years, Russia has experienced both ups and downs. Internal upheavals caused it to miss some important opportunities of the 20th century, but now it has a fair chance of winning the new century and becoming a major pillar of the new world. If Russia succeeds, it will make its way into the world not through the "window to Europe" cut by Peter the Great 300 years ago, but through a wide-open door.

Originally published in *Russia in Global Affairs*, April–June 2003, vol. 1, no. 2

Do We Need Reform of Russian Foreign Policy?

Yuriy Fyodorov

Foreign policy is both an indicator and an essential factor of the state of domestic affairs...

Not only the prestige of our country on the world scene, but also the political and economic situation in Russia depend on how competently and effectively we use our diplomatic resources.

Message of Russian President V. V. Putin to the Federal Assembly of the Russian Federation, April 3, 2001.

Introduction

The parliamentary and presidential election of 2003–2004 marked an essential milestone in Russian political history. For the first time since the collapse of the USSR the Russian President became firmly established as the absolute national leader. The Kremlin gained full control of both houses of parliament. Communists and their nationalist associates, who used to play an important and, as one can see, quite destructive role in the political life of the country for the entire previous decade, were sidelined. At the same time, the year 2003 posed complicated questions concerning key directions for Russia's further development. There are no direct answers to these questions so far. In particular, adherents of a political turn towards authoritarianism became more active. There are indicators that the strategic trend of Russian foreign policy is not irreversible. By the beginning of 2004, there was a halt, possibly even a rollback in the relations between Russia and the leading democratic states. This, in turn, again raises a question concerning the fundamental course of Russian foreign policy and the links between this policy and the dynamics of internal political development.

Crisis of the 1990s

During Vladimir Putin's first presidential term, Russia's international stance underwent fundamental changes. Most importantly, there was a replacement of the top political leaders in Russia at the turn of 1999–2000, which allowed the Russian position on the world scene to be strengthened, and the crisis that had affected Russian foreign policy in the second half of the previous decade to be overcome. This latter revealed itself in several major ways. First of all, as from the middle of the 1990s, and especially after the appointment of Yevgeniy

Primakov as Minister of Foreign Affairs, Russia was balancing on the verge of confrontation with the US and NATO and was on the threshold of a "cold war" from time to time. This confrontation peaked with the adventuristic transfer of Russian paratroops to Pristina in June 1999. This could have turned into a clash between the Russian troops and NATO armed forces, with unpredictable consequences.

Russia's inability to achieve its proclaimed strategic goals on the world scene was just as consequential. While running the risk of disrupting its relations with the developed democratic states, Moscow, nevertheless, failed to prevent both NATO expansion, its operation against Belgrade, and the withdrawal of the USA from the ABM Treaty. Neither integration in the post-Soviet space, nor the reinforcement of Russia as the leading force in the territory of the former Soviet Union took place. Steady support for Milosevic's regime finally led to the loss of Russian influence in the Balkans and weakened the role of the UN Security Council, and with it the role of Russia as a permanent member of it. This provides evidence of serious failures of a key component of the foreign policy process, namely of the ability to formulate national strategic goals to be achieved in the world arena.

The main point is that Russia's inadequate vision of the situation, combined with its great-power ambitions, resulted in it setting *a priori* unattainable goals. Inevitable failures were put down to hostile schemes of the West, rather than to Russia's own mistakes, of course. This approach distorted the perception of international realities even further. In their turn, western countries would increasingly interpret Russian foreign policy as a legacy of the traditional Soviet motivations: morbid mistrust; the imperial syndrome; the aspiration to set the USA against Europe; a wish to keep Central and Eastern Europe as zones of possible expansion, etc. Thus, a vicious cycle took shape, fraught with confrontation, which led Russian foreign policy down a blind alley.

Only normalization of relations with China was carried out successfully. The cessation of confrontation with China strengthened security on the Russian Far Eastern borders. However, rendering assistance to China in a military build-up hardly meets Russia's security objectives in the Far East, especially in the future. All attempts to create a true political partnership with Beijing, let alone a military one, as part of the Russian elite would want, turned out unsuccessful.

The situation reached breaking point at the end of the 1990s. Moscow raised the question of strong military "countermeasures" in response to the US withdrawal from the ABM Treaty and to NATO's invitation to the Baltic states to join the alliance. The question was raised of Russia's withdrawal from most—or even all treaties—on arms control, including the Treaty on Intermediate and Short-Range Missiles. There was mention of strengthening Russia's armed force groupings in western areas, right up to deployment of tactical nuclear weapons in the Kaliningrad region, as the Russian press sometimes wrote. Another proposition was accelerated military integration with Belarus. It was not accidental that in 2000 Margaret Thatcher noted, "With every day that passes, the conduct of Russia today comes to resemble more and more that of the Soviet Union."[1]

If such "countermeasures" had been taken, it would inevitably have led to a new round of military-political confrontation. The West could have started a new arms race, built a "sanitary border" along the Russian frontiers, and supported separatist forces in its regions. Yet even if the Russian leaders had restricted themselves to merely curtailing relations with the USA and NATO and militant rhetoric, the country would still have been moved to the margins of world politics. Most likely, the USA and NATO would simply have cut their relations with Moscow.

The Russian foreign policy crisis is caused by the mentality typical of a considerable part of the Russian elite in many respects. There was an increasing gap between Russia's great-power ambitions and the actual influence it could exert in the world arena. They equated influence, on the one hand, with security, on the other hand. The West was accused of undermining Russia's international positions and forcing it out of the regions where its traditional interests were concentrated.

For example, Primakov wrote:

> We all, leaders of the Armed Forces Council, pictured well for ourselves that with the end of the "cold war" the notion of "enemy" would disappear…The leaders of some western countries are acting with the purpose of not allowing Russia to play a special role in stabilizing the situation in the former Soviet republics, with the purpose of ruining the development of tendencies towards rapprochement with the Russian Federation.[2]

By putting the failures of Russian foreign policy down to conspiracy by enemies, this type of vision of world politics would aggravate mistrust towards the outside world. At the same time, the weakening of the country's positions in the world arena due to economic or other objective reasons was interpreted as a threat to be addressed using military force. Degradation of the conventional armed forces was leading to an overestimation of the role of nuclear weapons. However, the possession of nuclear weapons in itself, although it can neutralize the threat of large-scale aggression, will not translate into political influence. Ranking second in the world in terms of its nuclear potential, Russia was unable to prevent NATO expansion, the war against Milosevic's regime and its collapse, and other events, seen by Moscow as unwanted and dangerous.

---

1 "Thatcher Warns Over Russia," *The Daily Telegraph*, July 20, 2000, p.2.
2 Primakov, Ye., *Gody v bolshoy politike* [Years in big politics], Moscow, 1999, pp. 133, 135.

Furthermore, the depth and significance of differences in key interests and strategic cultures of the US, European states and Japan were strongly exaggerated. It was assumed that, after the end of the Cold War, the military-political unity of the West would come apart and world politics would be shaped by the interaction among "independent power centers": Russia, Europe (then in the process of integration), Japan, China and the US.

Soon after his appointment as head of the Russian Ministry of Foreign Affairs, Primakov claimed:

> After the end of the Cold War, the tendency of transition from a confrontational bipolar world to a multipolar one began to develop. The centripetal forces that used to draw a considerable part of the rest of the world to either of the two superpowers were abruptly weakened...Western European countries, which became independent from the US "nuclear umbrella," started displaying greater independence than before. Step by step, their inclination to the "Eurocenter" prevailed over the transatlantic orientation. Against the background of quickly strengthened positions of Japan, the bonds of its military-political dependence on the United States grew weak.[3]

The strategy based on such a vision (often called a "multipolar world concept") assumed the possibility of building a formal or informal coalition between Russia, China and, probably, integrated Europe, with the purpose of weakening the US positions in the world order. Besides, supporters of the concept assumed that Russia, although relatively weak, was able to have an impact on global developments by playing off disagreements among the other "centers."

The wrong political conclusion that resulted from the "multipolar" conception led to large-scale errors. For example, it was believed that the critical attitude on the part of some European countries to the US plans to deploy national ballistic missile defense could prevent the US withdrawal from the ABM Treaty. As a result of this, as well as a flawed assessment of how the different forces in the US ruling circles were aligned, Moscow refused to hold any serious negotiations with the Clinton administration on modification (acceptable to both states) of the ABM Treaty. This facilitated the withdrawal from the ABM Treaty for the Republican administration (perhaps even made it possible), while Moscow saw the ABM Treaty as the "cornerstone of strategic stability" at the time.

Another example: the weakening of Japanese–US military cooperation expected by supporters of the "multipolar concept." If that happened (never mind possible scrapping of the US–Japanese Security Treaty) then nuclear arming of Japan would be inevitable. This would cause a chain reaction in the

---

3 Primakov, Ye. M., "Mezhdunarodnyye otnosheniya nakanune XXI veka: problemy i perspektivy [International relations on the eve of the 21st century: problems and prospects]," *Mezhdunarodnaya Zhizn* [International affairs], 1996, no. 10, p. 3.

Asia-Pacific region, stimulate the nuclear military programs of China and the Democratic People's Republic of Korea, and push South Korea and Taiwan to get nuclear weapons. As a result, Russia would face a new situation in the Far East that would be less favorable to its national security.

The influence that the bearers of the mentality inherited from the collapsed USSR have had on the Russian bureaucratic system can be largely explained by the peculiarities of the country's transition from totalitarianism to democracy. With the exception of the events of September–October 1993, Russia managed to avoid any grave civil conflict and to preserve the state system. Yet there was a cost: in particular, the preservation of those "groups of interests" and lobbies in the elite, whose social status and position in the bureaucratic or economic system were based on confrontation with the West, albeit weakened since the Cold War time. During the 1990s, their influence was growing, thanks to President Yeltsin's weakening positions. He, in particular, would repeatedly explain opposition to the West on certain issues by the pressure exerted by the State Duma, where the dominating positions were taken by the left and nationalistic factions.

In fact, a renewed confrontation with the West would have stimulated the revanchist groups to occupy the key positions in Russian politics. There would have been a reallocation of scarce resources in favor of the army and the military industry, right up to the establishment of a mobilization-type directive economy. This, in turn, would have aggravated the economic crisis and rolled back the formation of market mechanisms. Such a development would have provoked resistance from a considerable part of the country's business and political elite, the leaders and the majority of the "new middle class." The inevitable political conflict would have resulted either in the establishment of an authoritarian regime and mass repressions, or disintegration of the country. Under either option, Russia would have found itself left far behind. Even if the democratic forces had finally won, valuable time—a crucial factor for Russia's revival—would have been lost.

The end of the deadlock

The situation that existed at the beginning of the current decade required a revision of Russia's international strategy. Immediately after Vladimir Putin took office, the Kremlin started indicating Moscow's wish to overcome the crisis in its relations with the West. Contacts with NATO leaders were resumed. A series of talks between the Russian leader and heads of the leading European states were held. The Russian–US summit in Ljubljana in June 2001 marked the onset of changes in Russian–US relations.

Moscow's support of the US anti-terrorist operation in Afghanistan proved the most important, though not the only, moment in the development of new relations between Russia and the USA. This was followed by the Kremlin's reserved (without the hysterics typical of the second half of the 1990s) reaction to the US withdrawal from the ABM Treaty. This enabled the Strategic Arms Reduction Treaty (START), which was vital for Russia, to be signed. The signing of the Treaty was not only of military importance, but also of great political consequence. It demonstrated that the elements of cooperation had prevailed in Russian–US relations over political differences.

A conceptual breakthrough followed at the Russian–US summit in May 2002. The Declaration on new strategic relations between Russia and the USA adopted at the summit emphasizes that the current situation in the security sphere differs radically from that of the Cold War period. Putin and Bush stated: "the period when Russia and the USA regarded each other as enemies or as a strategic threat is over." They rejected "the failed model of rivalry between the great powers, rivalry that could only escalate the conflict potential in Central Asia and in the South Caucasus." They specified the spheres for cooperation: fighting terrorism and regional instability, preventing proliferation of weapons of mass destruction and missiles, assisting the settlement of conflicts in the Middle East and South Caucasus.

The improvement in Russian–US relations helped overcome the deadlock in relations between Russia and NATO. Immediately after the Russian–US summit in May 2002, there was a top meeting of the Russia–NATO Council. This put an end to unproductive discussions on NATO expansion eastwards, which had poisoned the international climate in previous years. A foundation (though partial) was laid for the conceptual, legal and institutional framework of a new model of relations between Russia and western states.

The changes in Russian foreign policy in 2001–2002 were brought about not only by the striving to prevent a crisis in relations with the West, but also by an awareness of the common threats that Russia and the developed democratic states were facing. Among the most important of these threats are international terrorism, proliferation of weapons of mass destruction, instability caused by regional and local conflicts. The events of September 11, 2001 pushed both Moscow and Washington to rapprochement and moved the current disagreement into the background. Mr. Putin received a great chance to demonstrate a constructive approach to the most vital international problems.

Overcoming the crisis in Russian foreign policy and achieving pragmatic goals has been no easy matter. The inertia of the past decade was a great hindrance. In particular, a few directive documents prepared before were approved in 2000. These included the National Security Conception, Military Doctrine and Russian Foreign Policy Concept, all of them still bearing a noticeable trace of the confrontational approach. Although varying in details, these documents mentioned, among other things, a tendency towards the establishment of a "unipolar world" as the main threat to Russia's national security. Moreover, this outwardly vague thesis was specified in the Foreign Policy Concept. The strengthening of the global position of the USA as the main and the only "power center" was specifically defined as a threat to Russian security.

The document reads:

[N]ew challenges and threats to the national interests of Russia are emerging in international affairs. There is a growing trend towards the establishment of a unipolar world order, with economic and power domination by the United States.[4]

Another example: elaboration of START was hindered by the demand Russia put forward concerning mandatory elimination of nuclear warheads removed from the scrapped missiles. The paradox was that the demand was unacceptable not only to the USA, but to Russia as well. Its realization presupposed inspections of the entire "life cycle" of the nuclear supply—from its production to dismantling. This would have resulted in the disclosure of classified information concerning the production of nuclear weapons. No nuclear state could agree to that. A failure to sign the treaty would have called into question the purpose and feasibility of establishing new Russian–US relations aimed at overcoming the policy of the "guaranteed mutual destruction" inherited from the past. It was necessary to take fundamental decisions at the top political level to overcome these difficulties.

"The Primakov school"	Vladimir Putin
Vision of Russia	
A great power, one of the power centers in the "multipolar world."	A European country. An equal member of the western society.
Major world tendencies	
Two contending tendencies: formation of the "multipolar world" and US striving for domination on the world scene.	Internationalization and globalization. Competition for markets and investments. Rise of extremism and terrorism.
Major threats to Russia	
Formation of the "unipolar world." The US policy of global domination.	Terrorism, extremism, proliferation of weapons of mass destruction. Transnational organized crime.
Russia's key strategic goals	
"Strategic partnership" with China and India, as well as with the "rapidly integrating" Europe on the anti-American basis. Expectations of NATO collapse.	Strategic partnership with the US, NATO and European Union; good relations with China.

4 "Foreign Policy Conception of the Russian Federation," *Nezavisimoye Voyennoye Obozreniye*, 2000, no. 25.

In practice, since 2001 Russian foreign policy has been evolving in a direction opposite to that specified in the directive documents of 2000. In his speeches, the President has advocated a vision of world politics quite different from the views that prevailed in the second half of the 1990s.[5]

In contrast to the Primakov school, which reduced the whole of world politics to the primitive interaction of "power centers" according to the classical European scheme of "balance of forces" of the 17th–19th centuries, Putin defined a much more complex, realistic, and elaborate notion of international relations at the beginning of the 21st century. However, the directive documents in the spheres of foreign and domestic policies approved in 2000 were neither cancelled nor disavowed. This caused conceptual and doctrinal ambiguity, which was misused by adherents of the confrontational, or rather traditional, approach to relations with the West; the manifestation of the approach in question has badly affected both Russia's international position and its domestic situation.

Lessons of Iraq

The US–UK operation against the regime of Saddam Hussein has become an exceptionally hard test for the survivability of the Russian foreign policy strategy that was finally established by mid 2002. The preparation for the military operation against Baghdad, followed by the operation itself, made Moscow face a difficult choice. In the case of victory, the USA would have strengthened its role as the only global military power. Adjusting to this situation required fundamental political decisions, while opposition could have pushed Russia to the periphery of world politics. Yet the defeat of the US–British coalition would have caused a surge of the terrorist movement and inspired "rogue states," including those in the regions adjoining the Russian borders. The best way out of the situation would have been to prevent the war in Iraq. In that case the problem would have been resolved by itself. Yet, as soon as a military operation became inevitable, Russia should have shown its disagreement, but without provoking any deterioration in its relations with the USA. That was how China chose to act, for example.

From the very beginning of 2003, Moscow was sending contradictory signals to the world. On the one hand, the Russian leaders intensified their pressure on Iraq, trying to persuade it to comply with all UN requirements related

---

5 The idea of this table and its basic details were borrowed from Igor Zevelev's article "Rossiya i SShA v nachale novogo veka: anarkhiya—mat partnerstva" [Russia and the US at the turn of the new century: anarchy as the mother of partnership], *Pro et Contra*, vol. 7, no. 4, Fall, 2002, pp. 79–80. Certain concepts and wordings have been added by the author of this article.

to the search for weapons of mass destruction in Iraq. They also made it clear that the preservation of the cooperation with the US was more important for Russia than Saddam Hussein's destiny. Thus, in his speech of February 2003 in Kiev, Putin made the following statement with regard to the Iraq situation "We have actually achieved a good level in our interaction with the USA, and we appreciate this... The way we will construct the edifice of international security has more importance than Iraq itself."[6]

Similar motives were found, for example, in the article by the then Russian Minister of Foreign Affairs Igor Ivanov, published in the *Washington Post* just on the eve of the commencement of the US–British operation against Baghdad. It said that " Irrespective of what will happen to Iraq, Russia hopes that Moscow and Washington will act guided by the spirit of the Russian–US interaction, which was recorded in the joint declaration signed by Presidents Putin and Bush in Moscow in May."[7]

However, simultaneously with constructive efforts of that kind, the Russian Ministry of Foreign Affairs repeatedly spoke in a pointedly strict manner against the acceptance of a UN Security Council resolution, which directly or indirectly justified the violence against Baghdad. This could have had a point if the position of the Security Council had influenced the actions of the USA and Great Britain. However, these states decided to wage the war against Iraq without any sanction from the Security Council. In this situation, Russia's position only irritated the US establishment and undermined the potential of the Security Council. The latter was in direct opposition to Russia's interests. For Russia, its membership of the Security Council is a symbolic confirmation of its lost great-power status.

However, this kind of destructive policy met the interests of the powerful part of the Russian political and government elite, for which partnership with Saddam Hussein's regime was more important than interaction with the USA. Thus, former Chairman of the State Duma Gennadiy Seleznev said, without a shadow of embarrassment in 2002, that Russia considered Iraq to be a strategic partner in the Middle East, and the prospects of further development of Russian–Iraqi interaction were enormous.[8]

After the beginning of the military operation and right up to the fall of

---

6 "President V. V. Putin's Opening Address and Answers to Questions at the Meeting with Students and Professors of the Taras Shevchenko National University, Kiev, January 28, 2003," *Information Bulletin of the RF Ministry of Foreign Affairs*, January 30, 2003.

7 Ivanov, Igor "A Russian Resolve for Peace and Partnership," *The Washington Post*, March 15, 2003, A23.

8 Report of the Press-Service of the RF Federal Assembly State Duma "On the Meeting between the Chairman of the Russian State Duma G. N. Seleznev and Deputy Prime Minister of the Republic of Iraq Tariq Aziz," January 28, 2002.

Baghdad, Russia was insisting on the termination of the operations, withdrawal of the US–British troops from Iraq, and renewal of the discussion on the Iraq problem in the UN. In fact, what was proposed was a return to the *status quo ante*. There were no chances for such demands to be met. Moreover, hypothetical realization of that plan would have meant the victory of Saddam's regime, and that would have inspired extremist circles in the Islamic world.

At the same time, a shrill anti-American campaign was launched in Russia. Its organizers' political instincts, inherited from the Soviet past, were combined with the intentions of the careerists who detected a cardinal shift in the Kremlin's international policy on the eve and during the first days of the war in Iraq, and who made haste to become "more Catholic than the Pope himself." That campaign was aimed at the Russian President as well. As a matter of fact, the hysterical critics of the USA blamed Putin for the wrong policy of partnership with the Americans.

In addition to all other problems, breaking up Russian–US relations would have provided grounds for a sudden rise in military expenditure and, consequently, for cutting the economic reforms. It was not by accident that the State Duma, where militant left and national-bureaucratic figures dominated at that time, demanded increased military expenditure immediately after the military actions began in Iraq. Along with making irresponsible declarations, the Parliament postponed the ratification of START, which had taken Russian diplomacy such an effort to achieve.

The pressure of the revanchist circles impeded the development of a realistic approach to the war in Iraq. Yet, as early as April 1, 2003, Putin emphasized that Russia was not interested in the defeat of the US and Great Britain. A true signal for revising the Russian position was sent by Putin on April 3, 2003. He declared that Russia could not afford the luxury of getting directly involved in an international crisis. The President emphasized that, in solving any problems, Russia always used to interact with the United States. Changes in political goals, which started soon after that, allowed the crisis in Russian–US relations to be gradually alleviated. Russian support for Resolution No. 1483 issued by the UN Security Council, which also legalized the interim Iraqi administration formed by the US and Great Britain, played an important role.

Putin's Address to the Federal Assembly of May 16, 2003 was of fundamental consequence. In particular, President Putin defined a system of threats to the national security of Russia: "In the modern world relations among the states are largely determined by the existing serious actual and potential threats of global scale. We believe such threats to be international terrorism, proliferation of weapons of mass destruction, regional, territorial conflicts, the drug threat."[9]

---

9 http://www.president.kremlin.ru/text/appears/44623.shtml

This coincides almost completely with the US view of the threats to national security and, accordingly, creates an objective ground for constructive interaction between the two states. Just as Washington, Moscow gives serious consideration to the possibility of delivering preventive strikes on terrorist bases beyond its own territory. As a matter of fact, a refusal to take preventive steps in fighting terrorism will restrict its victims' possible actions to mere reactions, which may lead to casualties among civilians and the loss of initiative. It is remarkable that Putin did not repeat the declarations spread during the war in Iraq with regard to the alleged threats posed by the USA. Instead, he clearly specified the main point of his position on this crucial matter.

Consequently, by the summer of 2003 a reasonable and constructive policy prevailed in Russian foreign policy. At the initial stage of the Iraqi crisis, the Russian position was counterproductive. Once again the mechanism of political-diplomatic failures described above came out. The crisis in relations with the USA was combined with setting unattainable goals: preventing the war in Iraq, strengthening the role of the UN, etc. For a while, it was not recognized that support for a totalitarian regime suspected of spreading weapons of mass destruction met the interests of the extremist forces that threatened both the USA and Russia. Nevertheless, up to this time influential circles in Russia had been counting on the US failure in the post-war settlement in Iraq. For the USA, the Russian position on Iraq called into question the very concept of the strategic partnership with Russia and led to a reconsideration of attitudes towards Moscow.

There were other reasons behind the diplomatic failures of early 2003. Right up to the fall of Baghdad, the Russian position was based, as we can surmise, on the wrong assumption regarding a lengthy resistance of the Iraqi troops. Most Russian political figures and prominent experts in international law or foreign affairs expected the USA to "get stuck" in Iraq seriously and for a long time. There is evidence that the Russian Ministry of Defense forecast a protracted war in Iraq. Thus, according to information from the Russian press, they prepared a campaign on deployment of Russian naval ships to the Persian Gulf. They did not rule out direct interference in the military operations in Iraq either. The *Nezavisimaya Gazeta* newspaper, which is usually well informed about the plans of the Ministry of Defense, wrote at the beginning of April 2003:

> Observers think that the naval presence in the conflict area will enable us to follow the situation and, if required, to land troops and take part in the post-war reorganization. The assumptions of the Russian General Staff turned out to be correct: the war in Iraq is going to be protracted... There is a possibility that the Baltic group of ships will act together with the naval forces of Germany and France.[10]

---

10 Mukhin, Vladimir, "Flot Rossii gotov k pokhodu v Araviyskoye more" [Russian fleet is ready for the Arabian Sea campaign]," *Nezavisimaya Gazeta*, April 2, 2003, p. 1.

The assumption that Russian policy at the beginning of 2003 was based on the idea of a prolonged war explains some peculiarities of that policy. One such is the emphatically strict position of the Ministry of Foreign Affairs concerning a possible resolution by the UN Security Council, which might sanction the use of force against the Iraqi regime. In fact, if the military actions in Iraq had been longer than expected, and the losses of the US–British troops had exceeded the level acceptable for these countries, Washington and London would have started searching for a way out of the war. Consequently, they would have needed support from Moscow, Paris and Berlin. The most appropriate place for diplomatic negotiations would have been the UN Security Council. The Russian Ministry of Foreign Affairs would have solemnly declared that, in conformity with its warning, the violation of the UN Charter was fraught with defeat. The US global military position would have been shaken. This would probably have been considered as a factor favorable for enhancing the influence of Russia, France and Germany. Yet, actually the defeat of the US and Britain would not have meant a victory for those states, but rather signified a triumph of the Iraqi regime and similar "rogue regimes." However, this was not always realized by the Russian military establishment. In particular, the *Nezavisimoye Voyennoye Obozreniye* [*Independent Military Review*] wrote clearly that "according to our information, the military were surprised at President Putin's unexpected statement that Russia did not wish the USA to be defeated in the war."[11]

Unfortunately, it turned out that many Russian military analysts failed to assess the duration of the 2003 Iraqi campaign correctly. Nor did they understand the reasons behind the defeat of the Iraqi armed forces. For example, it is often explained by betrayal by the Iraqi military command. This version explains why the actual course of the war was essentially different from the forecasts made on the eve of the military operations. However, there is another important thing. Russian expert Aleksandr Golts wrote:

> The Russian military establishment just cannot afford to come up with any in-depth explanations for the changes taking place in the art of war at present. Indeed, in this case they would have to confess that Russia is not prepared to accept the challenge of the revolution in the art of war. In Russia, they prefer not to take it as an integrated whole. At best, they can see only some components of the entire system.[12]

The main point is that the revolution in the art of war is an indivisible complex of in-depth changes in the sphere of weapons, operative art, tactics, organ-

---

11 Sokut, Sergey, "Po prishtinskomu stsenariyu [According to the Pristina scenario]," *Nezavisimoye Voyennoye Obozreniye*, no. 13, April 11–17, 2003, p. 1.
12 Golts, Alexander, "Nepravilnaya voyna" [The wrong war]," in *Russia in Global Affairs*, vol. 1, no. 3, July–September 2003, p. 171.

ization of the armed forces and the "military philosophy" as a whole. When this approach was put into practice, it enabled the United States and Great Britain to smash Saddam Hussein's army quickly and with minimal casualties. In particular, the training of manpower capable of using complex contemporary weapons and military equipment systems efficiently, as well as acting independently and taking the initiative in rapidly changing combat conditions, has started to play a special role. This approach, in turn, requires switching to a professional, well-trained and mobile army. However, military reform has been in fact suspended in Russia.

Overestimating consequences of the "transatlantic crisis" was another source of diplomatic errors made in early 2003. Hence, the illusions with regard to the alleged forthcoming formation of the "multipolar world" and consequent expectations that a strategic "Russia–France–Germany" "triangle" would emerge. Perhaps, such concepts were adopted as the basis of the Russian policy for a certain period. Thus, an article by Russian Foreign Minister Igor Ivanov published in mid February of 2003 made it clear that the Russian, French and German cooperation could become a long-lasting phenomenon in world politics, "the significance of which goes beyond the Iraqi crisis." It read as follows:

> The other day, Russia, France and Germany made a joint statement regarding their joint opinion about the settlement of the Iraqi conflict. Many observers have assessed this initiative as a new phenomenon in world politics, the significance of which goes beyond the Iraqi crisis.... All these are components of the multipolar world order, which is to replace the former bipolar one characterized by its inflexibility, sluggishness and determinism.[13]

Some Russian experts started speaking in earnest about "NATO's partial dismantling," about the possibility—though some way down the line—of actual military integration within the framework of the European Union and its military cooperation with Russia, and about the emergence of Europe as a powerful counterbalance to the United States. Thus, prominent Russian political scientist Sergey Karaganov wrote in the summer of 2003 when the military actions in Iraq were over:

> All Europeans and the entire world need the European Union as a powerful party to make up for "the lack of controllability" and strengthen international stability. It is also necessary to prevent a situation when only one country of the Euro-Atlantic community—the US—has the capability and the will to combat new threats.[14]

---

13 Ivanov, Igor, "America Must Not Return to Cold War Attitudes," *Financial Times*, February 14, 2003.

14 Karaganov, S. "Shansy i ugrozy novogo mira [Chances and threats of the New World]," in *Russia in Global Affairs*, vol. 1, no. 2, April–June 2003, p. 17.

Such expectations turned out to be merely another demonstration of "wishful thinking," which is often peculiar to the body of Russian experts. In practice, what the Iraqi crisis demonstrated was the fragility of European integration in the military and foreign policy spheres. The fault line in the Euro-Atlantic community does not only run between the United States and a number of European countries; it runs between European countries themselves, as well. By no means could this situation enhance the formation of a unified European policy in the military sphere, which is facing great difficulties as it is. France and Germany's resolution to oppose the US strategic course has proved to be fundamentally exaggerated. Between European states and the US there still remains a large gap in the field of the creation of up-to-date military forces that fully utilize the advances of the revolution in military art. This leads to a dependence of Europe on the United States in the military sphere, as well as the interest of European countries in the preservation of NATO. The overcoming of the transatlantic crisis that started in the second half of 2003 proved, once again, that expectations of a long-term and deep fault line between Europe and the United States and, consequently, formation of the notorious "multipolar world" are baseless.

Yet, perhaps, the main lesson of the Iraqi crisis consists in the realization that attempts to revise the strategic line of foreign policy formulated by the Russian President are fraught with troublesome consequences. Actually, supposing Putin had failed to eliminate the crisis in Russian–US relations in the late spring-early summer of 2003, Russia would actually have been semi-isolated today. In particular, we must take into consideration the fact that transatlantic partnership, including in the military sphere, is of much more importance for the United States and, especially, for Europe, than relations with Russia.

"Post-Iraqi" problems

The overcoming of the crisis caused by the Iraqi war enabled us to maintain the course of cooperation with developed democratic countries. However, we had failed to achieve any tangible progress in implementing this course by the second half of 2003 and beginning of 2004. Moreover, there was a hiatus in relations between Russia and the leading countries of the West. In many respects, this is a result of the pressure exerted by the revanchist forces, as well as an unwillingness, or failure, on the part of a considerable section of the Russian political, military and academic establishment to abandon their Soviet-style approaches to foreign policy and safety.

However, all this is merely one aspect of the problem. In 2001–2002 it was important to prevent the severe crisis that was beginning to take shape in relations between Russia and the western countries. First of all, this mission required political will. The present-day problems, however, are related to the deepening and institutionalization of relations between Russia and its western partners, which are much more difficult to carry out. We need not only to reject outdated approaches but also to coordinate our opinions on a broad range of problems. Yet, the main thing is to develop efficient cooperation procedures, mechanisms and institutions. We need a better understanding of the fact that such cooperation is becoming more and more important for its participants. However, this fact is often prejudiced. As a result, the process of working out a positive agenda of relations between Russia and the leading western countries is time consuming and complicated. However, if this process is going to take too much time, it will endanger both the expedience and possibility of establishing new relations between Russia and the West.

Among the positive components of Russian foreign policy (including the policy pursued after the Iraqi war) we can mention the slow—but still progressing—building-up of partnership relations with the North Atlantic Community. A Russia–NATO framework document has been signed on rescuing crews of submarines in distress. A joint document containing detailed assessments of threats posed by terrorism to security in the Euro-Atlantic region has been approved, as have political modalities regarding peacemaking operations of the Russia–NATO Council. Under the Council's aegis, urgent security-related problems are being discussed, such as crisis regulation, counteracting the proliferation of weapons of mass destruction, and ballistic missile defense of the theater of military operations. A comprehensive plan of cooperation between Russia and NATO, comprising more than one hundred joint events, was approved in December 2003. Further development of cooperation in the field of military technology, interchange of information on military planning, improvement of troop interoperability in the cases of joint operations, discussion of mechanisms for the interchange of intelligence information for the purposes of anti-terrorist operations, etc. have been scheduled. Joint exercises (including on the territory of Russia) have been planned. These developments are in sharp contrast with the tense relations that were typical of the recent past.

Russian leaders consider NATO an important and promising partner. As President Putin emphasized, "for Russia, with its geopolitical position, the extension of equal interaction with NATO means actual implementation of the multiple-vector approach that has no alternative and which we are determined to pursue. It is unthinkable for us to be outside Europe..."[15]

Changes taking place in NATO have created conditions for the development of cooperation between the North Atlantic alliance and Russia. These changes also determine Russia's interest in the cooperation. Russian Foreign Ministry Ambassador-at-large A. Alekseyev wrote,

---

15 RF President V. V. Putin's Speech at the Russian–NATO Council session, May 28, 2002, www.president.kremlin.ru.

NATO's orientation towards transformation is of great importance for Russia. Undoubtedly, the alliance's determination to find responses to new threats and challenges in combination with respect for international law will enhance the cooperation between Russia and the Alliance. Russia and NATO's assessment of their needs in the sphere of security is identical in many respects. All principal lines of NATO's transformation have something in common with the basic areas of cooperation stipulated by the Rome Declaration. It appears that we can regard the adjustment of Russia and NATO's military potentials to today's realities as an important component of their departure from the military schemes of the Cold War period.[16]

Underestimation and even disregard of NATO on the part of Russia is counterproductive. The North Atlantic alliance is gradually transforming itself into a Euro-Atlantic security system and embracing larger territories. Russia has common borders with NATO in the Baltic region. The interest of Ukraine and the South Caucasian states in developing their contacts with NATO is growing. There are NATO troops in Afghanistan and some Central Asian countries. China also aspires to discuss security problems in the region with the Alliance. In other words, NATO is becoming a strategic actor in the geographical zone where Russia's essential interests are concentrated. It will be easier for Russia to solve security problems in the zone in cooperation with NATO, rather than by ignoring it. This appears especially relevant, considering Russia's need for economic and military resources to counteract destructive forces in the regions close to its borders.

At the same time, many Russians still regard NATO as a source of military threat. NATO's participation in resolving security-related problems in the former USSR territory is considered as a strategic challenge. Many people think we must parry it by building up our own military potential and strengthening our influence in the newly emerged independent states. A position such as this does not chime with Russia's interests, even when the latter are viewed from the traditional point of view. Attempts to obstruct the development of relations between NATO and the newly independent states are considered by the latter as encroachment upon their independence. As a result, these states merely become firmer in their aspirations to cooperate with NATO and join the alliance in the future.

The negative attitude to NATO is particularly typical of the military circles. The odious position formulated by the Russian military authorities in October 2003 confirms this attitude. They explicitly threaten to take certain countersteps if NATO's military doctrine is not amended. The booklet published by the Russian Federation's Defense Ministry in October 2003 emphasizes,

16 Alekseyev, A. P., "NATO na putyakh transformatsii [NATO on the way of transformation]," in *European Safety: Events, Assessments, Forecasts*, no. 9, Institute of Scientific Information for Social Sciences, Russian Academy of Sciences, Moscow, p. 3.

Russia...expects complete withdrawal of direct and indirect anti-Russian components from both military plans and political declarations of the NATO member nations...If NATO is going to survive as a military alliance with the current offensive posture, a cardinal reconstruction of the Russian military planning and principles of organization of the Russian Armed Forces including the amendment of the Russian nuclear strategy will be required.[17]

If such threats come true, the emerging cooperation between Russia and NATO will be undermined. It is unclear who is going to determine whether the "indirect anti-Russian components" have been completely withdrawn from political declarations of the NATO member nations, or whether the Alliance's current military doctrine has been properly amended to reduce its "offensive" character, and in what way. What is ignored is the fact that a change in their strategic policies by both NATO and Russia is a long-term and complicated process that requires mutual trust between the parties as its fundamentally important component. Any ultimatum demands may complicate and reverse the development.

Inconsistency is part and parcel of relations between Russia and the USA. Russia's political elite, as well as the foreign policy agency, emphasize their interest in partnership with the United States. At the same time, they urge the country's leaders to take steps that conflict with this policy. The actors that most actively pursue such actions come from those forces in the Russian establishment for whom confrontation with the USA is a tool of upholding or recovering their political status or achieving their economic goals.

Among other things, the inconsistency of Russian policy towards the USA is manifested in approaches to proliferation of weapons of mass destruction. The USA considers proliferation as a major threat to its national security. The US leaders assess other states' actions regarding this problem at least as one of the basic criteria in forming their own approach to such states, if not the main one. Russian top leaders have also emphasized on more than one occasion that proliferation of weapons of mass destruction poses one of the most hazardous threats to security. However, the Russian policy lacks adequate consistency and strictness towards any states exposed as violators of the nuclear nonproliferation regimes.

In particular, Russia has not joined the Proliferation Security Initiative advanced by the USA in the middle of 2003. The Initiative is aimed at preventing transportation of weapons of mass destruction (WMD) as well as their delivery means and related materials from and to countries suspected of pro-

---

17 *Aktualnyye zadachi razvitiya Vooruzhennykh Sil RF* [Urgent problems of the development of the Russian armed forces], Moscow, RF Ministry of Defense, 2003, pp. 16, 18.

liferation, including prevention by exerting pressure. The implementation of the Initiative would become an important practical step towards the prevention of proliferation of WMD. The main argument against the Initiative adduced by Russia is that it conflicts with the right to free passage stipulated in the UN Convention on the Law of the Sea. However, in the first place, the UN Convention was passed more than 20 years ago, when the threat of proliferation was not that critical. New political and social realities, as they emerge, always require appropriate correction of legal provisions. It is true for the problems of nonproliferation as well. Second, the Convention itself contains exceptions to the free passage right. They are related to the prevention of slave trading, piracy and drug trafficking. In other words, and in essence, the Convention allows coercive actions against ships suspected of dangerous activities. It is also important that 11 countries had joined the Initiative by the end of 2003 and about 50 states had announced their support. In other words, the Initiative will be implemented regardless of Moscow's acceptance of it.

Many analysts believe that the approach of the Russian diplomatic authorities to the nuclear crisis on the Korean Peninsula is not determined solely by their aim to thwart the extremely dangerous nuclear ambitions of Pyongyang, but also by the desire to uphold their own influence in the region. Among other things, they are flirting with the North Korean regime. In particular, the Russian Ministry of Foreign Affairs opposes discussion of the Korean "nuclear crisis" at a session of the UN Security Council. This runs counter to Russia's strategic goal of consolidating the role of the United Nations and its Security Council. Excluding the UN from the process of settling the crisis on the Korean Peninsula undermines the organization's role in safeguarding international security.

Russian–Iranian cooperation in the sphere of nuclear energy is a large obstacle in the way of relations between Russia and the USA. In spite of ample evidence of Iran's intentions to develop nuclear weapons, the Russian Federation's Nuclear Power Ministry, as before, is reluctant to cut down the Russian–Iranian nuclear cooperation. There is an obvious discrepancy between Russia's fundamental security interests that assume the need to prevent proliferation of weapons of mass destruction, and the economic interests of the nuclear industry. This discrepancy predetermines the inconsistency of Russia's position regarding a number of specific nonproliferation issues. If we fail to overcome this situation, Iran is going to remain a stumbling block in Russian–US relations in the future as well, in particular, considering that Tehran backs Hezbollah—one of the most dangerous Islamist terrorist organizations.

Moscow's unpreparedness to reach an agreement on these grave problems led to another outburst of the negative attitude to Russia in the US at the end of 2003. Analysts think that Washington initiated a process of reviewing its strategic approach to relations with Russia.

Russia's relations with the EU and the leading European states lost some of their dynamic nature in 2003. One of Russia's most important problems—that of the Kaliningrad transit—was solved in late 2002-early 2003. Unfortunately, attempts to facilitate the Schengen visa regime for Russian citizens, which poses a serious problem for Russia, are hopeless. The project of opposition to the US policy in Iraq, jointly with France and Germany, failed. The split of Europe into the "old" and "new" parts intensified doubts as to whether it was possible to turn the EU into an influential military and political power. The process of ratifying the adopted Treaty on Conventional Forces in Europe, which is of importance to Russia, has been blocked by Moscow's unwillingness to withdraw its troops from the Trans-Dniester region, Republic of Moldova, and reach an agreement with Georgia about the terms of closure of the Russian military bases. All this has substantially narrowed the sphere of interaction between Russia and the European states. In addition, difficulties in the adoption of the EU Constitution worry European countries much more than relations with Russia. It is most likely that the expansion of the European Union will make European states focus on relations within the framework of the Union even more, which is going to reduce their interest in developing political relations with Russia. The need to overcome the crisis in transatlantic relations will have the same result. At the same time, disagreements in the assessment of the economic and political consequences of the EU's expansion for Russia have been brought to the forefront of Russian–European relations. Moscow fears that the expansion will have negative consequences for Russia's economic interests in Central and Eastern Europe.

The aggravation of Russia's relations with the leading western powers is also related to the developments on the Russian domestic political scene. Developed democratic countries are worried about the intensification of authoritarian trends and the strengthening of the influence of the military and defense establishment. We can see from the history of the post-Soviet period that such groups are rarely interested in actual cooperation by Russia. The weekly *VPK: Voyenno-Promyshlennyi Kuriyer* [Military-Industrial Courier], which is close to the military circles, worded their expectations very clearly:

> It seems that the realities of 2004 are just going to intensify the tendencies of 2003...This opens up appropriate opportunities and chances. Within the framework of the emerging political construction, the defense and industrial complex as well as the Armed Forces have the right to consider that their immediate issues and needs will attract paramount attention on the part of both political and military authorities of the Russian Federation.[18]

---

18 Tuliyev, Mikhail, "Ustoychivost politicheskoy konstruktsii [Stability of political construct]", *VPK: Voyenno-Promyshlennyi Kuriyer*, no. 1 (18), January 14–20, 2004, p. 1.

Another reason for concern in the West is the success of the radical social-ist-revanchist movement "Rodina" ["Motherland"] established, as many people believe, with the assistance of the Kremlin administration. This organization enjoys the support of a considerable part of the marginalized strata. In particular, "Rodina"'s chaotic but aggressive ideology involves not only hostile anti-western rhetoric, but also a slogan calling for a reunion of the Russian population. Thus, Dmitriy Rogozin writes,

> We must make a point of the reunion issue, however unrealistic it may seem at present, and be creating corresponding conditions consistently upholding the chosen position, in the same way as it was demonstrated by Germany for 40 years, which ultimately led the nation to unification.[19]

So far, statements like this are nothing more than irresponsible rhetoric. However, if someone attempts to put the idea of "reunion of the separated Russian people" into practice, this could have a disastrous effect.

Difficulties in working out a positive agenda with regard to relations with developed democratic countries are also conditioned by the events taking place in the post-Soviet territories, and in particular, Russia's involvement in the situation in Georgia. On the one hand, Moscow supported the peaceful handover of power from Edward Shevardnadze to the opposition. Yet, on the other hand, it was another occasion when the Russian establishment faced the temptation to take advantage of the separatist public sentiments in a number of Georgian territories in order to put pressure upon the newly elected Georgian authorities. There were intensive talks with leaders of Abkhazia, South Ossetia and Adzharia, republics that are not controlled by Tbilisi. Adzharian leader Aslan Abashidze made a clear suggestion that, in case of any complications with the Georgian authorities, he would not hesitate to resort to the help of Russian forces deployed at the 12th Russian military base located on the outskirts of Batumi. In his turn, Russian Deputy Minister of Foreign Affairs Valeriy Loshchinin said that Moscow regarded Abashidze's activities as "the most important factor in stabilizing the situation in Georgia."[20]

The question of the Russian bases in Georgia has become a very vexed one. At the OSCE summit in Istanbul in 1999 Russia undertook to withdraw two military bases out of four by July 1, 2001 and come to an agreement with Tbilisi by the end of 2000 regarding the terms of withdrawal of the two remaining military bases. The former obligation was carried out, while the latter was not. It causes serious dissatisfaction in Georgia. The Russian military department insists that the bases are to remain in Georgia for some time, since their withdrawal and deployment at another location will incur heavy expenses.

---

19 Rogozin, D., *My vernem sebe Rossiyu* [We will recover Russia], Moscow, 2003, p. 70.
20 Quote from the *Yezhenedelnyi Zhurnal*, no. 47, December 1–7, 2003, p. 43.

This fact gives rise to serious doubts. According to the International Institute for Strategic Studies, there are about 3,000 servicemen, approximately 65 tanks, 200 armored personnel carriers and 140 gun mounts at the Russian bases in Georgia.[21] It is hard to agree that the transition of such a minor contingent and its deployment at a new place would incur heavy expenses. Moreover, the strength of the Russian Armed Forces is to be reduced within the next few years and some of the servicemen that are in Georgia now will be dismissed upon the termination of the term of their military service or upon retirement.

On the whole, the developments in the post-Soviet territories indicate several steady trends. Russia is lacking the political, economic and military resources to safeguard its own stability and security in the territory of the former Soviet Union, and establish its special status in these territories. However, Russia's declining status in the newly independent states, which results from the lack of resources, is often ascribed to the intrigues carried on by the USA and other western countries. The latter are suspected of trying to force Russia out of the area of its vital interests. The situation in the post-Soviet territories is often interpreted from the perspective of the zero-sum game. In other words, the development of relations between the West and post-Soviet independent states is regarded as Russia's strategic defeat. There are attempts to neutralize this perceived defeat by building up Russia's military presence and backing up the circles that are inclined to lean toward Moscow for any reasons. Under the circumstances, even the elites of those newly independent states loyal to Russia tend to develop their relationships with the North Atlantic alliance, United States and European countries. They regard them as forces capable of neutralizing the attempts by those influential Russian circles infected with imperial ambitions to gain dominance in the territory of the former USSR.

The West is not prepared to accept the restoration of the Russian empire in any form in the territory of the former Soviet Union. Europe and the United States are antipathetic to the aspirations of Russia to impose its military presence on the newly emerged independent states, when such countries do not want to have Russian troops on their territories. However, one can perceive this position of the West as going against Russian interests only if one assumes that the restoration of something similar to the former USSR serves these interests.

In practice, though, Russia's security interests include, in the first place, stability in the regions adjacent to the country's borders and efficient functioning of civil infrastructures and security systems on their territories. Provided these requirements are met, we can stop the flows of drugs, illegal migrants and weapons coming from the territories of the newly emerged independent states,

---

21 *The Military Balance 2003–2004*, IISS, Oxford University Press, 2003, p. 94.

as well as prevent formation of transnational criminal groups. In a number of cases, cooperation with the USA, NATO and the EU in the sphere of security and stability measures within the post-Soviet space would be essential. As a matter of fact, Russia is highly interested in the engagement of western countries and structures in resolving these problems, since neither Russia itself, nor the newly independent states are capable of coping with these difficulties independently, without substantial assistance from abroad. To adopt this strategy, however, we need to reject the stereotypes widely spread in the Russian political thinking.

★   ★   ★

One of the main conclusions of this analysis is that there has been an apparent gap between the fundamental goals pursued by President Putin and the practice of Russian foreign policy in the past years. As a result, Russia's foreign policy has become less dynamic and, in a sense, has become sluggish. This might have been the reason behind the recent dismissal of the Minister of Foreign Affairs. Indeed, the Ministry of Foreign Affairs must become a powerful tool for promoting the President's strategic policy aimed at effective cooperation with the community of developed democracies. Unless the cooperation develops, we are going to lose the positive potential accumulated by Russia in relations with these countries in 2001–2002, and our position on the world scene will be fundamentally weakened. It is important to bear in mind that any complication in these relations will impede the implementation of the in-depth liberal program of social and economic reforms proclaimed by President Putin.

Originally published in *Yaderny Kontrol* [Nuclear Control], vol. 10, no.2, 2004, pp. 57–72.

About the Contributors

ANDREI KOZYREV – Foreign Minister of the Russian Federation (1990–1996).

YEVGENY PRIMAKOV – Foreign Minister of the Russian Federation (1996–1998); Prime-Minister of the Russian Federation (1998–1999).

VLADIMIR PUTIN – President of the Russian Federation (2000–present).

IGOR IVANOV – Secretary of the Security Council of the Russian Federation (2004–present); Foreign Minister of the Russian Federation (1999–2004).

SERGEI IVANOV – Minister of Defense of the Russian Federation (2001–present); Secretary of the Security Council of the Russian Federation (1999–2001).

ANATOLY TORKUNOV – Rector, Moscow State Institute of International Relations (MGIMO-University).

ALEKSEI BOGATUROV – Director, Academic Educational Forum on International Relations.

ALEKSEI ARBATOV – Director, Center for International Security Studies, Institute of World Economy and International Relations, Russian Academy of Sciences; Deputy of the State Duma of the Federal Assembly of the Russian Federation (1993–2003).

ANDREI KOKOSHIN – Deputy of the State Duma of the Federal Assembly of the Russian Federation (1999–present); Director, Institute of International Security Studies, Russian Academy of Sciences.

SERGEI ROGOV – Director, Institute of the USA and Canada Studies, Russian Academy of Sciences.

VLADIMIR LUKIN – Representative of the President of the Russian Federation on Human Rights (2004–present); Ambassador of the Russian Federation in the United States (1992–1993); Deputy of the State Duma of the Federal Assembly of the Russian Federation (1993–2003); Vice-Speaker of the State Duma (1999–2003).

VYACHESLAV NIKONOV – President, "Polity" Foundation; Deputy of the State Duma of the Federal Assembly of the Russian Federation (1993–1995).

ALEKSEI SALMIN – President, "Russian Socio-Political Center"; Dean, School of Political Sciences, Moscow State Institute of International Relations (MGIMO-University).

ANDREI MELVILLE – Vice-Rector, Moscow State Institute of International Relations (MGIMO-University).

DMITRI TRENIN – Deputy Director, Carnegie Moscow Center; Senior Associate, Carnegie Endowment for International Peace.

SERGEI KARAGANOV – Chair of the Presidium, Council on Foreign and Defense Policy; Deputy Director, Institute of Europe, Russian Academy of Sciences.

YURIY FYODOROV – Professor of Political Science, Moscow State Institute of International Relations (MGIMO-University).

TATIANA SHAKLEINA – Chief, Department of Foreign Policy Studies, Institute of the USA and Canada Studies, Russian Academy of Sciences.

Index

C

Center for Strategic Development, 226

Charter on European Security, 166, 169

Chechnya, 246, 251, 275–276, 297–298, 307, 313, 350, 354, 357, 359–360, 393, 457

Chemical Weapons Convention, 38, 315

Chernobyl, 5

Chernomyrdin, Viktor, 427

China, xii, 50–51, 65–73, 100, 147, 149, 151, 181–182, 208, 264, 306–307, 321–323, 334–336, 343–344, 395, 397, 401–402, 411, 448–449, 464

    "One China" principle, 149

Chirac, Jacques, 256–257

Chubais, A., xii

Clinton, William, 286, 349

Cold War, 51, 196, 209, 213, 240, 244, 314, 320–321

COMECON, 430

Commonwealth of Independent States, x, 33–35, 48–49, 53, 55, 60, 62–63, 97–98, 123, 131, 134, 136, 140, 142–144, 167–168, 174, 203–204, 255, 262–263, 272–273, 301, 312, 344, 419–420, 423–424

    Agreement on the Establishment of the, **3–7**, 13

    Charter of the, 10, **13–25**, 34

    Collective Security Treaty of the (1992), **9–12**, 109, 344

    Commission for Human Rights, **23**

    Coordinating Consultive Committee, **21**

    Councils,

        Collective Security Council, 10

        Council of Commanders of Border Troops, **22**

        Council of Heads of Government, 18, **19–20**, 21

        Council of Heads of State, 16–18, **19–20**, 21–25

        Council of Member States, 16

        Council of Ministers of Defense, **22**

        Council of Ministers of Foreign Affairs, **21**

    Economic Court, **22**

    High Command of the United Armed Forces, **22**

    Inter-Parliamentary Assembly, **23–24**

    Ministry for Cooperation with Member Countries of the, 423

Comprehensive Nuclear Test Ban Treaty, 94, 101, 212, 253, 315

Concept of the World in the 21st Century, 249, 260

Concert of Europe, The First, 383–385, 398–402

Q

Quadrennial Defense Review, 351–352

R

Rice, Condoleeza, 354, 357–358, 362, 372

Rio Group, 59

Rodina, 482

Romania, 46

Rumsfeld, Donald, 358, 361–362

Russia-EU Industrialists' Roundtable, 177–178

Russian Association of International Research, 288

Russian Federation, miscellany of,

    Agreement on Customs Union (3), 155, 156

    Central Bank of Russia, 168, 172

    Constitution of the, 89, 102, 105, 119, 130, 143, 229–230

    Council of the, 102

    Defense Ministry of the, 124, 446

    Federal Assembly of the, 102, 145, 229, 235

    Foreign Policy Concept of the, **89–103**, 236–237, 239, 243, 267, 409, 424, 438, 469

    Government Commission of the, 178

    Migration Service of the, 422

    Military Doctrine of the, **105–127**

    Ministry of Foreign Affairs, 63, 102–103, 178, 287–288, 410, 416, 429–430, 446, 471, 474, 480, 484

    Ministry of Justice of the, 230

    National Security Concept of the, 89, 105, **129–146**, 237, 350

        New Version of the, **269–278**

    Nuclear Power Ministry of the, 480

    Russian Foreign Service, 36

    Security Council of the, 102, 145, 271, 446

    Supreme Council, 63

Russian–American Anti-Terrorist Group, 395

Russian–US Charter of Partnership and Friendship, 193

S

Schroeder, Gerhard, 359

Serbia, 47, 299

Sestanovich, Stephen, 197

Shanghai Five, 100, 147–149, 151–152, 181